THE HISTORY AND COINAGE OF THE ROMAN IMPERATORS 49–27 BC

THE HISTORY AND COINAGE OF THE ROMAN IMPERATORS 49–27 BC

David R. Sear

SPINK
London
1998

Published by Spink and Son Ltd
5, 6 & 7 King Street
St James's
London, SW1Y 6QS

ISBN 0 907605 98 2

British Library Cataloguing-in-Publication Data
A catalogue record for this book is available from the British Library

Set in 10/12pt Times by Columns Design Ltd, Reading
Printed in Great Britain at The University Press, Cambridge

Contents

Acknowledgements

I have the pleasant task of thanking the many friends and colleagues in the numismatic world who have extended their help at various stages in the long process of the production of this book. Cathy Lorber, Rick Witschonke and Peter Clayton all checked early versions of the manuscript and offered much useful comment. The final version is undoubtedly better for their valuable critiques, though it still contains many of my personal idiosyncrasies which I stubbornly refused to change. Obtaining suitable numismatic illustrations for such a detailed survey presented a real challenge, but the task was eased by the cooperation of Rick Witschonke (to whom a special debt of gratitude is owed for his unstinting efforts in this cause); Rick Ponterio; Reverend J. Alex Sherlock; Barry Rightman; Bill Rudman; and Paul Rabin. My gratitude is also extended to Michel Amandry of the Bibliothèque Nationale de France, and Andrew Burnett of the British Museum for their kind cooperation in the seemingly endless quest for images. Many of the better quality photographic reproductions in this book are the work of Andrew Daneman, formerly photographer for Numismatic Fine Arts and undoubtedly one of the most gifted members of his profession. Again, I am grateful to Cathy Lorber for making many of these illustrations available to me. Peter Clayton generously provided the interesting selection of topographical illustrations from his extensive photographic library, and the two maps were prepared by Terry Hardaker of Oxford, whose fine work will already be familiar to students and collectors from my earlier publications on Greek and Greek Imperial coinage.

This will be my first book under the aegis of Spink & Son and I would like to put on record what a pleasure it is to be able to rely on a professional of the calibre of Douglas Saville to see these complex projects through to publication. In the difficult early stages of the creation of The Roman Imperators I was much encouraged by Bobby Cox, formerly Chief Executive of B.T. Batsford, to whom I would like to express my gratitude. The same sentiments are extended to my close friends and associates Tory and Rob Freeman for their patience and understanding during the lengthy production process which frequently diverted my attention from pressing business commitments. Words cannot adequately express my appreciation of the forbearance of my wife Margaret during the many evenings and weekends which have had to be devoted to this work. The lot of an author's wife is not an easy one but I would like her to know how deeply her support has been valued over a period of time considerably greater than that covered by the interminable conflicts of the Roman Imperators.

Introduction

The inspiration for this book was provided by Ronald Syme's brilliant elucidation of the death throes of the Roman Republic and the birth of the Empire.[1] This study powerfully focuses attention on one of those remarkable eras in history when the conventions of law and order which had governed men's lives for generations were suddenly threatened. For a while it appeared to many supporters of the old order that civilization was descending into chaos. But something vital and different was to emerge phoenix-like from the ashes of the past, bringing about the rejuvenation of a system of government which had outlived its capability to control the complex challenges of a new age. The analogy with our own era is compelling, adding to the relevance of a fresh appraisal of the brief epoch during which supreme power resided in the hands of the Roman Imperators.

The leading personalities involved in an age of violent transition will often assume a 'larger than life' aspect to the succeeding generations of a more settled era. The fifth decade of our own century, during the cataclysm that was World War II, saw the spectacle of men such as Churchill and Roosevelt opposing the forces of evil personified by Hitler and Mussolini with the help of unlikely alliances, such as that with the Russian dictator Joseph Stalin. The upheavals of the late 18th and early 19th centuries brought to the fore Napoleon Bonaparte (possibly the last of the Imperators) on one side, and popular 'heroes' such as Horatio Nelson and the Duke of Wellington on the other. In American history who can compare in public recognition with Washington, Franklin, Jefferson and Lincoln, all of whom played principal roles in revolutionary times. So it was with the individuals who held centre-stage in the sixth and seventh decades of the final century before the commencement of the Christian era.

Our story opens in January of 49 BC with the celebrated crossing of the Rubicon by the 50-year-old proconsul Gaius Julius Caesar, a symbolic and irrevocable act which signalled the beginning of an era of civil conflict. That struggle, in a multitude of forms, was to last almost two decades, until the conquest of the Ptolemaic kingdom of Egypt by Caesar's 33-year-old heir Octavian. The intervening years were to witness a veritable bloodbath of Roman aristocracy, not to mention the wholesale slaughter of numberless soldiers in fiercely contested battles such as Thapsus and Munda. Often, great pains were taken to avoid representing these hostilities as civil war and to advertise them as struggles against the enemies of Rome. For example, in Caesar's quadruple triumph, celebrated in the capital in 46 BC, the recent victory over the Pompeians in north Africa became a war against King Juba of Numidia; and when Octavian declared war fourteen years later it was against Queen Cleopatra of Egypt. In both cases, of course, the true enemies had been fellow-Romans (the sons of Pompey, Cato and Scipio in the first instance, Mark Antony and his supporters in the second), but in order to heighten patriotic fervour it was deemed necessary to represent the struggle as being against a foreign aggressor, a transparent deception which nevertheless served its purpose very well.

At the end of it all the old order had been swept away and a single man (Octavian, soon to be called Augustus) stood at the pinnacle of power in the Roman state. Many brave and famous men (Cato, Cicero and Brutus among them) had perished defending what they believed to be a democratic system against the forces of tyranny. In reality, of course, they were merely defending their own highly privileged status within an oligarchy, though that should not be allowed to detract from the undoubted nobility of their motives. The Octavian of our story had been as cruel and ruthless as anyone during this period of violent transition but it would scarcely be just to censure him for that. A mere youth of eighteen when first thrust into the forefront of Roman politics at a time of desperate crisis and utter confusion his chances of survival, let alone success, were slim indeed. Had it not been for the magical name of Caesar, bequeathed to him in the dictator's will, it is doubtful if posterity would ever have heard of the young Gaius Octavius, descended from an equestrian family of Velitrae and fatherless at the age of four. But he had the good fortune to be related to the mighty Caesar through his mother Atia, who was the daughter of Caesar's sister Julia, and the great man clearly recognized the potential of this untried youth. His judgement proved sound indeed and 'the boy' (the name by which Antony referred to him at the beginning of their relationship) went on to bring to fruition many of the dictator's aspirations which he himself was destined never to realize. Once he had achieved supreme power Augustus (the name by which Octavian was known from January 27 BC) became the very model of the gentle and beneficent autocrat, the true father of his country, and continued so until his death in AD 14 at the age of seventy-seven.

The other principal Roman personality in our story is Marcus Antonius (better known by the Anglicized form as Mark Antony). A military man of dashing character, he was one of Caesar's most trusted lieutenants and was twenty years Octavian's senior. His is the real tragedy of this episode. He was the wrong man, in the wrong place, at the wrong time. Caesar's sudden death on the Ides of March 44 BC thrust his consular colleague Antony into a leadership role in the 'Caesarian' party, though at heart he probably remained a true Republican throughout his life. Initially, the Caesarians were very much a minority group, except amongst the military, and their primary aim was to bring to justice those who had perpetrated the savage crime against the late dictator. Octavian, of course, was also of this party though it took a year and a half for Antony to recognize him as any kind of equal in its leadership. Antony was seduced by the glamour of his new-found prominence and quickly set about strengthening his position without any clear idea of why he was doing it or what his long-term goals might be. In this he was the exact opposite of

Octavian who, only barely out of his teens, was having great difficulty in getting people to take him seriously whilst possessing a perfect vision of where his destiny was going to lead him. As the possessor of a relentless ambition, and the coolness of mind to calculate the odds under the most trying of circumstances, he had a huge advantage over his swashbuckling but emotionally vulnerable rival Antony.

The delicate balance of power between these two very different men gradually began to shift in Octavian's favour with Antony's increasing involvement with the alluring Cleopatra, queen of Egypt. Caesar had also had a relationship with this fascinating representative of the Greek Ptolemaic dynasty and she claimed her child born in 47 BC was the son of the dictator (this of course made him a prime target for elimination in the eyes of Caesar's adopted son Octavian). Cleopatra's true ambitions are hard to gauge. Octavian utilized her as the instrument of Antony's destruction and in consequence every aspect of her character has been vilified by a literary tradition whose aim was to glorify Octavian at the expense of his enemies. It seems reasonable to surmise that she was a calculating and opportunistic woman who saw in the good fortune of her intimate acquaintance with Rome's most powerful men a unique chance to restore the declining fortunes of her once-great kingdom. To attribute to her motives anything more sinister than that – such as the overthrow of the Roman Republic and the transfer of the centre of political power to Alexandria – is patently absurd, though it must have seemed real enough to a nervous Italian citizenry in 32 BC when Octavian's vitriolic propaganda was being disseminated. Unfortunately, as Antony fell increasingly under Cleopatra's spell (he even went through a form of marriage with her at Antioch in 37 BC) he seems to have become less effective as a political and military leader. This first became apparent in the disastrous failure of his Parthian invasion in 36 BC which seriously undermined his reputation. Cleopatra must have suffered the agonizing experience of seeing her dream slipping from her grasp. The end came with the debacle of the Actium campaign (summer 31 BC) which ended Antony's career and condemned the Ptolemaic kingdom of Egypt to early extinction. The melodramatic nature of Antony and Cleopatra's suicides in Alexandria the following year added to the lustre of the legend.

The rich variety of coin issues in these final years of the history of the Roman Republic is of extraordinary importance in the interpretation of the complex sequence of events. In cataloguing and describing the types in the greatest possible detail I have subdivided the 22-year period into six chapters, each commencing and ending at some important juncture in the story. An overview of the events covered by the chapter is followed by a catalogue of the coins in which the relevance of each individual type is discussed in depth. The listings are grouped according to the issuing authority as it is neither possible nor desirable to attempt a reconstruction of the precise sequence of all issues. Their inter-relationship may be better understood by referring to the chronological conspectus of issues in Appendix 1. In the main I have followed the chronology adopted by Michael Crawford,[2] but in some instances my opinion differs, in such cases the reasoning behind the reattribution has been fully explained. References are cited following the description of each type and variety, and the denomination, place of mintage, and date are stated with the greatest possible degree of accuracy in the light of the current state of our knowledge. Concordances are provided with the catalogue listings of Crawford, Babelon/RSC, Cohen/RSC, and RIC.

As an aid to the student and collector an attempt has been made to illustrate as many coins as possible, though the extreme rarity and poor striking of some issues has made it difficult to find suitable photographs. Line illustrations, most of them engraved by the gifted 19th century artist L. Dardel,[3] have in some instances been used to augment the photographic reproductions. To facilitate ease of reference indices have been provided covering Coin Legends, Types, and Mints, as well as a detailed index to the Historical Narrative. Current valuations may be found in the Table of Comparative Rarities and Values, where additional information is provided on Crawford's estimates of the numbers of obverse and reverse dies produced for each precious metal issue; Sydenham's rarity ratings; and the late 19th century valuations appearing in the works of Babelon and Cohen. To complete the picture Appendix 2 presents a comprehensive survey, with brief notes, of all the local coinages of the Imperatorial period. This is based on the listings in the monumental *Roman Provincial Coinage,* Volume 1, by Andrew Burnett, Michel Amandry, and Pere Pau Ripolles,[4] unquestionably one of the finest pieces of original numismatic research to appear this century. The 524 coin types listed in Appendix 2 more than double the total number of pieces catalogued in *The History and Coinage of the Roman Imperators, 49–27 BC.*

DAVID R. SEAR
Los Angeles
November 1997

Footnotes

1 *The Roman Revolution* (Oxford, 1939).
2 *Roman Republican Coinage* (Cambridge, 1974). The importance of this work for the period under consideration cannot be over-estimated.
3 Originally used to illustrate the works of Cohen and Babelon.
4 London and Paris, 1992.

Bibliography and Abbreviations

Primary sources

Appian	*Civil Wars*
Asconius	*Commentary on Cicero's Orations (pro Scauro)*
Caesar	*Civil War*
	Alexandrian War, African War, and Spanish War (by different authors)
Cicero	*Letters (ad Brutum, ad familiares)*
	Orations (in Verrem, pro Balbo, Philippics)
Cornelius Nepos	*Life of Atticus*
Dio Cassius	*Roman History*
Homer	*Odyssey*
Horace	*Odes*
	Epodes
	Satires
Livy	*The History of Rome*
Pliny the Elder	*Natural History*
Plutarch	*Parallel Lives (Sulla, Brutus, Cicero, Caesar, Antonius)*
Res Gestae	*Res Gestae Divi Augusti (Monumentum Ancyranum)*
Suetonius	*The Lives of the Caesars (Divus Iulius, Divus Augustus)*

Secondary sources

AIIN	*Annali dell'Istituto Italiano di Numismatica*
Amandry	M. Amandry, 'Le monnayage en bronze de Bibulus, Atratinus et Capito', *Revue Suisse de Numismatique* 65 (1986), pp. 73–85; 66 (1987), pp. 101–12; and 69 (1990), pp. 65–96
Amandry Corinth	M. Amandry, 'Le monnayage des duovirs corinthiens', *Bulletin de Correspondance Hellénique, Supp. XV* (1988)

AMC	C. H. V. Sutherland and C. M. Kraay, *Catalogue of the Coins of the Roman Empire in the Ashmolean Museum, Part I, Augustus* (1975)
AMNG	*Die antiken Münzen Nord-griechenlands* (ed. F. Imhoof-Blumer, 1898–)
Babelon	E. Babelon, *Description Historique et Chronologique des Monnaies de la République Romaine* (1885–6)
Beltran	A. Beltran, *Las monedas latinas de Cartagena* (1949)
BMCC	D. Allen, J. Kent and M. Mays, *Catalogue of the Celtic Coins in the British Museum* (1987–95)
BMCG	R. S. Poole, B. V. Head, P. Gardner, W. Wroth, G. F. Hill and E. S. G. Robinson, *Catalogue of the Greek Coins in the British Museum* (1873–1927)
BMCRE	H. Mattingly, *Coins of the Roman Empire in the British Museum, Vol. I, Augustus to Vitellius* (1923)
BMCRR	H. A. Grueber, *Coins of the Roman Republic in the British Museum* (1910; revised edition 1970)
BN	E. Muret and A. Chabouillet, *Catalogue des Monnaies Gauloises de la Bibliotheque Nationale* (1889)
Buttrey	T. V. Buttrey, 'The Triumviral Portrait Gold of the Quattuorviri Monetales of 42 BC', *ANSNNM 137* (1956)
CBN	J.-B. Giard, *Catalogue des Monnaies de l'Empire Romain, Vol. I, Auguste* (revised edition, 1988)
Cesano	S. L. Cesano, 'Le monete di Cesare', *RPAA* (1947–9), pp. 103-51
Chaves	F. Chaves, *Las monedas hispano-romanas de Carteia* (1979)
CIL	*Corpus Inscriptionum Latinarum* (1863–)
Cohen	H. Cohen, *Description Historique des Monnaies Frappées sous l'Empire Romain, Volume I* (2nd edition, 1880)
Crawford	M. H. Crawford, *Roman Republican Coinage* (1974)
	M. H. Crawford, *Roman Republican Coin Hoards* (1969)
De la Nauze	'Le Poids de l'anc. Livre romaine', *Mém. de l'Acad. roy. des Inscr., &c., vol. xxx* (1764), p. 382

Deroc	A. Deroc, 'Les monnaies coloniales de Forum Julii (Fréjus)', *Mélanges Colbert de Beaulieu* (1987), pp. 285–93
Dessau	H. Dessau, *Inscriptiones Latinae Selectae* (1892–1916)
Eckhel	J. Eckhel, *Doctrina numorum veterum* (1792–8)
FITA	M. Grant, *From Imperium to Auctoritas* (1946; reprinted with corrections, 1969)
Gabrici	E. Gabrici, *La Monetazione del Bronzo della Sicilia Antica* (1927)
Giard	J.-B. Giard, 'Le monnayage antique de Nimes', *Ecole Antique de Nimes* (1971–2), pp. 47–60
GM	F. Imhoof-Blumer, *Griechische Münzen* (1890)
GMI	A. M. Guadan, *La Moneda Iberica* (1980)
Grant	M. Grant, *The Army of the Caesars* (1974)
Hill	*The Monuments of Ancient Rome as Coin Types* (1989)
Huelsen	Ch. Huelsen (transl. by J. B. Carter), *The Roman Forum: its History and its Monuments* (2nd edition, 1909)
Hunterian	G. MacDonald, *Catalogue of Greek Coins in the Hunterian Collection, University of Glasgow* (1899–1905)
IG	*Inscriptiones Graecae* (1873–)
ILLRP	*Inscriptiones Latinae Liberae Rei Publicae* (1963–5)
KM	F. Imhoof-Blumer, *Kleinasiatische Münzen* (1901–2)
Kraft	K. Kraft, *Zur Münzpragung des Augustus* (1969)
Lenormant	C. Lenormant, 'Notice sur les deniers romains qui portent le nom de L. Valerius Acisculus, *Nouvelles Annales publiées par la section française de l'Institut Archéologique de Rome*, vol. ii (1838), pp. 142–69
Llorens	M. M. Llorens, *La ceca de Ilici* (1987)
LS	F. Imhoof-Blumer, *Lydische Stadtmünzen* (1897)
Lugli	G. Lugli, *Roma Antica: Il centro monumentale* (1946)
Mazard	J. Mazard, *Corpus Nummorum Numidiae Mauretaniaeque* (1955)
Melville Jones	J. Melville Jones, *A Dictionary of Ancient Roman Coins* (1990)
Meshorer	Y. Meshorer, *Ancient Jewish Coinage*, Vol. II (1982)

MG	F. Imhoof-Blumer, *Monnaies Grecques* (1883)
Mørkholm	O. Mørkholm, 'The Autonomous Tetradrachms of Laodicea ad Mare', *ANSMN 28* (1983), pp. 89–107
	O. Mørkholm, 'Ptolemaic Coins and Chronology: The Dated Silver Coinage of Alexandria', *ANSMN 20* (1975), pp. 7–24
NAH	L. Villaronga, *Numismatica Antigua de Hispania* (1979)
Newman	R. Newman, 'A Dialogue of Power in the Coinage of Antony and Octavian (44–30 BC)', *ANSAJN 2* (1990), pp. 37–63
OCD	S. Hornblower and A. Spawforth (eds), *The Oxford Classical Dictionary* (3rd edition, 1996)
RG	W. Waddington, E. Babelon, and T. Reinach, *Recueil Général des Monnaies Grecques D'Asie Mineure* (1904–12; partially revised 1925)
RIC	C. H. V. Sutherland, *The Roman Imperial Coinage, Volume I, 31 BC–AD 69* (revised edition, 1984)
RPC	A. Burnett, M. Amandry, and P. P. Ripolles, *Roman Provincial Coinage, Volume I* (1992)
RSC	H. A. Seaby, *Roman Silver Coins, Volume I, The Republic to Augustus* (3rd edition, 1978)
Scheers	S. Scheers, *Traité de Numismatique Celtique. II. La Gaule Belgique* (1977)
SNG Cop.	Sylloge Nummorum Graecorum, *The Royal Collection of Coins and Medals, Danish National Museum* (1942–79)
SNG Levante	E. Levante, Sylloge Nummorum Graecorum, Switzerland I, *Levante-Cilicia* (1986)
SNG v. Aul.	Sylloge Nummorum Graecorum, Deutschland, *Sammlung H. von Aulock* (1957–68)
Sutherland	C. H. V. Sutherland, *The Emperor and the Coinage: Julio-Claudian Studies* (1976)
	C. H. V. Sutherland (with Nekriman Olcay and K. E. Merrington), *The Cistophori of Augustus* (1970)
Svor. Crete	J. Svoronos, *La Numismatique de la Crete Ancienne* (1890)
Svor. Ptol.	J. Svoronos, *Ta Nomismata tou Kratous ton Ptolemaion* (1904)
Sydenham	E. A. Sydenham, *The Coinage of the Roman Republic* (1952)

Troxell	H. A. Troxell, 'The Coinage of the Lycian League', *ANSNNM 162* (1982)
v. Aul. Pisidia	H. von Aulock, *Münzen und Stadte Pisidiens* I & II (1977 and 1979)
Youroukova	Y. Youroukova, *Coins of the Ancient Thracians* (translated by V. Athanassov, 1976)

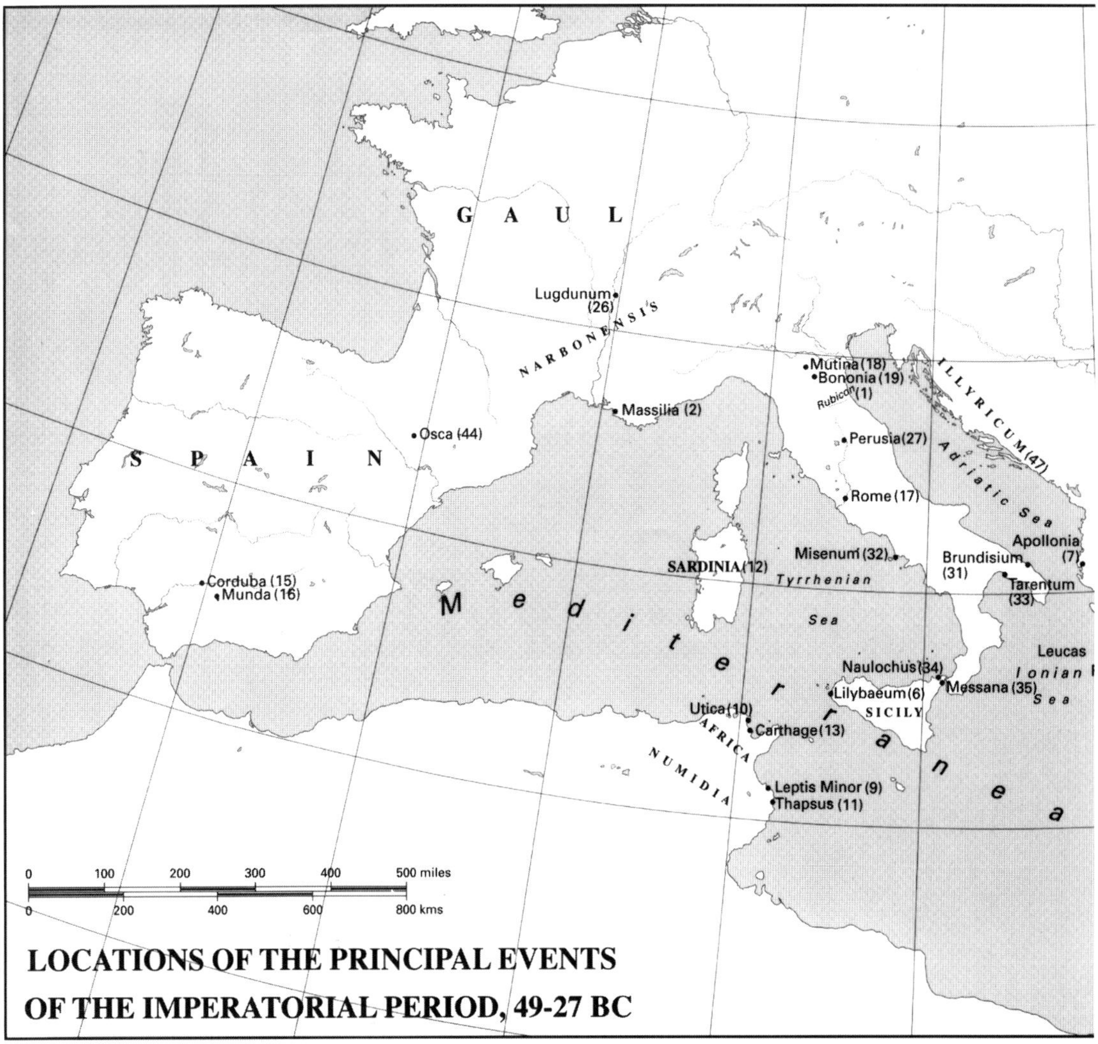

LOCATIONS OF THE PRINCIPAL EVENTS OF THE IMPERATORIAL PERIOD, 49-27 BC

KEY TO MAP

1 River Rubicon Caesar's crossing of this river in northern Italy in January 49 BC inaugurates the era of civil wars.

2 Massilia this city of southern Gaul delays Caesar's advance on Spain in 49 BC. Five years later, following the dictator's assassination, it is occupied by Sextus Pompey who has been a fugitive in Spain since the battle of Munda in 45 BC.

3 Pharsalus Caesar's victory over Pompey on 9 August 48 BC destroys the latter's power and leads ultimately to his murder on the Mediterranean coast of Egypt on 28 September.

4 Alexandria

Caesar enters the Egyptian capital following Pompey's death and is captivated by Queen Cleopatra's youthful charm (48 BC). He champions her cause against her brother and rival, Ptolemy XIII. Antony spends the winter of 41–40 BC with the Egyptian queen in the Ptolemaic palace. In 34 BC Alexandria witnesses Antony and Cleopatra's magnificent 'triumph'. This is followed by the celebrated 'Donations' by which the Roman Triumvir bestows on the Egyptian queen and her children an extensive array of royal titles and territories. An issue of denarii is made to commemorate the occasion. In early August 30 BC, with the Egyptian capital already in Octavian's hands, Antony and Cleopatra commit suicide, thus ending the civil war.

5 Zela

the site of Caesar's victory in August 47 BC over Pharnaces, son of Mithradates the Great of Pontus. The success of this lightning campaign gives rise to the famous Caesarian quotation *veni, vidi, vici,* "I came, I saw, I conquered".

6 Lilybaeum Caesar embarks from this western Sicilian port for Africa to confront the survivors of the Pompeian party (late 47 BC). Coins are struck for him at this time by his lieutenant A. Allienus.

7 Apollonia this city of Illyricum is used as a mint by the Pompeians following their flight from Italy early in 49 BC. It is the place of residence of the young Octavius at the time of Caesar's assassination five years later. In the early part of 43 BC denarii are struck here by Gaius, younger brother of M. Antony, whilst under siege by Brutus.

8 Ephesus this ancient city of Ionia is used as a mint by the Pompeians during the raising of troops in Asia prior to the battle of Pharsalus (49 BC). Antony is proclaimed the 'New Dionysus' here in the year following Philippi (41 BC) and thereafter he uses it as a mint on various occasions (41 and 39 BC). Antony and Cleopatra winter here in 33–32 BC at the commencement of the great military build-up which leads to Actium. In 28 BC Octavian strikes silver cistophori at Ephesus celebrating the restoration of peace and describing the victor of Actium and Alexandria as the 'Champion of the Liberty of the Roman People'.

9 Leptis Minor this port-city opens its gates to Caesar soon after his arrival in north Africa at the commencement of the war against the Pompeians.

10 Utica the provincial capital is the headquarters of the Pompeians during the war in Africa against Caesar and it serves as their principal mint in 47–46 BC. It may also be the mint for Q. Cornuficius' coinage issued in 42 BC.

11 Thapsus Caesar's brilliant victory here over the Pompeians on 6 February 46 BC seriously weakens his adversaries and the survivors flee to Spain to make one last stand.

12 Sardinia Caesar visits this western Mediterranean island in 46 BC on his way back to Rome following his victory at Thapsus. Eight years later Sextus Pompey's lieutenant Menodorus surrenders control of Sardinia to Octavian.

13 Carthage Rome's old rival is refounded as a Roman colony by Caesar in 46 BC, a century after its destruction following the Third Punic War.

14 Corinth this ancient and illustrious city of southern Greece, destroyed by Rome at about the same time as Carthage, is also refounded by Caesar as a colony (44 BC).

15 Corduba this Spanish city serves as the headquarters of the Pompeians during their final stand against Caesar in 46–45 BC.

16 Munda Caesar's final victory over the Pompeians is achieved here on 17 March 45 BC. It results in the total destruction of their cause, though Sextus Pompey survives to plague the dictator's heirs.

17 Rome Caesar is assassinated at a meeting of the Senate on the Ides (15th) of March 44 BC The Capitoline mint is the source of all the regular issues of Roman republican coinage down to the time of Octavian's closure of the establishment in 40 BC. The Capitoline mint may have been temporarily reopened by Octavian in 32 BC for the production of the CAESAR DIVI F, IMP CAESAR, and subsequent coinages down to the time of the constitutional settlement of January 27 BC.

18 Mutina Decimus Brutus is besieged by Antony in this northern Italian city in 44–43 BC but is relieved by Octavian and the consuls Hirtius and Pansa.

19 Bononia Antony, Octavian, and Lepidus meet in this northern Italian city in November 43 BC and establish the Second Triumvirate.

20 Smyrna Brutus and Cassius meet in this ancient city of Asia early in 42 BC to formulate their plans to oppose the triumviral government in Rome. Gold and silver coins are struck in the names of both tyrannicides on this occasion.

21 Xanthus Brutus' siege of this Lycian city leads to the mass suicide of its inhabitants (spring 42 BC).

22 Rhodes Cassius subdues this wealthy island-state in his drive to raise money for the war against the Triumvirs (42 BC).

23 Sardis the old Lydian royal capital is the site of the second meeting of Brutus and Cassius (summer 42 BC) which signals the commencement of the campaign which will lead to Philippi. As with the first meeting at Smyrna gold and silver coins are struck in the names of both tyrannicides to mark the occasion.

24 Neapolis this port-city of Macedon serves as the naval base of the Republicans during the Philippi campaign, with fleets under the command of Domitius Ahenobarbus and Staius Murcus (autumn 42 BC).

25 Philippi this Macedonian city is the site of two battles in October 42 BC which decide the fate of the Republic and result in the suicide deaths of both Cassius and Brutus.

26 Lugdunum only recently founded by Munatius Plancus this city of Gaul is the mint for two series of silver quinarii issued by Antony in 43 and 42 BC.

27 Perusia Octavian's siege of Lucius, younger brother of M. Antony, in this central Italian city ('Perusine War' 41–40 BC) results in the latter's surrender and disgrace, together with Antony's wife Fulvia.

28 Tarsus Antony's celebrated meeting with Cleopatra takes place in the Cilician capital in 41 BC amid the sumptuous luxury of the Egyptian queen's royal barge.

29 Athens Brutus gains support for the republican cause in this celebrated centre of democracy after fleeing Italy following the assassination of Caesar in March of 44 BC. Four years later Antony, en route to Italy, meets his wife Fulvia here and admonishes her for her part in the Perusine War. Later, from 39–37 BC, Antony and his new bride

Octavia make Athens their place of residence and coins are struck here in 38 BC. In May of 32 BC Antony and Cleopatra take up residence in the city during the great military build-up which will result in the battle of Actium the following year. Denarii are struck for Antony at this time, one of the two types also bearing the name of his lieutenant M. Junius Silanus. Octavian visits Athens late in 31 BC, following his victory at Actium, and is initiated into the Eleusinian Mysteries.

30 Corcyra the former republican admiral Ahenobarbus – a pirate in the Adriatic and Ionian Seas since Philippi – joins forces with Antony in the early summer of 40 BC and coins are struck on this island of western Greece in commemoration of the event.

31 Brundisium Antony and Octavian meet at this southern Italian port in the late summer of 40 BC and conclude the Pact of Brundisium. Octavian's sister, Octavia, is married to the eastern Triumvir to seal the alliance.

32 Misenum under the terms of the pact signed at this harbour-town in the summer of 39 BC Antony and Octavian give recognition to Sextus Pompey's status but do not admit him to the Triumvirate.

33 Tarentum Antony and Octavian conduct their last conference at this celebrated Greek city of southern Italy (late spring 37 BC). They sign a pact of mutual co-operation and renew the Triumvirate for a further 5-year term. Then they go their separate ways, never again to meet. The Antonian admirals Atratinus and Capito may have issued their 'fleet' coinage of reduced weight at Tarentum in the summer of 37 BC in commemoration of the accord.

34 Naulochus it is off the promontory of Naulochus, in north-eastern Sicily, that Agrippa achieves his memorable naval victory over Sextus Pompey on 3 September 36 BC. The latter's power is finally destroyed, and with the subsequent deposition from the Triumvirate of Lepidus Octavian now enjoys supremacy in the West.

35 Messana — Sextus Pompey's headquarters ever since his seizure of Sicily in 43 BC, Messana is plundered by troops under the command of Lepidus following the naval battle of Naulochus. The episode leads indirectly to the downfall of the third member of the Triumvirate.

36 Antioch — Antony meets Cleopatra in the Syrian capital and marries her according to the customs of the East, even though he is still married to Octavia (autumn 37 BC).

37 Cyprus — this former Ptolemaic possession is restored to the Egyptian kingdom by Caesar in 48 BC and the arrangement is confirmed by Antony following his marriage to Cleopatra at Antioch. The island reverts to provincial status following Cleopatra's downfall in 30 BC.

38 Chalcis — this small kingdom of Antilebanon, together with most of the coastal territory of Phoenicia and Palestine, is given by Antony to his new wife following their union in 37 BC.

39 Cyrenaica — in the 'Donations' of Alexandria (34 BC) this north African territory, together with Libya, is bestowed on Cleopatra Selene, daughter of Antony and the Egyptian queen. Following Octavian's conquest of the Ptolemaic kingdom four years later Cyrenaica reverts to its former provincial status.

40 Phraaspa — the capital of Media Atropatene, Phraaspa is besieged unsuccessfully by Antony at the commencement of his disastrous invasion of Parthia (36 BC).

41 Seleucia — the port of the Syrian capital of Antioch, Seleucia is the probable mint for the 'fleet' coinage issued in 38 BC by Antony's admiral Bibulus.

42 Lechaeum — Corinth's port on the Corinthian Gulf, Lechaeum may be the mint for the 'fleet' coinage issued in 38 BC by Antony's admiral Atratinus.

43 Piraeus — Athens' great harbour complex at Piraeus is the likely mint for the 'fleet' coinage issued in 38 BC by Antony's admiral Capito.

44 Osca
Octavian's general Cn. Domitius Calvinus issues denarii at this Spanish city in connection with his campaign against the Cerretani (39 BC).

45 Miletus
Sextus Pompey's long and colourful career is ended in this Ionian city of Asia when he is executed in 35 BC by Antony's lieutenant M. Titius.

46 Armenia
Antony deposes King Artavasdes and reduces his country to the status of a Roman province in retribution for his act of betrayal during the invasion of Parthia (34 BC). Armenia manages to regain its independence three years during the war between Antony and Octavian.

47 Illyricum
Octavian's surprisingly successful campaigns in this wild and mountainous region in 35–34 BC greatly enhance his military reputation.

48 Samos
Antony transfers his headquarters from Ephesus to the island of Samos in April 32 BC whilst his army crosses to Greece in readiness for the confrontation with Octavian. Octavian himself visits the island in the winter of 31–30 BC following his victory at Actium, but is obliged to make a hurried departure because of serious unrest in Italy.

49 Patrae
this northern Peloponnesian city at the mouth of the Gulf of Corinth serves as Antony and Cleopatra's headquarters over the winter of 32–31 BC and is almost certainly the mint for Antony's celebrated 'legionary' coinage.

50 Actium
the site of the celebrated naval victory of Agrippa over Antony (2 September 31 BC), off the western coast of Greece, which effectively ends the latter's political career and gives Octavian unquestioned authority over the entire Roman world. A rare issue of denarii is made, possibly in the Antonian camp at Actium, one variety bearing the name in monogram form of one of Antony's few remaining senior officers, the tyrannicide Decimus Turullius.

51 Methone
Agrippa's capture of this strategically important harbour-town in the southern Peloponnese (early 31 BC) threatens Antony's vital supply line of corn-ships from Egypt.

52 Leucas	Agrippa's capture of this large island south-west of Actium is a further blow to Antony as it enables Octavian's fleet to blockade the narrow entrance to the Ambracian Gulf and prevent the passage of the Antonian supply ships.
53 Paraetonium	Antony's attempt to prevent the capture of this town 150 miles west of Alexandria fails and results in the loss of his 40 remaining ships (summer 30 BC). This episode marks the end of any serious resistance to Octavian's conquest of Egypt.
54 Cyrene	in the summer and autumn of 31 BC L. Pinarius Scarpus, Antony's lieutenant in the Cyrenaica, strikes coins initially for Antony and then for Octavian, the later series belonging to the period following the battle of Actium.
55 Nicopolis	the city founded to commemorate the victory over Antony and Cleopatra in 31 BC, Nicopolis is built on the site of the military camp occupied by Octavian during the Actian campaign.

Prologue: the decline of senatorial authority and the birth of military autocracy in the late Republic

On 10 January 49 BC the army of the proconsul Gaius Julius Caesar was assembled on the northern banks of the little river Rubicon which marked the boundary between the province of Cisalpine Gaul and Italy proper. Through long years of campaigning Caesar had led his men to total victory in the Gallic War and had won their unswerving devotion to his cause. The Roman world was now poised to witness an event which would plunge it into a state of civil war, a conflict which would take no less than two decades to run its full course. The final act in the drama would be played out on 1 August 30 BC when Mark Antony, who had been championing Caesar's cause before the Senate at the time of the Rubicon crossing, took his own life in the Egyptian capital of Alexandria. This gave the supreme power in the Roman world to Caesar's heir, Octavian, and ushered in an era of autocracy which was to last half a millennium in the West, and one and a half millennia in the East. The republican form of government which had served Rome so well for nearly five hundred years had become an anachronism in an age which saw the city on the Tiber as the centre of a world empire encompassing almost the entire Mediterrranean basin.

Ironically, in hastening her rise to greatness Rome owed much to her old rival, the Phoenician colony of Carthage situated on the northern coastline of Africa to the west of Sicily. It was in the two great conflicts with Carthage, known as the First and Second Punic Wars (264–241 BC and 218–202 BC) that the Romans became masters of the art of warfare, at sea as well as on land. This was simply a matter of survival, for if Rome had not prevailed then Carthage would certainly have destroyed her and thereafter western European history would surely have taken a different course. But the Romans emerged from the initial conflict with a valuable new martial skill (naval warfare) and their first overseas provinces (Sicily, Sardinia and Corsica); and from the second with a superbly disciplined infantry force which was to prove more than a match for any of its opponents during the numerous wars of the 2nd century BC.

The Second Punic War had ended with the Roman victory over the Carthaginian leader Hannibal at the battle of Zama, 202 BC. The Roman forces were commanded by the 34-year-old Publius Cornelius Scipio (Scipio Africanus). It was his personal achievement that over a remarkably short period of time a citizen militia had been transformed into a virtually invincible fighting machine. As the conqueror of the mighty Hannibal Scipio became the first in a long line of military commanders whose deeds raised them above ordinary men. His prestige in Rome at the turn of the century was probably higher than that of any Roman before him and yet, with all his personal glory, he posed no threat to the established institutions of the Republic. Such threats were surely to come but more than a century was to pass before the political climate had changed sufficiently for the authority of a great soldier to be able to challenge that of the Conscript Fathers themselves.

The stage was now set for Rome's first military encounter with the mighty Greek kingdoms of the eastern Mediterranean, successor states to the vast empire conquered by Alexander the Great a century and a quarter before. Two of the three principal kingdoms (Macedon and Syria) were, at the beginning of the 2nd century BC, under the rule of strong and expansionist monarchs, respectively Philip V and Antiochus III, the Great. The other major kingdom, Egypt, was in a period of decline, the throne being occupied by a minor (Ptolemy V Epiphanes) with affairs of state left to the care of unscrupulous and incompetent ministers. Neither Philip nor Antiochus were friendly to the nascent Italian state which had just eclipsed the power of Carthage – as early as 215 BC Philip had even entered into an alliance with the Romans' sworn enemy Hannibal – and Rome was justifiably concerned that the kings of Macedon and Syria had designs on Egypt and its foreign possessions.

Embassies were sent from Rome to the Egyptian capital of Alexandria, in 200 BC and again in 196, in a vain attempt to curb the influence of Antiochus of Syria who had already laid claim to large areas of Ptolemaic territory. But it was with Philip of Macedon that the first military conflict came. After three years of somewhat inconclusive fighting in the Second Macedonian War the Roman general T. Quinctius Flamininus inflicted a crushing defeat on Philip V at the battle of Cynoscephalae (197 BC). At the Isthmian Games in the following year Flamininus, posing as the champion of liberty, proclaimed the 'Freedom of Greece' in a highly emotional and melodramatic ceremony. This instantly made him an object of veneration amongst the Greeks, a position never before enjoyed by a Roman. One cannot doubt Flamininus' sincerity in his philhellenism and it is unlikely in the extreme that he was placing self-aggrandizement over the legitimate interests of the Roman state. But his actions did have certain remarkable consequences, such as the establishment of cult worship in his name and, even more importantly from a numismatic standpoint, the issue of gold coins bearing his name and portrait. Never before had a living Roman been depicted on a coin, and another 152 years were to elapse before contemporary portraiture made its first appearance on the currency of the Roman Republic, just prior to Caesar's assassination. Yet, as in the case of Scipio Africanus, the extraordinary fame and glory achieved by Flamininus aroused no fears in republican Rome that he had designs on usurping the constitution. The victor of Cynoscephalae continued for some years as a loyal and successful commander, in accordance with the policies of the Senate, and later retired into the relative obscurity of Roman aristocratic life.

Cynoscephalae broke the power of the Macedonian monarchy, though Philip V retained his throne until his death in 179 BC. Rome's victory in the

Second Macedonian War made inevitable a trial of strength with Antiochus the Great of Syria, a conflict which was not long delayed. The Syrian king invaded Greece in 192 BC at the invitation of the Aetolians, but his advance was soon checked by the Romans and the theatre of war then shifted to Asia Minor. Here, Rome benefited from her alliances with the kingdom of Pergamum and the great maritime power of Rhodes, and the issue was finally decided in a pitched battle fought beneath the walls of the Lydian city of Magnesia ad Sipylum (189 BC). Scipio Africanus, conqueror of Hannibal, together with his brother Scipio Asiagenus achieved a momentous victory over the Syrian army. Antiochus was obliged to retire to his eastern territories, where he was murdered two years later, and the Seleucid kingdom ceased to be a major factor in the politics of the eastern Mediterranean area. The main beneficiary of Antiochus' downfall was Rome's faithful ally, the kingdom of Pergamum, the territories of which were vastly expanded through the acquisition of the former Seleucid possessions in western Asia Minor.

In the space of little more than a decade (202–189 BC) Rome had been catapulted into the position of a major Mediterranean power. Macedon was finally conquered in 168 BC when King Perseus, son of Philip V, was defeated by the general L. Aemilius Paullus. The country was then given a republican constitution and, eventually, was annexed as a Roman province in 146 BC. The same year saw the final destruction of Carthage, in the Third Punic War, and the creation of the province of Africa out of the former territories of Rome's old rival. The Roman commander on this occasion was Scipio Aemilianus, a son of Macedon's conqueror L. Aemilius Paullus, who had been adopted into the Cornelia family by the elder son of Scipio Africanus. A little later in the century King Attalus III of Pergamum secretly willed his kingdom to Rome, and on his death in 133 BC a large area of western Asia Minor had to be hastily organized as the province of Asia.

Inevitably, as novel political and religious ideas flowed into the city on the Tiber from the farthest reaches of the civilized world, the traditional values and institutions of Roman life were increasingly called into question. This process was to be a slow but inexorable one, and by the opening decades of the 1st century bc the political climate in Rome had evolved sufficiently for men to begin to think in terms of powerful individuals usurping the constitutional prerogatives of the Senate. This marked a real turning point in history for it signalled the first stirrings of the acceptance of the principle of autocratic government in the Roman world. Of enormous significance in this evolution were the military reforms carried out by Gaius Marius in the closing years of the 2nd century BC. By enlisting landless citizens (proletarii) in his army Marius solved the problem of the acute shortage of military manpower and, more significantly, created an army which owed its primary allegiance to its commander rather than to the elected magistrates of the Republic. Marius rapidly became the most influential man in the Roman world and held the consulship for an unprecedented five consecutive years (104–100 BC). His military reforms also made possible the rise of other powerful individuals: Pompeius Strabo, father of Pompey the Great, who distinguished himself in the Social War and then refused to disband his army in defiance of the government at Rome; and Cornelius Sulla who, also at the head of a loyal army of

Social War veterans, seized power in Rome in 88 BC and obtained for himself the coveted military command against Mithradates, king of Pontus. Later, on his return from the East in 83 BC, Sulla established an autocratic regime in the capital, enacted sweeping constitutional reforms, presided over a virtual reign of terror through his notorious proscription lists, and secured his own personal immunity through election to the office of dictator.

These critical years also witnessed the births and early careers of the two men who were destined to bring the transitional process to its logical conclusion by plunging the Republic into an era of civil war which was to see the end of Senatorial government in Rome. Gnaeus Pompeius Magnus (Pompey the Great) was born on 29 September 106 BC, the son of Gnaeus Pompeius Strabo, consul in 89 BC and a distinguished commander in the Social War. Six years later, on 13 July 100 BC, Gaius Julius Caesar entered the world in an unpretentious house in the somewhat disreputable Subura district of Rome, a short distance from the Forum Romanum. The paths followed by these two individuals to their final tragic destinies were very different ones. From its beginning the career of Pompey was highly unorthodox. He seems to have had little regard for the normal conventions of Roman aristocratic life, preferring instead to rely on the power and influence vested in him through the command of armies, a trait doubtless inherited from his father. In this respect he would seem to have been the true architect of the downfall of the republican constitution but, though his character was complex and enigmatic in the extreme, it is doubtful whether he possessed the vision and subtlety to conceive and carry through such a grand design. Rather, he filled the role of a magnificent figurehead of a movement away from republicanism which had been gathering momentum for some time, though it may be doubted whether this truly reflected his own personal views on the matter. Cicero's loyalty to him would seem to indicate that he projected quite a different image to his close associates. Whatever the truth of the matter, it was certainly not through the schemes of Pompey that the rule of the Senate was finally brought to an end, but rather through the genius of his arch rival Caesar whose very name has come down through the centuries as being synonymous with autocratic government.

By the time he was twenty-five, in 81 BC, Pompey had already raised his own army, assisted the dictator Sulla to achieve supreme power, and celebrated a triumph in Rome for his victories in Sicily and Africa. In comparison, Caesar appears to have accomplished little by the time he had reached the same age, in 75 BC, and the seemingly unremarkable young aristocrat attracted little attention as he pursued the traditional cursus honorum. At this stage of their careers none could have foreseen that a quarter of a century later the bitter political rivalry between these two men would erupt into a conflict which, ultimately, would bring about the downfall of the Roman Republic. Their paths did not cross in ernest until the latter part of the 60s BC when Caesar's involvement in the schemes of Licinius Crassus, a jealous rival of Pompey, marked the beginning of his own challenge to the supremacy of the famous general. At this time Pompey was achieving further glory in the East through his victories over the Mediterranean pirates and over Mithradates of Pontus. He took it upon himself to reorganize Rome's territories in the area,

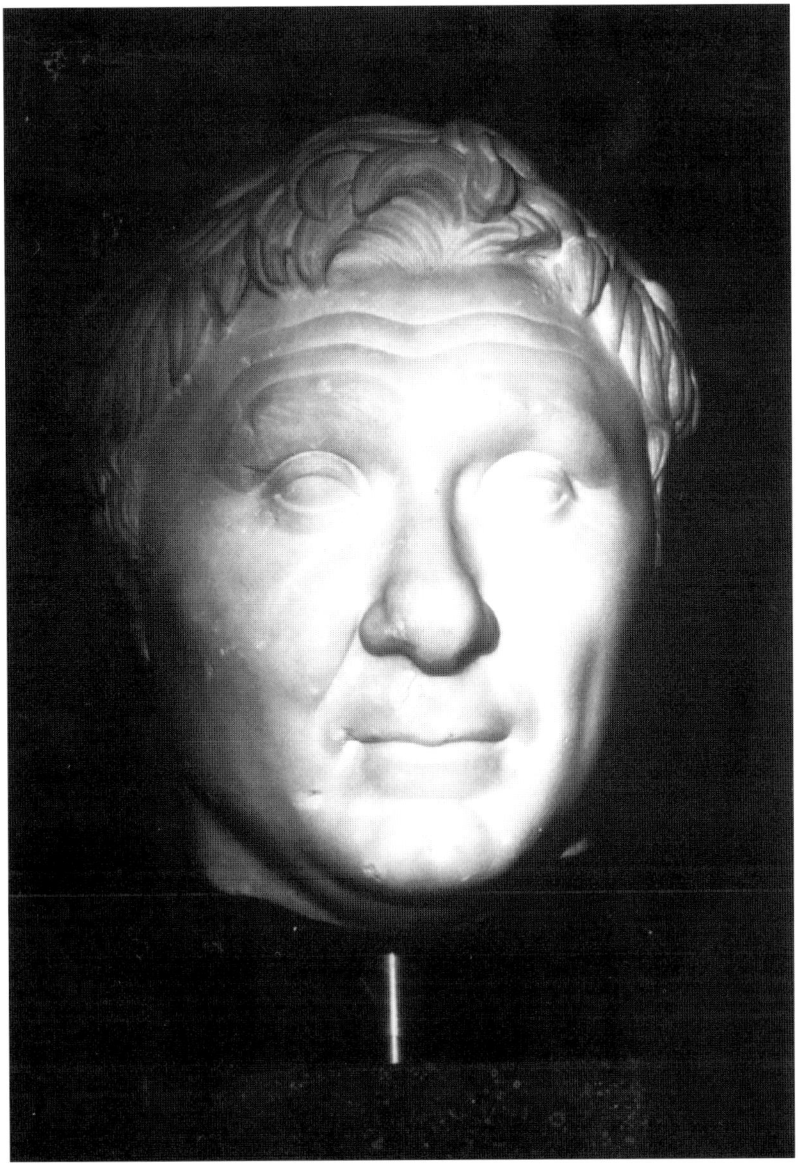

Few portrait busts of Pompey the Great survive, but his distinctive features, when compared to the coins, leave no doubt as to his identification. Marble bust, Ny Carlsberg Glyptotek, Copenhagen.

creating the new provinces of Syria and Cilicia out of the now defunct Seleucid kingdom and settling affairs in Judaea. These activities further aroused the suspicions of the conservative senatorial establishment, the optimates, who attempted to curb Pompey's power on his return to Italy in 62 BC.

In the meantime Caesar's career had been flourishing in Rome. 63 BC saw his election to the prestigious lifetime office of pontifex maximus, against optimate opposition, and the next year brought a praetorship followed by a successful military command in Spain. Caesar was now poised to occupy the highest magistracy of the Republic. In 59 BC he embarked on the first of his five consulships and at last it became possible for him to take the initiative in the political game being played out in Rome. He quickly saw the advantages to be gained by proposing an anti-optimate coalition between himself, Pompey and Crassus, thus bringing into being the First Triumvirate. Although not an officially constituted body, like the Second Triumvirate sixteen years later, this alliance between the three most powerful and influential men in Rome was a force to be reckoned with and one which could not easily be opposed, even by the Senate. It led to Caesar obtaining a five-year proconsular command in Gaul which was to provide him with the military prestige and resources which he needed to make his ultimate bid for supreme power a decade later.

This uneasy rapprochement between three politically ambitious men continued for some years. Each was distrustful of the motives and long-term goals of the others, but as long as there were three partners it was difficult for one to step too far out of line without risking the joint opposition of the other two. The delicate balance of power was fatally disrupted in 53 BC when Crassus, in desperate pursuit of military glory to rival that of his two colleagues, was defeated and killed near Carrhae during his invasion of Parthian Mesopotamia. Caesar and Pompey were left to face one another as rivals for supremacy in the Roman world. The final conflict between the conqueror of Gaul and the conqueror of Mithradates could not now be long delayed.

CHAPTER 1

Pharsalus – the Civil War between Caesar and Pompey and its aftermath, 49–47 BC

After Crassus' death the advantage in the rivalry between the two surviving Triumvirs seemed to rest firmly with Pompey. He was securely established in the capital, where he could easily enhance his already overwhelming influence amongst the Roman aristocracy, and his adherents seized every opportunity to portray the absent Caesar as a potential threat to the security of the state. Caesar's proconsular command in Gaul prevented him from setting foot in Italy to defend his own interests, but his trump card was his stalwart army of seasoned veterans who were enthusiastically devoted to their charismatic commander. In contrast, Pompey's army was stationed in distant Spain, their leader having chosen to remain in Rome rather than take up his proconsular command in 54 BC.

Matters came to a head in the opening days of the year 49 BC. Though he was clearly unprepared for the outbreak of war Pompey's hand was forced by the two consuls who, acting independently of the vacillating Senate, placed a sword in his hand and bade him, on their authority, to take command of the Republic's forces in Italy and lead them against Caesar. The young tribune Marcus Antonius (Mark Antony) had argued on Caesar's behalf before the Conscript Fathers, his eloquence contributing to their indecision. We thus meet for the first time one of the central characters in the great drama which was to be played out over the following two decades. The hasty action of the consuls L. Cornelius Lentulus and C. Claudius Marcellus was plainly a serious blunder. Not only did it place Pompey constitutionally in the wrong, but it gave Caesar the perfect opportunity to utilize his military superiority on the pretext of defending himself against an aggressor. Events then moved quickly. On 10 January Caesar crossed the Rubicon and advanced rapidly on Rome, thus precipitating the civil war by returning to Italian soil whilst still in possession of his proconsular military command. Caesar carried all before him and his adversary soon realized, if he had not known it from the start, that he would have to abandon not only Rome itself but quit Italy altogether. Accordingly, Pompey decided on an immediate evacuation to Greece where he could set about assembling an adequate army with which to oppose Caesar. He commanded the members of the Senate to accompany him and many of them dutifully did so, including M. Porcius Cato (Cato Uticensis) and, eventually, a reluctant and disillusioned Cicero.

Despite his abandonment of the capital Pompey's position was by no means desperate. He still had powerful forces at his disposal and Caesar would be hard pressed to challenge his opponent simultaneously on two fronts – in Spain as well as Greece. These thoughts would have been uppermost in Caesar's mind when he arrived in Rome, having just failed to cut off Pompey's embarkation from the port of Brundisium. The situation in the capital was chaotic, as most of the elected magistrates had fled with Pompey, and Caesar was obliged to spend valuable time in organizing a provisional government. Rome was placed under the authority of a praetor, the future Triumvir M. Aemilius Lepidus, and the 33-year-old noble, Mark Antony, was appointed commander-in-chief in Italy.

Realizing that time was of the essence, with Pompey busily gathering recruits for his army in the East, Caesar decided to strike first by launching a lightning attack on the Pompeian forces in Spain. With typical Caesarian humour he boasted to his friends that he was going to fight an army without a general and would return to fight a general without an army.[1] He hastened west, delayed briefly by the resistance of the Greek city of Massilia in southern Gaul, which had remained staunchly pro-Pompeian, and after initial setbacks forced the surrender of the generals Afranius and Petreius. Their legions were disbanded and in Further Spain Pompey's legate Varro was likewise obliged to submit to Caesar, thus eliminating for the time being the Pompeian threat in the West (August, 49 BC).

The victor now hurried back to Rome where he had been named dictator in his absence. After presiding over the magisterial elections for the coming year, in which he himself was designated as consul, and introducing measures to alleviate the financial hardships caused by the civil war, Caesar now turned his attention to his main task – the final trial of strength with Pompey. The 'general without an army' had not been idle during his year in Greece and had managed to put together and train a sizeable force of new recruits. However, the loss of his legions in Spain was a severe blow and he must have known that his hastily assembled army would be no match for Caesar's veterans in a pitched battle. Accordingly, as he received intelligence of his opponent's preparations at Brundisium he took up a strong defensive position on the coast of Illyricum near Dyrrhachium. Caesar's main weakness lay in his lack of naval power and he was forced to split his army in two in order to transport all his troops across the Adriatic. Had Pompey seized his opportunity at this point he might have gained a decisive victory over his weakened adversary but, as usual, he exercised great caution and made no move. Eventually, the second contingent of Caesar's army, under the command of Antony, succeeded in evading the Pompeian blockade and effected a juncture with their comrades in Epirus.

The two great leaders now confronted one another militarily for the first time. Caesar was anxious to utilize his advantage by giving battle, but Pompey could not be induced to risk an engagement. The stalemate continued for some time until Pompey made a sudden assault on Caesar's thinly stretched lines of blockade. Pompey had drawn first blood but he failed to press home his advantage. Caesar was able to withdraw into Thessaly, hoping thereby to encourage the enemy into some rash military action. The manœuvrings continued for some time and Caesar's lieutenant Domitius Calvinus failed in his attempt to intercept the forces of Metellus Scipio, governor of Syria, who was hastening to Pompey's aid. Calvinus could not prevent the union of the two Pompeian armies, and shortly thereafter Caesar and Pompey finally met on the field of battle near the Thessalian town of Pharsalus (9 August 48 BC). Encouraged by the timely arrival of reinforcements, and by his success at Dyrrhachium, the wary Pompey had at last been persuaded by his advisers to risk a pitched battle, confident that he now had the measure of his opponent. The result was an overwhelming victory for Caesar and his loyal veterans, many of whom had served under his banner for a full decade. Their superior fighting qualities more than compensated for Pompey's cavalry advantage on which he was pinning all his hopes, and by the end of the day the less disciplined Pompeian army had been totally routed and put to flight.

Pompey himself, experiencing for the first time in his long military career the anguish of defeat, fled to the coast and took ship to Egypt. He cherished the hope that his great prestige in the East, dating from his victory over Mithradates 15 years before, would enable him to re-establish his power and offer a renewed challenge to the victor of Pharsalus. However, the royal house of Egypt which, ironically, owed its very survival to Pompey through the actions of his legate Gabinius, was filled with alarm at the reported approach of mighty Caesar's defeated adversary. The young Ptolemy XIII and his advisers decided that the easiest way out of their predicament was to murder Pompey as soon as he set foot on Egyptian soil. In this way they hoped to gain Caesar's favour whilst eliminating the risk of Pompey's wrath should they have refused sanctuary to the eventual victor in the civil war. Thus, the famous general and imperator, Gnaeus Pompeius Magnus, met an ignominious end on the Mediterranean shore of the Ptolemaic kingdom of Egypt (28 September 48 BC). Caesar arrived on the scene soon afterwards and seemed genuinely grieved that his former colleague in the Triumvirate had suffered such a tragic fate. But in his heart he must have been grateful that a potentially dangerous and embarrassing situation had been averted by the independent action of others.

Thus ended the first phase of the civil war less than 21 months after Caesar's crossing of the Rubicon. Already one of the two principal contenders in the struggle had perished and Caesar seemed to have triumphed over all opposition to his supremacy in the Roman world. But Pompey was survived by two sons and many of his former adherents remained loyal to his memory. In addition, many citizens of the Republic felt uneasy concerning Caesar's long-term political ambitions and they awaited developments with apprehension.

The victor soon became embroiled in the machinations of Egyptian politics where the young Queen Cleopatra was involved in a struggle for supremacy with her brother Ptolemy XIII. Captivated by her youthful charm Caesar lent his support to Cleopatra enabling her to prevail over her rival, who perished by drowning in the course of his flight. The late king's younger brother, Ptolemy XIV, now became Cleopatra's junior colleague on the throne of Egypt. After dallying in the Land of the Nile for about 7 months Caesar was obliged to hasten to Asia Minor where Pharnaces, son of the late Pontic king Mithradates VI, had risen in revolt claiming the whole of his father's former realm. In a lightning campaign Caesar crushed his opponent at the battle of Zela (August 47 BC), an achievement which he later commemorated in his triumph with the famous motto *veni, vidi, vici* – 'I came, I saw, I conquered'.

But the conqueror's extended absence in the East had allowed the remnants of the Pompeian party to regroup in north Africa and to offer renewed opposition to his supremacy. Never a man to shrink from vital tasks, it is likely that Caesar would have preferred to proceed directly to Africa to confront his opponents rather than return to Rome. But during his sojourn in the East events had taken an ugly turn in Italy where Antony had been left in charge. Civil disorder had broken out, the result of widespread financial hardship which had been only partially alleviated by the dictator's emergency measures hurriedly enacted prior to his departure for Greece. Worse still, mutiny had broken out amongst some of the legions stationed in Campania. This potentially disastrous situation, the handling of which had proved to be quite beyond Antony's abilities, was easily defused by Caesar on his arrival in Rome. All interest which had accrued on loans from the outbreak of the war was cancelled, and the mutinous legions were quieted by the promise of vast booty to be divided following victory in Africa. Antony, who had been too preoccupied with the acquisition of confiscated private property to properly fulfil his mandate from Caesar, was treated with coldness by his commander and was to remain in disfavour for the next year or more. Caesar at last felt free to give his undivided attention to the growing power of the Pompeians in Africa where formidable forces were now arrayed against him. In addition to the legions commanded by Scipio these included the considerable army of King Juba of Numidia, an implacable enemy of Caesar who had defeated and killed the dictator's lieutenant Curio in 49 BC. The royal army boasted some thirty thousand men, many of them trained as Roman legionaries, and included at least sixty war-elephants: these, however, were eventually to prove fatal to the Pompeian cause. On leaving Rome Caesar first crossed to Sicily, which was to serve as his advanced base for the military operations, and quickly set about organizing his invasion force. With winter now fast approaching he embarked from Lilybaeum, in the far west of the island, with six legions and 2600 cavalry. Ahead of him lay Africa and four months of frustating campaigning before he finally succeeded in bringing the Pompeians to battle.

COINAGE OF THE PERIOD

A. Issues of Pompey and his Supporters

In the opening days of the year 49 BC the city on the Tiber was rife with rumours concerning the activities of Caesar, whose army was reported to be gathering on the northern Italian border. It was in this atmosphere of uncertainty and alarm that the moneyer Q. Sicinius was appointed by the pro-Pompeian government in Rome. The coinage of Sicinius was to be the last normal issue of silver denarii prior to the Caesarian occupation of the city. It ceased when the moneyer fled with the other Pompeians before Caesar's victorious advance.

1

1 Diademed head of Fortuna Populi Romani right, FORT–P R before and behind. *Reverse:* filleted palm-branch and caduceus in saltire, wreath above, Q SICINIVS below, III–VIR across field. *Silver denarius. Rome, early 49 BC.* (Crawford 440; Sydenham 938; BMCRR 3947; Babelon Sicinia 5).

The type clearly refers to Pompey himself, his past achievements, and his anticipated success against Caesar should matters come down to a trial of strength. The goddess Fortuna will surely smile kindly on the great general whose loyal service to Rome has already brought him honour and acclaim, symbolized by the palm-branch and wreath. Apparently contemporary with the coinage of Q. Sicinius was an exceptional issue produced in the name of Cn. Nerius, who was quaestor urbanus at the time of the outbreak of the civil war.

2

2 Bearded head of Saturn right, harpa at shoulder, NERI Q VRB before. *Reverse:* legionary eagle between two standards, L LENT on left, C MARC on right, COS in lower field. *Silver denarius. Rome, early 49 BC* (Crawford 441; Sydenham 937; BMCRR 3950; Babelon Neria 1).

The obvious military nature of this coinage would indicate that it was initiated after news of Caesar's crossing of the Rubicon had been received in Rome. At that point there could no longer be any doubt that the rivalry between Pompey and Caesar would have to be resolved by force of arms, and these types would, therefore, have been most appropriate to the occasion. An interesting feature is that the two consuls whose actions had inadvertently provided Caesar with the justification for invasion (L. Cornelius Lentulus and C. Claudius Marcellus) are both named on the reverse of this issue. Later, they were to resume the minting of silver denarii in their own names as part of the government in exile (see nos. 4–6).

With their retreat to Greece the Pompeians surrendered control of the production of coinage from the capital. All subsequent Pompeian coinages were produced by temporary provincial minting establishments which supplied money as and when the military situation required it. The mint of Rome now became a tool of Caesar and his party and thereafter it remained firmly in Caesarian hands, even after the dictator's assassination in 44 BC. The Pompeian moneyer Q. Sicinius, who had been active in Rome prior to the withdrawal (see no. 1), soon resumed his duties in exile.

3

3a

3b

3 Diademed head of Apollo right, star below, Q SICINIVS before, III VIR behind. *Reverse:* club of Hercules supporting lion's skin, the head in profile to right, arrow and bow in field on either side, C COPONIVS on right, PR S C on left. *Silver denarius. Military mint in the East, 49 BC* (Crawford 444/1a; Sydenham 939; BMCRR East 24; Babelon Sicinia 1).

3a Similar to 3, but the lion's scalp is facing instead of in profile. *Silver denarius. Military mint in the East, 49 BC* (Crawford 444/1b; Sydenham 939b; BMCRR East 29; Babelon Sicinia 2).

3b Similar to 3, but the head of Apollo is to left. *Silver denarius. Military mint in the East, 49 BC* (Crawford 444/1c; Sydenham 940; BMCRR East 30; Babelon Sicinia 4).

On this large issue Sicinius' name is linked with that of another Pompeian who had fled Rome on Caesar's approach, the praetor C. Coponius. In order to assert the validity of the issue the formula S C (*senatus consulto*) is added, indicating that the coins were struck under senatorial authority. This was not wholly untrue, as many of the Conscript Fathers had followed Pompey to Greece. But a Senate in exile had little claim to legitimacy when some of their number had remained in Rome and those who had fled were being replaced by Caesarian nominees. It is possible that the design indicates a mint or mints in the province of Asia as the source of this coinage. A club draped with a lion's skin appears as the standard obverse type on silver half cistophori and quarter cistophori of several important mints in the area, including Ephesus, Pergamum, Sardis, Tralles, and Apamea. Ephesus, as the residence of the proconsul, perhaps has the strongest claim. Grueber[2] suggests that the denarii of Sicinius and Coponius were intended for the use of the Pompeian fleet commanded by the latter, though the volume of the issue perhaps indicates a wider usage.

The exiled consuls Lentulus and Marcellus, whose names had already appeared on the emergency issue from Rome (see no. 2), also participated in the production of coinage to help finance Pompey's military recruitment in the East. The types of these silver denarii are of considerable interest and make reference to family history as well as to the current circumstances of the issues.

4

4 Triskeles, with winged head of Medusa at centre and ears of corn between the legs. *Reverse:* naked Jupiter standing facing, looking right, holding thunderbolt in right hand and eagle on left, LENT and MAR on left, COS and harpa (the latter sometimes omitted) on right. *Silver denarius. Military mint in the East, 49 BC* (Crawford 445/1; Sydenham 1029, 1029a; BMCRR Sicily 1, 3; Babelon Cornelia 64).

This denarius has traditionally been assigned to a Sicilian mint, but the circumstances of the hurried Pompeian withdrawal from Brundisium to Greece make this most unlikely. The obverse type should be regarded as nothing more than a reference to the family history of the consul Marcellus whose ancestor, M. Claudius Marcellus, captured Syracuse in 211 BC during the course of the Second Punic War. Jupiter, chief deity of the Roman pantheon, is the unifying element in the varied coinage produced in the names of the consuls Lentulus and Marcellus.

5

5 Head of Apollo right, with long hair, L LENT C MARC before, COS behind. *Reverse:* naked Jupiter standing facing, looking right, holding thunderbolt in right hand and eagle on left, star and Q on left, garlanded altar on right. *Silver denarius. Apollonia in Illyricum, 49 BC* (Crawford 445/2; Sydenham 1030; BMCRR East 21; Babelon Cornelia 65).

Cicero (*Ad Familiares,* xiii, 29) makes specific mention of silver coinage being struck at Apollonia at this time and describes the city as a headquarters of the Pompeians. The letter Q in the reverse field indicates that a quaestor was also involved in the production of these coins, though with the outcome of the imminent conflict in some doubt he obviously preferred to maintain his anonymity. Cicero, however, has revealed his identity and in Michael Crawford's words 'the coyly anonymous Quaestor … should be identified with T. Antistius'.[3]

6 Head of Jupiter right, with long beard. *Reverse:* cultus statue of the Ephesian Artemis facing, her hands extended with fillet hanging from each, L LENTVLVS on right, MAR COS (rarely C MARC COS) on left. *Silver denarius. Ephesus, 49 BC* (Crawford 445/3; Sydenham 1031, 1031b; BMCRR East 23; Babelon Cornelia 66–7).

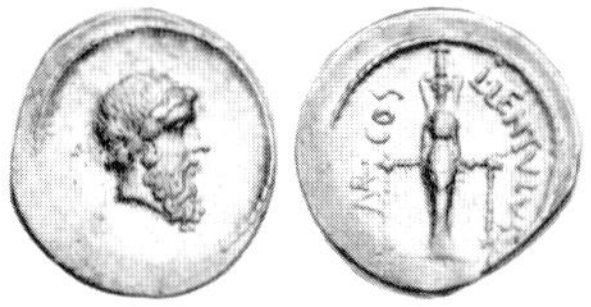

6

Caesar himself records (*De Bello Civili,* iii, 4, 1) that 'He [Pompey] had made up nine legions of Roman citizens – five which he had brought across from Italy; one of veterans, from Cilicia; one from Crete and Macedonia, of veterans who had settled in these provinces after their discharge by their previous commanders; and two from Asia, which Lentulus when consul had ordered to be enrolled'. Thus, we know that Lentulus was active in raising troops for Pompey in the province of Asia, and it seems probable that this denarius was issued at Ephesus in connection with these activities.

The series is completed by two issues bearing Pompey's own name – MAGN (Magnus). On these denarii he is associated with two of his lieutenants, the proquaestors Cn. Calpurnius Piso and Terentius Varro. Pompey himself uses the title of *proconsul* to give a semblance of legitimacy to his production of coinage. This is in marked contrast to the contemporary issues of Caesar who simply uses his own *cognomen* 'CAESAR' as the issuing authority and does not share the responsibility with any subordinate. With the civil war now under way Caesar clearly felt no need for the observance of constitutional niceties.

7 Bearded head of Numa Pompilius right, wearing diadem inscribed NVMA, CN PISO PRO Q behind. *Reverse:* prow of galley right, MAGN above, PRO COS below. *Silver denarius. Mint in Greece, 49–48 BC* (Crawford 446; Sydenham 1032; BMCRR Spain 62; Babelon Pompeia 8; Cohen 4).

7

Although Grueber assigned these issues to Pompey's supporters in Spain it seems much more likely that they were produced in Greece between the time of Pompey's arrival from Italy, early in 49 BC, and the fateful battle of Pharsalus on August 9th of the following year. The obverse type is personal to Piso, the Calpurnia *gens* claiming descent from Calpus, son of Numa Pompilius. The prow refers to Pompey's naval victories, in particular his successes against the pirates in 67 BC.

8 Diademed terminal bust of Jupiter right, VARRO PRO Q behind. *Reverse:* vertical sceptre between dolphin, on left, and eagle, on right, MAGN PRO / COS in two lines in exergue. *Silver denarius. Mint in Greece, 49–48 BC* (Crawford 447/1a; Sydenham 1033; BMCRR Spain 64; Babelon Pompeia 7; Cohen 3).

8

This issue appears to be contemporary with the coinage of Piso, though struck probably at a different mint in Greece. The symbolism of the reverse type is Pompey's illustrious military career and his famous victories by land and sea, notably in the wars against Mithradates of Pontus and the Mediterranean pirates. The terminal bust relates to the extraordinary powers bestowed on Pompey by the Senate extending over almost the whole of the Roman dominions. The proquaestor Varro should not be confused with the famous general and author M. Terentius Varro whose son he may possibly have been. A few specimens are known on which this obverse type is duplicated on the reverse (cf. BMCRR Spain 67–9). This may have been due to a shortage of reverse dies in an emergency situation, but as coins of this type are usually plated or of base metal the likelihood is that they are merely contemporary forgeries.

Before leaving the subject of coinage in the name of *Magnus Proconsul,* mention should be made of a remarkable gold aureus the precise chronology of which is still a subject of dispute but which undoubtedly predates our period by a good number of years. This excessively rare coin (Crawford 402, Sydenham 1028, BMCRR East 20, Babelon Pompeia 6, and Cohen 19) has as its obverse type a head of Africa accompanied by the inscription MAGNVS, whilst the reverse shows Pompey in a triumphal quadriga with PRO COS in the exergue. The most likely occasion for its issue is Pompey's triumph in 71 BC following his return from Spain after the collapse of the Sertorian revolt. The obverse makes reference to his African victory against the Marians a decade earlier. Although not belonging to the period under consideration this type possesses great significance through the unequivocal manner in which it illustrates the unorthodox nature of the power already wielded by Pompey so many years before the outbreak of the civil war with Caesar.

B. Issues of Caesar

With his crossing of the Rubicon and invasion of Italy Caesar would have had an immediate need of money for financing his military operations. This need was largely met by an unusually extensive issue of silver denarii of a single type.

9

9 Elephant walking right, trampling on dragon the head of which rears up before him, CAESAR in exergue. *Reverse:* emblems of the pontificate – simpulum, aspergillum, axe and apex. *Silver denarius. Military mint travelling with Caesar, 49–48 BC* (Crawford 443; Sydenham 1006; BMCRR Gaul 27; Babelon Julia 9; Cohen 49).

At least one obverse die has been noted on which the dragon is omitted, presumably the result of an engraver's error (Numismatic Fine Arts, Auction XXVII, 5 December 1991, lot 602).

It must remain a matter for conjecture whether this coinage commenced in Gaul, as part of Caesar's preparations for invasion, or whether it dates from his acquisition of bullion left behind in the public treasury by the panic-stricken Pompeians when they fled Rome. What does seem certain is that production of this type was kept separate from the regular issues of the Roman moneyers, thus emphasizing the extraordinary military nature of this coinage produced at a time of unprecedented crisis in the affairs of the Republic. It has already been noted that, unlike his rival, Caesar chose to take sole responsibility for the production of coinage despite the obvious unconstitutionality of so doing without possession of a qualifying magistracy and without official sanction from the Senate. Caesar saw this as no obstacle in this time of national crisis and did not hesitate to put into circulation silver denarii bearing nothing more than his own *cognomen* as the issuing authority. The types are also of interest and, presumably, represent Caesar's personal choice. The symbolism of the obverse can hardly be anything other than the triumph of good over evil, whilst the reverse alludes to Caesar's possession of the office of pontifex maximus. It is difficult to assess how long this important type remained in issue, but in all probability it served the needs of the Caesarian forces right up to the time of the final campaign leading to the battle of Pharsalus. Contrary to most other authorities Crawford describes the elephant as the reverse type, though without explaining his reasons for so doing.

The next issue in Caesar's name displays more variety, not only of type but also of denomination.

10 Diademed female head (Clementia?) right, wearing oak-wreath, numeral LII (= 52) behind. *Reverse:* trophy of Gallic arms, with horned helmet, oval shield and carnyx, axe surmounted by animal's head on right, CAE–SAR across lower field. *Gold aureus. Military mint travelling with Caesar, probably commencing after the battle of Pharsalus, 9 August 48 BC* (Crawford 452/1; Sydenham 1008; BMCRR 3953; Babelon Julia 25; Cohen 17).

10

11 Same as preceding. Silver denarius. Military mint travelling with Caesar, probably commencing after the battle of Pharsalus, 9 August 48 BC (Crawford 452/2; Sydenham 1009; BMCRR 3955; Babelon Julia 26; Cohen 18).

11

The gold aureus was the first coin of this denomination to be struck for almost a quarter of a century, since the type described above issued on the occasion of Pompey's triumph in 71 BC. It is ironic that Caesar's aureus was produced in connection with the only major military defeat of Pompey's career. The obverse type symbolizes the victor's policy of leniency towards his fellow citizens against whom he had fought, a policy which was eventually to contribute in no small measure to his own downfall three-and-a-half years later. It has long been recognized that the numeral '52' refers to Caesar's age at the time of the production of these coins, and as he was born on 13 July 100 BC the date of the issue is fixed to the 12-month period commencing 13 July 48. Pharsalus was just 4 weeks after Caesar's 52nd birthday. The reverse celebrates the long years of campaigning in Gaul during which Caesar established his reputation as a military commander of genius. It provides a suitable martial theme for the issue whilst avoiding reference to the current civil conflict, which would ill have served the cause of reconciliation.

12

12 *Obverse:* same as preceding. *Reverse:* trophy of Gallic arms, bearded captive seated right at base, CAE–SAR across central field. *Silver denarius. Military mint travelling with Caesar, probably commencing after the battle of Pharsalus, 9 August 48 BC* (Crawford 452/4; Sydenham 1010; BMCRR 3959; Babelon Julia 28; Cohen 19 variant).

13 Similar to 12, but the captive's head is turned to left, looking up at trophy. *Silver denarius. Military mint travelling with Caesar, probably commencing after the battle of Pharsalus, 9 August 48 BC* (Crawford 452/5; Sydenham 1011; BMCRR 3960; Babelon Julia 27; Cohen 19).

13

These issues, which are considerably rarer than no. 11, probably represent the activity of a secondary mint. The general theme, however, remains the same and dwells on Caesar's earlier military successes in Gaul and the mercy shown to his peers with differing political views, even those who had gone so far as to oppose him on the field of battle. The distinctive figure of a Gallic captive has sometimes been identified as Vercingetorix, the celebrated chieftain of the Arverni, who fell into Caesar's hands at the capture of Alesia in 52 BC and was exhibited in the dictator's magnificent triumph in Rome six years later. However, such an interpretation of the type must be regarded as fanciful. The Romans would hardly have accorded a living enemy the remarkable honour of being depicted on the coinage, albeit as a captive in bondage, and the figure is better regarded as symbolic of the defeated Gallic tribes.

14

14 Veiled female head (Vesta?) right, simpulum and numeral LII (= 52) behind. *Reverse:* trophy of arms, with horned helmet, round shield and sword, wreath on left, ancile on right, CAE–SAR across lower field. *Silver quinarius. Military mint travelling with Caesar, probably commencing after the battle of Pharsalus, 9 August 48 BC* (Crawford 452/3; Sydenham 1012; BMCRR 3961; Babelon Julia 29; Cohen 16).

Crawford[4] identifies the veiled head on obverse as that of Vesta, the Roman goddess of the hearth, whose rites were in the care of the pontifices (Caesar, it will be remembered, had held the office of pontifex maximus since 63 BC). In the reverse field is an ancile, a shield in the shape of a figure of eight, which was recognized as a cult object of Mars. Its appearance on this coin implies some reference to the Salian priesthood, though Caesar is not otherwise known to have had any connection with the Salii. The silver quinarius, or half denarius, had not been struck for many years following its short-lived revival in the opening decades of the 1st century BC. The coin had special associations with Gaul in the late republican period and it seems possible that this may have been a factor in Caesar's decision to resume production, it being especially appropriate to a series devoted to the commemoration of his Gallic victories. The Roman moneyers, presumably acting under Caesar's instructions, also began issuing the quinarius at this time marking the beginning of

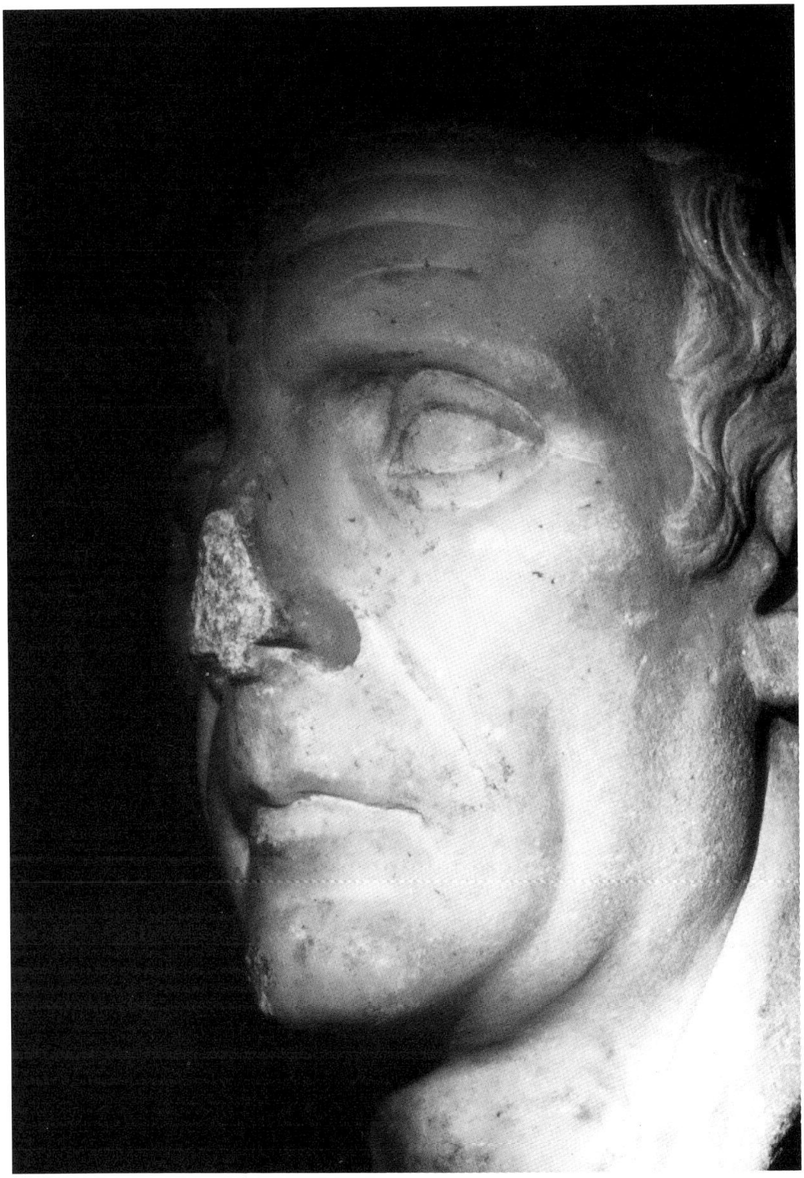

Caesar's receding hairline caused him concern and his enemies amusement, so Suetonius tells us. He therefore highly esteemed the honour granted him by the Senate of wearing a wreath at all times, a feature of his portrait coins. Marble bust, Ny Carlsberg Glyptotek, Copenhagen.

another brief revival of the denomination. This was to extend down to the end of the imperatorial period and into the opening years of the Augustan principate. Production of the half denarius was eventually discontinued by Augustus about 23 BC and thereafter was not issued again until after the downfall of the Julio-Claudian dynasty nine decades later.

15

15 Axe and simpulum, CAESAR on right, DICT on left. *Reverse:* jug and lituus, ITER below, all within laurel-wreath. *Gold aureus. Military mint travelling with Caesar in the East, probably in the course of his journey back to Rome from Alexandria, spring to autumn 47 BC* (Crawford 456/1a; Sydenham 1027; BMCRR East 36; Babelon Julia 15; Cohen 21).

15a Similar to preceding, but CAESAR on left and DICT on right. *Gold aureus. Military mint travelling with Caesar in the East, probably in the course of his journey back to Rome from Alexandria, spring to autumn 47 BC* (Crawford 456/1b – specimen cited from Berlin).

This very rare type, which is not accompanied by any corresponding issue of silver denarii, is dated by Caesar's second dictatorship (*dictator iterum*) to the period October 48 to October 47 BC. Its place of mintage is quite uncertain, but as Caesar was with Cleopatra in Egypt from October 48 BC until the following spring, and then travelled through Syria and Asia Minor on his way back to Rome (which he did not reach until the autumn), it seems reasonable to surmise that these aurei were struck somewhere in the East. They may, perhaps, be connected with the lightning military campaign against Pharnaces II of Bosporus culminating in Caesar's victory at the battle of Zela in August, 47 BC. The types, however, are scarcely martial, the priestly implements on obverse representing the college of pontifices (headed by Caesar as pontifex maximus), those on reverse the college of augurs to which he also belonged. The only reference to victory is in the wreath which surrounds the reverse type, possibly commemorating Zela.

C. Issues of the Roman Moneyers

When Caesar took possession of Rome early in 49 BC, following the flight of Pompey and his supporters, his urgent need of money was partially met by the production of denarii of the elephant/pontifical emblems type (see no. 9). This coinage was produced solely in the name of Caesar from a mint presumably located within his military camp. However, it was important that the normal production of coinage at the Capitoline mint should be resumed as quickly as possible and to this end Caesar instructed the moneyer Manius Acilius Glabrio, who was probably the son of the consul of 67 BC, to take over the position vacated by the pro-Pompeian Quintus Sicinius who had fled into exile (see no. 1, also nos. 3–3b). It cannot be determined whether Acilius already held the office of moneyer prior to Caesar's arrival in Rome, and decided to support the new regime, or whether he was actually Caesar's nominee. The reverse legend, which proclaims him as one of the *tresviri monetales* (college of three moneyers), may possibly indicate the former as being the more likely alternative. But whatever the origin of his appointment Acilius' coinage is a large and important one and must have played a vital role in the opening phase of Caesar's rule in Rome.

16

16 Laureate head of Salus right, SALVTIS upwards behind. *Reverse:* Valetudo standing left, resting left elbow on column and holding snake in uplifted right hand, MN ACILIVS III VIR VALETV around (MN and

TV ligatured). *Silver denarius. Rome, 49 BC* (Crawford 442/1a; Sydenham 922; BMCRR 3944; Babelon Acilia 8).

16a Similar to preceding, but **SALVTIS** downwards. *Silver denarius. Rome, 49 BC* (Crawford 442/1b; Sydenham 922; BMCRR 3943; Babelon Acilia 8).

16a

The theme of this issue is good health personified by the goddesses Salus and Valetudo. Mommsen (*Histoire de la monnaie romaine,* ii, p. 498) seems to have come up with the best interpretation of the types suggesting that they refer to the arrival in Rome, in 219 BC, of the Greek physician Archagathus who set up his practise at a cross roads named after the Acilia *gens*. In consequence of this, for some reason which is not entirely clear, the family claimed the notable distinction of having been responsible for the introduction of professional medicine into the city. This coin type, dwelling solely on the moneyer's family history and drawing attention to his constitutional authority through the inclusion of his official title, provides a nice balance to the contemporary and wholly unconstitutional issue in Caesar's name (see no. 9).

For the following year (48 BC) a full college of three moneyers was appointed. Rome was, of course, now firmly under Caesarian control and this is often reflected in the choice of coin types. A special feature of the coinage of this period was the reintroduction of the two fractional silver denominations, the quinarius (half denarius) and the sestertius (quarter denarius), which had not been struck since the opening decades of the 1st century BC.

17 Diademed female head (Clementia?) right, wearing oak-wreath. *Reverse:* Victory advancing right, her wings spread, holding caduceus in right hand and trophy of Gallic arms over left shoulder, **L HOSTILIVS SASERNA** (or **SASERN**) around. *Silver denarius. Rome, 48 BC* (Crawford 448/1a–b; Sydenham 951, 951a; BMCRR 3989, 3993; Babelon Hostilia 5).

17

This and the following two types were issued in the name of the moneyer Lucius Hostilius Saserna about whose subsequent career history is silent. His coinage concentrates on the theme of Caesar's conquests in Gaul and thus complements the military issues of Caesar himself which probably commenced after the battle of Pharsalus on August 9th (see nos. 10–14). Saserna's coinage should thus be regarded as belonging to the latter part of the year 48 BC. This obverse type would seem to be identical to Caesar's issues of aurei and denarii (nos. 10–13) though omitting the age-numeral '52'.

18 Head of captive Gallic warrior right, with long pointed beard and flowing hair, chain around his neck, Gallic shield behind. *Reverse:* naked Gallic warrior in galloping biga driven right by charioteer holding whip, he faces backwards and hurls spear with right hand and holds shield on left arm, **L HOSTILIVS** above, **SASERN** (or **SASERNA**) below. *Silver denarius. Rome, 48 BC* (Crawford 448/2a–b; Sydenham 952, 952a; BMCRR 3994; Babelon Hostilia 2).

18

This type clearly symbolizes Caesar's Gallic conquests during his proconsular command through the years 58–50 BC. The striking head on obverse has often, though rather fancifully, been identified as that of Vercingetorix, the celebrated chieftain of the Arverni (see the commentary following no. 13). The spirited reverse type is of interest for its depiction of the manner in which the Celtic aristocracy of Gaul, and presumably of Britain also, utilized their chariots in combat.

19

19 Head of female Gallic captive right, her hair long and dishevelled, Gallic trumpet (carnyx) behind. *Reverse:* cult statue of Diana (Artemis) facing, her right hand resting on head of stag leaping left at her feet and holding vertical spear in left, **L HOSTILIVS** on right, **SASERNA** on left. *Silver denarius. Rome, 48 BC* (Crawford 448/3; Sydenham 953; BMCRR 3996; Babelon Hostilia 4).

This interesting type would seem to refer to an incident in the early stages of the civil war between Caesar and Pompey. It will be remembered that shortly after taking possession of Rome Caesar had marched west to confront the Pompeian forces in Spain. His advance was briefly hampered by the stubborn resistance of the Greek city of Massilia (modern *Marseille*) on the southern coastline of Gaul and he was obliged to spend valuable time in organizing a siege by sea as well as by land. Having made the necessary arrangements he continued on his march to Spain leaving others to take care of the reduction of Massilia. Ultimately it fell into Caesarian hands and on his journey home following his success in Spain Caesar was able to visit the city. Although the inhabitants were spared the usual atrocities of retribution Massilia was nevertheless deprived of its extensive territories and ceased to exercise any independent political influence in western Mediterranean affairs. The reverse type of this denarius commemorates the episode through its depiction of an archaic statue of the Ephesian Artemis (Diana of the Ephesians). This deity was held in special reverence by the Greek citizens of Massilia (originally a colony of Phocaea founded *c.*600 BC) and the city possessed a splendid temple erected in honour of the goddess.

20

20 Mask of bearded Pan right, **PANSA** below. *Reverse:* Jupiter Axurus (or Anxurus) seated left, head facing, laureate and naked to waist, holding patera in extended right hand and resting on sceptre held in left, **C VIBIVS C F C N IOVIS AXVR** around. *Silver denarius. Rome, 48 BC* (Crawford 449/1a; Sydenham 947; BMCRR 3978; Babelon Vibia 18).

One obverse die has been noted on which the engraver has repeated the moneyer's praenomen by inserting the letter **C** *before* **PANSA** *(Numismatic Fine Arts Auction XXVII, 5 December 1991, lot 549). This coin is probably a hybrid combining a reverse die of Pansa's sole* *coinage with an obverse die of the joint issue with his colleague D. Junius Brutus (see no. 28).*

20a

20b

20a Similar to 20, but with shepherd's staff (pedum) behind mask of Pan, and the moneyer's name on reverse is in a straight line instead of curved round. *Silver denarius. Rome, 48 BC* (Crawford 449/1b; Sydenham 948; BMCRR 3980; Babelon Vibia 19).

20b Similar to 20a, but with syrinx (Pan-pipe) instead of pedum behind mask of Pan. *Silver denarius. Rome, 48 BC* (Crawford 449/1c; Sydenham 948a).

Gaius Vibius Pansa Caetronianus was the adoptive son of the C. Vibius Pansa who held the office of moneyer at the time of the Social War (*c.*90 BC). After his own moneyership he was first appointed governor of Bithynia (47–46 BC), then of Cisalpine Gaul (45 BC), and was designated by Caesar for the consulship in 43 BC – a good example of the possible rapidity of advancement in public life in Caesarian Rome. In the maelstrom of intrigue and political manœuvrings following Caesar's assassination Pansa embarked on his consulship with Aulus Hirtius as his colleague. Both consuls, however, perished in office following the raising of Antony's siege of Mutina despite their success in this operation. Rumour had it that Pansa, already wounded at Forum Gallorum, was a victim of Caesar's 19-year-old heir Octavian who saw an opportunity to take his place as consul. Unlike the coinage of Hostilius Saserna, the types of which are pure Caesarian propaganda, that of Pansa would seem to be principally concerned with his own family history. The obverse type of no. 20 and its variants represents nothing more than a pun on the moneyer's *cognomen* Pansa. It is, in fact, copied from the coinage of his adoptive father issued more than forty years before. The reverse, however, is of more interest. Jupiter Axurus (more correctly Anxurus) would seem to refer to some family connection with Tarracina the earlier name of which was Anxur. Situated on the west coast of Italy, about 100 kilometres (62 miles) south-east of Rome, the city possessed a famous shrine of Jupiter on its acropolis. Here the god was represented as a handsome youth just as he appears on the denarii of C. Vibius Pansa.

21 Head of young Bacchus or Liber right, wearing wreath of ivy tied with fillet, **PANSA** behind. *Reverse:* Ceres walking right, holding a lighted torch in each outstretched hand, plough before, **C VIBIVS C F C N** behind. *Silver denarius. Rome, 48 BC* (Crawford 449/2; Sydenham 946; BMCRR 3976; Babelon Vibia 16).

21

22

22a

22 *Obverse:* same as preceding. *Reverse:* Ceres in chariot drawn right by two snakes, holding reins in right hand and torch in outstretched left, C VIBIVS C F C N below and on right, reading outwards. *Silver denarius. Rome, 48 BC* (Crawford 449/3a; Sydenham 945; BMCRR 3973; Babelon Vibia 17).

22a Similar to preceding, but C VIBIVS C F C N on right and below, reading inwards. *Silver denarius. Rome, 48 BC* (Crawford 449/3b; Sydenham 945; BMCRR 3975; Babelon Vibia 17).

Crawford considers that Liber (an Italian deity equivalent to Bacchus) is perhaps a family type of the Vibii.[5] A similar head of the god appears on denarii of the moneyer C. Vibius Varus who held office in 42 BC (see no. 192). The type of Ceres (the Greek Demeter) bearing lighted torches is again inspired by the coinage of Pansa's adoptive father (cf. Crawford 342/3) and is illustrative of the goddess's search for her lost daughter Proserpina (Persephone) who had been abducted to the underworld by Hades.

23

23 Laureate head of Libertas right, wearing necklace of pendants and cruciform earring, LIBERTATIS behind. *Reverse:* Roma seated right, head facing, on pile of arms, crowned by Victory flying left, sword in sheath at her waist, her left foot set on globe, resting on sceptre held in right hand, C PANSA C F C N on left. *Silver denarius. Rome, 48 BC* (Crawford 449/4; Sydenham 949; BMCRR 3983; Babelon Vibia 20).

Unlike Pansa's other denarius types this one appears to be concerned with contemporary events. Libertas and victorious Roma must surely relate to the recent successes of Caesar in driving Pompey and his supporters from the capital and defeating the Pompeian generals in Spain. By this means Caesar had restored 'liberty' to the Roman people. Half a decade later Libertas was to appear on the coinage of the tyrannicides Brutus and Cassius who likewise claimed to have freed the Romans from oppression by the assassination of Caesar on the Ides of March, 44 BC.

24

24 Laureate and draped bust of Mercury right, wearing winged diadem. *Reverse:* tortoise, caduceus on right, C PANSA on left. *Silver sestertius. Rome, 48 BC* (Crawford 449/5; Sydenham 950; BMCRR 3986; Babelon Vibia 21).

Mercury (the Roman equivalent of the Greek Hermes), the winged messenger of the gods, was regarded as the protector of merchants and of commerce which, doubtless, was greatly facilitated by the restoration of the two fractional silver denominations, the sestertius and the quinarius. The tortoise on reverse alludes to Mercury's invention of the lyre for which he used the shell of the reptile as a sounding box. The silver sestertius, or quarter denarius, was originally introduced in the currency reform of *c.*211 BC. Discontinued after only a few years of issue (*c.*208 BC) the denomination did not reappear for well over a century. The passage of the *Lex Papiria* in 91 BC authorized the revival of the silver sestertius as well as the production of bronze coins on the semuncial weight standard. Sestertii of this period bear the inscription **E L P** which may be expanded to *ex lege Papiria* – 'in accordance with the Papirian Law'. Issue of the denomination then lapsed again for about four decades until the time of Caesar's rule in Rome when it was revived during the moneyership of C. Vibius Pansa. Unlike the silver quinarius (half denarius), also revived at about this time, the silver sestertius ceased to be issued with Caesar's downfall in 44 BC and was never again minted. When the sestertius reappeared about 18 BC, as part of Augustus' arrangements for his new imperial coinage, it was as a large base metal coin struck in orichalcum (brass).

25 Head of young Mars right, wearing crested helmet. *Reverse:* two carnyces (Gallic trumpets) in saltire, oval shield above, round shield below, **ALBINVS** (or **ALBINV**) on right, **BRVTI F** on left. *Silver denarius. Rome, 48 BC* (Crawford 450/1; Sydenham 941, 941a; BMCRR 3962; Babelon Postumia 11).

25

This type, like those of Hostilius Saserna, commemorates Caesar's success in the Gallic Wars. It was especially appropriate to this moneyer because of the various commands which he had held during these campaigns. The career of Decimus Junius Brutus is better known to us than most of the moneyers of this period. Probably the son of the D. Junius D.f. Brutus who was consul in 77 BC, he was later adopted by some member of the Postumia *gens*, possibly the moneyer A. Postumius Albinus who held the office *c.*81 BC. The young Brutus now changed his name to Decimus Postumius Albinus, though on his coins he still proclaims that he is 'the son of Brutus' (*Bruti filius*). In addition to his extensive service under Caesar in the Gallic Wars he was later appointed to command the Caesarian fleet during the blockade of Massilia (June, 49 BC). After serving as moneyer in the following year his loyalty to Caesar was rewarded first with the governorship of Transalpine Gaul and later the promise of the government of Cisalpine Gaul. He was even named in Caesar's will as the dictator's heir if Octavius should reject the inheritance. Despite all this Albinus, son of Brutus, still joined the conspiracy against Caesar in 44 BC and was one of the assassins on the Ides of March. He should not, of course, be confused with the more famous Marcus Junius Brutus who, with Cassius, was one of the leading conspirators. In the chaotic situation following Caesar's murder Decimus travelled to Cisalpine Gaul in order to raise an army to fight for the senatorial cause, but within a few months his position was challenged by Mark Antony who proceeded to blockade him in the city of Mutina (modern *Modena*). He was saved by the intervention of the consuls for 43 BC, Hirtius and Pansa (the latter his colleague as moneyer five years before), and Caesar's heir, Octavian. Antony withdrew to Transalpine Gaul and Decimus followed him, having been appointed by the Senate as supreme commander of the republican army. But the Caesarian veterans preferred not to fight against their former comrades and Decimus, finding himself deserted by his troops, fell into the hands of a Gallic chief who executed him on the instructions of Antony.

26

26 Head of Pietas right, wearing necklace and cruciform earring, **PIETAS** behind. *Reverse:* two right hands clasped and holding winged caduceus, **ALBINVS BRVTI F** around, below. *Silver denarius. Rome, 48 BC* (Crawford 450/2; Sydenham 942; BMCRR 3964; Babelon Postumia 10).

Caesar's well known policy of mercy in dealing with those of his fellow citizens who had opposed him is well illustrated by this type which combines the head of Pietas, personifying the ideals of duty and love of country, with joined hands, an instantly recognizeable symbol of friendship. The caduceus represents *felicitas,* the happiness resulting in prosperity and success which is the logical outcome of the dictator's enlightened thinking.

27

27 Bare head of the consul Aulus Postumius Albinus right, **A POSTVMIVS COS** around, behind and below. *Reverse:* **ALBINVS** (or **ALBINV** or **ALBIN**) / **BRVTI F** in two lines within wreath of corn-ears. *Silver denarius. Rome, 48 BC* (Crawford 450/3; Sydenham 943–943b; BMCRR 3966, 3967, 3972; Babelon Postumia 13, 14).

Having been received into the Postumia *gens* Decimus Brutus considered it his duty as moneyer to honour some illustrious member of his adoptive family. Unfortunately, the precise identity of the portrait head on obverse cannot be ascertained with any degree of certainty. The two principal candidates are the consuls of 151 BC and 99 BC. The claim of the former is largely based on sculptural parallels and is dismissed as unconvincing by Michael Crawford in *Roman Republican Coinage* (p. 466). It is just possible that the consul of 99 BC, rather than the moneyer of 81 BC, was the true adoptive father of Decimus Brutus, and if this were so then it would be natural for Decimus to depict him on his coinage. The late republican coinage contains numerous instances of ancestral portraiture, some of them only recently deceased (such as the two grandfathers of the moneyer Q. Pompeius Rufus in 54 BC). This was to be taken a step further by the Pompeians in Spain in 46–45 BC with the depiction of Pompey the Great, whose murder had taken place only two years before; and by Sextus Pompey, also in Spain, who issued denarii in 45–44 BC with the head of his elder brother, Cn. Pompeius Junior, who had only recently perished following Caesar's victory at Munda. Viewed in this context it could be considered only a logical progression that Caesar should have taken the decision to place his own portrait on the coinage at the beginning of the year 44 BC. Even though his assassination followed just eleven weeks later this step certainly opened the floodgates to contemporary portraiture on the Roman coinage, and thereafter non-portrait coins became the exception. The Roman state was clearly moving close to autocracy after almost half a millennium of republican government.

28

28 Mask of bearded Pan right, C PANSA below. *Reverse:* two right hands clasped and holding winged caduceus, ALBINVS BRVTI F around, below. *Silver denarius. Rome, 48 BC* (Crawford 451/1; Sydenham 944; BMCRR 3987; Babelon Vibia 22).

This remarkable issue combines an obverse type of the moneyer C. Vibius Pansa with a reverse of his colleague in the moneyership, Decimus Brutus. The coins are clearly not hybrids as the obverse varies from Pansa's sole coinage, the principal difference being the addition of his praenomen 'C' before 'PANSA'. It would thus seem that Pansa and Brutus were more closely associated in office than the other moneyer of 48 BC, Hostilius Saserna. In fact, it is tempting to suggest a sequence of issues for the coinage of this year: that of Pansa would seem to come first, with types which concentrate more on the moneyer's family than on contemporary events; Brutus would have struck next (though there was probably a lengthy period during which both moneyers were active, hence no. 28) with types which begin to place a greater emphasis on Caesar's past military achievements and his attitude towards his adversaries, i.e. propaganda types for the upcoming trial of strength with Pompey; and finally Hostilius Saserna whose types are wholly related to Caesar's military achievements in Gaul, including those of the preceding year, and whose coinage may be seen as complementing the military issues of Caesar himself which are attributed to the period following the battle of Pharsalus on 9 August 48 BC.

Caesar was absent from Rome for much of the following year (47 BC) but normal production of coinage from the Capitoline mint continued without interruption under the supervision of a full college of three moneyers. Two of these, Licinius Nerva and Antius Restio, issued the entire range of silver denominations (denarius, quinarius and sestertius) whilst the third, Plautius Plancus, produced denarii only.

29 Head of Medusa facing, with coiled snake on either side of face, L PLAVTIVS below. *Reverse:* Victory advancing right, head facing, her wings spread, conducting four rearing horses and holding palm-branch in left hand, PLANCVS (or PLANCV) below. *Silver denarius. Rome, 47*

29

29a

BC (Crawford 453/1a–b; Sydenham 959, 959a; BMCRR 4004, 4008; Babelon Plautia 15).

One obverse die has been noted on which the engraver has mistakenly spelt the moneyer's nomen **PAVTIVS**.

29a Similar to preceding, but without the snakes either side of Medusa's face, and sometimes the moneyer's *nomen* appears as **PLAVTIV**. *Silver denarius. Rome, 47 BC* (Crawford 453/1c–e; Sydenham 959b; BMCRR 4009; Babelon Plautia 14).

Lucius Plautius Plancus was the brother of the L. Munatius Plancus who was *praefectus Urbi* under Caesar in 45 BC and two years later, as proconsul of Gallia Comata, was the founder of the colony of Lugdunum (modern *Lyon*). Plautius Plancus had been born Gaius Munatius Plancus but had been adopted by a Lucius Plautius whose *praenomen* and *nomen* he thereupon assumed, retaining only the *cognomen* of his original name. The unusual elegance of the reverse type of his silver denarii suggests that the design was inspired by some specific work of art and this may, perhaps, be identified with the picture by the celebrated mid-4th century BC painter Nicomachus of Thebes which was placed in the Capitol by L. Munatius Plancus on the occasion of the celebration of his Gallic triumph in 43 BC. This notable picture may well have been in the possession of the moneyer during his period of office and have been reproduced as a coin type in celebration of Caesar's military successes in 48 and 47 BC. It could have become the property of his brother, Munatius Plancus, following Plautius' proscription by the triumviral government in 43 BC resulting in his execution and the confiscation of his property: there is certainly more than a hint of suspicion that Munatius bore some responsibility for Plautius' tragic end. The significance of the Medusa head on the obverse of these denarii still awaits a convincing explanation, though presumably it is in some way related to the history of the family into which the moneyer had been adopted.

30 Laureate head of Fides right, wearing earring and necklace, **FIDES** before, **NERVA** behind. *Reverse:* one-armed horseman galloping right, with his right hand dragging by the hair a naked warrior who holds sword and shield, **A LICINI** below, **III–VIR** across field. *Silver denarius. Rome, 47 BC* (Crawford 454/1; Sydenham 954; BMCRR 3999; Babelon Licinia 24).

The form of the moneyer's nomen on reverse is variable and may also appear as **LICIN**, **LICINIV**, *or* **LICINIVS**.

30

30a

30a Similar to preceding, but with A LICINIVS behind head of Fides on obverse, and with NERVA below the horseman on reverse, III VIR around. *Silver denarius. Rome, 47 BC* (Crawford 454/2; Sydenham 955; BMCRR 4002; Babelon Licinia 23).

Unlike his colleague Plautius Plancus nothing is known of the subsequent career of the moneyer Aulus Licinius Nerva. His choice of coin types seems to relate wholly to his ancestral history and the absence of a Caesarian theme may be explained by the dictator's extended stay in the East allowing the regular coinage of the Roman moneyers to resume their traditional pattern. But with civil war again looming this development was destined not to be of long duration. The distinctive reverse type of Nerva's denarii, featuring a one-armed warrior engaged in combat with a barbarian, clearly relates to some act of heroism on the part of an ancestor which would have been familiar to Romans of the mid-1st century BC. Unfortunately, we are not as well informed regarding the history of this moneyer's family. The head of Fides, personifying the ideals of loyalty and trustworthiness, here makes its sole appearance on the coinage of the Roman Republic and presumably complements the theme of the reverse type.

31 Head of Minerva right, wearing crested Corinthian helmet, NERVA behind. *Reverse:* Victory advancing right, holding wreath and palm-branch, A LICINI (or LICINIV) before. *Silver quinarius. Rome, 47 BC* (Crawford 454/3; Sydenham 956, 956a; BMCRR i, p. 515; Babelon Licinia 25).

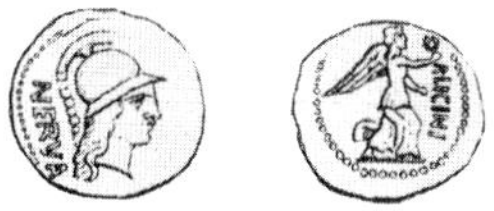

31

Caesar had reintroduced the silver quinarius (half denarius) denomination in his military coinage of 48–47 BC and two of the three Roman moneyers for the year 47 (Licinius Nerva and Antius Restio) followed suit. The issue, however, was a small one and the coins are rare today. Presumably they met some specific financial need or, alternatively, served a ceremonial purpose involving the distribution of money. On Nerva's quinarii the types – Minerva, goddess of war, and Victory – have a distinctly martial theme which can hardly be unconnected with Caesar's military activities in the East.

32 Laureate head of Apollo right, NERVA behind. *Reverse:* Victory advancing right, holding wreath and palm-branch, A LICINI (or LICIN) before. *Silver sestertius. Rome, 47 BC* (Crawford 454/4; Sydenham 957; BMCRR 4003; Babelon Licinia 26).

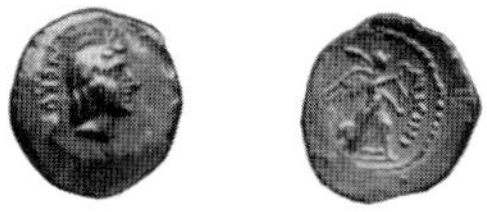

32

33

33 *Obverse:* same as preceding. *Reverse:* horseman galloping right, holding whip, A LICINI below. *Silver sestertius. Rome, 47 BC* (Crawford 454/5; Sydenham 958; BMCRR i, p. 516; Babelon Licinia 27).

Another restoration of the Caesarian period, the silver sestertius (quarter denarius) was first struck by the moneyer C. Vibius Pansa in 48 BC (see no. 24) after an interval of more than forty years since the previous issue. The types of Nerva's sestertii would seem to be agonistic, the reference being to the *Ludi Apollinares* the establishment of which as one of the five principal festivals of the Roman calendar (13 July) had taken place during the praetorship of an ancestor, P. Licinius Varus, in 208 BC. The galloping horseman of no. 33 is symbolic of the equestrian events in the games whilst Victory refers to success in the various contests. It links, of course, with the reverse of the quinarius (no. 31) where victory probably has a wider, i.e. military, significance.

34

34 Bare head of the tribune C. Antius Restio right, RESTIO behind. *Reverse:* Hercules, naked, advancing right, brandishing club held aloft in right hand and holding trophy in left, usually with lion's skin over left arm, C ANTIVS C F around, on right. *Silver denarius. Rome, 47 BC* (Crawford 455/1; Sydenham 970; BMCRR 4029; Babelon Antia 1).

35

35 Conjoined diademed heads of the Dei Penates right, DEI PENATES around, behind and below. *Reverse:* same as preceding. *Silver denarius. Rome, 47 BC* (Crawford 455/2; Sydenham 971; BMCRR 4032; Babelon Antia 2).

The issues of Gaius Antius Restio, son of Gaius, complete the series of moneyers' coins issued in Caesarian Rome down to the time of the outbreak of the second phase of the civil war between Caesar and the Pompeians. This moneyer was the son of the C. Antius Restio who held the office of tribune of the plebs in 68 BC and whose principal claim to fame was his authorship of a sumptuary law limiting the amount of money which could be spent by private individuals in the pursuit of public office. Needless to say this made him very unpopular with his peers. His son's portrayal of him on the coinage just two decades later was another important step towards the acceptance of contemporary portraiture on the Roman coinage. One may speculate that Restio was even encouraged by those closest to the dictator to select this particular obverse type for part of his denarius issue. The other obverse type for this denomination depicts the heads of the Dei Penates whose precise identity is made clear by the accompanying inscription. The town of Lavinium in Latium was a centre for the cult of these Roman household gods and their appearance may indicate that the moneyer's family originated from this place. The reverse of Hercules carrying a military trophy, which is common to both denarius obverse types, relates to the supposed origin of the Antia *gens* which claimed descent from Antiades, son of Hercules and Aglaia. A trophy was not one of Hercules' normal attributes and its representation here may well imply a reference to Caesar's various military exploits during his extended absence from Rome. Four years after his moneyership, in the latter part of 43 BC, Antius Restio was proscribed by the triumviral government of Antony, Octavian and Lepidus. He was fortunate that through the loyalty of one of his slaves he was able to escape to Sicily where Sextus Pompey, the younger son of Pompey the Great, was providing a safe haven for refugees from the proscriptions.

36 Diademed head of Diana right, wearing earring and necklace, bow and quiver over shoulder, **C ANTIVS** behind. *Reverse:* stag standing right, with garlanded antlers, **RESTIO** before. *Silver quinarius. Rome, 47 BC* (Crawford 455/3; Sydenham 972; BMCRR 4033; Babelon Antia 3).

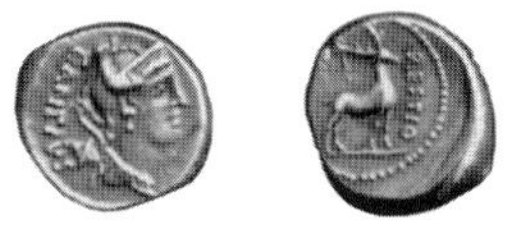

36

37 Head of ox facing, with garlanded horns, **C ANTIVS** below. *Reverse:* lighted altar, garlanded, **RES–TIO** across field. *Silver sestertius. Rome, 47 BC* (Crawford 455/4; Sydenham 973; BMCRR 4034; Babelon Antia 4).

37

38 Bust of Mercury right, wearing winged petasus, caduceus over shoulder, **C ANTIVS** behind. *Reverse:* same as preceding. *Silver sestertius. Rome, 47 BC* (Crawford 455/5; Sydenham 974; BMCRR i, p. 522; Babelon Antia 5).

38

39 Crested Corinthian helmet right, **C ANTIVS** around, behind and below. *Reverse:* owl standing right on shield, head facing, **RESTIO** behind. *Silver sestertius. Rome, 47 BC* (Crawford 455/6; Sydenham 975; BMCRR 4036; Babelon Antia 6).

39

The types of the fractional silver denominations of the moneyer C. Antius Restio concentrate on the general theme of major deities of the Roman pantheon and the sacrificial ceremonies performed in their honour. This preoccupation with the principal gods and goddesses of the state becomes a feature of the moneyers' coinage throughout the remainder of Caesar's dictatorship. Crawford[6] draws an interesting analogy with the coin types of the period of Sulla's supremacy in Rome, thirty-five years before, and suggests that both dictators were pursuing a deliberate policy of associating their personal cause with that of the *res publica* (the State) itself – 'an attitude which is incompatible with the collective ideology of oligarchic rule and which eventually finds expression in autocracy'.

CHAPTER 2

Thapsus and Munda – the final defeat of the Pompeians, 47–45 BC

Caesar's African invasion force, which we left as it was embarking from Lilybaeum in Sicily, soon ran into trouble in the shape of a storm which scattered the fleet. In consequence, when Caesar made landfall at Hadrumetum he had with him only 3000 infantry and 150 cavalry. Unaware of their commander's planned destination the rest of his ships began a desperate search for him as soon as the storm subsided, but some considerable time elapsed before they all succeeded in rejoining him. The situation was fraught with danger but, as usual, the Caesarian luck held and no serious move against him was made by the Pompeian commanders whose headquarters were far to the north, at Utica. Unable to take Hadrumetum with so few troops at his disposal Caesar moved down the coast to Leptis Minor which, thankfully, opened its gates to him. Now, with a harbour at his disposal, it was possible for the invader to strengthen his position as ships of his scattered fleet gradually began arriving, eventually followed by reinforcements from Sicily. Initially, the priority was to obtain supplies – difficult in this terrain and at this season – and on one occasion a large foraging party commanded by Caesar himself came close to disaster when it was surprised by the Pompeian commanders Labienus and Petreius. Only by brilliant manoeuvring was Caesar able to extricate his force from their dire predicament and to regain the security of their camp. Once his army had been sufficiently reinforced the principal objective became enticing the main force of the Pompeians into a pitched battle where the experience of his veteran legions would give Caesar a clear advantage.

Arrayed against Caesar in this campaign were all of his principal adversaries at this time, motivated either by their loyalty to the memory of Pompey or by fear of the rise of a powerful dictatorship which would threaten the continued existence of Rome's republican traditions. As we have seen, the two sons of Pompey, Gnaeus and Sextus, both survived their father's downfall at Pharsalus: they now became the focal point of the renewed opposition to the supremacy of the dictator. Gnaeus, however, did not remain in Africa for the duration of the war but instead occupied the Balearic Islands and thence crossed to Spain where pro-Pompeian sentiment still survived as a significant political factor. His younger brother Sextus remained in Africa though as he was only about 20 years of age he was not able to occupy a prominent position in the command structure of the Pompeian forces. The guiding spirit in the anti-Caesarian movement was Marcus Porcius Cato, later known as Cato Uticensis, the great-grandson of the famous Cato the Censor (234–149 BC). A rigid traditionalist in the mould of his illustrious ancestor, the corner-stone of Cato's philosophy was that he would prefer to die with the Republic rather than outlive it. The course which events were to take would give him the opportunity to realize this lofty aspiration which he did, in the grand manner, to the intense annoyance and frustration of his conqueror. Caesar rightly saw in the reputation of Cato's life and the dramatic circumstances of his death a potential super-martyr for the republican cause. Something of the depth of the dictator's feelings in this matter may be gauged by his later authorship of the *Anti-Cato* in angry response to Cicero's laudatory pamphlet *Cato*.

The universal respect which Cato commanded amongst his contemporaries enabled him to arbitrate in the rivalries and disputes which arose between the military leaders of the Pompeian party. Probably the general who came closest to matching Caesar's genius as a strategist was Titus Labienus, formerly Caesar's legate in Gaul though subsequently an ardent supporter of Pompey and his cause. But Labienus was a man of relatively low birth, his family having originated from the Picenum region of Italy, and this counted against him in the aristocratic hierarchy of the Pompeian leadership. Merely because of this brilliant tactician's lack of an illustrious ancestry Cato foolishly insisted on passing him over and bestowing the overall command on Q. Caecilius Metellus Pius Scipio. Although certainly the possessor of an awe-inspiring name, and formerly the father-in-law of Pompey himself, this did not, unfortunately for his cause, compensate for his total unfitness to confront an opponent of the calibre of Caesar. Other leaders of the Pompeian army in Africa included Afranius and Petreius, who had already unsuccessfully opposed Caesar in Spain prior to the battle of Pharsalus; P. Attius Varus, formerly governor of Africa, who had resumed control of his old province following Caesar's invasion of Italy in 49 BC; and Faustus Sulla, son of the dictator Sulla. A powerful, though unstable, ally was King Juba of Numidia who, if he could be counted on, added greatly to the manpower ranged against Caesar and could even contribute a large contingent of war-elephants.

Caesar now embarked on a series of ploys with the object of tricking his opponents into engaging in a pitched battle. Cato, although he remained at the provincial capital of Utica, constantly urged the greatest caution in being drawn into an engagement of Caesar's choosing. In consequence, weeks and months passed with little activity other than Caesar occasionally changing the location of his encampment. The impasse was finally broken when Caesar made a move against the important coastal city of Thapsus, cleverly creating a situation which, it appeared to the Pompeian command, they could turn to their advantage. Believing he had Caesar's army trapped on a narrow strip of land bounded by the sea on one side and a marshy salt lake on the other, Scipio made the fatal mistake of dividing his forces. Leaving Afranius and Juba to guard the southern end of the isthmus Scipio marched overnight around the salt lake to take up a blocking position at the other end, only a mile from the enemy encampment (6 February 46 BC). This was the opportunity for which Caesar had waited for months. With the enemy forces weakened by division, operating in difficult terrain without sufficient room to make use of their superiority in cavalry, and moreover preoccupied with the task of constructing field fortifications, they were in no position to offer effective resistance to the sudden and massive advance of Caesar's veteran legions. The ranks of Scipio's forces were quickly broken and dispersed and to add to the rout Juba's elephants, alarmed by the enemy archers and slingers, turned and charged back towards the Pompeian lines, trampling their own infantry in their path. On hearing of the disaster Afranius and Juba with the rest of the army turned tail and fled. Caesar's victory was complete, with minimum losses on his side, and many military tacticians regard Thapsus as the crowning glory of the dictator's brilliant career as a field commander. But on the darker side, Caesar on this occasion found himself unable to control his victorious soldiers who, frustrated by months of delaying tactics on the part of the enemy, exacted a terrible revenge on their vanquished opponents more than ten thousand of whom are reported to have perished after surrendering.

Events now moved quickly in marked contrast to the inactivity of the preceding months. Of the Pompeian leaders only Sextus Pompey, Labienus, and Varus survived to join Gnaeus Pompey in Spain. Scipio fled by ship but was overtaken by enemy forces and took his own life rather than surrender and become Caesar's prisoner. Afranius and Faustus Sulla were arrested and delivered up to the dictator but, somewhat uncharacteristically, he allowed them to be executed despite Afranius' former consular status. Like his soldiers Caesar's patience was obviously wearing thin and, after all, Afranius had already benefited from Caesar's clemency once following the campaign against the Pompeians in Spain in 49 BC. King Juba of Numidia, accompanied by the general Marcus Petreius, made good his escape from Thapsus to his capital city of Zama. Theatrical to the last, it was his intention to offer himself as a sacrifice on a huge pyre which had already been constructed against such an eventuality. The citizens of Zama were to be accorded the honour of sharing in their sovereign's dramatic self-immolation but there was a marked reluctance to take up this generous offer. So great was the reluctance, in fact, that the city gates were barred against them and Juba and his Roman ally had to content themselves with a duel-pact. Under the terms of this they were to dine together in some splendour at one of the king's country estates after which they were to solemnly engage in combat to the death, the victor promising to take his own life immediately afterwards. Juba killed Petreius in the duel and then committed suicide with the assistance of a slave.

But the most significant death at this time was that of Cato. Following the first news of the battle he had secured the defences of Utica in the hope that all was not lost and that he could provide a safe haven for large numbers of Pompeian refugees. When the enormous scale of the catastrophe became apparent Cato realized that he had no alternative but to take his own life, the prospect of falling into Caesar's hands being unthinkable. Accordingly, with quiet dignity he fell upon his sword in his private apartment and soon expired despite the best efforts of his doctor and slaves to save him. Although the people of Utica were not inclined to support Cato's political beliefs they had the highest regard for his integrity in the government of the place during a most troubled time. They gave him an honourable funeral and henceforth his name was forever linked with Utica and its people through the appellation 'Uticensis'. Caesar was furious at Cato's grand gesture realizing that he was far more dangerous as a martyr than as a living opponent. Generations later the name of Cato Uticensis was still revered as one of the greatest Roman patriots of all time.

The civil war appeared to be at an end at last allowing Caesar the freedom to devote his attention to other pressing matters in his inexorable progress towards the establishment of an autocracy at Rome. Whether this progress was the result of a conscious decision on his part we shall never know. He was not destined to survive sufficiently long to make it clear where he was ultimately headed. But the forces to which he gave an enormous impetus were to lead so soon to the firm establishment of a monarchical government and the demise of true senatorial authority that one can hardly doubt that this was Caesar's own goal.

Affairs had first to be settled in Africa. Most of the former Numidian kingdom of Juba was reorganized as a new Roman province – Africa Nova – under the governorship of Gaius Sallustius Crispus, better known as the historian Sallust. One of the more unlikely beneficiaries of the African War was a certain Publius Sittius, erstwhile friend of both Sulla and Cicero who, in order to escape his creditors and restore his financial fortunes, had taken up the life of a mercenary leader in Mauretania (64 BC). On the outbreak of hostilities between Caesar and the Pompeians in north Africa Sittius had offered assistance to the former and performed many valuable services, including the hunting down of Scipio after Thapsus. His reward was a principality centred on the city of Cirta (modern *Constantine* in Algeria) which he ruled until his assassination in 44 BC. The Mauretanian kingdom, under Caesar's allies Bocchus and Bogud, also benefited from Juba's downfall gaining territory from the former Numidian kingdom.

The dictator was now able to return to Rome though he interrupted his journey with a visit to Sardinia, one of the Republic's earliest overseas possessions (seized from the Carthaginians in 238 BC). On reaching the capital he immediately set about planning a magnificent quadruple triumph which was to surpass in spectacle anything ever seen before in the city on the Tiber. The four processions were held on separate days with each devoted to a specific theme: Caesar's victories in Gaul during his proconsular command, 58–51 BC; his victory over Ptolemy XIII of Egypt in 47 BC; that over Pharnaces of Pontus later in the same year; and finally his most recent success at Thapsus in north Africa. As triumphs could not be celebrated for victories over fellow-Romans the last was advertised as the defeat of an African aggressor, king Juba of Numidia, whose 4-year-old son, also called Juba, was one of the chief ornaments of the procession. The child was befriended by Caesar's 17-year-old great-nephew Octavius, destined eventually to become the Emperor Augustus, and through this valuable connection young Juba's future success was assured. He was eventually granted the kingdom of Mauretania and later was to marry Cleopatra Selene, the daughter of Queen Cleopatra VII of Egypt and Mark Antony. Many Roman aristocrats felt uneasy about this final element of the quadruple triumph as everyone was aware that Caesar's real adversaries at Thapsus were Scipio and Cato. Pictures depicting the deaths of these noble Romans were even exhibited in the procession, ostensibly because of their treason in allying themselves with an enemy of Rome but in reality as a warning to anyone contemplating opposition to the dictator. The message was not lost on the senators and, lacking a safe outlet, the pressure of discontent with Caesar's autocratic behaviour began to grow amongst the aristocracy of the capital, even including some individuals regarded by the dictator as his personal friends. The final phase of these lavish celebrations was a huge feast at which the entire population of the city dined bountifully at no fewer than twenty-two thousand tables. This was munificence on such a scale that it must have survived vividly in the public memory long after Caesar was no more. Doubtless, it contributed in no small measure to the goodwill later enjoyed by Octavian in Rome as the adopted son and heir of the Divine Julius.

One of the chief aims of the quadruple triumph was to reward the loyalty of Caesar's veterans many of whom had served under their remarkable commander for more than a decade. Of late, however, this loyalty had been wearing a little thin, *viz* the mutiny amongst the legions stationed in Campania prior to the African campaign. These men were anxious to receive the promised rewards for their many years of service, both in money and in land, and Caesar did not intend to disappoint the trust which had been placed in him for so long. As part of the celebrations there was a distribution of money to the veterans consisting of a payment of five thousand silver denarii to each legionary and ten thousand for the centurions. Even the spectators received a hundred denarii each. In order to facilitate the payment of these huge sums the Roman mint produced an unprecedented issue of gold aurei, each the equivalent of 25 denarii, bearing the names of Caesar and the praetor Aulus Hirtius (see no. 56). Numerous specimens of this coinage have survived down to the present day.

To satisfy the need for land on which to settle his veterans Caesar established many new colonies at this time not only in Italy, where acreage was becoming scarce, but also in the provinces. Such foundations had been made before – Narbo in Provence in 118 BC was the first successful example – but Caesar's activities in this direction provided the impetus which was to result in the enormous proliferation of provincial colonies in the early Roman imperial period. These foundations served a dual purpose for they also enabled Caesar to reduce the ever-growing numbers of the Roman proletariat, many of whom were without work and dependent on the corn-dole. Thus, Carthage was refounded as a colony at this time, exactly 100 years after the sack and destruction of Rome's old rival and the establishment of the province of Africa. Corinth, also destroyed by the Romans in the very same year (146 BC), was designated by Caesar to be the recipient of another colony, probably in connection with the dictator's plan to cut a canal through the Isthmus. This bold scheme was never completed in ancient times but as the capital of the Roman province of Achaea Corinth was to enjoy something of a revival of its ancient prestige and prosperity during the imperial era. Other important foundations dating from this phase of Caesar's activities included Carthago Nova and Tarraco in Spain, Arelate and Forum Iulii (modern *Fréjus*) in Gaul, and Sinope on the southern shores of the Euxine (Black Sea).

During this brief respite from campaigning Caesar threw himself wholeheartedly into the formulation of a wide-ranging programme of legislation affecting many aspects of the everyday life of the state. Unfortunately, fate decreed that in most instances the author of these proposed reforms would not be given sufficient time to oversee their enactment, and his violent death on the Ides of March, 44 BC, resulted in a period of renewed civil strife which rendered impossible any further progress in this direction. However, of the changes which Caesar was able to bring about the most significant was the introduction, on 1st January 45 BC, of the new Julian calendar. The accurate measurement of time was now regularized through the implementation of a system which has remained essentially unchanged down to the present day. Prior to this the Roman year had comprised only 355 days with the result that in order to keep the calendar in step with the seasons it had been necessary to insert an intercalary month every third year. This intercalation was, by tradition, left to the discretion of the pontifices, the priestly college of which Caesar himself had been the head (pontifex maximus) since 63 BC. Unfortunately, this body did not always take its responsibilities in this matter sufficiently seriously, and in the years between 52 BC and the beginning of the Thapsus campaign only one intercalation had taken place. This, perhaps, was scarcely surprising at a time when the chief pontiff was busy fighting military campaigns all over the Mediterranean arena, but it did mean that the calendar was now two months in advance of the seasons, a circumstance which must have occasioned considerable public inconvenience. Steps were now taken to find a permanent remedy to this unsatisfactory state of affairs and, acting with the guidance of the Alexandrian astronomer Sosigenes, Caesar added 67 days between November and December of 46 BC. This, in combination with an intercalation which had already taken place earlier in the year, brought the calendar into line with the next solar year (45 BC) and henceforth the length of each year was reckoned at $365\frac{1}{4}$ days. The additional 10 days over the former 355-day year were placed at the end of different months and every fourth year an extra day was inserted in February to correct the error. Even now, the new system was not properly established until AD 8, for after Caesar's death the pontifices mistakenly added the extra day every three years instead of four and Augustus was obliged to omit the intercalations of 5 BC, 1 BC, and AD 4 in order to bring the calendar into line again.

Caesar's considerable activities as a reformer were, however, to be interrupted by yet another challenge from the Pompeian party. It will be remembered that, following the battle of Thapsus, the survivors of the disaster had made their way to Spain to join forces with Gnaeus Pompey. Foremost amongst the refugees were Gnaeus' brother Sextus, the general Titus Labienus, and the former governor of Africa, P. Attius Varus. Because of the extreme unpopularity in the Iberian peninsula of Q. Cassius Longinus, Caesar's appointee as governor of Further Spain, the Pompeians determined that here was the ideal place for them to rally their forces and make a final stand against the dictator. Cassius had been replaced by Trebonius in 47 BC but the damage to the Caesarian cause had already been done. Gnaeus Pompey had been able to harness the forces of resentment to his own advantage and, strengthened by the arrival of the survivors from north Africa, he was soon able to field a considerable army comprising some thirteen legions. Caesar, distracted by his busy programme in the capital, was perhaps initially unaware of the seriousness of the situation in Spain. When he did give it his attention he despatched two of his generals, Q. Pedius and Q. Fabius, to deal with the revolt, but they had proved quite unequal to the task and it soon became clear that Caesar would have to take the field for a third time against the Pompeian opposition.

Caesar set out from Rome early in November, 46 BC, and on his arrival at the Spanish front four weeks later immediately took charge of the military operations. He knew there was no easy victory to be had here for there was considerable popular support for the Pompeian cause amongst the local population and in Labienus he was faced by a general of exceptional ability who had already demonstrated during the north African campaign that he could almost match Caesar's tactical skill. The Pompeians were based in Corduba (modern *Cordoba*) on the middle Baetis which, being strongly garrisoned by two legions, was not considered a serious target by the invader. Instead, as in north Africa, Caesar's aim was to bring the opposition to battle where the superiority of his legions would give him the advantage, even if outnumbered. Again, the opposition exercised extreme caution and for the first few months of the campaign Caesar had to content himself with besieging towns loyal to Gnaeus and constantly shifting his position to try and tempt his opponent into fighting. Gradually, as his strongholds fell one by one, the young Pompey began to feel cornered and on 17 March 45 BC, he was finally enticed into risking all in a pitched battle to be fought between the cities of Urso and Munda. Trusting in his luck and the invincibility of his troops Caesar had, on this occasion, given almost too much advantage to the enemy in order to force the issue. The slope of the ground favoured the Pompeians, an advantage which, given the numerical superiority of their forces, should have been enough almost to guarantee their success in the conflict. As it was, Caesar's military genius and the spirit and unswerving loyalty of his seasoned veterans were to be tested to the utmost in this, his last battle.

The bitter fighting continued for many hours with the eventual outcome remaining in serious doubt until the final stages of the battle. Sensing that he might have miscalculated the odds Caesar rallied his soldiers by performing acts of personal heroism in the midst of the fray. This gave his veterans fresh hope and they increased the pressure on their opponents to the point where they were able to thrust back the Pompeian left. This gave the Caesarian cavalry the opportunity to strike at their opponent's flank and rear, a move which finally broke the spirit of the Pompeian troops who began to retreat in disarray. The final losses were very high, especially on the Pompeian side, and of their leading commanders both Labienus and Varus fell in battle. Gnaeus Pompey made good his escape from Munda but was later apprehended and put to death. Only his younger brother Sextus survived. Given refuge by the people of the Lacetani tribe, the 21-year-old younger son of the great Pompey was later to embark on a freebooting career spanning almost a decade during which he was often to be a thorn in the side of Caesar's successors.

All opposition to Caesar's supremacy had now been effectively crushed and in September he returned to Rome to celebrate a triumph over the forces of rebellion aided by traitorous Romans. Somewhat uncharacteristically, Spain was harshly dealt with by the victor and the city of Corduba was sacked with great loss of life. The dictator was clearly irritated by the continued support which the province had given to the Pompeian cause and wished to teach it a severe lesson. It was now nearly five years since he had crossed the Rubicon and offered his first challenge to a Senate dominated by Pompey and his supporters. Those years had seen dramatic changes in the structure of the republican government, or at least in men's perception of the institutions by which they were governed. The years which followed were to bring even greater changes, though Caesar himself would not live to see the outcome of the great forces which he had set in motion.

COINAGE OF THE PERIOD

A. Issues of the Pompeians in North Africa

During the long build up of their forces in north Africa, spanning the greater part of the year 47 BC, a considerable coinage, mostly of silver denarii and quinarii, was produced by the Pompeians to help defray the costs of the growing military establishment under their command. This was augmented by a large output of denarii by King Juba of Numidia, with much rarer quinarii, sestertii and bronzes, mostly bearing the name and portrait of the Pompeian ally and presumably minted at his capital of Zama. The headquarters of the Pompeians was at the provincial capital of Utica, about 30 miles north-west of the site of Carthage, and it seems likely that this was the location of their principal mint. Most of the types were struck in the name of the Pompeian commander-in-chief, Q. Caecilius Metellus Pius Scipio, either solely or with two different legates, P. Licinius Crassus Junianus and M. Eppius. Somewhat surprisingly, Cato Uticensis himself authorized issues in his own name, though the types were merely a revival of those which had been used by the moneyer M. Porcius Cato more than four decades before.

40 Head of Jupiter right, hair and beard in ringlets, eagle's head left and horizontal sceptre below, METEL PIVS before, SCIP IMP behind. *Reverse:* curule chair flanked by ear of corn and dragon's head, scales balanced on cornucopiae above, CRASS IVN on right, LEG PRO PR on left. *Gold aureus. Utica, 47–46 BC* (Crawford 460/1; Sydenham 1047; BMCRR Africa p. 571; Babelon Caecilia 48).

41 Same as preceding. *Silver denarius. Utica, 47–46 BC* (Crawford 460/2; Sydenham 1048; BMCRR Africa 4; Babelon Caecilia 49).

41

The gold aureus denomination had been revived by Caesar the preceding year following his victory over Pompey at Pharsalus (see no. 10). Scipio's aureus is known only from a single surviving example preserved in the Paris collection. The interesting type is full of symbolism: the archaistic head of Jupiter, identified by the eagle's head below, is reminiscent of the bust of Jupiter Terminalis on the coinage of Pompey the Great (see no. 8) and may have been intended to revive memories of the fallen leader; the ear of corn, cornucopiae and scales celebrate the famed fertility of the province of Africa; the curule chair doubtless refers to Scipio's consulship in 52 BC in which he was the colleague of Pompey himself, who happened also to be his son-in-law;

whilst the dragon's head implies a rebuttal of Caesar's implication that the Pompeian cause represented the evil over which he would triumph (see no. 9). Crassus Junianus, whose name appears on the reverse in the subsidiary role of *legatus pro praetore*, is known to have been a friend of Cicero and in 51 BC held the office of tribune of the plebs. He fled to sea following the battle of Thapsus and it seems likely that he committed shipboard suicide in the same manner as his commander-in-chief.

42

42 Turreted head of the city-goddess of Utica right, ear of corn behind, caduceus before, prow below, uncertain rectangular object above, CRASS IVN on right, LEG PRO PR on left, laurel-wreath border. *Reverse:* military trophy flanked by lituus and jug, METEL PIVS on right, SCIP IMP on left. *Silver denarius. Utica, 47–46 BC* (Crawford 460/3; Sydenham 1049; BMCRR Africa 6; Babelon Caecilia 52).

This type features the head of the tutelary deity of the mint-city of Utica which was traditionally the earliest Phoenician settlement on the north African coast, possibly dating back to the 8th century BC. The Romans made it the capital of the province of Africa following the destruction of Carthage in 146 BC and it became the headquarters of the Pompeian resistance to Caesar during the period 47–46. Cato resided in the city during the last year of his life and committed suicide there following Thapsus. His name is forever linked with the place through the appellation 'Uticensis'. The symbols surrounding the head of the goddess appear to be emblematic of the exceptional fertility of the region in which Utica was situated and its importance as a port and naval base. The trophy on reverse, combined with symbols of the augurate, would seem to refer to Scipio's adoptive grandfather, Q. Caecilius Metellus Numidicus who, as consul in 109 BC, played a leading role in the military operations against Jugurtha of Numidia (Jugurthine War). Once again, the issue bears the additional name of the *legatus pro praetore* Crassus Junianus, but it will be noticed that this time the inscriptions are reversed with that of the commander-in-chief appearing on the reverse, doubtless to emphasize the significance of the type.

43

43 Lion-headed figure of the Genius of Africa (Sekhmet) standing facing, clad in long robes, holding *ankh* in right hand, G T – A either side of head, Q METEL PIVS on right, SCIPIO IMP on left. *Reverse:* Victory standing left, holding caduceus and shield, P CRASSVS IVN on right, LEG PRO PR on left. *Silver denarius. Utica, 47–46 BC* (Crawford 460/4; Sydenham 1050; BMCRR Africa 8; Babelon Caecilia 51).

This, probably the rarest of the denarii of Scipio, is certainly the most remarkable of the coin types issued by the Pompeians in north Africa. The curious lion-headed deity on obverse is identified by the accompanying letters 'G T A' as *Genius terrae Africae*, the Spirit of the land of Africa. The figure holds in her right hand the *ankh*, the symbol of life, and she is equated by Grueber[7] with Sekhmet, a goddess who personified 'the violent heat of the sun' and whose cult 'extended not only over the whole of Egypt and Zeugitana, but also to Libya'. Her appearance on a Roman denarius at this time bears eloquent testimony to the disruption to the normal practices of the

Republic caused by the civil war between Caesar and the Pompeians and to the far-flung theatres of that conflict. The reverse type of Victory is more conventional, though the goddess has the unusual attributes of a caduceus and a small circular shield (described by Crawford as a patera). She symbolizes the anticipated success of Pompeian arms against the forces of the dictator, hopes which were to be dashed on the field of Thapsus.

44

44 Laureate head of Africa right, clad in elephant's skin, ear of corn before, plough below, Q METELL on right, SCIPIO IMP on left. *Reverse:* naked Hercules standing facing, his right hand on hip, left resting on club draped with lion's skin and set on rock, EPPIVS on right, LEG F C on left. *Silver denarius. Military mint travelling with Scipio in Africa, 47–46 BC* (Crawford 461; Sydenham 1051; BMCRR Africa 10 (head of Africa large) and 12 (head small); Babelon Caecilia 50).

There is considerable variation in the size of the head of Africa on the obverse dies of this type.

Africa is here personified clad in her elephant's skin head-dress, a type the origins of which may be traced back to the effigy of the deified Alexander the Great which the satrap Ptolemy of Egypt placed on his initial issue of silver tetradrachms shortly after 323 BC. On this denarius she is accompanied by the subsidiary symbols of plough and corn-ear, clearly representative of the fertility of the soil of *provincia Africa*. The reverse type of Hercules admits of no such simple explanation and has been the subject of much speculation amongst scholars over the past century and a half. Perhaps the most likely interpretation is that Hercules is here equated with the great Phoenician deity of Melkart, the chief god of Tyre which was the mother city of Carthage. Melkart was much honoured in north Africa and the Numidian kings actually claimed descent from him. The type could, therefore, have been intended as a compliment to King Juba, a powerful ally of the Pompeians against Caesar. This issue bears the *nomen* of the legate Marcus Eppius who was a prominent supporter of the Pompeian cause from the time of the outbreak of the civil war in 49 BC. His title 'LEG F C' is of special interest as it occurs nowhere else on the coinage. The most likely expansion of the abbreviation is *legatus fisci castrensis* ('legate of the camp treasury') which would imply that the mint was a military one. Eppius survived Thapsus and we shall meet him again striking for Sextus Pompey in Spain (see nos. 234 and 234a).

45 Laureate head of Jupiter right, hair and beard in ringlets, Q METEL around, above and before, PIVS behind and below. *Reverse:* African

45

elephant walking right, SCIPIO above, IMP in exergue. *Silver denarius. Military mint travelling with Scipio in Africa, 47–46 BC* (Crawford 459; Sydenham 1046; BMCRR Africa 1; Babelon Caecilia 47).

Both stylistically and in volume this coinage stands apart from the rather limited issues in Scipio's name which can safely be attributed to the provincial capital of Utica (nos. 40–3). The inescapable conclusion is that this type, which is in the sole name of the commander-in-chief, is a product of the military mint operating within the security of Scipio's camp. It would appear to belong to the later stages of the campaign as the Pompeian army was moving around the province prior to being enticed into the fatal engagement at Thapsus.

46

46a

46b

46 Draped female bust (?Roma or Libertas) right, her hair collected into a knot behind, M CATO PRO PR before. *Reverse:* Victory seated right, holding patera in extended right hand, and palm-branch over shoulder in left, VICTRIX (TR ligatured) in exergue. *Silver denarius. Utica, 47–46 BC* (Crawford 462/1c; Sydenham 1052; BMCRR Africa 15; Babelon Porcia 9).

46a Similar to preceding, but on obverse the hair is bound with fillet, the legend starts below the bust, and with ROMA (MA ligatured) behind. *Silver denarius. Utica, 47–46 BC* (Crawford 462/1a; Sydenham 1053; BMCRR Africa 17; Babelon Porcia 10).

46b Similar to preceding, but on reverse Victory holds wreath instead of patera in extended right hand. *Silver denarius. Utica, 47–46 BC* (Crawford 462/1b; Sydenham 1053a; BMCRR Africa 18; RSC/Babelon Porcia 10a).

47

47 Head of Liber right, wreathed with ivy, his hair long, M CATO (AT ligatured) PRO PR around, below. *Reverse:* Victory seated right, holding patera, same as 46. *Silver quinarius. Utica, 47–46 BC* (Crawford 462/2; Sydenham 1054, 1054a; BMCRR Africa 19–20; Babelon Porcia 11).

It seems remarkable that the rigid traditionalist M. Porcius Cato would have consented to have his name inscribed on coins which were being issued wholly unconstitutionally, though it should be remembered that just half a decade later another staunch republican, M. Junius Brutus, was to go even further in the betrayal of his principles by placing his own portrait on the coinage. Cato strikes in his capacity as propraetor of Sicily, an appointment which was made by the Senate at the outset of the civil war but one which he was forced to abandon when Caesar's lieutenant C. Scribonius Curio invaded his province. The types require no special comment as they are merely copies of the issues of another M. Porcius Cato, possibly a cousin of Uticensis, who held the office of moneyer *c.*89 BC. The silver quinarius (half denarius) had been reintroduced by Caesar in 48–47 BC and the Pompeians were here following suit, though they were probably also influenced by the existence of quinarii in the prototype series.

B. Issues of the Pompeians in Spain

After the disaster of Thapsus the survivors of the Pompeian party joined Gnaeus Pompey in Spain and spent the remainder of the year 46 BC making preparations for a final trial of strength with Caesar. An interesting series of coins, mostly silver denarii, was produced at this time to help finance their activities. The portrait head of Pompey the Great, now deceased for almost two years, makes its first appearance on the Pompeian coinage at this time, the memory of the great leader being invoked to rally his supporters in one last effort to overcome their sworn enemy. Corduba (modern *Cordoba*) was the Pompeian headquarters in Spain and it seems reasonable to surmise that their minting establishment was located there, the security of the place being guaranteed by the presence of two legions.

48

48a

48 Head of Roma right, wearing crested helmet, M POBLICI (or POBLIC) LEG PRO around, before, PR behind, bead and reel border. *Reverse:* Hispania standing right, shield on her back, holding two spears over shoulder in left hand, and with right presenting palm-branch to Pompeian soldier standing left on prow, armed with sword, CN MAGNVS IMP around, below and on right. *Silver denarius. Corduba, 46–45 BC* (Crawford 469/1a–d; Sydenham 1035; BMCRR Spain 72; Babelon Pompeia 9; Cohen *Pompey the Great* 1).

48a Similar to preceding, but on obverse the legend is divided M POBLICI LEG before and PRO PR behind, and with border of dots. *Silver denarius. Corduba, 46–45 BC* (Crawford 469/1e; Sydenham 1035a; BMCRR Spain 75; RSC/Cohen *Pompey the Great* 1a).

This was the principal type of the Pompeian war-coinage in Spain prior to the battle of Munda. The issue bears the names of both Gnaeus Pompey Junior and his *legatus pro praetore,* Marcus Poblicius, who is otherwise unattested. The reverse type symbolizes the enthusiastic support of Further Spain for the Pompeian cause, whilst the appearance of the helmeted head of Roma on obverse is an expression of hope that the current campaign will lead to the final downfall of the dictator Caesar and the liberation of the republic from his monarchical rule.

49

49 Bare head of Pompey the Great right, **CN MAGNVS** (or **MAGN**) before, **IMP** (or **IMP F** or **IMP B:** behind. *Reverse:* Corduba, wearing turreted head-dress, standing right amidst heap of arms, holding transverse spear in left hand and with right grasping the hand of Pompeian soldier who has just disembarked from ship, the stern of which appears on right, **M MINAT / SABIN** in two lines in exergue, **PR Q** on left. *Silver denarius. Corduba, 46–45 BC* (Crawford 470/1a; Sydenham 1036, a–c; BMCRR Spain 77–9; Babelon Pompeia 10–11; Cohen *Pompey the Great* 5–8).

50

50 *Obverse:* same as preceding. *Reverse:* Spanish city-goddess, wearing turreted headdress, standing right, holding caduceus in left hand and with right presenting laurel-branch to Pompeian soldier who stands facing, resting on spear held in right hand, crowned by another city-goddess who stands left beside him, on right, holding trophy over left shoulder, **M MINAT / SABIN** in two lines in exergue, **PR Q** on left. *Silver denarius. Corduba, 46–45 BC* (Crawford 470/1c; Sydenham 1038, a-c; BMCRR Spain 82–3; Babelon Pompeia 14; Cohen *Pompey the Great* 11).

51

51 *Obverse:* same as preceding. *Reverse:* Spanish city-goddess, wearing turreted headdress, standing right, holding caduceus in left hand and with right grasping the hand of Pompeian soldier who stands facing, crowned by another city-goddess who stands left beside him, on right, holding trophy over left shoulder, **M MINAT / SABI** in two lines in exergue, **PR Q** on left. *Silver denarius. Corduba, 46–45 BC* (Crawford 470/1d; Sydenham 1039; BMCRR Spain 81; RSC/Cohen *Pompey the Great* 11d).

52

52 *Obverse:* same as preceding. *Reverse:* Pompeian soldier standing right, looking back at Spanish city-goddess, wearing turreted head-dress, who stands right behind him, her right hand raised in greeting, another city-goddess kneeling left before him, presenting shield, **M MINAT / SABI** in two lines in exergue, **PR Q** on left. *Silver denarius. Corduba, 46–45 BC* (Crawford 470/1b; Sydenham 1037, a–c; BMCRR Spain 80; Babelon Pompeia 12; Cohen *Pompey the Great* 9).

The types of this interesting series are full of symbolism. The obverse revives the memory of the great leader whose tragic death had occurred only two years before on the Mediterranean shores of Egypt; whilst the reverses celebrate the supportive attitude of the Spanish cities, whose sympathy for the Pompeian cause was already well established and had been strengthened in recent years by the abuses of Caesar's appointee as governor of Further Spain, Q. Cassius Longinus. The coins were issued by Gnaeus Pompey's lieutenant, M. Minatius Sabinus, who is described as *proquaestor* in the inscriptions but is otherwise unknown to history. The rarity of the series as a whole – Crawford records only five obverse and eight reverse dies – suggests that it was introduced only shortly before Munda and was abruptly terminated by Caesar's overwhelming victory which ended for ever the threat from the

Pompeian opposition. When Sextus Pompey, the only high-ranking survivor of Munda, resumed the production of coinage in Spain, possibly towards the end of the year 45 BC, it was with a portrait type of Pompey the Great in continuation of the pre-Munda series of Minatius Sabinus (see nos. 232–232c).

53

53 Laureate head of Janus, mark of value I above. *Reverse:* prow of galley right, CN MAG (MA ligatured) above, mark of value I before, IMP below. *Bronze as. Corduba, 46–45 BC* (RPC 486; Crawford 471; FITA pp. 22–4; Sydenham 1040; BMCRR Spain 84; Babelon Pompeia 15).

This Pompeian revival of the traditional bronze as is remarkable in a number of ways. The denomination had not been issued by the Roman Republic in almost four decades and the final issues had been on the semuncial weight standard, of about 11 grams, authorized by the *Lex Papiria* in 91 BC. The Spanish asses of Gnaeus Pompey Junior were struck on the old uncial standard (*c.* 22 grams) from metal doubtless obtained from the rich copper mines at Cotinae in Baetica. They began a tradition of Pompeian bronze issues which was continued by Sextus Pompey in Spain and, later, in Sicily. The types (Janus head/prow to right) were the traditional ones used on the first struck asses of the Roman Republic introduced in the great currency reform of *c.*211 BC.

C. Issues of Caesar for the African Campaign

Before embarking for Africa from the Sicilian port of Lilybaeum Caesar spent some time on the island organizing the invasion force with which he was going to confront Scipio and the other Pompeians. During this period (late 47 BC) a small issue of silver denarii was produced in Caesar's name by Aulus Allienus who had had been appointed proconsular governor of Sicily in the preceding year. The issue was an unusual one for Caesar's coinage in that it bore the name of one of his lieutenants in addition to his own, a feature which was more typical of the Pompeian series.

54

54 Diademed and draped bust of Venus right, C CAESAR IMP COS ITER around. *Reverse:* Trinacrus, naked but for mantle wrapped around left arm, standing left, his right foot set on prow, holding triskeles in right hand, his right elbow resting on knee, A ALLIENVS PRO COS around. *Silver denarius. Sicilian mint, possibly Lilybaeum, late 47 BC* (Crawford 457; Sydenham 1022; BMCRR Sicily 5; Babelon Julia 14; Cohen 1).

The Sicilian origin of this coinage is made clear by the appearance of Trinacrus, reputedly a son of Neptune and the eponymous deity of the island, who appears to have been conceived in order to account for the ancient name of the country – Trinacria. In reality, this name probably had its origins in the island's three promontories and its consequent triangular shape, which also accounts for the adoption of the three-legged triskeles as the symbol of Sicily. Venus here makes her initial appearance on Caesar's coinage. As the ancestress of the *gens* Julia through Iulus, grandson of Venus and Anchises, the goddess was especially revered by the dictator and was to play a prominent role on the coinage of his final years.

55

55 Diademed head of Venus right. *Reverse:* Aeneas, naked, advancing to front, body inclined to left, holding palladium on extended right hand and bearing his father Anchises, wearing long tunic and hood, on his left shoulder, CAESAR on right. *Silver denarius. Military mint travelling with Caesar in North Africa, 47–46 BC* (Crawford 458; Sydenham 1013; BMCRR East 31; Babelon Julia 10; Cohen 12).

This type doubtless represents Caesar's war coinage for the protracted campaign against the Pompeians in Africa culminating in the battle of Thapsus. Although not on a comparable scale to the 'elephant' coinage of 49–48 BC (see no. 9) the issue was, nevertheless, greater in extent than any subsequent issue in the dictator's name. The theme of the ancestry of Caesar and the *gens* Julia, already introduced on the rare Sicilian denarii of Allienus (see no. 54), is here carried a stage further by the representation of the Trojan prince Aeneas, the son of Venus and Anchises and the father of Ascanius (= Iulus). Aeneas bears his aged father on his shoulders as they leave the ruined city of Troy after its capture by the Greeks. He also carries the palladium, a statue of Athena which protected Troy and was later brought to Italy by Aeneas where it eventually became the protector of the city of Rome. The type was doubly appropriate for the African campaign because of the relationship between Aeneas and Dido, princess of Tyre, who was the foundress of the Phoenician colony of Carthage.

D. Caesar's Special Issues for the Quadruple Triumph

A vital element of the lavish celebrations in Rome following Caesar's return after his victory at Thapsus was the distribution of large sums of money to his loyal troops, many of whom had served under his command for more than a decade. With five thousand denarii going to each legionary and ten thousand for the centurions there must have been an extraordinarily heavy demand placed on the Capitoline mint to produce sufficient quantities of new coinage. The problem was partially solved by Caesar's decision to authorize the large-scale production of gold aurei, each the equivalent of 25 silver denarii, the first mass production of this denomination in the history of the Roman coinage.

56

56 Veiled female head (Vesta?) right, C CAESAR COS TER around. *Reverse:* emblems of the augurate and pontificate – jug between lituus on left, and axe on right, A HIRTIVS PR around, on left and below. *Gold aureus. Rome, early 46 BC* (Crawford 466; Sydenham 1017–1018a; BMCRR 4050–54; Babelon Julia 22–3; Cohen 2–3).

This issue is securely dated to 46 BC by its reference, in the obverse inscription, to Caesar's third consulship (COS TER = *Consul tertium*). Aulus Hirtius who, as praetor, was responsible for overseeing the production of this remarkable coinage, was a close personal friend of Caesar and had served as his legate in Gaul. A man of wide-ranging talents, Hirtius was renowned as a connoisseur of fine food and wine. In the literary field he completed Caesar's *Gallic War* by authoring the eighth and final book in the period immediately following the dictator's assassination, and he was probably also responsible for the *Alexandrian War* describing the events in Egypt in the autumn of 48 BC. With Antony temporarily out of favour because of his mishandling of the situation in Italy during Caesar's absence in the East, Hirtius at this time was probably the most influential member of the Caesarian party in Rome. It is scarcely surprising, therefore, that his name should appear on this extraordinary issue of gold coinage. The types require little comment. The theme is peaceful and dwells on Caesar's possession of various priestly offices. The veiled female head on obverse is probably that of Vesta, the Roman goddess of the hearth, whose rites were in the care of the pontifices, the chief of whom (pontifex maximus) was Caesar himself. A similar head had already appeared on a silver quinarius of Caesar issued in 48 BC following the victory at Pharsalus (see no. 14). The great pressure under which the mint was working at this time is evidenced by the extremely variable quality of the die-engraving and technical execution of this coinage, a highly unusual phenomenon for Roman gold. This has even led numismatists of the past to see in some versions of the obverse head an attempt to represent the facial features of Caesar himself, though there seems little likelihood of this occurring deliberately as early as 46 BC.

57 Head of Ceres right, wearing wreath of corn, DICT ITER before, COS TERT behind. *Reverse:* emblems of the augurate and pontificate – simpulum, aspergillum, jug and lituus, AVGVR above, PONT MAX below, D on right. *Silver denarius. Utica (?), early 46 BC* (Crawford 467/1a; Sydenham 1023; BMCRR Africa 21; Babelon Julia 16; Cohen 4).

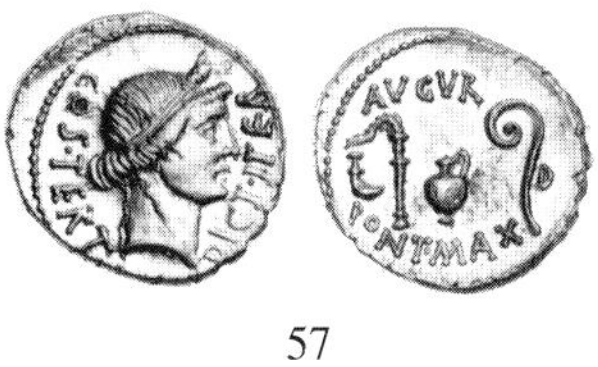

57

57a

57a Similar to preceding, but with M instead of D in reverse field to right. *Silver denarius. Utica (?), early 46 BC* (Crawford 467/1b; Sydenham 1024; BMCRR Africa 23; Babelon Julia 16; Cohen 4).

This extensive issue of denarii would seem to represent another measure on the part of Caesar to ease the burden on the Capitoline mint in the period prior to the distribution of vast sums of money at the quadruple triumph. Curiously, the inscriptions on these coins omit the actual name of the dictator and neither is there any mention of a lieutenant acting on behalf of the commander-in-chief in his absence. However, the titles clearly refer to Caesar – his dictatorships, his consulships, and his possession of various priestly offices. The head of Ceres, goddess of agriculture, is symbolic of the grain-producing wealth of Africa the supply of which to Rome had been interrupted by the civil war. Attention is drawn to the extraordinary nature of the issue by the appearance of either the letter 'D' (*donativum* = largess) or the letter 'M' (*munus* = gift) in the reverse field. This accords well with the intended use of the coins for the payment of Caesar's loyal veterans, both prior to the quadruple triumph and during the celebration itself. The actual place of mintage remains uncertain. Utica, capital of the province of Africa, seems a likely choice on the basis that it had already been used as a mint by the Pompeians and, following Thapsus, became the administrative centre for the reorganization of the region.

E. Issues of Caesar for the Spanish Campaign

The final Pompeian challenge to Caesar's supremacy – that of Gnaeus and Sextus Pompey, Titus Labienus and Attius Varus – necessitated the production of yet another large-scale emergency coinage to help defray the costs of the campaign. As on the Caesarian coinage for the African campaign the obverse is occupied by a head of Venus, ancestress of the *gens* Julia, this time accompanied by a small Cupid identifying her as Venus Genetrix to whom Caesar had lately dedicated a temple in the Forum Julium. The reverses revert to the old theme of Caesar's victories in Gaul. Doubtless, they were intended to revive memories of 'the good old days' in the hearts of his seasoned veterans who were now being called upon to face the Pompeian threat for the third time in only two and a half years. Their patience was probably wearing thin with this persistent foe and Caesar may have been concerned over the question of maintaining discipline during a protracted campaign. Of the two types, no. 59 is noticeably scarcer than no. 58 and there are differences in style and fabric which may be indicative of separate minting establishments, or different periods of issue, or both. In the absence of further evidence it seems best to regard the entire series simply as the product of Caesar's military mint during the course of the 4-month campaign against the Pompeians in Spain. Production may have continued after Munda as Sextus Pompey remained active in the peninsula and even initiated a new series of silver and bronze coins (see nos. 232–4).

58 Diademed head of Venus right, wearing triple-drop earring and necklace of pendants, Cupid at her shoulder behind. *Reverse:* trophy of Gallic

58

arms with two seated captives at base, the one on left a female in attitude of dejection, the one on right a bearded male with hands bound behind him, CAESAR in exergue. *Silver denarius. Military mint travelling with Caesar in Spain, late 46-early 45* BC (Crawford 468/1; Sydenham 1014; BMCRR Spain 89; Babelon Julia 11; Cohen 13).

59 Diademed bust of Venus left, with slight drapery, wearing single-drop earring and with star in hair behind, Cupid at her shoulder before, sceptre over shoulder behind, lituus on left. *Reverse:* trophy of Gallic arms with two captives at base, the one on left a kneeling male with hands bound behind him, the one on right a seated female in attitude of dejection, CAESAR in exergue. *Silver denarius. Military mint travelling with Caesar in Spain, late 46-early 45* BC (Crawford 468/2; Sydenham 1015; BMCRR Spain 86; Babelon Julia 12; Cohen 14).

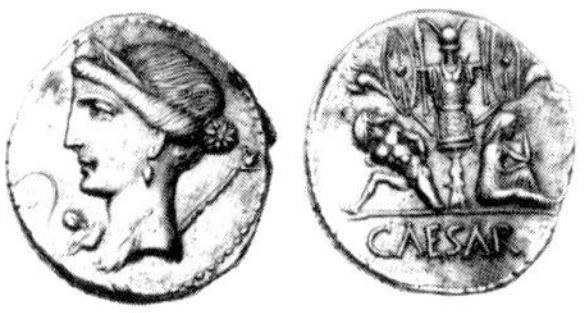

59

F. Caesar's Special Issues for the Spanish Triumph

Although his victory at Munda had been achieved against Roman adversaries, Caesar nevertheless did not hesitate to celebrate a triumph on his return to Rome and even granted a like honour to his lieutenants Pedius and Fabius. This was contrary to normal precedent, and even though a segment of the quadruple triumph in the preceding year had been devoted to a celebration of the victory over the Pompeians at Thapsus this had been advertised as the defeat of an African enemy, king Juba of Numidia. Clearly, the dictator's patience with opposition was close to being exhausted and he was no longer prepared to show deference to the sensibilities of the Roman aristocracy. Although Caesar held the Spanish war to have been the quelling of rebellion, many citizens must have given deep thought to the true reality of this sinister development in the affairs of Rome. For if this were rebellion against whom was it directed? Certainly not against the legitimate governing body of the state, the Senate. Rather, it was against the authority of one man who had seized power more than four years before and was showing no inclination whatsoever to relinquish it. In fact, this episode may well have been a significant contributory factor in the genesis of the plot against the dictator's life which was to lead to his assassination before another year had passed. Several exceptional issues of coinage appear to be associated with this late phase of Caesar's dictatorship prior to the introduction of portrait coinage at the beginning of the year 44 BC.

60 Draped bust of Victory right, wing visible behind shoulder, C CAES behind, DIC TER before. *Reverse:* sacrificial jug with handle, L PLANC

60

60a

61

on left, **PRAEF VRB** (**VR** ligatured) on right. *Gold aureus. Rome, autumn 45 BC* (Crawford 475/1a; Sydenham 1019, 1019a; BMCRR 4118–19; Babelon Julia 19; Cohen 31).

60a Similar to preceding, but on reverse **PR** instead of **PRAEF**, and **VR** not ligatured. *Gold aureus.* Rome, autumn 45 BC (Crawford 475/1b; Sydenham 1019b; BMCRR 4122; Babelon Julia 18; Cohen 30).

61 Same as 60. *Gold half-aureus, or quinarius.* Rome, autumn 45 BC (Crawford 475/2; Sydenham 1020; BMCRR 4123; Babelon Julia 20; Cohen 32).

Although Crawford[8] regards this issue as belonging early in the year 45 BC, on the basis of the title *Dictator Tertium*, it seems preferable to follow Grueber's[9] view that the series was produced specially for Caesar's Spanish triumph in October. The third dictatorship dates from April 46 BC, but instead of remaining valid for the normal period of one year the extraordinary powers were now extended for an unprecedented term of ten years, an ominous indication of Caesar's future plans. Therefore, the use of *Dictator Tertium* after April 45 BC appears to present no special problems as Caesar certainly held the office of dictator at this time and '**DIC TER**' accurately recorded the most recent occasion of its renewal. Moreover, there was already a precedent in Caesar's own coinage for the retention of the dictatorial title beyond the period to which it strictly applied. The denarii struck in Africa in 46 BC following Thapsus (see nos. 57 and 57a) still styled Caesar *Dictator Iterum* even though his second annual appointment had technically expired in October 47 BC. It is hard to escape the conclusion that Caesar's cavalier attitude towards the niceties of constitutional convention was reflected in the official titles appearing on his coinage. After all, many of his issues accorded him no title whatsoever and simply substituted his own *cognomen* of '**CAESAR**' as the issuing authority: there could be no clearer statement than this of the dictator's disdainful attitude towards the republican constitution.

The prominence of the winged goddess Victoria on the obverse of these gold coins is surely commemorative of some significant military success, and that can hardly be anything other than Caesar's victory at Munda resulting in the deaths of his principal adversaries and the final collapse of the Pompeian cause. That the series was produced specially for the Spanish triumph is made even more likely by the inclusion of a half-aureus, or gold quinarius, the sole appearance of this denomination in the republican period. In later times the gold quinarius, and its counterpart in silver, came to be associated with the distribution of largess on occasions of public celebration and it may well be that the tradition had its origins with Caesar's triumph in October, 45 BC. Another exceptional issue of the period, the orichalcum dupondius (?) of C. Clovius (see nos. 62 and 62a), probably served much the same purpose and represented a low value donation piece for distribution to the populace during the triumphal procession. L. Munatius Plancus, whose name appears on the gold aurei and quinarii, was one of the more colourful of the minor political personalities of the imperatorial and early imperial age. Brother of the L. Plautius Plancus who had occupied the office of moneyer in 47 BC (see nos. 29 and 29a), Munatius Plancus was one of six *praefecti Urbi* appointed by Caesar late in 46 BC to administer affairs at home during his absence in Spain. C. Clovius may have been another of these officials. As the issue of gold coins for the Spanish triumph was produced in his name Plancus must have occupied a prominent position in the Caesarian faction in Rome. This is borne out by Caesar 's nomination of him to the governorship of Transalpine Gaul in 44 BC and to the consulship for 42 BC. During his governorship he founded the colony of Lugdunum (modern *Lyon*) in 43 BC and ultimately gave his support to Mark Antony during the complex political manœuvrings of the immediate post-Caesarian period. After a long period of friendship he eventually quarrelled with Antony over Cleopatra's intended participation in the war against Octavian and went over to the opposing camp (32 BC). Finding favour with Caesar's heir, it was on Plancus' suggestion that Octavian received the title of 'Augustus' on 16 January 27 BC. Five years later Plancus occupied the office of censor, and on his death he was buried in a monumental tomb at Caieta, about 80 miles south-east of Rome. We shall meet him again striking coins for Antony in Greece in 40 BC (see nos. 252–5). The type of a capis, or one-handled jug, appears to be personal to the urban prefect and may relate to his membership of the priestly college of the *Epulones*. It occurs again on Plancus' coinage for Mark Antony.

62

62 Draped bust of Victory right, wing visible behind shoulder, **CAESAR DIC TER** before. *Reverse:* Minerva walking left, carrying in her right hand a trophy over right shoulder, and with her left holding spears and shield ornamented with Gorgon's head from which issue rays, snake with head erect at her feet, **C CLOVI** on left, **PRAEF** on right. *Orichalcum dupondius (?). Rome, autumn 45 BC* (RPC 601; Crawford 476/1a; FITA pp. 7–11; Sydenham 1025; BMCRR 4125; Babelon Julia 17; Cohen 7).

62a Similar to preceding, but with the addition of a star on obverse behind head of Victory. *Orichalcum dupondius (?). Rome, autumn 45 BC* (RPC 601; Crawford 476/1b; FITA pp. 7–11; Sydenham 1026; BMCRR 4127; Babelon Julia 17; Cohen 7).

This issue would seem to be closely associated with the gold aurei and quinarii of L. Plancus and there appears to be no compelling reason to regard it as anything other than a complementary coinage produced in Rome for distribution at Caesar's Spanish triumph.[10] The issue of *aes* at this time was a great novelty as regular production had ceased four decades before and was not destined to be resumed until the Augustan reform of *c.*19–18 BC. The idea probably originated with the Pompeian coinage of asses issued in Spain prior to the battle of Munda (see no. 53). These, however, were of the traditional type for this denomination (Janus head/prow) and conformed to the old uncial weight standard of about 22 grams. Caesar's coinage, however, was of totally novel design and was struck in orichalcum (brass), the first time this metal had been used for currency in the West. This makes the denomination difficult to determine, but an approximate weight standard of 15 grams would seem to indicate a dupondius. The bust of Victory and the warlike figure of Minerva convey a clear message that this was a special coinage issued for the celebration of a military success. Not a great deal is known of C. Clovius (or Cluvius), the prefect entrusted with the production of this most unusual coinage. We are not even sure of the precise nature of his prefectship, though it is tempting to assume that he was another of the six *praefecti Urbi* appointed by Caesar before he set out for Spain.[11] In 44 BC we find him as governor of Cisalpine Gaul and there appear to be later references to him in the age of Augustus.

G. Issues of the Roman Moneyers

The final years of Caesar's supremacy in Rome were busy ones for the Capitoline mint and full colleges of three moneyers were appointed for each of the years 46 and 45 BC. All six moneyers struck the entire range of denominations in silver (denarius, quinarius and sestertius) though the bulk of the production was, of course, of denarii. Both years saw Caesar involved in major campaigns against the Pompeian opposition and the coinage of the moneyers was substantially augmented by the dictator's own issues, already described above. Demand was especially high at the time of the quadruple triumph in 46 BC, following the African campaign, and the exceptionally large issues of Cordius Rufus and T. Carisius were clearly intended to meet a major part of that need. It is noticeable that the types of the moneyers' coins in this period show an increasing tendency to allude to Caesar himself rather than to the mint-magistrate's own ancestry. Clearly, if only subtly, a transition was taking place here. But the process was moving inexorably towards the revolutionary changes which were to be introduced on the coinage at the beginning of the fateful year 44 BC.

63 Conjoined heads of the Dioscuri right, wearing laureate pilei surmounted by stars, **RVFVS III VIR** behind and below. *Reverse:* Venus Verticordia standing left, holding scales in right hand and transverse sceptre in left, Cupid hovering behind her left shoulder, **MN CORDIVS** (**MN** ligatured) on right. *Silver denarius. Rome, 46 BC* (Crawford 463/1a; Sydenham 976; BMCRR 4037; Babelon Cordia 2).

63

63a Similar to preceding, but the pilei are decorated with fillet instead of laurel-wreath, and sometimes the moneyer's *nomen* appears as **CORDIV** or **CORDI**. *Silver denarius. Rome, 46 BC* (Crawford 463/1b; Sydenham 976a–c; BMCRR 4039; Babelon Cordia 1).

63a

This denarius coinage in the name of Manius Cordius Rufus is on a scale commensurate with the state's requirements at the time of Caesar's quadruple triumph when, it will be remembered, five thousand denarii were paid to each legionary soldier and ten thousand to each centurion. Other than his coinage, Rufus is known only from an inscription found at Tusculum (*ILLRP* 414) recording that he held the office of praetor. The obverse type of this denarius also indicates his Tusculan origin as there was a special cult of Castor and Pollux at this ancient city of Latium situated about 15 miles south-east of Rome. The reverse type of Venus was doubtless intended to be complimentary to Caesar, and the head of the goddess appears on another of this moneyer's denarius types (see no. 65).

64 Crested Corinthian helmet right, surmounted by owl, **RVFVS** behind. *Reverse:* the aegis, with head of Medusa at centre, **MN CORDIVS** (**MN** ligatured) around. *Silver denarius. Rome, 46 BC* (Crawford 463/2; Sydenham 978; BMCRR 4042; Babelon Cordia 4).

64

65 Diademed head of Venus right, wearing cruciform earring and necklace, **RVFVS S C** behind. *Reverse:* Cupid riding on the back of dolphin right which he guides with bridle, **MN CORDIVS** (**MN** ligatured) below. *Silver denarius. Rome, 46 BC* (Crawford 463/3; Sydenham 977; BMCRR 4040; Babelon Cordia 3).

65

These subsidiary types of Rufus' coinage honour two of the principal female deities of the Roman pantheon – Minerva, goddess of war, and Venus. The allusion is clearly to the dictator: his military successes, especially the most recent at Thapsus; and the ancestry of the *gens* Julia through Iulus, grandson of Venus and Anchises. An interesting feature of no. 65 is the appearance of the formula **S C** (*senatus consulto*) on obverse indicating that the issue was a special one struck under senatorial authority. The reason for this is unclear but it must be related to the exceptional demands being made on the mint at this time to provide sufficient coinage to meet the expenses of the quadruple triumph. It may have been discovered that there was a shortfall in the quantity of coinage originally authorized necessitating an emergency measure by the Conscript Fathers to provide additional supplies.

66 Radiate head of Sol right, **MN** (ligatured) **CORDIVS** (or **CORDI**) behind and below. *Reverse:* eagle standing left, looking right, wings extended, **RVFVS** in exergue. *Silver quinarius. Rome, 46 BC* (Crawford 463/4b–d; Sydenham 979, 979a; BMCRR 4044; RSC/Babelon Cordia 5b, 5c).

66

66a

66a Similar to preceding, but the eagle stands to right, looking left. *Silver quinarius. Rome, 46 BC* (Crawford 463/4a; Sydenham 979b; BMCRR vol. I, p. 525, note 1; Babelon Cordia 5).

Caesar's restoration of the silver quinarius (half denarius) in 48–47 BC led to a brief revival of this small denomination which had never been established as a regular part of the republican monetary system. Production of the quinarius and its half, the silver sestertius, by the moneyers of 46 and 45 BC could well have been associated with the dictator's two military triumphs, following Thapsus and Munda, in which these exceptional coins would have fulfilled some special ceremonial purpose. The types of Cordius Rufus' quinarii honour two of the principal male deities of the Roman pantheon – the sun god Sol, whose head is depicted wearing his crown of rays; and Jupiter, who is represented by his attendant eagle.

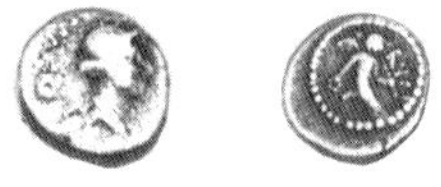

67

67 Diademed head of Venus right, MN (ligatured) CORDIVS (or CORDI) behind. *Reverse:* Cupid walking right, holding wreath and palm-branch, RVFVS (or RVFV or RVFI or RVF) on right. *Silver sestertius. Rome, 46 BC* (Crawford 463/5a–b; Sydenham 980, 980a–b; BMCRR 4045, 4048; Babelon Cordia 6, 7).

68

68 Crested Corinthian helmet right, MN CORDIVS (MN ligatured) behind and below. *Reverse:* Cupid walking right, holding wreath and palm-branch, RVFVS (or RVFI or RVF) on right. *Silver sestertius. Rome, 46 BC* (Crawford 463/6a; Sydenham 981, 981a; BMCRR 4049; Babelon Cordia 8, 9).

68a Similar to preceding, but the reverse legend RVFVS is to left of Cupid. *Silver sestertius. Rome, 46 BC* (Crawford 463/6b).

The sestertii of this moneyer echo two of his denarius types (nos. 64 and 65) in honouring Minerva and Venus. It is interesting to note that Cupid, the child of Venus, is depicted with the usual attributes of the goddess Victory (wreath and palm-branch) thus emphasizing the allusion to Caesar's successes against his adversaries.

Little appears to be known of Titus Carisius, the principal colleague of Cordius Rufus in the monetary triumvirate for 46 BC, though he may have been the father of the P. Carisius who was *legatus pro praetore* under Augustus in Spain and who issued an extensive coinage from the newly founded colony of Augusta Emerita (modern *Mérida*) in 25–23 BC. As in the case of Rufus, part of the denarius coinage of T. Carisius was produced under senatorial sanction, using the formula S C (*senatus consulto*), suggesting an emergency augmentation of the issue to meet the special needs of Caesar's quadruple triumph.

69

69 Head of the Sibyl Herophile right, her hair bejewelled and enclosed in a sling. *Reverse:* Sphinx seated right, T CARISIVS (or CARISIV) above and/or before, III VIR in exergue. *Silver denarius. Rome, 46 BC* (Crawford 464/1; Sydenham 983, 983a–b; BMCRR 4060–62; Babelon Carisia 10, 11).

This attractive type was doubtless intended to be complimentary to Caesar by drawing attention to the supposed Trojan origin of the Julia *gens* (through

Venus and Aeneas). The city of Gergis in the Troad, close to ancient Troy, claimed to be the birthplace of the Sibyl Herophile, a priestess endowed with prophetic powers. Her tomb was also stated to be in the temple of Apollo at Gergis and coins of the city struck in the 4th and 3rd centuries BC depict her facing head with a seated Sphinx on reverse.[12] Attalus I of Pergamum (241–197 BC) removed the inhabitants of Gergis to a new location near the sources of the river Caicus, and early in the 2nd century BC the former territory of Gergis was given by the Romans to Ilium, the city built on the site of ancient Troy.

70

70 Head of Juno Moneta right, with slight drapery, wearing cruciform earring and necklace, MONETA behind. *Reverse:* implements for coining money – anvil die with garlanded punch die above, tongs on left, hammer on right, T CARISIVS (or CARISIV) above, all within laurel-wreath. *Silver denarius. Rome, 46 BC* (Crawford 464/2; Sydenham 982, 982a-b; BMCRR 4056; Babelon Carisia 1).

This celebrated type refers directly to the office of moneyer at a time when the mint was the focus of attention as it worked under enormous pressure endeavouring to meet the abnormally high demand for currency occasioned by the distribution of cash to thousands of veterans at the dictator's quadruple triumph. The obverse type refers to the location of the mint which was situated on the Capitol next to the temple of Juno Moneta. The reverse depicts the actual implements employed by the mint workers in their task of striking the coin blanks. The reverse (punch) die is shown above the anvil containing the obverse die. Also depicted are the hammer with which the punch die was struck and the tongs for handling the heated blanks prior to striking.

71

71a

71b

71 Head of Roma right, wearing helmet with plain crest and decorated at side with feather, ROMA behind. *Reverse:* cornucopiae resting on globe between sceptre, on left, and rudder, on right, T CARISI (or CARIS or CARISIV) below, all within laurel-wreath. *Silver denarius. Rome, 46 BC* (Crawford 464/3c; Sydenham 984, 984a–b; BMCRR 4066, 4069; Babelon Carisia 4, 5).

71a Similar to preceding, but Roma's helmet has ornate crest of chevron pattern. *Silver denarius. Rome, 46 BC* (Crawford 464/3a; Sydenham 984, 984a–b; BMCRR 4065, 4068; Babelon Carisia 4, 5).

71b Similar to preceding, but the helmet has dragon's head instead of crest. *Silver denarius. Rome, 46 BC* (Crawford 464/3b; Sydenham 984, 984a–b; BMCRR 4064, 4067; Babelon Carisia 4, 5).

This type symbolizes the world dominion exercised by Rome extending over both land and sea, the former represented by the magistrate's sceptre, the latter by the ship's rudder; and the universal prosperity enjoyed under her beneficent rule indicated by the horn of plenty atop the celestial globe. Once again the reference is to the dictator, not the moneyer, and reflects the hope that with Caesar's recent victory over the Pompeians at Thapsus peace and prosperity can now be restored following the disruption of three years of civil conflict.

72

72 Draped bust of Victory right, wearing diadem of pearls, wings visible behind shoulders. *Reverse:* Victory in galloping biga right, holding wreath in extended right hand, T CARISI in exergue. *Silver denarius. Rome, 46 BC* (Crawford 464/4; Sydenham 986; BMCRR 4073; Babelon Carisia 2).

73

73 Draped bust of Victory right, wings visible behind shoulders, S C behind. *Reverse:* Victory in galloping quadriga right, holding wreath in extended right hand, T CARISI in exergue. *Silver denarius. Rome, 46 BC* (Crawford 464/5; Sydenham 985; BMCRR 4070; Babelon Carisia 3).

One reverse die has been noted on which the engraver has mistakenly spelt the moneyer's nomen ***CARSI*** *(Paris).*

These two types, featuring the goddess of victory on both obverse and reverse, are clearly in celebration of Caesar's recent success in the African campaign which, together with his earlier conquests, was about to be acclaimed in the quadruple triumph. The second version, which adds the formula S C (*senatus consulto*) to the obverse design, would seem to indicate an emergency supplement to Carisius' output of denarii necessitated by Caesar's urgent need for extra supplies of coinage with which to pay his veterans (see no. 65 for the corresponding issue of Cordius Rufus).

74

74 Draped bust of Victory right, wings visible behind shoulders, palm-branch over left shoulder. *Reverse:* Roma seated left on pile of arms, holding short sword in right hand and resting on sceptre held in left, her right foot set on helmet, T CARISI on right. *Silver quinarius. Rome, 46 BC* (Crawford 464/6; Sydenham 987; BMCRR 4075; Babelon Carisia 6).

The rare half denarius of Carisius again dwells on the theme of Caesar's victories. Roma is shown at rest having, through her dictator, overcome the enemies of the state by military conquest. In contrast, the types of the silver sestertii concentrate on honouring the principal deities of the Roman pantheon, a topic more prominent on the coinage of Carisius' colleague, Cordius

Rufus. A bearded head of Bacchus' attendant Silenus (usually identified as Pan) appears in combination with a panther, the animal sacred to the god of wine; whilst Diana in her role as the huntress is shown with her hound.

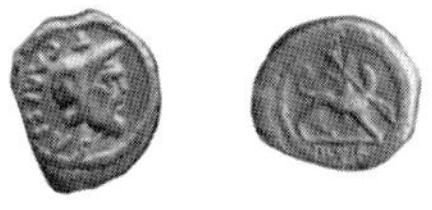
75

75 Bearded head of Silenus right, **T CARISIVS** behind, above, or below. *Reverse:* panther walking right, holding thyrsus, **III VIR** in exergue. *Silver sestertius. Rome, 46 BC* (Crawford 464/7a,b; Sydenham 988, 988a; BMCRR 4076; Babelon Carisia 12, 13).

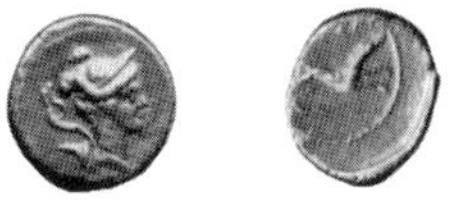
76

76 Diademed head of Diana right, bow and quiver over shoulder visible behind. *Reverse:* hound running right, **T CARISI** (or **CARIS** or **CAR** or **CA**) above. *Silver sestertius. Rome, 46 BC* (Crawford 464/8a; Sydenham 989; BMCRR 4077; Babelon Carisia 7).

76a Similar to preceding, but the reverse legend (**T CA**, **T CARIS**, or **T CARISI**) is in exergue. *Silver sestertius. Rome, 46 BC* (Crawford 464/8b; Sydenham 989a; BMCRR vol. I, p. 531, note 1; Babelon Carisia 8, 9).

The remaining member of the monetary triumvirate for 46 BC was Gaius Considius Paetus who is otherwise unknown to history. His denarii were not issued in such large quantities as those of his two colleagues and he would seem to be the odd man out in other respects, *viz* the absence of an issue corresponding to the special *senatus consulto* types of Cordius Rufus and T. Carisius (see nos. 65 and 73) and the absence of the title *triumvir* (**III VIR**) in his coin inscriptions. This probably indicates that Paetus was the junior member of his monetary college and that his coinage belongs to the latter part of the year, after the quadruple triumph, when the pressure on the mint had significantly diminished.

77

77a

77b

77 Laureate head of Apollo right within laurel-wreath. *Reverse:* curule chair, **C CONSIDIVS** above, **PAETVS** in exergue. *Silver denarius. Rome, 46 BC* (Crawford 465/1a; Sydenham 990; BMCRR 4080; Babelon Considia 4).

77c

77a Similar to preceding, but with border of dots instead of laurel-wreath on obverse. *Silver denarius. Rome, 46 BC* (Crawford 465/1b; Sydenham 990a; BMCRR 4083; Babelon Considia 3).

77b Similar to preceding, but with **A** behind head of Apollo, and **C CONSIDI** above curule chair, **PAETI** in exergue. *Silver denarius.* Rome, 46 BC (Crawford 465/2a; Sydenham 991; BMCRR 4084; Babelon Considia 2).

77c Similar to preceding, but without border of dots on obverse. *Silver denarius. Rome, 46 BC* (Crawford 465/2b; Sydenham 991a; BMCRR 4086; RSC/Babelon Considia 2a).

Crawford[13] suggests that this reverse type may refer to 'the privilege accorded to Caesar after his victory at Thapsus to sit in the Senate on a curule chair between the Consuls'. The letter 'A' appearing on the obverses of two of the varieties (nos. 77b and 77c) is presumably intended to emphasize the identity of the deity depicted. Especially noticeable on this issue is the rendering of the moneyer's name in two cases, the nominative (CONSIDIVS PAETVS) and the genitive (CONSIDI PAETI). The same peculiarity, though less pronounced, may be observed also on certain issues of Paetus' two colleagues, Cordius Rufus (CORDIVS RVFVS, CORDI RVFI) and T. Carisius (T CARISIVS, T CARISI).

78

78a

78 Laureate and diademed head of Venus right, PAETI behind. *Reverse:* Victory in galloping quadriga left, holding wreath in right hand and long palm-branch and reins in left, C CONSIDI in exergue. *Silver denarius. Rome, 46 BC* (Crawford 465/3; Sydenham 992; BMCRR 4087; Babelon Considia 6).

78a Similar to preceding, but head of Venus is to left. *Silver denarius. Rome, 46 BC* (Crawford 465/4; Sydenham 993; BMCRR 4090; Babelon Considia 7).

79

79 Bust of Minerva right, wearing crested Corinthian helmet and aegis. *Reverse:* Victory in galloping quadriga right, holding wreath in right hand and long palm-branch and reins in left, C CONSIDI in exergue. *Silver denarius. Rome, 46 BC* (Crawford 465/5; Sydenham 994; BMCRR 4091; Babelon Considia 5).

Both of these types refer unequivocally to the dictator's recent military success against the Pompeians in Africa. Venus, especially sacred to Caesar and his family, is complemented by Minerva (Athena), goddess of war, whose head, wearing the distinctive Corinthian-type helmet, recalls the gold coinage of Alexander the Great himself. The unifying element of both types is Victory driving her chariot at full speed into the fray of battle.

80

80 Laureate and diademed head of Venus right, PAETI behind. *Reverse:* Victory walking right, bearing trophy with both hands, C CONSIDI on right. *Silver quinarius. Rome, 46 BC* (Crawford 465/7b; Sydenham 996a; BMCRR 4095; Babelon Considia 8).

80a Similar to preceding, but head of Venus is diademed only, and with PAETVS instead of PAETI and CONSIDIVS instead of CONSIDI. *Silver quinarius. Rome, 46 BC* (Crawford 465/7a; Sydenham 996, misdescribed; BMCRR 4094, misdescribed; RSC/Babelon Considia 8a).

80b Laureate and diademed head of Venus right, PAETI behind. *Reverse:* Victory walking left, bearing trophy with both hands, C CONSIDI (or CONSIDIV or CONSIDIVS) on left. *Silver quinarius. Rome, 46 BC* (Crawford 465/6b–d; Sydenham 995a, misdescribed, and 996b; BMCRR 4096; RSC/Babelon Considia 9–9b).

80b

80c Similar to preceding, but head of Venus is diademed only and with PAETVS instead of PAETI behind; C CONSIDIVS on reverse. *Silver quinarius. Rome, 46 BC* (Crawford 465/6a; Sydenham 995; BMCRR 4093; RSC/Babelon Considia 9c).

81 Winged bust of Cupid right, C CONSIDIVS (or CONSIDI or CONSID or COSNVS) below. *Reverse:* double cornucopiae on globe. *Silver sestertius. Rome, 46 BC* (Crawford 465/8a; Sydenham 997, 997a; BMCRR 4097–8; Babelon Considia 10).

81

81a Similar to preceding, but the head of Cupid is very small, with C CONSIDIVS (or CONSIDI) below. *Silver sestertius. Rome, 46 BC* (Crawford 465/8b; Sydenham 997b–c; Babelon Considia 11).

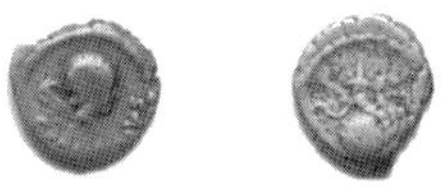

81a

Like the denarii, the fractional silver denominations of this moneyer concentrate on the theme of Caesar, his military successes and their consequences. Venus is again prominent and Cupid, youthful son of the goddess, appears on the sestertius. Victory bearing a military trophy commemorates Thapsus whilst the double cornucopiae surmounting the celestial globe is symbolic of the prosperity of the Roman world, the restoration of which has been made possible by Caesar's defeat of the enemies of the state (see also no. 71).

The college of three moneyers appointed for the following year (45 BC) consisted of Lucius Papius Celsus, Lollius Palicanus, and Lucius Valerius Acisculus. Their issues were on a significantly smaller scale than those of their immediate predecessors, the volume of whose coinage had been expanded to accommodate the dictator's need for additional supplies of currency at the time of the quadruple triumph. All three moneyers struck the full range of silver denominations – denarius, quinarius, and sestertius. Collectively, their coinage represents the last normal republican issue from the Capitoline mint prior to the fundamental changes introduced by Caesar at the beginning of 44 BC which, within a few years, were to lead to the complete cessation of regular production.

82 Head of Juno Sospita right, clad in goat's skin tied at neck. *Reverse:* she-wolf standing right, holding in her mouth a stick which she is about to place on a brazier to right of which stands eagle fanning the flames with its wings, L PAPIVS in exergue, CELSVS III VIR above. *Silver denarius. Rome, 45 BC* (Crawford 472/1; Sydenham 964; BMCRR 4018; Babelon Papia 2).

82

One reverse die has been noted on which the engraver has mistakenly spelt the moneyer's cognomen ***CEESVS***.

83 Laureate head of Triumphus right, trophy over left shoulder visible behind, TRIVMPVS below. *Reverse:* same as preceding. *Silver denarius.*

83

Rome, 45 BC (Crawford 472/2; Sydenham 965; BMCRR 4023; Babelon Papia 3).

One obverse die has been noted on which the engraver has mistakenly spelt the name of the deity **TRIΛMPVS**.

84

85

84 Bust of Victory right, wings visible behind shoulders. *Reverse:* girl standing right, feeding from her dress a snake which is erect before her, **L PAPIVS** on left, **CELSVS** on right. *Silver quinarius. Rome, 45 BC* (Crawford 472/3; Sydenham 966; BMCRR 4025; Babelon Papia 4).

84a Similar to preceding, but without the moneyer's *cognomen* **CELSVS** on reverse. *Silver quinarius. Rome, 45 BC* (Crawford 472/3; Sydenham 966a; BMCRR 4027; RSC/Babelon Papia 4a).

85 Head of Mercury right, wearing winged petasus, caduceus over left shoulder visible behind, **CELSVS** before. *Reverse:* lyre (no legend). *Silver sestertius. Rome, 45 BC* (Crawford 472/4b; Sydenham 967; BMCRR 4028; Babelon Papia 5).

85a Similar to preceding, but with **L PAPI** to right of lyre on reverse. *Silver sestertius. Rome, 45 BC* (Crawford 472/4a; Sydenham 969; BMCRR vol. I, p. 520, note 2; Babelon Papia 7).

85b Similar to preceding, but with **CELSVS** instead of **L PAPI** on reverse. *Silver sestertius. Rome, 45 BC* (Crawford 472/4c; Sydenham 968; BMCRR vol. I, p. 520, note 2; Babelon Papia 6).

L. Papius Celsus is known only from his coinage though it seems likely that he was the son of the Lucius Papius who had held the office of moneyer about three and a half decades before (cf. Crawford 384). Both moneyers indicated their origin by the depiction of Juno Sospita, the goddess clad in a goat's skin, who was especially sacred to the inhabitants of Lanuvium (modern *Lanuvio*), an ancient Latin city in the Alban Hills about twenty miles south-east of Rome. Celsus' coinage has other Lanuvine types: the girl feeding a snake, which relates to an annual ceremony in which a young virgin descended into the grotto below the temple of Juno Sospita to feed the sacred serpent; and the she-wolf and eagle kindling a fire, which appears to illustrate the legend of the foundation of the city as recorded by Dionysius of Halicarnassus in his *Roman Antiquities* (i. 59) written during the reign of Augustus. The former had already appeared as a coin type on the denarii of another son of Lanuvium, L. Roscius Fabatus, whose issues are dated to *c.*64 BC (cf. Crawford 412). The obverse types of nos. 83 (Triumphus) and 84 (Victory) would appear to be commemorative of the previous year's great events, though an alternative interpretation would be that these coins make reference to Munda and the triumph staged in Rome in the autumn of 45 BC in celebration of the dictator's final victory over the Pompeians. The appearance of Mercury on the sestertius conforms to the usual Caesarian pattern for this denomination of honouring the principal deities of the Roman pantheon. Mercury, the Roman equivalent of the Greek Hermes, was a patron of both artists and merchants. On this type he is linked with the lyre, the musical instrument utilizing a tortoise-shell for its sound box, which was said to have been invented by the god. Mercury was again to appear on sestertii of the following year issued by the moneyer P. Sepullius Macer (see no. 170).

Lollius Palicanus, colleague of Celsus in the moneyership for 45 BC, seems to have been the son of the Marcus Lollius Palicanus who held the office of tribune of the plebs in 71 BC and the praetorship several years later. The coin types of the younger Palicanus appear to refer both to his father's career and to contemporary events in Caesarian Rome.

86 Diademed head of Libertas right, wearing earring and necklace, **LIBERTATIS** behind. *Reverse:* view of the Rostra in the Roman Forum, ornamented with ships' beaks and surmounted by subsellium (tribune's bench), **PALIKANVS** (or **PALIKANI** or **PALIKANVS** with **NV** ligatured) above. *Silver denarius. Rome, 45 BC* (Crawford 473/1; Sydenham 960, 960a; BMCRR 4011; Babelon Lollia 2).

86

This type would seem to make reference to the tribunate of the elder Palicanus, father of the moneyer, during which vigorous efforts were made to restore the rights and privileges of the *tribuni plebis*, representatives of the common people, which had been severely curtailed during the dictatorship of Sulla. The appearance of Libertas, personification of the freedom of the individual citizen, was also relevant to contemporary events as Caesar was regarded as the 'Liberator' of the state following his final destruction of the Pompeian opposition at Munda. The depiction on the reverse is of the Rostra, the celebrated speakers' platform in the Roman Forum. This structure received its name from the beaks (rams of war-galleys), captured from the neighbouring city of Antium, with which the platform was adorned in 338 BC.

87 Laureate head of Honos right, **HONORIS** behind. *Reverse:* curule chair, sometimes garlanded and/or surmounted by wreath, between two ears of corn, **PALIKANVS** above. *Silver denarius. Rome, 45 BC* (Crawford 473/2a–d; Sydenham 961; BMCRR 4014; Babelon Lollia 1).

87

The allusion here would again appear to be to the career of the elder Palicanus and to his political advancement, though merit and 'honour', to the curule magistracy of the praetorship (*c.*69 BC). However, as in the case of the previous type there may be a double meaning. The curule chair could refer to the special privileges granted to Caesar following his victory at Thapsus giving him the extraordinary right to attend meetings of the Senate seated on a curule chair between the consuls (cf. the denarius type of C. Considius Paetus, no. 77).

88 Diademed head of Felicitas right, wearing earring and necklace, **FELICITATIS** behind. *Reverse:* Victory in galloping biga right, holding wreath in right hand, **PALIKANI** in exergue. *Silver quinarius. Rome, 45 BC* (Crawford 473/3; Sydenham 962; BMCRR 4016; RSC/Babelon Lollia 3a).

88

The unequivocal message of this type is the 'happiness' (*Felicitas*) of the Roman people occasioned by Caesar's victory at Munda over the Pompeians, the enemies of the state. This is the only appearance of the goddess Felicitas on the coinage of the Roman Republic.

89 Urn without handles (olla). *Reverse:* tessera nummularia with ring attached, **PALIK** on right, **ANVS** on left. *Silver sestertius. Rome, 45 BC* (Crawford 473/4; Sydenham 963; BMCRR 4017; Babelon Lollia 4).

89

An enigmatic type which has been the subject of a variety of interpretations, the sestertius of Lollius Palicanus has been explained by Crawford[14] as representing on the obverse a money-container and on the reverse a *tessera nummularia*. This was a bronze ticket, or tag, with which the money-changers (*nummularii*) marked the bags of coins the contents of which they had counted and certified as being of good metal and weight. The reason for the appearance of this interesting type is not clear but may be related to measures, not otherwise attested, taken by Caesar to strengthen public confidence in the currency during this prolonged period of civil conflict when so many of the coins in circulation were emanating from mints other than the official establishment in Rome.

The other member of the monetary triumvirate for the year 45 BC was Lucius Valerius Acisculus about whom little else has been recorded. The types of his denarii are more varied than those of his colleagues and have given rise to much scholarly speculation, but most probably relate, if only by allusion, to the achievements of the dictator who now occupied a position of virtually unchallenged supremacy in Rome and her provinces.

90

90a

90 Head of Apollo right surmounted by star, his hair tied with band, double-headed pick (*acisculus*) behind, ACISCVLVS behind and below, border of dots. *Reverse:* Europa seated on bull walking right, holding with both hands her veil which billows out in a semicircle above her head, L VALERIVS (or VALERIV) in exergue. *Silver denarius. Rome, 45 BC* (Crawford 474/1a; Sydenham 998; BMCRR 4099; Babelon Valeria 17).

90a Similar to preceding, but with laurel-wreath border on obverse. *Silver denarius. Rome, 45 BC* (Crawford 474/1b; Sydenham 998a; BMCRR 4102; Babelon Valeria 16).

The interpretation of this attractive reverse type has exercised the minds of many numismatists dating back to Charles Lenormant.[15] The generally accepted view that the female figure is that of Valeria Luperca (sister of the early Roman consul Publicola and the heroine of a legend related by Plutarch) has not gone unchallenged and has recently been firmly rejected by Crawford[16] who prefers to see Europa riding on the bull. In mythology, Zeus fell in love with this Phoenician princess and, turning himself into a bull, enticed her to ride on his back whereupon he swam out to sea and took her to Crete where she bore him several children. Is it too fanciful to see in this type a reference to Queen Cleopatra of Egypt who, at Caesar's invitation in 46 BC, had crossed the sea to join him in Rome where she remained until his assassination? The significance of Apollo's appearance on the obverses of this, and the following two types, remains obscure: the star is an indication of divinity.

91 *Obverse:* same as 90a. *Reverse:* human-headed owl, wearing crested Corinthian helmet, walking right, carrying spear and shield, L VALERIVS in exergue, laurel-wreath border. *Silver denarius. Rome, 45 BC* (Crawford 474/2a; Sydenham 999; BMCRR 4105; RSC/Babelon Valeria 18a).

91a Similar to preceding, but the owl carries two spears and shield. *Silver denarius. Rome, 45 BC* (Crawford 474/2b; Sydenham 999a; BMCRR 4106; Babelon Valeria 18).

91a

91b Similar to preceding, but the legend (L VALERIVS) is behind the owl instead of in exergue. *Silver denarius. Rome, 45 BC* (Crawford 474/2c; Sydenham 999b; BMCRR 4108; Babelon Valeria 19).

91b

This curious reverse symbolizes Minerva, goddess of war and patroness of wisdom, who was the Roman equivalent of the Greek Athena. The primary reference is to Caesar's successes in the field, but this unusual form of representation of the goddess with the emphasis placed on her attendant bird, the owl, may be intended to draw attention to other aspects of the dictator's accomplishments – his innovativeness as an administrator and perhaps even to his brilliance as an orator and an author. The laurel-wreaths surrounding the types (also to be seen on nos. 92 and 92a, and on the obverses of nos. 90a, 93 and 95) are a further reference to the honours bestowed on Caesar following his victories at Thapsus and Munda.

92

92a

92 *Obverse:* same as 90a. *Reverse:* head of Sibyl right, her hair bejewelled and enclosed in a sling, L VALERIVS before, laurel-wreath border. *Silver denarius. Rome, 45 BC* (Crawford 474/3a; Sydenham 1000; BMCRR 4109; Babelon Valeria 14).

92a Similar to preceding, but without legend on reverse. *Silver denarius. Rome, 45 BC* (Crawford 474/3b; Sydenham 1001; RSC/Babelon Valeria 15a).

The graceful head of a Sibyl (presumably the Sibyl Herophile) on this type invites comparison with the issue of T. Carisius, moneyer in the preceding year (see no. 69). The purpose, as before, was probably to draw attention to the supposed Trojan origin of the Julia *gens* and its illustrious son, the dictator C. Julius Caesar.

93

93 Laureate head of Jupiter right, double-headed pick (*acisculus*) behind, ACISCVLVS behind and below, laurel-wreath border. *Reverse:* snake-legged ('anguipedic') giant, with his right hand grasping a thunderbolt which has pierced his side, his left hand raised, L VALERIVS in exergue. *Silver denarius. Rome, 45 BC* (Crawford 474/4; Sydenham 1003; BMCRR 4114; Babelon Valeria 21).

This appealing type illustrates the battle of the Gods against the Giants, the obvious symbolism being Caesar's victories over his enemies, foremost amongst whom were the Pompeians. A similar representation had appeared on a denarius issued some seven decades earlier by the moneyer Cn. Cornelius Sisenna (cf. Crawford 310). The theme of this epic struggle was a popular one in art and was an obvious choice as a coin type to flatter the vanity of the dictator. Its equation of Caesar with the supreme deity (possibly augmented by the reverse type of no. 90) doubtless caused consternation in the ranks of the traditional Republicans whose protests may have led to an abrupt termination of the issue, hence its surprising rarity today.

94

94 Radiate head of Sol right, double-headed pick (*acisculus*) behind, ACISCVLVS behind and below. *Reverse:* Luna in galloping biga right, holding whip in extended right hand, L VALERIVS in exergue. *Silver denarius. Rome, 45 BC* (Crawford 474/5; Sydenham 1002; BMCRR 4110; Babelon Valeria 20).

The celestial deities representing the Sun and the Moon are mutually complementary. Sol suggests a reference to eastern affairs, possibly Caesar's military successes in Egypt and Asia Minor in 48–47 BC with perhaps even the hint of an allusion to the presence of the young Cleopatra in Rome. Moreover, with the final removal of the Pompeian threat the dictator was now planning a campaign against Parthia with the object of avenging the disastrous defeat of Crassus eight years before and recovering his lost legionary standards.

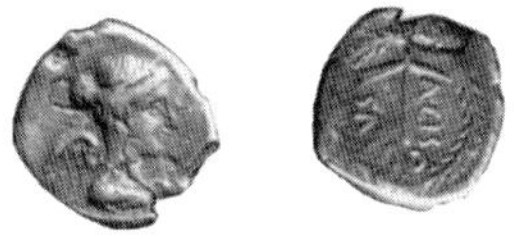

95

95 Bust of Victory right, wings visible behind shoulders. *Reverse:* double-headed pick (*acisculus*), ACISCVLVS around, laurel-wreath border. *Silver quinarius. Rome, 45 BC* (Crawford 474/6; Sydenham 1004; BMCRR 4116; Babelon Valeria 22).

As usual, Victory is featured prominently on the quinarius and refers to Caesar's triumph over his Pompeian adversaries. The *acisculus*, a punning allusion to the moneyer's *cognomen* which is used as a subsidiary symbol on the obverses of all his denarii, appears as a principal type on both of the fractional denominations. The obverses of the sestertii give further emphasis to Caesarian themes already well established on the coins of the moneyers: prosperity and material abundance, as symbolized by the double cornucopiae, had already appeared the previous year on a sestertius of Considius Paetus (see no. 81); and the supposed Trojan origin of the Julia *gens* had been commemorated by the depiction of the Sibyl Herophile on a denarius of Titus Carisius (see no. 69) as well as on denarii of Acisculus' own coinage (see no. 92).

96 Double cornucopiae bound with fillet. *Reverse:* double-headed pick (*acisculus*), ACISCVLVS around. *Silver sestertius. Rome, 45 BC* (Crawford 474/7; Sydenham 1005; BMCRR 4117; Babelon Valeria 23).

97 Head of Sibyl right, laurel-branch before. *Reverse:* same as preceding. *Silver sestertius. Rome, 45 BC* (Crawford 474/8; RSC/Babelon Valeria 23a).[17]

96

CHAPTER 3

The Ides of March and Philippi – the death of Caesar and the downfall of the Republican cause, 44–42 BC

The final act in the Caesarian drama was about to be played out. Five years had now elapsed since the crossing of the Rubicon and Caesar's initial challenge to the supremacy of Pompey. Those years had witnessed the dictator's meteoric rise to a position of virtually unchallenged dominion in Rome and her provinces and a corresponding decline in the authority of the Senate which was, in the main, still under the control of the old nobility. This decline in senatorial authority had, of course, been an ongoing process spanning many decades, but the political convulsions initiated by Caesar's invasion of Italy in 49 BC had surely set the seal on the fate of Rome's republican government.

On his return to Rome in September, 45 BC, following the final victory over the Pompeians at Munda, Caesar was at last able to turn his attention to the future and his own role in the government of the state. What his perception of that role was we can only surmise, for he now had only six months to live and the final outcome of the complex sequence of events following his sudden and violent removal from the political scene probably bore little resemblance to Caesar's own ultimate ambitions if, indeed, he even had a clear idea of where his destiny was leading him. Caesar was a maestro of opportunism and it may well be that there never was such a thing as a great master plan in his mind, rather a brilliant ability always to turn the current situation to his advantage. If he perceived the possibility of establishing a permanent autocracy then his concept of this would surely have been based on the great Hellenistic monarchies of the post-Alexandrine age, the last surviving representative of which he had recently become acquainted with during his stay in Egypt (48–47 BC). Such an idea would have been abhorrent to Romans of all classes, not just the old aristocracy, and had Caesar survived the Ides of March it is conceivable that he might have transferred his residence to the East where kingship and the divinity of a ruler were long-established traditions. Cleopatra, the queen of Egypt and the living representative of a 300-year-old dynasty of god-kings, was with Caesar in Rome at this time and the importance of her influence should not be underestimated. Her political ambitions were clearly to be revealed a decade later when her influence over Mark Antony led to his adoption of the trappings of oriental monarchy and, ultimately, the betrayal of his

Roman supporters. Caesar, had he lived, might have been tempted down the same path, though one suspects that Cleopatra's hold over the dictator's affections was of a more transitory kind.

Whatever his long-term goals one thing was assured: Caesar had no immediate plans to resign his extraordinary powers and restore the full authority of the Senate. This he made clear in a number of ways. Instead of initiating the process of disbanding his army, now that the struggle with the Pompeians was over, he actually began making preparations for a war against Parthia. Doubtless, Caesarian propaganda emphasized that it was now time to avenge the disastrous defeat of Crassus in 53 BC, and the loss of his legionary standards, and to restore Roman military prestige in the eyes of the Republic's principal foreign adversary. But had Caesar been able to return to Rome as the conqueror of Parthia his popularity and authority would have been so much enhanced that it would have been virtually impossible for the aristocracy to oppose whatever constitutional changes he then wished to enact. The new year (44 BC) saw further startling developments. In addition to embarking on his third consecutive consulship (his fifth) Caesar was declared dictator for life (*dictator perpetuus*), an unprecedented step which must have caused disappointment and alarm amongst large numbers of the aristocracy who were now looking for a return to constitutional government. But perhaps the greatest blow to those who cherished hopes of Caesar's early retirement from the political arena (the path chosen by Sulla thirty-five years before) was the appearance of the dictator's portrait on the silver denarii minted by all four of the newly appointed college of moneyers. This was a truly revolutionary step and must have been viewed as such by contemporaries. Portraits of the recently deceased Pompey had appeared on denarii issued in Spain prior to Munda (see nos. 49–52) and ancestral portraiture had appeared with some regularity on the coins of the moneyers over the preceding decade. But the actual depiction of the current head of state, even if the constitutionality of his position was open to question, would certainly have been viewed by some as tantamount to a recognition of his kingship and even his divinity.

In this unhealthy climate of stifled anger and resentment on the part of a frustrated senatorial opposition the plot against Caesar's life gradually took form. Suetonius[18] records that more than sixty conspirators were implicated in the cabal and, in illustration of the general discontent with the dictatorial regime, quotes a line of graffiti which had been scrawled on the pedestal of the statue of L. Junius Brutus, Rome's first consul in 509 BC – 'If only you were alive now!' He also records a verse which appeared one day on the base of Caesar's own statue – 'Brutus was elected Consul when he sent the Kings away; Caesar sent the Consuls packing, Caesar is our King today'. Whether accurately reported or not, these sentiments surely represent the mood of the capital in the opening weeks of the year 44 BC. Foremost in the conspiracy were M. Junius Brutus, son-in-law of Cato (the martyr of Thapsus); C. Cassius Longinus, a survivor of Crassus' defeat by the Parthians in 53 BC and later a supporter of Pompey, but pardoned by Caesar in 47 BC; and Decimus Junius Brutus, a Caesarian officer especially favoured by the dictator, who had held the office of moneyer in 48 BC (see nos. 25–8). These three men were all to play significant roles in the political manoeuvrings of the early years of the post-Caesarian period. Doubtless, many individual motives were at work amongst the three score conspirators but all were probably united in the belief that they were performing the duty of patriotic citizens in ridding the state of a dangerous tyrant. Cicero was not of their number but nevertheless steadfastly regarded the tyrannicides as heroes.

On the evening of 14 March Caesar dined at the house of his *magister equitum* (master of horse) M. Aemilius Lepidus, Decimus Brutus being one of the company. If the writings of the 2nd century AD author Appian of Alexandria[19] are to be given credence, one of the topics of conversation amongst Lepidus' guests was the type of death to be preferred over all others. Portentously, Caesar alone expressed the desire for a sudden death and one may wonder at the feelings of Decimus Brutus on hearing the words spoken by his benefactor and intended victim. Later that night the dictator's wife, Calpurnia, had a nightmare in which she saw her husband wounded and bleeding. Not surprisingly, this dream had such a profound effect on her that she begged Caesar not to attend the Senate meeting the following day, a plea to which he was inclined to yield. However, Decimus Brutus was within earshot of the enactment of this touching domestic scene and quickly realized that today's meeting represented the last opportunity for the conspirators to have access to the dictator before he returned to the security of his military camp prior to the departure for the East. Accordingly he persuaded Caesar to go ahead with the original plan, pointing out that it would scarcely be politic to show disrepect to the Conscript Fathers on the eve of setting out for a foreign war. So the dictator's fate was sealed. As he sat in the Senate chamber, supposedly in the company of friends, his colleague in the consulship, Mark Antony, was detained outside and engaged in conversation by Gaius Trebonius. With their daggers concealed the other conspirators gathered around the dictator whose suspicions were still not aroused. By a pre-arranged plan one of their number began arguing with Caesar over the matter of his brother's banishment. In the heat of the dispute he seized the dictator's robe whereupon the other assassins fell upon their defenceless victim whose final act was to resign himself voluntarily to his inevitable fate. He fell under a rain of dagger blows at the foot of Pompey's statue. The act was clearly an immense tragedy for Rome. The state was in the midst of a complex constitutional transition and the sudden loss of a statesman and soldier of Caesar's brilliance, at the very height of his powers, could only lead to the direst consequences in terms of human suffering and political dislocation. Fourteen years of bloody conflict would now ensue before another man could stand at the same pinnacle of supreme authority as Caesar had done at the dawn of the Ides of March, 44 BC.

Rome was stunned by the loss of its great leader. Caesar, like Abraham Lincoln nineteen centuries later, 'now belonged to the ages'.[20] But those remaining had to make quick decisions upon which much might depend now that the brutal actions of a few moments had totally transformed the situation and apparently undone all that Caesar had striven to achieve over the preceding half decade. Would, as the assassins fondly believed, the Republic now miraculously recover from the assaults made on the constitution by the late dictator? Or would the forces that had been set in motion prove too strong to be effectively controlled by the old aristocracy which, over so many years, had demonstrated only weakness and ineptitude in its handling of the most important element in the political equation – the army.

The first few hours following the murder were ones of utter confusion for everyone in the city, but especially for those most prominent in political life. Caesar's lieutenant Antony, now the sole consul, had been prevented from coming to his colleague's assistance in the Senate-chamber and had fled back to his house, obviously fearing for his own life. But the assassins had no plans to harm anyone other than the principle object of their hatred, thinking that the removal of the dictator himself would be sufficient to fully achieve their ends. In this belief they were, of course, hopelessly deluded. They had failed to take into account those men whose own political ambitions had been aroused through their association with Caesar. But their greatest blunder was their failure to appreciate the significance of Caesar's army of battle-hardened veterans, a powerful and influential body of men to whom many promises had been made regarding cash settlements and land grants.

We have already caught fleeting glimpses of the elder of the two dominant characters in the post-Caesarian phase of our story: the time has now come to examine his background in a little more detail. Marcus Antonius, better known to the modern world as Mark Antony, was born on 14 January 83 BC. A somewhat rakish youth was followed by a distinguished cavalry command during which he saw service in the East under Aulus Gabinius, governor of Syria (57–54 BC). He then joined Caesar who was in the midst of his conquest of Gaul and soon became one of the great general's most trusted lieutenants. As a young tribune he argued on Caesar's behalf before the Senate at the time of the Rubicon crossing in 49 BC, and a little later was appointed commander-in-chief in Italy during Caesar's various absences in connection with the civil war against Pompey and the subsequent eastern campaigns. His failure in 47 BC to control the civil disorder in the capital and quell the mutiny amongst the legions stationed in Campania had angered Caesar. The dictator was obliged to waste valuable time restoring the situation when the activities of the Pompeians in Africa required his urgent attention. After this episode Antony fades from the picture for some time but he must have succeeded in redeeming himself for he was designated as Caesar's colleague in the consulship for the fateful year 44 BC.

After they had finished plunging their daggers into the dictator's lifeless body the conspirators left the Senate-house expecting to be greeted as liberators by a wildly enthusiastic and grateful populace. In this expectation they were disappointed for almost total silence reigned in the empty streets. Confused by this unforeseen turn of events they decided to repair to the safety of the Capitol to await developments. They were gradually losing the initiative which they had gained by their sudden and wholly unexpected act. Now would have been the time for them to take control of the situation and proclaim the full restoration of constitutional government. Had they acted swiftly and authoritatively they might have had a chance to carry the day and prolong the rule of the Senate, but the fleeting moment of opportunity was quickly lost.

Meanwhile, Antony was desperately trying to gain information regarding the extent of the conspiracy and the amount of popular support which it commanded. As it gradually became clear that he had not been marked out as the conspirators' next victim his confidence began to return and he was further encouraged by a message from the assassins suggesting that, as the surviving consul, he should convene a meeting of the Senate to discuss the new state of affairs. To this he agreed but subsequent negotiations failed to establish a mutually acceptable location for the tryst. Antony was understandably suspicious of the invitation to the conspirators' stronghold on the Capitol whilst they, in turn, were unwilling to accept his suggestion of the Temple of Tellus which was close to the consul's house. In the end the meeting of the Senate did take place in the Temple of Tellus but without Caesar's murderers in attendance. The senators who were present at this extraordinary session had not taken part in the conspiracy but nevertheless their sympathies lay with their absent colleagues rather than with the adherents of the late dictator. However, their hand was forced by the presence of large numbers of Caesar's veterans who, angered at their commander's murder, surrounded the temple as soon as they heard that the Senate was in session there. Doubtless, Antony was anxious to have their support to strengthen his hand in dealing with the Conscript Fathers and had spread word of the meeting through his agents. Intimidated by the unruly soldiers outside the doors of the meeting chamber the Senate felt obliged to refrain from passing any resolutions which were hostile to the dictator's memory. The annulment of his acts would have invalidated his promises of grants of land to discharged soldiers and no one was willing to risk the consequences of such an action. However, by ratifying his acts the Senate was implying its acceptance of the constitutionality of Caesar's position and it followed that the next step should have been the authorization of the punishment of his murderers. This was a course of action they were most unwilling to take and, as a way out of their predicament, Cicero proposed a general amnesty which was eagerly adopted by the timorous assembly who went even further by decreeing a public funeral in honour of the murdered dictator.

As Caesar's consular colleague Antony was granted the privilege of delivering the funeral oration and he had no intention of letting slip this unique opportunity to gauge the mood of the people. The ceremony took place five days after the dictator's murder, a most uneasy period in the city during which no one could be sure in whose hands the political power truly lay. Antony was clearly at his best in manipulating the emotions of the large crowd which had gathered for the occasion and in turning the rising tide of mass hysteria to his own advantage. Under the terms of the will the sum of 300 sestertii (*i.e.* 75 denarii or 3 gold aurei) was bequeathed to every citizen resident in the city and the late dictator's private gardens were given over to the people to be used as a public park. As his heir and the inheritor of the bulk of his property Caesar named his great-nephew the 18-year-old Gaius Octavius whom he adopted as his son. The young man was thus able to take the magical name of Caesar and, later, following the dictator's deification, could style himself *divi filius* ('son of god') a title of which he was to make the fullest use throughout his long life. This aspect of the will was to be of the very greatest future consequence for had he not been adopted by his great-uncle it is most unlikely that the young Octavius could ever have aspired to play a leading role in

Roman politics. A poignant moment was reached when Decimus Brutus, one of the assassins, was named in the will as Caesar's alternative choice to be his heir should Octavius decline the adoption.

The climax to the proceedings was reached when Caesar's body was brought into view of the crowd still wrapped in his blood-stained robe. Antony seized the moment and solemnly proclaimed his personal willingness to honour the vow which he, and all the senators, had taken to defend Caesar and to avenge any conspiracy against him. However, this he was unable to do because of the Senate's recent proclamation of an amnesty. On hearing this the crowd was aroused to fury and it was not just the body of Caesar that was burned that momentous day – the Senate-house and the homes of the conspirators were all consigned to the flames at the hands of the raging mob. The terrified Senate was rendered powerless, Caesar's assassins fled the city, and Antony was left in undisputed command of the situation.

Rioting continued for some time after the funeral and in the absence of effective governmental authority it seemed likely that the situation would only grow worse. Accordingly, the Senate found itself obliged to accede to Antony's request to be allowed to organize a military force, with himself as its commander, in order to restore law and order. Antony's 'bodyguard' was drawn from the large number of Caesarian veterans in the city whose loyalties naturally lay with their late commander's trusted lieutenant and colleague in the consulship rather than with a group of politicians whose sympathies had always been pro-Pompeian. Antony's hand was thus strengthened, for once the disturbances had been put down the military force remained in existence and under his personal command enabling him to dictate his own terms to the Senate. Caesar's arrangements for the following year were now changed. Instead of Antony proceeding to his assigned province of Macedonia, once his consulship ended, it was decreed that he should take up a six-year command in Cisalpine Gaul and Gallia Comata with four legions, to be transferred from Macedonia, at his disposal. This was to be his power base for the inevitable trial of strength with the tyrannicides Brutus and Cassius who had fled to the East following Caesar's funeral and were now posing as the champions of republicanism against the evil forces of dictatorship.

It was while this drama was being played out that Caesar's heir, C. Octavius, arrived in Rome from Apollonia in Illyricum where he had been sent by the dictator to complete his education. The grandson of Caesar's sister, Julia, his father had died when he was only four years old and his upbringing had been entirely in the hands of his mother, Atia, Caesar's niece. The young man's good looks and quiet modesty had already earned him many friends and although he was not yet nineteen at the time of his arrival in the capital (June, 44 BC) his new name of C. Julius Caesar Octavianus certainly made him a force to be reckoned with. This was a fact which Antony did not immediately grasp, and his scornful dismissal of him as 'the boy' proved to be one of his biggest political miscalculations.

The first opponent with whom Antony had to deal was the tyrannicide Decimus Brutus, who had been named in Caesar's will as his second choice as heir. Decimus had taken possession of the province of Cisalpine Gaul soon after the dictator's assassination and was hurriedly recruiting an army with which to support the cause of the Senate. In this he showed more foresight than most of his co-conspirators who seem not to have recognized the vital role which would have to be played by the military if traditional republican government was to be restored. Cassius, in Syria, was too far away and too preoccupied with establishing his own authority to have any influence on the course of events in Rome and Italy; whilst Brutus, in Macedonia, decided for whatever reason that this was not a propitious moment to act. Another interested spectator was Sextus Pompey, the younger son of Pompey the Great, who had survived the final downfall of the Pompeian cause at Munda and was currently occupying Massilia with an army and, more significantly, a fleet under his command.

On his departure from Rome with his 'bodyguard' Antony's plan was to meet the four legions which he had summoned from Macedonia and with this powerful force under his command seek out and destroy Decimus Brutus before he could become too well established. It would seem he felt no apprehension over leaving the young Octavian in the city, but immediately following the consul's departure 'the boy' set about raising his own military force from retired veterans who had been settled by the late dictator in Campania. Many were happy to serve again under the magical name of Caesar, even if its bearer was an untried lad of nineteen, and Octavian soon found himself at the head of a considerable military force. Antony learned of these unexpected developments with some concern, but a much greater blow was to follow – the desertion of two of the Macedonian legions to Caesar's heir. Despite these serious setbacks Antony continued with his planned attack on Decimus Brutus who, confronted with the prospect of almost certain defeat against his powerful adversary, decided to shut himself up in the walled city of Mutina (modern *Modena*) in Cisalpine Gaul. The ensuing siege was still in progress at the commencement of the new year (43 BC) when two new consuls, Aulus Hirtius and Gaius Vibius Pansa Caetronianus, took office in Rome. Both of these individuals we have met before: Hirtius as the praetor responsible for the remarkable issue of gold aurei struck for Caesar's quadruple triumph in 46 BC (see no. 56); and Pansa as moneyer in 48 BC (see nos. 20–4) when, by a remarkable coincidence, one of his colleagues in office was none other than Decimus Brutus himself.

Naturally, the Senate was anxious to come to the aid of its champion and to raise Antony's siege of Mutina. The problem, of course, was the lack of an army of sufficient size for the accomplishment of this task. Under these circumstances it was scarcely surprising that the Conscript Fathers, under the leadership of Cicero, should seek the help of Octavian. It is, perhaps, less obvious why Caesar's adopted son should have chosen to aid one of the dictator's principal assassins, especially as that individual had been so trusted that he had been named as alternative heir in Caesar's will. It says much for the political maturity of the young Octavian that he was able to supress his natural feelings of antagonism towards Decimus Brutus in order to achieve the larger goal of forcing Antony to accept him as an equal partner in the leadership of the Caesarian party. Thus, the curious alliance of Octavian and the Senate came into being, and a formidable military force was able to march north from Rome under the triple-command of Caesar's heir and the two consuls. Battle was joined initially at Forum Gallorum, about nine miles southeast of Mutina, and Pansa sustained a serious wound during the course of the short engagement. Antony was then worsted at Mutina and was obliged to raise the siege and effect a hurried withdrawal from the area (21 April 43 BC). Hirtius, however, was killed at the moment of victory and Pansa died shortly after, leaving Octavian in sole command of the victorious army. Instead of pursuing his defeated adversary and delivering the death-blow Octavian chose to remain at Mutina. It is likely that his soldiers, having performed their designated task on behalf of their young commander, had no desire to inflict further harm on their former comrades. After all, the troops on both sides in this brief war were Caesarian veterans and Octavian probably considered that it would be foolhardy to try to persuade his men to take further action, even if he had wished to do so himself. He had now achieved his object of acquiring Antony's respect and was probably already thinking in terms of an alliance with him. The future of the Caesarian cause was still uncertain as long as Marcus Brutus and Cassius remained at large in the East, and both were busily recruiting and training formidable armies with which to oppose Caesar's successors.

Decimus Brutus, freed at last from the threat of Antony, was now appointed supreme commander of the republican army by the Senate. Unlike Octavian, he foolishly determined to pursue Antony into Transalpine Gaul with the object of destroying his former tormentor. But the Caesarian veterans refused to march under his command, preferring instead to accept the authority of Caesar's adopted son, and Decimus was obliged to undertake his mission with a much reduced force. This was eventually to lead to his downfall, for Antony, having crossed the Alps, succeeded in winning the support of various western provincial governors: M. Aemilius Lepidus, Caesar's former *magister equitum* and now governor of Gallia Narbonensis and Nearer Spain; C. Asinius Pollio of Further Spain; and L. Munatius Plancus, proconsul of Gallia Comata and, as urban prefect under Caesar, the issuer of gold aurei and quinarii in 45 BC (see nos. 60–1). Finding themselves in opposition to this formidable coalition, Decimus' troops deserted him and joined the enemy. Their unfortunate commander took flight, hoping to make good his escape to Marcus Brutus in Macedonia. However, he was betrayed and captured by a Celtic chief who had him executed at the request of Antony, a sad end indeed for a man who had been held in such high regard by Caesar.

In the first heady days following the arrival in Rome of news of the victory at Mutina the Senate, mistakenly believing itself delivered from the Antonian curse, hastily passed a series of ill-conceived measures many of which the Conscript Fathers were soon to regret. In addition to appointing Decimus Brutus to the supreme military command they deliberately snubbed the young Octavian, believing that his usefulness was now at an end and that he could safely be ignored. They went further by legitimizing the commands of Brutus in Macedonia and Cassius in Syria, conferring on them a *maius imperium* over all provincial governors in the East, and even made contact with Sextus Pompey in Massilia offering him the title of commander of the fleets of the Republic. Antony was declared a public enemy, together with all the soldiers who supported him, and the same treatment was later meted out to Lepidus when he joined forces with Antony in Gaul. The soldiers of Octavian, now fully realizing the fickleness of the Roman Senate, sent a deputation to Rome demanding that their commander should be granted one of the vacant consulships. The Senate hesitated and Octavian replied by marching on Rome (July 43 BC). The matter was quickly settled: Octavian and his uncle Pedius were elected consuls for the remainder of the year (19 August) and the senators began to realize the full extent of their folly. A law was now passed outlawing Caesar's assassins (the *Lex Pedia*), the recent measures against Antony and Lepidus were rescinded, and Octavian made preparations to march north at the head of an army now comprising eleven legions.

In accordance with a pre-arranged plan the three Caesarian leaders – Antony, Octavian and Lepidus – met at Bononia early in November. The result of this momentous meeting was the establishment of the Second Triumvirate, in effect a triple-dictatorship with each of the participants holding the rank of *triumvir reipublicae constituendae* – Triumvir for the regulation of the Republic. Unlike the First Triumvirate of Caesar, Pompey and Crassus in 60 BC, which had been a private arrangement between the three men, the new alliance was given full legal status by the passing of the *Lex Titia* on 27 November. Under the terms of this law the three Triumvirs were given sweeping powers in the enactment of legislation and the appointment of magistrates and governors, their rank being superior to all other officials, including consuls. In addition, they were granted specific provinces: Cisalpine and Transalpine Gaul for Antony; Sicily, Sardinia and Africa for Octavian; and Spain and Gallia Narbonensis for Lepidus. They were to hold these extraordinary powers for a term of five years, until the end of 38 BC, though it must have been universally recognized that the likelihood of such authority ever being voluntarily laid aside was slight indeed. A five-year term of supreme authority, which could be renewed indefinitely at the pleasure of its holder, was coming very close indeed to the concept of monarchy. Therefore, it should not occasion surprise, and probably did not do so at the time, that the depiction on the coinage of the portraits of the principal contenders for political power – a revolutionary concept when it had been introduced by Caesar less than two years before – now became normal practice. Indeed, the regular issues of the Roman moneyers, which had supplied the requirements of the Republic for so long, were now threatened with extinction as more and more of the financial needs of the generals were being met by provincial mints and by minting establishments moving with the armies and operating within the security of the military camps.

The republican traditionalists knew that they had lost, even though there was still a glimmer of hope while Brutus and Cassius survived in the East. But things had now gone so far that even if the tyrannicides were successful in overcoming the triumviral regime could even they be trusted to restore the constitutional rule of the Senate? If Brutus and Cassius were to return as victorious heroes to Rome might not they, too, be tempted down the same path of personal glory? The Republic was dead and men such as Cicero knew that it was so. They looked with apprehension to the future and their worst fears were soon to be fully justified.

The Triumvirs' most immediate need was for money with which to pay the huge military establishment under their command. Accordingly, their very first act was to revive the spectre of proscriptions which had made the dictatorship of Sulla such a hated episode in the annals of Roman history. Scenes of unspeakable horror ensued in Rome as the wealthy opponents of the Triumvirs were mercilessly hunted down and executed, ostensibly for their political crimes but in reality because of the value of their possessions which were confiscated by the triumviral government. No less than three hundred senators and two thousand knights perished in this bloodbath, a truly heinous crime for which each of the Triumvirs must bear a heavy burden of guilt. Many others escaped with their lives, though not their property, by fleeing to Sicily where Sextus Pompey, himself included on the list of those proscribed, had seized several cities following his departure with his fleet from Massilia. Of the victims of the proscriptions undoubtedly the most illustrious was Marcus Tullius Cicero, the great orator and statesman, who had been prominent in political life for decades. His inclusion on the deadly list was due primarily to the *Philippics*, a series of speeches to the Senate delivered between September 44 BC and April 43 BC in which he was bitterly critical of Antony. This sealed his fate and he met his death with courage and dignity on 7 December 43 BC, just a few weeks short of his sixty-fourth birthday.

With their coffers at least partially replenished by the proceeds of the proscriptions the Triumvirs could now turn their attention to the final obstacle standing between them and political and military supremacy in the Roman world. As we have seen, following Caesar's funeral the assassins were obliged to beat a hasty retreat from Rome in order to escape the wrath of the populace which had been deliberately stirred up against them by Antony in his oration. Of the two principal tyrannicides, M. Junius Brutus had eventually established himself in Macedonia whilst C. Cassius secured his base in distant Syria. The two were to work independently towards the same goal of vanquishing Caesar's successors and re-establishing senatorial authority in Rome, their forces to be eventually combined for the final confrontation with Antony and Octavian.

Brutus, prior to his arrival in Macedonia, had gained considerable support for his cause in Athens. He soon managed to set about raising an army which was later strengthened by the addition of the legions of Vatinius, proconsul of Illyricum, who was won over to his side. Further successes followed, including the capture of C. Antonius, brother of Mark Antony, who was attempting to gain possession of his assigned province of Macedonia (March 43 BC); the submission of a number of Thracian chieftains; and a highly successful campaign against the Bessi which resulted in his salutation as *imperator*. In the meantime Cassius was consolidating his position in Syria where, with the assistance of Staius Murcus, governor of Syria, and his predecessor in this office, Caecilius Bassus, he had successfully defeated the attempt of Antony's nominee, Dolabella, to take possession of his province (July 43 BC). Cassius' hand had been strengthened by his acquisition of four legions, under the command of A. Allienus, which had been despatched by Queen Cleopatra of Egypt to assist Dolabella against Caesar's murderer. This force had been intercepted and induced to join the republican cause.

The time was now ripe for the two tyrannicides to meet and discuss future plans and on Brutus' proposal the conference took place at the Asian city of Smyrna. The result was a continuation of vigorous military action on the part of both leaders as well as extortion on the grand scale from communities in Asia Minor and Syria. Brutus besieged the Lycian city of Xanthus driving its inhabitants to mass suicide, whereupon the other cities of the region submitted to his demands for contributions to his cause. The citizens of Rhodes were also reluctant to involve themselves in the coming Roman civil war with the result that Cassius subdued them and extracted the vast sum of 8000 talents (about 48 million silver drachmas) from the island-state. There were numerous other instances of such exactions and there seemed little to choose between the tactics adopted by the Caesarians in the West and the republican leaders in the East. One of the measures taken by Cassius was to have grave future consequences for Rome's eastern provinces. Quintus Labienus, son of the Pompeian general Titus Labienus, had been sent into Parthia to solicit the aid of King Orodes II on behalf of the republican cause. Although the hoped-for assistance never materialized Labienus did return to Syria more than a year after the battle of Philippi. He came, however, at the head of a Parthian army in company with Orodes' son, Pacorus, and proceeded to devastate Syria and parts of Asia Minor before his eventual defeat by Antony's legate, P. Ventidius.

In the summer of 42 BC a second meeting between Brutus and Cassius took place at the old Lydian capital of Sardis. Their forces were now united, the troops enthusiastically hailing both commanders as *imperator*, and plans were made for the coming military confrontation with the Triumvirs. The situation looked promising for the Republicans. In addition to their formidable legionary force (which probably outnumbered the Caesarian army in available manpower at Philippi) they enjoyed complete naval superiority with powerful fleets under the command of Cn. Domitius Ahenobarbus and Staius Murcus based at the Macedonian port of Neapolis. In September Brutus and Cassius led their army of nineteen legions across the Hellespont into Europe and moved west along the *via Egnatia* to Philippi. Here, a little to the west of the city, they took up a strong defensive position in readiness for the long-awaited contest which would decide the fate of the Republic.

Antony and Octavian had crossed to Greece leaving Lepidus to take care of affairs in Italy. The Triumvirs were experiencing numerous difficulties at this time. Sextus Pompey, the ranks of his supporters swelled by the influx of refugees from the proscriptions, had become more aggressive and now had the whole of Sicily under his control. Octavian had attempted to check his power by sending a naval force against him under the command of Salvidienus Rufus, but this had been defeated in an engagement off Rhegium. There was still a serious shortage of funds, despite the recent seizures of property, and new taxation burdens added to the hatred already felt for the Caesarian leaders. On top of all this the incredible stresses of the past two years were beginning to take their toll on Octavian's health. His delicate constitution was to remain a problem throughout his long life and he was frequently subject to serious bouts of illness which sometimes appeared to be life-threatening. On this occasion he fell ill soon after making the crossing from Brundisium and was obliged to remain at Dyrrhachium while Antony marched eastwards along the *via Egnatia* to confront the encamped armies of Brutus and Cassius at Philippi.

At this point the odds certainly appeared to be in the Republicans' favour. The armies of Brutus and Cassius occupied separate camps, both in good defensive positions, and they had access to fresh supplies from their fleet stationed at nearby Neapolis. This gave them the option of playing a waiting game while hunger and the onset of winter – it was already October – took their toll on the army of the Triumvirs. Antony, however, was a military tactician of great innovation and daring and it is clear that he had learned much from his years of service under the greatest strategist of them all, the late dictator. He commenced the construction of a causeway across the marsh which protected the southern approaches to the republican encampments. Cassius was obliged to respond, drawing off a large number of troops to thwart the further advance of the causeway. With the strength of the opposing army thus weakened by division Antony launched a lightning attack on Cassius' camp which he succeeded in storming and occupying for a time before falling back to his former position. Cassius was so demoralized by this sudden and unexpected reverse that he lost hope, believing in his despair that the same fate had befallen Brutus, and he committed suicide. In reality, Brutus' soldiers had responded to the emergency by launching a counter-attack on Octavian's camp which they succeeded in capturing and briefly occupying. Octavian himself was present in the camp, having recovered sufficiently to undertake the journey from Dyrrhachium, and was lucky to escape with his life.

Although militarily the first battle of Philippi had no significant outcome, the loss of Cassius was a devastating blow from which the Republicans could scarcely hope to recover. For the following three weeks Brutus remained inactive, a policy which might have brought success to his cause had he not allowed himself to be persuaded by others to risk all in a pitched battle. The second battle of Philippi was fought on 23 October 42 BC and resulted in the total rout of the republican army. Octavian, still weak from his illness, had played little part in the bitterly contested engagement, though his loyal troops had fought with great heroism in the absence of their commander. Brutus himself escaped from the field of battle with a few close companions but, realizing that all was now lost, fell upon his own sword in a scene immortalized by Shakespeare in *Julius Caesar* – 'This was the noblest Roman of them all' (Act v, scene v, 68).

The initial phase of the post-Caesarian civil wars was now at an end. The Triumvirs were victorious and there was no longer any serious opposition to their supremacy in the Roman world. Fate had, perhaps, been kind in not allowing Cicero to live to see this day. What remained was a protracted period of growing rivalry between the two principal Caesarian leaders, Antony and Octavian, extending over a period of eleven years. Occasional skirmishes eventually culminated in the inevitable trial of strength, the naval battle of Actium which was to mark one of the great turning points in world history. In a sense Philippi also marked the end of the Triumvirate which, from now on, was in reality a Duumvirate. Lepidus, always the junior partner in the coalition, now subsided into obscurity and was virtually ignored by his colleagues, though he continued to hold the title of Triumvir until his deposition by Octavian in 36 BC.

In the period immediately following Philippi Antony undoubtedly held the upper hand in his relationship with Octavian who, it will be remembered, was scarcely able to participate in the campaign which led to the final downfall of the republican cause. Antony utilized the strength of his position to obtain the Eastern command which, he thought, would be the key to his ultimate supremacy. Octavian was left with the more difficult, and potentially dangerous, task of settling vast numbers of veterans in Italy who were no longer required for military service. But this gave him control of Rome and his keen political sense told him that the city on the Tiber was the true key to empire. Morever, he possessed something precious to which Antony, whatever his achievements, could never aspire – the magical name of Caesar. Further, on 1 January 42 BC the Senate had recognized Julius Caesar as a god (*Divus Iulius*) and in consequence the 20-year-old Octavian was now *divi filius* – 'son of god'. These were things which must constantly have been gnawing away at the back of Antony's mind.

COINAGE OF THE PERIOD

A. Issues of the Roman Moneyers in Honour of Caesar

In the closing months of Caesar's life the Senate, clearly under pressure, had decreed that the dictator's portrait should appear as the obverse type on the silver denarii issued by the college of moneyers appointed for the year 44 BC.[21] Further, the number of moneyers comprising the college was now increased from the traditional three (triumvirate) to four (quattuorvirate), the reasons for this change being unclear. The depiction of Caesar's portrait was, of course, a truly revolutionary development in the history of the Roman coinage, the first time that the effigy of a living individual had been allowed to appear on the currency of republican Rome. Whether it implied an acceptance of Caesar's role as monarch is, however, open to serious doubt as this would surely have been too great a leap at this juncture. Rather, it was viewed as simply yet another honour bestowed on the victorious military leader whose wishes, or vanities, could not easily be denied in the current political climate. Other honours had included his right to wear a wreath of laurel and a purple robe, as well as to sit upon a gilded chair. But these were the accoutrements of a *triumphator*, not a king, and it is likely that the senators' intention was that Caesar's depiction on the coinage should be viewed in the same light. Caesar's intentions, however, may well have been different and the message conveyed to the man in the street must certainly have been that great changes were afoot in the government of the Roman world.

One of the principal difficulties in the classification of Caesar's portrait denarii of 44 BC is the differentiation between issues made before and after the Ides of March. Crawford[22] places those issues inscribed CAESAR DICT QVART, CAESAR IMP, CAESAR IM P M, CAESAR DICT PERPETVO, and CAESAR DICT IN PERPETVO during the period of the dictator's lifetime;

and those with **CAESAR IMPER** and **CAESAR PARENS PATRIAE** after the assassination. This chronology has been adhered to in the following listing. Antony soon gained control of the situation in Rome so it seems likely that there was only a short break – if indeed there was any interruption at all – in the production of coins bearing Caesar's name and effigy. Changes in design followed later in the year, with some denarii still bearing a Caesarian obverse whilst others depicted a temple dedicated to Caesar's clemency (**CLEMENTIAE CAESARIS**). A new departure was the substitution of Mark Antony's portrait for that of the slain dictator. Antony thus became the second living Roman to be depicted on the coinage, though for the time being there was no accompanying legend.

98

98 Wreathed head of Caesar right, lituus and **CAESAR DICT** behind, **QVART** before. *Reverse:* Juno Sospita in galloping biga right, brandishing spear and holding shield, **M METTIVS** in exergue. *Silver denarius. Rome, January 44 BC* (Crawford 480/2a,b; Sydenham 1057; BMCRR 4135; Babelon Julia 31; Cohen 36).

The lituus behind Caesar's head may curve either to left or to right.

99 Similar to preceding, but **M METTIVS** is below horses instead of in exergue. *Silver denarius. Rome, January 44 BC* (Crawford 480/2c; RSC/Cohen 36a).

This, Caesar's first portrait type, appears to have been issued during the first half of January and is probably contemporary with the denarius of Aemilius Buca depicting Sulla's dream (see no. 164). The use of *dictator quartum* indicates that it predates Caesar's receipt of the title *dictator perpetuus*. The lituus symbolizes his membership of the priestly college of augurs, whilst the reverse type indicates that the moneyer, Marcus Mettius, was from Lanuvium where the goddess Juno Sospita was held in special reverence (cf. also the issues of L. Papius Celsus in the preceding year, nos. 82–4). This Mettius may be the same man who, as Caesar's legate 14 years earlier, had been sent as an emissary to Ariovistus at the commencement of the Gallic War. He had been detained as a prisoner by the king of the Suebi but was later rescued by Caesar.

100

100 Wreathed head of Caesar right, lituus and simpulum behind, **CAESAR IMP** (**MP** sometimes ligatured) before. *Reverse:* Venus standing left, holding Victory on extended right hand and sceptre in left, her left arm resting on shield set on globe, **M METTIVS** behind, variable control-letter (**G**, **H**, **I**, **K**, or **L**) in field to left. *Silver denarius. Rome, January–February 44 BC* (Crawford 480/3; Sydenham 1056; BMCRR 4143–8; Babelon Julia 32; Cohen 34).

The issue of this type probably extended from mid-January into the earlier part of February, prior to the introduction of the **CAESAR DICT PERPETVO** legend which, though it was not used by Mettius, did supersede **CAESAR IMP** on the coinage of his colleague Sepullius Macer. The addition of the simpulum behind Caesar's head was indicative of his office as pontifex maximus which, contrary to normal practice, he held in addition to his augurship. As the ancestress of the *gens* Julia Venus had already featured prominently on Caesarian issues and was to appear as the principal reverse type in this final phase of the dictator's coinage. The small globe beneath her shield on this type represents world dominion, most appropriate symbolism for the coinage of a great military dictator. A peculiarity of the issues of Mettius, not shared by any of his three colleagues in the monetary college, was the use of control-letters on the reverse dies of his Venus coinage. This practice, common on republican issues in the early decades of the 1st century, had not been utilized for many years and the reason for its revival by Mettius at this time is unclear. Curiously, the five control-letters (G–L) used on this type follow on from the other set of five (A–E) which appear on that part of Mettius' coinage which is attributed by Crawford to the period *following* Caesar's assassination (see no. 101). Crawford's chronology would appear to be correct but the seeming anomaly of the control-letter sequence awaits a convincing explanation.

101

101 Wreathed head of Caesar right, CAESAR before, IMPER behind. *Reverse:* similar to preceding, but with control-letter A, B, C, D, or E in left field. *Silver denarius. Rome, March–April 44 BC* (Crawford 480/17; Sydenham 1055; BMCRR 4137–42; Babelon Julia 33; Cohen 35).

The obverse dies of this type show signs of hasty execution which has led Crawford to assign them to the period immediately following the Ides of March. The indications of Caesar's augurship and his membership of the college of pontifices no longer appear in association with his portrait, but the reverse dies still bear the curious sequence of control-letters which had characterized Mettius' earlier series. The CAESAR IMPER coinage of Mettius is paralleled by a similar issue of Sepullius Macer (see no. 108) though in the latter case there are, of course, no control-letters on the reverse dies.

102

102 Wreathed head of Caesar right, CAESAR IM before, large crescent dividing P M behind. *Reverse:* Venus standing left, holding Victory on extended right hand and resting on sceptre held in left, L AEMILIVS behind, BVCA before. *Silver denarius. Rome, January–February 44 BC* (Crawford 480/4; Sydenham 1060; BMCRR 4152; Babelon Julia 34; Cohen 22).

Lucius Aemilius Buca appears to have been a distant relative of the dictator Sulla, a connection celebrated by his first denarius type which makes no direct reference to Caesar (see no. 164). It is recorded[23] that he testified on behalf of another Sullan relative, M. Aemilius Scaurus, at the latter's trial in 54 BC for misconduct during his government of Sardinia. Buca appears to have been the only one of the four moneyers in 44 BC not to have issued coins after the death of Caesar unless, as seems unlikely, his quinarii and sestertii belong to the period subsequent to 15 March. He is also alone in being the only one to use the new moneyers' title IIII VIR on his coinage. The obverse legend of this denarius records Caesar's possession of the office of pontifex maximus, held since 63 BC. Crawford[24] suggests that the large crescent, taken in conjunction with the star depicted on the coinage of Sepullius Macer, indicates 'a belief in the imminence of a new age'. The issue appears to be contemporaneous with the CAESAR IMP coinages of M. Mettius (see no. 100) and Sepullius Macer (nos. 106, 106a) and may thus be tentatively dated to the period mid-January to early February.

103

103 Wreathed head of Caesar right, **CAESAR DICT** before, **PERPETVO** behind. *Reverse:* fasces and winged caduceus in saltire, clasped hands in the angle to left, globe above, axe below, and **L BVCA** to right. *Silver denarius. Rome, February–March 44* BC (Crawford 480/6; Sydenham 1063; BMCRR 4157; Babelon Julia 37; Cohen 25).

The obverse legend records Caesar's new title of 'dictator for life' (*dictator perpetuus*) which appears to have been granted towards the middle of February. This, and parallel issues by Sepullius Macer (see nos. 107, a–e) and Cossutius Maridianus (nos. 111 and 111a), may thus be dated to the final month of the dictator's life. The highly symbolic reverse type brings together a number of themes: the pontificate (fasces and axe); *felicitas* (caduceus); *concordia* (clasped hands); and world dominion (globe).

104

104 *Obverse:* same as preceding. *Reverse:* Venus seated right, holding Victory on extended right hand and transverse sceptre in left, **L BVCA** behind. *Silver denarius. Rome, February–March 44* BC (Crawford 480/7a; Babelon Aemilia 16; Babelon Julia 36 variant).

104a

104a Similar to preceding, but the obverse legend is divided **CAESAR** before, **DICT PERPETVO** behind. *Silver denarius. Rome, February–March 44* BC (Crawford 480/7b; Sydenham 1062; BMCRR 4155; Babelon Julia 36; Cohen 24).

The seated Venus is a most unusual pose for this goddess and one which is not to be found on any other denarius of the Roman Republic.

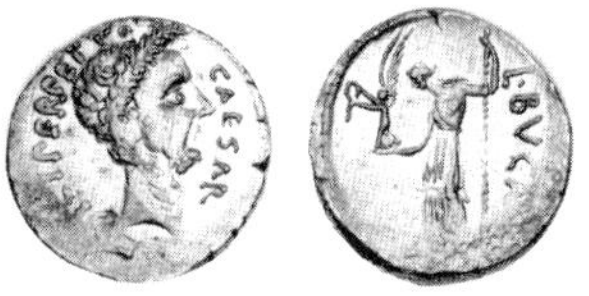

105

105 *Obverse:* same as preceding. *Reverse:* Venus standing left, holding Victory on extended right hand and resting on sceptre held in left, **L BVCA** behind. *Silver denarius. Rome, February–March 44* BC (Crawford 480/8; Sydenham 1061; BMCRR 4154; Babelon Julia 35; Cohen 23).

This duplicates the reverse type used by Buca in his earlier issue (see no. 102) though the moneyer's name has been simplified by the omission of the *nomen*.

106

106 Wreathed head of Caesar right, large star (of six rays) behind, **CAESAR IMP** (**MP** sometimes ligatured) before. *Reverse:* Venus standing left, holding Victory on extended right hand and resting on sceptre held in left, **P SEPVLLIVS** behind, **MACER** before. *Silver denarius. Rome, January–February 44* BC (Crawford 480/5a; Sydenham 1071a; BMCRR 4167; RSC/Cohen 41a).

106a

106a Similar to preceding, but the star behind Caesar's head is of eight rays, and with star also at the base of Venus' sceptre on reverse. *Silver denarius. Rome, January–February 44* BC (Crawford 480/5b; Sydenham 1071; BMCRR 4165; Babelon Julia 46; Cohen 41).

Publius Sepullius Macer, who was probably the most prolific in coin production of the four moneyers who held office in 44 BC, is otherwise quite unknown. He does not seem to have participated in the brief initial issue at the beginning of January, but thereafter produced an extensive coinage up to the time of Caesar's murder on 15 March. His activity continued in the post-Caesarian months and his later issues included the CLEMENTIAE CAESARIS temple type (see no. 110) and the first portrait coin of Mark Antony (no. 142). This denarius is contemporary with the CAESAR IMP coins of Mettius (see no. 100) and the CAESAR IM P M coins of Buca (no. 102) and may thus be tentatively dated to the period mid-January to early February. Crawford[25] suggests that the large star, taken in conjunction with the crescent depicted on the coinage of Aemilius Buca, indicates 'a belief in the imminence of a new age'.

107 Wreathed head of Caesar right, CAESAR before, DICT PERPETVO behind. *Reverse:* Venus standing left, holding Victory on extended right hand and resting on sceptre held in left, shield on ground to right, P SEPVLLIVS behind, MACER (upwards) before. *Silver denarius. Rome, February–March 44 BC* (Crawford 480/9; Sydenham 1073a; BMCRR 4172).

107a

107a Similar to preceding, but MACER reads downwards on reverse. *Silver denarius. Rome, February–March 44 BC* (Crawford 480/10; Sydenham 1073; BMCRR 4169; Babelon Julia 48; Cohen 38).

107b Similar to preceding, but without shield on reverse, and usually with star at base of Venus' sceptre. *Silver denarius. Rome, February–March 44 BC* (Crawford 480/11; Sydenham 1072; BMCRR 4168; Babelon Julia 49; Cohen 40).

107b(1)

107c Wreathed and veiled head of Caesar right, CAESAR before, DICT PERPETVO behind. *Reverse:* same as 107. *Silver denarius. Rome, February–March 44 BC* (Crawford 480/12).

107d *Obverse:* same as preceding. *Reverse:* same as 107a. *Silver denarius. Rome, February–March 44 BC* (Crawford 480/13; Sydenham 1074; BMCRR 4173; Babelon Julia 50; Cohen 39).

107b(2)

107e *Obverse:* same as preceding. *Reverse:* same as 107b. *Silver denarius. Rome, February–March 44 BC* (Crawford 480/14; Sydenham 1074a; BMCRR 4175; RSC/Cohen 39/40).

107d

The large number of variations on this type are indicative of the volume of the coinage, all the more remarkable in view of its brief period of issue (mid-February to mid-March). Specimens are often carelessly struck indicating that the mint was working under great pressure, just as it had been at the time of the quadruple triumph in 46 BC. With the contemporary issues of Aemilius Buca (see nos. 103–5) and Cossutius Maridianus (nos. 111 and 111a), though the latter were on a much smaller scale, the volume of production in the 4-week period preceding the Ides of March is impressive indeed. The reason for this must be sought in Caesar's projected Parthian War for which large quantities of coinage would have been required to pay the army. It will be remembered that the dictator was on the point of departing for this campaign when he was struck down by the assassins. An interesting feature of some of the obverses of Macer's coinage in this period (seen also on the contemporary issues of Maridianus) is the veil worn by Caesar. This is connected with his possession of the prestigious office of pontifex maximus which he had held

107e

for the past two decades. The small star seen at the base of the sceptre on some varieties of the reverse is symbolic of the divinity of Venus.

108 Wreathed head of Caesar right, CAESAR before, IMPER behind. *Reverse:* Venus standing left, holding Victory on extended right hand and resting on sceptre held in left at base of which is star, P SEPVLLIVS behind, MACER before. *Silver denarius. Rome, March–April 44 BC* (Crawford 480/18; Sydenham 1070; BMCRR 4164; Babelon Julia 47; Cohen 42).

108

Like the denarii of Mettius with CAESAR IMPER (see no. 101) the obverse dies of this type show signs of hasty execution, and Crawford has assigned them to the period immediately following the dictator's murder. Macer's issue is, however, considerably smaller than that of his colleague (Crawford records only 8 reverse dies compared with 40 for Mettius).

109 Wreathed and veiled head of Caesar right, lituus below chin, apex behind, CAESAR before, PARENS PATRIAE behind. *Reverse:* horseman (*desultor*) on horseback galloping right, a second horse at his side in background, wearing conical cap and holding whip in right hand, wreath and palm-branch behind, P SEPVLLIVS above, MACER below. *Silver denarius. Rome, April–May 44 BC* (Crawford 480/20; Sydenham 1075; BMCRR p. 549, Type II; Babelon Julia 51; Cohen 43).

109

The title *Parens Patriae* ('Parent of his country') was first bestowed on Cicero for his part in exposing the Catiline conspiracy in 63 BC. Caesar had only received the distinction in the final months of his life, but its commemoration here is on an issue which is clearly subsequent to the Ides of March. A denarius with similar obverse, though with different reverse type, was struck by Cossutius Maridianus (see no. 112). The late dictator's membership of the two priestly colleges, the augurs and the pontifices, is indicated by the lituus and apex on either side of his portrait. The reverse represents a departure from the types employed in the earlier part of the year while Caesar was still alive. It depicts a *desultor*, a participant in an equestrian event which formed part of the games celebrated regularly at Rome. The rider has two horses under his control and presumably was required to switch from one to the other while the animals were in motion. The wreath and the palm would refer to the prizes awarded to the victor. It is tempting to see in the introduction of this type a reference to the Parilian games celebrated on 21 April of each year. In 44 BC the Parilia turned into a celebration of Caesar's victory at Munda, Antony doubtless taking full advantage of the opportunity to stir up public sentiment in support of the Caesarian cause. The same reverse was used in combination with two other obverse types: the temple dedicated to Caesar's clemency, 'CLEMENTIAE CAESARIS' (see no. 110); and the first portrait of Mark Antony (see no. 142). These would clearly seem to bear the stamp of Antonian propaganda in the first critical months of his regime in Rome.

110 Tetrastyle temple with globe in pediment, CLEMENTIAE CAESARIS (AR sometimes ligatured) around, below. *Reverse:* horseman (*desultor*) galloping right, same as 109. *Silver denarius. Rome, April–May 44 BC* (Crawford 480/21; Sydenham 1076; BMCRR 4176–7; Babelon Julia 52; Cohen 44).

110

There is one obverse die with CAESARES *and another with* CAESAREIS.

Plutarch[26] records that near the end of Caesar's life the Senate, grateful for the leniency which he had so often shown to its members, had decreed that a temple should be erected in honour of the dictator's *clementia*. It is questionable whether this temple was ever built, and this coin type, which was almost certainly part of Antony's campaign to popularize Caesar's memory, can hardly be taken as evidence of its existence.

111

111 Wreathed and veiled head of Caesar right, CAESAR before, DICT PERPETVO behind. *Reverse:* Venus standing left, holding Victory on extended right hand and resting left arm on shield set on globe, C MARIDIANVS behind. *Silver denarius. Rome, February–March 44 BC* (Crawford 480/16; Sydenham 1067; BMCRR 4185; Babelon Julia 41; Cohen 9).

111a

111a Similar to preceding, but the obverse legend reads CAESAR before, DICT IN PERPETVO behind. *Silver denarius. Rome, February–March 44 BC* (Crawford 480/15; Sydenham 1068; BMCRR 4186; Babelon Julia 42; Cohen 10).

Gaius Cossutius Maridianus, the fourth member of the monetary triumvirate for 44 BC, is otherwise unknown to history, though he may have been related to the L. Cossutius Sabula who had held the office of moneyer three decades before (cf. Crawford 395). His status appears to have been a little different from that of his three colleagues. His coinage begins late (probably about mid-February) and this may explain why, unlike the other moneyers, there were no quinarii or sestertii issued in his name. This would seem to suggest that the rare fractional denominations of the moneyers were usually struck at the beginning of the year, perhaps in connection with public distributions of money during the new-year's celebrations. Maridianus was also the only member of his monetary college to use his official title in one of his coin inscriptions – A A A F F, abbreviated from IIII VIR A A A F F (*quattuorvir aere argento auro flando feriundo*), 'one of four men for the casting and striking of bronze, silver, and gold' (see no. 112). The expansion of the obverse legend from CAESAR DICT PERPETVO to CAESAR DICT IN PERPETVO is not paralleled on the contemporary issues of Aemilius Buca and Sepullius Macer.

112

112 Wreathed and veiled head of Caesar right, lituus below chin, apex behind, CAESAR before, PARENS PATRIAE behind. *Reverse:* C COSSVTIVS and MARIDIANVS arranged in form of cross, A–A–A–F F in the four angles. *Silver denarius. Rome, April 44 BC* (Crawford 480/19; Sydenham 1069; BMCRR 4187, 4190; Babelon Julia 43; Cohen 8).

There is one obverse die with **PARE:S** *for* **PARENS** *and another with the* **TR** *of* **PATRIAE** *ligatured.*

The obverse type is the same as that used briefly by P. Sepullius Macer (see no. 109) and the issue is clearly posthumous, presumably belonging to mid-April. The remarkable reverse type, already referred to above, represents the first occurrence of the full title of the moneyer's office on the coinage of the Roman Republic. After the **PARENS PATRIAE** issues of Maridianus and Macer there was no further production in 44 BC of coins bearing the portrait of the slain dictator. This is hardly surprising given the complexities of the political situation in the second half of the year, with Antony giving his attention to the elimination of the threat from Decimus Brutus in the north, Octavian attempting to establish himself as a serious contender for power, and the Senate still hoping for the defeat of the Caesarian faction and the restoration of constitutional republican government. In any case, coin production in the opening months of the year had been on a large scale, possibly in anticipation of the Parthian War, and there was no longer any real need for the moneyers to remain active. In the following year, however, there was a brief revival of Caesarian portraiture by one member of the new college of moneyers.

113 Wreathed head of Caesar right (no legend). *Reverse:* female figure (Venus or Pax) standing left, holding caduceus in extended right hand and resting on sceptre held in left, **L FLAMINIVS** on right, **IIII VIR** on left. *Silver denarius. Rome, August 43 BC* (Crawford 485/1; Sydenham 1089; BMCRR 4201; Babelon Julia 45; Cohen 26).

113

It is unlikely that the obviously pro-Caesarian coinage of L. Flaminius Cilo would have been issued before Octavian's occupation of Rome in the late summer of 43 BC, in the aftermath of Antony's discomfiture at Mutina. The types are clearly a revival of the Caesarian coinage of the opening months of the preceding year though without an inscription to identify the portrait on the obverse. Also, the goddess holds a caduceus instead of a small figure of Victory, but her pose, with bowed head, is identical to that on the coins of Mettius, Buca, Macer, and Maridianus. The portraiture of Caesar shows a remarkable degree of idealization which, in the absence of an inscription, gives an unmistakable impression of divinity. This characteristic is by no means attributable to the whims of individual die-engravers but was part of a carefully orchestrated policy on the part of Octavian which was to lead to the Senate's recognition of Caesar as a god on 1 January 42 BC. Little appears to be known of Flaminius though he may be the 'Cillo' who was proscribed by the triumviral government late in the year. If so, then the pro-Caesarian sentiments of his coinage did little to help his cause. His other denarius type, with head of Venus / Victory in biga (see no. 171) – also clearly Caesarian – accords him the title of *pri(mus) fl(avit)*, indicating that he was the first of his monetary college to strike. As the possessor of this distinction he may well have acted as superintendent of operations for the entire production of coinage in this year, and would thus have been held responsible for the types of his colleagues' issues which certainly failed to convey any idea of support for the Caesarian cause (see nos. 172–174b).

114

114 Wreathed head of Caesar right, CAESAR before, IMP behind. *Reverse:* Mars, naked but for helmet, standing facing, his body inclined to right, head facing left, resting on spear held in right hand and holding sword in scabbard away from his body in left, P CLODIVS on left, M F on right. *Silver denarius. Rome, 42 BC* (Crawford 494/16; Sydenham 1123; BMCRR 4280; Babelon Julia 56; Cohen 37).

The most remarkable feature of the monetary college of 42 BC was its regular production of gold coins, the first occasion in the history of the republican coinage that the moneyers had been called upon to perform such a task. The proscriptions were the source of the bullion required for this unprecedented coinage and its purpose was to help defray the costs of the huge military build-up prior to the final confrontation with the republican leaders Brutus and Cassius at Philippi. The certain identification of L. Livineius Regulus, P. Clodius, L. Mussidius Longus, and C. Vibius Varus as the monetary college during this critical year in the history of the Republic rests on the work of Theodore Buttrey.[27] In addition to their production of aurei these moneyers were responsible for a considerable output of denarii, and a few of these bore portraits of the late dictator. This type, issued by Publius Clodius, son of Marcus, of whom we have no certain knowledge, uses an obverse that returns to the realistic style of portraiture of Caesar's lifetime issues, in marked contrast to the idealized effigies employed on Flaminius' denarii in 43 BC. Parallel issues were produced with the names and portraits of two of the Triumvirs, Antony and Octavian (see nos. 148 and 155). The type of Mars, god of war, was certainly appropriate to a time when preparations were under way for the war against the republican forces in the East.

115

115 Wreathed head of Caesar right, laurel-branch behind, caduceus before (no legend). *Reverse:* bull charging right, L LIVINEIVS above, REGVLVS below. *Silver denarius. Rome, 42 BC* (Crawford 494/24; Sydenham 1106; BMCRR 4274; Babelon Julia 57; Cohen 27).

Nothing is known of Lucius Livineius Regulus other than the information which is provided by his varied coinage of aurei and denarii. This suggests that he was the son of the praetor of the same name who was a friend of Cicero and whose portrait is depicted on several of Regulus' coin types (see nos. 175–80). There is no obvious interpretation of the reverse type of the denarius reviving the memory of Caesar. Crawford[28] suggests that it may be connected with an incident related by Suetonius which took place place during the Thapsus campaign: 'Religious scruples never deterred him [Caesar] for a moment. At the formal sacrifice before he launched his attack on Scipio and King Juba, the victim [a bull] escaped; but he paid no heed to this most unlucky sign and marched off at once.'[29] L. Livineius Regulus, the praetor, is known to have served under Caesar in the African War, a fact recorded by the unknown Roman author of the commentary on the campaign: 'He [Caesar] went on from Hadrumetum the same day, leaving Livineius Regulus there with a legion, and made for Utica.'[30] The symbolism of the subsidiary symbols (laurel-branch and caduceus) on either side of Caesar's head is also uncertain, though they probably relate to the peace and prosperity which he had hoped to restore to the Roman world by his victories over the enemies of the state, only to have the opportunity snatched from him by the republican assassins whose leaders the Triumvirs were now preparing to confront.

116 Wreathed head of Caesar right (no legend). *Reverse:* cornucopiae on globe, between rudder (on left) and caduceus and apex (on right), **L MVSSIDIVS LONGVS** around (variously disposed: sometimes in semicircle above, sometimes above and to right, sometimes to left and below). *Silver denarius. Rome, 42 BC* (Crawford 494/39; Sydenham 1096–1096c; BMCRR 4237–41; Babelon Julia 58; Cohen 29).

116

Like his three colleagues in the monetary college of 42 BC Lucius Mussidius Longus is unknown to history. The obverse type of his denarius in honour of the deceased dictator has no inscription or subsidiary symbols accompanying the portrait, though there is no attempt here to idealize or deify the effigy. The themes of the highly symbolic reverse type are Caesar's mastery of both land and sea (the cornucopiae on globe and the rudder), his possession of the office of pontifex maximus, represented by the apex, and the *felicitas* which he had brought to the Roman people, signified by the caduceus. The inference, of course, was that Caesar's heirs, the Triumvirs Antony, Octavian and Lepidus, had now assumed the dictator's mantle and would continue his enlightened policies as soon as they had disposed of the threat posed by his assassins Brutus and Cassius.

Curiously, the other member of this monetary college, C. Vibius Varus (also unrecorded by the ancient sources), issued no coins in commemoration of Caesar's memory, though it is unlikely that this omission had any political significance. Varus did strike denarii with the portraits of Antony and Octavian, though without identifying inscriptions, in addition to aurei in the names of all three Triumvirs.

The portrait of Caesar as a coin type was a powerful tool of propaganda for Antony and Octavian in the period leading up to the decisive military confrontation with the republican leaders at Philippi in October, 42 BC. In addition to the denarii produced by the Roman moneyers, listed above, some of these representations occurred on the issues of military mints under the direct control of the imperators (see nos. 118, 123, and 135). A denarius of Octavian even depicts the late dictators gilded curule chair, appropriately inscribed **CAESAR DIC PER** (see nos. 137, 137a). After Philippi it was Octavian who made most use of his connection with Caesar. In order to counter Antony's powerful position as the vanquisher of the tyrannicides at Philippi and subsequently the master of Rome's wealthy eastern provinces, it was necessary for Octavian to make maximum use of his close association with Caesar. He was, after all, the late dictator's adoptive son and the bearer of his illustrious name. Perhaps most importantly of all he was the son of a god – *divi filius*. Octavian was to utilize to the full this powerful advantage which he possessed over Antony, and the coinage was to play a vital role in this war of propaganda which was to lead inexorably to the watery arena of Actium for its final resolution.

B. Special Issue Celebrating Caesar's Fifth Consulship

Caesar celebrated his fifth consulship on 1 January 44 BC, an event which occasioned a special issue of gold aurei presumably intended for distribution to notables at the time of the consular ceremonies. The obverse legend also records his fourth dictatorship (DIC QVAR, *dictator quartum*), a title which was used up to the middle of February and which is also to be found on Caesar's initial issue of portrait denarii by the moneyer M. Mettius (see nos. 98–9). This coinage is unusual in that, unlike Caesar's earlier gold issues from the mint of Rome (see nos. 56 and 60–1), it does not bear the name of the lieutenant responsible for its production. Nevertheless, there seems to be no compelling reason to doubt its attribution to the Capitoline mint.

117

117 Diademed bust of Venus right, with shoulders bare, CAES DIC behind, QVAR before. *Reverse:* COS QVINC in one line within laurel-wreath. *Gold aureus. Rome, January 44 BC* (Crawford 481/1; Sydenham 1021; BMCRR 4129; Babelon Julia 30; Cohen 20).

C. Military Issues of Antony

Following his embarrassing defeat at Mutina (21 April 43 BC) Antony effected a rapid withdrawal across the Alps to southern Gaul where, despite the weakness of his position, he succeeded in persuading the governor of Gallia Narbonensis and Nearer Spain, M. Aemilius Lepidus, to join forces with him (29 May). With the strength of their combined armies behind him Antony could again feel secure and his position was further improved in the late summer when his cause was espoused by L. Munatius Plancus, the proconsul of Gallia Comata. In the meantime Octavian had made himself master of Rome by marching on the capital after the Senate, believing itself freed from the Caesarian threat, had foolishly tried to snub him. Antony now saw the wisdom of entering into negotiations with the young Caesar and messages passed back and forth between Gaul and Rome. The end result was a meeting in early November between Antony, Octavian and Lepidus at Bononia (modern *Bologna*) in Cisalpine Gaul. This resulted in the formation of the Second Triumvirate, the constitutionality of which was established by the *Lex Titia* passed on 27 November. With the arrival of the Triumvirs in Rome the full horror of the proscriptions was unleashed as the Caesarian leaders set about trying to raise the necessary funds for the coming military confrontation with Brutus and Cassius.

At some point during the early stages of this complex sequence of events (possibly as early as the final phase of the siege of Decimus Brutus in Mutina) Antony established a mint within the security of his military camp. Its initial product was a denarius combining his own portrait with that of Caesar, thereby asserting his leadership of the Caesarian party at a time when he was beginning to feel threatened by Octavian. Doubtless the propaganda was aimed at his soldiers, the loyalty of whom might be suspect now that Caesar's adopted son had become a factor in the political power game.

118 Bare head of M. Antony right, bearded, lituus behind, M ANTON (or ANTO) IMP before (NT ligatured). *Reverse:* wreathed head of Caesar right, capis behind, CAESAR DIC before. *Silver denarius. Military mint travelling with Antony in Cisalpine Gaul, April 43 BC* (Crawford 488/1; Sydenham 1165, 1165a; BMCRR Gaul 53; Babelon Antonia 4; Newman 43.1; Cohen 2).

118

The symbols of the augurate appearing behind the heads serve to emphasize the link between Antony and the slain dictator and thus to strengthen his claim to be Caesar's true successor. Antony is depicted unshaven as an indication of mourning, a feature which was to characterize the numismatic portraiture of both Antony and Octavian until Caesar's murder had been avenged at Philippi. This is the first occurrence of Antony's name on a coin, his earlier issue from Rome having been anepigraphic (see no. 142). The title of *imperator*, which serves as the authority for the striking of this coin, was assumed by both Antony and Octavian at the time of the war around Mutina.

After crossing the Alps with the remnants of his army Antony made camp a short distance from the numerically superior force commanded by M. Aemilius Lepidus. The Senate believed that Lepidus would crush Antony's exhausted and demoralized army and free the State from the domination of the Caesarian faction. However, Antony had already been in secret communication with the governor of Narbonensis and had come to an agreement with him, doubtless promising a share in any future Caesarian government as an incentive. With the connivance of the two commanders the soldiers of both armies – former comrades under Caesar's standards – were allowed to fraternize and make common cause, whereupon Lepidus wrote to the Conscript Fathers informing them that he had no choice but to accept the *fait accompli*. The Senate responded by declaring Lepidus a public enemy, the same treatment which had been meted out to Antony earlier in the year. The new alliance was commemorated by an issue of silver denarii and quinarii.

119 Emblems of the augurate – lituus, capis and raven, M ANTON COS (NT ligatured) above, IMP below. *Reverse:* emblems of the pontificate – simpulum, aspergillum, axe and apex, M LEPID COS IMP around, on left. *Silver denarius. Military mint travelling with Antony and Lepidus in Transalpine Gaul, June 43 BC* (Crawford 489/1; Sydenham 1157; BMCRR Gaul 32; Babelon Antonia 8; Newman 43.2; Cohen 4).

119

119a

119a Similar to preceding, but with M ANTON IMP (NT ligatured) above type on obverse, and M LEPID IMP on reverse. *Silver denarius. Military mint travelling with Antony and Lepidus in Transalpine Gaul, June 43 BC* (Crawford 489/2; Sydenham 1156; BMCRR Gaul 31; Babelon Antonia 10; Newman 43.3; Cohen 2).

The types draw attention to the priestly colleges of which the two leaders were members. Antony was an augur, whilst Lepidus had been elected to the prestigious office of pontifex maximus in 44 BC in succession to Caesar himself. He had obtained this position though the influence of Antony who was grateful for the military assistance which Lepidus had given him in the uncertain days following the dictator's assassination. Given this close association of the two men in the recent past it is scarcely surprising that they came to an amicable agreement in Gaul in the late spring of 43 BC. The inscriptions of the first variety include reference to the proconsular commands of both leaders, whilst on the second their military rank as *imperatores* is considered sufficient authority for the striking of coinage. Lepidus was to retain the office of pontifex maximus until his death three decades later. It was then bestowed on the Emperor Augustus and thereafter became one of the inherited imperial titles down to the late 4th century AD.

120

120 Emblems of the augurate – lituus, capis and raven, M ANT IMP (ANT ligatured) above. *Reverse:* emblems of the pontificate – simpulum, aspergillum, axe and apex, LEP IMP above. *Silver quinarius. Military mint travelling with Antony and Lepidus in Transalpine Gaul, June 43 BC* (Crawford 489/3; Sydenham 1158/1158a; BMCRR Gaul 33; Babelon Antonia 13; Newman 43.4; Cohen 3/5).

The minor varieties of obverse and reverse legend recorded by some authorities are not included by Crawford and are probably best regarded as misreadings.

The silver quinarius, or half denarius, had always been a popular denomination in Gaul so it is not surprising to find it issued as part of the coinage commemorating the alliance between Antony and Lepidus. This variety has the same types as the denarius and doubtless belongs to the same period of issue.

121

121 *Obverse:* same as preceding. *Reverse:* Victory standing right, crowning trophy (no legend). *Silver quinarius. Military mint travelling with Antony and Lepidus in Transalpine Gaul, summer 43 BC* (Crawford 489/4; Sydenham 1159; BMCRR Gaul 36; Babelon Antonia 7; Newman 43.5; Cohen 82).

This quinarius provides clear evidence of the superiority enjoyed by Antony in his 'partnership' with Lepidus. The obverse is unchanged from the previous issue but the governor of Narbonensis is now ignored, his place on the reverse being taken by a representation of Victory which was traditional on this denomination. Crawford records almost four times the number of dies for this variety in comparison with the one bearing both names, so its issue may have continued throughout the summer.

122 Winged bust of Victory right, her hair drawn back and collected into a knot behind, one long plait arranged in a loop along the top of her head (no legend). *Reverse:* lion walking right, LVGV/DVNI in exergue and above, A on left, XL on right. *Silver quinarius. Lugdunum, autumn 43 BC* (Crawford 489/5; Sydenham 1160; BMCRR Gaul 40; cf. Babelon Antonia 32; RPC 512; Newman 43.6; Cohen Fulvia 4).

122

This exceptional type was struck at *colonia Copia Felix Munatia Lugdunum* (modern *Lyon*), a city which was destined for greatness under the Roman Empire and which had only recently been founded by L. Munatius Plancus, proconsular governor of Gallia Comata. Plancus, it will be remembered, had given his support to Antony once it had become apparent that the latter's fortunes had been restored by his alliance with Lepidus. Antony's name is not mentioned on the coin but the date-numeral A XL ('year 40') undoubtedly refers to his age at the time of the issue.[31] A similar type was struck the following year, this time including Antony's name and titles and recording his age as 41 (see no. 126). The bust of Victory on the obverse has been the subject of much speculation, many numismatists seeing in its features a portrait of Antony's wife, Fulvia. The head is certainly distinctive in its facial features and in the treatment of the hair and there are several other issues of the period exhibiting similar effigies: a denarius of the moneyer L. Mussidius Longus issued in 42 BC (see no. 186); and an aureus of C. Numonius Vaala of 41 BC (see no. 321). All of these types fall within the period of Fulvia's lifetime (died 40 BC) and strong evidence in support of the identification comes from a series of bronze coins[32] issued from the mint of

Eumenea in Phrygia (*provincia Asia*) at the time of Antony's journey to the East in 41 BC. As a token of respect to the Triumvir the name of Eumenea was changed to Fulvia in honour of his wife, and on the obverses of the coins struck on this occasion Fulvia is depicted as Nike (Victory) in precisely the same manner as on the Roman issues of 43–41 BC. The lion on the reverse of this quinarius (and no. 126) is thought to relate either to the mint city of Lugdunum, of which it may have been the emblem, or to Antony himself. In the latter case it would be a zodiacal sign referring to the period of Antony's birth, just as the capricorn was later used on the coinage of Augustus. It would seem that at this time the moon, rather than the sun, was used to compute the appropriate sign.[33] A lion was to appear again as an Antonian reverse type on an aureus struck at Athens in 38 BC (see no. 266).

123 Bare head of M. Antony right, bearded, lituus behind, M ANTON (or ANTO) IMP R P C before and below (NT ligatured). *Reverse:* wreathed head of Caesar right, capis behind, CAESAR DIC before. *Silver denarius. Military mint travelling with Antony in Cisalpine*

123

Gaul, November 43 BC (Crawford 488/2; Sydenham 1166, 1166a; BMCRR Gaul 55, 57; Babelon Antonia 5–6; Newman 43.7; Cohen 3).

This issue would appear to be a revival of the type struck by Antony in the spring during the war around Mutina (see no. 118). After his Gallic adventures Antony, accompanied by his ally Lepidus, was now back in Cisalpine Gaul to meet with his former opponent Octavian. The conference between the three men at Bononia, in early November, set the seal on the formation of the Second Triumvirate, an event commemorated by this issue. It clearly belongs to the period immediately following the agreement at Bononia as the form of the triumviral titulature (R P C) had not yet been expanded to the normal III VIR R P C. A distinctive feature of this coinage is the portrait of Antony which has a strangely elongated form, giving it something of the appearance of a caricature. Presumably, Antony's retinue at this time lacked the services of a die-engraver competent in the art of portraiture.

124

125

124 Bare head of M. Antony right, bearded, lituus behind, M ANTONIVS III VIR R P C around. *Reverse:* bare head of Octavian right, bearded, C CAESAR III VIR R P C around. *Gold aureus. Military mint travelling with Antony in Cisalpine Gaul or Italy, November–December 43 BC* (Crawford 492/1; Sydenham 1162; BMCRR Gaul 47; Babelon Antonia 39; Newman 42.1; Cohen 4).

125 *Obverse:* same as preceding. *Reverse:* bare head of Lepidus right, aspergillum and simpulum behind, M LEPIDVS III VIR R P C around. *Gold aureus. Military mint travelling with Antony in Cisalpine Gaul or Italy, November–December 43 BC* (Crawford 492/2; Sydenham 1161; BMCRR Gaul 46; Babelon Antonia 36; Newman 42.2; Cohen 1).

These aurei, celebrating the establishment of the Triumvirate, were produced by the military mint located in Antony's camp. Under these circumstances it is scarcely surprising that their types are aimed at minimizing the importance of Octavian by omitting all reference to his membership of the priestly colleges of augurs and pontifices. In marked contrast, Antony's augurship and Lepidus' office as pontifex maximus are both emphasized by the addition of priestly emblems behind their portraits. Because the inscriptions lack the imperatorial title (IMP) Newman[34] suggests that these coins were struck after the Triumvirs had entered Rome when the designation would no longer have been appropriate. The equivalent issue from Octavian's military mint (see no. 133) does have the imperatorial title and, if Newman is correct, would thus predate Antony's coinage.

126

126 Winged bust of Victory right, her hair drawn back and collected into a knot behind, one long plait arranged in a loop along the top of her head, III VIR behind, R P C before. *Reverse:* lion walking right, ANTONI above, IMP in exergue, A on left, XLI on right. *Silver quinarius. Lugdunum, 42 BC* (Crawford 489/6; Sydenham 1163; BMCRR Gaul 48; Babelon Antonia 32; RPC 513; Newman 42.3; Cohen Fulvia 3).

This type revives the exceptional Lugdunese quinarius struck in the previous autumn (see no. 122) on which Antony was not actually named, though a date-numeral indicating his age (40) appeared on the reverse. The new issue includes both his name and the imperatorial and triumviral titles (IMP, III VIR R P C) though because of lack of space on the small dies the reference to the mint itself had to be omitted. Antony's age is now given as 41 (A XLI) so the coin post-dates his birthday on 14 January 42 BC. However, its precise period of issue within the year remains uncertain. It is tempting to associate it with the victory over Brutus and Cassius at Philippi in October, though it was probably struck earlier. As in the case of the original type Antony was almost certainly not present in the city at the time of the issue, the coinage simply being struck in his honour. For the possibility of Victory being endowed with the features of Antony's wife, Fulvia, see the commentary on no. 122 above.

127

127 Bare head of M. Antony right, bearded, lituus behind (no legend). *Reverse:* radiate head of Sol right, M ANTONIVS III VIR R P C around. *Silver denarius. Military mint travelling with Antony in Italy, spring–summer 42 BC* (Crawford 496/2; Sydenham 1170; BMCRR East 87; Babelon Antonia 29; Newman 42.4; Cohen 68).

With money flowing into their coffers from the proceeds of the proscriptions the Triumvirs could now give their undivided attention to preparations for the campaign against the tyrannicides, Brutus and Cassius, who had been equally industrious in extorting wealth from the rich communities of the East for the recruiting and training of a powerful army to fight for the republican cause. Because of its close stylistic affinities to certain issues of the Roman moneyers in 42 BC, especially the denarius struck for Antony by C. Vibius Varus (see no. 149), it seems likely that this type was produced by the Triumvir's military mint while his army was still encamped outside Rome. Indeed, it does not seem beyond the realms of possibility that the same die-engraver who worked for Varus at the Capitoline mint was induced to travel outside the city to Antony's camp to produce dies for this military issue. Antony may have been especially pleased with the portrait (of outstanding style for this period endowing its subject with an almost regal dignity) and have given orders initially for the artist to work exclusively on his coinage and later to transfer his activities to the military mint. This hypothesis would also explain the surprising rarity of the corresponding issue of Varus for Octavian (see no. 158) which would have been cut short by Antonys actions. The resulting shortfall in issues from the Capitoline mint honouring Octavian was perhaps made good by additional types produced by the moneyers P. Clodius and L. Livineius Regulus (see nos. 156 and 157). The head of the sun god Sol, symbolic of the East, looks forward to the approaching campaign against the Republicans which would require the triumviral armies to cross from Italy to Greece and perhaps even to Asia.

128

128 Bare head of M. Antony right, bearded, M ANTONI behind, IMP (MP sometimes ligatured) before. *Reverse:* distyle temple containing large disk bearing radiate and draped bust of Sol facing, III – VIR – R P C to left, below, and to right. *Silver denarius. Military mint travelling with Antony in Greece, autumn 42 BC* (Crawford 496/1; Sydenham 1168; BMCRR Gaul 60, 62; Babelon Antonia 34; Newman 42.5; Cohen 12).

The reappearance of IMP in Antony's titulature suggests that this issue is subsequent to the second battle of Philippi (23 October), though as the Triumvir is still bearded it must have been struck quite soon after the deaths of Brutus and Cassius before orders had been given for the modification of the portrait. With Caesar's murder now avenged both Antony and Octavian could shave the beards which they had worn as a sign of mourning. The curious reverse type continues the eastern theme, symbolized by the sun god, which had commenced on the military issues in Italy prior to the crossing of Antony and Octavian to Greece (see no. 127). A similar type occurs at a later date on the bronze coinage of the colony of Buthrotum in Epirus issued during the reign of Augustus.[35] This may indicate Antony's presence in the area in the period immediately following Philippi.

129

129 Bare head of M. Antony right, beardless, lituus and IMP behind. *Reverse:* radiate head of Sol right, M ANTONIVS III VIR R P C around. *Silver denarius. Military mint travelling with Antony in Greece and Asia, late 42–early 41 BC* (Crawford 496/3; Sydenham 1169; BMCRR East 89, 91; Babelon Antonia 31; Newman 42.6; Cohen 70).

This is a revival of the type struck in Italy before the Philippi campaign (see no. 127). The addition of the imperatorial title (IMP), the beardless effigy of Antony, and the inferior style of the engraving clearly mark this out as a military issue subsequent to the victory over Brutus and Cassius. There is much variation in the size of the heads, both of Antony and of Sol, and a number of different artists must have been employed in an attempt to improve the appearance of these coins. If, as has been suggested, Antony was especially fond of the type struck before his departure from Rome then it is not surprising that he should have ordered its resumption after Philippi. However, given this scenario it is easy to understand his disappointment with the quality of the new issue, hence the experimentation with different die-engravers. The smaller heads would appear to belong to the earlier part of the issue and to draw their inspiration from the temple of Sol type (no. 128). The larger heads seem to be the precursors of the typical heavy portraits of Antony's later years and may even have been struck in Asia at the beginning of his journey to the East.

As the true architect of the victory over the Republicans Antony's dominance over his triumviral colleagues seemed assured. He was able to dictate the terms of the post-war settlement which gave him control not only of Rome's wealthy eastern provinces but also the strategically important territories of Old Gaul (Gallia Narbonensis) and Gallia Comata with their large armies of seasoned veterans. Had he found some pretext to move against Octavian now there would have been little to prevent him from achieving total supremacy in the Roman world. But Caesar's heir, despite the disadvantages of youth, lack of military experience, and weak health, had now earned Antony's respect and the older Triumvir was content to immerse himself in the luxuries of the East and to enjoy the fruits of his success. He was soon to establish his fatal relationship with Cleopatra, queen of Egypt, a liaison which was to have a profound influence on the course of events over the following decade. For better or worse Antony's future was now irrevocably linked with the affairs of the East leaving Octavian to quietly establish himself as the master of Rome. And the coinages of the Triumvirs, like their destinies, were soon to follow quite separate paths.

D. Military Issues of Octavian

Octavian's first military coinage, like that of Antony, was associated with the war around Mutina in the spring of 43 BC. What is normally described as his initial issue of denarii depicts the equestrian statue which the Senate had voted in his honour in January (see no. 131). However, there is another denarius type which, though it has always been ascribed to Julius Caesar, has never been satisfactorily explained in the context of the dictator's coinage.

130 Head of Venus right, wearing fillet, her hair collected into a knot behind (no legend). *Reverse:* trophy of Gallic arms with chariot at base on left, and shield, two spears and carnyx on right, CAESAR (or C CAESAR) on left, IMP on right. *Silver denarius. Military mint travelling with Octavian in Italy or Cisalpine Gaul, spring 43 BC* (Crawford 482/1; Sydenham 1016; BMCRR Spain 70; Babelon Julia 13; Cohen *Julius Caesar* 15).

130

While the types appear to be purely Caesarian in character the distinctive style and considerable rarity of the issue, together with the unique form of the legend, make it hard to find a satisfactory place for it within the sequence of Caesar's military coinages.[36] These are normally inscribed with the dictator's *cognomen* 'CAESAR' alone, the addition of the imperatorial title and the *praenomen* being found only on the very rare Sicilian issue made in 47 BC by Caesar's lieutenant Allienus (see no. 54). The only denarii inscribed CAESAR IMP to be issued directly under the dictator's authority were the portrait coins by the Roman moneyers Mettius and Sepullius Macer struck in the final months of Caesar's life (see nos. 100 and 106), while CAESAR IMPER occurs immediately following the Ides of March (see nos. 101 and 108). There would have been no occasion for a military coinage at this time unless Caesar was planning a special issue for the forthcoming Parthian War, but the types of such an issue would surely not have looked back to the Gallic War for their inspiration. An attribution of these coins to the early days of Octavian's authority in Italy would appear to resolve these difficulties. Before marching against Antony in company with the consuls Hirtius and Pansa Octavian had already raised his own loyal army of retired Caesarian veterans who had been settled in Campania. Under these circumstances it would have been quite logical for the young man who had just inherited the magical name of Caesar to wish to reward the loyalty of his veteran troops by reviving memories of the famous campaigns in which they had first served under his adoptive father. Moreover, the two varieties of the legend would seem to support this attribution as CAESAR IMP was one of the last forms employed by Caesar before his assassination, thus linking Octavian with the memory of the slain dictator, whilst C CAESAR IMP appears on Octavian's very first issue of portrait denarii which, presumably, succeeded the Venus/trophy coinage.

131

131 Bare head of Octavian right, bearded, C CAESAR IMP around. *Reverse:* equestrian statue of Octavian left, his right hand raised, S C in exergue. *Silver denarius. Military mint travelling with Octavian in Cisalpine Gaul, spring–summer 43 BC* (Crawford 490/1; Sydenham 1318; BMCRR Gaul 81; Babelon Julia 63; Newman 43.8; Cohen 246).

The head of Octavian here appears for the first time on the coinage, a portrait which would eventually come to monopolize the obverses of the Roman precious metal currency until the death of Augustus almost six decades later. This initial issue probably belongs to the period between Antony's defeat at Mutina, in April of 43 BC, and Octavian's decision to march on Rome in the summer to impose his will on a vacillating Senate. Like Antony, Octavian appears unshaven as a sign of mourning for the late dictator, a portrait characteristic which would be retained until the deaths of Brutus and Cassius at Philippi. The reverse depicts the equestrian statue which the Conscript Fathers had voted in honour of Caesar's heir at the beginning of the year. His troops were needed to bolster the army of the consuls in their mission to raise Antony's siege of Decimus Brutus in Mutina, and by such flattery the Senate hoped to persuade the young man to do their bidding. Octavian agreed, but only because he had his own agenda, and on his return to the capital in August he had the authority, backed by overwhelming military force, to dictate his own terms to a cowering republican government. It is likely that on this occasion he required the promise of an equestrian statue to be made good, for the type appears again (though facing the other way) on a denarius struck at the end of the year, soon after the establishment of the Triumvirate (see no. 134). The formula *S(enatus) C(onsulto)*, 'by decree of the Senate', undoubtedly refers to the statue itself rather than to the constitutional validity of the coin issue. This was a military coinage produced on Octavian's own authority and it unlikely that it had been officially sanctioned, even though the issuer was ostensibly acting as the Senate's champion in its confrontation with Antony.

132

132 Bare head of Octavian right, bearded, C CAESAR COS PONT AVG around (NT and AV usually ligatured). *Reverse:* wreathed head of Caesar right, C CAESAR DICT PERP PONT MAX around (NT and MA ligatured). *Gold aureus. Military mint travelling with Octavian in Italy, late summer–autumn 43 BC* (Crawford 490/2; Sydenham 1321, 1321a; BMCRR Gaul 74, 75; Babelon Julia 64; Newman 43.9; Cohen 2).

This impressive issue of aurei, unmatched in Antony's coinage in Gaul, dates from the time of Octavian's election as consul on 19 August 43 BC with his uncle, Q. Pedius, as colleague. The Senate had been forced to acquiesce in the young man's elevation to Rome's highest office when he had marched on the city from the north at the head of an army composed of eight legions. The coinage would have been required for the payment of this impressive force while Octavian was settling affairs in the capital prior to his return to Cisalpine Gaul and the establishment of the Triumvirate. The reverse honours his adoptive father, the late dictator, slain in the Senate-house only eighteen months before. His portrait on this issue would have been popular with the soldiers, most of whom were Caesarian veterans, and the type served to strengthen Octavian's claim to be Caesar's true successor. In this regard it was in response to Antony's issue of denarii in Cisalpine Gaul a few months earlier (see no. 118). The obverse inscription records Octavian's consulship (COS), the first of thirteen which he would hold throughout his long life, as well as his membership of the priestly colleges of the pontifices (PONT) and the augurs (AVG). He would not hold the prestigious office of pontifex maximus, possessed by his adoptive father, until the death of the incumbent, Lepidus, in 13/12 BC. The portraiture on this issue is of superior style, suggesting perhaps that an engraver from the Capitoline mint was seconded to the staff of Octavian's military establishment in his camp outside the city. This artist probably remained with Octavian when he marched north, for his work appears to be recognizeable in the issue of aurei struck later in the year to commemorate the formation of the Triumvirate (see no. 133).

133 Bare head of Octavian right, bearded, C CAESAR IMP III VIR R P C PONT AV (or AVG) around (NT sometimes ligatured, AV always so). *Reverse:* bare head of M. Antony right, bearded, M ANTONIVS IMP (or IM) III VIR R P C AVG around (AV ligatured). *Gold aureus. Military mint travelling with Octavian in Cisalpine Gaul, November–December 43 BC* (Crawford 493/1; Sydenham 1167; BMCRR Gaul 59; Babelon Julia 77; Newman 43.12; Cohen 3).

133

This aureus type accords Octavian and Antony the full triumviral title of III VIR R P C (*triumvir reipublicae constituendae*) and was struck within the former's military camp following the historic meeting at Bononia early in November, 43 BC. The third member of the Triumvirate, M. Aemilius Lepidus, is pointedly ignored, there being no corresponding issue bearing his name and portrait. Octavian's superiority is also subtly indicated by the inclusion of the priestly titles of both Triumvirs. Here, the younger man enjoyed a distinct advantage by virtue of his membership of both the principal colleges (the pontifices and the augurs) whilst Antony could boast only an association with the latter. These slights were answered in the issue from Antony's mint (see nos. 124–5) on which all reference to Octavian's membership of the priestly colleges is omitted, whilst Antony's augurship and Lepidus' possession of the office of pontifex maximus are emphasized by the representation of priestly emblems behind their portraits. The neatly engraved dies with good portraiture which characterize Octavian's aurei in celebration of the Triumvirate are perhaps by the same hand as his preceding issue (see commentary on no. 132).

134

134 Bare head of Octavian right, bearded, C CAESAR III VIR R P C around. *Reverse:* equestrian statue of Octavian right, his right hand raised, S C in exergue. *Silver denarius. Military mint travelling with Octavian in Cisalpine Gaul, November–December 43 BC* (Crawford 490/3; Sydenham 1316; BMCRR Gaul 63; Babelon Julia 65; Newman 43.10; Cohen 243).

This revives Octavian's first portrait denarius, issued in the spring or summer (see no. 131), though with the triumviral title replacing the imperatorial and the equestrian statue shown facing the other way. It thus corresponds to Antony's issue with Caesar's portrait on reverse (see no. 123) which is also a revival of his first military portrait type (no. 118). At some point Octavian appears to have become concerned over the possible propaganda advantage being gained by Antony through his depiction of the late dictator. The result was another type, also with Caesar's portrait on reverse, though with no identifying legend, this presumably being considered superfluous on a coin issued by his adoptive son. Production can only have been on a very limited scale as the type is presently represented by only a single surviving specimen.

135 *Obverse:* same as preceding. *Reverse:* wreathed head of Caesar right (no legend). *Silver denarius. Military mint travelling with Octavian in Cisalpine Gaul, November–December 43 BC* (Crawford 490/4; Sydenham 1324; Newman 43.11; RSC/Cohen 6a).

In the months leading up to the battle of Philippi the extensive issues of the Roman moneyers were augmented by the military coinages of Antony (see no. 127) and Lepidus (nos. 139–140a), and the following types produced by the mint accompanying Octavian.

136

136 Bare head of Octavian right, bearded, CAESAR III VIR R P C around. *Reverse:* equestrian statue of Octavian left, holding lituus in right hand, the horse decorated with phalarae around its neck, S – C divided by rostrum (beak of war-galley) left in exergue. *Gold aureus. Military mint travelling with Octavian in Italy, spring–summer 42 BC* (Crawford 497/1; Sydenham 1319; BMCRR Gaul 95; Babelon Julia 66; Newman 42.7; Cohen 245).

This is yet another depiction of the equestrian statue voted by the Senate in January of 43 BC in honour of Octavian (see also nos. 131 and 134). The presence of the augur's staff (lituus) in the rider's right hand refers to Octavian's augurship and challenges Antony's exclusive use of this symbolism as a sign of authority.[37] The rostrum in exergue indicates the location of the statue in the Roman Forum. It was erected in the vicinity of the Rostra, the celebrated speakers' platform which received its name from the beaks or rams of captured enemy war-galleys with which it was adorned. The phalerae (military ornaments) which appear around the horse's neck probably relate to honours bestowed on Octavian for his victory at Mutina. In this case they would represent another artful slight of Octavian's triumviral colleague who had been his opponent in this campaign. An unusual feature of this aureus, shared by the two following denarius types, is the form of Octavian's name which is rendered simply as CAESAR instead of the usual 'C CAESAR'. The probable intention was to strengthen the connection between Octavian and his adoptive father to the detriment of Antony's claim to be Caesar's true successor.

137 *Obverse:* same as preceding. *Reverse:* curule chair surmounted by wreath and inscribed CÆSAR DIC PER (AR usually also ligatured; sometimes PR for PER). *Silver denarius. Military mint travelling with Octavian in Italy, spring–summer 42 BC* (Crawford 497/2a–c; Sydenham 1322; BMCRR Gaul 76; Babelon Julia 89; Newman 42.8; Cohen 55).

137

137a Similar to preceding, but the curule chair is inscribed CAESAR DIC PER (or PE). *Silver denarius. Military mint travelling with Octavian in Italy, spring–summer 42 BC* (Crawford 497/2d; RSC/Cohen 55a, c).

137a

This type goes even further in stressing the close link between Octavian and Caesar. The gilded *sella curulis*, inscribed with the dictator's name and title, and the wreath placed on the empty seat are both symbolic of the extraordinary honours which the Senate had bestowed on the dictator during his lifetime. Since 1 January 42 BC he had been officially recognized as a god (*Divus Iulius*) thus making Octavian *divi filius*, 'son of god', a title which was to be of inestimable value in the young man's relentless pursuit of political supremacy in the Roman world.

138 Draped bust of youthful Mars right, wearing crested helmet ornamented with plume, spear over left shoulder visible behind, CAESAR III VIR R P C around (AR sometimes ligatured). *Reverse:* legionary eagle between two standards, trophy in background, S – C either side of eagle's shaft. *Silver denarius. Military mint travelling with Octavian in Greece, autumn 42 BC* (Crawford 497/3; Sydenham 1320; BMCRR Gaul 96, 98; Babelon Julia 67; Newman 42.9; Cohen 248).

138

The strong military flavour of this type would seem to place it in the period either immediately preceding or following the battle of Philippi on 23 October. The youthful aspect of Mars, god of war, is probably complimentary to the young Octavian, whilst the S C (*senatus consulto*, 'by decree of the Senate') refers to the measure by which Caesar's heir had gained official command of an army rather than to the constitutional validity of the coin issue. A substantial proportion of the coinage was now being produced by military mints, this being one of the legacies of the civil war commencing with the issues of Caesar and Pompey in 49 BC. The strict legality of these coinages was certainly open to question, though with the fate of the Republic itself now hanging in the balance the constitutionality of the currency was not high on anyone's political agenda. The victory of the Caesarians at Philippi ensured that there was going to be a fundamental change in the way in which the state was governed. Within just a few years the Capitoline mint in Rome would be closed down altogether, thus ending two and a half centuries of tradition dating back to the era preceding the First Punic War.

E. Military Issue of Lepidus

From the time that he joined forces with Mark Antony in Gaul (29 May 43 BC) Marcus Aemilius Lepidus, Caesar's former master of horse and now governor of Gallia Narbonensis and Nearer Spain, surrendered effective control of his army and appears to have been content to play a subordinate role to his more charismatic ally. In return for Lepidus' loyalty in the difficult period prior to the establishment of the Second Triumvirate Antony allowed the pontifex maximus a nominal position in the conduct of affairs, insisting that he should participate in the new arrangement worked out with Octavian at Bononia in November of 43 BC. Doubtless, Antony considered that Lepidus' involvement in the triumviral government would give him a distinct advantage over Octavian, knowing that he could count on his junior partner's loyalty and support against Caesar's adopted son in the event of a serious dispute arising between the Caesarian leaders.

On the special issues of gold aurei struck to commemorate the formation of the Triumvirate, those produced by Antony's military mint honour all three members of the new regime (see nos. 124–5), whilst those issued from Octavian's camp mention Antony alone (see no. 133). Lepidus did not participate at all in this coinage, though this is hardly surprising if, as seems likely, he and Antony shared the same camp. The one military issue which may be ascribed to Lepidus is principally of silver denarii, though a single specimen of the aureus has been recorded.[38]

139 Bare head of Lepidus right, LEPIDVS PONT MAX III V R P C around (NT and MA ligatured). *Reverse:* bare head of Octavian right, CAESAR IMP III VIR R P C around (MP ligatured). *Gold aureus. Military mint travelling with Lepidus in Italy, spring–summer 42 BC* (Crawford 495/1; Sydenham 1323, note; BMCRR Africa, p. 579, note 2; Babelon Aemilia 34; Cohen 1).

140

140 Similar to preceding, but sometimes VIR (ligatured) instead of V on obverse, and sometimes the MP of IMP is not ligatured on reverse. *Silver denarius. Military mint travelling with Lepidus in Italy, spring–summer 42 BC* (Crawford 495/2a–c; Sydenham 1323, 1323a; BMCRR Africa 29–31; Babelon Aemilia 35; Newman p. 60 and pl. 7, C; RSC/Cohen 2–2b and 2d).

One revers die has been noted with IMA (MA ligatured) instead of IMP.

140a

140a Similar to 139, but the reverse legend commences C CAESAR. *Silver denarius. Military mint travelling with Lepidus in Italy, spring–summer 42 BC* (Crawford 495/2d; BMCRR Africa, p. 579, note 2; RSC/Cohen 2c).

Lepidus, rather than Octavian, would appear to be the author of this coinage as it publicizes his possession of the office of pontifex maximus whilst ignoring the rare distinction of membership of both the pontifices and augurs enjoyed by Caesar's adopted son. The issue possesses some puzzling features. If, as Crawford[39] suggests, it was 'struck from the proceeds of the proscriptions in preparation for the campaign of 42' then why does it ignore Antony? An alternative occasion for the issue is, however, hard to come up with. Grueber (BMCRR) and Sydenham both ascribe it to 40 BC or later, the former regarding it as an African coinage of Lepidus after he had been granted the government of that region by Octavian, the latter considering it a Gallic issue of Octavian. This late a date (after the Perusine War) appears unlikely, though the problem of Antony's absence remains.

Almost two decades before the probable date of this issue M. Aemilius Lepidus had served as a moneyer in Rome, striking denarii of three types (cf. Crawford 419).

F. Issue of C. Antonius as Proconsular Governor of Macedonia

Gaius Antonius, younger brother of Mark Antony, had served as a legate of Caesar in 49 BC, though he had been obliged to surrender to a Pompeian fleet which blockaded him on the island of Curicta in the Adriatic. In 44 BC he was elected praetor urbanus and in the difficult months following the dictator's assassination he assisted Mark Antony in establishing his ascendancy in post-Caesarian Rome. Towards the end of the year the Senate appointed Gaius to the proconsular governorship of Macedonia, a decision which was reversed soon afterwards when the Conscript Fathers gave their support instead to the tyrannicide M. Junius Brutus. Undaunted by this set-back, Gaius Antonius proceeded to try and take possession of his province as soon as he had laid down his praetorship. He got no further than Apollonia in Illyricum in which city he was besieged by Brutus, eventually falling into his rival's hands (March, 43 BC). He remained a prisoner of Brutus for some considerable time, his execution taking place early in the following year, probably in reprisal for the death of Cicero who had been proscribed by the Triumvirs.

141 Draped bust of the Genius of Macedonia right, wearing cap (causia), C ANTONIVS M F PRO COS around. *Reverse:* emblems of the pontificate – two simpula and axe, PONTIFEX below. *Silver denarius. Apollonia in Illyricum, January–March 43 BC* (Crawford 484/1; Sydenham 1286; BMCRR East 37; Babelon Antonia 148; Cohen 1).

141

This rare coinage was doubtless struck while C. Antonius was being besieged in Apollonia by M. Junius Brutus. The issue thus anticipates Gaius' governorship which he was destined never to take up. The obverse symbolizes the province which was the bone of contention between the two men. As a coin type it invites comparison with the denarius issued about a dozen years before by the moneyer Cn. Plancius, who had a close personal association with Macedonia (cf. Crawford 432). The reverse commemorates C. Antonius' election in 44 BC to the priestly college of the pontifices through the influence of the pontifex maximus, the dictator Julius Caesar.

G. Issues of the Roman Moneyers in Honour of Antony

Antony's portrait first appeared on the coinage not long after Caesar's murder, on an issue of the Roman moneyer P. Sepullius Macer which can probably be dated to the period late April to early May, 44 BC (see no. 142). Subsequent Antonian issues, in 43 BC, are the products of the military mints travelling with his armies in Transalpine and Cisalpine Gaul, both prior to the establishment of the Second Triumvirate in November (see nos. 118–22) and following this momentous event (nos. 123–5). The beginning of the year 42 BC saw the firm establishment of the triumviral regime in Rome. With the publication of the proscription lists great wealth began to flow into the treasury, the proceeds of confiscated property seized from those who had been condemned to death for their political allegiances. As a result the four moneyers appointed for 42 BC were able to produce an extensive coinage, including an unprecedented issue of gold aurei many of which bore the names and portraits of the three Triumvirs. This enabled the Caesarian leaders to meet the expenses of the huge army which they were assembling for the coming trial of strength with Brutus and Cassius. With this important issue portraiture on the coinage was well on its way to becoming an established norm and, as we shall see, even the republican leaders were not immune to its seductive appeal despite its monarchical implications.

142

142 Veiled head of M. Antony right, bearded, lituus below chin, capis behind (no legend). *Reverse:* horseman (*desultor*) on horseback galloping right, a second horse at his side in background, wearing conical cap and holding whip in right hand, wreath and palm-branch behind, P SEPVLLIVS above, MACER below. *Silver denarius. Rome, April–May 44 BC* (Crawford 480/22; Sydenham 1077; BMCRR 4178; Babelon Antonia 2; Cohen 74).

This, the first portrait of Antony to appear on the coinage, belongs to a series issued by the moneyer P. Sepullius Macer which includes two other obverse types linked by the same reverse. One of these has a posthumous portrait of Caesar with the title PARENS PATRIAE (see no. 109), the other a temple dedicated to Caesar's clemency (see no. 110). Although the obverse is unepigraphic the features are clearly those of the 39-year-old surviving consul who is depicted unshaven as a sign of mourning for the slain dictator. This was to remain a characteristic of the numismatic portraiture of Antony (and Octavian) until Caesar's murder had been avenged at the battle of Philippi two and a half years later. The subsidiary symbols on obverse are emblematic of Antony's membership of the priestly college of augurs, the capis taking the place of the apex on the posthumous portrait of Caesar which indicated his additional membership of the college of pontifices, a rare distinction shared by Octavian but not by Antony. The depiction on reverse of the horseman engaged in competition (*desultor*) seems to link this issue to the Parilian games celebrated on 21 April, thus suggesting a period of issue for this type of late April to May, 44 BC. The Rome mint was not to strike again in honour of Antony until 42 BC, after the establishment of the Second Triumvirate.

143 Bare head of M. Antony right, bearded, M ANTONIVS III VIR R P C around. *Reverse:* Hercules seated facing on rock, lion's skin draped over lap, his legs turned towards left, holding vertical spear in right hand and parazonium in left, shield ornamented with Gorgon's head at his side to right, L REGVLVS on left, IIII VIR A P F on right. *Gold aureus. Rome, 42 BC* (Crawford 494/2a; Sydenham 1103; BMCRR 4255; Babelon Antonia 21; Buttrey, p. 67 and pls. v–vi, 48.1–7; Cohen 25).

143a Similar to preceding, but on reverse L REGVLVS to right, and IIII VIR A P F to left. *Gold aureus. Rome, 42 BC.* (Crawford 494/2b; Sydenham 1103a; BMCRR 4256; Babelon Antonia 22; Buttrey, p. 67 and pl. vi, 48.8–14; Cohen 25).

143a

The triumviral title III VIR R P C (*triumvir reipublicae constituendae*, 'Triumvir for the regulation of the Republic'), borne by Antony, Octavian and Lepidus, had already been proclaimed on military issues in Cisalpine Gaul at the end of the preceding year (see nos. 123–5 and 133–5). The extensive moneyers' coinage for 42 BC marked the sole appearance of this title on the issues of the Capitoline mint which, like the Republic itself, was rapidly approaching its demise. Soon it would cease operation altogether, interrupting centuries of tradition as the principal source of coinage for the State, until its resurrection two decades later as a vital element of the reformed imperial currency system of Augustus. This type, struck by Livineius Regulus in honour of Antony, has an unconventional representation of the hero Hercules, presumably in his role as ancestor of the Antonii. The moneyer's title is also of special interest. He is described as IIII VIR A P F (*quattuorvir auro publico feriundo*, 'one of four men for the striking of public gold'), a specific reference to the extraordinary nature of this coinage, marking the first occasion on which the mint magistrates had been called upon to issue gold coins as a regular part of the currency.

144

144 Bare head of M. Antony right, bearded, M ANTONIVS III VIR R P C around. *Reverse:* winged male figure standing left, naked and wearing radiate crown, bow and quiver over shoulder, holding caduceus in right hand and cornucopiae in left, his right foot resting on globe to left of which is eagle perched on a cippus, shield at his feet to right, P CLODIVS

M F IIII VIR A P F around. *Gold aureus. Rome, 42 BC* (Crawford 494/5; Sydenham 1118; BMCRR 4276; Babelon Antonia 19; Buttrey, p. 65 and pl. iv, 45; Cohen 73).

The significance of the composite deity featured on the reverse of this aureus has been the subject of much scholarly speculation. The attributes of Sol (radiate crown), Apollo (bow and quiver), Victory (wings), Felicitas (caduceus and cornucopiae), Jupiter (eagle) and Mars (shield) are all associated with a naked male figure representing Genius. The type should probably be interpreted as being personally complimentary to Antony as the dominant member of the Triumvirate.

145

145 Bare head of M. Antony right, bearded, M ANTONIVS III VIR R P C around. *Reverse:* Mars, naked but for crested helmet, standing right, his left foot set on shield, resting on vertical spear held in right hand and holding sword in scabbard in left, L MVSSIDIVS T F LONGVS IIII VIR A P F around, commencing above. *Gold aureus. Rome, 42 BC* (Crawford 494/8b; Sydenham 1097; BMCRR 4226; Babelon Antonia 25; Buttrey, p. 68 and pl. viii, 51.4–11; Cohen 21).

145a Similar to preceding, but the reverse legend commences in exergue, and the MV of MVSSIDIVS is ligatured. *Gold aureus. Rome, 42 BC.* (Crawford 494/8a; Babelon Antonia 24; Buttrey, p. 68 and pl. viii, 51.1–3; Cohen 21).

Mars was obviously appropriate to a time of preparation for war and the moneyer Mussidius Longus employs the same reverse type on aurei issued for Octavian and Lepidus (see nos. 152 and 161). Crawford[40] suggests that the type may allude to the plans of the Triumvirs to prosecute the Parthian War projected by Caesar in the final months of his life.

146

146 Bare head of M. Antony right, bearded, M ANTONIVS III VIR R P C around. *Reverse:* cornucopiae tied with fillet, L MVSSIDIVS on left, LONGVS on right. *Gold aureus. Rome, 42 BC* (Crawford 494/14;

Sydenham 1100; BMCRR 4230; Babelon Antonia 23; Buttrey, p. 64 and pls. ii–-iii, 42; Cohen 20).

This type looks forward to the restoration of prosperity in the Roman world, symbolized by the horn of plenty, following the anticipated victory of the Triumvirs over the Republicans and the consequent end of civil conflict. As in the case of Longus' other triumviral aureus type (Mars) this reverse is common to all three of the Caesarian leaders (see also nos. 153 and 162).

147 Bare head of M. Antony right, bearded, M ANTONIVS III VIR R P C around. *Reverse:* two right hands clasped, C VEIBIVS above, VAARVS below. *Gold aureus. Rome, 42 BC* (Crawford 494/11; Sydenham 1141; BMCRR p. 587; Babelon Antonia 27; Buttrey, p. 63 and pl. i, 39).

147

The unity of the triumviral government is here emphasized. Gaius Vibius Varus, like his three colleagues in the monetary college of 42 BC, is otherwise unknown to history. The same reverse type occurs on aurei issued for Octavian (see no. 154) and Lepidus (no. 163).

148 Bare head of M. Antony right, bearded, M ANTONIVS before, III VIR R P C behind. *Reverse:* Mars, naked but for helmet, standing facing, his body inclined to right, head facing left, resting on spear held in right hand and holding sword in scabbard away from his body in left, P CLODIVS on left, M F on right. *Silver denarius. Rome, 42 BC* (Crawford 494/17; Sydenham 1121; BMCRR 4278; Babelon Antonia 20; Cohen 72).

148

P. Clodius struck parallel issues in the names of the late dictator (see no. 114) and the Triumvir Octavian (no. 155). An additional denarius type (see no. 156) was exclusive to Octavian and may have been intended to help compensate for the termination of Varus silver coinage bearing the portrait of Caesars heir. As in the case of the aureus of Mussidius Longus (no. 145) the appearance of the god of war, armed in readiness for battle, was most appropriate to the circumstances of the time.

149 Bare head of M. Antony right, bearded (no legend). *Reverse:* Fortuna standing left, holding Victory on extended right hand and cornucopiae in left, C VIBIVS behind, VARVS before. *Silver denarius. Rome, 42 BC* (Crawford 494/32; Sydenham 1144; BMCRR 4293; Babelon Antonia 26; Cohen 4).

149

Fortuna holding a small figure of Victory represents an expression of confidence that good luck and success will attend the Triumvirs in their forthcoming military confrontation with the Republicans. Varus also struck this type with the portrait of Octavian, though specimens of the latter issue are much rarer (see no. 158). On the evidence of stylistic similarity it seems possible that the die-engraver responsible for the triumviral portraits was later transferred from the Capitoline to Antonys military minting establishment in his camp outside the city (see note to no. 127).

The other two moneyers for 42 BC, Livineius Regulus and Mussidius Longus, issued no denarii with Antony's portrait. However, they did strike silver in honour of Caesar, who was now officially recognized as a god (see nos. 115 and 116), and Regulus issued one type for Octavian (see no. 157), possibly to help compensate for the termination of Varus silver coinage bearing the portrait of Caesars heir. M. Aemilius Lepidus is ignored on the moneyers' silver issues, perhaps indicating that even at this early stage it was clearly recognized that he was playing only a subsidiary role in the triumviral government.

H. Issues of the Roman Moneyers in Honour of Octavian

Although the 19-year-old Octavian had already made himself master of Rome by the late summer of 43 BC he is not featured on any of the moneyers' issues for this year. His influence, however, is apparent in the revival of Caesar's portrait on the denarius coinage of L. Flaminius Cilo (see no. 113). The first coinage in Octavian's name was produced by a military mint travelling with him at the time of the Mutina campaign against Antony in the spring of 43 BC (see nos. 130 and 131). The establishment of the Second Triumvirate towards the end of the year, followed by the acquisition of vast wealth through the proscriptions, enabled the Caesarian leaders to commission an unprecedented coinage of gold aurei from the Capitoline mint to be struck by all four moneyers appointed for 42 BC. Thus, the name and portrait of Octavian (Gaius Caesar) appears for the first time on the coinage of Rome alongside those of his triumviral colleagues Antony and Lepidus.

150 Bare head of Octavian right, with slight beard, C CAESAR before, III VIR R P C behind. *Reverse:* Aeneas running right, bearing his father Anchises on his shoulders, L REGVLVS before, IIII VIR A P F behind. *Gold aureus. Rome, 42 BC* (Crawford 494/3b; Sydenham 1104; BMCRR 4257; Babelon Julia 83; Buttrey, p. 67 and pl. vii, 49.3 & 5–8; Cohen 444).

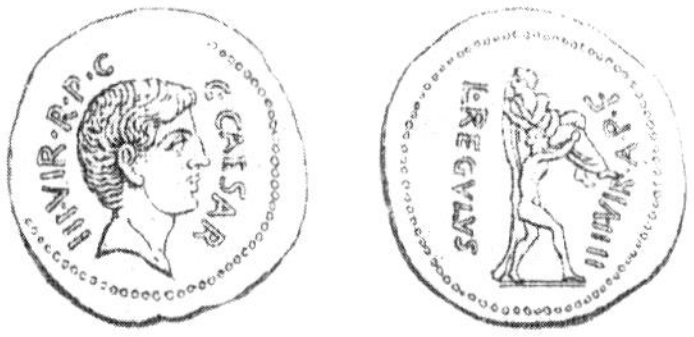

150a

150a Similar to preceding, but on reverse L REGVLVS is behind Aeneas and IIII VIR A P F before. *Gold aureus. Rome, 42 BC* (Crawford 494/3a; Sydenham 1104a; BMCRR 4258; Babelon Julia 83; Buttrey, p. 67 and pl. vii, 49.1–2 & 4; Cohen 444).

The reverse type honours Octavian's ancestry through his adoptive father, Gaius Julius Caesar. The Trojan prince Aeneas, son of Venus and Anchises, is depicted bearing his aged father on his shoulders as they leave the ruined city of Troy following its capture by the Greeks. Aeneas was the father of Ascanius (= Iulus) from whom the *gens* Julia claimed its descent. The type was doubtless intended to revive memories of Caesar's large issue of denarii, in 47–46 BC, for the campaign against the Pompeians in north Africa (see no. 55). As on the corresponding issues of Antony and Lepidus the obverse legend proclaims the triumviral title *triumvir reipublicae constituendae* ('Triumvir for the regulation of the Republic'); whilst the reverse has the moneyer's title *quattuorvir auro publico feriundo* ('one of four men for the striking of public gold').

151

151 Bare head of Octavian right, with slight beard, C CAESAR III VIR R P C around. *Reverse:* Venus seated three-quarter face to left on cippus, holding dove on extended right hand, her left arm encircling Cupid who hovers at her side, P CLODIVS M F IIII VIR A P F around. *Gold aureus. Rome, 42 BC* (Crawford 494/6a; Sydenham 1119; BMCRR 4277; Babelon Julia 80; Buttrey, p. 65 and pl. iv, 46.1; Cohen 412).

151a Similar to preceding, but the reverse legend is more compactly spaced, commencing above and ending on right. *Gold aureus. Rome, 42 BC* (Crawford 494/6b; Buttrey, p. 65 and pl. iv, 46.2).

Venus Genetrix had been prominent on the issues of the Caesarian moneyers, and her head had appeared on Caesar's military denarii struck in 46/45 BC for the Munda campaign (see nos. 58–9). As the supposed ancestress of the Julia *gens* Venus was an obvious choice as reverse type for these aurei of Octavian, the young Triumvir's constant objective being to stress his close association with his adoptive father. The composition is of unusual elegance and may have been inspired by some noted piece of sculpture.

152

152 Bare head of Octavian right, with slight beard, C CAESAR III VIR R P C around. *Reverse:* Mars, naked but for crested helmet, standing right, his left foot set on shield, resting on vertical spear held in right hand and holding sword in scabbard in left, L MVSSIDIVS T F LONGVS IIII

VIR A P F around, commencing above. *Gold aureus. Rome, 42 BC* (Crawford 494/9b; Babelon Julia 85; Buttrey, pp. 68–9 and pl. ix, 52.4–7, 52.10 and 52.12; Cohen 468).

152a Similar to preceding, but the reverse legend commences in exergue, and the MV of MVSSIDIVS is ligatured. *Gold aureus. Rome, 42 BC.* (Crawford 494/9a; Sydenham 1098; BMCRR 4227; Buttrey, pp. 68–9 and pl. viii, 52.1–3, pl. ix, 52.11 and 52.13).

Mars was obviously appropriate to a time of preparation for war and the moneyer Mussidius Longus employs the same reverse type on aurei issued for Antony and Lepidus (see nos. 145 and 161). Crawford[41] suggests that the type may allude to the plans of the Triumvirs to prosecute the Parthian War projected by Caesar in the final months of his life.

153

153 Bare head of Octavian right, with slight beard, C CAESAR III VIR R P C around. *Reverse:* cornucopiae tied with fillet, L MVSSIDIVS on left, LONGVS on right. *Gold aureus. Rome, 42 BC* (Crawford 494/15; Sydenham 1101; BMCRR 4231; Babelon Julia 84; Buttrey, pp. 64–5 and pl. iii, 43; Cohen 467).

This type looks forward to the restoration of prosperity in the Roman world, symbolized by the horn of plenty, following the anticipated victory of the Triumvirs over the Republicans and the consequent end of civil conflict. As in the case of Longus' other triumviral aureus type (Mars) this reverse is common to all three of the Caesarian leaders (see also nos. 146 and 162).

154

154 Bare head of Octavian right, with slight beard, C CAESAR III VIR R P C around. *Reverse:* two right hands clasped, C VEIBIVS above, VAARVS below. *Gold aureus. Rome, 42 BC* (Crawford 494/12; Sydenham 1142; BMCRR 4292; Babelon Julia 88; Buttrey, p. 63 and pl. i, 40; Cohen 540).

The unity of the recently established triumviral government is here emphasized, perhaps in an attempt to counter its growing unpopularity in Italy due to the proscriptions. With Brutus and Cassius assembling their powerful forces in Asia the security of the Caesarian regime in Rome must have seemed quite uncertain at this juncture. The same reverse type occurs on aurei issued for Antony (see no. 147) and Lepidus (no. 163).

155 Bare head of Octavian right, with slight beard, CAESAR before, III VIR R P C behind. *Reverse:* Mars, naked but for helmet, standing facing, his body inclined to right, head facing left, resting on spear held in right hand and holding sword in scabbard away from his body in left, P CLODIVS on left, M F on right. *Silver denarius. Rome, 42 BC* (Crawford 494/18; Sydenham 1122; BMCRR 4279; Babelon Julia 78; Cohen 410).

155

P. Clodius struck parallel issues in the names of Caesar (see no. 114) and Mark Antony (no. 148). With the trial of strength with the republican forces now imminent the god of war is here invoked, as on the aureus of Mussidius Longus (no. 152), to bring success to the Caesarian cause.

156

156 *Obverse:* same as preceding. *Reverse:* Pietas standing left, holding branch in extended right hand and resting on sceptre held in left, P CLODIVS behind, M F before. *Silver denarius. Rome, 42 BC* (Crawford 494/19; Sydenham 1124; BMCRR 4282; Babelon Julia 81; Cohen 411).

This rare type, which is exclusive to Octavian, lays emphasis on the filial loyalty of the young Triumvir which places on him a special obligation to avenge the late dictator's brutal assassination. This type and the next may have been issued to compensate for the termination of Varus silver coinage bearing the portrait of Caesars heir.

157 Bare head of Octavian right, with slight beard, C CAESAR before, III VIR R P C behind. *Reverse:* Victory, naked to the hips, standing right, holding wreath in extended right hand and palm-branch over her shoulder in left, L LIVINEIVS before, REGVLVS behind. *Silver denarius. Rome, 42 BC* (Crawford 494/25; Sydenham 1107; BMCRR 4260; Babelon Julia 82; Cohen 443).

157

Another type struck solely for Octavian, the reference is clearly to the trial of strength between the Caesarian forces of the Triumvirs and the republican army led by Brutus and Cassius. Octavian's portrait bears only slight traces of a beard, and it is unclear whether Victory appears in hopeful anticipation of a successful outcome to the conflict or whether she is in actual commemoration of Philippi.

158

158 Bare head of Octavian right, with slight beard (no legend). *Reverse:* Fortuna standing left, holding Victory on extended right hand and cornucopiae in left, C VIBIVS behind, VARVS before. *Silver denarius. Rome, 42 BC* (Crawford 494/33; Sydenham 1145; cf. BMCRR p. 588, Type ii var., though this is a coin of Antony misdescribed; cf. Babelon Julia 86, another misdescribed Antony; Cohen 539).

Fortuna holding a small figure of Victory represents an expression of confidence that good luck and success will attend the Triumvirs in their forthcoming military confrontation with the Republicans. Varus also struck this type with the portrait of Antony (see no. 149) for whom the issue appears to have been much larger than that bearing Octavians effigy. Antonys hypothesized activities with regard to the die-engraver responsible for this coinage, possibly resulting in his transfer to the Triumvirs military mint outside Rome, may provide an explanation of the surprising rarity of Octavian's type (see note to no. 127). Additional issues by the moneyers P. Clodius and Livineius Regulus (see nos. 156 and 157) may have been intended to make good the resulting shortfall in coinage honouring Octavian.

I. Issues of the Roman Moneyers in Honour of Lepidus

Other than his appearance on his own military issue, probably struck in Italy in the months preceding Philippi (see nos. 139–40), the portrait of Lepidus occurs only on gold aurei produced at the Capitoline mint by the *quattuorviri monetales* of 42 BC. Lepidus enjoyed a full share in this remarkable coinage with his triumviral colleagues Antony and Octavian, though it is noteworthy that not a single issue of silver denarii was struck with his name and portrait. This would seem to be a sure indication of his junior status in the Triumvirate even in this early phase of its existence. A curious feature of Lepidus' aurei is the direction of his portrait. This faces to the left on coins issued by three of the four moneyers,[42] whilst the heads of Antony and Octavian are invariably turned to the right. The reason for this differentiation is unclear, unless it was intended as a subtle hint of Lepidus' inferior status.

159

159 Bare head of Lepidus right, M LEPIDVS III VIR R P C around. *Reverse:* the Vestal virgin Aemilia, veiled and draped, standing left, holding simpulum in extended right hand and transverse sceptre in left, L REGVLVS IIII VIR A P F around. *Gold aureus. Rome, 42* BC (Crawford 494/1; Sydenham 1105; BMCRR 4259; Babelon Aemilia 36; Buttrey, p. 66 and pls. iv-v, 47; Cohen 3).

The Vestal virgin Aemilia had a double significance for Lepidus, both as the legendary ancestress of the Aemilia *gens* and because of the Triumvir's office of pontifex maximus in which he had succeeded the slain dictator in 44 BC. It thus complements Regulus' types for Antony and Octavian, both of which make reference to the origins of their respective *gentes* (see nos. 143 and 150). The titulature of both the Triumvir and the moneyer are the same as on the equivalent issues of Antony and Octavian. This type is unique in the series in its depiction of Lepidus' head facing to right, in conformity with the effigies of his two colleagues. In contrast, Lepidus' aurei struck by Clodius, Longus, and Varus all show his portrait turned to left.

160

160 Bare head of Lepidus left, M LEPIDVS III VIR R P C around. *Reverse:* female figure standing facing, looking right, holding sceptre and cornucopiae, uncertain object at her feet to right, P CLODIVS M F IIII VIR A P F around. *Gold aureus. Rome, 42* BC (Crawford 494/4; Sydenham 1120; BMCRR p. 584, Type iii; Buttrey, p. 65 and pls. iii–iv, 44).

The enigmatic reverse type of this extremely rare issue still awaits a satisfactory explanation. Even the identity of the female figure remains in doubt. Grueber[43] and Sydenham[44] both favour the goddess Concordia, whilst Buttrey[45] sees Felicitas, citing Lepidus' completion in 44 BC of the temple of Felicitas on the site of the old Senate-house. Crawford's[46] view is that Fortuna is depicted. In reality, none of these suggestions carries much weight and the situation is further complicated by the uncertainty of the object at the goddess's feet, variously described as an owl, a wineskin, or a cuirass. Presumably, the insignificance of Lepidus' position in the power structure of the Caesarian party rendered it more difficult (or rather of no great importance) to select an appropriate coin type. Unlike the portraits of his two triumviral colleagues Lepidus' head is turned to left on the aurei struck for him by P. Clodius, a curious feature also found on the issues of L. Mussidius Longus and C. Vibius Varus.

161 Bare head of Lepidus left, M LEPIDVS III VIR R P C around. *Reverse:* Mars, naked but for crested helmet, standing right, his left foot set on

161

shield, resting on vertical spear held in right hand and holding sword in scabbard in left, L MVSSIDIVS T F LONGVS IIII VIR A P F around, commencing above. *Gold aureus. Rome, 42 BC* (Crawford 494/7b; Sydenham 1099; BMCRR 4228; Babelon Aemilia 38; Buttrey, p. 68 and pl. vii, 50.2–4; Cohen 2).

161a Similar to preceding, but the reverse legend commences in exergue, and the MV of MVSSIDIVS is ligatured. *Gold aureus. Rome, 42 BC* (Crawford 494/7a; Buttrey, p. 68 and pl. vii, 50.1).

Mars was obviously appropriate to a time of preparation for war and the moneyer Mussidius Longus employs the same reverse type on aurei issued for Antony and Octavian (see nos. 145 and 152). Crawford[47] suggests that the type may allude to the plans of the Triumvirs to prosecute the Parthian War projected by Caesar in the final months of his life. Once again, Lepidus' head faces in the opposite direction to those of his two colleagues, possibly a subtle indication of the inferiority of his status in the Triumvirate.

162

162 Bare head of Lepidus left, M LEPIDVS III VIR R P C around. *Reverse:* cornucopiae tied with fillet, L MVSSIDIVS on left, LONGVS on right. *Gold aureus. Rome, 42 BC* (Crawford 494/13; Sydenham 1102; BMCRR 4232; Babelon Aemilia 37; Buttrey, pp. 63–4 and pls. i–ii, 41; Cohen 1).

This type looks forward to the restoration of prosperity in the Roman world, symbolized by the horn of plenty, following the anticipated victory of the Triumvirs over the Republicans and the consequent end of civil conflict. As in the case of Longus' other triumviral aureus type (Mars) this reverse is common to all three of the Caesarian leaders (see also nos. 146 and 153).

163 Bare head of Lepidus left, M LEPIDVS III VIR R P C around. *Reverse:* two right hands clasped, C VEIBIVS above, VAARVS below. *Gold*

163

aureus. Rome, 42 BC (Crawford 494/10; Sydenham 1143; BMCRR p. 588, Type i, var. *b*; Babelon Aemilia 39; Buttrey, p. 63 and pl. i, 38).

The unity of the recently established triumviral government is here emphasized, perhaps in an attempt to counter its growing unpopularity in Italy due to the proscriptions. With Brutus and Cassius assembling their powerful forces in Asia the security of the Caesarian regime in Rome must have seemed quite uncertain at this juncture. The same reverse type occurs on aurei issued for Antony (see no. 147) and Octavian (no. 154).

J. Regular Issues of the Roman Moneyers

The fateful year 44 BC saw the first appointment of a college of four moneyers (quattuorvirate) in place of the traditional triumvirate. M. Mettius, L. Aemilius Buca, P. Sepullius Macer, and C. Cossutius Maridianus comprised this group which had the doubtful honour of presiding over the first coin issues of republican Rome to bear the portrait of a living individual. What their personal feelings were concerning the monarchical implications of this revolutionary step we shall never know. But the issues continued for some time following Caesar's assassination on the Ides (15th) March and Macer even produced one type bearing the veiled portrait of Mark Antony, the first effigy of the later Triumvir to appear on the coinage (see no. 142). It would seem that the issues of this quattuorvirate had ceased by May, which is hardly to be wondered at given the unusually heavy volume of coinage in the opening months of the year and the extraordinarily confused political situation in the capital following the sudden and violent termination of the dictatorial regime.

Most of the issues of the moneyers' college of 44 BC have already been covered in this survey (see nos. 98–112 and 142). However, in addition to their extensive production of coinage honouring Caesar, and the single variety of Antony, there are also a few rare types which make no direct reference to the Caesarian government in Rome.

164 Diademed head of Venus right, L BVCA behind. *Reverse:* Sulla reclining right against rock, Luna descending left from mountain on right, veil floating above her head and holding lighted torch in right hand, Victory with spread wings standing facing in background, holding staff in raised right hand. *Silver denarius. Rome, January 44 BC* (Crawford 480/1; Sydenham 1064; BMCRR 4160; Babelon Aemilia 12).

164

Lucius Aemilius Buca appears to have been a distant relative of the dictator Sulla. It is recorded[48] that he testified on behalf of another Sullan relative, M. Aemilius Scaurus, at the latter's trial in 54 BC for misconduct during his government of Sardinia. Of the four moneyers of the college of 44 BC Buca was alone in striking a denarius with personal types which lacked any specific reference to Caesar's dictatorial regime. The issue may well be contemporary with Caesar's first portrait type produced by the moneyer M. Mettius in the first half of January (see nos. 98 and 99). The remarkable reverse type has been interpreted as representing the famous dream which Sulla experienced in 88 BC in the course of his advance on Rome to attack Marius. Plutarch[49] relates that when Sulla was at Nola in Campania a goddess appeared to him in his sleep and placed thunder in his hand, bidding him strike down his enemies whom she called by name. This he did and they were consumed to ashes. In this elaborate coin type the goddess is depicted as Luna and the slumbering Sulla is urged on by Victory to confront his adversaries. There seems little doubt that the issue belongs to the period of Caesar's lifetime as it is highly unlikely that Buca would have initiated such a type following the dictator's assassination. In addition to being an ancestral type of the moneyer it should, perhaps, also be regarded as symbolic of Caesar's own destiny in overcoming the rivalry of the Pompeian faction. The depiction of Venus on the obverse would have been just as appropriate for Caesar as for Sulla.

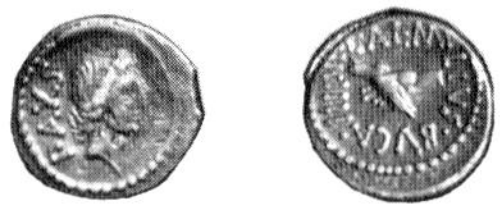
165

165 Diademed head of Pax right, PAXS behind. *Reverse:* clasped hands, L AEMILIVS BVCA IIII VIR around. *Silver quinarius. Rome, January 44 BC* (Crawford 480/24; Sydenham 1065; BMCRR 4162; Babelon Aemilia 18).

The theme of this rare half denarius is peace and harmony in the Roman world resulting from Caesar's final triumph over his adversaries. Pax, the goddess of peace, who was to feature so prominently on the coinage of the Empire, here makes her first certain appearance on the Roman currency. The clasped hands on reverse are symbolic of *concordia* and a little later the same image was to reappear as a subsidiary symbol on the reverse of one of Buca's denarii (see no. 103).

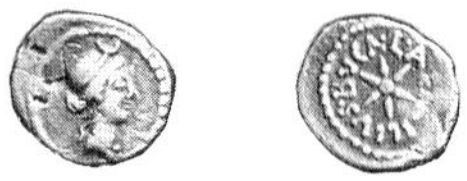
166

166 Diademed head of Luna right, crescent above. *Reverse:* star of six rays, L AEMILIVS BVCA around. *Silver sestertius. Rome, January 44 BC* (Crawford 480/26; Sydenham 1066; BMCRR 4163; Babelon Aemilia 19).

This type should be associated with Buca's denarius featuring Sulla's dream (see no. 164). The head of the moon-goddess Luna now appears as the obverse type, her identity being made clear by the crescent-moon above. The large star on reverse may be symbolic of Venus whose head appears as the obverse type of the denarius. The same symbol may sometimes be seen at the base of Venus' sceptre on several of Caesar's portrait issues (see nos. 106a, 107b, 107e and 108).

167

167 Head of Juno Sospita right, clad in goat's skin, snake erect behind. *Reverse:* Victory in galloping biga right, holding whip, M METTI in exergue. *Silver quinarius. Rome, January 44 BC* (Crawford 480/23; Sydenham 1058; BMCRR 4149; Babelon Mettia 1).

There is a clear connection between this half denarius type of M. Mettius and Caesar's first portrait denarius issued by the same moneyer in the opening weeks of the year (see nos. 98 and 99). Mettius' Lanuvine origin is again celebrated by the appearance of the goddess Juno Sospita, though here she is promoted to the obverse of the coin. The figure of Victory hurrying to battle in her chariot can hardly refer to anything other than Caesar's recent military successes in Spain, though perhaps the type also looks forward to the dictator's projected campaign against the Parthians.

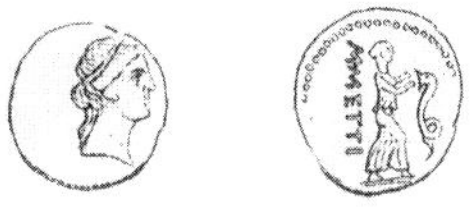

168

168 Diademed head of Venus right. *Reverse:* girl standing right, feeding snake erect before her, M METTI on left. *Silver sestertius. Rome, January 44* BC (Crawford 480/28; Sydenham 1059; BMCRR, p. 544; Babelon Mettia 2).

The reverse of this extremely rare issue revives a type first used two decades before by the moneyer L. Roscius Fabatus (cf. Crawford 412) and subsequently by one of the moneyers of 45 BC, L. Papius Celsus (see no. 84). Like Mettius, both were unquestionably sons of Lanuvium. The type relates to certain annual rites associated with the worship of Juno Sospita by which a girl was selected from the community to descend into the grotto beneath the goddess's temple. Her task was to feed the sacred serpent and if she survived the ordeal then this was taken as proof of her virginity and there was much rejoicing in her family. The head of Venus on obverse is clearly complimentary to Caesar, the goddess being the ancestress of the *gens* Julia through Iulus, grandson of Venus and Anchises.

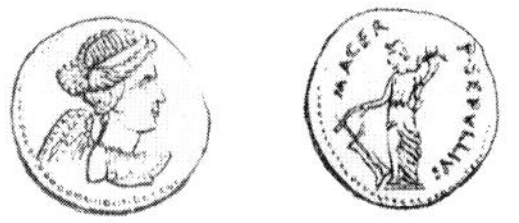

169

169 Diademed and draped bust of winged Victory right. *Reverse:* Fortuna standing left, holding rudder and cornucopiae, P SEPVLLIVS MACER around. *Silver quinarius. Rome, January 44* BC (Crawford 480/25; Sydenham 1078; BMCRR, p. 550; Babelon Sepullia 9).

Another type of great rarity, this half denarius features the goddesses of victory and fortune, a powerful combination of divine help which had never deserted Caesar in all his exploits from the time he had crossed the Rubicon five years before. His good fortune was, however, about to run out as the conspirators formulated their plans to rid the Republic of what they perceived to be a deadly threat. The figure of Fortuna, which was later to become so familiar on the money of imperial Rome, here makes her first appearance on the coinage bearing her standard attributes of rudder and cornucopiae. A bust of the goddess had already appeared in 49 BC on a denarius of the moneyer Q. Sicinius, a supporter of Pompey (see no. 1).

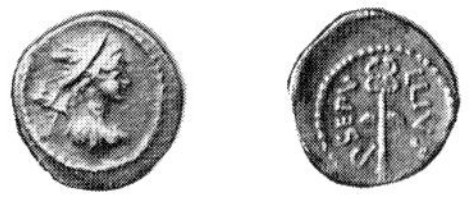

170

170 Draped bust of Mercury right, wearing winged petasus, caduceus over shoulder. *Reverse:* winged caduceus, P SEPVLLIVS around. *Silver sestertius. Rome, January 44* BC (Crawford 480/27; Sydenham 1080; BMCRR 4183; Babelon Sepullia 11–12).

Mercury was the Roman equivalent of the Greek Hermes. He was the winged messenger of the gods and was widely regarded as the protector of merchants and of commerce. Caesar's restoration in 48 BC of the fractional silver denominations, sestertius and quinarius, doubtless facilitated trade and the head of Mercury was a frequent obverse type on quarter denarii issued by the Caesarian moneyers (see nos. 24, 38, and 85). The caduceus, the winged staff of Mercury, was also symbolic of *felicitas* and was featured as a prominent element of the reverse design of one of the most remarkable of Caesar's lifetime portrait denarii (see no. 103).

Unlike his three colleagues the fourth member of the monetary college of 44 BC, Gaius Cossutius Maridianus, struck no quinarii or sestertii. Moreover, his denarius issues with Caesar's portrait did not commence before about mid-February and this would seem to indicate that the fractional silver denominations of the other moneyers belong to the earliest phase of the coinage, perhaps being struck for distribution at the new-year festivities.

Not surprisingly, moneyers' issues for the turbulent year 43 BC are on a restricted scale and only three members of the college can be identified – L. Flaminius Cilo, P. Accoleius Lariscolus, and Petillius Capitolinus. Denarii only were struck, the fractional silver which had been such a feature of the regular Roman coinage of Caesar's regime now being abandoned. Flaminius proclaims himself as striking first in his college and his issues include a portrait denarius of Julius Caesar (see no. 113), albeit without inscription. This could hardly have been struck before Octavian's military occupation of Rome in the late summer, following his success over Antony at Mutina, so it would seem that the entire moneyers' coinage for this year fell within the period August–December.

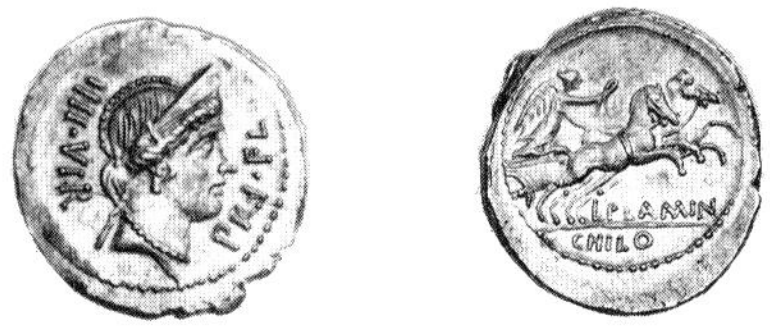

171

171 Diademed head of Venus right, IIII VIR behind, PRI FL before. *Reverse:* Victory in galloping biga r., holding wreath, L FLAMIN (or FLAMINI) below, CHILO in exergue. *Silver denarius. Rome, August 43 BC* (Crawford 485/2; Sydenham 1088; BMCRR 4198; Babelon Flaminia 2).

Little is known of the personal history of this moneyer though he may be the 'Cillo' who was proscribed by the triumviral government at the end of the year. If so, then the pro-Caesarian sentiments of his coinage clearly did little to help his cause. The title of *pri(mus) fl(avit)* on obverse indicates that he was the first of his monetary college to strike and as the possessor of this distincton he may well have acted as superintendent of operations for the entire production of coinage in this year. The form of his *cognomen* is of interest as it includes the aspirate (*Chilo* instead of *Cilo*), this being a feature of certain moneyers' names from the beginning of the 1st century BC. On the denarii issued by an ancestor of the same name more than sixty years before the spelling is simply 'CILO' (cf. Crawford 302).

172

172a

172 Draped bust of Diana Nemorensis right, P ACCOLEIVS behind, LARISCOLVS before. *Reverse:* Triple cult statue of Diana Nemorensis facing, supporting on their hands and shoulders a beam, above which are five cypress trees, the figure on left holding poppy, that on right holding lily. *Silver denarius. Rome, September–December 43 BC* (Crawford 486/1; Sydenham 1148; BMCRR 4211; Babelon Accoleia 1).

172a Similar to preceding, but with long lock of hair falling down Diana's neck on obverse. *Silver denarius. Rome, September–December 43 BC.* (Crawford 486/1; Sydenham 1148a; BMCRR 4214; RSC/Babelon Accoleia 1a).

This remarkable type relates to the place of origin of the moneyer's family, the town of Aricia, 16 miles south-east of Rome at the foot of the Alban Hills. The place was chiefly celebrated for the temple of Diana Nemorensis, the ruins of which are still visible today in the woods beside Lake Nemi. The priest of the goddess was called the *Rex Nemorensis*, or 'king of the grove', and the cult seems to have been shrouded in mystery and magic. Strangely, the priesthood was restricted to runaway slaves who acquired their position by killing their predecessor in combat. This followed a formal challenge consisting of a violation of the sacred grove through the plucking of a branch. Aricia was the birthplace of Octavian's mother, Atia, who died in 43 BC during her son's consulship. She was accorded the honour of a public funeral and as this exceptional coin type relating to her native town belongs to this exact time it is hard to escape the conclusion that there must be some connection. As Crawford[50] rightly points out 'his (*i.e.* Lariscolus') appointment as moneyer will have taken place in 44 and hence have owed nothing to Octavian'. However, in this year of political dislocation might it not have been possible for a son of Aricia to have been appointed to the office of moneyer through the influence of the young Caesar, the new master of Rome, who wished to honour the birthplace of his recently deceased mother. As the moneyers' coinage does not seem to have commenced until the latter part of the year there would have been plenty of time for Octavian to pull the necessary strings for one of the appointments to the quattuorvirate to be changed.

173 Head of Jupiter right, CAPITOLINVS behind. *Reverse:* the Capitoline temple of Jupiter, represented as a richly decorated hexastyle edifice, PETILLIVS below. *Silver denarius. Rome, September–December 43 BC* (Crawford 487/1; Sydenham 1149; BMCRR 4217; Babelon Petillia 1).

173

174

174a

174b

174 Eagle, its wings spread, standing right on thunderbolt, PETILLIVS above, CAPITOLINVS below. *Reverse:* hexastyle temple, similar to preceding, but without legend. *Silver denarius. Rome, September–December 43 BC* (Crawford 487/2a; Sydenham 1150; BMCRR 4220; Babelon Petillia 2).

174a Similar to preceding, but with S – F on either side of temple. *Silver denarius. Rome, September–December 43 BC* (Crawford 487/2b; Sydenham 1151; BMCRR 4222; Babelon Petillia 3).

174b Similar to preceding, but with F – S on either side of temple. *Silver denarius. Rome, September–December 43 BC* (Crawford 487/2c; Sydenham 1152; BMCRR 4224; Babelon Petillia 4).

The celebrated temple of Jupiter, Best and Greatest, on the Capitoline Hill (*Aedes Iovis Optimi Maximi Capitolini*) was of very early foundation, though the original tetrastyle structure of the Tuscan order was burned to the ground on 6 July 83 BC. It was eventually rebuilt, hexastyle of the Corinthian order, and dedicated in 69 BC by the consul Q. Lutatius Catulus. It is this second version of the temple which is depicted on the denarii of Petillius Capitolinus issued in the closing months of 43 BC. It would appear that this moneyer's family had some hereditary connection with the temple and the college of Capitolini, though Crawford[51] considers that his coin types were selected merely to provide punning allusions to his *cognomen*. The scholiast of Horace[52] relates that there was a man of this name who was accused of having stolen the god's crown, but because he was a friend of Octavian the charges were dismissed. It seems likely that this fortunate individual and the moneyer were one and the same person, in which case he certainly possessed some official role in the custodianship of the Capitoline Temple as Horace's tale also states that he was in charge of the sanctuary at the time of the theft. The letters 'S F' (sometimes reversed) which flank the temple on nos. 174a and 174b are generally interpreted as *sacris faciundis*, 'appointed to take care of sacred things', *i.e.* an allusion to the functions undertaken by certain members of the Petillia *gens*.

The monetary quattuorvirate for 42 BC (L. Livineius Regulus, P. Clodius, L. Mussidius Longus, and C. Vibius Varus) was appointed by the newly constituted triumviral government of Antony, Octavian and Lepidus. Its activities were extensive and remarkable. For the first time in the history of the republican coinage the moneyers were called upon to oversee the regular production of gold coins. Although many of these aurei were issued in the names of the three Triumvirs, with their portraits (see. nos. 142–7, 150–4, and 159–63), a few bore the personal types of the moneyers and made no direct reference to the Caesarian regime. Denarii were also struck with personal types, and these greatly outnumbered the triumviral varieties which were issued in honour of Antony, Octavian, and the late dictator (see nos. 148–9, 155–8, and 114–16). Lepidus was pointedly ignored in the silver series and, as in the preceding year, no fractional silver coins (quinarii and sestertii) were struck at all. The half denarius was destined to be revived in certain military issues of the triumviral period, but the silver sestertius ceased as a denomination of the Roman coinage with Caesar's assassination in 44 BC.

175 Bare head of the praetor L. Livineius Regulus right, **REGVLVS** behind, **PR** before. *Reverse:* curule chair dividing six fasces, three on either side, **L LIVINEIVS** above, **REGVLVS** in exergue. *Gold aureus. Rome, 42 BC* (Crawford 494/26; Sydenham 1108; BMCRR 4263; Babelon Livineia 9).

176 Same as preceding. *Silver denarius. Rome, 42 BC* (Crawford 494/27; Sydenham 1109; BMCRR 4264; Babelon Livineia 10).

177 Similar to preceding, but the head is smaller and lacks the accompanying legend. *Silver denarius. Rome, 42 BC* (Crawford 494/28; Sydenham 1110; BMCRR 4267; Babelon Livineia 11).

176

Although history records nothing of the moneyer Lucius Livineius Regulus his coinage is of considerable interest and provides tantalizing glimpses of his family history which go some way to establishing his identity. The distinctive portrait head which dominates the obverses of his aurei and denarii is identified as that of another L. Regulus who held the office of praetor. This may well have been his father who, with his brother Marcus, was a friend of Cicero, and who served under Caesar in the Thapsus campaign of 46 BC. Another ancestor, this time a *praefectus Urbi*, is referred to on no. 180. Traditionally it has been thought that the moneyer himself was the holder of this office, but this view is rightly rejected by Crawford[53] who states 'neither the history of the times nor constitutional practice permits the view that the moneyer was himself Praefectus Urbi in or about 42 BC'. The reverse types of Regulus' coinage concentrate on the themes of public games in the circus, corn-distributions, and the celebration of curule offices held by ancestors.

177

178 Small bare head of the praetor L. Livineius Regulus right (no legend). *Reverse:* modius, with corn-ear on either side, **L LIVINEIVS** above, **REGVLVS** in exergue. *Silver denarius. Rome, 42 BC* (Crawford 494/29; Sydenham 1111; BMCRR 4269; Babelon Livineia 13).

178

This reverse refers to one of the responsibilities undertaken by the aediles, the *cura annonae* which entailed the maintenance and distribution of Rome's corn-supply. Its relevance to the moneyer himself is unclear, though Crawford[54] makes the interesting suggestion that sometimes the office of moneyer served as a substitute for an aedileship and that in such cases the coin types advertise what the moneyer would have provided to the public if he had been elected aedile. The same is true of the following type where the reverse graphically illustrates the contests staged in the arena in the public games which were also under the jurisdiction of the aediles.

179

180

179 *Obverse:* same as preceding. *Reverse:* scene of combat between gladiators and wild beasts: in the foreground a gladiator advances to left and attacks a leaping lion with his spear; in the background another combatant stands to right and defends himself with sword and shield against a leaping panther; in field to left a wounded boar is seated to right; L REGVLVS in exergue. *Silver denarius. Rome, 42 BC* (Crawford 494/30; Sydenham 1112; BMCRR 4271; Babelon Livineia 12).

180 *Obverse:* similar to preceding, but the head is larger, and with L REGVLVS behind, PR before. *Reverse:* curule chair flanked by two fasces, REGVLVS F above, PRAEF VR in exergue. *Silver denarius. Rome, 42 BC* (Crawford 494/31; Sydenham 1113; BMCRR 4261; Babelon Livineia 8).

As stated above, it unlikely in the extreme that the moneyer himself was the holder of the office of *praefectus Urbi*, the type more likely referring to another ancestor.

181 Radiate head of Sol right. *Reverse:* crescent moon surmounted by semicircle of five stars, P CLODIVS / M F in two lines below. *Gold aureus. Rome, 42 BC* (Crawford 494/20b; Sydenham 1114; BMCRR 4284; Babelon Claudia/Clodia 16).

181a

182

181a Similar to preceding, but with quiver behind head of Sol. *Gold aureus. Rome, 42 BC* (Crawford 494/20a; Sydenham 1114a; BMCRR 4285; Babelon Claudia/Clodia 16).

182 Same as preceding. *Silver denarius. Rome, 42 BC* (Crawford 494/21; Sydenham 1115; BMCRR 4287; Babelon Claudia/Clodia 17).

183 Laureate head of Apollo right, lyre behind. *Reverse:* Diana Lucifera standing facing, looking right, bow and quiver at shoulder, holding long lighted torch in each hand, P CLODIVS on right, M F on left. *Gold aureus. Rome, 42 BC* (Crawford 494/22; Sydenham 1116; BMCRR p. 586; Babelon Claudia/Clodia 14).

184

184 Same as preceding. *Silver denarius. Rome, 42* BC (Crawford 494/23; Sydenham 1117; BMCRR 4290; Babelon Claudia/Clodia 15).

Like the other members of the monetary quattuorvirate of 42 BC we have no certain knowledge of the identity of Publius Clodius, son of Marcus. His personal coin types admit of no obvious explanation other than the general belief in the imminence of a new age suggested by the celestial types of Sun and Moon and their related deities Apollo and Diana.

185

185b

185 Head of Ceres right, wreathed with corn. *Reverse:* L MVSSIDIVS / LONGVS in two lines within wreath of corn-ears tied above. *Gold aureus. Rome, 42* BC (Crawford 494/44a; Sydenham 1090; BMCRR 4233; Babelon Mussidia 1).

185a Similar to preceding, but with L MVSSIDI / LONGI on reverse. *Gold aureus. Rome, 42* BC (Crawford 494/44b; Sydenham 1090b; BMCRR vol. I, p. 576, note 1; Babelon Mussidia 2).

185b Similar to preceding, but with L MVSSIDI / LONGVS and wreath tied below. *Gold aureus. Rome, 42* BC (Crawford 494/45; Sydenham 1090a; BMCRR 4234; Babelon Mussidia 3).

185c Similar to preceding, but the head of Ceres is diademed instead of wreathed, and with L MVSSID / LONGI within wreath tied above. *Gold aureus. Rome, 42* BC (Crawford 494/46; Sydenham 1091; BMCRR 4235).

In addition to his triumviral portrait aurei, and denarii in honour of the late Julius Caesar, Lucius Mussidius Longus produced an interesting range of personal coin types in gold and silver. The aurei feature Ceres, Roman goddess of agriculture, and perhaps reflect early concerns for Rome's corn-supply in the light of Sextus Pompey's activities in Sicily and his control of the seas. The triumviral government would want to allay citizens' fears that the city might be threatened with famine as a result of their current inability to deal with the menace of Pompey the Great's renegade son.

186

186 Winged and draped bust of Victory right, her hair drawn back and collected into a knot behind, one long plait arranged in a loop along the top of her head. *Reverse:* Victory in galloping biga right, **L MVSSIDIVS** above, **LONGVS** below. *Silver denarius. Rome, 42 BC* (Crawford 494/40; Sydenham 1095; BMCRR 4229; Babelon Mussidia 4).

The theme of military victory which dominates this type clearly refers to the conflict with the republican leaders Brutus and Cassius culminating in the battle of Philippi. Whether the issue was in anticipation of the event or commemorative of it we can only speculate, but as the battle was fought late in the year the former alternative seems the more likely. The bust of Victory on obverse has been the subject of much speculation, many numismatists seeing in its features a portrait of Antony's wife, Fulvia. The head is certainly distinctive in its facial features and in the treatment of the hair and there are several other issues of the period exhibiting similar effigies – quinarii of Antony issued at Lugdunum in 43 and 42 BC (see nos. 122 and 126), and an aureus of C. Numonius Vaala of 41 BC (see no. 321). All of these types fall within the period of Fulvia's lifetime (died 40 BC) and strong evidence in support of the identification comes from a series of bronze coins[55] issued from the mint of Eumenea in Phrygia (*provincia Asia*) at the time of Antony's journey to the East in 41 BC. As a token of respect to the Triumvir the name of Eumenea was changed to Fulvia in honour of his wife, and on the obverses of the coins struck on this occasion Fulvia is depicted as Nike (Victory) in precisely the same manner as on the Roman issues of 43–41 BC.

187

187 Diademed and veiled head of Concordia right, **CONCORDIA** behind. *Reverse:* clasped hands holding caduceus, **L MVSSIDIVS LONGVS** around, below. *Silver denarius. Rome, 42 BC* (Crawford 494/41; Sydenham 1092; BMCRR 4236; Babelon Mussidia 5).

The message here is the unity of the Triumvirs in their resolve to defeat the republican forces led by Caesar's two principal assassins. The theme of *concordia* carries over on to the next type, the reverse of which depicts the shrine of Venus Cloacina which stood on the north side of the Forum above the Cloaca Maxima, one of Rome's oldest sewers. The platform of this shrine still exists in the Forum. The type may be interpreted as conveying the concept of purification following the treacherous murder of the dictator by men who had professed to be his friends.

188

188a

188 *Obverse:* same as preceding. *Reverse:* shrine of Venus Cloacina consisting of circular platform surmounted by two statues of the goddess, each resting right hand on cippus, the platform inscribed CLOACIN and ornamented with trellis-pattern balustrade, flight of steps and portico on left, L MVSSIDIVS LONGVS around, above. *Silver denarius. Rome, 42 BC* (Crawford 494/42a; Sydenham 1093; BMCRR 4242; Babelon Mussidia 6).

188a Similar to preceding, but with star below Concordia's chin on obverse. *Silver denarius. Rome, 42 BC* (Crawford 494/42b; Sydenham 1093a; BMCRR 4244; Babelon Mussidia 6).

188b Similar to preceding, but with crescent below Concordia's chin. *Silver denarius. Rome, 42 BC* (Crawford 494/42c; Sydenham 1093b; BMCRR 4246; Babelon Mussidia 6).

The reverse depicting the shrine of Venus Cloacina also occurs in combination with the facing head of Sol as the obverse type. The depiction of the sun god, taken in combination with the celestial symbols of star and crescent appearing below Concordia's chin on the two preceding types, is strongly suggestive of the imminence of a new age. Sol may also refer to Rome's eastern possessions which, as soon as the anticipated victory over the tyrannicides was achieved, would come under the authority of the triumviral government.

189

189a

189 Radiate and draped bust of Sol three-quarter face to right. *Reverse:* shrine of Venus Cloacina, same as preceding. *Silver denarius. Rome, 42 BC* (Crawford 494/43a; Sydenham 1094; BMCRR 4248; Babelon Mussidia 7).

189a Similar to preceding, but on reverse the platform is inscribed CLOAC, and each of the statues of Venus rests its right hand on bird standing on cippus. *Silver denarius. Rome, 42 BC* (Crawford 494/43b; Sydenham 1094a; BMCRR 4252; RSC/Babelon Mussidia 7a).

This survey of the coin types of the college of moneyers for 42 BC concludes with those issued by C. Vibius Varus about whose personal history the ancient sources are silent. Like his colleagues, this moneyer's aurei and denarii exhibit considerable variety, with two types in gold and three in silver.

190

191

190 Laureate head of Apollo right. *Reverse:* Venus standing left, her back turned towards the spectator, viewing herself in mirror held in left hand, column behind her, C VIBIVS on left, VARVS on right. *Gold aureus. Rome, 42 BC* (Crawford 494/34; Sydenham 1137; BMCRR 4300; Babelon Vibia 27).

191 Bust of Roma left, wearing crested helmet with plume on each side, holding spear in right hand, shield decorated with star on left arm. *Reverse:* winged Nemesis standing right, looking down at her right hand with which she draws out fold of drapery from her breast, C VIBIVS on right, VARVS on left. *Gold aureus. Rome, 42 BC* (Crawford 494/35; Sydenham 1136; BMCRR 4299; Babelon Vibia 25).

The representation of Apollo on the first of these aureus types closely resembles the head on the contemporary gold and silver of P. Clodius (see nos. 183 and 184). Venus, ancestress of the *gens* Julia, is obviously intended to be complimentary to the memory of the late dictator and to his heir, the young Triumvir Octavian. In this instance Apollo may also be associated with the *gens* Julia (cf. Crawford's commentary[56] on the coinage of the moneyer L. Julius Caesar who held office *c.*103 BC). The second, and rarer, aureus type of Varus has a highly distinctive design on which the winged goddess Nemesis makes her sole appearance on the coinage of the Republic. Nemesis was associated with the concept of righteous retribution and her invocation was thus highly appropriate to the circumstances of the time, as the Triumvirs prepared for their final reckoning with Caesar's assassins.

192

192 Head of young Bacchus or Liber right, wreathed with ivy and grapes. *Reverse:* panther springing left towards garlanded altar surmounted by bacchic mask, thyrsus resting diagonally in background, C VIBIVS in exergue, VARVS on right. *Silver denarius. Rome, 42 BC* (Crawford 494/36; Sydenham 1138; BMCRR 4295; Babelon Vibia 24).

Bacchus was the name by which the Romans generally referred to the Greek deity Dionysus. He was also equated with Liber Pater, the Italian god of fertility and wine. His appearance on this denarius seems to be related to the family traditions of the Vibii and to have no particular relevance to the historical circumstances of the issue. A similar head had appeared six years earlier on denarii of the Caesarian moneyer C. Vibius Pansa Caetronianus (see nos. 21–22a). The reverse type is complementary to the obverse, the panther being the animal especially associated with Bacchus and the thyrsus being the god's distinctive staff.

193 Laureate head of bearded Hercules right. *Reverse:* Minerva standing right, resting on spear held in right hand and holding Victory on extended left, shield on ground at her left side, C VIBIVS on right, VARVS on left. *Silver denarius. Rome, 42 BC* (Crawford 494/37; Sydenham 1139; BMCRR 4301; Babelon Vibia 23).

193

194 Bust of Minerva right, wearing crested Corinthian helmet and aegis. *Reverse:* Hercules, naked, standing left, resting right hand on club set on ground and holding lion's skin over left arm, C VIBIVS on right, VARVS on left. *Silver denarius. Rome, 42 BC* (Crawford 494/38; Sydenham 1140; BMCRR 4303; Babelon Vibia 26).

194

These two scarce and attractive types honouring Minerva and Hercules allude to the forthcoming struggle with the republican forces led by Brutus and Cassius. The goddess of war, the consort of Jupiter, and the legendary hero are invoked as powerful allies of the Triumvirs in their quest to avenge the murder of Caesar.

K. Emergency Issues of the Senate in 43 BC

The precise circumstances of the issue of two aureus types in the joint names of the praetors Lucius Cestius and Gaius Norbanus are quite uncertain and have exercised the minds and ingenuity of numerous scholars over the years. Their date of issue has been variously ascribed to the period of Caesar's absence from Rome for the Spanish campaign of 46–45 BC, at which time he appointed a number of *praefecti Urbi* to take care of affairs in the capital; to the confused period immediately following Caesar's assassination in March, 44 BC, when the Senate was briefly free to exercise its independent authority; and to the equally uncertain time the following summer when the Senate, mistakenly believing itself freed of the Caesarian curse following Antony's defeat at Mutina, was making preparations for the defence of the capital against a possible attack by Octavian. The latest of these dates appears to be the least erroneous, the unlikelihood of 'PR' being used as an abbreviation for *praefecti [Urbi]* rather than *praetor* eliminating the first possibility, and the extreme uncertainty of the Senate's position following the Ides of March making the second suggestion equally untenable. Crawford's[57] view, which is accepted here, is that the issue probably belongs to the early months of 43 BC during the brief senatorial alliance with Octavian whilst preparations were under way for the confrontation with Antony which culminated in the war around Mutina.

195 Draped bust of Africa right, wearing elephant's skin head-dress. *Reverse:* curule chair, its front legs ornamented with sculptured eagles, surmounted by crested Corinthian helmet right, L CESTIVS above, C NORBA in exergue, PR in lower right field, S C in lower left. *Gold aureus. Rome, January–April 43 BC* (Crawford 491/1a; Sydenham 1153; BMCRR 4191; Babelon Cestia 1).

195

195a

196

195a Similar to preceding, but with two confronted snakes instead of helmet on the curule chair, and with EX S C in lower left field. *Gold aureus. Rome, January–April 43 BC* (Crawford 491/1b; Sydenham 1154; BMCRR 4192; Babelon Cestia 2).

196 Draped bust of Sibyl (?) right, her head bound with fillet, the hair gathered into knot behind, C NORBANVS above, L CESTIVS below, PR before. *Reverse:* Cybele, turreted, enthroned left on car drawn left by two lions, holding patera and resting left arm on drum, S C in upper field. *Gold aureus. Rome, January–April 43 BC* (Crawford 491/2; Sydenham 1155; BMCRR 4193; Babelon Cestia 3).

The identities of the two praetors are by no means well established. L. Cestius appears to have left no record other than his coins, unless he is the Cestius who was proscribed by the triumviral government at the end of the year and, like Cicero, met his end at this time.[58] C. Norbanus may be equated with the C. Norbanus C.f. Flaccus who held the consulship in 38 BC with Appius Claudius Pulcher as his colleague. Crawford[59] also regards him as the moneyer who held office *c.*83 BC (Crawford 357/1) though the interval of four decades seems unusually long.

The interpretation of the types is no less problematical. This coinage was clearly an exceptional one and if, as proposed above, it was produced by the Senate in an emergency situation for the payment of troops required to raise Antony's siege of Mutina then we might expect the types to be in honour of the particular legions involved. With this in mind the head of Africa could refer to units withdrawn from that province, but the significance of the other head, tentatively identified as Sibyl, still remains obscure. The curule chair might be intended as a gesture towards the sentiments of soldiers loyal to the Caesarian cause: the late dictator's gilded *sella curulis* had appeared on a number of issues during his lifetime (see nos. 77 and 87) and would do so again on Octavian's early triumviral coinage the following year (see no. 137). It would, of course, be ironic indeed for such a type to be placed on a senatorial issue of coinage intended for Caesarian troops going to the assistance of one of the dictator's assassins, just as it was ironic for these soldiers to be engaged in such an enterprise in the first place. But the entire political situation in Italy at this time was one of confusion and ambiguity, as the various contenders for power in the post-Caesarian world jostled for advantage, and we should not be surprised if this is reflected on the coinage. The Caesarian connotation is, perhaps, made less obvious by the appearance of a Corinthian helmet or two snakes atop the curule chair, both being symbols of Minerva, goddess of war. Like so many aspects of this enigmatic coinage the depiction of the Asian mother-goddess Cybele admits of no obvious explanation, though Crawford[60] proposes that she may be associated with the concept of victory (cf. the denarius type of C. Fabius issued *c.*102 BC, Crawford 322/1)

L. Issues of M. Brutus

The coinage of the republican leaders Brutus and Cassius appears not to have commenced prior to the occasion of their meeting at Smyrna on the west coast of Asia Minor early in 42 BC. Following this meeting the two 'liberators' began a systematic programme of extortion from the wealthy communities of Asia Minor in order to finance the final build-up of their military power prior to the inevitable confrontation with the Caesarian leaders which would decide the fate of the Roman world. These extortions provided the bullion with which the tyrannicides' subsequent coinage was produced, just as in Italy the proscriptions of the triumviral government were furnishing the necessary wealth to underwrite their war coinage.

197

198

197 Simpulum between sacrificial axe and knife, BRVTVS below. *Reverse:* jug and lituus, LENTVLVS / SPINT below. *Gold aureus. Military mint, probably at Smyrna, early 42 BC* (Crawford 500/6; Sydenham 1309; BMCRR East, p. 483; Babelon Junia 40).

198 Same as preceding. *Silver denarius. Military mint, probably at Smyrna, early 42 BC* (Crawford 500/7; Sydenham 1310; BMCRR East 80; Babelon Junia 41; Cohen 6).

The likely occasion for this issue was the meeting of Brutus and Cassius at Smyrna early in 42 BC. Brutus' name is rendered in the form of his *cognomen* alone, without title, just as it had appeared on his coinage as moneyer more than a decade earlier (cf. Crawford 433/1–2). For this reason it seems probable that this was the earliest issue to be struck in honour of the tyrannicide, though Cassius would seem to have reached Smyrna first and commenced the production of coinage in anticipation of his colleague's arrival (see nos. 217 and 218). The coins also bear the name of the legate P. Cornelius Lentulus Spinther, a former adherent of Pompey who was one of Cassius' principal lieutenants. His inscription is placed below symbols of the augurate, the priestly college to which he was elected in 57 BC. The symbols on obverse are those of the college of pontifices of which Brutus was a member. Spinther's name is also found on a contemporary series of aurei and denarii struck for Cassius (see nos. 220–3).

199

199 Head of Libertas right, LEIBERTAS before. *Reverse:* lyre between quiver and filleted laurel-branch, CAEPIO BRVTVS PRO COS around. *Silver denarius. Military mint travelling with Brutus in Lycia, spring to early summer 42 BC* (Crawford 501/1; Sydenham 1287; BMCRR East 38; Babelon Junia 34; Cohen 5).

The reverse draws its inspiration from the contemporary silver hemidrachms of the Lycian League and the issue is clearly connected with Brutus' military activities in this region of southwestern Asia Minor subsequent to his meeting with Cassius at Smyrna. *Libertas* was the principal theme of the Republicans' coinage and the head of the allegorical personification of the freedom of the individual citizen appears as the obverse type, together with an identifying inscription. Brutus' nomenclature is now expanded and includes the proconsular title. The object to the left of the lyre on reverse is usually described as a plectrum, but Troxell[61] points out that it is almost certainly a quiver of the common cylindrical type with conical lid which often has a central projection. It is of common occurrence on the coinage of the Lycian League, as is the filleted laurel-branch which appears to the right of the lyre. All three objects are, of course, symbolic of Apollo whose head monopolizes the obverses of the Lycian League coinage.

200 Veiled and draped bust of Libertas right, L SESTI before, PRO Q behind. *Reverse:* tripod between sacrificial axe and simpulum, Q CAEPIO BRVTVS PRO COS around. *Gold aureus. Military mint travelling with Brutus in southwestern Asia Minor, spring to early summer 42 BC* (Crawford 502/1; Sydenham 1289; BMCRR East, p. 472; Babelon Junia 36; Cohen 10).

201

201 Similar to preceding, but the obverse legend runs around the head instead of being divided. *Silver denarius. Military mint travelling with Brutus in southwestern Asia Minor, spring to early summer 42 BC* (Crawford 502/2; Sydenham 1290; BMCRR East 41; Babelon Junia 37; Cohen 11).

202

202 *Obverse:* same as preceding. *Reverse:* Victory walking right, holding wreath and palm-branch, Q CAEPIO BRVTVS PRO COS around. *Silver quinarius. Military mint travelling with Brutus in southwestern Asia Minor, spring to early summer 42 BC* (Crawford 502/3; Sydenham 1291; BMCRR East 46; Babelon Junia 38; Cohen 12).

When Brutus besieged Xanthus in Lycia in 42 BC these Lycian pillar tombs were already almost three centuries old. The later Roman theatre before them was curtailed out of respect for the earlier monuments.

203

203 Quaestorial chair, against which rests diagonal staff, modius below, L SESTI above, PRO Q in exergue. *Reverse:* tripod between simpulum and apex, Q CAEPIO BRVTVS PRO COS around. *Silver quinarius. Military mint travelling with Brutus in southwestern Asia Minor, spring* *to early summer 42 BC* (Crawford 502/4; Sydenham 1292; BMCRR East 47; Babelon Junia 39; Cohen 13).

The form of Brutus' name and titles links this group of coinage issued under the proquaestor L. Sestius to no. 199, a type which is clearly associated with the tyrannicide's campaigns in Lycia. The themes of Libertas and Apollo (the latter represented by the tripod) dominate the types of this series, whilst one of the quinarii – a most unusual denomination for an eastern issue – also makes the traditional reference to victory, undoubtedly appropriate to the circumstances under which it was struck. The obverse of the other half denarius refers to the office of quaestor through its depiction of the magistrate's chair (*subsellium*), his staff (*virga viatoris*), and the modius or grain measure. The subsidiary types in the reverse fields of nos. 200, 201 and 203 are symbolic of Brutus' membership of the college of pontifices. L. Sestius Quirinalis, son of the Pompeian partisan P. Sestius, was devoted to his commander Brutus but later succeeded in gaining the favour of Augustus who made him consul suffectus in 23 BC. He was the recipient of one of Horace's Odes (*Carmina*, i. 4), Q. Horatius Flaccus also having served under Brutus' standards as a *tribunus militum*. Doubtless during this tumultuous period Sestius and Horace formed an enduring friendship.

204

204 Head of Apollo right, his hair in ringlets and bound with both taenia and laurel-wreath. *Reverse:* trophy, composed of helmet, cuirass and two shields, one of which has incurved sides ('figure-of-eight'), two captives, male and female, seated back to back at base, both in attitude of despair, Q CAEPIO BRVTVS IMP around. *Silver denarius. Military mint travelling with Brutus in Lycia, early summer 42 BC* (Crawford 503/1; Sydenham 1293; BMCRR East 52; Babelon Junia 35; Cohen 8).

Like no. 199, this very rare type is closely associated with the contemporary hemidrachms of the Lycian League.[62] The date, however, is somewhat later as the proconsular title has now given way to that of *imperator* indicating that the issue was probably made shortly before the second meeting of the tyrannicides at Sardis in the summer of 42 BC. The highly distinctive Apollo head on obverse, with its unusual combination of taenia and laurel-wreath, is virtually identical to those appearing on the local silver currency. The trophy on reverse is symbolic of Brutus' extensive military operations both in Thrace and in Lycia.

205 Draped bust of Apollo right, lyre before, C FLAV HEMIC LEG PRO PR around. *Reverse:* Victory standing left, holding palm-branch in left hand and with right crowning trophy, set in ground before her, composed of helmet, cuirass, two swords and shield with incurved sides (figure-of-eight), Q CAEP BRVT IMP around. *Silver denarius. Military mint travelling with Brutus in Lycia, early summer 42 BC* (Crawford 504/1; Sydenham 1294; BMCRR East 55; Babelon Junia 49; Cohen 7).

205

Another rare type, linked with the preceding through its depiction of Apollo and a trophy (note the distinctive 'figure-of-eight shield') and the form of Brutus' name and title. The style and treatment of the subject is, however, completely different and the military nature of the coinage is emphasized by the addition of the name of the *legatus pro praetore* responsible for the issue. The precise identity of this legate has not been established, though several Flavii are attested for this period. His *cognomen* is quite uncertain and Crawford rejects the usually proposed form of Hemicillus. A 'Flavius Noster', possibly the issuer of these coins, is mentioned by Brutus in his correspondence to Cicero[63] and to Atticus[64]; whilst another Flavius features in Plutarch's[65] account of Brutus' last hours ('Then after a little he uttered the names of each of his friends whom he had seen killed defending him in the battle, and he sighed most heavily when he came to Labeo and Flavius, the first of whom was his legate and the second his chief of engineers'). If these all refer to the same man, and he is indeed the *C Flav Hemic* of the coinage, then it would seem that Plutarch has mistakenly transposed the ranks of Brutus' two champions. Yet another Flavius, this time with the correct *praenomen* Gaius, is mentioned by Appian[66] as an enemy of Octavian and a casualty of the Perusine War between the Triumvir and Lucius Antony (41–40 BC), though in this instance the connection with Brutus' *legatus pro praetore* must be regarded as less likely.

206

207

206 Laureate head of Libertas right, M SERVILIVS behind, LEG before. *Reverse:* trophy, composed of helmet, cuirass, two spears, and shield with incurved sides ('figure-of-eight'), Q CAEPIO on left, BRVTVS IMP on right. *Gold aureus. Military mint, probably at Sardis, summer 42 BC* (Crawford 505/4; Sydenham 1314; BMCRR East 85; Babelon Junia 47; Cohen 9).

207 Same as preceding. *Silver denarius. Military mint, probably at Sardis, summer 42 BC* (Crawford 505/5; BMCRR East, pp. 484–5, note 1; Babelon Junia 48; RSC/Cohen 9a).

The second meeting of Brutus and Cassius, at Sardis in the summer of 42 BC, seems to have been the occasion for this issue produced by the legate M. Servilius. Other types were struck in the name of Cassius in commemoration of his naval exploits against the Rhodians (see nos. 224–6). The coinage honouring Brutus was on a somewhat smaller scale, the denarius in particular being of extreme rarity. The reverse type continues to dwell on the theme of Brutus' military successes in Thrace and, later, in Lycia, and the familiar 'figure-of-eight' shield is featured on the trophy. Libertas, which was to be the watchword at the first battle of Philippi, again appears as the obverse type. Her head is accompanied by the name of Marcus Servilius who was personally involved in the Lycian campaign and may have been present at the fall of Xanthus and Patara to Brutus.

208

208 Bare head right of L. Junius Brutus, consul 509 BC, **L BRVTVS PRIM COS** around, all within oak-wreath. *Reverse:* bare head right of M. Junius Brutus, the tyrannicide, **M BRVTVS IMP** around, above, **COSTA LEG** around, below, all within oak-wreath. *Gold aureus. Military mint travelling with Brutus and Cassius in western Asia Minor or northern Greece, late summer to autumn 42 BC* (Crawford 506/1; Sydenham 1295; BMCRR East 57; Babelon Junia 43; Cohen 16).

We now reach the final and unquestionably the most remarkable phase of Brutus' coinage. The revolutionary changes made by the republican leadership at this time are regarded by many as a complete betrayal of the lofty principles which were their professed reason for slaying Caesar and making war on his heirs. Although Cassius' name does not appear on any of these late issues there can be no doubt that he was in agreement with what was being done, for Brutus could hardly have acted independently in such a matter. The reasons for the sudden appearance of Brutus' own portrait on the coinage in the final months before Philippi have to be sought in the circumstances of the time. It is, perhaps, too easy to condemn this action in terms of a final surrender to the seductive attractions of self-aggrandizement. Even if he had harboured secret desires for personal glory, which would certainly not be unnatural, this would hardly have been the time to make these ambitions public. Rather, we should view this as a counter to the Triumvirs' massive publicity campaign, most prominent in which were the unprecedented issues of portrait gold coins produced by the college of Roman moneyers for 42 BC (see nos. 143–7, 150–4, and 159–63). With the day of final reckoning fast approaching it would be hard to condemn the Republicans for indulging in the same tactics as their adversaries and attempting to capitalize on the illustrious name and family traditions of Brutus, a descendant of the very founder of the Roman Republic four hundred and sixty-seven years before. Small wonder that at this time Brutus finally abandons his adoptive name of Quintus Caepio Brutus and reverts to the full splendour of his original name, Marcus Junius Brutus. On this beautiful aureus his portrait is accompanied by that of his renowned ancestor Lucius Junius Brutus, first consul of the Republic. Both heads are encircled by the *corona civica* of oak traditionally awarded to those who had displayed their patriotism by saving the lives of comrades in the heat of battle or by rescuing the Republic itself at times of great peril. The issue also bears the name of the legate Pedanius Costa about whom little is known other than his obvious adherence to the republican cause and to Brutus in particular.

209 Laureate head of Apollo right, COSTA before, LEG behind. *Reverse:* trophy, composed of helmet, cuirass, shield with incurved sides ('figure-of-eight'), and two spears, BRVTVS IMP around. *Silver denarius. Military mint travelling with Brutus and Cassius in western Asia Minor or northern Greece, late summer to autumn 42 BC* (Crawford 506/2; Sydenham 1296; BMCRR East 59; Babelon Junia 42; Cohen 4).

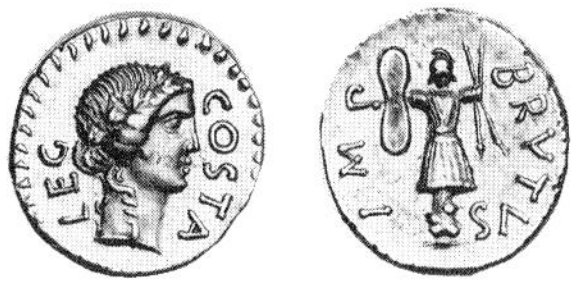

209

This denarius would appear to be contemporary with the preceding portrait aureus as it bears the name of the same legate, Pedanius Costa. The reverse type is almost identical to the aurei and denarii issued at Sardis a month or two earlier (see nos. 206 and 207), though the two spears and the distinctive 'figure-of-eight' shield have been transposed. Another difference is that the 'Q CAEPIO' has now disappeared from Brutus' name, and although the *praenomen* 'M' is not present here as it is on the portrait aureus we can assume that the change is related to the tyrannicide's reversion to his original name of Marcus Junius Brutus.

210 Diademed head of Libertas right, LEIBERTAS before. *Reverse:* stem of prow and anchor in saltire (no legend). *Silver quinarius. Military mint travelling with Brutus and Cassius in western Asia Minor or northern Greece, late summer to autumn 42 BC* (Crawford 506/3; Sydenham 1288; BMCRR East 39; Babelon Junia 33; RSC 5a).

210

Although anonymous there can be little doubt that this rare half denarius was struck by Brutus. The obverse inscription and design link it with one of the denarius types (see no. 199) and the theme of 'Libertas' dates back to the tyrannicide's much earlier coinage as moneyer (cf. Crawford 433/1). More difficult to determine is the precise occasion for the issue. Crawford[67] states 'formal details and stylistic similarities link 3 [*i.e.* the quinarius] with 2' [*i.e.* the preceding denarius of Costa] and he may well be correct in this observation. In any case, for sake of convenience I have placed the issue here in the closing phase of the Republicans' coinage prior to Philippi. The nautical theme of the reverse may be complimentary to Cassius whose own coinage dwells on his naval victory resulting in the capture of Rhodes. Equally, it could be a more general reference to the overwhelming naval superiority enjoyed by the Republicans over the Caesarians.

211 Bare head of Brutus right, BRVTVS behind, IMP before, all within laurel-wreath. *Reverse:* combined military and naval trophy, composed of helmet, cuirass, curved sword with two spears, and shield with incurved sides ('figure-of-eight'), two prows, back to back, and two shields at base, small L above the prow on left, oar (?) above that on right, CASCA on left, LONGVS on right. *Gold aureus. Military mint travelling with Brutus and Cassius in western Asia Minor or northern Greece, late summer to autumn 42 BC* (Crawford 507/1b; Sydenham 1297; BMCRR East 62; Babelon Junia 46).

211

211a Similar to preceding, but without the small **L** in reverse field. *Gold aureus. Military mint travelling with Brutus and Cassius in western Asia Minor or northern Greece, late summer to autumn 42 BC* (Crawford 507/1a; Sydenham 1297a; BMCRR East, p. 479, note; Babelon Junia 45; Cohen 14).

Now that Brutus had taken the bold and irrevocable step of placing his own effigy on the coinage (see no. 208) two additional portrait types were produced by the 'liberators' in gold and silver as a prelude to the final trial of strength with the Triumvirs at Philippi. The symbolism of the reverse type of this beautiful aureus is quite clear, being a joint celebration of the military achievements of Brutus, in Thrace and Lycia, and the naval exploits of Cassius against the Rhodians. The diminutive letter '**L**' appearing in the reverse field of the majority of the recorded specimens has been variously interpreted as an engraver's signature or representing 'Libertas' or 'Lycia'. Any of these alternatives is certainly possible, but the last seems to be the most plausible given the military nature of the accompanying type. The laurel-wreath border on obverse continues the theme of Brutus' initial aureus type where both portraits are surrounded by the *corona civica* of oak. The change to a wreath of laurel may be without significance other than a variation on a decorative element of the design. Some, however, may have viewed it as having more sinister implications of regal ambition on the part of Brutus, and although it is doubtful that such suspicions had any basis in reality this kind of numismatic iconography may have weakened the Republicans' claims to be the champions of liberty and democracy in the struggle against tyranny as personified by the triumviral regime.

Publius Servilius Casca Longus, whose name also appears as the responsible lieutenant on the following denarius type, was one of the leading conspirators against Caesar and was actually the first to plunge his dagger into the dictator on the Ides of March. His brother Gaius played a lesser role in the conspiracy and both subsequently left Italy to join the republican forces. They saw extensive service in the East and Publius was even entrusted with command of Brutus' fleet. At Philippi the brothers fought bravely but when it became clear that all was lost following the second battle they emulated their commander-in-chief by committing suicide.

212

212 Laureate head of bearded Neptune right, trident below, **CASCA** behind, **LONGVS** before. *Reverse:* Victory walking right on broken sceptre, holding broken diadem with both hands and palm-branch over shoulder in left, **BRVTVS** behind, **IMP** before. *Silver denarius. Military mint travelling with Brutus and Cassius in western Asia Minor or northern Greece, late summer to autumn 42 BC* (Crawford 507/2; Sydenham 1298; BMCRR East 63; Babelon Junia 44; Cohen 3).

This remarkable reverse type graphically symbolizes the anticipated defeat of the forces of tyranny which were aiming at the destruction of Rome's republican constitution and its replacement by an autocratic form of government. It is ironical indeed that while Casca's denarius depicts Victory breaking the diadem of royal power his aureus shows Brutus' portrait surrounded by a similar symbol of regal or even divine status. Neptune, god of the sea, is honoured on the denarius doubtless in celebration of Cassius' naval exploits against the Rhodians and perhaps also in connection with the overwhelming superiority in maritime power enjoyed by the Republicans over the Caesarians prior to Philippi. The type could also be interpreted as being complimentary to Casca himself in his role as commander of Brutus' fleet.

213 Laureate, veiled and draped female bust right, her head surmounted by polos, L PLAET CEST behind. *Reverse:* sacrificial axe and simpulum (or culullus), BRVT IMP below. *Gold aureus. Military mint travelling with Brutus and Cassius in western Asia Minor or northern Greece, late summer to autumn 42 BC* (Crawford 508/1; Sydenham 1299; BMCRR East, p. 479; Babelon Junia 50; Cohen 1).

214

214 Same as preceding. *Silver denarius. Military mint travelling with Brutus and Cassius in western Asia Minor or northern Greece, late summer to autumn 42 BC* (Crawford 508/2; Sydenham 1300; BMCRR East 66; Babelon Junia 51; Cohen 2).

What appears to have been the final issue of coinage in the name of the tyrannicide Marcus Junius Brutus prior to the fateful battle of Philippi was made by his lieutenant Lucius Plaetorius Cestianus who is otherwise unknown to history. Crawford[68] regards him as the likely son of the L. Plaetorius L.f. who was responsible for a small issue of denarii about 74 BC in his capacity as quaestor (Crawford 396). The priestly emblems on reverse clearly relate to Brutus' membership of the college of pontifices but the significance of the obverse type is less clear. Previous cataloguers have frequently recognized the female head as that of Ceres, the Roman goddess of agriculture, and if this were so then it might indicate that Cestianus, like his father, held the office of quaestor. The identification of the deity is, however, far from certain and Crawford suggests the Greek goddess Artemis (Diana). She may, perhaps, be indicative of the place of mintage but the question has to be regarded as still unresolved.

215 Bare head of Brutus right, BRVT above, IMP before, L PLAET CEST around, behind. *Reverse:* pileus (cap of Liberty) between two daggers, their points downwards, EID MAR below. *Gold aureus. Military mint travelling with Brutus and Cassius in western Asia Minor or northern Greece, late summer to autumn 42 BC.* (Unlisted in all the standard works of reference: two specimens have, however, been published by

215

H.A. Cahn, the first in *Proceedings of the International Numismatic Congress in Paris, 1953*, p. 213; the second in *Quaderni Ticinese XVIII*, 1989, pp. 211–32, no. 4a).

216

216 Same as preceding. *Silver denarius. Military mint travelling with Brutus and Cassius in western Asia Minor or northern Greece, late summer to autumn 42 BC* (Crawford 508/3; Sydenham 1301; BMCRR East 68; Babelon Junia 52; Cohen 15).

Arguably the most famous of all the coin types of ancient Rome, the *Eidibus Martiis* coinage of Brutus – probably his final issue before Philippi – is an unashamed celebration of the very act of tyrannicide. This was certainly as far as the Republicans could possibly go in their condemnation of all that the late dictator had stood for and in their provocation of his heirs, the triumviral leaders Antony and Octavian. So extraordinary is this type that it was renowned even in ancient times and actually receives mention by the historian Dio Cassius[69] who wrote in the early decades of the 3rd century AD. The two daggers representing the weapons of the assassins flank a pileus, the cap of Liberty, which was the special head-dress of the twins Castor and Pollux (the Dioscuri). The divine brothers, patrons of Rome, were believed to have intervened on the battlefield in one of Rome's direst military crises – the battle of Lake Regillus in 496 BC when the forces of the Latin League were defeated. Thus, the pileus serves to characterize the assassination of Caesar as a profoundly patriotic act, perhaps even divinely authorized. The symbolism of the design was made even more powerful by Brutus' descent from the Republic's founder and first consul, L. Junius Brutus, who in 509 BC swore on a bloody dagger to expel the Tarquin kings from Rome. The implied parallel with Caesar's assassins was clearly part of Brutus' justification for his involvement in the brutal act on the 'Ides of March' 44 BC, for violence against a fellow citizen was a capital crime under Roman law but the right of regicide might cancel the offence. However, so direct a reference to an act of questionable morality was probably imprudent at best and is arguably unique in the history of the Roman coinage.

Although it has long been thought that the Brutus 'EID MAR' issue consisted entirely of silver denarii recent decades have seen the appearance of two purported examples of the gold aureus. Both of these remarkable finds were published by Herbert Cahn (in 1953 and 1989), but in his 1974 publication *Roman Republican Coinage* Michael Crawford decided not to include the aureus and in the Appendix[70] states 'The aureus of Brutus with EID MAR is in my view false, *pace* H.A. Cahn, *Congres 1953*, 213; the formal reasons advanced by Cahn for accepting the piece are without weight and the piece itself invites suspicion; there is a cast of the example published by Cahn in the ANS, labelled "Forgery, Athens"; another example is listed in D. Christianus, *Catalogus Numismatum Antiquorum* (Copenhagen, n.d.) p. 4, no. 10, in the company of seven other Republican gold coins, all false (information from T.V. Buttrey), yet another is rightly in the BM forgery trays'. Crawford's views on the specimen published in 1989 have not been made known, but as the piece is a great deal more convincing than the previously published example it has been decided to include it here, albeit with some misgivings.

M. Issues of C. Cassius

The coinage of the other principal tyrannicide, C. Cassius Longinus, is on a noticeably smaller scale than that of Brutus, with only three major types in gold and four in silver as opposed to seven aurei and ten denarii for Brutus. In addition, Brutus has three quinarius types, a denomination which is unknown for Cassius. The reason for this disparity is that Cassius' issues are in the main confined to the two occasions when the leaders met in western Asia Minor, at Smyrna early in 42 BC and at Sardis in the summer, events which were celebrated by joint issues of coinage. Brutus' mint, on the other hand, produced additional coinages in the periods following these meetings, the first in connection with his military operations in Lycia (see nos. 199–205), the second during the tyrannicides' final campaign which culminated in Philippi (see nos. 208–16).

The only issue of Cassius which appears to have been produced independently of Brutus comprises two aurei struck by his legate Marcus Aquinus. This coinage would seem to predate the meeting at Smyrna, a conclusion strengthened by Cassius' designation as *proconsul* (PR COS) on the first variety, the sole instance of the use of this title on the tyrannicide's coinage. The titulature then changes to *imperator* for the succeeding issue of Aquinus and this form of legend (C CASSI, or CASSEI, IMP) is subsequently retained for the remainder of Cassius' coinage.

217

218

217 Diademed head of Libertas right, LIBERTAS (TA ligatured) below, M AQVINVS LEG behind. *Reverse:* tripod surmounted by the *cortina* (cauldron) and two laurel-branches, fillet hanging on either side, C CASSI on left, PR COS on right. *Gold aureus. Military mint, possibly at Smyrna, early 42 BC* (Crawford 498/1; Sydenham 1302; BMCRR East 71; Babelon Cassia 12; Cohen 2).

218 Similar to preceding, but with IMP instead of PR COS to right of tripod on reverse. *Gold aureus. Military mint, possibly at Smyrna, early 42 BC* (Crawford 499/1; Sydenham 1303; BMCRR East 72; Babelon Cassia 13; Cohen 1).

The reverse type of no. 218 was subsequently adopted for one of Lentulus Spinther's denarii associated with the meeting of the tyrannicides at Smyrna (see no. 219). A date just prior to this momentous occasion would thus seem reasonable for Aquinus' aurei. Cassius may have reached Smyrna first and commenced the production of coinage in advance of his colleague's arrival, hence the lack of a corresponding issue for Brutus. Libertas personified the ideals of the 'liberators' in their fervent desire to rid Rome of the scourge of monarchical rule. Her head dominates the obverses of Cassius' coinage and also appears on many of Brutus' issues. The tripod on reverse symbolizes Apollo in his role as the god of prophecy. Doubtless the tyrannicides were anxious to invoke the support of this important deity in their life-and-death struggle with what they perceived to be the forces of evil. Another suggested interpretation of this type is a reference to Cassius' membership of the priestly college of the *quindecimviri sacris faciundis* ('fifteen men for the performing of sacred ceremonies'). One of the responsibilities of this important college was the custody of the celebrated Sibylline Books in which prophecies were made concerning the future of the state. The change of Cassius' titulature from *proconsul* to *imperator* prior to his meeting with Brutus is of some interest as it carries an implication that Cassius wished to assert his seniority over his colleague. The first issues of Brutus struck for him at Cassius' mint during the meeting at Smyrna are without title (see nos. 197 and 198) and he is only styled *imperator* shortly before the second meeting of the tyrannicides at Sardis in the summer of 42 BC (see nos. 204 and 205). Of the legate Marcus Aquinus, author of this first coinage of Cassius, we have no certain knowledge unless he may be equated with the M. Aquinius who fought against Caesar in the Thapsus campaign and was afterwards pardoned by the dictator.[71]

219

219 Tripod surmounted by the *cortina* (cauldron) and two laurel-branches, fillet hanging on either side, C CASSI on left, IMP on right. *Reverse:* jug and lituus, LENTVLVS / SPINT below. *Silver denarius. Military mint, probably at Smyrna, early 42 BC* (Crawford 500/1; Sydenham 1308; BMCRR East 79; Babelon Cassia 14; Cohen 7).

The obverse of this rare denarius is a close copy of the reverse of the aureus of M. Aquinus already described (see no. 218). It bears the name of another of Cassius' legates, P. Cornelius Lentulus Spinther, whose issues in the names of both Brutus (see nos. 197–8) and Cassius appear to have been made on the occasion of the meeting of the two republican leaders at Smyrna early in 42 BC. The jug and lituus are symbolic of Spinther's membership of the priestly college of augurs to which he was elected in 57 BC.

220

220 Diademed head of Libertas right, LEIBERTAS before, C CASSI IMP behind. *Reverse:* same as preceding. *Gold aureus. Military mint, probably at Smyrna, early 42 BC* (Crawford 500/2; Sydenham 1306; BMCRR East 76; Babelon Cassia 15; Cohen 3).

221 222 223

221 Same as preceding. *Silver denarius. Military mint, probably at Smyrna, early 42 BC* (Crawford 500/3; Sydenham 1307; BMCRR East 77; Babelon Cassia 16; Cohen 4).

222 Similar to preceding, but the bust of Libertas is veiled and draped. *Gold aureus. Military mint, probably at Smyrna, early 42 BC* (Crawford 500/4; Sydenham 1304; BMCRR East 73; Babelon Cassia 17; Cohen 5).

223 Same as preceding. *Silver denarius. Military mint, probably at Smyrna, early 42 BC* (Crawford 500/5; Sydenham 1305; BMCRR East 74; Babelon Cassia 18; Cohen 6).

These aurei and denarii struck for Cassius by his lieutenant Lentulus Spinther represent the principal coinage in the name of the tyrannicide and are to be associated with the meeting of Brutus and Cassius at Smyrna. The head of Libertas had already appeared as an obverse type on the gold coinage struck by Cassius' legate Aquinus (see nos. 217 and 218) and was to be seen again on the tyrannicide's aurei and denarii struck on the occasion of the second meeting of the republican leaders at Sardis (see nos. 224–6).

224 225 226

224 Laureate head of Libertas right, C CASSI IMP behind. *Reverse:* aplustre, the branches terminating in flowers, M SERVILIVS on left, LEG on right. *Gold aureus. Military mint, probably at Sardis, summer 42 BC* (Crawford 505/1; Sydenham 1311; BMCRR East 82; Babelon Cassia 20; Cohen 8).

225 Same as preceding. *Silver denarius. Military mint, probably at Sardis, summer 42 BC* (Crawford 505/2; Sydenham 1312; BMCRR East 83; Babelon Cassia 21, Cohen 9).

226 Laureate head of Libertas right, C CASSEI IMP behind. *Reverse:* crab holding aplustre in its claws, untied diadem and rose below, M SERVILIVS on left, LEG on right. *Silver denarius. Military mint, probably at Sardis, summer 42 BC* (Crawford 505/3; Sydenham 1313; BMCRR East 84; Babelon Cassia 19; Cohen 10).

The final issue of coinage in the name of C. Cassius was made by the legate M. Servilius on the occasion of the meeting of Brutus and Cassius at the old Lydian capital of Sardis. At this time (summer 42 BC) their forces were permanently united in readiness for the inevitable trial of strength with the Triumvirs. Coins were struck for Brutus (see nos. 206 and 207) as well as Cassius, but the latter's issues were on a larger scale and the types are full of symbolism. The theme is the commemoration of Cassius' celebrated victory over the Rhodian fleet which resulted in his occupation of the island and the pillaging of its wealth for the benefit of the republican cause. The first type (aureus and denarius) depicts an aplustre, the curved decorative extension of the stern post of a galley. Its extremities are ornamented with a floral motif which probably represents the rose of Rhodes. The second type, in silver only, is more elaborate and features a crab, the civic badge of the island of Cos in whose waters the opposing armadas met. It holds in its claws an aplustre symbolizing that Cos was the key to success in the contest between the Roman and Rhodian fleets. Beneath the crab are the Rhodian rose and an untied regal diadem representing the victor's prize. Plutarch[72] records that when Cassius took possession of Rhodes he was saluted by the citizens as their lord and king but rejected the offer with disdain, stating 'I am neither lord nor king, but I have punished and killed the man who would have been both'. Marcus Servilius, the legate responsible for this remarkable issue, was praised by Cicero[73] as 'a man of great bravery' (*vir fortissimus*) and certainly saw much action during the various campaigns of the republican leaders.

With this series the coinage of the tyrannicide C. Cassius Longinus comes to an end. All subsequent issues of the Republicans in the remaining months before Philippi were struck in honour in M. Junius Brutus whose illustrious name and overall popularity were doubtless considered to be a greater asset to the cause than anything which his dour colleague could offer. Although a man of superior military skills and greater experience than Brutus, Cassius' violent temper and sarcastic tongue, combined with a reputation for ruthlessness in dealing with defeated adversaries, made him less attractive as a popular leader and was probably responsible for his disappearance from the coinage at this critical time. His surprising suicide in the early stages of the conflict at Philippi might possibly have been due to a depressed state of mind resulting from this decline in his personal prestige. Regretfully, as Cassius did not share in the remarkable final phase of the Republicans' coinage, when his colleague was experimenting with the revolutionary and potentially politically damaging concept of portraiture, we have been denied the opportunity of possessing the likeness of this celebrated leader, a man who could have altered the entire subsequent course of Roman history.

N. Issues of Q. Cornuficius

While events in Italy and the East were moving inexorably towards the final confrontation between the Triumvirs and the republican leaders at Philippi a lesser drama was being played out in north Africa. Here, Quintus Cornuficius (sometimes called Cornificius), governor of Africa Vetus and a supporter of

The entrance to the old Mandraki Harbour on Rhodes, captured by Cassius, now guarded by the Knights' Fort St Nicolas. The Colossus of Rhodes, one of the Seven Wonders of the Ancient World, was said to bestride the harbour mouth here before it was toppled in an earthquake in 226 BC.

the republican cause, was engaged in a struggle for regional supremacy with Titus Sextius, governor of Africa Nova, whose loyalties lay with the triumviral government in Rome. Initially, the war appeared to be going Cornuficius' way and early military successes even encouraged him to invade his adversary's territory. But over-confidence was eventually to bring about his downfall and the issue was finally decided near Utica in the early summer of 42 BC when the army of Cornuficius was surrounded by the superior forces of Sextius. In the ensuing massacre the governor of Africa Vetus was slain leaving his rival as master of both the African provinces.

Quintus Cornuficius had enjoyed a distinguished career during the dictatorship of Caesar whose favour he had won in 48 BC through his recovery of Illyricum and its defence against the Pompeian fleet. A grateful Caesar had rewarded him with the praetorship and he was also appointed to the priestly college of augurs. The governorship of Cilicia followed in 46 BC and two years later he took up his post in Africa Vetus. Although this was subsequent to the dictator's assassination the appointment had probably been made by him. Cornuficius' loyalty to Caesar, if it ever existed, certainly did not extend to his successors and the governor of Africa Vetus refused to hand over his command to Antony's nominee for the post, Calvisius Sabinus. Instead, he held his province for the Senate and at the end of 43 BC he was proscribed by the triumviral government which reassigned the territory to Sextius, hence the war between the two African governors. In the literary field Cornuficius also achieved some prominence and his accomplishments as an orator and a poet gained for him the respect and even the close friendship of Cicero.[74]

During the struggle against Sextius, in the early months of 42 BC, Cornuficius produced an attractive coinage of gold aurei and silver denarii, all of great rarity today. Three obverse types are combined with the same reverse depicting Cornuficius in priestly robes being crowned by the goddess Juno Sospita. The accompanying legend accords him the titles of both *augur* and *imperator*, though it is uncertain when he took the imperatorial title. We must assume that it was in connection with victories achieved in the opening phase of the war with Sextius.

227

228

227 Bearded head of Jupiter Ammon left. *Reverse:* Q. Cornuficius, veiled and in priestly robes, standing facing, holding lituus in right hand, crowned with wreath by Juno Sospita who stands left, wearing goat's skin head-dress and holding shield and spear in left, a crow perched on her shoulder, Q CORNVFICI AVGVR IMP around, below (partially in exergue). *Gold aureus. North African mint, possibly Utica, spring to early summer 42 BC* (Crawford 509/1; Sydenham 1352; BMCRR Africa, p. 577; Babelon Cornuficia 1).

228 Same as preceding. *Silver denarius. North African mint, possibly Utica, spring to early summer 42 BC* (Crawford 509/2; Sydenham 1353; BMCRR Africa 26; Babelon Cornuficia 2).

229 Draped bust of Africa right, wearing elephant's skin head-dress, two spears behind. *Reverse:* same as preceding. *Gold aureus. North African mint, possibly Utica, spring to early summer 42 BC* (Crawford 509/3 – unique specimen in Zagreb).

230

231

230 Same as preceding. *Silver denarius. North African mint, possibly Utica, spring to early summer 42 BC* (Crawford 509/4; Sydenham 1355; BMCRR Africa 28; Babelon Cornuficia 4).

231 Head of Ceres left, wreathed with corn. *Reverse:* same as preceding. *Silver denarius. North African mint, possibly Utica, spring to early summer 42 BC* (Crawford 509/5; Sydenham 1354; BMCRR Africa 27; Babelon Cornuficia 3).

The three obverses of Cornuficius' coinage all relate to his province of Africa Vetus (*i.e.* the 'old' province of Africa). It will be remembered that Africa Nova, the 'new' African province, had been created by Caesar in 46 BC out of the former Numidian kingdom of Juba. Ammon was an Egyptian/ Libyan deity who came to be equated with the Greek Zeus and Roman Jupiter. His head had appeared frequently on Greek coins of the Cyrenaica and on the large bronzes of the Ptolemaic kings of Egypt. The distinctive head of Africa had its origins in the early tetradrachms of Ptolemy I of Egypt (late 4th century BC) which depicted a beardless portrait of Alexander the Great clad in an elephant's skin. In subsequent issues the youthful features of the Macedonian king were gradually feminized until the head came to be regarded as that of the goddess who personified Africa. The female deity of no. 231, her head wreathed with ears of corn, is usually identified as Ceres, the Roman goddess of agriculture, who was the equivalent of the Greek Demeter. Her daughter Proserpina (Persephone) is another possibility. Crawford prefers to see her as Tanit, the principal goddess of Carthage.

The elaborate reverse type shows the governor of Africa Vetus in the robes of an augur, a member of the prestigious Roman priesthood which specialized in predicting the outcome of important ventures such as military actions or long and hazardous journeys (hence the English words 'augur' and 'augury'). He holds the lituus, a curved ceremonial staff which was used by the augurs to delineate an area in which the observation of birds was to take place. Cornuficius is crowned by the goddess Juno Sospita who was especially revered by the inhabitants of Lanuvium (modern *Lanuvio*), an ancient Latin city in the Alban Hills about twenty miles south-east of Rome. Her appearance on these coins clearly indicates that Cornuficius' family originated from this place and he may well have been born there. The raven (*cornix*) which is perched on Juno's shoulder was sacred to the goddess, having featured in a story related by Livy[75] which dates from the time of Hannibal's presence in Italy in the early stages of the Second Punic War (217 BC). The place of mintage of Cornuficius' coinage has not been firmly established but the provincial capital of Utica seems a likely location. Just four years before Utica had operated as a Pompeian mint in the period prior to Caesar's victory at Thapsus (see nos. 40–3 and 46–7).

O. Issues of Sextus Pompey in Spain and Southern Gaul

Sextus Pompeius Magnus Pius, the younger son of Pompey the Great and Mucia, was born about 67 BC. Because of his youth he had not played a prominent role in the great conflict between Caesar and the Pompeians extending over the years 49–45 BC and we have only caught the occasional glimpse of him down to the time of the final Pompeian defeat at Munda on 17 March 45 BC. His elder brother, Gnaeus Pompey, had survived the Spanish disaster but was captured during his flight and put to death. Sextus Pompey was now the sole survivor of the principal members of the formerly dominant Pompeian party which had offered such dogged resistance to Caesar's meteoric rise to political supremacy in the Roman world.

After escaping from Munda Sextus, still only twenty-two, led the perilous life of a fugitive enduring many hardships until he found refuge with the people of the Lacetani tribe in northern Spain. While Caesar remained in the peninsula meting out harsh punishment to the rebellious province the son of Pompey was able to do little more than lead the life of a bandit and a pirate. But with the dictator's departure for Rome Sextus took a bolder line and from the remnants of the army which had contended so valiantly at Munda he was gradually able to assemble an effective fighting force. By the employment of guerrilla tactics this new Pompeian army achieved appreciable success against the Caesarian generals Carrinas and Pollio until the son of Pompey eventually gained control of Further Spain. More than this, he even managed to assemble a sizeable fleet, an asset which was to be of inestimable value in his future dealings with political rivals. But by now the Ides of March had come and gone and the political situation in Rome had taken on a whole new complexion. Sextus' stature was such that both sides in the rivalry between the Caesarians and the Republicans were anxious to secure his alliance and a reconciliation with the government in Rome was arranged by the future Triumvir M. Aemilius Lepidus (summer 44 BC). It looked as though his days as an exile were at an end, but although he now left Spain he did not return to the capital and merely transferred his residence to the port of Massilia (modern *Marseille*) in southern Gaul. Here he anchored his fleet and encamped his army, deeming it wiser to play the role of an interested spectator of events in distant Rome.

His caution proved to be well founded. In April of 43 BC the Senate, emboldened by the news of Antony's discomfiture at Mutina, bestowed on Sextus the grandiose title of Commander-in-Chief of the Fleet and of the Sea Coasts (*praefectus classis et orae maritimae*). But in August the Conscript Fathers were forced by the victorious Octavian to do a *volte-face* and under the terms of the *Lex Pedia* the late dictator's assassins were condemned and Sextus was outlawed once again. If he had ever cherished the notion of returning to Rome to lead the life of an aristocrat then this development surely marked the end of his aspirations. As the year drew to a close the newly-established Triumvirate of Antony, Octavian and Lepidus published its notorious proscription lists prominent on which was the name of Sextus Pompeius. But the outlaw had already decided it was time for action and had set sail for from Massilia to Sicily where he soon established a base from which he was able to raid and blockade the Italian mainland. He may have regreted his decision not to to play a more active role in the critical period of complex political manœuvrings which saw the downfall of the senatorial cause and the establishment of the Triumvirate, but the opportunity was now lost. Sextus' presence in Sicily provided a sanctuary for fugitives from the proscriptions and subsequent upheavals in Italy and the numbers of his supporters rapidly swelled. Again, he played no part in the momentous events of the year 42 BC though he did defeat the attempt of Octavian's general Salvidienus to dislodge him from his island stronghold. His position in Sicily was now firmly established and he awaited the outcome of the life-and-death struggle between the Caesarians and the Republicans which was finally decided in favour of the former on the field of Philippi.

The coinage of Sextus Pompey falls into three distinct phases. The first was during his freebooting career in Spain following Munda (45–44 BC); the second belongs to his stay in Massilia prior to his appointment by the Senate as Commander-in-Chief of the Fleet (44–43 BC); and the third and most prolific period of production was in Sicily between the time of his defeat of Salvidienus and the Pact of Misenum (42–39 BC). The first two series fall within the period presently under consideration, whilst the third will be covered in Chapter 4 (see nos. 332–336).

232 Bare head of Pompey the Great right, **SEX MAGNVS** before, **IMP B** behind. *Reverse:* Pietas standing left, holding palm-branch in right hand and transverse sceptre in left, **PIETAS** behind. *Silver denarius. Spanish mint, 45–44 BC* (Crawford 477/1a; RSC/Cohen *Pompey the Great* 12b).

232a Similar to preceding, but with **SEX MAGN** before head of Pompey the Great, and **IMP SAL** behind. *Silver denarius. Spanish mint, 45–44 BC* (Crawford 477/1b; Sydenham 1042; BMCRR Spain 93; Babelon Pompeia 18; Cohen *Pompey the Great* 14).

232a

232b Similar to preceding, but with **SEX MAGN** before head of Pompey the Great, and **PIVS IMP SAL** behind. *Silver denarius. Spanish mint, 45–44 BC* (Crawford 477/3a; Sydenham 1042a; BMCRR Spain, p. 371 note; Babelon Pompeia 17; Cohen *Pompey the Great* 13).

232c Similar to preceding, but without **SAL**. *Silver denarius. Spanish mint, 45–44 BC* (Crawford 477/3b; Sydenham 1041; BMCRR Spain, p. 370; Babelon Pompeia 16; Cohen *Pompey the Great* 12).

This rare issue is the successor of the pre-Munda coinage struck at Corduba by Sextus' elder brother Gnaeus Pompey Junior (see nos. 49–52) though is of noticeably inferior style. One of the six recorded obverse dies (the first used for no. 232) had actually been re-cut from one employed for Gnaeus' coinage.[76] The exact date of Sextus' issue is, however, uncertain. Crawford favours late 45 BC and it is certainly unlikely that the younger son of Pompey would have been in a position to produce coinage much earlier than this. However, a later date may be preferable, perhaps even after the Ides of March, when Sextus would have felt more confident in the production of coinage in opposition to the Caesarian regime. Despite its brevity this series appears to comprise two distinct parts, one – presumably the earlier – omitting the name 'Pius' (Sextus Magnus Imperator), the other including it (Sextus Magnus Pius Imperator). The reverse type of Pietas (the battle-cry at Munda[77]) refers in general to Sextus' family loyalty and in particular to his vow to avenge the violent deaths of his father and elder brother, as well as to his own assumption of the *cognomen* 'Pius'. The abbreviation **SAL** which occurs on some of the obverse dies of this coinage is interpreted by Babelon and Grueber (BMCRR) as *salutatus*. Crawford, however, prefers to see it as the mint mark of Salpensa, a city situated in the south of the peninsula some 20 miles south-east of Hispalis. Despite the obvious attraction of being able to identify the place of origin with such precision the present writer feels that such a prominent mint mark would be unprecedented on a denarius issue of this period. Furthermore, the lettering of **SAL** is of the same size and form as the rest of the inscription which would seem to be a sure indication that the word should rather be regarded as an integral part of the obverse legend.

233

233 Bare head of Gnaeus Pompey Junior left, **SEX MAGNVS SAL** (**AL** ligatured) **IMP** around. *Reverse:* Pietas standing left, holding palm-branch in right hand and transverse sceptre in left, **PIETAS** behind. *Silver denarius. Spanish mint, 45–44 BC.* (Crawford 477/2; Sydenham 1043; BMCRR Spain 94; Cohen *Pompey the Great* 15).

The portrait on this variety is more youthful than the others in the series and there seems little doubt that it represents Sextus' elder brother, Gnaeus Pompey Junior, who perished soon after the defeat at Munda. Comparison with the head of Gnaeus appearing on the reverse of the aureus of Sextus struck several years later (see no. 332) shows similar features, though the style of the Sicilian issue is far superior. Especially characteristic is the prominent brow. The left facing head provides a further differentiation from his father's portrait and probably denotes the junior status of the younger Pompey (see note preceding no. 159 regarding Lepidus' portraits on his aurei of 42 BC). Sextus had vowed to wreak vengeance for the destruction of his family at the hands of Caesar and his adherents so it is hardly surprising that he should depict his martyred brother in addition to his father on his initial issue of coinage.

234

234 Laureate head of Janus, altar partially or fully visible between, **MAGNVS** (**MA** sometimes ligatured), **MAGNV** or **MAGN** above, **PIVS IMP F** below. *Reverse:* prow of galley right, **EPPIVS** above, **LEG** below. *Bronze as. Spanish mint, 45–44 BC* (RPC 487; Crawford 478/1a; FITA pp. 22–4; Sydenham 1045, 1045a; BMCRR Spain 104, 106; cf. Babelon Pompeia 19; cf. Cohen *Pompey the Great* 2).

234a Similar to preceding, but without altar or legend on obverse, and with mark of value **I** above the Janus head. *Bronze as. Spanish mint, 45–44 BC* (Crawford 478/1b; BMCRR Spain 108 – description corrected from die-duplicate in Hannover).

This type represents Sextus' continuation of the production of Pompeian bronzes in Spain[78] initiated by his elder brother prior to Munda (see no. 53). Like the earlier issue, these coins appear to be based on the old uncial weight standard of *c*. 22 grams which on the regular republican coinage had been abandoned in favour of the lighter semuncial standard under the terms of the *Lex Papiria* in 91 BC. Gnaeus' issue had been in the name of the imperator alone, but Sextus' coinage also bears the name of a lieutenant, the legate Eppius with whom we have already met in connection with his issues for the Pompeians in north Africa (see no. 44). Marcus Eppius was one of the few to have survived both Thapsus and Munda. Of his subsequent career we have no certain knowledge.

235

235 Bare head of Pompey the Great right, **NEPTVNI** behind, trident before, dolphin right below. *Reverse:* galley with billowing sail and bank of rowers moving to right, star in upper field to left, **Q NASIDIVS** (or **NASIDIV**) below. *Silver denarius. Massilia, 44–43* BC (Crawford 483/2; Sydenham 1350; BMCRR Sicily 21; Babelon Pompeia 28, 29; Cohen *Pompey the Great* 20).

236 Bare head of Pompey the Great left, **NEPTVNI** behind, trident before, dolphin left below. *Reverse:* four galleys without sails about to engage in combat, two moving to right, two to left, **Q NASIDIVS** below. *Silver denarius. Massilia, 44–43* BC (Crawford 483/1; Sydenham 1351; BMCRR Sicily, p. 565; Babelon Pompeia 30; Cohen *Pompey the Great* 21).

236

The first of these two types was struck in some quantity whilst the second is of great rarity. Their polished style and neat execution is in marked contrast to the relatively crude products of the Spanish mint and the issue clearly has a different origin. They are unique amongst the coins of Sextus Pompey in being anonymous, other than the name of the naval commander Q. Nasidius which appears on the reverse. The absence of the title 'Commander-in-Chief of the Fleet and of the Sea Coasts' bestowed on Sextus by the Senate in April of 43 BC would appear to indicate a date prior to this award. In consequence it seems likely that the issue belongs to the period of Sextus' sojourn at the port-city of Massilia in southern Gaul, an attribution which is reinforced by the strong naval theme of the types themselves.

Quintus Nasidius had already been associated with Massilia earlier in his career, having been sent by Pompey the Great in 49 BC to relieve the siege of the city by Caesar's legate Decimus Brutus, a task in which he failed. Later, he had command of the Pompeian fleet in north Africa and following the disaster at Thapsus he hastened to Spain where he joined the Pompeian forces led by Gnaeus Pompey Junior. These coins provide the only evidence of his later service under Sextus and it would seem that he held the chief command of the imperator's formidable fleet. It is not surprising, therefore, that we should find Nasidius striking these types during Sextus' lengthy stay at Massilia. Some years later the Pompeian admiral was to recognize the futility of the cause and desert to Antony in the East. The Triumvir made him a junior admiral in his own fleet and he saw service at the fateful battle of Actium on 2 September 31 BC, after which nothing further is heard of him.

Although Sextus' name does not appear on this issue the inscription NEPTVNI, together with the symbols trident and dolphin, may be taken to refer to him or at least to his position of naval supremacy in western Mediterranean waters. Following his later successes against Octavian he is attested as having been hailed as 'Son of Neptune'[79] and even 'Neptunius dux'.[80] Some time towards the close of the year 43 BC the *praefectus classis et orae maritimae*, now outlawed by a Senate cowering before the will of Octavian and soon to be proscribed by the Triumvirs, set sail from Massilia and headed south-east for the shores of Sicily. Here, the most successful phase of his career was to begin. With the extra revenues made available by his blockading activities, augmented by the contributions of grateful refugees from the proscriptions, the coinage of Sextus Pompey assumed a much greater importance and was produced in all three metals on a scale far in excess of his earlier issues (see nos. 332–6).

CHAPTER 4

Philippi to the Parthian War – Antony's ascendancy and the growing dissension of the Triumvirs, 42–36 BC

The second battle of Philippi, 23 October 42 BC, marked the end of an era in the history of the Roman people. With the deaths of Brutus and Cassius the flickering flame of the republican cause was finally extinguished. Sextus Pompey and his adherents now represented the only significant challenge to the Caesarian Triumvirate. But the younger son of the great Pompey was little more than a renegade and a pirate. He was the lone survivor of a once-great cause the real hopes of which had already been dashed by the military genius of Caesar on the battlefields of Pharsalus, Thapsus and Munda.

Political supremacy was now simply a matter of rivalry between the three Caesarian leaders. In reality, this was only a two-horse race for Lepidus was very much the junior partner in the alliance, a position which he had occupied from the earliest days of the Triumvirate. Thus, a mere thirty-one months after the daggers had rained down on the *dictator perpetuus* on the Ides of March Caesar's cause had finally triumphed over all serious opposition. Already it had come down to a contest between the two principal Caesarians, the 41-year-old Mark Antony, an experienced and charismatic military leader who had learned his craft at the side of Caesar himself, and the untried 21-year-old Octavian, heir to the dictator and his magical name. Although the young man lacked his triumviral colleague's long experience in the command of men and had the added disadvantage of a delicate constitution, he had, nevertheless, already exhibited remarkable political guile for one so young and was able to inspire the loyalty and affection of a close circle of friends possessing widely diverse talents.

It is remarkable, indeed, that a further eleven years were to elapse before the question of supremacy was finally settled by force of arms. The true lesson of this delay is that Antony, for all his popular swashbuckling image, did not have his heart in playing the leading role in a political revolution which was to result in the destruction of republicanism and its replacement by autocracy. That was Octavian's burning ambition and therein lay the reason for his ultimate success against what must have appeared at the time as insuperable odds. In this he was truly Caesar's heir, ideologically as well as legally. Antony had merely become caught up in the great movement through his personal attachment to Caesar and his own natural abilities as a leader of men. At Philippi he had genuinely grieved over the body of his former friend Brutus.

But he had fought against the tyrannicide with all his ability, not so much because Brutus represented the 'republican' cause but rather because he had betrayed Caesar's friendship. Octavian, on the other hand, was coldly indifferent to Brutus' fate. Had Antony possessed even a small part of his fellow-Triumvir's sense of destiny then he would surely have eliminated him within a year or two of Philippi. It would have been quite easy for him to do so at this time and few would have bothered to raise their voices in protest. As it was, he let the opportunity slip. Gradually, as the years passed by, Octavian, with patience and cunning, built the momentum of his relentless drive to political supremacy. He was already taking the first steps along that long road which was to lead him to the imperial throne.

But in the period immediately following Philippi the political future looked bleak indeed for the late dictator's 21-year-old heir. Because of ill-health he had played no meaningful role in the epic battle which had destroyed the republican cause. In consequence, he had no bargaining chips in the subsequent negotiations in which Rome's territory was divided up between the victorious Triumvirs. With no one in a position to oppose his will Antony had a free hand in these arrangements, a situation of which he took full advantage. His share was to be the wealthy territories of the East where the mischief caused by the recent activities of Brutus and Cassius needed to be set right. Additionally, however, he retained a powerful presence in the West where he continued to control Gallia Comata and added Narbonensis to his possessions at the expense of poor Lepidus. The junior Triumvir also lost his authority over Spain which was now ceded to Octavian as partial compensation for the temporary loss of Sicily to the renegade Sextus Pompey. Octavian's ace – though it could hardly have been perceived as such at the time – was the possession of Italy, and with it, Rome herself. Northern Italy was to be enlarged by the addition of Gallia Cisalpina. This region had formerly been a separate province, part of the southern boundary of which was delimitated by the river Rubicon. Africa alone was reserved for Lepidus whose days as a member of the Caesarian elite were clearly numbered.

Octavian, after a toilsome return journey to Rome much delayed by frequent bouts of illness, now confronted the full enormity of the task allotted him in the post-Philippi arrangements. Huge numbers of veterans, the survivors of some twenty-eight legions, were to be settled on land confiscated from communities throughout Italy. Hatred for the young Triumvir was to reach alarming proportions, threatening his very life, and even the soldiers on whose behalf he was acting became angry and frustrated with the delays in the granting of their rights. Civil strife was widespread, with rioting in the streets of many Italian cities, and it began to look as if Octavian might not survive long enough to become a serious rival to Antony's dominance of the post-Caesarian political scene. One might suspect with good reason that the possibility of such an outcome had been in the back of Antony's mind all along and that such a turn of events would rid him of the irksome presence of 'the boy' without the embarrassing necessity of personal intervention.

As the year progressed, opposition to Octavian's regime in Italy came to be focused on Mark Antony's younger brother, Lucius, egged on by his assertive sister-in-law, the Triumvir's wife Fulvia. Lucius Antony was one of the two consuls elected to hold office in 41 BC and was thus ideally placed to capitalize on the young Triumvir's difficulties in endeavouring to fulfil his obligations to the soldiery. The situation gradually deteriorated to the point where armed conflict between Consul and Triumvir was becoming a real possibility. Octavian, alarmed at his plight, even sent an embassy to Mark Antony who was in Syria, but with no positive results. Although he would not renege on his negotiated agreement with his colleagues the senior Triumvir was clearly playing a waiting game in the hope that events would somehow turn in his favour. In this hope he was to be disappointed.

Surrounded by enemies and with few choices of action open to him Octavian appeared to be on the brink of disaster. But, as usual, his luck held. Following some initial skirmishes in what came to be called the Perusine War Lucius Antony, confident in the expectation that his army would soon be reinforced by the might of his brother's Gallic legions, shut himself up in the strong city of Perusia and prepared to endure a short siege. However, the Antonian generals Pollio and Ventidius, in Cisalpine and Transalpine Gaul, were now faced with a difficult dilemma. If they supported the cause of their commander-in-chief's brother and wife against his triumviral colleague, with whom he had a signed treaty, then they might be risking their future careers and even their lives. In the absence of any directives from the East Pollio and Ventidius decided to remain aloof and in so doing they sealed the fate of Lucius Antony and Fulvia. The siege of Perusia dragged on for some months. Eventually it became clear to the defenders that they were supporting a lost cause and in February of 40 BC the city capitulated to Octavian. Not wishing to further antagonize his eastern colleague the Triumvir pardoned Lucius Antony and even appointed him to the governorship of Spain, where he died soon afterwards. Another opportune death at this time was that of Fufius Calenus, Antony's governor in Gaul, which allowed Octavian to take control of both the province and the legions. This was a most significant addition to his territory and to the military establishment under his command. It represented a major adjustment to the balance of power established after Philippi and he could hardly have expected Antony to accept the change without concessions on his own part. The day of reckoning was soon to come for Antony was now sufficiently alarmed by developments in the West to deem it necessary to visit Italy and demand an explanation of the recent tumultuous events.

Caesar's heir had survived what had probably been his moment of acutest danger in his entire career. The forces potentially ranged against him at the time of the Perusine War were awesome indeed. In addition to the Gallic legions of Pollio and Ventidius the coastlines were controlled by hostile fleets. In the Adriatic was Domitius Ahenobarbus, the former republican admiral, who was currently operating independently as a pirate in command of seventy ships and two legions; and in the Tyrrhenian Sea Sextus Pompey was supreme, his fleet recently augmented by that of another former republican admiral, Staius Murcus. Had there been any sense of common purpose amongst the Antonian and republican forces resulting in a unity of command then Octavian would surely not have survived this episode. But the young Caesar was the beneficiary of the inaction of others and as a result was able to extricate himself from a seemingly hopeless situation. Another factor at work here may have been the soldiers' perception that Octavian was, after all, working in their interests and to fight against him might well harm their own future prospects of a just settlement on retirement. Just as he had done at the time of the downfall of the senatorial cause and the establishment of the Triumvirate in 43 BC Sextus Pompey again remained inactive during a sequence of events which were to have a profound effect on the future.

With Antony's fleet approaching Brundisium in the late summer of 40 BC it would be appropriate here to review the Triumvir's activities in the East since he had taken leave of Octavian following Philippi. His task was to review the situation in Rome's eastern territories in the light of the recent activities there of Cassius and Brutus. Punishments would need to be meted out to those who had actively supported the republican cause and the whole complex system of client kings and Roman provinces required close scrutiny and reorganization where necessary. Another pressing need was to raise additional revenues, some of which would be required to fund his much-vaunted war against Parthia. Antony's design was that success in this crucial enterprise, first envisaged by Caesar himself, would give him total mastery of the Roman world and would enable him to set Octavian aside at his pleasure. Unfortunately, preoccupation with unexpected developments in the West would require the great military adventure to be delayed for a further half decade.

Antony's first stop was at Ephesus where he was hailed by the citizens as a new Dionysus. After a lengthy stay he embarked on an extensive tour of Asia Minor during the course of which he had his first encounter with Herod, son of the Idumaean Antipater and a Roman citizen for the past six years. Herod succeeded in making a most favourable impression on the Triumvir and this meeting was to mark the beginning of his remarkable career. Antony ultimately established him on the Judaean throne and even protected him from Cleopatra who coveted his kingdom. After Antony's downfall he managed to gain Octavian's confidence and thus secured possession of his throne for life. Antony's Asian perambulations during 41 BC eventually brought him to Tarsus, capital of Cilicia. Here, another meeting was to take place which would have a profound effect on the remainder of the Triumvir's life and would ultimately bring him to his final tragic destiny. Cleopatra VII, queen of Egypt for the past decade and formerly Caesar's mistress, had been accused of giving support to Cassius at the time of his occupation of Syria in 43 BC. The charge was groundless for Cleopatra had merely been attempting to assist the Caesarian Dolabella to take possession of Syria when the four legions which she had sent were intercepted by Cassius and induced to transfer their loyalty to the republican cause. However, she obeyed the summons of the mighty Triumvir perceiving an opportunity to establish a close relationship with the most powerful man in the Roman world, just as she had done seven years before with Caesar. They had, of course, met before, the first occasion being in Egypt in 55 BC when Antony was a young cavalry officer on the staff of Gabinius at the time of the restoration to the Egyptian throne of Cleopatra's father, Ptolemy XII. She was just a girl of fourteen whilst Antony was twenty-eight. A decade later he must have seen her frequently when she was living in Rome as Caesar's mistress. But it is unlikely that they would have had the opportunity, or even the desire, to form a relationship at this time. Now, everything was different.

The famous scene of the Egyptian queen, adorned as Aphrodite, sailing in her golden barge up the river Cydnus to Tarsus has been made vivid in the contemporary mind by Joseph Mankiewicz's 1963 Hollywood epic *Cleopatra*. Indeed, the whole story of their association had already been immortalized by Shakespeare in his *Antony and Cleopatra* written about 1607. The occasion of the meeting of the queen and the Triumvir at the Cilician capital was undoubtedly a spectacular one and set the tone for the entire course of their future relationship which was to last for eleven years. Although she came as the accused party she declined her judge's dinner invitation and instead played host herself aboard her sumptuous vessel where she could be fully in control of the situation. Her total innocence in the matter of the charges resulted in their immediate dismissal, though one may speculate that the outcome would probably have been the same even if she had been rash enough to lend assistance to Cassius. Cleopatra extracted from Antony the promise to come and spend the winter months with her in Alexandria, an offer which he was hardly likely to refuse. It was ironic, indeed, that while he was dallying in the luxury of the Egyptian court unbeknown to him his wife Fulvia was in the forefront of an armed rising against Octavian aimed at the removal of the young Triumvir for the benefit of her husband. Neither did he show her any gratitude for her efforts when they met a few months later in Athens.

Following their tryst in Tarsus Cleopatra and Antony went their separate ways, she directly back to Egypt to prepare for her lover's coming, he on to Syria and Palestine where there was more work to be done confirming the status of client kings and raising additional revenues. But these matters did not long delay him and the onset of winter found him cosily installed in the royal apartments of the Ptolemaic palace. Thus, the eastern Triumvir spent some considerable time enjoying the enchantment of this earthly paradise. But the outside world would not go away and his revelries were brought to an abrupt end in early March (40 BC) when alarming news arrived of a Parthian invasion of Syria. It will be remembered that in the winter of 43/42 BC Quintus Labienus, son of the Pompeian general Titus Labienus, had been sent into Parthia by Cassius to solicit the aid of King Orodes II on behalf of the republican cause. Unfortunately for Brutus and Cassius the hoped-for assistance never materialized and the battle of Philippi in October 42 BC left the emissary marooned in foreign territory. However, in the winter of 41/40 BC Labienus did return to Syria at the head of a Parthian army in company with Orodes' son, Pacorus. Antony's appointee as governor of Syria, Decidius Saxa, was unable to oppose the invasion as the two legions under his command were composed of troops enlisted by Cassius and they immediately went over to the enemy. Labienus and Pacorus proceeded to devastate Syria and Cilicia and then divided their forces, Labienus moving west into Asia Minor and Pacorus south through Syria and down the Phoenician coast to Palestine. Antony quickly came to realize that he should have taken more time and care in his selection and confirmation of client kings as few of them offered any kind of resistance to the invaders. In Judaea the Parthians gave their support to the Hasmonaean Antigonus Mattathias who was installed on the throne in place of the High-Priest Hyrcanus. Herod made a daring escape via his fortress of Masada and eventually found his way to Egypt from where, with Cleopatra's help, he set sail for Rome to seek aid from Antony.

When Antony left Alexandria in March of 40 BC he quickly learned of the disaster which had befallen Saxa and decided to make directly for Asia Minor. He left behind a pregnant queen of Egypt who he would not meet again for more than three years. In due course she gave birth to twins, a boy who was later to be named Alexander Helios, and a girl, Cleopatra Selene. A second son would be born to the couple in 36 BC, Ptolemy Philadelphus. These new additions to the Egyptian royal family joined Ptolemy Caesar (nicknamed Caesarion), born in the summer of 47 BC, who Cleopatra claimed was the son of Caesar himself. The existence of this last child must have been of considerable concern to the dictator's adoptive son, Octavian, and although the Triumvir always maintained that the queen's claim was spurious he nevertheless wasted no time in having the unfortunate youth put to death following his rivals' downfall in 30 BC.

With inadequate military forces at his disposal and dispatches arriving daily regarding the disastrous outcome of the Perusine War Antony decided that Asia Minor would have to be left to its fate for the time being. Accordingly, he made for Athens where his wife Fulvia was awaiting his arrival with some trepidation. Following the fall of Perusia she had been allowed to go free by Octavian and Antony was bitterly critical of what he regarded as the folly of her actions. It seems that her formerly indomitable spirit was broken during this confrontation, for she could not understand why she was being so vehemently censured when her sole object had been the advancement of her husband's interests. Doubtless, Antony was distracted by the catastrophic turn of recent events, but the true reason for his harshness perhaps lay deeper, in feelings of guilt regarding his recent infidelities. Whatever the truth of this, he left his spouse in a state of utter despair and her death soon afterwards must surely have been hastened by Antony's cruel treatment of her.

Also present in Athens were envoys from Sextus Pompey, the master of Sicily and possessor of a powerful fleet. They were naturally anxious to exploit any possible hostility between the two principal Triumvirs and they proposed an alliance should it be necessary for Antony to go to war with Octavian. Antony received them graciously but was non-committal, for he had probably not yet learned of Octavian's seizure of his Gallic legions following the death of Calenus. However, by the time he reached Corcyra he was certainly aware of this dramatic development and at this stage did not hesitate to ally himself with a former adversary, the republican admiral Ahenobarbus. Following Philippi this colourful individual had turned to piracy and, with a not inconsiderable fighting force composed of some seventy ships and two legions, he was currently terrorizing the ports of the Adriatic. Antony's general Pollio had made contact with Ahenobarbus and persuaded him to throw in his lot with the Triumvir who, at this critical juncture, was overjoyed to have his forces augmented in this way.

Thus, in the summer of 40 BC, the fleet of Antony and Ahenobarbus appeared off Brundisium which immediately shut it gates against them. The Triumvir may well have thought that this was Octavian's doing and merely represented the first step in an inevitable war between them. In reality, the townsfolk had been terrified at the arrival of the pirate Ahenobarbus who, just the previous year, had attacked the city and laid waste its territory. The ships of Sextus Pompey were also active in the area, eager to come to Antony's assistance if required, and if things were not bad enough for Octavian one of his most trusted generals, his friend Salvidienus who commanded the newly acquired Gallic legions, was engaged in secret communications with Antony with the object of changing his allegiance.

Having heard of his triumviral colleague's arrival at Brundisium Octavian hurried south at the head of a sizeable force of veterans. The two armies encamped opposite one another and it became clear from the outset that there was no desire on the part of the soldiers, many of them former comrades, to engage in yet another civil war. The spirit of compromise was in the air, much to the disappointment of Sextus Pompey's representatives, and the two sides decided to try and work out an amicable settlement of their differences. After lengthy negotiations, conducted by Pollio on behalf of Antony and Maecenas for Octavian, a comprehensive agreement was reached whereby Octavian retained possession of the Gallic provinces but in return restored five of his lost legions to Antony and conceded equal recruiting rights in Italy. As a gesture of friendship at the outset of the talks Antony had despatched the controversial Ahenobarbus to Bithynia as governor and had instructed Sextus Pompey to return to Sicily. In reciprocation, Octavian formerly acknowledged Ahenobarbus' new status (he had previously been condemned as an outlaw). The only reference to the third member of the Triumvirate, Aemilius Lepidus, in the Pact of Brundisium was a confirmation of his possession of the politically troubled and strategically insignificant region of north Africa. Otherwise, the rest of the Roman world was divided between Antony in the East and Octavian in the West.

The treaty was signed in early October of 40 BC and the seal was set upon the new accord by the arrangement of a marriage between Antony and Octavian's sister, Octavia. Fulvia had died in Sicyon soon after Antony's departure for Brundisium and Octavia's husband, C. Marcellus, had also conveniently expired earlier in the year. Following the conclusion of their business the two Triumvirs journeyed to Rome amidst great rejoicings. Both appeared to have benefited from the peaceful settlement of their differences and the soldiery and the civilian population were overjoyed to have been spared the horrors of yet another internecine conflict. An unfortunate corollary to the new mood of friendship and co-operation in the Caesarian leadership was the matter of Salvidienus' betrayal of Octavian's friendship. Antony felt in honour bound to reveal to his colleague the treachery of his trusted general and Salvidienus, who had already been designated for the consulship in the coming year, was brought to Rome and denounced as a traitor before a meeting of the Senate. He was immediately executed, a tragic end indeed for one who had perhaps stood as high as Marcus Agrippa in Octavian's esteem.

There was one notable exception to the universal mood of celebration – Sextus Pompey. The hopes of the great Pompey's younger son had been dashed by the unexpected reconciliation of the two Triumvirs and he now decided to exact a terrible revenge for his disappointment. The pirate of Messana stepped up his blockade of Italian ports and Rome was threatened with the spectre of famine. Fully aware that nothing destroys the popularity of a government faster than empty stomachs, Antony and Octavian prepared to take action against the renegade. Unfortunately, such a war would require the imposition of additional tax burdens and this proposal led to riots in the streets of the capital. Reluctantly, the Triumvirs had to accept the unpleasant necessity of opening negotiations with Sextus. At first his demands were quite outrageous, such as his replacement of Lepidus as the third member of the Triumvirate, but eventually the conditions were modified and a treaty was signed in the summer of 39 BC (Pact of Misenum). In recognition of his agreement not to interfere with Rome's food supply, Sextus was recognized as possessing authority over Sicily, Corsica and Sardinia. In addition, he was awarded the government of the Peloponnese which was to be surrendered to him by Antony. A further concession was the pardoning of all those who had sought exile with him since the proscriptions of late 43 BC. Although on the face of it this seemed a magnanimous act on the part of the Triumvirs, in fact it worked very much in their favour as it deprived Sextus of many of his most able adherents who naturally chose to return to their homes.

Affairs in the East had been demanding Antony's urgent attention ever since his departure from the area in the spring of 40 BC. Without doubt this had been an important factor in his decision to come to terms with Octavian at Brundisium and following the conclusion of the accord the general P. Ventidius was dispatched to Asia Minor and Syria with orders to confront the Parthian invaders and drive them from Roman territory (early 39 BC). This he accomplished with remarkable efficiency, destroying both the Roman renegade Labienus and Pacorus, son of the Parthian king Orodes II, during a series of brilliant campaigns in 39 and 38 BC. He then moved on to attack Samosata on the Euphrates at which point Antony, understandably alarmed at the military reputation being acquired by his lieutenant, arrived on the scene himself to take charge of affairs. There were stories of the general's acceptance of a bribe but this may have been merely a rumour spread to justify his removal from command. Ventidius returned to Rome to enjoy a splendid triumph (November 38 BC). His death soon afterwards was followed by a public funeral, a rare distinction. Antony at this time was residing with his new bride in Athens, having travelled to Greece at the end of 39 BC following the birth of their first child, the elder Antonia. During this early phase of their marriage Antony and Octavia appear to have found great happiness together and the Triumvir was content to direct affairs from Athens while he enjoyed the conjugal bliss of a quiet domestic life with a faithful and virtuous spouse.

It may be doubted whether Antony and Octavian had any real confidence in the agreement which had been reached with Sextus Pompey in the summer of 39 BC. Not surprisingly, problems soon began to arise and once again the grain ships bound for Rome were delayed or even prevented from reaching their destination. The impending end of the short-lived entente was marked by

Octavian's repudiation of his wife Scribonia, sister of Sextus' father-in-law L. Scribonius Libo. The marriage had taken place in 40 BC at a time when Octavian was endeavoring to conciliate Sextus who was courting Antony's alliance prior to the meeting of the Triumvirs at Brundisium. Scribonia became the mother of Octavian's only child, his daughter Julia, and the divorce took place on the very day of the baby's birth in 39 BC. Although reputedly possessing a quarrelsome disposition Scribonia had undoubtedly been ill-used as a pawn in the power game being played out in the crisis years of 40 and 39 BC. She subsequently remained devoted to her daughter's interests and actually outlived her former husband, the last recorded mention of her being early in the reign of Tiberius (AD 16). Freed from this irksome bond Octavian now took to wife Livia Drusilla, the former wife of Tiberius Claudius Nero who obligingly divorced her to facilitate the nuptials. The ceremony took place on 17 January 38 BC, just three days after Livia had given birth to her second son, Nero Claudius Drusus. The elder child, named Tiberius Claudius Nero after his father, had been born in 42 BC. Both boys were to be brought up in the household of Octavian and Tiberius was to be his eventual successor on the imperial throne. At the time of her marriage to Octavian Livia was a few days short of her twentieth birthday. Beautiful, intelligent and well-connected as a member of the old republican aristocracy, she represented a true love match for Octavian and it is surprising that their 52-year union remained childless.

War now appeared to be the only option open to the Triumvirs to provide a lasting solution to the problem of Sextus Pompey. Octavian invited Antony to a crisis meeting at Brundisium in the spring of 38 BC. For whatever reason – perhaps illness – the western Triumvir did not keep the tryst and Antony returned immediately to Athens, angered at what he interpreted as a slight. This unfortunate episode led to renewed tension between the leaders and meant that Octavian was now obliged to take unilateral action against the troublesome ruler of Sicily. The results of the conflict between Octavian and Sextus in 38 BC were inconclusive. An early advantage was gained by the Triumvir when Menodorus, a freedman of Pompey the Great and one of Sextus' principal lieutenants, surrendered Sardinia together with his fleet and an army composed of three legions. Fortunes were soon reversed, however, when Octavian's projected invasion of Sicily ended in disaster before it had even begun. The Triumvir was bringing part of his fleet from Tarentum through the Straits of Messana to rendezvous with his other ships which were heading south from their anchorage in the Bay of Naples. At this critical point Sextus suddenly descended on him and, utilizing the element of surprise, won an easy victory. As night descended there was a rapid deterioration in the weather resulting in a violent storm and much of Octavian's fleet was driven on to the rocks and destroyed. He was lucky to have survived himself and had Sextus pressed home his advantage at this point the whole future course of history might have been changed. As it was, Octavian's prestige suffered a serious setback as a result of this catastrophe and the near-fatal episode represented another low point in the young man's career. It was to take months of careful rebuilding to restore the damage inflicted on that fateful day, but Octavian was destined ultimately to gain his revenge.

The five-year term of the Triumvirate expired in November of 38 BC. Although technically the arrangement lapsed at this time in reality nothing changed, for control of the army still resided in the hands of the Triumvirs. Antony, with plans for his great Parthian expedition now well advanced in his mind, was anxious to have the powers officially renewed for a further half decade and in addition he needed more soldiers to supplement the legions under his command. Octavian, too, required his eastern colleague's help in the struggle against Sextus Pompey, though his trusted lieutenant Agrippa was already actively engaged in the construction of a powerful new fleet to replace the ships lost in the Straits of Messana. A conference between the two men had become a matter of some urgency, but both held back. Antony was still smarting over Octavian's failure to attend their proposed meeting the previous spring and in addition was justifiably annoyed that the equal rights of recruitment in Italy, agreed as a term of their pact in October 40 BC, had not resulted in any augmentation of his military establishment in the East. For his part, Octavian was deeply mistrustful of his colleague. He believed he had uncovered evidence of secret negotiations between Antony and Lepidus which threatened his control of the West.

Such was the mood of the two principal Triumvirs when Antony appeared off Tarentum with a fleet of 300 ships in the late spring of 37 BC, the year of the first consulship of M. Vipsanius Agrippa. The chances of an immediate renewal of their accord seemed slim indeed. Were it not for their mutual need of an agreement, and the vital presence of Octavia to mediate between them, it seems unlikely that anything meaningful would have been achieved at all. But common sense ultimately prevailed and for the last time the two Caesarian leaders sat together at the conference table and attempted to iron out their differences. They agreed to renew the Triumvirate and to deprive Sextus Pompey of the rights which had been granted him under the Misenum Pact two years before. In a renewed spirit of co-operation they were to furnish each other help in their various enterprises. To this end Antony lent a fleet of 120 ships, together with the services of the admirals L. Sempronius Atratinus and M. Oppius Capito, for service against Sextus;[81] whilst Octavian gave promise of twenty thousand men (four legions) to strengthen Antony's military etablishment prior to his invasion of Parthia. After the conclusion of the Pact of Tarentum the Triumvirs proceeded to Rome where they solemnly renewed their powers for another five-year term.

Antony now made preparation for his departure for the East. He and Octavian had been colleagues in the leadership of the Caesarian party for some five and a half years. During this time they had seen a great deal of one another, except for Antony's extended absence in the East following Philippi and his recent sojourn in Athens with Octavia. How well each had really understood the other's motives and ambitions is hard to say, but one may suspect that with his coldly analytical nature the younger man possessed a much clearer vision of his ultimate objectives and how he was going to overcome the inevitable opposition. Throughout this earlier phase of their association Antony had the upper hand, the result of his twenty years seniority and the enormous enhancement to his military prestige earned through his brilliant victory at Philippi. All this was soon to change. When Antony bad farewell to

Octavian, following the renewal of their triumviral powers, in the late summer of 37 BC neither man could have realized that fate had ordained that they would never meet again. Seven more years were to elapse before Octavian became undisputed master of the world but during this time the Caesarian leaders were destined to take quite separate paths. The younger man remained in the city on the Tiber, the capital of Rome's vast empire, cunningly contriving his ultimate triumph. The elder fell increasingly under the spell of the queen of Egypt and ultimately paid the price for his devotion to life's pleasures. One cannot but admire the single-mindedness of purpose which motivated Caesar's adopted heir, still only thirty-two years of age at Actium; but one should also feel compassion for the very human weaknesses of Antony who, finding himself in a situation not of his own creation, played a difficult hand to the best of his ability with great panache and in consequence has been judged one of history's most engaging losers.

With Antony's departure for the East Octavian was now free to pursue his war against Sextus Pompey. Throughout the summer and autumn of 37 BC the consul Agrippa tirelessly devoted all his energies to the completion of Octavian's new fleet and to the training of its crews composed of twenty thousand freed slaves pressed into service. He even devised a special grappling device fired from a catapault to facilitate the capture and boarding of an enemy ship. As no harbour was available large enough to accommodate the training manœuvres of such a large fleet a whole new naval complex was constructed at Lakes Lucrinus and Avernus near Puteoli in the Bay of Naples connected by canal to the sea. Eventually, by the following summer (36 BC) everything was ready for the attack on Sextus' base in Sicily. Octavian and Agrippa had devised a complex strategy involving a three-pronged invasion of the island: Lepidus, from north Africa, would attack the southern coast; Statilius Taurus, with the 120 ships contributed by Antony, would sail from Tarentum and head for the eastern coast; whilst Octavian and Agrippa would bring the new fleet south from Puteoli with the idea of engaging Sextus in a major naval battle. Operations commenced on 1 July. Lepidus was successful in landing twelve legions and quickly overran the western half of the island. So far so good. But on 3 July a violent storm hit the area of southern Italy and Sicily, and although Taurus was able to get safely back to his base at Tarentum Octavian was not so fortunate and sustained heavy damage to his fleet. Neptune again seemed to be favouring Sextus, but worse was to come.

Having effected repairs to his ships Octavian resumed operations the middle of the following month (August). Initially, things went well. Agrippa defeated a squadron of the enemy fleet off Mylae, but Octavian was then surprised by Sextus whilst he was attempting to ferry his legions across the Straits to Tauromenium. The Triumvir foolishly decided to risk a naval engagement and it almost cost him his life. Unable to match Sextus' superior seamanship Octavian suffered a disastrous defeat and came close to being captured by his adversary, barely managing to escape in the gathering dusk. He spent the night in a state of suicidal despondency, shivering on the shore of the mainland with but a single fellow survivor for company. But Octavian's darkest hour had truly come just before the dawn, for from this moment of utter despair his fortunes began to change and his star went into the ascendant. Coincidentally, at the same time in the East the seemingly invincible Antony was about to suffer the first serious military reverse of his career. As if by some predetermined plan the fortune of one Triumvir began to rise as the other commenced its fall.

Despite his success in this engagement Sextus was fully aware of the seriousness of his situation. Lepidus was advancing with a large legionary force from the west of the island while Agrippa had succeeded in capturing Tyndaris on the north coast. The three legions landed by Octavian at Tauromenium prior to his naval disaster were under the command of L. Cornificius and after a forced march across the northern slopes of Mt. Aetna they succeeded in reaching Tyndaris without mishap. Sextus was now penned up in the north-eastern corner of the island facing an army of overwhelming strength. His only hope was to risk all in a great naval battle. On 3 September 36 BC the two fleets engaged off the promontory of Naulochus and Sextus proved to be no match for Agrippa's brilliant tactics. His fleet, and with it his political power, were sunk in the waters of the Tyrrhenian Sea. Sextus fled back to Messana with only seventeen of his original 200 ships and then set sail for Asia where he hoped to find refuge with Antony. But his timing was bad for the eastern Triumvir was in the midst of his Parthian invasion and would soon be trying to extricate himself from his own catastrophe.

An important corollary of the downfall of Sextus Pompey was the deposition of the third member of the Triumvirate. Marcus Aemilius Lepidus had now held his exalted rank for seven years and although he had been ignored by his colleagues almost from the outset a suitable occasion had not yet arisen for him to be set aside. Neither Antony nor Octavian regarded Lepidus as a threat to their supremacy and each may have though it useful to have him as a countercheck to the other's ambitions. Now, his own pent up frustrations were to lead him into a course of action which would bring about his ruin.

It will be remembered that in the recent war against Sextus Lepidus had effected a successful landing in south-western Sicily with a legionary force of considerable size while his allies' fleets were being scattered by storms. As a result he found himself at the head of a much larger army than that of Octavian when the time came to accept the surrender of Sextus' forces in Messana following the battle of Naulochus. In fact, Octavian was still detained at Naulochus when Lepidus persuaded the Sextian commander Plinius to surrender to him rather than wait for the arrival of his triumviral colleague. This placed Lepidus in command of some twenty-two legions and he allowed the troops to plunder the city which had been Sextus' base ever since his occupation of Sicily in 43 BC. Disturbed by news of these developments Octavian quickly arrived on the scene to demand an explanation of his colleague's actions. Apparently, this was the moment for which Lepidus had been waiting, and perhaps even planning. Emboldened by the overwhelming size of his army, and motivated by resentment over his years of subordination, he began to dictate terms to Octavian requiring the restoration of his full rights as an equal partner in the Triumvirate. But Octavian was not to be intimidated. Lepidus had now foolishly committed himself and was to be totally undone when his vast army, lacking respect for its commander and with no reason for loyalty to his cause, deserted *en masse* to Octavian who had secretly infiltrated his opponent's camp with agents. It was all over now for Lepidus who had to throw himself on his former colleague's mercy. Caesar's heir, after deposing him from the Triumvirate, graciously allowed him to retire to Italy where he lived as a state prisoner at the coastal town of Circeii, some sixty miles south of Rome, for almost a quarter of a century. He still retained the prestigious office of pontifex maximus to which he had secured election in 44 BC in succession to Caesar. Following the former Triumvir's death in 13 BC the title was taken by Augustus and thereafter became an integral part of the imperial titles and powers assumed by the emperors on their accession.

In one short campaign Octavian had rid himself of two troublesome, if relatively unimportant, rivals. The real significance of this development was that Octavian now found himself master of the entire western portion of the Roman dominions, just as Antony controlled the East. A final showdown was now more inevitable than ever, but still it was to take another half decade for matters to come to a head. After settling affairs in his newly acquired territories Octavian proceeded to Rome which he entered on 13 November. Everywhere along the way he was greeted as a saviour, so great had been the concern over the disruption to everyday life in Italy caused by the piratical activities of Sextus Pompey. Honours were showered on the victor, perhaps his first real taste of popularity amongst the citizenry since he had come to power seven years before. Naulochus was to be commemorated by the erection of a triumphal arch and other memorials, and Octavian received the right to wear the wreath of the conqueror, the same honour which had been granted to Caesar. Significantly for the future, the Triumvir received the tribunician right of sacrosanctity, a privilege was he was later to develop into one of the cornerstones of the imperial office itself.

Following his departure from Italy in the late summer of 37 BC Antony, in company with his wife Octavia, had set out for the East. But the Triumvir was now tiring of his virtuous spouse to whom he had been married for almost three years. The couple had travelled only as far as Corcyra when Antony decided to send his wife back to Rome on the pretext that she was with child and that with all the preparations for the upcoming Parthian war she would have the benefit of a safer and quieter environment with her brother. Unbeknown to Octavia her husband, desirous of seeing Cleopatra again after a separation of some three and a half years, had written to the Egyptian queen and requested her to meet him in the Syrian capital of Antioch. Antony had clearly decided to adopt a new policy in his relationship with his fellow-Triumvir whom, it seems, he felt he could no longer trust in the light of so many unfulfilled promises in their numerous treaties.

So it was was that Antony and Cleopatra met again in the autumn of 37 BC for the first time since he had taken leave of her at Alexandria early in 40. Their extended separation had convinced the Triumvir that he felt a deep emotional attachment to this remarkable woman, a feeling which presumably was reciprocated. Their marriage took place soon afterwards and was according to the customs of the East. The union was not recognized under Roman law which still regarded Octavia as Antony's sole spouse. But Antony was now consort of the queen of Egypt, with all that that implied, and he immediately restored to the Ptolemaic realm certain territories which it had formerly possessed, such as the kingdom of Chalcis, most of the coastal territory of Phoenicia and Palestine, and the island of Cyprus. In addition, he acknowledged the paternity of the twins born to Cleopatra in 40 BC and re-named them Alexander Helios and Cleopatra Selene. The following year (36 BC) Cleopatra would give birth to another son, Ptolemy Philadelphus, named after one of Egypt's greatest kings, Ptolemy II, son of the dynastic founder. The child's name was significant for it symbolized Cleopatra's ambition to restore her kingdom to its former territorial boundaries, and beyond. Antony and Cleopatra themselves were identified as Dionysus and Aphrodite to their Greek subjects, Osiris and Isis to the Egyptians. All of this must have provoked more than a few raised eyebrows in the West, though at this stage most observers would have interpreted Antony's actions as being in Rome's interests in establishing a more secure basis for the government of the lands of the eastern Mediterranean.

At the same time that his western colleague was busy planning his Sicilian war Antony was poised to embark on the greatest military enterprise of his career, the same enterprise that Caesar was about to undertake at the time of his assassination eight years before – the conquest of Parthia. Success in this ambitious venture was vital to Antony's plans, for it would elevate his reputation to the level of Caesar or even Alexander himself, the great conqueror of Persia who had swept all before him on his eastern advance three centuries before. If he could return as the conqueror of Parthia Antony's authority in the entire Roman world would be unassailable and he would have nothing to fear from any potential rival, including Octavian. Cleopatra, however, was opposed to the enterprise. Perhaps she feared that if her new husband were to attain such renown she would lose much of her influence over him and his eyes would again be turned to the West. Or perhaps she realized that he was taking on more than he had the ability to achieve and the consequences of failure could be catastrophic.

In formulating the plans for his invasion Antony gave careful attention to the question of the loyalty and ability of the client kings who would be responsible for controlling many of the eastern territories during his absence on a foreign war which might be of some considerable duration. The Triumvir had learned his lesson from his earlier mistakes in confirming long-established but unsuitable rulers in their possession of regions which were vital to Rome's interests: now he elevated Amyntas to the throne of Galatia which, with additional lands, gave this talented leader authority over the entire central part of Asia Minor; Archelaus, son of Antony's paramour Glaphyra, was made ruler of Cappadocia; Polemo was given an extensive domain comprising the old kingdom of Pontus augmented by Lesser Armenia; and Herod's occupation of the Judaean throne was confirmed and given the backing of Roman military force. The wisdom of his decisions in the matter of client kings was later to receive powerful endorsement when Octavian retained all of Antony's principal appointments following Actium and even extended their spheres of influence.

But the key to Antony's campaign was the kingdom of Armenia which, under its ruler Artavasdes, had long been an ally of the Parthians. In 37 BC

Canidius Crassus invaded Armenia and defeated Artavasdes who thereupon professed his espousal of the Roman cause. This doubtful alliance was deemed sufficiently secure by Antony who, following the plan originally devised by Caesar, intended to utilize Armenia as an advanced base for his invasion. Why he was so badly fooled we can only speculate. Perhaps his judgement was affected by his frustration over the delays in getting this vital campaign under way.

At length, in the spring of 36 BC Antony set out from Syria at the head of a mighty army composed of sixteen legions of veteran troops, ten thousand Gallic and Spanish cavalry, and thirty thousand auxiliaries. In command of such a force, and with more thorough preparation, Caesar might well have been successful in this bold enterprise. But Antony did not possess the tactical skill of his mentor and in any case his groundwork had been hopelessly inadequate for a campaign of this complexity. As the Romans advanced deep into enemy territory Antony found that his progress was being delayed by the heavy wagons of the baggage train. These contained not only vital food supplies but also the elaborate siege equipment which was crucial to the success of the campaign. At this point the Triumvir made a strategic error which was to have devastating consequences. He resolved to press on towards his first objective, the fortress-city of Phraaspa, capital of Media Atropatene, whilst the key responsibility of protecting the baggage train was entrusted to an escort of just two legions augmented by a large force of Armenian cavalry under the command of their king. The Parthian army, doubtless benefiting from intelligence supplied by Artavasdes, managed to avoid the main Roman force and descended on the baggage train. The Armenians now treacherously abandoned their charge leaving only the two legions to protect the huge convoy. The escort was cut to pieces and their standards carried off as trophies to add to those lost by Crassus in 53 BC.

With his siege equipment lost and food supply seriously diminished Antony had fallen at the first hurdle. He attempted to take Phraaspa with improvised equipment but the attack was easily repulsed. With the season growing late and the onset of winter imminent Antony was forced to admit failure. All he could do was to accomplish a retreat as speedily as possible with the minimum of losses to his man-power. As usual, Antony displayed his finest qualities in adversity and the retreat to the Armenian frontier was achieved in an agonizing twenty-seven days. The army marched in square formation and was constantly under attack from the Parthians. Casualties were heavy. Numbing cold, hunger, thirst and disease all took their toll on the exhausted legions, but throughout the horror of it all Antony marched side by side with his men and shared all their privations. The Parthian king Phraates IV, who had only recently succeeded his father Orodes II on the Arsacid throne, must have been well pleased with the success of the strategy which he had devised to thwart the much-vaunted but ill-executed Roman invasion. Phraates was later to negotiate an amicable agreement with Augustus whereby all the military standards lost by Crassus in 53 BC and by Antony's invasion force seventeen years later were restored to the Romans (20 BC). Parthia was not to be troubled again by a full-scale Roman invasion until the time of the Emperor Trajan a century and a half later.

On reaching Armenia the Romans were in no position to take revenge on Artavasdes. Retribution would have to be delayed to some future occasion. In the meantime, Antony held his temper and obtained food supplies for his starving men. Then, the march began again across the snowy landscape to Syria. More losses were sustained and by the time the safety of the Roman province was reached Antony had lost more than one-third of his entire invasion force. In reponse to a message dispatched during the retreat, which had somehow miraculously reached its destination, Cleopatra arrived by ship on the Syrian coast bringing vital supplies of clothing and other necessities for the army. Once he had seen his men safely settled into winter quarters Antony returned with Cleopatra to Alexandria to take stock of the new situation.

The year 36 BC had marked a major turning point in the affairs of the various contenders for power in post-Caesarian Rome. Both Sextus Pompey and the third Triumvir Lepidus had seen their political careers destroyed, whilst even the two principal Triumvirs had come close to ruin – Antony during his agonizing retreat from Parthia, Octavian when he was disastrously defeated by Sextus' fleet in the Straits of Messana. But by the end of the year the balance of power between Antony and Octavian had, for the first time, shifted decisively in the latter's favour. He had defeated Sextus Pompey, who was now to become a minor thorn in Antony's side, and had deposed the Triumvir Lepidus, thereby creating in reality a Duumvirate. He stood at the head of forty-five legions whilst Antony's military establishment had been seriously weakened by the Parthian War. But most significantly of all, Antony's prestige as a military commander had been critically undermined by the recent disaster. Many now began to wonder whether, after all, Caesar's adoptive son was the true successor to the great dictator and provided the one hope for bringing the interminable civil strife to an end. This was undoubtedly true, but the price to be paid was the destruction of the Republic and the subjugation of Rome to the rule of an autocrat.

COINAGE OF THE PERIOD

A. Issues of Antony

After he had taken leave of Octavian towards the close of 42 BC Antony proceeded to Asia where he was to begin his task of reorganizing affairs in the East. Initially, he fixed his residence at Ephesus, the seat of the proconsular governor, and it was probably from the Ephesian mint that Antony issued a handsome series of gold aurei and silver denarii celebrating both the Triumvirate and the consulship, in 41 BC, of Antony's younger brother Lucius. Prior to this, however, during the course of his journey to the provincial capital, Antony's military mint had produced several other coinages. These probably fall at the beginning of the new year as the reverses commemorate the consulship of L. Antonius Pietas with the inscription PIETAS COS.

237 Bare head of M. Antony right, lituus behind, M ANTONIVS IMP III VIR R P C around. *Reverse:* Pietas standing left, holding *turibulum* (lighted censer) and cornucopiae surmounted by two storks, PIETAS –

COS (TA sometimes ligatured) across field. *Gold aureus. Military mint travelling with Antony in Asia, early 41 BC* (Crawford 516/4; Sydenham 1171, 1171a; BMCRR Gaul 65, 66; Babelon Antonia 45; Newman 41.13; Cohen 78).

238 Same as preceding. *Silver denarius. Military mint travelling with Antony in Asia, early 41 BC.* (Crawford 516/5; Sydenham 1172; BMCRR Gaul 67, 68; Babelon Antonia 46; Newman 41.14; Cohen 79).

238

239 *Obverse:* same as preceding. *Reverse:* Fortuna standing left, holding rudder behind her in right hand and cornucopiae in left, **PIETAS COS** below. *Silver denarius. Military mint travelling with Antony in Asia, early 41 BC.* (Crawford 516/3; Newman 41.12; RSC/Cohen 77a).

240

241

240 Bare head of M. Antony right, **ANT AVG IMP III V R P C** around (**ANT** and **AV** ligatured). *Reverse:* similar to preceding, but with stork standing at feet of Fortuna to left. *Gold aureus. Military mint travelling with Antony in Asia, early 41 BC.* (Crawford 516/1; Sydenham 1173; BMCRR Gaul 69; Babelon Antonia 43; Newman 41.10; Cohen 76).

241 Same as preceding. *Silver denarius. Military mint travelling with Antony in Asia, early 41 BC.* (Crawford 516/2; Sydenham 1174; BMCRR Gaul 70; Babelon Antonia 44; Newman 41.11; Cohen 77).

There would appear to be two distinct series here differentiated by fabric as well as type. The link is provided by no. 239 which exhibits the small, compact fabric typical of nos. 237 and 238 (as well as sharing the same obverse) whilst the reverse anticipates the type of nos. 240 and 241 which are typically struck on large, spread flans. It would seem logical to place the series with compact flans first as these most closely resemble the issues given to the period following Philippi (see nos. 128 and 129) and, like them, do not include the augural title (**AVG**) in the inscription.[82] Those with spread flans, on other hand, show a marked similarity to the extensive series attributed to Antony's sojourn in Ephesus (see nos. 242 ff.) and do include the augural title. Lucius Antony bore the *cognomen* 'Pietas' in recognition of his fraternal loyalty,[83] a devotion which he was to demonstrate amply later in the year when he headed an armed uprising in Italy against the authority of Octavian. The reverse types illustrate the theme of Pietas and both principal varieties include as an adjunct the stork, a bird which was an emblem of family piety.[84] On the later issue the deity holds the ship's rudder of Fortuna, goddess of good fortune, thus heralding an auspicious tenure of office for the new consul. Unfortunately for the first magistrate the events of 41 BC were to prove otherwise.

During his lengthy stay in Ephesus Antony is reported to have exacted large sums from the wealthy cities of Asia to finance his extravagances.[85] Part of this fortune appears to have been utilized for the production of the extensive coinage which is usually attributed to the Ephesian mint. These attractive aurei and denarii were issued in the names of three of Antony's lieutenants, M. Barbatius Pollio, M. Cocceius Nerva, and L. Gellius Poplicola. As we shall see, there are good reasons for considering this as the actual sequence of issue, with Barbatius striking first and Gellius last. However, we may question whether the entire series should be regarded as the product of a single mint. The influence of the style of Antonian portraiture initiated on this important coinage may be observed on many of the Triumvir's later issues.

242

243

242 Bare head of M. Antony right, M ANT IMP AVG III VIR R P C M BARBAT Q P around (MP and AV ligatured). *Reverse:* bare head of Octavian right, CAESAR IMP PONT III VIR R P C around. *Gold aureus. Ephesus, spring–early summer 41 BC* (Crawford 517/1a; Sydenham 1180; BMCRR East 98; Babelon Antonia 50; Newman 41.1; Cohen 7).

One obverse die has RARRAT for BARBAT (Crawford 517/1b).

243 Same as preceding. *Silver denarius. Ephesus, spring–early summer 41 BC* (Crawford 517/2; Sydenham 1181; BMCRR East 100; Babelon Antonia 51; Newman 41.2; Cohen 8).

BARBAT is sometimes blundered: the forms BARRAT, RARRAT, RARBAT, and BARBT have all been noted; also III VIR R R P C sometimes occurs on reverse (Crawford 517/2 note).

244 *Obverse:* same as preceding. *Reverse:* bare head of Lucius Antony right, L ANTONIVS COS around. *Silver denarius. Ephesus, summer 41 BC* (Crawford 517/3; Sydenham 1182; BMCRR East, p. 491; Babelon Antonia 49; Newman 41.3; Cohen 3).

The issue of M. Barbatius Pollio honouring Antony's triumviral colleague on reverse is by far the largest and most important in this series.[86] Barbatius bears the curious title of *quaestor pro praetore*, abbreviated to 'Q P', a distinction shared by his colleague L. Gellius. The style and fabric of both denominations are uniform throughout and there can be no doubt that the entire coinage belongs to one mint (presumably Ephesus). The rare denarius depicting Lucius Antony (no. 244) is probably best regarded as a hybrid piece with a reverse die belonging to the coinage of M. Nerva.

245 Bare head of M. Antony right, M ANT IMP AVG III VIR R P C M NERVA PROQ P around (MP, AV, and NE ligatured). *Reverse:* bare head of Lucius Antony right, L ANTONIVS COS around. *Gold aureus. Ephesus, summer 41 BC* (Crawford 517/4a; Sydenham 1184; BMCRR East 106; Babelon Antonia 47; Newman 41.4; Cohen 1).

245a

246

245a Similar to preceding, but without III before VIR in obverse legend. *Gold aureus. Ephesus, summer 41 BC* (Crawford 517/4b).[87]

246 Same as 245. *Silver denarius. Ephesus, summer 41 BC* (Crawford 517/5a; Sydenham 1185; BMCRR East 107; Babelon Antonia 48; Newman 41.5; Cohen 2).

246a Same as 245a. *Silver denarius. Ephesus, summer 41 BC* (Crawford 517/5b; BMCRR East, p. 492, note 3; RSC/Cohen 2a).

247

247 Similar to 246, but with capis behind head of M. Antony on obverse. *Silver denarius. Military mint travelling with Antony in Asia Minor, late summer 41 BC* (Crawford 517/5c; Sydenham 1186; BMCRR East 108; RSC/Cohen 2b).

One reverse die has ANTONNIVS for ANTONIVS (Crawford 517/1c note).

248 *Obverse:* same as 246. *Reverse:* bare head of Octavian right, lituus behind, CAESAR IMP PONT III VIR R P C around. *Silver denarius. Military mint travelling with Antony in Asia Minor, autumn 41 BC* (Crawford 517/6; Sydenham 1183; BMCRR East, p. 491; cf. Babelon Antonia 52, lituus omitted in error; Newman 41.6; RSC/Cohen 6a).

M. Cocceius Nerva, who bears the singular title of *proquaestor pro praetore*, appears to have been the second in the sequence of three Antonian lieutenants who issued coinage at this time. Half a decade later he was to hold the consulship with L. Gellius Poplicola, the same man who succeeded him as moneyer. A distant descendant was the Emperor Nerva, holder of the imperial office almost a century and a half later. Antony's departure from Ephesus seems to have taken place during the period of production of Nerva's coinage which was almost exclusively devoted to honouring the Triumvir's brother, the consul Lucius Antony.[88] The denarius with the augural symbol of a capis (one-handled jug) behind the head of M. Antony (no. 247) is of a different style and fabric[89] from Nerva's other issues which more closely resemble the coins of Barbatius. Thus, it would seem logical to regard this variety as the product of a military mint attempting to imitate the style of the preceding Ephesian issues during Antony's progress through Asia Minor. No corresponding aureus has been recorded and the denarii are noticeably scarcer than those struck at the provincial capital, indicating that the issue was of no long duration.

249

250

249 Bare head of M. Antony right, capis behind, M ANT IMP AVG III VIR R P C L GELL Q P around (MP and AV ligatured). *Reverse:* bare head of Octavian right, lituus behind, CAESAR IMP PONT III VIR R P C around. *Gold aureus. Military mint travelling with Antony in Asia Minor, autumn 41 BC* (Crawford 517/7; Sydenham 1187; BMCRR East, p. 493; Babelon Antonia 53; Newman 41.7; Cohen 9).

250 Same as preceding. *Silver denarius. Military mint travelling with Antony in Asia Minor, autumn 41 BC* (Crawford 517/8; Sydenham 1188; BMCRR East 109; Babelon Antonia 54; Newman 41.8; Cohen 10).

L. Gellius Poplicola was the last of the three moneyers to strike for Antony during the course of his sojourn in Asia Minor in 41 BC. Earlier in his career Gellius had been a partisan of Brutus but had acted treacherously towards the republican leaders and eventually deserted to Antony who entrusted him with high command. He held the consulship in 36 BC, with M. Cocceius Nerva as his colleague, and was one of Antony's principal admirals at Actium, commanding the right wing of the Antonian fleet. Like Barbatius, he bears the unconventional title of *quaestor pro praetore* (Q P) and honours Antony's triumviral colleague Octavian on his coinage. There are no issues bearing the name and portrait of Lucius Antony. In contrast to the later coinage of Nerva (see no. 247), assigned here to Antony's period of travel following his departure from Ephesus, the issues of Gellius include aurei as well as denarii and there is an improvement in the quality of the dies. The inference is that they may have been struck at one of Antony's cities of residence, perhaps even at Tarsus where he was to have his famous encounter with Cleopatra. The augural symbol of a capis (one-handled jug) behind the head of M. Antony, first encountered in this series on the later coinage Nerva, is repeated on the issues of Gellius. Another augural symbol, the lituus, is added behind the head of Octavian on reverse. The omission of any reference to Lucius Antony may be connected with the situation in Italy where the consul had placed himself at the head of a movement to oust the unpopular Octavian. Preliminary news of this had doubtless already been received by the eastern Triumvir and under the circumstances it would scarcely have been politic for him to be seen honouring his triumviral colleague's enemy, even though that enemy was his own brother. Alternatively, this feature of Gellius' coinage may have no greater significance than does the absence of Lucius from the regular issues of Barbatius and the similar absence of Octavian from the coinage of Nerva.

251 Bare head of M. Antony right, M ANTON IMP III VIR R P C AVG around. *Reverse:* bare head of Octavian right, CAESAR IMP PONT III VIR R P C around (NT sometimes ligatured, and sometimes VR for VIR and R C for R P C). *Silver denarius. Military mint travelling with Antony in Syria (?), autumn 41 BC* (Crawford 528/3; Sydenham 1194; BMCRR East 123, 126, 127; Babelon Antonia 40; Newman 41.9; RSC/Cohen 2–2c).

251

This issue in the joint names of the Triumvirs is hard to place. Crawford attributes it to the period following the Pact of Brundisium (October 40 BC) but stylistically it appears to have closer affinities to the coinages of Barbatius, Nerva, and Gellius. It differs from them in lacking the name of an Antonian lieutenant in the obverse legend and in the appearance of ligatures in Octavian's inscription rather than Antony's. On balance, it seems best to regard it as representing a late phase of Antony's coinage in Asia Minor in 41 BC, perhaps struck while he was passing through Syria and Palestine *en route* to Cleopatra in Alexandria.[90]

252 Lituus, on left, beside capis (one-handled jug), on right, M ANTON IMP AVG III VIR R P C around. *Reverse:* sacrificial jug with handle between vertical thunderbolt, on left, and caduceus, on right, L PLANCVS PRO COS around. *Gold aureus. Military mint travelling with Antony and Plancus in central Greece, early summer 40 BC* (Crawford 522/1; BMCRR East, p. 496, note; Babelon Antonia 58; Newman 39.3; Cohen 23).

253 Same as preceding. *Silver denarius. Military mint travelling with Antony and Plancus in central Greece, early summer 40 BC* (Crawford 522/2; Sydenham 1190; BMCRR East 116; Babelon Antonia 59; Newman 39.4; Cohen 24).

253

254 Similar to preceding, but with reverse legend L PLANCVS IMP ITER. *Gold aureus. Military mint travelling with Antony and Plancus in central Greece, early summer 40 BC* (Crawford 522/3; BMCRR East, p. 496, note; Newman 39.1).

255 Same as preceding. *Silver denarius. Military mint travelling with Antony and Plancus in central Greece, early summer 40 BC* (Crawford 522/4; Sydenham 1191; BMCRR East 118; Babelon Antonia 57; Newman 39.2; Cohen 22).

255

The aurei in this issue are known only from three specimens which were formerly in the Paris cabinet. They were lost in the great theft of 1831 but fortunately their precise weights had been recorded in an article published in 1764.[91]

In L. Munatius Plancus we renew our acquaintance with one of the more colourful of the minor political personalities of the imperatorial and early imperial age. We first met him as the issuer of gold aurei and quinarii struck for Caesar in the autumn of 45 BC on the occasion of the dictator's Spanish triumph (see nos. 60–1). Following the Perusine War of 41–40 BC Plancus abandoned his army and escaped with Antony's wife Fulvia to Greece where they awaited the Triumvir's arrival from the East. Having regained Antony's favour he accompanied him to Italy and was subsequently given the prestigious governorship of Asia and, later, that of Syria. After a long period of friendship he eventually quarrelled with Antony over Cleopatra's intended participation in the war against Octavian and went over to the opposing camp (32 BC). Finding favour with Caesar's heir, it was on Plancus' suggestion that Octavian received the title of 'Augustus' on 16 January 27 BC.

The distinctive type of a tall one-handled jug appears to be personal to Plancus as it had already appeared on his coinage for Caesar. It may relate to his membership of the priestly college of the *Epulones*[92] whose function was to supervise certain sacred banquets. The flanking symbols of thunderbolt and caduceus relate to Jupiter and *felicitas* and convey the promise that happiness and prosperity will be restored to the Roman people through the invincible strength of Antony and his legions, the victors of Philippi. The lituus and capis on obverse are, of course, symbolic of the Triumvir's status as an augur. The precise circumstances of the issue remain doubtful. Despite the two distinct varieties of reverse legend, naming Plancus as *proconsul* and *imperator iterum*, the entire coinage appears to form a homogeneous group and we may reasonably speculate that it was struck while Antony and Plancus were leading their army north-west from Athens to the Epirote coast, *en route* to their confrontation with Octavian. The view that it was produced by Plancus as proconsul of Asia following the Pact of Brundisium[93] appears much less likely as such an issue would not have served any practical purpose after the reconciliation of the triumviral leaders.

256

256 Bare head of M. Antony right, lituus behind. *Reverse:* caduceus between two cornuacopiae, all resting on globe, M ANT IMP above (ANT or NT sometimes ligatured, MP always ligatured), III VIR R P C below. *Silver denarius. Corcyra (?), summer 40 BC* (Crawford 520/1; Sydenham 1189; BMCRR East 114, 115; Babelon Antonia 35; Newman 40.1; RSC/Cohen 66–66b).

This small issue in the sole name of the Triumvir was struck from finely engraved dies and an attribution to a mint in western Greece would seem in order. One possibility is the island of Corcyra which served as a naval base for Antony prior to his departure for Brundisium. The symmetrical reverse type is symbolic of the restoration of commerce and prosperity throughout the Roman dominions[94] made possible by Antony's famous victory at Philippi which had brought to an end the bitter civil conflict with the republican faction. The lituus behind the Triumvir's head indicates his membership of the priestly college of augurs, a prestigious honour which receives extensive publicity on the Antonian coinage.

257 Bare head of M. Antony right, lituus behind, ANT IMP III VIR R P C around. *Reverse:* prow of galley right, star above, CN DOMIT AHENOBARBVS IMP around. *Gold aureus. Corcyra (?), summer 40 BC* (Crawford 521/1; Sydenham 1178; BMCRR East 111; Babelon Antonia 55; Newman 40.2; Cohen 9).

257

258 Same as preceding. *Silver denarius. Corcyra (?), summer 40 BC* (Crawford 521/2; Sydenham 1179, 1179a; BMCRR East 112, 113; Babelon Antonia 56; Newman 40.3; RSC/Cohen 10–10c).

258

The number of rays comprising the star on reverse varies on both denominations: seven, twelve, fourteen, and sixteen have all been recorded.

The reconciliation of the former republican admiral Cn. Domitius Ahenobarbus with the Triumvir Antony was arranged by the general Asinius Pollio who had recently reached the Adriatic coast following his abandonment of Lucius Antony's cause at Perusia. A supporter of Pompey in the earlier part of his career, Ahenobarbus accompanied Brutus to Macedonia following Caesar's assassination and was given command of the republican fleet in the Adriatic. Here he achieved some notable successes until the battle of Philippi left him without a cause. At this point he turned to piracy and became the scourge of the Adriatic ports (see nos. 338–9 for his coinage during this period). With a considerable fighting force at his disposal, comprising some seventy ships and two legions, he became a significant political factor in the summer of 40 BC when the two principal Triumvirs appeared to be on the brink of war. Pollio's success in winning him over to the Antonian side was an important coup and significantly strengthened Antony's hand in his subsequent negotiations with Octavian. After the Pact of Brundisium, one of the terms of which formally reinstated his civic rights, Ahenobarbus was appointed governor of Bithynia. He remained loyal to Antony almost to the end, but because of his bitter opposition to Cleopatra's personal involvement in the war against Octavian he finally deserted just prior to Actium and succumbed to a fever shortly afterwards.

Ahenobarbus' coinage for Antony is stylistically very close to the previously described issue in the sole name of the Triumvir (see no. 256) and it seems reasonable to surmise that both were produced by the same mint. Nos. 257 and 258 must have been struck somewhere along the coastline of the Adriatic and Ionian Seas and this would seem to strengthen the proposed attribution to Corcyra. The Triumvir's name and titles are rendered almost identically on both series, though the issue in his sole name includes his *praenomen* 'M'. The symbolism of the reverse type on nos. 257 and 258 is obvious and continues the nautical theme from Ahenobarbus' independent coinage issued the previous year (see nos. 338 and 339).

259

259 Bare head of M. Antony right, **M ANTONIVS IMP III VIR R P C** around. *Reverse:* head of Octavia right, her hair tied in knot behind with one long plait arranged in loop along top of head (no legend). *Gold aureus. Southern or central Italian mint, late 40 BC* (Crawford 527/1; BMCRR East, p. 499; Babelon Antonia 33; Newman 40.6).

The attribution of this remarkable aureus has been the subject of much scholarly debate, some preferring to see in the anonymous female portrait the likeness of Antony's third wife, Fulvia, others his fourth wife, Octavia. Fulvia had died in disgrace at Sicyon in 40 BC, soon after her husband's departure for Italy. She had been deeply implicated in the embarrassing episode of the Perusine War and it would be difficult indeed to discover an appropriate occasion for the issue of such a piece in her honour. In contrast, Antony's subsequent marriage to his triumviral colleague's sister was an occasion for great public rejoicing. It brought with it the promise of peace to a nation which had suffered too much civil conflict and in consequence it would have been fitting to celebrate the nuptials with a special issue of coinage.[95] Production must have been very limited, however, as today the type is represented by a single surviving specimen preserved in the Berlin cabinet. The coin formed part of a hoard uncovered in 1883 at Castagneto, near Volterra in central Italy.

260 Bare head of M. Antony right, **M ANTON IMP III VIR R P C**. *Reverse:* bare head of Octavian right, **CAESAR IMP III VIR R P C** around. *Gold aureus. Southern or central Italian mint, late 40–early 39 BC* (Crawford 528/1b; Sydenham 1192; BMCRR East 120; Babelon Antonia 37; Newman 40.4).

260a Similar to preceding, but with star below head of Antony on obverse. *Gold aureus. Southern or central Italian mint, late 40–early 39 BC* (Crawford 528/1a; Newman 40.4).

261

261 Same as preceding. *Silver denarius. Southern or central Italian mint, late 40–early 39 BC* (Crawford 528/2a; Sydenham 1193; BMCRR East 121; Babelon Antonia 38; Newman 40.5; Cohen 1).

261a Same as 260. *Silver denarius. Southern or central Italian mint, late 40–early 39 BC* (Crawford 528/2b; Sydenham 1193a; Babelon Antonia 38; Newman 40.5; RSC/Cohen 1b).

The reconciliation with Octavian at Brundisium is commemorated by Antony on this issue of aurei and denarii. It represents a revival of the types he had previously struck in the East (see nos. 242–3, 249–50, and 251). The significance of the star which appears below the elder Triumvir's head on some varieties is not immediately apparent but may relate to the dawn of a new age heralded by the re-establishment of accord between the two principal Caesarian leaders. For the corresponding issue by Octavian, see nos. 301–304a.

262

262 Head of M. Antony right, wearing ivy-wreath, lituus below, M ANTONIVS IMP COS DESIG ITER ET TERT around, all within ivy-wreath border. *Reverse:* draped bust of Octavia right above cista mystica flanked by two interlaced snakes with heads erect, III VIR on left, R P C on right. *Silver cistophorus = three denarii. Ephesus,*[96] *summer–autumn 39 BC* (RPC 2201; Sydenham 1197; BMCRR East 133; Babelon Antonia 60; Newman 39.5; Cohen 2).

263

263 Conjoined heads right of M. Antony and Octavia, the Triumvir wearing ivy-wreath, M ANTONIVS IMP COS DESIG ITER ET TERT around. *Reverse:* Dionysus standing left, holding cantharus and thyrsus, on cista mystica flanked by two interlaced snakes with heads erect, III VIR on left, R P C on right. *Silver cistophorus = three denarii. Ephesus, summer–autumn 39 BC* (RPC 2202; Sydenham 1198; BMCRR East 135; Babelon Antonia 61; Newman 39.6; Cohen 3).

This remarkable issue of silver cistophori from Asia, the first for about a decade, commemorates the marriage of Antony and Octavia and celebrates the Triumvir's divine status as the 'New Dionysus', an honour which had been bestowed on him at the time of his arrival in Ephesus in 41 BC.[97] The cistophorus had been the traditional monetary denomination of the Pergamene kingdom since the early part of the 2nd century BC and when the Romans acquired the territory on the death of Attalus III in 133 BC they continued production of the cistophorus to serve the needs of the newly constituted *provincia Asia.* In weight it was the equivalent of three Roman denarii, a relationship which had doubtless been intended from the inception of the coinage because of Rome's special relationship with the later Pergamene kings. Antony's titulature of 'imperator and consul designate for the second and third times' fixes the period of issue to the latter part of 39 BC, after the Pact of Misenum in July (when the consular designations were agreed for the next eight years) and before Antony's second imperatorial acclamation which probably took place in the winter of 39–38 BC. Although Octavia is not named on either type there can be no doubt over the identification of her portrait given the firm chronology of the issue.[98]

264

264 Laureate janiform head, beardless, with features resembling M. Antony, **L ATRATINVS AVGVR** around, below. *Reverse:* prow of galley right, **ANTONIVS** above, **IMP** below. *Bronze as. Uncertain mint in Asia (?), 40–39 BC.* (Crawford 530/1; RPC 2226; Amandry, p. 85 and pl. 17; FITA pp. 37–9 and pl. ii, 9; Sydenham 1254; BMCRR East, p. 501; Babelon Antonia 65; Cohen 3).

The circumstances which led to this curious issue are quite uncertain, as is its place of mintage, though the chronology can be established with reasonable accuracy from the obverse inscription. Lucius Sempronius Atratinus was elected to the priestly college of augurs in 40 BC and was appointed consul designate at the time of the Pact of Misenum in the summer of 39 BC (an office he did not actually hold until 34). No mention is made on this coin of Atratinus being *consul designatus* whereas his augurship is advertised prominently. We may thus infer that it was issued before July 39 BC. The reverse inscription would appear to indicate that Antony had not yet received his second imperatorial acclamation. The origin of this coinage has been considered by a number of scholars resulting in attributions ranging from Brundisium and Sicily in the West to Asia in the East. Although the traditional republican types of Janus head and prow seem to favour a western mint, the two known provenances (Troas and Ionia) are suggestive of a more easterly origin. In his later participation in the 'fleet coinage' (see nos. 279–84 and 291–3) Atratinus' 'heavy series' has been tentatively attributed to Lechaeum, the port of Corinth,[99] though it is unlikely that this has any bearing on the place of mintage of the present type. The weight standard is the semuncial which had been sanctioned under the terms of the *Lex Papiria* as long ago as 91 BC. But recent issues of *aes* in the West had been on the heavier uncial standard[100] and this could be interpreted as further evidence of an eastern origin for the asses of *L. Atratinus Augur*.

265 Bare head of M. Antony, bearded, right, lituus behind, M ANT IMP (or IM) III V R P C around (MP ligatured). *Reverse:* naked male figure (Jupiter?) standing facing, looking right, cloak over left shoulder, holding sceptre and branch, P VENTIDI on right (NT ligatured), PONT IMP on left (NT ligatured). *Silver denarius. Military mint travelling with P. Ventidius in Cilicia or northern Syria, autumn–early winter 39 BC* (Crawford 531/1a–b; Sydenham 1175; BMCRR Gaul 73; Babelon Antonia 63; Newman 39.7; RSC/Cohen 75–75a).

265

This very rare issue, for which only two obverse and two reverse dies have been recorded, was produced by Antony's lieutenant Publius Ventidius, a native of Picenum. The history of this remarkable individual goes back to his childhood in the Social War when, having been captured at Asculum, he was led through the streets of Rome as an ornament in the triumph of Pompeius Strabo, father of Pompey the Great (89 BC). Ridiculed as a muleteer in the early part of his career he eventually attracted the attention of Caesar who recognized his talents and promoted him to the rank of tribune. Having obtained a seat in the Senate he sided with Antony following the Ides of March and was instrumental in extricating the Caesarian leader from his plight at the siege of Mutina in 43 BC. A grateful Antony rewarded him with the consulship later in the year and in 42 gave him command of the legions in Gallia Narbonensis.

Despite his humble origin Ventidius was now recognized as one of the Republic's foremost generals. In the dispute between Lucius Antony and Octavian in 41–40 BC he chose not to intervene, being uncertain of Antony's position in the affair, and after the fall of Perusia he rejoined the Triumvir in the East. Here the situation was even more chaotic than in the West for while Antony had been dallying with Cleopatra in Alexandria Rome's eastern frontier had been violated by a Parthian invasion force under the joint leadership of the Roman renegade Quintus Labienus and Pacorus, son of the Parthian king Orodes II. This critical turn of events was to provide Ventidius with the opportunity to immortalize his name in the annals of Roman military history. The invaders easily defeated the Antonian governor Decidius Saxa, whose legions still retained strong republican sympathies, whereupon Syria and neighbouring Cilicia were quickly overrun. Labienus was later to extend his conquests right across southern Asia Minor as far as the Carian coast. Distracted by the prospect of a military confrontation with Octavian Antony was unable to confront the disastrous situation in person, but once their differences had been resolved at Brundisium at the end of 40 BC the Triumvirs lost no time in coming to grips with the crisis in the East. Ventidius was dispatched with orders to oppose the invaders and drive them from Roman territory, no trivial assignment for a general of his advanced years. Nevertheless, he achieved notable victories over the enemy at the Cilician Gates and at Mt. Amanus in 39 BC, eliminating Labienus in the process; and in the following year he defeated them again at Gindarus in Cyrrhestica where the Arsacid Crown prince Pacorus perished in the battle. Ventidius then proceeded to besiege Antiochus of Commagene in the fortress-city of Samosata on the Euphrates. This was enough for Antony who now appeared on the scene in person to relieve his energetic lieutenant of his command. It was clear that the Triumvir was becoming nervous that too much military glory was accruing to his subordinate. The victorious general returned to Rome where he was granted a magnificent triumph through the very streets that had seen him paraded as a captive half a century before. But the strain of the campaign had proved too much for the old warrior and he died soon afterwards. The fame he had achieved at the very end of his career earned him the rare distinction of a public funeral.

The denarii issued by P. Ventidius, according him the title of *imperator* and bearing the name and portrait of Antony, have received much attention from scholars. One school of thought connects them with the events of the Perusine War of 41–40 BC,[101] but this theory is based on false premises and must be discounted in favour of an attribution to Ventidius' campaigns in the East in 39–38 BC. The precise occasion is uncertain. Gindarus, in 38 BC, was certainly Ventidius' crowning achievement, but his imperatorial acclamation would almost certainly have followed his victories the previous year resulting in the defeat and death of Labienus, the disgraceful and shameful *Parthicus imperator*. It seems logical to place Ventidius' coinage at this time, perhaps while he was in winter quarters planning his campaign for the coming season. The curious style of the two known obverse dies, with their bearded portraits and outdated titulature, has been ingeniously explained by Newman[102] as resulting from the local copying of an earlier issue of Antony (such as no. 127) carried with him by Ventidius when he left Italy in the spring of 39 BC. The identity of the naked male figure on reverse is uncertain though the pose is reminiscent of Jupiter. In the reverse inscription Ventidius advertises his membership of the priestly college of the pontifices who supervised the ceremonies connected with the state religion of Rome. In driving the foreign invaders from Roman territory and defeating the traitorous Labienus Ventidius was perhaps invoking the divine assistance of the chief of the Roman deities.

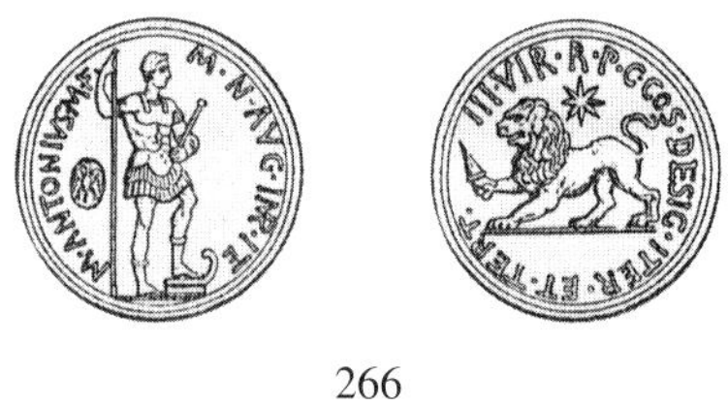

266

266 M. Antony, in military attire, standing right, resting on spear held in right hand and holding sword in left, his left foot set on prow of galley, **M ANTONIVS M F M N AVG IMP ITE** (?) around (**MP** and **TE**

The Hellenistic Odeion at Alexandria was an essential element of any cultured city where plays could be performed and readings take place. Antony wintered with Cleopatra in Alexandria in 41/40 BC.

ligatured). *Reverse:* lion prowling left, holding sword in its raised right forepaw, star above, III VIR R P C COS DESIG ITER ET TERT around. *Gold aureus. Athens, summer (?) 38 BC* (Crawford 533/1; BMCRR East, p. 505; Babelon Antonia 68; Newman 38.2; Cohen 15).

Unfortunately, the only known example of this extraordinary type was lost in the great theft from the Paris cabinet in 1831. This is all the more regretable since its obverse legend would appear to contain the only reference to Antony's second imperatorial acclamation (IMP ITE). The reading, however, is based solely on a sketch made by Morelli prior to the coin's loss and the accuracy of this drawing has been called into question by most modern scholars. The other coins in the series (see nos. 267–8a) all record the third acclamation (IMP TER or TERT), probably assumed after Ventidius' victory at Gindarus in the early summer of 38 BC, and it has to be admitted that it would not be difficult to mistake 'ITE' for 'TER', especially as we are unaware of the state of preservation of the piece. In all other respects, however, the illustration looks to have been very carefully rendered and until the matter can be settled by the discovery of a second specimen it cannot be disproved that 'IMP ITE' was the correct reading. If so, then the coin would be slightly earlier than the other types in the series and perhaps records an acclamation received for Ventidius' victory at Mt. Amanus the previous year.

The iconography of this aureus is quite remarkable. The full-length military figure of Antony depicts him in the majestic pose of the commander-in-chief of the Roman army and navy (the latter represented by the prow at his feet). The reverse has a crouching lion holding a sword and is surmounted by a radiate star – the rising sun of the Orient. Lions had already featured on the Antonian coinage on two issues of silver quinarii struck at Lugdunum in Gaul in 43 and 42 BC (see nos. 122 and 126). In the commentary on the first of these the suggestion was made that the lion represents the zodiacal sign of Leo and refers to the period of Antony's birth, just as the capricorn was later used on the coinage of Augustus. If this interpretation is to be accepted then the reverse type would be symbolic of the Triumvir as a strong and fearless warrior who is about to embark on the conquest of Rome's eastern rival, the kingdom of Parthia. There appears to be little doubt that Athens, the city of residence of Antony and Octavia during this period, was the place of mintage of this and the two following types. All exhibit the same characteristic of including the Triumvir's patronymics in the obverse inscription (M F M N, *son of Marcus*[103], *grandson of Marcus*[104]), and the denarius has his full-length standing figure, like the aureus, though depicted as a priest rather than a soldier.

267

267 M. Antony, veiled and wearing the priestly robes of an augur, standing right, holding lituus in right hand, M ANTONIVS M F M N AVGVR IMP TERT around (MP and RT ligatured). *Reverse:* radiate head of Sol right, III VIR R P C COS DESIG ITER ET TERT (or TER) around. *Silver denarius. Athens, summer 38 BC* (Crawford 533/2; Sydenham 1199; BMCRR East 141; Babelon Antonia 80; Newman 38.3; RSC/Cohen 13–13a).

Unlike the aureus no doubts exist regarding the reading of the obverse legend on the denarius of this series. As noted above it seems likely that Antony's third imperatorial acclamation (IMP TERT) resulted from Ventidius' victory at Gindarus, so this type and the next may safely be attributed to the summer of 38 BC and to the Athenian mint. This was prior to the Triumvir's decision to take a personal hand in the conduct of operations on the eastern frontier, a campaign which resulted in the succeeding issue of denarii (see nos. 269–72). Antony's depiction in the priestly robes of an augur emphasizes the importance which he placed on the possession of this religious office. The word 'augur', frequently unabbreviated, features prominently on most of the Triumvir's remaining coin issues right down to Actium. It was as though he was trying to stress his adherence to republican traditions in the face of Octavian's revolutionary drive towards an autocratic system of government for the Roman world. The head of the sun god Sol is, of course, symbolic of the East and had already appeared on denarii of Antony issued in 42–41 BC (see nos. 127 and 129). It symbolizes the renewal of the Triumvir's personal concern for eastern affairs after the distraction caused by his extended stay in Italy which had taken up the second half of 40 BC and almost the whole of the following year.

268

268 Bare head of M. Antony right, M ANTONIVS M F M N AVGVR IMP TER around. *Reverse:* head of Octavia right, her hair tied in knot behind with one long plait arranged in loop along top of head, COS DESIGN ITER ET TER III VIR R P C around. *Gold aureus. Athens, summer 38 BC* (Crawford 533/3a; Sydenham 1200; BMCRR East 144; Babelon Antonia 69; Newman 38.4; Cohen 1).

268a Similar to preceding, but with TERT for TER on obverse, and DESIG for DESIGN and TERT for TER on reverse; also, all the letter 'E's in the legends on both sides have the form 'II', and with M Γ for M F on obverse. *Gold aureus. Athens, summer 38 BC* (Crawford 533/3b; Sydenham 1201; BMCRR East, p. 508; Babelon Antonia 70 and vol. ii, pp. 592–3; Cohen 1).

The form of Antony's titulature on these aurei links them to nos. 266–7 and to the period of the Triumvir's residence in Athens with his wife Octavia. The substitution of 'II' for 'E' in the legends of no. 268a seems to represent a provincial variation on the form of the fifth letter of the Latin alphabet. It is to be found only on one pair of dies, doubtless the work of a local Athenian engraver.[105] This was to be the final appearance of Octavia on the precious metal coinage of her husband who, after taking leave of her at Corcyra in the late summer of 37 BC, was to renew his intimacy with Cleopatra at the Syrian capital of Antioch and go through a form of marriage with the Egyptian queen before the close of the year.

269

269 Bare head of M. Antony right, M ANT AVGVR III VIR R P C around. *Reverse:* trophy composed of helmet and cuirass, a curved sword attached to the right arm, a shield with incurved sides ('figure-of-eight') attached to the left, sword or dagger strapped to the waist, two round shields and two spears at base, IMP – TER across field. *Silver denarius. Military mint travelling with Antony in northern Syria, late summer–autumn 38 BC* (Crawford 536/1; Sydenham 1203; BMCRR East 148; Babelon Antonia 76; Newman 38.1; Cohen 16).

270

270 Bare head of M. Antony right, ANT AVGVR III VIR R P C around. *Reverse:* similar to preceding, but the trophy has 'figure-of-eight' shields attached to both arms, and without the sword or dagger at waist. *Silver denarius. Military mint travelling with Antony in northern Syria, late summer–autumn 38 BC* (Crawford 536/4; Sydenham 1202; BMCRR East 147; cf. Babelon Antonia 77, with M ANT for ANT, presumably in error; RSC/Cohen 17a).

271 *Obverse:* as 269. *Reverse:* trophy composed of helmet and cuirass, a curved sword attached to the right arm, a 'figure-of-eight' shield to the left, sword or dagger strapped to the waist, prow left at base of trophy to left, round shield to right, IMP – TER across field. *Silver denarius. Military mint travelling with Antony in northern Syria, late summer–autumn 38 BC* (Crawford 536/2, citing specimen in Vienna; RSC/Cohen 18d).

272

272 Bare head of M. Antony right, ANT AVGV (or AVG, AV sometimes ligatured) III VIR R P C. *Reverse:* same as preceding. *Silver denarius. Military mint travelling with Antony in northern Syria, late summer–autumn 38 BC* (Crawford 536/3; Sydenham 1204; BMCRR East 149; Babelon Antonia 78; RSC/Cohen 18–18c).

The martial theme and coarser execution of this series clearly differentiates it from the preceding group ascribed to the Athenian mint (nos. 266–8a). It seems reasonable to attribute it to Antony's expedition to northern Syria to take command of Ventidius' army at the siege of Samosata. Antony's third imperatorial acclamation (*Imperator tertio*) probably records Ventidius' victory at Gindarus in the early summer of 38 BC so this military coinage may be dated to the latter part of the year. The symbolism of the reverse type is of considerable interest as it appears to revive memories of Brutus' coinage struck four years earlier in Asia Minor. Although the primary intention was to commemorate the success of Antonian arms against the Parthian invasion force of Pacorus and Labienus it is difficult to avoid comparison with Brutus' coinage depicting a trophy with 'figure-of-eight' shield, sometimes with prows at base (see especially nos. 206–7, 209, and 211). The reason for the appearance of a prow on nos. 271 and 272 is not easily explained in an Antonian context, unless it merely draws attention to the strength of the eastern Triumvir's naval forces at a time when relations with Octavian were especially strained. The western Triumvir had failed to attend their proposed meeting at Brundisium in the spring and, incensed at what he interpreted as a deliberate slight, Antony is believed to have opened secret negotations with Lepidus. In this mood of anger and resentment might not the eastern Triumvir have begun to have regrets about Philippi and the suicide of his former friend, Marcus Brutus?

We may now move on to consider the remarkable and enigmatic series of Antonian bronze coins known collectively as the 'fleet coinage'. Few issues of the period have given rise to such widely diverse theories concerning their place of mintage, their chronology, and their purpose. Traditionally they have been associated with the Pact of Tarentum (summer 37 BC) under the terms of which Antony loaned his western colleague some 120 ships together with the services of two admirals, L. Sempronius Atratinus and M. Oppius Capito. This association certainly exists, and the later phase of the coinage ('light series') may well have been produced after the conclusion of the Pact. But several important factors have to be born in mind: firstly, this is an Antonian coinage, not a joint coinage of the two principal Triumvirs (the obverse legends refer to Antony alone); secondly, although the denominations are Roman the evidence of provenance is overwhelming that the coins circulated in the East and were in fact intended for the Greek-speaking areas of the Roman world (hence the Greek numerals Α, Β, Γ and Δ as marks of value); and finally, the earlier phase of the coinage ('heavy series') includes issues struck by a third Antonian admiral, L. Calpurnius Bibulus, who did not remain in the West with his two colleagues following the conclusion of the Pact of Tarentum and whose name does not appear on any of the issues of the 'light series'. All of this seems to point to the 'fleet coinage' having been initiated in the East, probably in the late summer of 38 BC, where it was issued simultaneously in six denominations by three admirals at their respective naval stations. Its commencement may be associated with Antony's military activities when he left Athens for the frontier region of northern Syria to take over the command from his general Ventidius. We know nothing of the details of these operations, but they could well have included some vital role for the fleet. The 'light series' would then have been a limited revival of the original coinage, struck in the following year (37 BC) to celebrate the new accord between the triumviral colleagues. It comprises only three denominations and was issued in the names of the two admirals who remained with Octavian after Antony's departure for the East in the late summer.

The 'fleet coinage' was of a truly revolutionary character and anticipates many of the changes introduced by Augustus two decades later in his sweeping reform of the Roman *aes* coinage. The largest denomination is the sestertius, or quarter denarius, traditionally a tiny silver coin but now struck for the first time in bronze. It bears both the Roman mark of value (HS) and the Greek letter-numeral Δ (= 4 asses). Next comes an unusual denomination, the tressis (3 asses), with mark of value Γ; the dupondius (2 asses), marked Β; and the as itself, marked Α. The series is completed by two fractional denominations, the semis, or half as, with its traditional mark of value S; and the quadrans (quarter as), marked with three pellets indicating that it was worth 3 unciae. Each denomination has its own distinctive obverse and reverse type, and the sestertius, tressis, dupondius, and as all have distinguishing symbols in the reverse field. The types and subsidiary symbols remain constant throughout the entire coinage (though Atratinus' issues usually include a lituus in the reverse field), so the only major differentiation between the three series is provided by the reverse legend which gives the name and titles of the responsible naval commander – L BIBVLVS M F PR DESIG, L ATRATINVS AVGVR COS DESIG, and M OPPIVS CAPITO PRO PR PRAEF CLASS F C.

273 Bare head of M. Antony right, facing draped bust of Octavia left, M ANT IMP TER COS DES ITER ET TER III VIR R P C (ANT and MP ligatured) around. *Reverse:* two standing figures (Antony and Octavia?) in quadriga of hippocamps right, HS in left field, Δ and

273

274

square object (astragalus?) below, L BIBVLVS M F PR DESIG around. *Bronze sestertius. Naval base of Bibulus in Syria (at Seleucia?), late summer–autumn 38 BC* (RPC 4088; Amandry p. 78, A; Sydenham 1255; BMCRR East, p. 510; Babelon Antonia 81).

274 Conjoined bare heads of M. Antony and Octavian right, facing draped bust of Octavia left, M ANT IMP TER COS DES ITER ET TER III VIR R P C (ANT and MP ligatured) around. *Reverse:* three galleys under sail right, Γ and triskeles below, L BIBVLVS M F PR DESIG around. *Bronze tressis. Naval base of Bibulus in Syria (at Seleucia?), late summer–autumn 38 BC* (RPC 4089; Amandry p. 78, B; Sydenham 1256; BMCRR East, p. 511).

275

275 *Obverse:* as 273. *Reverse:* two galleys under sail right, caps of the Dioscuri in upper field to left and to right, B below, L BIBVLVS M F PR DESIG around. *Bronze dupondius. Naval base of Bibulus in Syria (at Seleucia?), late summer–autumn 38 BC* (RPC 4090; Amandry p. 78, C; Sydenham 1257; BMCRR East, p. 512; cf. Babelon Antonia 83).

276 Conjoined heads of M. Antony and Octavia right, M ANT IMP TER COS DES ITER ET TER III VIR R P C (ANT and MP ligatured) around. *Reverse:* galley under sail right, A and head of Medusa (?) below, L BIBVLVS M F PR DESIG around. *Bronze as. Naval base of Bibulus in Syria (at Seleucia?), late summer–autumn 38 BC.* (RPC 4091; Amandry p. 79, D; Sydenham 1258; BMCRR East, p. 513).

277 Bare head of M. Antony right, M ANT IMP TER COS DES ITER ET TER III VIR R P C (ANT and MP ligatured) around. *Reverse:* forepart of galley right, L BIBVLVS M F PR DESIG around. *Bronze semis. Naval base of Bibulus in Syria (at Seleucia?), late summer–autumn 38 BC* (RPC 4092; Amandry p. 79, E; Sydenham 1259; BMCRR East 150; Babelon Antonia 85; cf. Cohen 97).

277

278 Janiform head (of M. Antony and Octavian?), M ANT IM TER COS DES ITER ET TER III VIR R P C (ANT ligatured) around. *Reverse:* stem of prow, three pellets in field, L BIBVLVS M F PR DESIG around. *Bronze quadrans. Naval base of Bibulus in Syria (at Seleucia?), late summer–autumn 38 BC* (RPC 4093; Amandry p. 80, F; cf. Sydenham 1260; cf. BMCRR East, p. 514).

278

L. Calpurnius Bibulus, son of M. Bibulus (Caesar's colleague in the consulship of 59 BC) and stepson of M. Junius Brutus, supported the republican cause after Caesar's assassination, was proscribed by the Triumvirs, and was present at the battle of Philippi in 42 BC. Pardoned by Antony, he rapidly achieved prominence in the circle of the eastern Triumvir's closest advisers and acted as a mediator in the delicate negotiations between the triumviral colleagues. Following in his father's footsteps he became a naval commander, in which role he was responsible for the production of part of Antony's 'fleet coinage' in the latter part of 38 BC. These coins have mostly been found in the East (Cyprus, Syria, Phoenicia, and Judaea) which would indicate that the fleet commanded by Bibulus was probably stationed on the Syrian coast at this time, perhaps at Seleucia (the port for Antioch). The reverse inscription accords him the title *praetor designatus* and he went on to hold the praetorship in 35 BC and the governorship of Syria from 34 until his death two years later.

279

279 Bare head of M. Antony right, facing draped bust of Octavia left, M ANT IMP TER COS DES ITER ET TER III VIR R P C (ANT and MP ligatured) around. *Reverse:* two standing figures (Antony and Octavia?) in quadriga of hippocamps right, HS in left field, Δ and square object (astragalus?) below, lituus above hippocamps' heads, L ATRATINVS AVGVR COS DESIG around. *Bronze sestertius ('heavy series', ca. 36 mm/21 gm). Naval base of Atratinus in Greece (at Lechaeum?), late summer–autumn 38 BC* (RPC 1453; Amandry p. 80, A; Sydenham 1261; Babelon Antonia 73; Cohen 5).

For another coin of this type, see no. 291 ('light series').

280

280 Conjoined bare heads of M. Antony and Octavian right, facing draped bust of Octavia left, M ANT IMP TER COS DES ITER ET TER III VIR R P C (ANT and MP ligatured) around. *Reverse:* three galleys under sail right, Γ and triskeles below, lituus above the prows, L ATRATINVS AVGVR COS DESIG around. *Bronze tressis. Naval base of Atratinus in Greece (at Lechaeum?), late summer–autumn 38 BC.* (RPC 1454; Amandry p. 81, B; Sydenham 1262; BMCRR East, p. 515).

281

282

281 *Obverse:* as 279. *Reverse:* two galleys under sail right, caps of the Dioscuri in upper field to left and to right, B below, lituus above or before the prows, L ATRATINVS AVGVR COS DESIG around. *Bronze dupondius ('heavy series', ca. 27 mm/12 gm). Naval base of Atratinus in Greece (at Lechaeum?), late summer–autumn 38 BC* (RPC 1455; Amandry p. 82, C; Sydenham 1263; BMCRR East, p. 516; Babelon Antonia 74; cf. Cohen 7).

For another coin of this type, see no. 292 ('light series').

282 Conjoined heads of M. Antony and Octavia right, M ANT IMP TER COS DES ITER ET TER III VIR R P C (ANT and MP ligatured) around. *Reverse:* galley under sail right, A and head of Medusa (?) below (the A is sometimes above the galley to left of the sail), lituus sometimes above prow, L ATRATINVS AVGVR COS DESIG around. *Bronze as ('heavy series', ca. 24 mm/9.5 gm). Naval base of Atratinus in Greece (at Lechaeum?), late summer–autumn 38 BC* (RPC 1456; Amandry p. 82, D; Sydenham 1264; BMCRR East, p. 516).

For another coin of this type, see no. 293 ('light series').

283 Bare head of M. Antony right, M ANT IMP TER COS DES ITER ET TER III VIR R P C (ANT and MP ligatured) around. *Reverse:* forepart of galley right, S above, L ATRATINVS AVGVR COS DESIG around. *Bronze semis. Naval base of Atratinus in Greece (at Lechaeum?), late summer–autumn 38 BC* (RPC 1457; Amandry p. 83, E).

284 Janiform head (of M. Antony and Octavian?), M ANT IMP TER COS DES ITER ET TER III VIR R P C (ANT and MP ligatured) around. *Reverse:* stem of prow (sometimes resembling lituus), three pellets in field, L ATRATINVS AVGVR COS DESIG around. *Bronze quadrans. Naval base of Atratinus in Greece (at Lechaeum?), late summer–autumn 38 BC* (RPC 1458; Amandry p. 83, F).

We have already met with L. Sempronius Atratinus in connection with an earlier issue of asses made for Antony, possibly in Asia in 40–39 BC (see no. 264). This individual had been elected to the priestly college of augurs in 40 BC and appointed consul designate at the time of the Pact of Misenum in the summer of the following year, though he did not actually hold the supreme magistracy until 34 BC when Antony resigned in his favour. His participation in the 'fleet coinage' extended over both the 'heavy series' and the later 'light series', the latter possibly struck in southern Italy after the conclusion of the accord known as the Pact of Tarentum in the summer of 37 BC. The evidence of provenance points to Atratinus' fleet having been stationed in Greece at the time of the commencement of the 'fleet coinage', and Corinth is suggested as the possible site of his headquarters by the authors of *Roman Provincial Coinage* (p. 285). If their surmise is correct then the port of Lechaeum on the Corinthian Gulf would be the most likely place for Atratinus' mint. After the establishment of the Roman *colonia* of Corinth in 44 BC there was a rapid growth in the importance of the harbour at Lechaeum, and in the 1st century AD it was linked to Corinth's forum by a paved street. Issues of local coinage – at Sparta in the Peloponnese, and later at the Sicilian mints of Entella and Lilybaeum[106] – attest to the varied career of this Antonian lieutenant, both during his period of command in Greece and whilst he was assisting Octavian against Sextus Pompey in accordance with the terms of the Pact of Tarentum.

285

285 Bare head of M. Antony right, facing draped bust of Octavia left, M ANT IMP TERT COS DESIG ITER ET TER III VIR R P C (NT, MP,

TE, and RT all ligatured) around. *Reverse:* two standing figures (Antony and Octavia?) in quadriga of hippocamps right, HS in left field, Δ and square object (astragalus?) below, M OPPIVS CAPITO PRO PR PRAEF CLASS F C around. *Bronze sestertius ('heavy series', ca. 37 mm/31 gm). Naval base of Capito in Greece (at Piraeus?), late summer–autumn 38 BC* (RPC 1462; Amandry p. 102, A; Sydenham 1265; BMCRR East 152).

For another coin of this type, see no. 294 ('light series').

286

286 Conjoined bare heads of M. Antony and Octavian right, facing draped bust of Octavia left, M ANT IMP TERT COS DESIG ITER ET TER III VIR R P C (NT, MP, TE, and RT all ligatured) around. *Reverse:* three galleys under sail right, Γ and triskeles below, M OPPIVS CAPITO PRO PR PRAEF CLASS F C around. *Bronze tressis. Naval base of Capito in Greece (at Piraeus?), late summer–autumn 38 BC* (RPC 1463; Amandry p. 102, B; Sydenham 1266; BMCRR East 154; Babelon Antonia 90; Cohen 1).

287 *Obverse:* as 285. *Reverse:* two galleys under sail right, caps of the Dioscuri in upper field to left and to right, B below, M OPPIVS CAPITO PRO PR PRAEF CLASS F C around. *Bronze dupondius ('heavy series', ca. 26 mm/15 gm). Naval base of Capito in Greece (at Piraeus?), late summer-autumn 38 BC* (RPC 1464; Amandry p. 103, C; Sydenham 1267; BMCRR East 155–7; Babelon Antonia 88; Cohen 12).

For another coin of this type, see no. 295 ('light series').

288

288 Conjoined heads of M. Antony and Octavia right, M ANT IMP TERT COS DESIG ITER ET TER III VIR R P C (NT, MP, TE, and RT all ligatured) around. *Reverse:* galley under sail right, A and head of Medusa (?) below, M OPPIVS CAPITO PRO PR PRAEF CLASS F C around. *Bronze as ('heavy series', ca. 22 mm/8 gm). Naval base of Capito in Greece (at Piraeus?), late summer–autumn 38 BC* (RPC 1465; Amandry p. 104, D; Sydenham 1268; BMCRR East 164).

For another coin of this type, see no. 296 ('light series').

289

289 Bare head of M. Antony right, M ANT IMP TERT COS DESIG ITER ET TER III VIR R P C (NT, MP, TE, and RT all ligatured) around. *Reverse:* forepart of galley right, S above, M OPPIVS CAPITO PRO PR PRAEF CLASS F C around. *Bronze semis. Naval base of Capito in Greece (at Piraeus?), late summer–autumn 38 BC* (RPC 1466; Amandry p. 105, E; Sydenham 1269; BMCRR East, p. 520; Babelon Antonia 86; Cohen 98).

290

290 Janiform head (of M. Antony and Octavian?), M ANT IMP TERT COS DESIG ITER ET TER III VIR R P C (NT, MP, TE, and RT all ligatured) around. *Reverse:* stem of prow, three pellets in field, M OPPI CAP PRAEF CLASS F C around. *Bronze quadrans. Naval base of Capito in Greece (at Piraeus?), late summer–autumn 38 BC* (RPC 1467; Amandry p. 106, F; cf. Sydenham 1270; cf. BMCRR East, p. 520).

Little is known of the Antonian admiral M. Oppius Capito, though he seems to have occupied an important position in the eastern Triumvir's inner circle of officers. His coins are more numerous than those of his colleagues and he is the only one of the three to include the title *praefectus classis* ('prefect of the fleet') in his inscriptions. Like Atratinus, Capito's coins are found principally in Greece, and given their relative abundance it seems logical to associate them with Antony and Octavia's normal place of residence at this time, the city of Athens. A large part of the Antonian fleet was doubtless anchored at Piraeus, the great harbour complex of Athens, and Capito's mint may well have been located there.

Three of the denominations of the 'fleet coinage' – sestertius, dupondius, and as – belong to two apparently separate issues, the 'heavy series' (which includes the other denominations) and the 'light series'. The former was struck in the names of all three admirals, Bibulus, Atratinus, and Capito, whilst Bibulus is omitted from the 'light series' which appears to be later in date. It is tempting to associate this dramatic reduction in size and weight with a change in the location of the fleet, perhaps resulting from Antony's journey west in the late spring of 37 BC to confer with Octavian. The result of their meeting was the Pact of Tarentum, by one of the terms of which the eastern Triumvir lent to his colleague part of his fleet (approximately 120 ships) together with the services of the admirals Atratinus and Capito. This might well have been the occasion for the partial revival of the 'fleet coinage' on a lighter weight standard, with Tarentum as the likely mint. It is interesting that when Augustus carried out his reform of the *aes* coinage almost two decades later it was precisely these three denominations (sestertius, dupondius, and as) which were introduced.

291

291 Bare head of M. Antony right, facing draped bust of Octavia left, M ANT IMP TER COS DES ITER ET TER III VIR R P C (ANT and MP ligatured) around. *Reverse:* two standing figures (Antony and Octavia?) in quadriga of hippocamps right, HS in left field, Δ and square object (astragalus?) below, lituus above hippocamps' heads, L ATRATINVS AVGVR COS DESIG around. *Bronze sestertius ('light series', ca. 27 mm/12 gm). Tarentum (?), summer 37 BC* (RPC 1459; Amandry p. 83, A; Sydenham 1261; BMCRR East 151).

For the equivalent coin of the 'heavy series', see no. 279.

292

292 *Obverse:* as preceding. *Reverse:* two galleys under sail right, caps of the Dioscuri in upper field to left and to right, B below, lituus above or before the prows, L ATRATINVS AVGVR COS DESIG around. *Bronze dupondius ('light series', ca. 23 m/7.5 gm). Tarentum (?),* *summer 37 BC* (RPC 1460; Amandry p. 84, B; Sydenham 1263; Babelon Antonia 75; cf. Cohen 8).

For the equivalent coin of the 'heavy series', see no. 281.

293 Conjoined heads of M. Antony and Octavia right, M ANT IMP TER COS DES ITER ET TER III VIR R P C (ANT and MP ligatured) around. *Reverse:* galley under sail right, A and head of Medusa (?) below, lituus sometimes above prow, L ATRATINVS AVGVR COS DESIG around. *Bronze as ('light series', ca. 20 mm/5 gm). Tarentum (?), summer 37 BC* (RPC 1461; Amandry p. 84, C; Sydenham 1264).

For the equivalent coin of the 'heavy series', see no. 282.

294 Bare head of M. Antony right, facing draped bust of Octavia left, M ANT IMP TERT COS DESIG ITER ET TER III VIR R P C (NT, MP, TE, and RT all ligatured) around. *Reverse:* two standing figures (Antony and Octavia?) in quadriga of hippocamps right, HS in left field, Δ and square object (astragalus?) below, M OPPIVS CAPITO PRO PR PRAEF CLASS F C around. *Bronze sestertius ('light series', ca. 26 mm/13 gm). Tarentum (?), summer 37 BC* (RPC 1468; Amandry p. 106, A; Sydenham 1265; BMCRR East 153; Babelon Antonia 89; Cohen 13).

For the equivalent coin of the 'heavy series', see no. 285

295 *Obverse:* as preceding. *Reverse:* two galleys under sail right, caps of the Dioscuri in upper field to left and to right, B below, M OPPIVS CAPITO PRO PR PRAEF CLASS F C around. *Bronze dupondius ('light series', ca. 22 mm/7.5 gm). Tarentum (?), summer 37 BC* (RPC 1469; Amandry p. 107, B; Sydenham 1267; BMCRR East 158–63).

For the equivalent coin of the 'heavy series', see no. 287.

296

296 Conjoined heads of M. Antony and Octavia right, M ANT IMP TERT COS DESIG ITER ET TER III VIR R P C (NT, MP, TE, and RT all ligatured) around. *Reverse:* galley under sail right, A and head of Medusa (?) below, M OPPIVS CAPITO PRO PR PRAEF CLASS F C around. *Bronze as ('light series', ca. 15 mm/4 gm). Tarentum (?), summer 37 BC* (RPC 1470; Amandry p. 108, C; Sydenham 1268; BMCRR East 165–71; Babelon Antonia 87; Cohen 11).

For the equivalent coin of the 'heavy series', see no. 288.

After taking leave of his western colleague in the late summer of 37 BC Antony returned to the East. Here, his destiny awaited him in the person of

Queen Cleopatra of Egypt and the long-projected invasion of Parthia which held the key to his ultimate success or his final ruination. At this critical point in history the future course of events in the Roman world truly hung in the balance. As it was, fate was to smile on Octavian and to turn its back on Antony. With the probable exception of the following rare type there were to be no further issues of coinage by the eastern Triumvir until well after the Parthian debacle in 36 BC. By this time Octavian's star was firmly in the ascendant by virtue of his victory over Sextus Pompey and the removal of Lepidus from the political scene.

297

297 Bare head of M. Antony right, ANTONIVS AVGVR COS DES ITER ET TERT around. *Reverse:* Armenian tiara, bow and arrow in saltire in background, IMP TERTIO III VIR R P C around. *Silver denarius. Antioch, or military mint travelling with Canidius Crassus in Armenia, autumn 37 BC* (Crawford 539/1; Sydenham 1205; BMCRR East 172; Babelon Antonia 94; Newman 35.1; Cohen 19).

The interpretation of this celebrated Antonian type has exercised the minds of scholars for many years. It has been variously attributed to the time of Antony's conquest of Armenia in 34 BC (by Babelon); to the bestowal of Lesser Armenia on Polemo of Pontus, placed by Grueber (in BMCRR) in 35 BC, though the actual date of this event has not been firmly established; again to the campaign of Antony against Artavasdes of Armenia, which Sydenham wrongly dates to 35 BC instead of 34; to 36 or 35 BC by Crawford, who states 'the types of this issue apparently reflect Antonius' Armenian expedition of 36', though he fails to elaborate on which expedition he has in mind (36 BC was the year of Antony's full-scale invasion of Parthia and the harrowing Roman retreat following the failure before Phraaspa);[107] and most recently to 35 BC by Newman, who, after giving sound reasons for rejecting the arguments of earlier writers, states without conviction that the coin 'must be dated to 35 and must have some connection to the Armenian campaign, but not necessarily the one against Artavasdes'. All this seems rather unsatisfactory. What we know for sure is that the Triumvir's titulature fixes the period of issue between the third imperatorial acclamation and the assumption of the second consulship, *i.e.* from the summer of 38 BC to the end of 35. This eliminates any connection with Antony's campaign in 34 resulting in the deposition of Artavasdes and the organization of Armenia as a Roman province. The preceding year (35 BC) had been devoted to repairing the damage done to the eastern Triumvir's army and to his military reputation by the debacle in Parthia, and to the final elimination of Sextus Pompey in Asia Minor. The whole of 36 BC was lost to the disastrous invasion of Parthia and the agony of the slow wintertime retreat, and could hardly have provided the opportunity for the celebration of a success in Armenia by an issue of coinage. That success could only have been the invasion of the country by Antony's general Canidius Crassus, undertaken in the autumn of 37 BC as a prelude to the Triumvir's attack on Parthia in the spring of the following year. Canidius' campaign was a brilliant success, resulting in the defeat of the Parthian ally Artavasdes and his professed transfer of loyalties to Rome. Such an achievement would certainly have warranted an issue of coinage, though whether it was produced for Antony by his lieutenant at a military mint in Armenia, or whether the Triumvir struck it himself at his headquarters in Antioch, is difficult to determine. The fine style of the engraving would tend to favour the latter option. Ironically, Canidius' success ultimately led to Antony's undoing, for the new royal 'ally' was to betray the Romans at a most critical juncture of the invasion resulting in the destruction of the vital baggage train and the loss of two entire legions.

B. Issues of Octavian

The weakness of Octavian's position in the immediate post-Philippi period is clearly demonstrated by his coinage which, in marked contrast to the victorious Antony's extensive issues in Asia (see nos. 237–51), is on a very limited scale. The only coins which may be attributed to 41 BC – the troubled year of Lucius Antony's consulship and the outbreak of the Perusine War – are two scarce denarius types, one with the name of Octavian's legate L. Cornelius Balbus, the other commemorating the erection of an equestrian statue.

298

298 Bare head of Octavian right, usually with slight beard, C CAESAR III VIR R P C around. *Reverse:* club left, BALBVS / PRO PR above and below. *Silver denarius. Military mint travelling with Octavian in Italy, late 41 BC* (Crawford 518/1; Sydenham 1325a; BMCRR Gaul 83; Babelon Julia 91, Cornelia 78; Newman 41.15; Cohen 417).

Lucius Cornelius Balbus, a native of the Spanish city of Gades (modern *Cadiz*), achieved prominence even in an age of noteworthy personalities. Usually distinguished as 'Balbus Major' he served with distinction in the war against Sertorius in the 70s and received Roman citizenship in 72 BC through the influence of Pompey. Following his move to Rome he became enormously wealthy and influential and was an intimate friend of both Pompey and Caesar, though he was always closer to the latter under whom he served for a time in Gaul. In 56 BC he was defended by Cicero against the charge of illegal usurpation of the citizenship[108] and acquitted. Although nominally neutral following the outbreak of civil war in 49 BC he clearly favoured the cause of the dictator whom he openly served after Pompey's downfall at Pharsalus. Obviously a man of acute political foresight Balbus supported the shaky cause of Caesar's youthful heir in the turbulent period following the 'Ides of March'. His eventual reward was the consulship, the first time in Roman history that the chief magistracy had been held by a foreign-born citizen. This took place in 40 BC following the accord reached by Antony and Octavian at the Pact of Brundisium signed in early October. Balbus' colleague in his brief tenure of the consulship was Antony's general P. Canidius Crassus, destined to be one of the few individuals sentenced to death by Octavian a decade later following the end of the civil war. Balbus himself probably died in the year of Actium (31 BC). He is mentioned as having been present the previous year at the deathbed of Cicero's confidant Pomponius Atticus.[109] With him on this occasion was Marcus Agrippa, the son-in-law of Atticus. Such was the wealth of Cornelius Balbus that in his will he was able to bequeath to every citizen of Rome the sum of 25 silver denarii, the equivalent of one gold piece.

The precise occasion for Balbus' production of denarii on behalf of Octavian is hard to determine, though it seems reasonable to associate the issue with the young Triumvir's military activities at the time of the outbreak of the Perusine War. Balbus strikes as propraetor, an office he may well have held the year prior to his consulship, whilst the club of Hercules makes reference to his Gaditane origin.[110] Obverse die linkages prove that the following type should be associated with Balbus' signed denarii, though the issue was made solely in the Triumvir's name.

299

299 Bare head of Octavian right, usually with slight beard, C CAESAR III VIR R P C around. *Reverse:* equestrian statue of Octavian galloping left, his right hand extended, POPVL IVSSV in exergue and on right. *Silver denarius. Military mint travelling with Octavian in Italy, late 41 BC* (Crawford 518/2; Sydenham 1317; BMCRR Gaul 79; Babelon Julia 97; Newman 41.16; Cohen 227).

This equestrian statue is quite different from the one depicted two years earlier on Octavian's initial issue of portrait denarii (see no. 131). It appears again on a gold aureus of Octavian belonging to the closing phase of the triumviral rivalry (see no. 394) and in all likelihood represents the monument erected in Rome to honour Caesar's heir following the battle of Philippi.

300

300 Bare head of Octavian right, with slight beard, C CAESAR III VIR R P C around. *Reverse:* thunderbolt, Q SALVIVS IMP (MP sometimes ligatured) COS DESIG (or DESG, sometimes with G above) around. *Silver denarius. Military mint travelling with Octavian in Italy, early 40 BC* (Crawford 523/1; Sydenham 1326–6b; BMCRR Gaul 86–8; Babelon Julia 92–3; Newman 40.7; Cohen 514).

The Q. Salvius of this brief issue may be identified with Quintus Salvius Salvidienus Rufus, the boyhood friend and confidant of Octavian who, despite his humble origins,[111] quickly rose to prominence under the triumviral government and was given a succession of important military commands. In 42

BC Octavian made him admiral of his fleet and instructed him to attack Sextus Pompey in Sicily. Despite being worsted by his adversary in an engagement off Rhegium Salvidienus was granted the title of *imperator* which appears on this coin. The following year he played a prominent role in the Perusine War which led to his appointment to the governorship of Gaul early in 40 BC. In this vital post, which carried with it the command of a large legionary force, Salvidienus was the successor of Antony's lieutenant Fufius Calenus. It was a measure of Octavian's total confidence in his general that he would elevate him to such an influential and politically sensitive position, for it was certain that a change of this magnitude in the balance of military manpower would not go unchallenged by Antony. But Octavian went even further and designated his lieutenant to hold the supreme magistracy in 39 BC (hence the *consul designatus* in the reverse legend). Unfortunately, the episode was to have a tragic outcome. Salvidienus proved to be unworthy of his friend's trust and entered into secret negotiations with Antony who was returning to Italy from the East to settle accounts with his young triumviral colleague. Clearly, Salvidienus must have believed that the end of Octavian's political career was at hand and wanted to secure his own future by coming to terms with the powerful victor of Philippi. But he had miscalculated, and when the Triumvirs made peace at Brundisium in the autumn of 40 BC Antony felt obliged to reveal to Octavian the faithlessness of his lieutenant. Salvidienus was recalled to Rome and denounced before the Senate which declared him a public enemy. His death quickly followed, whether by execution or by his own hand is not known, and a potentially brilliant career came to an abrupt and pathetic end.

The most likely occasion for Salvidienus' issue of denarii for Octavian was during the aftermath of the Perusine War in the early months of 40 BC, just prior to his departure to take up the governorship of Gaul. The Triumvir's titulature and portrait style are similar to the issues ascribed to the earlier part of the war (see nos. 298–9). Some light has been thrown on the significance of the reverse type by the discovery in the neighbourhood of Perusia of sling bullets bearing a thunderbolt and the inscription **Q SAL IM**.[112] The thunderbolt appears to be connected with some legend of prophecy associated with Salvidienus' youth.

301 Bare head of Octavian right, with slight beard, **CAESAR IMP** around. *Reverse:* bare head of M. Antony right, **ANTONIVS IMP** around. *Gold aureus. Southern or central Italian mint, late 40–early 39 BC* (Crawford 529/1; Sydenham 1327; BMCRR Gaul 90; Babelon Julia 62; Newman 39.8; Cohen 5).

301

This aureus, and the following silver denarii and quinarii, represent Octavian's coinage in commemoration of the Pact of Brundisium signed by the Triumvirs in October of 40 BC. For the corresponding issue of Antony, see nos. 260–1. Unlike their Antonian counterparts, Octavian's aurei and denarii lack the triumviral title in their inscriptions. This has sometimes given rise to speculation that the series should be attributed to an earlier period, prior to the formation of the Triumvirate in November of 43 BC. Stylistically, however, the coins would seem to belong to the era of the Perusine War and its aftermath, and in any case the hoard evidence clearly indicates a date of issue no earlier than 40/39 BC. The quinarii, although unmatched by corresponding issues in the Antonian series, have to be related to the new triumviral accord by virtue of their types. The denomination had special associations with the Gallic provinces and these coins may have been struck at the time of Octavian's visit to Gaul towards the end of 39 BC. It would have been particularly important for the young Triumvir to stress the new harmony in a region which had so recently witnessed his questionable appropriation of the Antonian military establishment and the treasonous behaviour of his appointee as governor, Salvidienus Rufus. Indeed, the theme of *concordia* would have possessed even greater significance at this time than earlier in the year, for the agreement with Sextus Pompey had been negotiated in the summer (Pact of Misenum) bringing with it the hope of more settled conditions in the western Mediterranean area.

302

302 Bare head of Octavian right, with slight beard, CAESAR IMP around. *Reverse:* caduceus, ANTONIVS IMP (counter-clockwise) around. *Silver denarius. Southern or central Italian mint, late 40–early 39 BC* (Crawford 529/2a; Sydenham 1327a; BMCRR Gaul 93; Babelon Julia 60; Newman 39.9; Cohen 6).

302a

302a Similar to preceding, but the legend on reverse reads clockwise. *Silver denarius. Southern or central Italian mint, late 40–early 39 BC* (Crawford 529/2c; Sydenham 1327a; BMCRR Gaul 92; Babelon Julia 60; Newman 39.9; RSC/Cohen 6a).

302b Similar to 302, but the legend on reverse is ANTON IMP. *Silver denarius. Southern or central Italian mint, late 40–early 39 BC* (Crawford 529/2b; Sydenham 1327b; BMCRR Gaul, p. 409, note 1; Babelon Julia 61; Cohen 5).

303

303 Bare head of M. Antony right, ANTONIVS IMP around. *Reverse:* caduceus, CAESAR IMP (counter-clockwise) around. *Silver denarius. Southern or central Italian mint, late 40–early 39 BC* (Crawford 529/3; Sydenham 1328; BMCRR Gaul 94; Babelon Antonia 15; Newman 39.10; Cohen 5).

304

304 Veiled and diademed head of Concordia right, III VIR R P C around. *Reverse:* clasped right hands holding caduceus, M ANTON C CAESAR around. *Silver quinarius. Military mint travelling with Octavian in Gaul, late 39 BC* (Crawford 529/4b; Sydenham 1195; BMCRR East 128, 130; Babelon Antonia 42; RSC/Cohen 67, 67a).

There is much variation in the size of Concordia's head on this issue.

304a Similar to preceding, but the legend on reverse is M ANTON C CAESAR IMP. *Silver quinarius. Military mint travelling with Octavian in Gaul, late 39 BC* (Crawford 529/4a, citing specimen in Copenhagen; Newman 39.11; RSC/Cohen 67b).

A remarkable feature of this entire series is the prominence accorded by Octavian to his triumviral colleague. Whereas Antony's coinage in celebration of the Brundisium agreement mentions his younger partner merely in a subsidiary role, Octavian strikes a denarius bearing Antony's portrait alone with his own name relegated to the reverse (no. 303). Further, the quinarii give

Antony's name precedence over that of Octavian. If, as seems likely, the coins were struck in Gaul then Octavian may have been adopting a deliberately conciliatory attitude in a region which had so recently been under the control of Antony's generals. All of this should be taken as strong evidence of the dominant position still enjoyed by Antony at this time. That pre-eminence was to endure for several years more, but all the time the politically astute young Caesar was employing all his guile to strengthen his position at the expense of the older man and almost imperceptibly the balance of power began to shift.

305 Wreathed head of the deified Julius Caesar right, star (*sidus Iulium*) before forehead, **IMP DIVI IVLI F TER III VIR R P C** around. *Reverse:* **M AGRIPPA COS / DESIG** in two lines across field. *Gold aureus. Military mint travelling with Agrippa in Gaul or with Octavian in Italy, 38 BC* (Crawford 534/1; Sydenham 1329; BMCRR Gaul 102; Babelon Julia 130; Newman 38.5; Cohen 33).

305

306 Wreathed head of Julius Caesar right facing bare head of Octavian left, **DIVOS IVLIVS** behind the dictator's head, **DIVI F** behind that of the triumvir. *Reverse:* same as preceding. *Silver denarius. Military mint travelling with Agrippa in Gaul or with Octavian in Italy, 38 BC* (Crawford 534/2; Sydenham 1330; BMCRR Gaul 100; Babelon Julia 129; Newman 38.6; Cohen 5).

306

307 Bare head of Octavian right, with slight beard, **IMP CAESAR DIVI IVLI F** around. *Reverse:* same as preceding. *Silver denarius. Military mint travelling with Agrippa in Gaul or with Octavian in Italy, 38 BC* (Crawford 534/3; Sydenham 1331; BMCRR Gaul 103; Babelon Julia 131; Newman 38.7; Cohen 545).

307

This important coinage was the first to bear the name of Octavian's principal lieutenant and the military architect of his future greatness, Marcus Vipsanius Agrippa. A contemporary and boyhood friend of the Triumvir, Agrippa was born of an obscure but prosperous family. He was at Octavian's side from the very beginning of the future emperor's political career, at the time of Caesar's assassination, and remained totally devoted to his friend's interests throughout the remaining thirty-two years of his life. It was through Agrippa's military genius, at sea as well as on land, that the threat of Sextus Pompey was finally removed at Naulochus in 36 BC and the decisive victory achieved over Antony and Cleopatra at Actium five years later.

Given Agrippa's unique relationship with Octavian it is scarcely surprising that this coinage should exhibit so many interesting features. Iconographically, the obverse of one of the denarii (no. 306) is remarkable for its depiction of confronted portraits. It may be surmised that the design was influenced by the 'dynastic' aureus of Sextus Pompey struck several years earlier in Sicily (see no. 332). The obverse legend uses the curiously archaic form **DIVOS** for **DIVVS** in identifying the portrait of the deified dictator, the same characteristic which is to be observed on the contemporary bronze coinage struck by Octavian in Italy (see nos. 308–9). Of greater significance was Octavian's adoption for the first time of the *praenomen imperatoris* (**IMP CAESAR**) in place of the traditional form in which it appears as a *cognomen*

(CAESAR IMP). This was to be important for the future development of imperial nomenclature as it personalized the position of the holder as overall head of the military, a prerequisite for any autocratic ruler. Following its use by Augustus the *praenomen imperatoris* lapsed for a while until the latter part of Nero's reign (*c.*AD 66). It was eagerly adopted by the rulers of the next imperial dynasty, the Flavian, and thereafter was employed regularly to denote the supreme authority of the emperor. The aureus (no. 305) shows a rejuvenated head of Julius Caesar, symbolizing his deification.[113] Associated with this portrait is a depiction of the *sidus Iulium*, or 'Julian star', the comet which appeared in the heavens shortly after the dictator's assassination. Such an occurrence was, of course, immediately interpreted as a sign of his coming apotheosis, a most fortuitous turn of events for the Caesarians. The same feature occurs on one of the contemporary Italian bronze types of Octavian, though here it appears before the portrait of the young Triumvir (see no. 309). The obverse legend is rather clumsily constructed on this aureus – *Imperator, Divi Iuli filius, tertio, triumvir reipublicae constituendae*. Although the portrait is that of Caesar the legend refers to Octavian (though he is not actually named) and appears to record his third imperatorial acclamation. It seems likely that this was granted in recognition of Agrippa's victories as governor of Gaul in 38 BC.

Unlike many of the issues of this period the series bearing the name of Marcus Agrippa can be placed in its precise chronological context. Octavian's lieutenant is named as 'consul designate', a title he bore in 38 BC in anticipation of his first consulship the following year.[114] Production of this coinage is generally assigned to a mint in Gaul in connection with Agrippa's extensive military activities there as governor, and this attribution is in all likelihood correct. But the possibility that it was struck by Octavian himself cannot be dismissed. The Triumvir was also quite active militarily during 38 BC, in southern Italy where he was endeavouring to put an end to the Pompeian menace in Sicily. He had actually achieved some success in this venture before suffering his near-fatal setback in the Straits of Messana. If the series was issued by the Triumvir then he would have been paying his friend a remarkable compliment by devoting the reverses of all three types to a simple inscription honouring the consul designate. A factor which could be interpreted as being in favour of the attribution to Octavian's mint is the remarkable iconography of the series, with its strong emphasis on the superiority of the younger Triumvir's claim to authority through his unique distinction of being *divi filius* – son of Rome's most recent deity, *Divus Iulius*.[115] Here we can surely detect the subtle hand of Octavian himself, though detailed instructions could have been sent to Agrippa in Gaul regarding the precise form which this coinage was to take. The same message comes through clearly on the following bronze issues which undoubtedly emanated from an Octavianic mint, possibly in southern Italy.

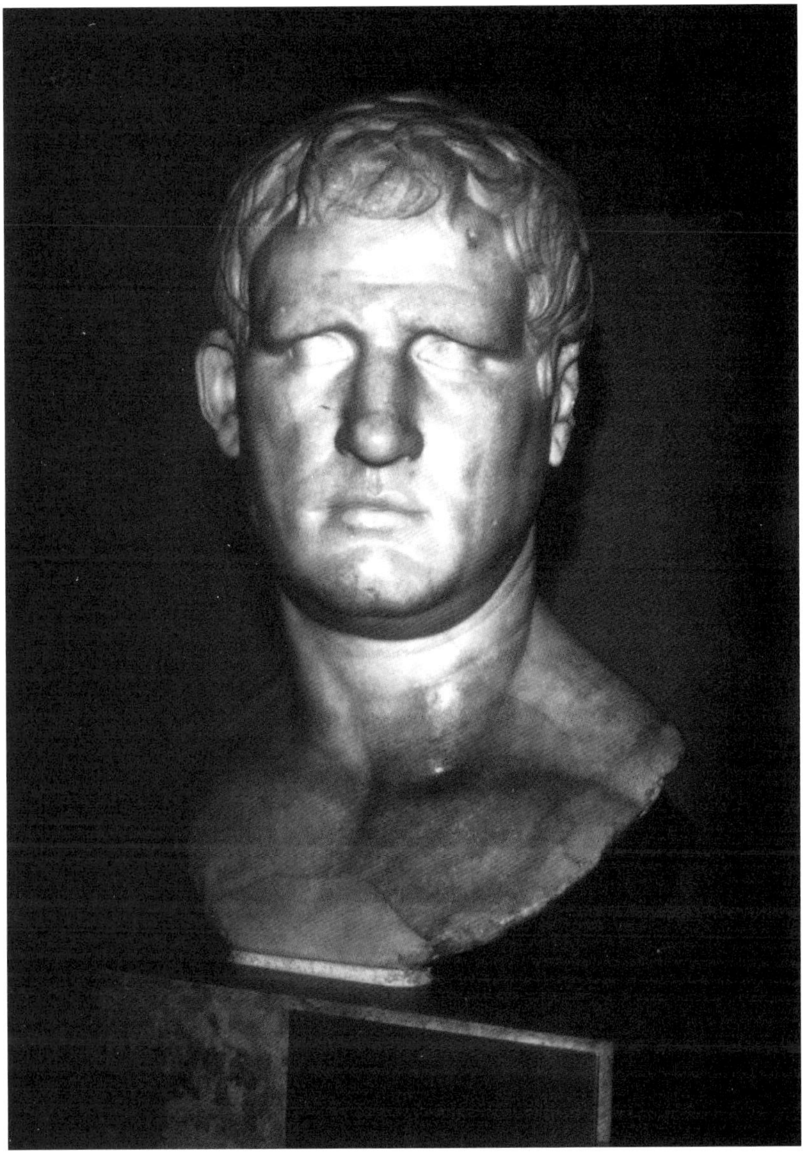

Designated as Augustus' heir before his death in 12 BC, this marble portrait bust of Agrippa well exemplifies the career military man. Ny Carlsberg Glyptotek, Copenhagen.

308 Bare head of Octavian right, with slight beard, CAESAR before, DIVI F behind. *Reverse:* wreathed head of Julius Caesar right, DIVOS before, IVLIVS behind. *Bronze sestertius or dupondius. Southern Italian mint (?), 38 BC* (RPC 620; Crawford 535/1; FITA pp. 49–50 and pl. i, 14; Sydenham 1335; BMCRR Gaul 106; Babelon Julia 98–9; Cohen 3–4).

308

309

309 Bare head of Octavian right, with slight beard, star (*sidus Iulium*) before, DIVI F behind. *Reverse:* DIVOS / IVLIVS in two lines within laurel-wreath. *Bronze sestertius or dupondius*. Southern Italian mint (?), 38 BC. (RPC 621; Crawford 535/2; FITA pp. 47–9; Sydenham 1336; BMCRR Gaul 108; Babelon Julia 101; Cohen 95).

Unlike Antony's 'fleet coinage' these handsome bronzes of Octavian bear no indication of their denomination. Grueber[116] calls them sestertii whilst Amandry[117] considers them to be dupondii. Either could be correct. The weight standard appears to be between 19 and 20 grams[118] which is closest to the tressis in the 'fleet coinage' (heavy series). On the evidence of provenance and style the former attributions to Gallic mints (Nemausus and Lugdunum) can no longer be considered tenable, though many of the ancient imitations of these types may have been produced in Gaul. An Italian origin now seems well established, though the actual location of the mint must remain a matter for speculation. Octavian was certainly active in the south of the peninsula during 38 BC and it is possible that these issues were connected with his campaign against the renegade Sextus Pompey. Tarentum was the port of embarkation for Octavian on his ill-fated voyage through the Straits of Messana and it has already been suggested that the same city may have been the mint for the revived Antonian 'fleet coinage' of Atratinus and Capito issued in the summer of the following year (see nos. 291–6). Whatever its precise origin the 'Divos Iulius' *aes* coinage may be viewed as supplementary to the gold and silver issues bearing the name of Marcus Agrippa as consul designate (see nos. 305–7), with which it shares a number of important characteristics already specified above. The propaganda value of the types and legends is obvious. The young Triumvir is depicted as the son and heir of the god Julius whose apotheosis was foretold by the miraculous appearance of a comet. What could Antony possibly boast to rival such a genealogy?

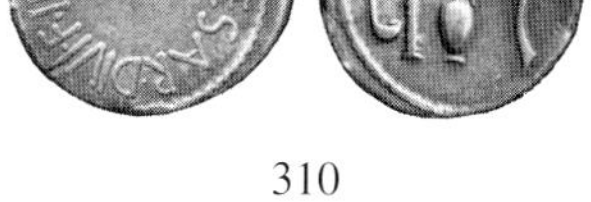

310

310 IMP CAESAR DIVI F III VIR R P C around empty field. *Reverse:* emblems of the augurate and pontificate – simpulum, aspergillum, jug and lituus (no legend). *Silver denarius. Southern or central Italian mint, summer 37 BC* (Crawford 537/1; Sydenham 1332; BMCRR Gaul 113; Babelon Julia 135; Newman 37.1; Cohen 128/337).

311 IMP CAESAR / DIVI F in two lines within laurel-wreath. *Reverse:* tripod with cauldron, COS ITER ET TER DESIG around. *Silver denarius.*

Southern or central Italian mint, summer 37 BC (Crawford 537/2; Sydenham 1333; BMCRR Gaul 115; cf. Babelon Julia 136; Newman 37.2; RSC/Cohen 111).

311

These two types are clearly linked with numbers 312 and 313 and the group as a whole must be attributed to the period immediately preceding and following the signing of the Pact of Tarentum and the renewal of the Triumvirate in the summer of 37 BC. No. 310 is of a curious design, the legend occupying the obverse of the coin and the type appearing on the reverse. The combination of augural and pontifical symbols was intended to revive memories of Octavian's adoptive father, the late dictator, who had used a similar reverse on an issue of denarii struck a decade earlier in north Africa (see nos. 57 and 57a). Octavian's superiority over his triumviral colleague, who could boast only membership of the college of augurs and could not claim to be the son of a deity, is thus given subtle emphasis. The appearance of the tripod on no. 311 refers to Apollo and marks the beginning (at least in the iconography of his coinage) of Octavian's long and important association with this deity. Curiously, the inscription omits all mention of the triumviral title, though it reappears on an almost identical type struck immediately after the renewal of the Triumvirate (see no. 313).

312

313

312 Bare head of Octavian right, bearded, **IMP CAESAR DIVI F III VIR ITER R P C** around. *Reverse:* emblems of the augurate and pontificate – simpulum, aspergillum, jug and lituus, **COS ITER ET TER DESIG** around, above and on right. *Silver denarius. Southern or central Italian mint, summer 37 BC* (Crawford 538/1; Sydenham 1334; BMCRR Gaul 116; Babelon Julia 140; Newman 37.3; Cohen 91).

313 Tripod with cauldron, **IMP CAESAR DIVI F III VIR ITER** around, **R P C** on cauldron. *Reverse:* **COS ITER ET / TERT DESIG** in two lines within laurel-wreath. *Silver denarius. Southern or central Italian mint, summer 37 BC* (Crawford 538/2; Sydenham 1333a; BMCRR Gaul, p. 415; Babelon Julia 137; Newman 37.4; Cohen 88).

The inclusion of the title *triumvir iterum* in the obverse inscriptions of these two types indicates that they are commemorative of the renewal of friendly relations between Antony and Octavian which resulted in the extension of the Triumvirate for a second five-year term. The close association of this issue with nos. 310 and 311 shows that all four types may confidently be dated to the summer of 37 BC.

One final Octavianic type, existing in both gold and silver denominations, may be included in the issues attributable to the period 42–36 BC. Once again the young Triumvir stresses his close association with Divus Iulius, this time by depicting the temple dedicated to the new deity. The fact that this edifice did not exist at the time of the issue acted as no deterrent to the use of such a powerful piece of propaganda. Although the late dictator had received deification on New Year's Day, 42 BC, work did not actually commence on the *Templum Divi Iuli* for a further eleven years. Lack of senatorial enthusiasm, if not outright opposition, doubtless contributed to this delay, but in any case Octavian was probably too preoccupied with the struggle for political supremacy to push the project through. Once building had commenced the temple was completed within a couple of years, it being dedicated by Octavian with great ceremony on 18 August 29 BC. Constructed on the site of Caesar's cremation in 44 BC it stood between the Basilica Aemilia and and the temple of Castor in the Roman Forum.

314 Bare head of Octavian right, bearded, **IMP CAESAR DIVI F III VIR ITER R P C** around. *Reverse:* tetrastyle temple of Divus Julius, containing his statue as augur, holding lituus, **DIVO IVL** inscribed on architrave, star (*sidus Iulium*) in pediment, lighted altar on left, **COS ITER ET TER DESIG** around. *Gold aureus. Southern or central Italian mint, spring to early summer 36 BC* (Crawford 540/1; Sydenham 1337; BMCRR Africa 32; Babelon Julia 138; Newman 37.5; Cohen 89).

315

315 Same as preceding. *Silver denarius. Southern or central Italian mint, spring to early summer 36 BC* (Crawford 540/2; Sydenham 1338; BMCRR Africa 33; Babelon Julia 139; Newman 37.6; RSC/Cohen 90, 90a).

*The '**D**' of **DESIG** is reversed on one die.*

315A

315A Galley with rowers sailing right, **IMP CAESAR** above. *Reverse:* Victory standing left, holding wreath, palm-branch, and rudder, **DIVI F** behind. *Silver quinarius. Southern or central Italian mint, spring to early summer 36 BC* (Sydenham 1339; BMCRR Africa 38; Babelon Julia 132; Cohen 94).

This coinage was produced in readiness for the attack on Sextus Pompey in Sicily in the summer of 36 BC. Substantial additional supplies of currency would have been required to help defray the cost of the great naval and military build-up prior to the commencement of hostilities, hence the production of gold as well as silver. The bearded Octavian makes his final appearance on the coinage. With the defeat of the last of the Pompeians the Triumvir reverted to being clean-shaven, a visible sign that the late dictator had at last been avenged on his old enemies. The identity of the temple on the reverse of the aureus and denarius is left in no doubt by the prominent inscription **DIVO IVL[IO]** on the architrave and the *sidus Iulium*, or 'Julian star', in the pediment. The conspicuous altar which appears to the left of the temple doubtless represents the temporary shrine erected in Caesar's honour on the very spot where his funeral had taken place.[119] The enigmatic quinarius type has received a variety of attributions and Crawford appears to have regarded it as post-Actian. However, the distinctive form of Octavian's titulature would seem to place it at this time and the strongly maritime theme of the types may be explained in the context of the vigorous preparations for the war against Sextus and the anticipated naval victory.

With this issue we come to the end of the initial phase of Octavian's coinage. Spanning seven years, from its inception in the spring of 43 BC, production had been on a limited scale, reflecting the weakness of the young man's position in the early period of his rivalry with Antony. The issues which followed, the precise chronology of which has been the subject of much scholarly debate, mark a complete change. In place of the tentative young political upstart the coinage now reveals a mature leader of destiny, the heir of the Hellenistic world as well as the master of Rome. In volume the later coinage of Octavian is equally impressive and the CAESAR DIVI F and IMP CAESAR issues provide a clear link to the majesty of the early imperial coinage of Augustus.

C. Issues of the Roman Moneyers

The final phase of the republican coinage at Rome is represented by the issues of six monetary magistrates. In 41 BC the regular quattuorvirate was appointed to oversee minting activities, but in the following year only two moneyers held office and thereafter the Capitoline mint appears to have ceased production altogether. With the downfall of the republican cause on the field of Philippi, in October of 42 BC, political power was concentrated in the hands of the two principal Caesarians, Antony and Octavian, and their military mints were to provide the bulk of the state's (or rather the army's) currency requirements over the following decade or so.

The four moneyers who held office during the troubled year 41 BC were C. Clodius Vestalis, M. Arrius Secundus, C. Numonius Vaala, and L. Servius Rufus. The scarcity of their issues suggests only a brief period of activity and this accords well with the situation in Italy where Octavian was maintaining only a precarious hold on power, surrounded as he was by forces opposed to his authority. This was the year of the consulship of Antony's brother, Lucius, and the Perusine War which could easily have resulted in the western Triumvir's demise at the age of only twenty-two.

316

316 Head of Flora right, with drapery at neck, wearing floral wreath, lily at her shoulder behind, C CLODIVS before, C F behind. *Reverse:* veiled female figure (Vestal virgin) seated left, holding two-handled bowl, VESTALIS behind. *Gold aureus. Rome, 41 BC* (Crawford 512/1; Sydenham 1134; BMCRR 4195; Babelon Claudia/Clodia 12).

317

317 Same as preceding. *Silver denarius. Rome, 41 BC* (Crawford 512/2; Sydenham 1135; BMCRR 4196; Babelon Claudia/Clodia 13).

This moneyer is the only one of his college about whom we possess any certain knowledge outside the evidence provided by the coinage itself. On the authority of two inscriptions from *Forum Clodii* in southern Etruria[120] we know that later in his career he went on to hold the proconsular command in Crete and Cyrene. His denarii are noticeably commoner than those of his three colleagues and must have provided the bulk of the moneyers' issues for the year 41 BC. The reverse type of a seated Vestal, one of the six *sacerdotes Vestales* (the sole female priesthood in Rome), may represent nothing more than a punning allusion to the moneyer's *cognomen*. Grueber and Crawford, however, both attempt more precise identifications, the former describing her as Claudia Quinta, the Vestal virgin who was instrumental in bringing the image of Cybele (Magna Mater) from Asia Minor to Rome in 204 BC, the latter preferring Claudia, daughter of Appius Claudius Pulcher (consul 143 BC), another noted Vestal, who protected her father against an *intercessio* (veto) following his unauthorized triumph. The obverse type depicting Flora, the Italian goddess of flowering or blossoming plants, probably relates to the foundation of the festival of the Floralia during the consulship in 240 BC of an ancestor of the moneyer, C. Claudius Centho.[121] It is tempting to see in the appearance of this minor deity a celebration of the 200th anniversary of this event.

318

319

320

318 Diademed head of Fortuna Populi Romani right, with drapery at neck, F P R above, M ARRIVS behind, SECVNDVS before. *Reverse:* vertical spear (*hasta pura*) between wreath, on left, and rectangular phalera, on right (no legend). *Gold aureus. Rome, 41 BC* (Crawford 513/1; Sydenham 1083; BMCRR 4209; Babelon Arria 1).

319 Young male head right, bare and with slight beard, M ARRIVS behind, SECVNDVS before. *Reverse:* same as preceding. *Silver denarius. Rome, 41 BC* (Crawford 513/2; Sydenham 1084; BMCRR 4210; Babelon Arria 2).

320 *Obverse:* similar to preceding, but without SECVNDVS before the head. *Reverse:* two soldiers advancing right, the foremost holding spear in left hand and with right reaching back to grasp one of the two standards held by his companion, SECVNDVS in exergue. *Silver denarius. Rome, 41 BC* (Crawford 513/3; Sydenham 1085; BMCRR p. 569; Babelon Arria 3).

The rare coinage of Marcus Arrius Secundus is of considerable interest and the types appear to throw some light on his lineage about which nothing is otherwise known. The youthful head on the denarii is usually described as that of an ancestor, possibly Quintus Arrius who may have been the father of the moneyer. Quintus was involved in the costly and embarrassing episode of the Servile War in which an army of gladiators, slaves, and free peasants, led and inspired by the Thracian gladiator Spartacus, succeeded in defying the might of the republican generals over a period of several years (73–71 BC). Spartacus' Celtic lieutenant Crixus was defeated by the praetor Quintus Arrius in 72 BC, one of the few Roman successes in the war until Spartacus was finally overcome by M. Licinius Crassus. The victory over Crixus may have provided the inspiration for the types of the coinage of Marcus Arrius Secundus. The extremely rare denarius (no. 320) perhaps illustrates an actual episode in the battle, with Quintus rallying his men by casting a standard into the ranks of the enemy to encourage the legionaries to advance to its recovery. The *dona militaria* ('military gifts'), featured on the reverses of the aureus and the other denarius, represent the honours which would have been awarded to Quintus for his success against the rebel forces. Depicted are the *hasta pura*, the spear presented for killing an enemy soldier in single combat, so-called because it had never wounded anyone; the corona (wreath), bestowed for outstanding bravery on the field of battle; and a rectangular phalera, a metal ornament usually worn on the breastplate of the cuirass as a mark of distinction. The obverse of the aureus shows the head of 'The Fortune of the Roman People', identified by the abbreviation F P R. In 71 BC the Roman Senate had given thanks to this deity for the deliverance of the state from the spectre of civil war, a sentiment which was equally appropriate three decades later in the year following Philippi.

A curious feature of the denarii of the three moneyers Arrius Secundus, Numonius Vaala, and Servius Rufus is the similarity of the portrait heads appearing on the obverses to certain prominent political figures, both living and recently deceased. In each case the similarity is close enough to have provoked scholarly comment, but sufficiently different to allow dissent and doubt in the identification. It has to be admitted that the youthful head on the coins of Secundus, already tentatively identified as that of Quintus Arrius, bears more than a passing resemblance to the young Octavian. Similarly, the portrait on Vaala's denarii (see no. 322) recalls the likeness of Julius Caesar, whilst that on the coinage of Rufus (see no. 324) has been widely accepted as displaying the facial features of M. Junius Brutus. The reason for this phenomenon, which can hardly be coincidental, must be sought in the confused political situation prevailing in Italy throughout the year 41 BC. The final outcome of the power struggle between Octavian and the consul Lucius Antony (egged on by the eastern Triumvir's politically ambitious wife Fulvia) was to remain in doubt until the latter part of the year. A difficult choice, therefore, confronted the three moneyers.[122] Each clearly had strong political sympathies but to express them in too unequivocal a manner might have had serious repercussions, not just for their future careers but even for their safety. The problem seems to have been solved by the adoption of deliberately ambiguous types featuring portraits which could be interpreted either as those of ancestors or, if it proved safe to do so, as those of Caesar and his adoptive son (for Vaala and Secundus) or Brutus in the case of Rufus. The last would appear to be a curious choice, given the recent defeat of the republicans, but Brutus and Antony had once been good friends and even so soon after Philippi it was probably clearly perceived by those with republican sympathies that the rule of Antony would be infinitely preferable to that of the young Caesar. If Antony's brother prevailed in the civil war in Italy then Rufus would surely not be censured by the eastern Triumvir for using a portrait resembling his old friend and recent opponent on the battlefield; whilst if Octavian proved victorious then he could plead that the head was merely that of an ancestor.

321

322

321 Winged head of Victory right, her hair drawn back and collected into a knot behind, one long plait arranged in a loop along the top of her head. *Reverse:* soldier advancing left, with sword and shield, attacking a palisaded earthwork (*vallum*) behind which are two similarly armed defenders, C NVMONIVS on right, VAALA in exergue. *Gold aureus. Rome, 41 BC* (Crawford 514/1; Sydenham 1086; BMCRR 4215; Babelon Numonia 1; Cohen Fulvia 2).

322 Mature male head right, bare and with slender neck, C NVMONIVS before, VAALA behind. *Reverse:* similar to preceding, but without C NVMONIVS on right. *Silver denarius. Rome, 41 BC* (Crawford 514/2; Sydenham 1087; BMCRR 4216; Babelon Numonia 2).

Another shadowy figure from this troubled period, C. Numonius Vaala employs the same reverse type for both gold and silver denominations. The interesting scene, depicting an attack on a military camp, is usually taken to illustrate an act of heroism performed by some ancestor, though it could equally well be nothing more than a punning allusion to the *cognomen* Vaala[123] (from *vallum*, meaning a palisade). As already mentioned (see commentary on Arrius Secundus following no. 320) the distinctive male head recalls the likeness of Julius Caesar[124] and possibly indicates the moneyer's espousal of Octavian's cause in the confrontation with Lucius Antony. If this is so then the obverse of the aureus comes as something of a surprise. The head of Victory may be interpreted as commemorating the recent defeat of the republicans at Philippi, but the form of the effigy is highly individual and displays precisely the same characteristics as the supposed portraits of Mark Antony's wife Fulvia (see nos. 122 and 126, the quinarii of Antony issued at Lugdunum in 43 and 42 BC, and no. 186, the denarius of L. Mussidius Longus of 42 BC). Fulvia, ever-ambitious on her husband's behalf, was very much the moving spirit behind her brother-in-law's challenge to Octavian's authority in Italy. The appearance of her likeness on this aureus may be taken as an indication that Vaala was 'hedging his bets' on the outcome of the Perusine War.

323

324

323 Conjoined heads of the Dioscuri right, each wearing laureate pileus surmounted by star, L SERVIVS before, RVFVS behind. *Reverse:* aerial view of the citadel and walls of Tusculum, with gateway in foreground inscribed TVSCVL. *Gold aureus. Rome, 41 BC* (Crawford 515/1; Sydenham 1081; BMCRR 4204; Babelon Sulpicia 9).

324 Bare male head right, bearded, L SERVIVS before, RVFVS behind. *Reverse:* the Dioscuri, naked, standing facing side by side, each holding spear and with sword strapped to waist (no legend). *Silver denarius. Rome, 41 BC* (Crawford 515/2; Sydenham 1082; BMCRR 4205; Babelon Sulpicia 10).

Unlike his three colleagues in the monetary college of 41 BC L. Servius Rufus has different obverse and reverse types for his aurei and denarii, though the theme of the Dioscuri is present on both denominations. The remarkable depiction on the aureus of the ancient Latin city of Tusculum[125] is clearly in celebration of the moneyer's place of origin, though nothing else is known of him. Castor and Pollux, the Dioscuri, are also illustrative of Rufus' Tusculan ancestry. At the battle of Lake Regillus in 496 BC the twin deities miraculously brought victory to the Romans over the Latins who were led by the Tusculan dictator Octavius Mamilius, son-in-law of Rome's last king Tarquinius Superbus. Given that the portrait head on the denarius is often identified as that of Brutus[126] (see commentary on Arrius Secundus following no. 320) and that the moneyer seems to have had strong republican sympathies, it is tempting, though perhaps merely fanciful, to see some subtle comparison between the characters and roles of the Brutus and Octavius of early republican times and their contemporary counterparts.

The following year (40 BC) was to be the last in which the triumviral government allowed a college of moneyers to produce currency at the Capitoline mint. It may well be that Octavian was angered by the activities of the preceding college, especially with regard to the probable depictions of Fulvia and Brutus, and decided to bring this important tool of propaganda entirely under his own control. Accordingly, only two monetary magistrates were appointed for 40 BC and the types of their issues were carefully monitored. With the Perusine War behind him Octavian's authority in Italy was now more firmly established and opposition to his regime could no longer be so openly expressed.

325

327

327a

325 Bare head of Octavian right, with slight beard, **DIVI** behind, **IVLI F** before. *Reverse:* Fortuna standing left, holding rudder and cornucopiae, **TI SEMPRON GRACCVS IIII VIR Q D** around. *Gold aureus. Rome, 40 BC* (Crawford 525/1; Sydenham 1126; BMCRR 4313; Babelon Sempronia 12; Cohen 522).

326 *Obverse:* as preceding. *Reverse:* legionary eagle (*aquila*) between military standard on left, and plough and measuring rod (*decempeda*) on right, **TI SEMPRON** above, **GRACCVS** below, **IIII VIR** on right, **Q DESIG** on left. *Silver denarius. Rome, 40 BC* (Crawford 525/2; Sydenham 1127; BMCRR 4314; Babelon Sempronia 13; Cohen 523).

327 Wreathed head of Caesar right (no legend). *Reverse:* similar to preceding, but with **TI SEMPRONIVS** above, **GRACCVS** below, **Q DESIG** on left, and **S – C** in field. *Silver denarius. Rome, 40 BC* (Crawford 525/3; Sydenham 1128; BMCRR 4316; cf. Babelon Sempronia 11; Cohen 48).

327a Similar to preceding, but the **S – C** is on obverse, either side Caesar's neck, and sometimes **DESI** or **DES** for **DESIG** on reverse. *Silver denarius. Rome, 40 BC* (Crawford 525/4a–c; Sydenham 1129, 1129a; BMCRR 4319–20; Babelon Sempronia 10; RSC/Cohen 47–47b).

Tiberius Sempronius Graccus strikes as *quaestor designatus* but is otherwise unknown to history. Despite being one of only two monetary magistrates appointed to hold office in 40 BC he uses the conventional designation **IIII VIR** (*quattuorvir*) on his issues depicting Octavian. The title disappears, however, on the denarii with the portrait of Caesar and is replaced by the formula **S C** (*senatus consulto*, 'by decree of the Senate'). This suggests an emergency augmentation of the issue to meet the special needs of Octavian's settlement of legionary veterans following the Perusine War. The actual process of this settlement is graphically illustrated by the reverse type of the denarii. The emblems of military life (eagle and standard) are replaced by the plough and the *decempeda*, the ten-foot surveyor's rod used to divide up the allotments of land granted to the soldiers on their retirement. On a different theme, the aureus honours the goddess Fortuna through whose favour the young Caesar finally emerged victorious from the dangers of the civil war which could so easily have cut short his career and changed the course of history.[127]

Of special interest is the first occurrence on the coinage of Octavian's title *divi filius* ('son of god'), here given in its fuller form of *divi Iuli filius*. Several years later it reappeared on the military issue of aurei and denarii bearing the name of Marcus Agrippa on reverse (see nos. 305–7). Thereafter, it became a regular part of the titulature of the Triumvir and, eventually, of the Emperor Augustus. Its introduction at this point was due to Octavian's desire to stress the legitimacy of his claim to power, especially important following the episode of the Perusine War in which his authority had been seriously challenged. He was the son and adopted heir of the divine Julius and he now intended to make full use of the immense propaganda value of this unique distinction.

328 Bare head of Octavian right, with slight beard, **DIVI** before, **IVLI F** behind. *Reverse:* bull-calf walking left, **Q VOCONIVS** above,

VITVLVS in exergue. *Gold aureus. Rome, 40 BC* (Crawford 526/1; Sydenham 1130; BMCRR 4306; Babelon Voconia 3; Cohen 546).

329

330

331

329 Wreathed head of Caesar right, **DIVI IVLI** before, lituus behind. *Reverse:* as preceding. *Silver denarius. Rome, 40 BC* (Crawford 526/2; Sydenham 1132; BMCRR 4308; Babelon Voconia 2; Cohen 46).

330 Bare head of Octavian right, with slight beard, **DIVI F** behind, lituus before. *Reverse:* bull-calf walking left, **Q VOCONIVS** above, **VITVLVS Q / DESIG** in exergue, **S – C** in field. *Gold aureus. Rome, 40 BC* (Crawford 526/3; Sydenham 1131; BMCRR 4307; Babelon Voconia 4; Cohen 547).

331 Wreathed head of Caesar right (no legend). *Reverse:* similar to preceding, but **DESIGN** for **DESIG** in exergue. *Silver denarius. Rome, 40 BC* (Crawford 526/4; Sydenham 1133; BMCRR 4311; Babelon Voconia 1; Cohen 45).

Of the history and origin of the moneyer Quintus Voconius Vitulus we have no certain knowledge other than the information imparted by his coinage. This would suggest that he was nominated to the quaestorship during his term of office as moneyer as only on his later issues is he accorded the title *quaestor designatus*. Like his colleague Sempronius Graccus the coinage of Vitulus is entirely devoted to honouring Divus Julius and his adoptive son Octavian. Unlike Graccus, however, his reverse type is of a purely personal nature (a surprising concession by Octavian) and represents a punning allusion to his *cognomen* (*vitulus* = bull-calf). The appearance of the augur's staff (lituus) in association with the heads of both Caesar and Octavian not only emphasizes their membership of the priestly college of augurs but also focuses attention on the closeness of their relationship. Antony utilized his possession of the augurship as an effective tool of propaganda and this represents an early challenge by his young colleague to his extensive use of this powerful symbolism.

With the issues of Graccus and Vitulus the long series of republican moneyers' coinage at Rome comes to a close. It would not be resumed for about two decades, and then only on a temporary basis which would not extend beyond the reign of Augustus. Its cessation only four years after the assassination of Caesar is of great significance as it shows just how far the transition from democracy to autocratic rule had already gone. While coinage was still being produced in the names of minor magistrates it could be argued that at least some semblance of the traditional form of government still existed. But the moneyers of 41 BC had taken full advantage of the autocrat's temporary loss of authority and in so doing had sealed their fate. The angry Triumvir resolved to do away with this irksome institution and, following one final issue in which the restoration of his power was made fully manifest, he summarily abolished a tradition which stretched back almost two and a half centuries. Henceforth, all state coinage would be under the direct control of either the eastern or western Triumvir,[128] and within a decade that power would be concentrated in the hands of Octavian alone.

D. Issues of Sextus Pompey in Sicily

The peregrinations of Sextus Pompey (younger son of Pompeius Magnus and the unworthy sole inheritor of a once great cause) finally brought him to Sicily where he was to enjoy the most successful phase of his swashbuckling career. In April of 43 BC the Senate, mistakenly believing itself freed from the threat of domination by the Caesarians, had bestowed on Sextus the imposing title of *praefectus classis et orae maritimae* ('Commander-in-Chief of the Fleet and of the Sea Coasts'). But just four months later the Conscript Fathers were forced by Octavian to rescind this promotion[129] and as the year drew to a close the newly-constituted triumviral government gave Sextus' name a prominent place on its proscription lists. While all this was taking place in Rome the *praefectus classis* himself was safely anchored in the harbour of Massilia in southern Gaul. On receiving word of the Senate's abrogation of his commission and the hostility of the Caesarian regime Sextus at last decided to make his move. He set sail from Massilia and headed for Sicily, which he intended to occupy and use as his base for harassing the Italian mainland. *En route* to Sicily he secured control of Corsica and Sardinia by leaving garrisons on these islands. By the spring of 42 BC Sextus was firmly established in Sicily and was providing a safe haven for refugees from the triumviral proscriptions. Not only did this provide him with additional wealth but it gave him the services of some of Rome's most eminent men.[130] Alarmed at these developments Octavian despatched a naval squadron, under the command of Salvidienus Rufus, with the object of checking the growing power and influence of the troublesome buccaneer. But Salvidienus was worsted in an engagement off Rhegium, and for the time being the Caesarians were too distracted by the impending trial of strength with the republican leaders Brutus and Cassius to pay any further attention to Sextus.

The most likely period of issue for Sextus' extensive and interesting Sicilian coinage is the time of his greatest prosperity, *i.e.* from his defeat of Salvidienus in 42 BC to the signing of the Pact of Misenum with Antony and Octavian three years later. His issues in gold and silver all record the title *imperator iterum* (IMP ITER) and Neptune provides a common theme on all three denarius types. Sextus received his second imperatorial acclamation as a result of the victory over Octavian's admiral[131] and on the same occasion he was hailed as 'son of Neptune' by his men. Although the Pact of Misenum appeared to favour the interests of Sextus, under its terms the refugees from the proscriptions were pardoned by the Triumvirs and allowed to return to their homes without penalty. This deprived Sextus of both resources and talent. Although he retained control of Sicily down to 36 BC his final years were much troubled by conflicts with the triumviral government in Rome and under these circumstances it would have become increasingly difficult for the master of Sicily to produce precious metal currency. His issues in this final period may have been restricted to the bronze asses, found in such numbers on the island, which show a marked decline in style as the series progresses (see no. 336).

332 Bare head of Sextus Pompey right, with close beard, MAG PIVS behind, IMP ITER before, all within oak-wreath. *Reverse:* bare heads of Pompey the Great right and Gnaeus Pompey Junior left, face to face, the latter bearded, lituus behind the father, tripod behind his son, PRÆF above, CLAS ET ORÆ / MARIT EX S C (MAR ligatured) below. *Gold aureus. Uncertain Sicilian mint, 42 BC* (Crawford 511/1; Sydenham 1346; BMCRR Sicily 13; Babelon Pompeia 24; Cohen *Sextus, Pompey, and Gnaeus* 1).

332

This remarkable 'dynastic'[132] type provides us with the only reliable portraits of the two sons of Pompey the Great. That of the elder, Gnaeus, may be compared with the left facing head appearing on a denarius of Spanish mintage belonging to Sextus' initial issue of coinage in 45–44 BC (see no. 233). Although the Sicilian die-engraver was far more accomplished than his Spanish counterpart the similarities of the two heads are sufficient to permit a reasonably certain identification of the earlier portrait. In marked contrast to the sensitive features of his elder brother the effigy of Sextus reveals just what we might have expected from our knowledge of his character and career. His is the quintessential portrait of the rough but cunning buccaneer, a man born of a noble house but now fallen on hard times because of Caesar and his followers. Octavian was the great-nephew and heir of the dictator so he and Sextus could never be anything but implacable foes, their rivalry one which would have to be fought to the death. The wreath of oak which surrounds his portrait is the *corona civica* or civic crown, traditionally awarded to those who had saved the lives of fellow-citizens. By defeating Octavian's admiral Salvidienus in 42 BC Sextus could justly claim to be the saviour of those who had sought refuge with him in Sicily to escape the horrors of the triumviral proscriptions. This victory is commemorated by the *imperator iterum* (IMP ITER) in the obverse legend, whilst the inscription on reverse proclaims him 'Commander-in-Chief of the Fleet and of the Sea Coasts', the honour bestowed on him by the Senate in April of the preceding year. The symbols behind the heads on reverse indicate the priestly colleges to which Sextus' father and brother belonged, the lituus signifying Pompey's membership of the augurs, the tripod his son's affiliation with the *quindecimviri sacris faciundis* ('fifteen men for the performing of sacred ceremonies').

333 Diademed head of Neptune right, trident over shoulder, MAG PIVS (MA usually ligatured) behind, IMP ITER (TE sometimes ligatured) before. *Reverse:* naval trophy set on anchor, top of trident visible above, heads of marine monsters (Scylla and Charybdis) at base, PRÆF CLAS ET ORÆ MARIT EX S C (MAR always ligatured, TE sometimes) around. *Silver denarius. Uncertain Sicilian mint, 42 BC*

333

(Crawford 511/2a–c; Sydenham 1347; BMCRR Sicily 15–16; Babelon Pompeia 21; RSC/Cohen 1–1d).

334

334 Bare head of Pompey the Great right, augural symbols capis (one-handled jug) and lituus behind and before, MAG PIVS IMP ITER around, above. *Reverse:* Neptune, naked but for chlamys on left arm, holding aplustre and resting right foot on prow, standing left between figures of the Catanaean brothers Anapias and Amphinomus running in opposite directions, bearing their parents on their shoulders, PRÆF above, CLAS ET ORÆ / MARIT EX S C (MAR ligatured) in two lines in exergue. *Silver denarius. Uncertain Sicilian mint, 42–40 BC* (Crawford 511/3a; Sydenham 1344; BMCRR Sicily 7; Babelon Pompeia 27; Cohen *Pompey the Great* 17).

334a

334a Similar to preceding, but on reverse the legend in exergue reads ORÆ MARIT ET / CLAS EX S C (MAR ligatured) in two lines. *Silver denarius. Uncertain Sicilian mint, 40–39 BC* (Crawford 511/3b; Sydenham 1345; BMCRR Sicily 11; Babelon Pompeia 25; Cohen *Pompey the Great* 18).

334b Similar to preceding, but on reverse the legend in exergue reads ORÆ MARIT ET / CLAS S C (MAR ligatured) in two lines. *Silver denarius. Uncertain Sicilian mint, 40–39 BC* (Crawford 511/3c; BMCRR Sicily, p. 561 note; Babelon Pompeia 26; RSC/Cohen *Pompey the Great* 18a).

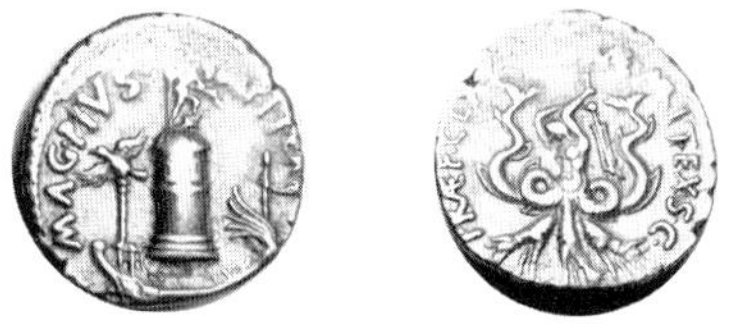

335

335 The Pharos (lighthouse) of Messana, represented as a cylindrical tower showing windows and balcony in its upper part and surmounted by a statue of Neptune standing right, holding trident and rudder, left foot set on prow, galley moving left in foreground at foot of lighthouse, legionary eagle in its prow, filleted sceptre in stern, MAG PIVS IMP ITER around. *Reverse:* the marine monster Scylla wielding rudder with both hands raised above her head, her upper body represented as that of a maiden, the lower part terminating in fish-tails and the foreparts of three dogs, PRÆF CLAS ET ORÆ MARIT EX S C (MAR always ligatured, TE sometimes) around. *Silver denarius. Uncertain Sicilian mint, 42–40 BC.* (Crawford 511/4a-b; Sydenham 1348; BMCRR Sicily 18; Babelon Pompeia 22; RSC/Cohen 2, 2a).

335a Similar to preceding, but on reverse the legend reads PRÆF CLAS ET ORÆ MARIT S C (MAR ligatured). *Silver denarius. Uncertain Sicilian mint, 42–40 BC* (Crawford 511/4c; RSC/Cohen 2b).

335b

335b Similar to preceding, but on reverse the legend reads PRÆF ORÆ MARIT ET CLAS S C (MAR always ligatured, TE sometimes). *Silver* *denarius. Uncertain Sicilian mint, 40–39 BC* (Crawford 511/4d; Sydenham 1349; BMCRR Sicily 20; Babelon Pompeia 23; RSC/Cohen 3, 3a).

The Sicilian denarii of Sextus Pompey appear to fall within the period 42–39 BC. It seems unlikely that he would have continued using the inferior title of *praefectus classis et orae maritimae* ('Commander-in-Chief of the Fleet and of the Sea Coasts') once his status as ruler of Sicily, Sardinia, Corsica, and the Peloponnese had been officially recognized by the Triumvirs under the terms of the Pact of Misenum. There are two principal varieties of reverse legend, one reading PRÆF CLAS ET ORÆ MARIT [EX] S C, the other PRÆF ORAE MARIT ET CLAS [EX] S C. The first would seem to be the earlier as it is the only form occurring on the aureus (no. 332) and the Neptune/naval trophy denarius (no. 333), both of which appear to be commemorative of Sextus' defeat of Salvidienus in 42 BC. The other denarius types (nos. 334 and 335) were issued with both forms of legend, the second being the scarcer in each case. This would indicate that the Pompey/Catanaean brothers and the Pharos/Scylla denarii were produced contemporaneously, perhaps at Catana and Messana respectively, with the second variety of legend being introduced late in the issue. The brothers Anapias and Amphinomus were renowned for having rescued their parents during an eruption of Mount Aetna, bearing them to safety on their shoulders. As well as being a possible indication of the place of mintage the type illustrates the theme of 'Pietas' in connection with Sextus' assumption of the name Pius. The marine monster Scylla, appearing on the reverse of no. 335, represents the dangers of the ocean, so deadly to Sextus' enemies but of no concern to the 'son of Neptune' himself. The legend of Scylla is Homeric[133] in origin where she is described as having twelve feet and six heads and inhabiting a cave in the cliff opposite the whirlpool Charybdis. From this lair she preyed upon unsuspecting sea-creatures and passing ships, devouring any sailors who came within her reach. The form of this monster depicted on Sextus' coinage is of a slightly more palatable kind, her upper body being in the guise of an alluring maiden. This derives from a later version of the legend in which Scylla, originally human, is represented as the unfortunate victim of the sorceress Circe, her rival for the affections of the marine god Glaucus.

The final issue to be considered in Sextus Pompey's Sicilian coinage is the extensive series of bronze asses, all of the same basic type but varying greatly in style.

336

336 Laureate head of Janus, with features resembling Pompey the Great, MAGN (or MAGNVS or MAGNV, the MA ligatured) above.

Reverse: prow of galley right, **PIVS** above, **IMP** below. *Bronze as. Uncertain Sicilian mint, or mints, 43–36 BC* (RPC 671; Crawford 479; FITA pp. 22–4; Sydenham 1044–1044b; BMCRR Spain 95–103; Babelon Pompeia 20; Cohen *Pompey the Great* 16).

This extensive coinage continues the tradition of Pompeian bronze issues begun in Spain under Gnaeus Pompey Junior and carried on after Munda by Sextus himself (see nos. 53 and 234). Indeed, the earliest issues of this type are generally attributed to Sextus' mint in Spain,[134] though it is by no means certain that production began prior to his arrival in Sicily in the latter part of 43 BC. The flans all exhibit rounded edges in marked contrast to the earlier coins of undoubted Spanish mintage which have bevelled edges. The considerable variation in style which is to be observed on coins of this type may be explained by the extended period over which they were struck, perhaps as long as seven years. Moreover, several mint establishments possessing varying degrees of competency could have been involved in their production. Like the earlier Pompeian bronze issues these asses were struck on the old uncial weight standard of about 22 grams which, for the regular republican coinage, had been abandoned in favour of the lighter semuncial standard in 91 BC, under the terms of the *Lex Papiria*. The types (Janus head/prow to right) were the traditional ones used on the first struck asses of the Roman Republic introduced in the great currency reform of *circa* 211 BC. They were to be the last coins of this type, for with the downfall of Sextus' regime in the West and the failure of Antony's Parthian invasion in the East the completion of the transition from republic to empire was now at hand, bringing with it fundamental changes in many aspects of Roman life, including the currency.

E. Issue of L. Staius Murcus

One of the minor figures of this tumultuous age Lucius Staius Murcus, who seems to have had some connection with the central Italian town of Sulmo[135] (modern *Sulmona*), served as Caesar's legate from 48–46 BC and was praetor in 45. Following the dictator's assassination the Senate appointed him proconsul of Syria where, together with Marcius Crispus, he besieged the Pompeian renegade Caecilius Bassus in Apamea. On the arrival in Syria of the republican leader Cassius (43 BC) Murcus did not hesitate to hand over control of his legions and in return was given command of a fleet. He quickly demonstrated his ability as a naval tactician, eventually joining forces with Domitius Ahenobarbus to gain mastery of the seas around Greece in readiness for the final trial of strength with the Caesarians. After the republican catastrophe at Philippi the two admirals picked up many of the survivors and then cruised the Ionian Sea awaiting developments. Eventually, Murcus decided to throw in his lot with Sextus Pompey in Sicily. It was a bad mistake. The son of Pompey, grateful enough for his ships, soon quarrelled with the former republican admiral and had him executed on a charge of conspiracy (40/39 BC). Ahenobarbus was to fare better. After a brief period of piratical activity he offered his services to Antony, eventually becoming one of the eastern Triumvir's most trusted lieutenants.

337

337 Head of Neptune right, trident over shoulder behind. *Reverse:* Murcus standing left, holding sword and with right hand raising female figure (Roma?) who kneels right before him, trophy in background between them, MVRCVS IMP in exergue. *Silver denarius. Mint travelling with Murcus in the Ionian Sea, 41 BC* (Crawford 510; Sydenham 1315; BMCRR East 86; Babelon Statia 1).

The poor style and execution of these rare coins identifies them as belonging to an emergency issue. There can be little doubt that they were produced in the months following Philippi, perhaps even on board Murcus' flagship in the Ionian Sea. The types are appropriate enough, though the symbolism of the reverse seems overly optimistic given the circumstances of the times. With Brutus and Cassius removed from the political equation there now seemed little hope of the remnants of the republican leadership being able to rescue Rome from the domination of the Caesarian party, even though they still controlled a significant naval force. Murcus' imperatorial title probably stems from the successful outcome of his siege of Bassus in Apamea (43 BC).

F. Issues of Cn. Domitius Ahenobarbus

The coinage of Ahenobarbus in the name of Antony, struck possibly at Corcyra in the summer of 40 BC, has already been described (see nos. 257–8). This was preceded by an independent issue of aurei and denarii attributable to the time when, with seventy ships and two legions under his command, he found himself deprived of a cause following the republican defeat at Philippi. Although he uses the title *imperator*[136] as his authority for coining Ahenobarbus was leading a life of piracy at this time and was the scourge of the Adriatic ports. The precise location of the mint, or mints, involved in the production of this coinage is impossible to ascertain and even the identities of the two individuals portrayed on the obverses are quite uncertain. It seems reasonable to attribute both types to 41 BC, though they could have been struck in the early part of the following year prior to Ahenobarbus' espousal of the Antonian cause.

338 Bare male portrait head right, with heavy features, AHENOBAR before. *Reverse:* view of the tetrastyle temple of Neptune, showing front and left hand side wall, NE–PT across upper field, CN DOMITIVS L F IMP around, below. *Gold aureus. Uncertain mint in the region of the Adriatic or Ionian Sea, 41–40 BC* (Crawford 519/1; Sydenham 1176; BMCRR East 93; Babelon Domitia 20; Cohen 1).

338

339

339 Bare male portrait head right, with slight beard and slender features, AHENOBAR before. *Reverse:* prow right, surmounted by military trophy, CN DOMITIVS IMP around, below. *Silver denarius. Uncertain mint in the region of the Adriatic or Ionian Sea, 41–40 BC* (Crawford 519/2; Sydenham 1177; BMCRR East 94; Babelon Domitia 21).

Given the circumstances of the issue it is scarcely surprising that both reverse types should exhibit a strong nautical theme. Scholars have attempted to associate the temple of Neptune with the sanctuary which stood in the Campus Martius in Rome.[137] But the date of the foundation of this structure has been contested, some believing that it may have been the work of Cn. Domitius Ahenobarbus (consul 192 BC), others preferring to attribute its construction to the consulship of Antony's partisan in 32 BC. The latter opinion – unlikely in any case in view of the circumstances of the consulship of Ahenobarbus and Sosius – would seem to eliminate the proposed identification of the aureus type, unless the imperator was commemorating a vow to construct such a temple if the god of the sea would deliver him safely from his present difficulties. Another possibility is that Ahenobarbus was depicting a temple at one of the ports where his fleet was stationed along the coastlines of the Adriatic or Ionian Sea. There were many such temples in the coastal cities of this region and the accomplished style and neat execution of the issue suggest that it was produced at an established centre rather than in a military camp or on board ship. It would be pointless, however, to speculate on the precise location of the temple and the mint.

The denarius type is obviously commemorative of Ahenobarbus' naval victory over Domitius Calvinus in early October, 42 BC, the occasion on which he was saluted *imperator*. But the identity of the portrait head appearing on the obverse is less clear, the same problem with which we are confronted in the case of the very different effigy depicted on the aureus. The way the legends are disposed on both denominations, with AHENOBAR alone appearing before the portrait heads, suggests the representation of an ancestor in each case. The depiction of the imperator himself on one of the denominations is not impossible but seems unlikely in the light of the evidence. In such a case one would have expected to see the full name and title appearing on the obverse, rather than being divided between obverse and reverse with the *cognomen* alone accompanying the head. Having established this, however, we are left with the problem of identifying the ancestors. The Ahenobarbi had been prominent in later republican history and several strong candidates spring to mind. One may be the issuer's own father, Lucius Domitius Ahenobarbus, Cicero's *princeps iuventutis* of 70 BC.[138] This man had been an implacable opponent of Caesar and had died trying to reach safety following the Pompeian defeat at Pharsalus in 48 BC. Other notables include the Gnaeus already referred to above, consul in 192 BC and later legate to L. Cornelius Scipio in the war against Antiochus III of Syria; another Gnaeus, consul in 122 BC and proconsul in Gaul, who defeated the Allobroges and Arverni and captured the latter's king Bituitus to adorn his triumph; and his son, another Gnaeus, who was one of the founders of Narbo, the first Roman colony in Gaul (founded 118 BC) and later pontifex and consul (in 96 BC). Doubtless, two of these luminaries are honoured on the coinage of their piratical descendant, though which ones we cannot say for sure.

G. Issue of Quintus Labienus

In the winter of 43/42 BC Quintus Labienus, son of the Pompeian general Titus Labienus, was ordered by Cassius Longinus to cross into Parthia and attempt to gain the active support of King Orodes II for the republicans in their struggle against the triumviral government in Rome. This was a dangerous assignment and one which was unlikely to bring much credit to the envoy even if he succeeded in executing his difficult commission. With the recent downfall of the Seleucids the Arsacids were now competing directly with Rome for influence and control in this sensitive border region and treating with the enemy would be construed by many – Caesarian and republican alike – as a traitorous act.

Labienus accomplished the first part of his task by winning the confidence of Orodes and his son Pacorus, but the Arsacid king held back from direct military intervention at this stage. The downfall of the republicans at Philippi in October of 42 BC left Labienus marooned in Parthia without a cause but, nothing daunted, he persuaded Pacorus to join him in a military adventure. The plan was to take advantage of the temporary Roman military weakness in the East occasioned by the recent defeat of the republicans and the consequent demoralized state of the eastern legions. Another critical factor which invited intervention by an opportunist foreign power was the eastern Triumvir's dalliance with the queen of Egypt. Because of his eagerness to enjoy the attractions of Alexandria over the winter of 41/40 BC Antony had failed to make adequate provision for the security of the eastern provinces by effecting much-needed changes in the system of client kings. In consequence, when Labienus and Pacorus suddenly descended on Roman Syria at the head of a Parthian army early in 40 BC their success was rapid and dramatic. Antony's governor, L. Decidius Saxa, did not possess the loyalty of his legions who had so recently marched under the standards of Brutus and Cassius. He was soon defeated and his army willingly joined Labienus, thus swelling the ranks of the invasion force.

The situation became critical for the Romans. Antony, isolated in distant Egypt, could do little but remain a helpless spectator to the catastrophe which was overtaking his territories. Of no use whatsoever were the client kings many of whom actively supported the invaders. With Syria and Cilicia already under their control Labienus and Pacorus divided their forces, the former heading west into Asia Minor, the latter south through Syria and down the Phoenician coast to Palestine. By this time Antony had taken ship for Athens leaving the eastern provinces to their fate for the time being. The meeting of the Triumvirs at Brundisium in the late summer of 40 BC led to the renewal of their accord and Antony was at last free to give his attention to the expulsion of the Parthian invaders and the destruction of their ally, the disgraceful Roman renegade Quintus Labienus. The eastern Triumvir sent his trusted general P. Ventidius to deal with the situation, a task which he performed in an exemplary fashion. Labienus, who had been roaming unmolested in Roman territory over the past year and was now in Caria, was surprised by Ventidius' sudden appearance in Asia early in 39 BC. He was pursued eastwards as far as Cilicia where he encamped on the Taurus slopes to make his stand. But his fortifications were easily stormed by the Antonian general whose troops were fresh from a victory over the Parthian cataphracts. Labienus lost his nerve and fled, only to be overtaken and put to death. His Parthian ally Pacorus suffered a similar fate at Ventidius' hands the following year and the eastern crisis was finally over.

340

341

340 Bare head of Labienus right, with slight beard, Q LABIENVS PARTHICVS IMP around. *Reverse:* horse standing right, with bridle and saddle, to which bow-case and quiver are attached (no legend). *Gold aureus. Uncertain mint in Syria or south-eastern Asia Minor, early 40 BC* (Crawford 524/1; Sydenham 1356; BMCRR East 131; Babelon Atia 2; Cohen 1).

341 Same as preceding. *Silver denarius. Uncertain mint in Syria or south-eastern Asia Minor, early 40 BC* (Crawford 524/2; Sydenham 1357; BMCRR East 132; Babelon Atia 3; Cohen 2).

Specimens of this extraordinary issue are of considerable rarity today and it is likely that they were all struck on a single occasion, perhaps for the purpose of a donative (or even a bribe) to the legions of Decidius Saxa. As Crawford[139] points out the *imperator* in the legend should not be regarded as qualifying *Parthicus*. The latter actually represents the issuer's *cognomen*[140] assumed in recognition of his success in obtaining Parthian assistance in the defence of the republic against the forces of tyranny. The imperatorial title itself may have been for the defeat of Antony's appointee as governor of Syria. The reverse type is illustrative of the celebrated Parthian light cavalry, the scourge of Rome's legions in the past and destined to be so again when Antony invaded Parthia in 36 BC.

H. Issue of Cn. Domitius Calvinus

A loyal partisan of Caesar from the time of the outbreak of the civil war in 49 BC Gnaeus Domitius Calvinus had already enjoyed a varied and controversial career spanning more than a decade. He is first heard of as legate to L. Valerius Flaccus in Asia (62 BC), was tribune in 59, and praetor three years later. He celebrated his first consulship in 53 BC, but the means by which he obtained the highest magistracy caused such scandal that the episode may have led to his exile in 51 Calvinus commanded the Caesarian centre at Pharsalus and two years later (46 BC) was present at Thapsus. But he also had his share of reverses, being defeated by Pharnaces II of Bosporus in 48 BC, and at sea by Cn. Domitius Ahenobarbus in 42 whilst attempting to ferry reinforcements for the triumviral army across the Adriatic at the time of Philippi. His second consulship was in 40 BC and the following year Octavian despatched him to Spain where the Cerretani were in revolt. His success in this command resulted in him being saluted *imperator* by his troops, an event recorded on his coinage. On his return to Rome he celebrated a triumph (36 BC) and was responsible for the restoration in marble of the *Regia*[141] in the *Forum Romanum*.

342 Bare male head right, with short curly hair and close beard, OSCA behind. *Reverse:* simpulum, aspergillum, axe and apex (emblems of the pontificate), DOM COS ITER IMP around, below and on right. *Silver denarius. Osca, 39 BC* (Crawford 532; Sydenham 1358; BMCRR Spain 109).

342

Remarkably, this coinage makes no reference to the western Triumvir Octavian to whose favour Domitius Calvinus owed his Spanish command. The omission remains unexplained though it must have been sanctioned by Rome. The obverse type is a close copy of the earlier Iberian silver coinage of Osca (*argentum oscense*), though with the name of the mint clearly proclaimed in Latin letters behind. The city of Osca was the site of Calvinus' headquarters during his campaigns against the Cerretani. The reverse type resembles the initial issue of denarii of Julius Caesar a decade earlier (see no. 9) and celebrates the issuer's membership of the priesty college of pontifices. The accompanying legend does not mention his pontificate,[142] though it does record his second consulship (40 BC) and his imperatorial title granted in 39 BC. The latter doubtless provided the occasion for the production of this most unorthodox coinage.

with the title King of Kings; Alexander Helios was to be ruler of Armenia, Media, and Parthia; Ptolemy Philadelphus was to receive the Egyptian territories in Syria and Cilicia and overlordship of the client kings in Asia Minor; whilst even Cleopatra Selene was not forgotten, her share being the Cyrenaica and Libya.

These dispositions were, of course, of a nominal nature only and had no material effect on the administration of Rome's eastern territories. However, they provided valuable ammunition for Antony's enemies in Rome as evidence of the increasing influence of Egypt's queen over the Triumvir. The Donations, together with the staging of the Armenian triumph in the Egyptian capital rather than Rome, could easily be utilized to promote the rumour that Antony's ultimate plan was to remove the seat of government from the city on the Tiber to distant Alexandria. Antony's undoing was at hand and Cleopatra, ignorant and perhaps careless of Italy's sensibilities, was to be the unwitting cause of his ruin.

During these years (35 and 34 BC) Octavian had not been idle. He clearly perceived that in order to achieve recognition as Antony's equal, and ultimately his superior, in all respects it was vital that he should gain for himself a solid military reputation as a commander of conspicuous ability and bravery. He determined that a series of campaigns in Illyricum would have the added advantage of boosting his popularity at home, for it was from the north-east that Italy's security was most seriously threatened by the tribal peoples of the mountainous interior. Accordingly, as soon as campaigning was possible at the close of the winter of 36–35 BC Octavian set out for the north-west Balkans and personally led one prong of the invasion force. His carefully planned strategy, involving operations by the fleet as well as the army, brought success on all fronts and the crowning achievement of the first year was the capture of the strategic stronghold of Siscia situated on an island between the rivers Savus and Colapis. The following year saw the pacification of the peoples of the Dalmatian coast and its hinterland and throughout the course of the war the young Triumvir displayed personal bravery of a high order, an aspect of his character which had not previously been seen. Although more ambitious military operations in this vitally important region would have to be postponed to later years the contrast between Octavian's meticulously devised campaigns and the disaster of Antony's Parthian invasion was not lost on many observers.

By the brilliant success of his military operations in Illyricum and by extensive building activities in Rome Octavian had raised the level of his prestige and popularity in readiness for the final confrontation with Antony which he knew could not now be long delayed. But first the groundwork had to be laid through a war of propaganda and early in 33 BC, the year of his second consulship, Octavian set events in motion by a speech delivered before the Senate in which he made a scathing attack on his triumviral colleague's conduct of affairs in the East. Doubtless he felt bitter over Antony's cruel treatment of his sister, but little that Octavian did was born of passion and we should see in his actions the initial phase of a carefully contrived plan to diminish Antony's still considerable reputation before finally bringing him to battle. As the year progressed the denunciations became more heated and flowed with equal vehemence from both sides. Neither was short of ammunition in this war of words. Octavian could point to Antony's shameful conduct in his relations with Octavia and his reputation for excessive drinking; his dangerous intimacy with a foreign queen and his recognition of her eldest child as the son of Caesar; his disloyalty to Roman sentiments and custom in staging a military triumph in the capital of an alien state; and finally the outrageous spectacle of the Donations of Alexandria by which authority over Roman territory had been granted to Cleopatra and her children. The eastern Triumvir, with perhaps greater justification though to lesser effect, could complain of Octavian's failure to comply with the terms of their various treaties, particularly where they applied to the raising of military recruits in Italy and the transfer of legions to the East in exchange for ships; and of the highly autocratic manner in which he had unilaterally deposed the third member of the Triumvirate, M. Aemilius Lepidus, following the war against Sextus Pompey. He even made the remarkable declaration that he was in favour of laying down his extraordinary powers and assisting in the restoration of the Republic, but that Octavian stood in the way of this desirable development.

Antony had spent – some would say wasted – a good part of the year 33 BC on the eastern border of Armenia meeting with the king of Media. The new Roman ally was fearful of being attacked by the Parthians if Antony withdrew his legions from Armenia for service in the upcoming confrontation with Octavian. To reassure him Antony retained the Roman troops in the province until the autumn, but with the rapidly deteriorating situation he was then obliged to concentrate his army at Ephesus where he and Cleopatra had determined to spend the winter of 33–32 BC. Antony now realized that his popularity and following in Rome, still surprisingly extensive, were being seriously undermined by Octavian's vitriolic propaganda. Accordingly, he dispatched a document to the consuls designate, Cn. Domitius Ahenobarbus and C. Sosius, both of whom were ardent partisans of the eastern Triumvir. It was addressed to the Senate and contained a detailed account and justification of his *acta*, including the highly controversial Donations of Alexandria, and requested that the measures which he had taken should be given official sanction by the Conscript Fathers.

As the year 33 BC drew to a close so did the current term of the Triumvirate which had now been in existence for a full decade. This military dictatorship had accustomed men to the realities of autocratic government, though authority was still wielded through such traditional offices as imperator and proconsul in deference to republican sensibilities. It was left to Augustus at a later time to define the status and make palatable the concept of imperial rule in Rome. Nothing, of course, was changed by the official lapse of the triumviral office at the end of 33. Both remaining Triumvirs continued to exercise the same powers and enjoy the same privileges as before. The only perceptible difference was that while Antony still styled himself 'Triumvir' Octavian ceased to do so at this point, preferring instead to rely on his personal *auctoritas* and his tribunician sacrosanctity. The young man was now strong enough to stand alone, free of the formal requirements of the republican constitution, just as his great-uncle had done more than a decade before.

Octavian departed from the city without ceremony before the new Antonian consuls took office on 1 January 32 BC. It had been expected that Ahenobarbus and Sosius would take this opportunity to present Antony's letter to the assembled Senate, but the document remained unread. The reason for this is not hard to discover. If the question of the legality, or even the prudence, of the Donations of Alexandria were brought up for open discussion then Antony's enemies were sure to exploit the occasion to stir up public feelings against the eastern Triumvir. Instead, Sosius, the more volatile of the two consuls, made an impassioned speech before the Conscript Fathers in which he extolled the virtues of Antony whilst bitterly criticizing Octavian. Not surprisingly, this scathing oratory quickly brought matters to a head. Octavian, who had been busy gathering a substantial body of veterans and other supporters, returned to Rome and entered the Senate-house surrounded by a powerful bodyguard. He took his seat between the two consuls and proceeded to address the assembly which was obliged to remain in obedient silence while he vilified his triumviral colleague and strongly censured the consul Sosius for his recent speech. Octavian informed the senators that he would soon be able to present to them incontrovertible evidence of Antony's serious wrongdoings and that they should reconvene on a fixed day for this purpose. This was more than enough for Ahenobarbus and Sosius who, together with more than 300 senators who still supported Antony's cause, fled the city and and the country to join the eastern Triumvir at his winter residence in Ephesus. The situation was reminiscent of the flight of the consuls and senators to Greece seventeen years before when the supporters of Pompey had hurriedly departed the city on the news of Caesar's approach.

So the spring of 32 BC saw Antony's magnificent entourage in Asia still further embellished by the addition of both consuls and a sizeable contingent of Roman senators; whilst in Rome Octavian (by what authority is uncertain) had already appointed two substitute consuls, M. Valerius and L. Cornelius Cinna. Octavian himself was designated for the consulship (his third) the following year with Antony as his colleague. It was clear to all that these arrangements would have to be changed as in all likelihood the two consuls designate would soon be at war.

Even though his principal opponents in the Senate had now departed Octavian was still not sure of the loyalty of many of the remaining Conscript Fathers. He appeared before them again contrasting his own selfless devotion to the cause of the Roman people with Antony's questionable activities in the East, special emphasis being placed on his triumviral colleague's reckless adventure in Parthia and on the disgraceful allocation of Roman territory to various members of Egypt's royal family. The weakened Senate meekly accepted Octavian's pronouncements and dutifully expressed its support for his position. Undoubtedly it would have done the same for Antony if he had been standing before them backed by a large military presence in the city. The support of the Senate was all well and good and formed a necessary part of his plan, but the western Triumvir knew that it was vital for him to be perceived as the leader of a popular nationalist movement in which men's passions were ignited in enthusiastic support of a just cause, the righteousness of which was beyond all moral question. Only thus could he challenge Antony for sole mastery of Rome and her empire.

Antony and Cleopatra wintered in 33/32 BC *at Ephesus. The sea has now receded some 10 km and the famous Temple of Artemis, one of the Seven Wonders of the Ancient World, lies 5 km to the east (right of the photo).*

Events now began to take a favourable turn for Octavian. In April Antony transferred his headquarters to Samos and spent a few weeks enjoying the pleasures of the island while his huge army was being transported across the Aegean to Greece. The following month he moved on to Athens where he and Cleopatra held court in some splendour to the delight of the Greeks. His generals and closest Roman advisers were now becoming seriously alarmed at the extent of the queen's influence over their commander-in-chief and a mood of pessimism began to set in. Their fears were confirmed when, not long after his arrival in Athens, the Triumvir wrote to his wife in Rome announcing their divorce. The loyal Octavia, heartbroken and weeping, finally left Antony's house together with her two young daughters. Her distress was truly moving and did great harm to Antony's reputation amongst the people of Rome. Octavian, righteously indignant at this shameful and unjust treatment of his sister, resolved to turn his rival's diplomatic blunder to his own advantage. There could be little doubt that Octavia's divorce was tantamount to a declaration of war by Antony against his former triumviral colleague.

Cleopatra's hand was clearly to be seen in his dramatic development. So it was interpreted by two of Antony's principal supporters, L. Munatius Plancus and his nephew M. Titius, and they reacted by deserting the Antonian court and fleeing to Octavian. Theirs was merely the first of many such defections. An important consequence of the arrival of the two former Antonians in Rome was the intelligence they brought with them regarding a will recently drawn up by the eastern Triumvir. According to their story this had been secretly carried to Rome and deposited for safekeeping with the six Vestal Virgins in the temple of Vesta in the Forum. They also claimed to have detailed knowledge of the contents of this important document and Octavian was most encouraged by what he heard. It appeared to be exactly what he had been waiting for, a weapon which could be used to unite Italy and the western provinces in their hatred of the Egyptian queen and to turn the coming civil war into a crusade of the Roman people against a foreign potentate whose insidious methods and evil ambitions knew no bounds. Cleopatra was to be used as the instrument of Antony's destruction. Whether she deserved such a cruel fate and whether her aspirations really went beyond a desire to revive the declining fortunes of her kingdom is hard to ascertain. The truth lies deeply buried beneath layers of Caesarian propaganda aimed at vilifying every aspect of her character.

The will was forcibly removed from the care of the Vestals. Octavian, having familiarized himself with its contents in private, read it out to the assembled Senate and its terms were quickly made public. Antony again asserted the legitimacy of the alleged paternity of Ptolemy Caesar, bequeathed great legacies to Cleopatra's children and, most damaging of all, commanded that following their deaths his body should be buried beside that of the Egyptian queen in Alexandria. Here was clear evidence (or so it was alleged by the Caesarians) that Antony planned to transfer the seat of government to the East, just as Alexander had done almost three centuries before when he turned his back on Macedonia and established his residence at Babylon. Unfortunately for Antony his recent celebration of his Armenian triumph in the Egyptian capital instead of Rome, together with the subsequent distribution of territories to the Ptolemaic royal family, appeared to give real credence to these allegations. Perhaps there was even an element of truth in them. In any case, the publication of Antony's will had an immediate and dramatic effect on the Italian people. At last Octavian found himself in the position which he had sought for so long, the heroic leader of Italy and the West against the insidious forces of the East, led and personified by Queen Cleopatra of Egypt. The coming hostilities would not be a civil war against Antony: he was merely to be pitied for having fallen under the evil spell of the oriental sorceress, for why else would he be betraying the interests of his fatherland.

Many years later Augustus recorded in his own account of the events of his long career that 'all Italy of its own accord swore an oath of allegiance to me and chose me as its leader in the war which I won at Actium'.[143] How spontaneous was this outpouring of patriotic fervour and how much it owed to the work of Octavian's agents is hard to gauge, but there can be little doubt that feelings ran high on this issue and many Romans must have felt that they had been betrayed by Antony. By the late autumn communities all over the country appeared to be uniting in their support of Octavian's leadership and

The Temple of Vesta in the Roman Forum where Octavian illegally seized Antony's will from the Vestals and made public the (alleged) evidence that Antony intended to turn to the East for a centre of government.

Caesar's heir now felt himself empowered to take drastic actions against his former triumviral colleague. Antony was formally deposed from the powers and rank of the Triumvirate,[144] just as Lepidus had been four years before, and he was further deprived of the right to hold the consulship the following year (31 BC), his place being taken by M. Valerius Messalla Corvinus. In a solemn ceremony before the temple of Bellona war was now declared on the queen of Egypt. All reference to Antony was carefully omitted in this declaration of a *iustum bellum*, but if he were to continue his support of Rome's enemy then clearly he would have to suffer the terrible consequences.

Antony received intelligence of these dramatic developments whilst in winter quarters in Greece. It was only what he had been expecting. His rival was master of Italy and the West, a position which in reality had been conceded to him a full decade before, following Philippi, and Antony may well have rued his decision at that time to abandon effective control of the fatherland. But all his efforts had now to be concentrated on preparations for the war and Antony busied himself at his headquarters in Patrae at the mouth of the Gulf of Corinth. The forces at his disposal were impressive indeed, probably greater in numbers than anything which his opponents could range against him, and he had a reliable line of supply in the fleet of Egyptian corn-ships provided by Cleopatra. The land army comprised some nineteen legions which still accounted for a total manpower of about seventy thousand infantry and twelve thousand cavalry despite heavy losses in the Parthian invasion. This force was under the command of Antony's trusted lieutenant Canidius Crassus. Even more formidable was the fleet of over five hundred warships. One full squadron of this, consisting of sixty ships, had been provided by Cleopatra. At its head stood the queen's magnificent flagship appropriately named *Antonia*.

But any numerical superiority which Antony may have enjoyed was more than offset by the confidence of Octavian's forces resulting from their recent successes on land in Illyricum and at sea against Sextus Pompey. In addition, they had been inspired with a passionate belief in the cause for which they were fighting – the defence of the homeland against a foreign menace – and this gave them an overwhelming psychological advantage. Antony's legions, on the other hand, had been badly mauled in the debacle of the Parthian invasion, whilst his magnificent and newly-equipped fleet was largely untried and lacked a commander of the brilliance of Marcus Agrippa. But most important of all, Antony's men were deeply mistrustful of their leader's relationship with the queen of Egypt and of the role which she was playing in the war. Antony himself they would gladly have followed to the ends of the earth, but were they fighting for him or for an enemy of Rome who would be the true beneficiary of any victory which they might achieve over their fellow Romans in Octavian's legions. This nagging concern was felt from the rank and file of Antony's army right up to its highest command. The odour of desertion was in the air.

Although the battle of Actium, fought on 2 September 31 BC, marked the end of the war, in reality the issue had already been decided by the various military actions which preceded it. The battle itself was something of a non-event and an anticlimax to what had been the most spectacular military build-up in Roman history. Hostilities were set in motion in the early months of 31 BC when Octavian and his army crossed to Epirus and advanced southwards towards the Ambracian Gulf. Here they set up their camp at Mikalitsi on the northern of the two promontories which flanked the narrow entrance to the gulf. Antony's main encampment was on the southern promontory, at Actium. Octavian's crossing to Greece and rapid deployment of his army had been facilitated by a diversionary naval operation undertaken by Agrippa in the south. The Caesarian admiral had captured Methone in Messenia at the extreme south-west of the Peloponnese. This was the southernmost of the towns garrisoned by Antony along the coastline of the Ionian Sea. Its loss was a serious blow as it gave Agrippa an excellent base from which he could attack the corn-ships from Egypt which were the lifeline of Antony's huge army. But worse was to follow for Agrippa then took Leucas, situated on an island to the south-west of Actium, thereby enabling his fleet to blockade the narrow entrance to the Ambracian Gulf and prevent the passage of Antonian supply ships. The subsequent capture of Patrae and Corinth cut the enemy off from their lines of supply in southern Greece.

Antony realized that he was gradually losing control of the situation and determined to mount an all out attack on Octavian's camp. The strategy was to isolate the Caesarians on the northern promontory by mounting a simultaneous assault from both north and south with the object of cutting off their water-supply. Antony and his army crossed the narrow strip of water and established themselves before Octavian's encampment. He then deployed a powerful cavalry force on the northern side of the Caesarian position by sending it around the Ambracian Gulf. The plan was not a bad one but its chances of success quickly evaporated in the face of treachery. At this critical juncture two of Antony's principal allies, the client kings Rhoemetalces of Thrace and Deiotarus of Paphlagonia, went over to Octavian taking with them their vital contingents of cavalry. A second sortie was led by the Triumvir himself but with the same result. This time Amyntas was the traitor and with him went his two thousand Galatian horse. With the very real prospect of a disastrous defeat now staring him in the face Antony gave up the assault on the enemy camp and withdrew his army across the mouth of the Ambracian Gulf to Actium.

With their lines of supply cut and their camp under virtual siege the great Antonian army began to suffer the effects of famine and disease. Desertions were now on a massive scale and included many of Antony's oldest and most high-ranking supporters – Ahenobarbus, who was gravely ill and had not long to live; Quintus Dellius; M. Junius Silanus; and the ex-Republican M. Licinius Crassus who was rewarded with the consulship for the following year. Canidius, one of only three Romans of consular status still remaining loyal to Antony, advised a withdrawal to Macedonia where the issue with Octavian could be decided by a pitched battle. Given the condition and the morale of the army at this point it is doubtful whether Antony's generalship would have prevailed in such an engagement. Others preferred to risk all on a naval battle where the odds seemed to be a good deal more favourable. Despite significant losses in various engagements with Agrippa the Antonian fleet was still at least equal in strength to that of the Caesarians, and in Sosius it had an experienced admiral of proven ability. In Antony's war council it was the latter view which prevailed. The naval solution had been strongly supported by Cleopatra, though by this time the Egyptian queen was doubtless motivated more by concerns for the security of her kingdom than for her husband's victory over Octavian. Perhaps she believed that some kind of negotiated settlement could still be made with the enemy which would allow her to continue ruling over the Ptolemaic realm with Antony as her consort. Morale in the Antonian camp was at a very low ebb. Defeated on land and deserted by many of his most trusted and able lieutenants, Antony began preparations for the great naval engagement which would decide not only his own fate but the entire future course of history in the Roman world. But in reality the issue had already been decided. Antony was a seriously disheartened, perhaps even broken man long before the sun rose on the morning of 2 September 31 BC.

We can only speculate over what actually occurred in the battle of Actium. No impartial narrative exists and in such cases it may be assumed that the tradition is seriously distorted, being hopelessly biased in favour of the victors at the expense of the vanquished. Even Antony's intentions are not clear. Did he really believe that he could still inflict such a crushing defeat on the enemy that it would be possible to overcome all the reverses of the preceding months and emerge triumphant as the sole master of the Roman world. Or did he plan merely to escape from the Caesarian blockade and return to Egypt with the bulk of his forces with the object of buying additional time for the formulation of a new strategy. It seems likely that Cleopatra would have favoured the latter course, for although she would hardly have wanted Antony to be defeated she may equally have been alarmed at the prospect of him becoming undisputed master of Rome. Once he was back in the capital her hold over her husband might well have been seriously diminished. Her real hope was probably to see Antony achieve a significant naval victory and thereby be able to negotiate with Octavian from a position of strength with the object of establishing a permanent and peaceful division of territory. She would then be able to pursue her dream of strengthening and expanding the Ptolemaic kingdom of Egypt with Antony as her consort. But none of this was to be.

The unreliable nature of the surviving evidence makes it difficult to reconstruct the actual course of the battle but the following summary is probably reasonably close to the truth. During the morning Antony's ships emerged from their anchorage and took up station to the landward of Octavian's galleys which stood well out at sea. All were awaiting the veering of the wind to the north-west which normally occurred about mid-day. On board Antony's huge fleet there may have been as many as forty thousand legionaries, a number doubtless matched by Octavian's armada which was under the sole command of Marcus Agrippa. Octavian had placed all his trust in the great admiral, the oldest and most loyal of his friends, whilst he himself played no active role in the conduct of the battle. He was certainly wise to do so. As the direction of the wind changed both fleets began to manœuvre to gain an advantageous position for engagement. There was certainly some serious fighting at this stage of the battle with losses on both sides, but Antony's ships seem to have fared worse with possibly as many as fifteen captured or sunk. Even his own flagship was grappled and he was unable to free it – a serious blow to his prestige. At this point something extraordinary happened. A large part of the Antonian fleet – his centre and left – quit the battle and returned to harbour. The majority of the ships of his right also gave up the fight and surrendered to the enemy. The treachery of the Antonian fleet had clearly been well organized though the individual responsible is unknown. We may suspect the admiral Sosius for he was afterwards pardoned by Octavian despite his outburst in the Senate twenty months before.[145] The deciding factor as far as the legionaries was concerned may well have been Antony's order to have the sails kept aboard the ships during the battle. This was not normal practice and Antony explained that he needed them in order to pursue Octavian's ships down wind and drive them away from their camp which would then be left unprotected and vulnerable to siege. The soldiers were suspicious and when the rumour began to spread that their commander was contemplating flight with Cleopatra the conspiracy seems to have spread like wildfire throughout the army.

The treacherous surrender of the major part of Antony's fleet had rendered his position hopeless. His flagship was disabled and he was left with a mere forty ships under his command. There was now no alternative but to signal Cleopatra with instructions to detach her squadron with all haste and make ready to set sail for Egypt. The plan was undoubtedly pre-arranged in the eventuality that the battle would go against them, though they could scarcely have foreseen such a disastrous outcome to the engagement. Even the war-chest – a treasure of vast size – had been taken aboard several of Cleopatra's vessels in the greatest secrecy. To consign such a valuable cargo to ships involved in a great battle might seem a huge risk to run, but they could hardly have left it ashore given the very real possibility that they would not be able to return to the camp to recover it. Some, of course, have interpreted this as evidence of Antony's perfidy, suggesting that it had been his intention all along to abandon his comrades in arms because of his infatuation for the queen of Egypt. Such a theory need scarcely be given any serious credence for without his loyal legions what hope could Antony have for survival (as subsequent events were so tragically to prove). Ironically, it was his men's suspicion of his intention to betray them which led to their own treachery and the certainty of Antony's defeat at Actium. When Canidius attempted a rapid evacuation of the military camp following the naval defeat the soldiers refused to obey his commands and instead opened negotations with Octavian. Perhaps it was at this stage that they discovered the absence of the war-chest and regarded this as absolute confirmation of their worst suspicions. A week later they surrendered and Canidius was obliged to flee for his life, eventually finding his way to Alexandria. The orderly withdrawal of the army to Egypt seems to have been part of the contingency plan in case of an unsatisfactory outcome to the naval battle, but the scheme had not anticipated the mass treachery of the Antonian legions which was the downfall of the Triumvir's cause.

Antony brought his partial squadron alongside Cleopatra's ships and went aboard the *Antonia*. The small fleet then set sail for Alexandria. An illustrious career had come to a dismal end and the haunting picture of the defeated Triumvir seated alone on the prow of the Egyptian flagship, his head buried in his hands, has a poignancy which spans the centuries and still arouses our compassion. On their arrival in Egypt Cleopatra busily set about making plans for their future. These ranged from the defence of Egypt againt Octavian, which clearly was an impossibility, to wild schemes such as the seizure of the Spanish silver mines and the establishment of a rebel state in the peninsula, much as Sertorius had done half a century before; and the founding of a new kingdom in the Far East where they could live free of Rome's interference. But Antony had lost the will to carry on and had retired to a house on the sea shore where he was living the life of a recluse. His was a tragic destiny indeed for one who could so easily have been master of the world. And so they waited for the inevitable end, Cleopatra trying to coax her consort out of his melancholia, he feeding his depression through constant reflection on the mistakes of the past. She did manage to get him to quit his hermit's existence and rejoin her in the palace but was unable to spur him on to any kind of military venture. He was right, of course, for their situation was quite hopeless. Had he endeavoured to lead an army against Octavian his soldiers would simply have gone over to the enemy, as coming events were to demonstrate, so the only real alternatives were suicide or to await the coming of the executioner.

His victory at Actium gave Octavian the prize that he had been relentlessly pursuing for the past thirteen years – sole mastery of the Roman world. But after almost two decades of civil wars the mood of revolution was still very much in the air and it would only be by a long and painstaking process that the 32-year-old heir of Julius Caesar would be able to gain full control of the situation. There were now huge numbers of veteran soldiers to be settled, both Antonian as well as Caesarian, and one of Octavian's first actions was to send Agrippa back to Italy to assist Maecenas with the difficult task. He then moved east, first to Athens, where he was initiated into the Eleusinian Mysteries, and then on to Samos, the stepping-stone to Asia. At this point he received an urgent message from Agrippa asking him to return to Italy as quickly as possible. Serious problems had arisen with the veterans who, fearing that they would no longer be considered in the division of Egypt's vast wealth, had become mutinous and were threatening the security of the country. Octavian took ship to Brundisium – at great personal risk in the stormy seas of winter-time – in order to take charge of the situation and give his personal assurance to the soldiers that their long years of loyal service would be rewarded as soon as the conquest of Egypt was complete. This they were prepared to accept and Octavian was at last able to give his full attention to the final obstacle – the elimination of Cleopatra and Ptolemy Caesar and the acquisition of the immense Ptolemaic treasure.

The invasion of Egypt took place in the summer of 30 BC, almost a year after Actium. It was planned as a two-pronged attack, with Octavian himself advancing through Syria and approaching the country from the east, whilst the assault on the western frontier was entrusted to his lieutenant Cornelius Gallus who was destined to be appointed the first prefect of the new province of Egypt. Antony's lieutenant in the Cyrenaica, L. Pinarius Scarpus, had already taken the precaution of transferring his allegiance to Octavian and with it the four legions under his command. Gallus now advanced on the coastal town of Paraetonium, about 150 miles to the west of Alexandria, and the capture of the place finally provoked Antony to attempt some kind of military relatiation. However, his naval operation to relieve Paraetonium ended in disaster and resulted in the loss of his forty remaining ships. The relentless advance continued, the pincer movement gradually closing in on Alexandria for the kill. Antony communicated to his former triumviral colleague that he would be willing to commit suicide in exchange for Cleopatra's life. But he was no longer in a bargaining position and there was no response from Octavian. Cleopatra, desperate for the survival of her children, tried a different line. She submitted her sceptre and diadem, the symbols of her royalty, to Octavian with the request that he should crown one of her sons in her place. But Octavian had other plans for Egypt and they most certainly did not include the perpetuation of the Ptolemaic dynasty.

The enemy forces reached the outskirts of the Egyptian capital at the end of July. In anticipation of Octavian's arrival Cleopatra had taken refuge on the upper floor of her mausoleum which was still under construction at the time. She was attended by her two most trusted handmaids, Iras and Charmion. In the ground floor chamber of the building she had collected the fabled treasure of the Ptolemies, the key to Octavian's future in enabling him to fulfil all his financial commitments. This was the one trump card she still had left to play and she had taken the precaution of surrounding the treasure with highly inflammable material. One wrong move on Octavian's part and his future would literally go up in the smoke of Cleopatra's royal pyre. As for Antony, theatrical to the last he was intent on meeting a soldier's end in battle against ovewhelming odds. He did in fact launch a surprise attack on Octavian's advance guard as it approached Alexandria and thereby achieved a brief reprieve for the city. But on the following day (1 August), being unable to find anyone willing to fight alongside him, he finally gave up the hopeless struggle and returned to the doomed royal capital. On entering the city he received a message that Cleopatra, in despair, had already taken her own life. She probably wished to hasten his end so that he would not have to face the humiliation of capitulation to Octavian. As she had doubtless intended he took this as a signal for his own suicide and forthwith fell upon his sword. But the wound was not instantly fatal and when he was informed shortly afterwards that Cleopatra still lived he pleaded to be taken to her at the mausoleum. The only means of access to the upper chamber was through a window and it was only with the greatest difficulty that Cleopatra and the two girls were able to haul up the stretcher bearing the dying man. Thus, in the arms of the woman for whom he had sacrificed everything Marcus Antonius the Triumvir expired at the age of fifty-three (1 August 30 BC).

While this little drama was being played out the Roman army took possession of the city and Octavian installed himself in the royal palace. He lost no time in ordering a search for Cleopatra and, because the treasure was not yet in his hands, gave strict orders that she must be taken alive. The queen was soon located shut up in her mausoleum together with her handmaids and the body of Antony. But she refused to surrender and threatened the destruction of the treasure if they attempted to take her by force. The following day, however, the Romans succeeded in apprehending her peaceably before she was able to carry out her threat. Her attention had been distracted by Cornelius Gallus who held her in a lengthy conversation through a grating at the ground floor level of the building. In the meantime several of his companions scaled the walls and gained access to the upper chamber through the same window which had so recently admitted the dying Antony. Cleopatra was taken back to her palace and Octavian took possession of the fabulous riches of the Egyptian kingdom. His financial problems were finally at an end.

All that now remained was the delicate question of how to deal with Cleopatra. She had been at war with Rome and lost. For that crime there could be no punishment other than death. But how was this to be achieved, for a Roman imperator could not order the execution of a woman. The solution of this dilemma exercised all of Octavian's ingenuity. He knew that she ardently desired to have one of her children succeed her on the Egyptian throne – she had communicated as much to him while he was still advancing on Alexandria. He also knew that she abhorred the prospect of being taken as a captive to Rome and exhibited to the mob as the principal ornament of his triumphal procession. Accordingly, he determined on a private interview with the queen in which he would subtly deprive her of her reasons for wishing to live. There have been many, both at the time and in the succeeding centuries, who would have given anything to be the proverbial 'fly on the wall' during this remarkable encounter of the representatives of two great civilizations at this electric moment of transition. But the first emperor of Rome and the last queen of Egypt met alone. Because of the subsequent course of events it may fairly be assumed that Octavian informed Cleopatra of his intention to abolish the kingdom and to reduce the country to the status of a Roman province. It was hardly necessary to state the implications of this decision for her eldest son. She had long feared this outcome and had even attempted to ensure the safety of Ptolemy Caesar by sending him to some remote destination in the Indian sea. With her last reason for living thus removed Octavian must have hinted at his intention of taking her to Rome. This was enough, and Octavian knew he could now leave it to Cleopatra to accomplish the act which he was constrained by convention from ordering himself.

So it was that on 10 August 30 BC the queen of Egypt was left alone with Iras and Charmion in her private apartments. She had arranged – and Octavian undoubtedly knew of it – that a poisonous snake (an asp) should be smuggled into the palace in a basket of figs. The melodramatic nature of the reported circumstances of Cleopatra's death has often led to doubt being cast on the traditional account, but the special significance of the asp to Egyptian royalty lends great credence to the story. The small hooded serpent was native to Egypt and Libya and its head appeared as an ornament on the crown of Egypt. Its function was to protect from harm the line of the sun-god Re, deity of the royal after-life in the old Egyptian religion which had been so eagerly adopted by the Greek Ptolemies. The unique distinction of the asp was that it conferred deification on the recipient of its venom.

The three women prepared themselves for their destinies, for the handmaids were to share the fate of their royal mistress. There was to be no interference from the representatives of the foreign power which now occupied Cleopatra's palace, her city, and her kingdom. Once she was suitably arrayed in her gorgeous royal robes she lay on her couch of gold and placed the asp to her breast. The serpent quickly accomplished its deadly work and Iras and Charmion followed suit. In a mock show of distress and concern the Romans then burst into the chamber and the famous words were uttered by an officer and by the dying servant: 'Is this well done, Charmion?' 'Aye, 'tis very well.'

The Ptolemaic kingdom of Egypt was no more. In its place Octavian established the Roman province of *Aegyptus* under the government of a *praefectus* of equestrian rank (Cornelius Gallus was the first to hold the office). The prefect of Egypt was directly answerable to Octavian and the whole country was organized as a private estate, a status very different from that of any other Roman province. In effect, Octavian viewed himself as the direct successor of the Ptolemaic rulers and doubtless he was regarded as such by his Egyptian subjects, though their 'king' now resided elsewhere. Roman senators were strictly excluded from visiting the former Ptolemaic kingdom unless they had Octavian's personal permission to do so.

Cleopatra had been most obliging in arranging for her own demise without any blame attaching to the conqueror of her kingdom. But before the episode of the *Bellum Alexandrinum* could be considered closed it was necessary for Octavian to give direct orders for a number of executions. The list was mercifully short: Ptolemy Caesar, the 17-year-old supposed son of the dictator by Cleopatra; Marcus Antonius Junior ('Antyllus'), elder son of the Triumvir by Fulvia; D. Turullius and Cassius of Parma, the last two surviving assassins of Caesar; and Antony's lieutenant P. Canidius who had remained loyal even after Actium. The three children of Cleopatra by Antony were spared and were brought up in the household of the virtuous Octavia. Nothing is known of the subsequent fate of the two boys, but Cleopatra Selene was married to Juba II, king of Mauretania, and their son Ptolemy inherited his father's throne in AD 23. His murder by the Emperor Caligula in AD 40 brought to an ignominious end the illustrious Ptolemaic line.

The tragedy of Antony and Cleopatra had run its course and with their suicides two decades of civil war were finally at an end. Octavian, backed by an immense military establishment, could now assume sole authority in the Roman world. This, of course, signalled the passing of any lingering hopes there may have been for the restoration of senatorial rule in Rome. Inevitable though the process of transition from republic to autocracy had been, the actual death throes of the old order had developed into a surprisingly protracted, painful, and costly experience for the Roman people. Many brave individuals had stood firm against the impending change, and men such as Cato Uticensis, Cicero, and M. Junius Brutus had chosen to die honourably by their own hand rather than live under the rule of tyrants. Even Antony himself had strong republican sympathies and had he not been caught up in the glamour of life as a close associate of Caesar it is doubtful if he would ever have filled the role of a revolutionary leader. But the wholly unexpected turn of events on the 'Ides of March' had thrust him into the position of successor to the dictator and heir to his aspirations and enterprises.

Octavian, on the other hand, was Caesar's true heir in every sense. It would, indeed, have been better for all concerned if the dictator had lived another ten years and been able to hand over the reigns of power to a mature Octavian. But at the time of his great-uncle's assassination he was an unknown and untried youth of eighteen years whilst Antony, two decades his senior, could boast a long and successful career of military service. Furthermore, Antony was the surviving consul in a situation of grave public emergency and as such men looked to him to take a leadership role in the uncertain days and weeks which lay ahead. Thus, he may almost involuntarily have become the head of the 'Caesarian' party, but one may speculate whether his heart was truly in it. His sorrow at the suicide of his former friend Brutus, following the battle of Philippi, was genuine indeed; and his wife Fulvia was bitterly frustrated by his ingratitude and apparent lack of ambition when he chastised her for playing a prominent part in the Perusine War which could so easily have resulted in Octavian's early downfall.

Antony and Octavian were never comfortable with one another as colleagues in the Triumvirate and the wonder is that their rivalry, which had existed from the very outset of their relationship, took so long to resolve. On Antony's side it was probably due to that lack of political motivation which had so disappointed his third wife, whilst Octavian in the early years of their association needed all his ingenuity merely to survive the seemingly endless succession of trials and tribulations with which he was obliged to contend. But by dogged determination and with the help of loyal and gifted friends, such as Marcus Agrippa and Gaius Maecenas, he gradually began to gain the upper hand in the triumviral partnership. The real turning point was the year 36 BC when Octavian managed to dispose of both Sextus Pompey and Lepidus whilst Antony's invasion of Parthia ended in disastrous failure, a setback from which he never fully recovered. Thereafter, with Antony falling increasingly under the spell of the Egyptian queen it was only a matter of time before Octavian achieved his ultimate victory.

Thus, Caesar's heir – still only thirty-three years of age at the time of his conquest of Egypt – at last stood alone at the pinnacle of political power, though the authority which he wielded had yet to be properly defined in constitutional terms. That was to be one of the achievements of the coming decades, for Octavian (soon to be called Augustus) was destined to live a further forty-four years before finally handing over a firmly established monarchy to his stepson, the Emperor Tiberius.

COINAGE OF THE PERIOD

A. Issues of Antony

The momentous events of 36 BC had marked the beginning of the shift in the balance of power which, half a decade later, was to lead to the total ruin of Antony's cause and the final triumph of Caesar's heir. Following the catastophic failure of his much-vaunted invasion of Parthia the eastern Triumvir produced no significant issues of Roman coinage for several years. The deficiency was perhaps partially made good by the production in Syria or Phoenicia of Greek tetradrachms bearing the heads of both Antony and Cleopatra, an issue the commencement of which appears to coincide with a gap in the series of dated 'posthumous Philip' tetradrachms of the Antioch mint.[146] The eastern Triumvir resumed his coinage in 34 BC in connection with the punitive campaign against Artavasdes of Armenia.

343 Bare head of M. Antony right, **M ANTONI M F M N AVG IMP TERT** around. *Reverse:* bare head of Mark Antony Junior (M. Antonius Antyllus) right, **COS ITER ΔESIGN TERT III VIR R P C** around. *Gold aureus. Military mint travelling with Antony in Syria or Armenia, spring–summer 34 BC* (Crawford 541/1; Sydenham 1206; BMCRR East 173; Babelon Antonia 92; Newman 34.1; Cohen 2).

343

344 Bare head of M. Antony right, **ANTON AVG IMP III COS DES III III V R P C** around. *Reverse:* bare head of Mark Antony Junior (M. Antonius Antyllus) right, **M ANTONIVS M F F** around. *Gold aureus. Military mint travelling with Antony in Syria or Armenia, spring–summer 34 BC* (Crawford 541/2; Sydenham 1207; BMCRR East 174; Babelon Antonia 91; Newman 34.2; Cohen 1).

344

This issue is securely dated by its reference to Antony's second consulship in 34 BC. Also recorded is his designation to a third consulship which he was destined to hold jointly with Octavian in 31. Circumstances were to dictate otherwise. The dies of this extremely rare issue are delicately engraved, and the use of **Δ** instead of **D** in **DESIGN** on no. 343 betrays the hand of a Greek die-cutter who was unfamiliar with the Latin alphabet. The spring and summer of this year were devoted to Antony's campaign of revenge against the Armenian king Artavasdes who had been instrumental in the failure of the Triumvir's Parthian invasion two years before. Artavasdes was duly brought to heel and deposed from his throne. His future role was to be the chief exhibit in Antony's magnificent triumph in Alexandria later in the year. On the evidence of these aurei it would appear that Antony's eldest son, the nine-year-old Marcus Antonius Junior,[147] accompanied his father on this relatively harmless adventure. The Triumvir's son by Fulvia, the young Mark Antony was betrothed to Octavian's infant daughter Julia at the time of the Pact of Tarentum (summer, 37 BC). Following Actium he assumed the toga of manhood (*toga virilis*) and was sent by his father to Octavian with peace overtures which were, of course, rejected. Following Octavian's capture of Alexandria in 30 BC the unfortunate boy, still only thirteen years of age, was on the list of necessary executions, a fate which he shared with Cleopatra's eldest son, the seventeen-year-old Ptolemy Caesar (Caesarion). On these coins his portrait shows a remarkable resemblance to his father, a fact which would certainly have helped seal his fate. His name appears only on the second variety. The curious ending of the accompanying inscription may best be expanded to *Marci filii filius*[148] ('Marcus Antonius the son, son of Marcus').

345 Bare head of M. Antony right, Armenian tiara behind, **ANTONI ARMENIA DEVICTA** around. *Reverse:* diademed and draped bust of Cleopatra right, stem of prow before, **CLEOPATRAE** (sometimes **CLEOPAT**, **CLEOPATR**, or **CLEOPATRA**) **REGINAE REGVM FILIORVM REGVM** around. *Silver denarius. Alexandria, autumn 34 BC* (Crawford 543; Sydenham 1210–1210b; BMCRR East 179; Babelon Antonia 95; Newman 34.3; RSC/Cohen 1–1e).

345

On one die **ARMENTA** *appears for* **ARMENIA** *(BMCRR East 182), and on another* **SESINAE** *for* **REGINAE** *(Babelon Antonia 95 var).*

This remarkable type clearly illustrates the extent of Cleopatra's influence over Antony in the years following the failure of his invasion of Parthia. The appearance on a Roman coin of the portrait and titles of a foreign head of state certainly represented an unprecedented departure from convention and would have provided valuable ammunition for Octavian in his war of propaganda against the eastern Triumvir. The occasion for the issue can hardly have been anything other than the celebrated and enigmatic 'Donations of Alexandria' which took place following Antony's Armenian triumph through the streets of the Egyptian capital in the autumn of 34 BC. Antony appears as the vanquisher of Armenia following the success of his punitive campaign against Artavasdes earlier in the year. But the grandiose title of *Armenia Devicta* sounds a hollow note in the light of the failure of the Triumvir's grand design for the conquest of Parthia. Even more imposing is the titulature of Cleopatra, though the legend is clumsily rendered in Latin and not easily interpreted. For the first and last time on the Roman coinage the royal title of *Regina* appears applied to a living individual. 'Of Cleopatra, Queen of Kings and of her Sons who are Kings' would seem to be the most satisfactory translation, though not all elements of this are present. The connection with the granting of honours and titles to Cleopatra and her childen in the ceremony of the 'Donations' is obvious and the coins may have been struck for distribution to soldiers and citizenry on this occasion. The prow-stem before Cleopatra's bust symbolizes the importance of the Egyptian naval contingent to the forces of the eastern Triumvir. Many of the surviving specimens of this type show evidence of careless engraving and shoddy execution and this, together with the imprecise form of the Latin, is consistent with their production by a mint which was unaccustomed to striking Roman coinage (*i.e.* Alexandria).[149] An additional factor favouring an attribution to the Egyptian capital is Cleopatra's appearance on the anvil (*i.e.* the obverse) die, whilst her Roman consort is relegated to the reverse.[150]

346

347

346 Bare head of M. Antony right (artist's signature 'P' concealed in the hair behind the ear), ANTON AVG IMP III COS DES III III V R P C around. *Reverse:* M SILANVS AVG / Q PRO COS in two lines across field. *Silver denarius. Athens, summer 32 BC* (Crawford 542/1; Sydenham 1208; BMCRR East 175; Babelon Antonia 97; Newman 33.1; Cohen 71).

347 *Obverse:* as preceding. *Reverse:* ANTONIVS / AVG IMP III in two lines across field. *Silver denarius. Athens, summer 32 BC* (Crawford 542/2; Sydenham 1209; BMCRR East 177; Babelon Antonia 96; Newman 33.2; Cohen 2).

This issue has usually been assigned an earlier date.[151] However, an inscription from Athens[152] indicates that M. Junius Silanus held his office of *quaestor pro consule* in that city, and as Antony did not arrive there from Samos until May of 32 BC it seems reasonable to date the coins to the summer of that year. The Triumvir's titulature accords perfectly with this date as his third consulship was designated for the following year. M. Junius Silanus had a most varied career. In the political confusion of the immediate post-Caesarian years he supported in rapid succession his brother-in-law Aemilius Lepidus, Mark Antony, and finally Sextus Pompey, before returning to Rome under the terms of the Pact of Misenum in 39 BC. In the triumviral rivalry his support initially went to Antony under whom he served in Greece during the military build-up prior to the Actian campaign. It was at this time that his issue of coinage was made in the eastern Triumvir's name, though just prior to Actium he went over to Octavian in company with the historian Quintus Dellius, author of an important account of Antony's Parthian War. Like so many of Antony's principal officers Silanus was appalled at the extent to which Cleopatra's influence had grown. His reward was the consulship in 25 BC which he held in partnership with the Emperor Augustus himself. His coinage shows that, like both of the Triumvirs, he had been elected to the priestly college of augurs. Although his name appears only on the first variety (no. 346) the types are clearly linked and there seems little doubt that Silanus was responsible for the entire coinage. The repetition of Antony's name and part of his titles on the reverse of the second variety (no. 347) seems unnecessary and faintly absurd. The reason for it remains unexplained. Another curious feature of this issue is the appearance of an engraver's signature ('P') concealed in Antony's hair just behind his ear. This is the only such occurrence in the entire Roman republican coinage. It is so well concealed that it went unnoticed until 1920 when it was pointed out in an Italian sale catalogue.[153]

The last major coinage issued by the Triumvir Marcus Antonius, prior to his downfall at Actium on 2 September 31 BC, was the celebrated 'legionary' series. The volume of this coinage was truly prodigious and specimens are occasionally found in hoards of the Severan period, some two and a half centuries after the pieces originally entered circulation. This was because the 'legionary' denarii had early acquired a reputation (partially deserved) for having been struck in debased metal and for that reason had not disappeared from circulation during the latter part of Nero's reign (after AD 64) when that emperor reduced the weight, but probably not the fineness, of the denomination. Soon afterwards Vespasian (AD 69–79) even countermarked some specimens of the Antonian denarii in order to maintain their legality in circulation. When Trajan (in AD 107) decided to demonetize the precious metal coinage issued prior to Nero's currency reform of AD 64 he produced a fascinating series of 'restoration' coins, bearing the emperor's name, reviving some of the principal denarius types of the republican period together with a number of aurei honouring some of his imperial predecessors. Significantly, the denarii did not include a restoration of Antony's 'legionary' type for the very good reason that these coins still remained in circulation in appreciable numbers. More than half a century later, during the joint reign of Marcus Aurelius and

Lucius Verus (AD 161–169), a restoration of the type honouring *legio VI* was produced, though the motivation behind this very specific revival remains obscure.

Antony knew that his army and navy would both have vital roles to play if he was to prevail over Octavian in the struggle for mastery of the Roman world. Accordingly, the two branches of the armed forces receive equal attention on the coinage which was produced specifically for military pay during the long months of preparation prior to the final conflict. Naval symbolism had occurred before on Antony's coinage, notably on the aurei and denarii struck for him by Ahenobarbus in 40 BC (see nos. 257 and 258), and on the extensive bronze 'fleet coinage' produced by the admirals Bibulus, Atratinus, and Capito in 38–37 BC (see nos 273–96). The type of a legionary *aquila* between standards, which was to become so familiar on the coinage of imperial Rome, had been utilized only twice before in the period of the civil wars.[154] Its initial occurrence was on a denarius minted in Rome by the quaestor urbanus Cn. Nerius soon after Caesar's crossing of the Rubicon at the beginning of 49 BC (see no. 2); whilst almost eight years later the young Triumvir Octavian had used it on a denarius struck in connection with the Philippi campaign (see no. 138). Now the type was to become familiar to all on Antony's massive pre-Actium coinage and the deep impression which it made on the Roman consciousness at this time was doubtless responsible for the frequency of its occurrence on the coins of the emperors.

Twenty-three legions are honoured, three of them with additional types giving their names as well as their numbers (*XII Antiqua*, *XVII Classica*, and *XVIII Lybica*). Many of these units would have been raised by Antony in the East as his supply of Italian recruits had been virtually cut off by Octavian. Under the terms of their triumviral agreements both leaders were supposed to have equal acccess to Italian enlistees but because of the distrust which existed between them Octavian, who had full control of the fatherland, never allowed his eastern colleague to exercise his rights in this regard. Following the surrender of the Antonian army at Actium many of the legions were disbanded. Others were incorporated into Octavian's army, hence the name *Gemina* ('Twin') which was applied to several of the legions at this time. On the Antonian 'legionary' coinage the praetorian cohorts (**CHORTIVM PRAETORIARVM**) and the cohort of *speculatores* (**CHORTIS SPECVLATORVM**) also receive mention. Although silver denarii formed the bulk of the issues gold aurei have been recorded for the *cohortes praetoriae* and for *legiones II, IV, VI, XII, XIII, XIV*, and *XIX*. The style and fabric of the coins is uniform throughout suggesting that the entire series was issued from a single centrally-located mint. As production probably did not commence before the latter part of 32 BC, by which time Antony was already in Greece, it seems logical to seek a mint in this region rather than farther afield.[155] It would be tempting to see the 'legionary' series as the successor of Silanus' coinage at Athens (see nos. 346–7), but the fabric is so different that another mint must be sought. A likely choice would be Antony's headquarters at Patrae, near the mouth of the Gulf of Corinth, where he was to spend the winter of 32/31 BC making final plans for the deployment of troops and naval forces. Actium itself seems an improbable location because of the potential vulnerability of a site so close to the enemy encampment.

348 Galley right, with rowers, a mast with fluttering banners placed at the prow, ANT AVG above, III VIR R P C below. *Reverse:* legionary eagle (*aquila*) between two standards (*signa*), LEG-PRI across lower field either side of eagle's shaft. *Silver denarius. Patrae (?), autumn 32–spring 31 BC* (Crawford 544/13; Sydenham 1215; BMCRR East 189; Babelon Antonia 104; Newman 32.1; Cohen 26).

348

This is by far the rarest of the Antonian 'legionary' denarii with only three or four specimens known. *legio prima* is distinct from Octavian's *legio I* (raised by Caesar) and must have been an Antonian regiment which was disbanded or lost its separate identity after Actium.

349 349A

349 Similar to preceding, but with LEG–II on reverse either side of eagle's shaft. *Silver denarius. Patrae (?), autumn 32–spring 31 BC* (Crawford 544/14; Sydenham 1216; BMCRR East 190; Babelon Antonia 105; Newman 32.1; Cohen 27).

349A Same as preceding. *Gold aureus. Patrae (?), autumn 32–spring 31 BC* (Numismatic Fine Arts auction, 13 May 1991, lot 20: unpublished in all the principal works of reference).

An Antonian legion which was disbanded or lost its separate identity after Actium.

350 Similar to preceding, but with LEG–III on reverse. *Silver denarius. Patrae (?), autumn 32–spring 31 BC* (Crawford 544/15; Sydenham 1217; BMCRR East 193; Babelon Antonia 106; Newman 32.1; Cohen 28).

350

The regiment honoured here is probably *legio III Gallica*. This legion was raised by Caesar and is known to have served with Antony in the East. Another possibility is *legio III Cyrenaica* which may have been raised by Antony himself.

351 Similar to preceding, but with LEG–IV. *Gold aureus. Patrae (?), autumn 32–spring 31 BC* (Crawford 544/2; Sydenham 1218; BMCRR East 187; Babelon Antonia 109; Newman 32.1; Cohen 31).

352 Same as preceding. *Silver denarius. Patrae (?), autumn 32–spring 31 BC* (Crawford 544/17; Sydenham 1219; BMCRR East 195; Babelon Antonia 108; Newman 32.1; Cohen 30).

352

353 Similar to preceding, but with LEG–IIII. *Silver denarius. Patrae (?), autumn 32–spring 31 BC* (Crawford 544/16; Sydenham 1220; BMCRR East 194; Babelon Antonia 107; Newman 32.1; Cohen 29).

Legio IV, later called *Scythica*, was probably raised by Antony himself. Surprisingly, it managed to retain its identity in Octavian's military reforms following Actium.

354

354 Similar to preceding, but with LEG–V. *Silver denarius. Patrae (?), autumn 32–spring 31 BC* (Crawford 544/18; Sydenham 1221; BMCRR East 196; Babelon Antonia 110; Newman 32.1; Cohen 32).

Legio V Alaudae was originally raised by Caesar in Transalpine Gaul in 52 BC, and was reconstituted by Antony following the dictator's death in 44 BC.

355 Similar to preceding, but with LEG–VI. *Gold aureus. Patrae (?), autumn 32–spring 31 BC* (Crawford 544/3; Sydenham 1222; BMCRR East 188; Babelon Antonia 112; Newman 32.1).

356

356 Same as preceding. *Silver denarius. Patrae (?), autumn 32–spring 31 BC* (Crawford 544/19; Sydenham 1223; BMCRR East 197; Babelon Antonia 111; Newman 32.1; Cohen 33).

Another Caesarian legion raised in 52 BC, this time in Cisalpine Gaul, *legio VI Ferrata* was reconstituted by Lepidus in 44 BC and the following year was taken over by Antony, just prior to the establishment of the Second Triumvirate.

357

357 Similar to preceding, but with LEG–VII. *Silver denarius. Patrae (?), autumn 32–spring 31 BC* (Crawford 544/20; Sydenham 1224; BMCRR East 198; Babelon Antonia 113; Newman 32.1; Cohen 34).

An Antonian legion which was disbanded or lost its separate identity after Actium.

358

358 Similar to preceding, but with LEG-VIII. *Silver denarius. Patrae (?), autumn 32–spring 31 BC* (Crawford 544/21; Sydenham 1225; BMCRR East 199; Babelon Antonia 114; Newman 32.1; Cohen 35).

On one obverse die the N *of* ANT *is retrograde. RSC 35a also records the form LEG–IIX, but the authority is not recorded.*

An Antonian legion which was disbanded or lost its separate identity after Actium.

359

359 Similar to preceding, but with LEG–IX. Silver denarius. Patrae (?), autumn 32-spring 31 BC *(Crawford 544/23; Sydenham 1227; BMCRR East 201; Babelon Antonia 116; Newman 32.1; Cohen 37).*

360 Similar to preceding, but with LEG–VIIII. *Silver denarius. Patrae (?), autumn 32–spring 31 BC* (Crawford 544/22; Sydenham 1226; BMCRR East 200; Babelon Antonia 115; Newman 32.1; Cohen 36).

An Antonian legion which was disbanded or lost its separate identity after Actium.

360

361 Similar to preceding, but with LEG–X. *Silver denarius. Patrae (?), autumn 32–spring 31 BC* (Crawford 544/24; Sydenham 1228; BMCRR East 202; Babelon Antonia 117; Newman 32.1; Cohen 38).

361

Legio X, later called *Gemina*, was another of the units which originated in 59 BC or earlier. Like *legio VI Ferrata* it was reconstituted by Lepidus in 44 BC and the following year was acquired by Antony, just prior to the establishment of the Second Triumvirate.

362 Similar to preceding, but with LEG–XI. *Silver denarius. Patrae (?), autumn 32–spring 31 BC* (Crawford 544/25; Sydenham 1229; BMCRR East 203; Babelon Antonia 118; Newman 32.1; Cohen 39).

362

An Antonian legion which was disbanded or lost its separate identity after Actium.

363 Similar to preceding, but with reverse legend LEG XII ANTIQVAE around, above the legionary eagle and standards. *Silver denarius. Patrae (?), autumn 32–spring 31 BC* (Crawford 544/9; Sydenham 1231; BMCRR East 222; Babelon Antonia 120; Newman 32.1; Cohen 40).

363

364 Similar to preceding, but with LEG–XII across lower field on reverse, either side of eagle's shaft. *Gold aureus. Patrae (?), autumn 32–spring 31 BC* (Crawford 544/4, citing specimen in Oxford).

365 Same as preceding. *Silver denarius. Patrae (?), autumn 32–spring 31 BC* (Crawford 544/26; Sydenham 1230; BMCRR East 204; Babelon Antonia 119; Newman 32.1; Cohen 41).

365

Legio XII Fulminata was raised by Caesar in 58 BC and, having been reconstituted in 44/3 BC, it passed into the service of Antony in the East. The *cognomen Antiqua* is otherwise unattested.

366 Similar to preceding, but with LEG–XIII on reverse. *Gold aureus. Patrae (?), autumn 32–spring 31 BC* (Crawford 544/5 and Sydenham 1232, both citing specimen in Hersh Collection).

367 Same as preceding. *Silver denarius. Patrae (?), autumn 32–spring 31 BC* (Crawford 544/27; Sydenham 1232a; BMCRR East 205; Babelon Antonia 121; Newman 32.1; Cohen 42).

367

An Antonian legion which was disbanded or lost its separate identity after Actium.

368 Similar to preceding, but with LEG–XIV. *Gold aureus. Patrae (?), autumn 32–spring 31 BC* (Crawford 544/6; Sydenham 1234 note; BMCRR East, p. 528, note; Babelon Antonia 124; Newman 32.1; Cohen 45).

369 Same as preceding. *Silver denarius. Patrae (?), autumn 32–spring 31 BC.* (Crawford 544/29; Sydenham 1234; BMCRR East 208; Babelon Antonia 123; Newman 32.1; Cohen 44).

369

370

370 Similar to preceding, but with LEG–XIIII. *Silver denarius. Patrae (?), autumn 32–spring 31 BC* (Crawford 544/28; Sydenham 1233; BMCRR East 207; Babelon Antonia 122; Newman 32.1; Cohen 43).

An Antonian legion which was disbanded or lost its separate identity after Actium.

371

371 Similar to preceding, but with LEG–XV. *Silver denarius. Patrae (?), autumn 32–spring 31 BC* (Crawford 544/30; Sydenham 1235; BMCRR East 210; Babelon Antonia 125; Newman 32.1; Cohen 47).

An Antonian legion which was disbanded or lost its separate identity after Actium.

372

372 Similar to preceding, but with LEG–XVI. *Silver denarius. Patrae (?), autumn 32–spring 31 BC* (Crawford 544/31; Sydenham 1236; BMCRR East 211; Babelon Antonia 126; Newman 32.1; Cohen 48).

An Antonian legion which was disbanded or lost its separate identity after Actium.

373

373 Similar to preceding, but with reverse legend LEG XVII CLASSICAE around, above the legionary eagle and standards. *Silver denarius. Patrae (?), autumn 32–spring 31 BC* (Crawford 544/10; Sydenham 1238; BMCRR East 223; Babelon Antonia 128; Newman 32.1; Cohen 50).

374

374 Similar to preceding, but with LEG–XVII across lower field on reverse, either side of eagle's shaft. *Silver denarius. Patrae (?), autumn 32–spring 31 BC* (Crawford 544/32; Sydenham 1237; BMCRR East 212; Babelon Antonia 127; Newman 32.1; Cohen 49).

An Antonian legion which was disbanded or lost its separate identity after Actium. The *cognomen Classica* seems to relate to special naval duties assigned to this regiment by the eastern Triumvir.

375

375 Similar to preceding, but with reverse legend LEG XVIII LYBICAE around, above the legionary eagle and standards. *Silver denarius. Patrae (?), autumn 32–spring 31 BC* (Crawford 544/11; Sydenham 1240; BMCRR East 225; Babelon Antonia 130; Newman 32.1; Cohen 53).

376

376 Similar to preceding, but with LEG–XVIII across lower field on reverse, either side of eagle's shaft. *Silver denarius. Patrae (?), autumn 32–spring 31 BC* (Crawford 544/33; Sydenham 1239; BMCRR East 213; Babelon Antonia 129; Newman 32.1; Cohen 51).

Babelon Antonia 131, citing Morell, records the variant form LEG–XIIX, but in the absence of recent confirmation it has to be regarded as suspect.

An Antonian legion which was disbanded or lost its separate identity after Actium. The *cognomen Lybica* suggests that it was raised in north Africa.

377 Similar to preceding, but with LEG–XIX on reverse. *Gold aureus. Patrae (?), autumn 32–spring 31 BC* (Crawford 544/7; Sydenham 1242 note; BMCRR East, p. 528, note; Babelon Antonia 134; Newman 32.1; Cohen 56).

378 Same as preceding. *Silver denarius. Patrae (?), autumn 32–spring 31 BC* (Crawford 544/35; Sydenham 1242; BMCRR East 214; Babelon Antonia 133; Newman 32.1; Cohen 55).

379 Similar to preceding, but with LEG–XVIIII. *Silver denarius. Patrae (?), autumn 32–spring 31 BC* (Crawford 544/34; Sydenham 1241; Babelon Antonia 132; Newman 32.1; Cohen 54).

378

An Antonian legion which was disbanded or lost its separate identity after Actium.

379

380 Similar to preceding, but with LEG–XX. *Silver denarius. Patrae (?), autumn 32–spring 31 BC* (Crawford 544/36; Sydenham 1243; BMCRR East 215; Babelon Antonia 135; Newman 32.1; Cohen 57).

Octavian's *legio XX* (later called *Valeria Victrix*) may have been raised after Actium, in which case it could have contained some elements of Antony's disbanded twentieth.

380

381 Similar to preceding, but with LEG–XXI. *Silver denarius. Patrae (?), autumn 32–spring 31 BC* (Crawford 544/37; Sydenham 1244; BMCRR East 216; Babelon Antonia 136; Newman 32.1; Cohen 58).

Like *legio XX*, this regiment may have been raised after Actium, in which case it could have contained some elements of Antony's disbanded twenty-first.

381

382 Similar to preceding, but with LEG–XXII. *Silver denarius. Patrae (?), autumn 32–spring 31 BC* (Crawford 544/38; Sydenham 1245; BMCRR East 217; Babelon Antonia 137; Newman 32.1; Cohen 59).

An Antonian legion which was disbanded or lost its separate identity after Actium. Augustus' *legio XXII Deiotariana* did not exist until 25 BC when it was formed out of two regiments raised by the late King Deiotarus of Galatia who had modelled his army on the Roman legions.

382

383 Similar to preceding, but with LEG–XXIII. *Silver denarius. Patrae (?), autumn 32–spring 31 BC* (Crawford 544/39; Sydenham 1246; BMCRR East 219; Babelon Antonia 138; Newman 32.1; Cohen 60).

An Antonian legion which was disbanded or lost its separate identity after Actium. Its number was never used again. When Augustus reorganized the Roman army he reduced its total strength to twenty-eight legions, but *XXII* was the highest number borne by any regiment until Trajan raised his *legio XXX Ulpia Victrix*. The reason for this apparent aberration was that it probably represented the thirtieth legion in the Roman military establishment at that time.

383

Other Antonian 'legionary' denarii have been recorded with numbers ranging from *XXIV* to *XXX*. These must be regarded as extremely suspect and it is doubtful whether any genuine specimens exist.[156] As already mentioned, no legion in imperial times ever bore a number higher than *XXII*, with the sole exception of Trajan's thirtieth, and it is improbable that Antony would have raised any regiments with numbers higher than *XXIII*.

384 Galley right, with rowers, a mast with fluttering banners placed at the prow, ANT AVG above, III VIR R P C below. *Reverse:* legionary eagle (*aquila*) between two standards (*signa*), CHORTIVM PRAETORIARVM around, above. *Gold aureus. Patrae (?), autumn 32–spring 31 BC* (Crawford 544/1; Sydenham 1212; BMCRR East 183; Babelon Antonia 101; Newman 32.1; Cohen 8).

385

385 Same as preceding. *Silver denarius. Patrae (?), autumn 32–spring 31 BC* (Crawford 544/8; Sydenham 1213; BMCRR East 184; Babelon Antonia 102; Newman 32.1; Cohen 7).

The praetorian cohorts had their origins in the small escorts which accompanied the generals on campaign. The name derives from the commander's tent (*praetorium*), a name which was later applied to the commandant's house in a permanent fort. At the time of Actium Antony probaby had at least four praetorian cohorts and these are honoured on this interesting adjunct to the 'legionary' coinage. In his reorganization of the military establishment in the years following Actium Augustus established a permanent body of nine praetorian cohorts, three in Rome itself, the remainder dispersed among neighbouring towns. They were regarded as élite troops and this was reflected in their living conditions and remuneration (more than three times the rate of pay for legionaries). The praetorian prefects, first appointed by Augustus in 2 BC, were to exercise enormous political power in Rome in the centuries to follow.

386

386 Galley right, with rowers, a mast with fluttering banners placed at the prow, ANT AVG above, III VIR R P C below. *Reverse:* three standards, each decorated with two wreaths and model of a prow, CHORTIS SPECVLATORVM around, above. *Silver denarius. Patrae (?), autumn 32–spring 31 BC* (Crawford 544/12; Sydenham 1214; BMCRR East 185; Babelon Antonia 103; Newman 32.1; Cohen 6).

Antony here commemorates his special cohort of *speculatores*. In late republican times men of this designation served in the legions as scouts, messengers, and collectors of military intelligence (*i.e.* spies).[157] Ten *speculatores* were normally assigned to each legion, but Antony took the important step of forming a separate cohort of *speculatores* with special responsibilties for carrying out the personal instructions of the commander-in-chief. Augustus developed this concept and in imperial Rome the mounted speculatorian cohort became an inner corps of the praetorian guard charged with the vital task of protecting the emperor's person. The denarii issued by Antony in honour of his cohort of *speculatores* differ in one important detail from the remainer of the 'legionary' coinage. Three standards are shown on the reverse in place of the usual legionary *aquila* between two standards. To each of these speculatorian standards two wreaths and a miniature depiction of the prow of a galley are attached. The naval reference is of particular interest as it appears to refer to one of the specialized roles of the *speculatores* as lookouts on board ship where they occupied a turret (*specula*) at the stern of the vessel.

With the conclusion of his vast 'legionary' coinage, produced to pay an army which was destined to remain largely inactive throughout the campaign of Actium, the eastern Triumvir's career was rapidly drawing to its close. One final issue of portrait denarii was struck by Decimus Turullius, one of the assassins of Caesar thirteen years before and ironically one of the few senior officers still remaining loyal to Antony at this time.

387

387 Bare head of M. Antony right, M ANTONIVS AVG IMP IIII COS TERT III VIR R P C around. *Reverse:* Victory standing left, holding wreath tied with fillet in right hand and palm-branch over shoulder in left, D TVR (TVR ligatured) in lower field to right, all within wreath of laurel. *Silver denarius. Actium (?), summer 31 BC* (Crawford 545/1; Sydenham 1211; BMCRR East 227; Babelon Antonia 146; Newman 31.1; Cohen 11).

388

388 Similar to preceding, but without the legend on reverse. *Silver denarius. Actium (?), summer 31 BC* (Crawford 545/2; Sydenham 1211a; BMCRR East 228; Babelon Antonia 147; Cohen 81).

Like so many of the minor characters of this tumultuous era Decimus Turullius had a most chequered career, emerging as one of the conspirators against Caesar, in whose assassination he was an active participant, and ending as a close adherent of Antony, Caesar's colleague in the consulship on the Ides of March. Although Turullius' alliances, like those of Ahenobarbus and others, may appear contradictory, in reality they speak more of the gradual change in Antony's position than of any shift in their own political sympathies. Antony had only become the leader of the Caesarian party by a chance of fate – suddenly thrust into that role by the events of 15 March 44 BC – and as the years passed he gradually reverted to his true character, that of a Roman noble with strong republican loyalties. His own nature thus contained the seeds of his ultimate failure and downfall. But his position had been so dominant in the early years of the Triumvirate that he might still have prevailed in spite of himself had it not been for his fatal obsession with the queen of Egypt.

The precise circumstances of this issue remain obscure. Stylistically appealing, bespeaking the hand of a Greek artist, they provide our final glimpse of this great but tragic figure. Antony's features for the first time betray the stresses and disappointments of the past decade and a half of political upheaval and the frustrations of having to deal with a youthful rival who possessed such a remarkable single-mindedness of purpose. The obverse titulature is of particular interest as it records Antony's third consulship. He and Octavian had been designated to hold a joint consulship in 31 BC (their third in each case) but Octavian had deposed him at the end of the preceding year following the publication in Rome of Antony's will. The eastern Triumvir's place as chief magistrate of the republic had been taken by M. Valerius Messalla Corvinus, but this did not prevent him from claiming what he considered to be his rightful office and recording it on his coinage. Had Antony prevailed at Actium Octavian and Corvinus would have been deposed and the consular *fasti* would have been rewritten. As it was Antony's 'third consulship' remained a fiction recorded only on the denarii of Turullius and those of Pinarius Scarpus in the Cyrenaica (see nos. 389–91).

The legend also celebrates Antony's fourth imperatorial acclamation (IMP IIII). The third acclamation had been seven years before, for Ventidius' victory at Gindarus, but the occasion for his fourth is uncertain. He was still IMP III on the denarii of M. Junius Silanus issued in the summer of 32 BC (see no. 346) which indicates that the fourth acclamation must be related to the Actian campaign. There was precious little in the way of military success which Antony could claim as justification for another acclamation, but by this time he was clutching at straws and his entire titulature on this issue could be regarded as spurious.[158] The elegant figure of Victory on reverse, recalling numerous Greek prototypes, is equally ambiguous. Perhaps the type celebrates the anticipation of success against Octavian rather than its accomplishment, in which case the fourth imperatorial acclamation could be viewed in the same light. Antony may have hoped that the appearance of Victory on this coinage (possibly struck in his camp at Actium) would inspire his soldiers to accomplish the success which was being predicted.

It is noteworty that Turullius' name appears only inconspicuously in monogram form on the first variety and is absent altogether on the second. As one of the last two surviving assassins of Caesar[159] he was clearly anxious to avoid drawing attention to himself at a time when Octavian seemed poised to assume the mantle of sole authority in the Roman world. But despite these precautions his fate was already sealed. He was captured following Actium and Octavian sent him for execution to the island of Cos where, twelve years earlier as a naval commander under Cassius Longinus, he had felled the trees of a grove sacred to Asklepios in order to obtain timber for ships. Thus in a single act was achieved the punishment of a tyrannicide and the propitiation of an angry god.

One final Antonian issue remains to be considered – that of L. Pinarius Scarpus in the Cyrenaica. When the eastern Triumvir was assembling his forces for the final confrontation with Octavian in Greece he held eleven legions in reserve. Four of these were in the Cyrenaica where Scarpus was charged with the task of countering Octavian's African army under the command of Cornelius Gallus and protecting Egypt from invasion from the west. In the months prior to Actium Scarpus struck several denarius types in Antony's name, presumably to supplement a deficient supply of coinage for the payment of his legions.

389

389 Head of Jupiter Ammon right, M ANTO COS III IMP IIII around, commencing behind the head. *Reverse:* legionary eagle (*aquila*) between two standards (*signa*), LEG–VIII across lower field either side of eagle's shaft, SCARPVS above, IMP on right. *Silver denarius. Cyrene, summer 31 BC* (Crawford 546/1; Sydenham 1279; BMCRR Cyrenaica 1; Babelon Antonia 100; Cohen 80).

390 *Obverse:* as preceding. *Reverse:* Victory walking right, holding wreath in extended right hand and palm-branch over shoulder in left, ANTONIO / AVG before, SCARPVS (or SCARPV) IMP (the last three letters variously arranged, the MP sometimes ligatured) behind. *Silver*

390

391

denarius. Cyrene, summer 31 BC (Crawford 546/2; Sydenham 1280; BMCRR Cyrenaica 2; Babelon Antonia 98; RSC/Cohen 1–1b).

391 Similar to preceding, but with obverse legend M ANTONIO COS III IMP IIII, commencing above the head instead of behind. *Silver denarius. Cyrene, summer 31 BC* (Crawford 546/3; Sydenham 1280a; BMCRR Cyrenaica 3; Babelon Antonia 99; RSC/Cohen 1c–d).

This series clearly belongs to the period immediately preceding Actium as it borrows elements of the types and legends of both the 'legionary' coinage (cf. nos. 348–86) and the denarii of Turullius (nos. 387–8). The first type (no. 389), for which only one reverse die has been recorded, honours *Legio VIII*, one of the four legions under Scarpus' command in the Cyrenaica. It is an almost exact copy of Antony's 'legionary' type with the addition of Scarpus' name and imperatorial title.[160] Why this particular legion should have been singled out is unclear. It is possible that the original intention had been to produce types in honour of all four units, but after a few had been struck for *Legio VIII* the decision was made to issue a single type featuring the goddess Victoria. Like the coins of Turullius, which doubtless provided the inspiration, this second type was used in anticipation of Antony's success over the forces of Octavian. The theme of victory was continued on Scarpus' later coinage for Octavian (see nos. 411–15), though here it celebrates the reality of the Caesarian victory at Actium. Jupiter (or Zeus) Ammon had featured prominently on both the early Cyrenaican coinage and, later, on the large bronzes of Ptolemaic Egypt.[161] The adoption of the type by Antony's lieutenant was, therefore, most appropriate and it appears on the obverses of all his issues for the eastern Triumvir. Following Actium, however, it was soon abandoned in favour of the open hand of conciliation. Interestingly, Antony's name appears in the dative case,[162] indicating the dedicatory nature of the coinage, and some of the later issues for Octavian exhibit the same characteristic (see nos. 412–15). Once again, Antony's third consulship and his fourth imperatorial acclamation are recorded, as on the coins of Turullius. The appearance of the Triumvir's name on both the obverse and reverse of nos. 390–1 seems an unnecessary duplication. In this feature they resemble the denarii issued by Junius Silanus the previous summer (see no. 347).

The identity of Lucius Pinarius Scarpus is of some interest. Although relatively little is known of him it would appear that, like Octavian, he was a great-nephew of Caesar himself and was actually mentioned as a beneficiary in the dictator's will.[163] He reappears at Philippi as a Caesarian general serving under Antony[164] after which we lose sight of him again for about a decade. During this time we must assume that he remained with Antony in the

East as just prior to Actium he was given his important command in the Cyrenaica. His timely desertion to Octavian's cause marked the end of any lingering hopes Antony may have cherished of being able to put up a spirited resistance to the invasion of Egypt. Scarpus' coins, both for Antony and later for Octavian, accord him the title of *imperator*, but we have no precise knowledge of how or when he earned this distinction. Neither do we possess any information relating to his subsequent history, but we need not doubt that his illustrious cousin permitted him to retire in peace and live out the remainder of his days under Rome's new imperial government.

B. Issues of Octavian

Much confusion has surrounded the subject of Octavian's coinage during the latter part of the triumviral period and a brief review of recent scholarly opinion seems in order. Michael Crawford, in *Roman Republican Coinage* (published 1974), excludes these issues altogether, though in *Coinage and Money under the Roman Republic* (1985) he dates the series as a whole to the years 34–30 BC. C. H. V. Sutherland (*The Emperor and the Coinage,* 1976) states that on the basis of hoard evidence the CAESAR DIVI F and IMP CAESAR issues must have been roughly contemporary in circulation with Antony's 'legionary' coinage and that production probably began in 31 BC and extended down to the beginning of 27. He also recognizes the Italian origin of the series, a position which had been adopted long before by H.A. Grueber in *Coins of the Roman Republic in the British Museum* (1910) though subsequently rejected by Mattingly. Sutherland asserts that the change in legend in all likelihood occurred in 29 BC, based on the evidence of Dio Cassius' statement (lii. 41) that at this time Octavian was granted the permanent right to use the *praenomen imperatoris* as his legitimate appellation. However, in espousing this view he fails to take into account Octavian's extensive earlier use of the *praenomen imperatoris* (see nos. 307 and 310–15, spanning the years 38–36 BC) which would certainly validate its appearance on the IMP CAESAR coinage prior to 29 BC. In these observations Sutherland appears to have been influenced by the chronology adopted much earlier by Harold Mattingly, though the author of *Coins of the Roman Empire in the British Museum*, volume I (published 1923) was basing his views on the mistaken belief that the coinage was of eastern mintage and therefore could not have commenced before Octavian's victory at Actium in September 31 BC.

In his revision of volume I of *The Roman Imperial Coinage* (1984) Sutherland amended his earlier opinion by dating the introduction of the CAESAR DIVI F series to 32 BC, thus making it roughly contemporary with the commencement of Antony's 'legionary' coinage. A more radical view was adopted by Jean-Baptiste Giard (*Catalogue des Monnaies de l'Empire Romain I*, revised edition, 1988) who, following Konrad Kraft's *Zur Münzpragung des Augustus* (1969), places the entire issue of CAESAR DIVI F and IMP CAESAR types in 29 BC in connection with Octavian's triple triumph. The principal difficulty with this interpretation is that it deprives Octavian of coinage over an unacceptably long period of time (about seven years). The idea that after 36 BC the western Triumvir required no additional supplies of money until the year following the conquest of Egypt can hardly be given serious credence. It is my contention that the key to understanding the chronology of Octavian's post-36 BC coinage lies in the correct interpretation of the enigmatic denarius type with portrait head on obverse and circular shield on reverse (see nos. 392–3). This has been give a strange assortment of attributions in the standard works of reference,[165] but the youthfulness of Octavian's features on the anepigraphic obverse and the form of the legend on reverse (IMP CAESAR DIVI F) all point to an intermediate issue (probably in 35 or 34 BC) bridging the gap between the temple of Divus Julius type of 36 BC (see nos. 314–15) and the introduction of the CAESAR DIVI F series. This I would place in 32 BC, more or less contemporary with the commencement of Antony's 'legionary' coinage, extending down to the invasion and conquest of Egypt in 30 BC. The series can be further subdivided between issues which appear to be pre-Actian (32–31 BC) and post-Actian (31–30 BC) based on the messages conveyed by their types. Then, following the acquisition of the vast Ptolemaic treasury in the summer of 30 BC, CAESAR DIVI F would have been succeeded by the IMP CAESAR coinage which was required to pay off the legionary veterans and to help defray the enormous cost of the triple triumph in August 29 BC.

392

392 Bare head of Octavian right (no legend). *Reverse:* round shield, with three concentric circles of studs and central boss, IMP above, CAE–SAR on either side, DIVI F below. *Silver denarius. Mint in northern Italy or travelling with Octavian in Illyricum, 35/34 BC* (RIC 543a; CBN 1017; AMC 1; BMCRE 309 = BMCRR Gaul 119; Babelon Julia 133; Cohen 126).

393 Similar to preceding, but Octavian's head is to left. *Silver denarius. Mint in northern Italy or travelling with Octavian in Illyricum, 35/34 BC* (RIC 543b; CBN 1021; BMCRE 313 = BMCRR Gaul 123; Babelon Julia 134; Cohen 127).

As previously noted, this type seems to provide the key to the elucidation of the final phase of Octavian's coinage. The anepigraphic obverse with its youthful head of the Triumvir facing in either direction foreshadows the iconography of the subsequent CAESAR DIVI F and IMP CAESAR coinages, whilst the legend corresponds precisely to the form used on the preceding issues of 37–36 BC (see nos. 310–315), though without the triumviral and consular titles.[166] Octavian's extensive campaigning in Illyricum in 35 and 34 BC provide the obvious reason for the issue, hence the military flavour of the reverse type, and the minting could have taken place in either year (or both). There is no evidence for determining the place of mintage, though northern Italy seems likely given the theatre of war. Less probable is a military mint moving with the Triumvir on campaign. The coins do have an Italian 'feel', though this is more perceptible on the succeeding CAESAR DIVI F series.

394 Bare head of Octavian right (no legend). *Reverse:* equestrian statue of Octavian galloping left, his right hand extended, CAESAR DIVI F below. *Gold aureus. Italian mint (possibly Rome), autumn 32–summer*

394

395

31 BC (RIC 262; CBN 82; AMC 200; BMCRE 594 = BMCRR 4325; Babelon Julia 103; Cohen 73).

395 Bare head of Octavian right (no legend). *Reverse:* Venus standing right, half-turned from spectator and with drapery covering only her lower thighs, holding helmet and transverse sceptre and resting left arm on column, at base of which to left is shield with star device, CAESAR – DIVI F across field. *Silver denarius. Italian mint (possibly Rome), autumn 32–summer 31 BC* (RIC 250a; CBN 19; AMC 197; BMCRE 599 = BMCRR 4333; Babelon Julia 108; Cohen 62).

396 Similar to preceding, but Octavian's head is to left. *Silver denarius. Italian mint (possibly Rome), autumn 32–summer 31 BC* (RIC 250b; CBN 24; AMC 199; BMCRE 601 = BMCRR 4334; Babelon Julia 109; Cohen 63).

397

398

397 Diademed head of Venus right, wearing necklace of pendants (no legend). *Reverse:* Octavian, in military attire, hurrying left, his cloak billowing out behind, his right hand extended and holding transverse spear in left, CAESAR – DIVI F across field. *Silver denarius. Italian mint (possibly Rome), autumn 32–summer 31 BC* (RIC 251; CBN 1; AMC 196; BMCRE 609 = BMCRR 4327; Babelon Julia 105; Cohen 70).

398 Similar to preceding, but Octavian holds globe in his extended right hand. *Silver denarius. Italian mint (possibly Rome), autumn 32–summer 31 BC* (RIC –; CBN 5; BMCRE p. 100, note *; BMCRR pp. 9–10, note 3; Babelon Julia 106; Cohen 71).

399

399 Bare head of Octavian right (no legend). *Reverse:* Pax standing left, holding olive-branch in right hand and cornucopiae in left, CAESAR DIVI F around. *Silver denarius. Italian mint (possibly Rome), autumn 32–summer 31 BC* (RIC 252; CBN 26; AMC 194; BMCRE 605 = BMCRR East 236; Babelon Julia 115; Cohen 69).

400 Diademed head of Pax right, olive-branch before, cornucopiae behind (no legend). *Reverse:* Octavian, in military attire, walking right, his right hand raised in *adlocutio* and holding spear over shoulder in left, CAESAR – DIVI F across field. *Silver denarius. Italian mint (possibly Rome), autumn 32–summer 31 BC* (RIC 253; CBN 6; AMC 193; BMCRE 611 = BMCRR 4329; Babelon Julia 107; Cohen 72).

400

401 Bare head of Octavian right (no legend). *Reverse:* Mercury, naked, seated right on rock upon which is spread his cloak, petasus slung on his back, holding lyre with both hands, CAESAR – DIVI F across field. *Silver denarius. Italian mint (possibly Rome), autumn 32–summer 31 BC* (RIC 257; CBN 73; AMC 201; BMCRE 596 = BMCRR 4335; Babelon Julia 116; Cohen 61).

401

These types would appear to constitute Octavian's elusive pre-Actian coinage, the western Triumvir's answer to Antony's 'legionary' series. Taken as a whole they represent a very substantial output, certainly enough to have served Octavian's needs prior to the naval battle which determined the outcome of the war. The question of where they were struck has exercised the minds of scholars over several generations, but the Italian origin of these and succeeding issues in the CAESAR DIVI F and IMP CAESAR coinages appears now to have been adequately substantiated. Whether a single mint was responsible for the entire output and whether that establishment was the Capitoline mint itself are questions which remain to be determined. We shall probably never have the answers for sure, but there is certainly a marked uniformity in the neat engraving and polished execution of the coins which immediately suggests Rome as the source of these issues. It is true that no college of moneyers had been appointed over the preceding eight years or so, but doubtless the machinery of the mint was still in place and most of the engravers and artisans would probably have remained in the city following the closure in 40 BC. Thus, the refurbishment of the facility on the Capitol, next to the temple of Juno Moneta, should not have presented any insuperable problems. The issue would certainly have been an extraordinary one, without precedent in the republican series, but these were extraordinary times and it must be remembered that patriotic fervour was running high in the face of the threat from the foreign queen and her traitorous Roman lackey. It has been argued that it would have been more convenient for Octavian to have the mint located at or near his naval headquarters at Brundisium. However, it would scarcely have been any less convenient to have the mint situated at its traditional site in Rome as this would have saved the irksome necessity of having to transport bullion, minting equipment, and experienced personnel across the country.

In marked contrast to the monotony of the Antonian 'legionary' series the types of the pre-Actian CAESAR DIVI F coinage exhibit great inventiveness and are of considerable interest. In this they foreshadow the diversity of the imperial coinage to follow. The aureus (no. 394) repeats a type which had originally appeared on a denarius of 41 BC (see no. 299). The spirited equestrian representation of Octavian probably depicts the statue which had been erected in Rome to honour the young Triumvir's participation in the battle of

Philippi. Taken together with the denarii featuring Venus, ancestress of the Julia *gens* and special guardian deity of the now deified dictator, these types convey a powerful message of Octavian's divine heritage and of his role as the true inheritor of the Caesarian tradition. Adding to the interest of this series is the cleverly contrived antithetical relationship[167] of two pairs of types (nos. 395/6 with 397/8, and 399 with 400), together with another pairing in the post-Actian phase of the CAESAR DIVI F coinage (see nos. 406–9) and yet another in the succeeding IMP CAESAR coinage (see nos. 425–7). The first of these pairings depict head of Octavian on obverse and figure of Venus on reverse, and head of Venus on obverse and figure of Octavian on reverse; similarly, 399 and 400 have Octavian head/Pax standing and Pax head/Octavian standing respectively. Taken together, these types may be interpreted as holding out the promise that Caesar's heir, now a proven military leader in his own right, will bring peace to the war-ravaged state through his imminent victory over the foreign aggressor Cleopatra and her misguided Roman allies. This theme is further emphasized by the remaining type (no. 401) which, through its depiction of Mercury[168] on reverse, pledges a restoration of both commerce and the arts[169] as a result of Octavian's final triumph. It was a promise that was destined to be amply fulfilled over the decades to follow. At this point there was a dramatic change in the type content of the CAESAR DIVI F coinage. In place of the Caesarian propaganda we now see an exultant celebration of Octavian's momentous victory at Actium.

402

403

402 Bare head of Octavian right (no legend). *Reverse:* Victory in galloping biga right, holding wreath in right hand and long palm-branch and reins in left, CAESAR DIVI F in exergue. *Gold aureus. Italian mint (possibly Rome), autumn 31–summer 30 BC* (RIC 260; CBN 78; BMCRE 592 = BMCRR 4323; Babelon Julia 113; Cohen 67).

403 Similar to preceding, but Victory holds the long palm-branch in her right hand and reins in left (no wreath), and the exergual line appears only below the horses' hind-hooves. *Gold aureus. Italian mint (possibly Rome), autumn 31–summer 30 BC* (RIC 261; BMCRE 593 = BMCRR 4324).

404 Bare head of Octavian left (no legend). *Reverse:* empty triumphal quadriga moving slowly right, the car ornamented with figures on its front and side panels and surmounted by miniature galloping quadriga, CAESAR DIVI F in exergue. *Gold aureus. Italian mint (possibly Rome), autumn 31–summer 30 BC* (RIC 259; CBN 80; BMCRE 590 = BMCRR 4321; Babelon Julia 120; Cohen 77).

405

405 Similar to preceding, but the empty triumphal quadriga is moving to left. *Gold aureus. Italian mint (possibly Rome), autumn 31–summer 30 BC* (RIC 258; CBN 81; BMCRE 591 = BMCRR 4322; Babelon Julia 119; Cohen 76).

406 Bare head of Octavian right (no legend). *Reverse:* Victory standing left on globe, holding wreath in extended right hand and palm-branch in left, CAESAR – DIVI F across field. *Silver denarius. Italian mint (possibly Rome), autumn 31–summer 30 BC* (RIC 254a; CBN 35; AMC 191; BMCRE 602 = BMCRR 4338; Babelon Julia 111; Cohen 65).

407

407 Similar to preceding, but Octavian's head is to left. *Silver denarius. Italian mint (possibly Rome), autumn 31–summer 30 BC* (RIC 254b; CBN 36; AMC 192; BMCRE 603 = BMCRR 4339; Babelon Julia 110; Cohen 64).

408 Similar to preceding, but Victory stands to right on globe. *Silver denarius. Italian mint (possibly Rome), autumn 31–summer 30 BC* (RIC 255; CBN 41; BMCRE 604 = BMCRR 4340; Babelon Julia 112; Cohen 66).

409 Winged bust of Victory right, undraped, her hair drawn back and collected into knot behind (no legend). *Reverse:* Octavian, as Neptune, standing left, naked but for cloak hanging from shoulders behind, his right foot set on globe, holding aplustre in right hand and resting on sceptre held in left, CAESAR – DIVI F across field. *Silver denarius. Italian mint (possibly Rome), autumn 31–summer 30 BC* (RIC 256; CBN 12; AMC 190; BMCRE 615 – BMCRR 4341; Babelon Julia 117; Cohen 60).

409

410 Victory standing right on prow of galley, holding wreath in extended right hand and palm-branch over shoulder in left (no legend). *Reverse:* Octavian in triumphal quadriga right, the car ornamented with figures on its front and side panels, holding branch in right hand and reins in

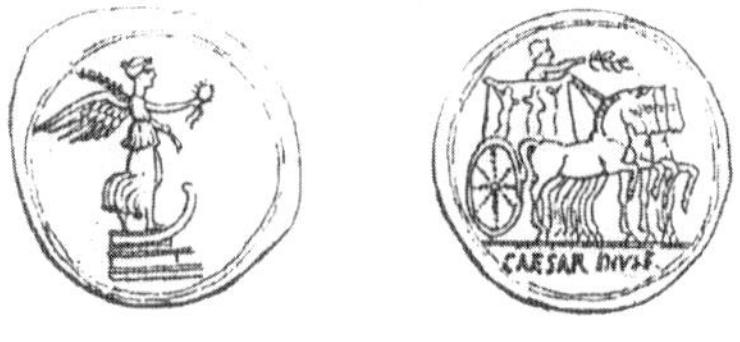

410

left, **CAESAR DIVI F** in exergue. *Silver denarius. Italian mint (possibly Rome), late summer 30 BC* (RIC 263; BMCRE 616 = BMCRR 4342; Babelon Julia 118; Cohen 75).

The victory over Antony and Cleopatra having at last been achieved Octavian's coinage immediately began to reflect the jubilant mood of the Caesarians as they prepared to enjoy the fruits of their success. More than thirteen years had elapsed since the assassination of Caesar and during this time his heir had flirted with disaster on numerous occasions in his quest to assume the dictator's mantle and bring his revolutionary schemes to fruition. For much of this time the young Octavian had been in the shadow of his more popular triumviral colleague, the gregarious Mark Antony. But he had never lost sight of his ultimate goal and with the unwitting help of the queen of Egypt he eventually succeeded in undermining Antony's position to the point where he was able to go on to the offensive and, from a position of strength, force a military solution to their rivalry.

So it was that Octavian's coinage of 31–30 BC was filled with the imagery of victory. The goddess herself is everywhere. Her winged bust appears as an obverse type whilst her full-length figure is shown speeding into battle in her chariot, standing on a celestial globe[170] (the symbol of world dominion), and even atop the prow of one of Octavian's galleys. Two of these types exhibit the curious antithetical relationship already encountered on the pre-Actian **CAESAR DIVI F** coinage. Nos. 406–8 depict Octavian on obverse and Victory on reverse, whilst 409 has Victory on obverse and Octavian (as Neptune) on reverse. Yet another such pairing is to be found on the **IMP CAESAR** coinage of 30–29 BC (see nos. 425–7). The aurei with an empty triumphal quadriga on reverse (see nos. 404–5) convey a promise of the lavish celebrations planned by Octavian for the people of Rome following the settlement of affairs in the East. However, almost two years were to elapse following Actium before the victor could make good his pledge and bring the magnificent spectacle of his triple triumph to the streets of the capital. The representation of Octavian as Neptune, god of the sea, in combination with the bust of Victory (no. 409) is a clear reference to the naval battle itself. There were to be other instances of Octavian appearing in the guise of a deity, a sure sign that he was actively encouraging the notion of his own divinity. After twelve years of being *divi filius* Caesar's heir was now aspiring to be a god in his own right, at least in the eyes of his eastern subjects.

Of special interest is the concluding type in this series (no. 410). It seems probable that the reverse depiction of Octavian in a triumphal quadriga commemorates his victorious entry into Alexandria at the beginning of August

On the rear wall of the Ptolemaic temple of the goddess Hathor at Dendera is the only relief in Egypt of Cleopatra, here seen making offerings to the gods with her son Caesarion.

30 BC. The great naval victory at Actium the previous year had of course paved the way for the invasion of Egypt, hence the obverse type of Victory on a prow.[171] The conqueror holds a branch in his right hand, in all likelihood

symbolizing the promise of a new era of peace and reconciliation made possible by this final victory. The issue was small and specimens are very rare today. This is because it was almost immediately replaced by a type which, though otherwise identical in every respect, now bore the new legend **IMP CAESAR** below the quadriga (see no. 416). I have already suggested that the occasion for the change from **CAESAR DIVI F** to **IMP CAESAR** was the acquisition of the vast Ptolemaic treasury following the conquest of Egypt. This type would appear to support my view.

An intriguing addendum to Octavian's post-Actian coinage is provided by the issues of the former Antonian general L. Pinarius Scarpus. It will be recalled that in the period prior to the battle this distant cousin of Octavian had been appointed by Antony to the command of four legions in the Cyrenaica with the task of countering Octavian's African army under Cornelius Gallus and protecting Egypt from invasion from the west. News of Antony's defeat soon reached Cyrene and, lest his own fate be dictated by his commander-in-chief's downfall, Scarpus lost no time in transferring his allegiance (and his legions) to the victor.

411

411 Head of Jupiter Ammon right, **AVGVR** behind, **PONTIF** before. *Reverse:* Victory standing right on globe, holding wreath in extended right hand and palm-branch in left, **IMP – CAESAR** (**AR** ligatured) / **DIVI – F** across field. *Silver denarius. Cyrene, autumn 31* BC (Crawford 546/4; RIC 535; CBN 897; AMC 326; Sydenham 1281; BMCRE 690 = BMCRR Cyrenaica 4; Babelon Julia 141; Cohen 125).

This would appear to have been the initial issue produced by Scarpus following his defection to the Caesarians as it continues the principal type of Jupiter Ammon/Victory which he had been striking for Antony (see nos. 390–91). The issuer's name is conspicuous by its absence, indicating that at this stage the defector was unsure of Octavian's attitude and thought it best to strike solely in the name of his new commander-in-chief. We know from the comments which he made during the Actian campaign[172] that Octavian liked the fruits of treason but despised the traitors themselves. Scarpus' contribution of four legions doubtless ensured his survival, but nothing is known of his subsequent career so his perfidy does not seem to have earned him high public office. The reverse type is of interest as it is unquestionably draws its inspiration from the contemporary **CAESAR DIVI F** coinage of Octavian (see no. 408).[173] The addition of the *praenomen imperatoris* on Scarpus' issue provides further evidence of the common usage of this form prior to 29 BC. Prominently featured on the obverse are Octavian's priestly titles of *augur* and *pontifex*. This is in marked contrast to the references to consulship and imperatorial acclamation on the earlier issues for Antony.

412 Open right hand, **IMP CAESARI** above, **SCARPVS IMP** below. *Reverse:* Victory standing right on globe, holding wreath in extended right hand and palm-branch in left, **DIVI F** on right, **AVG PONΓ** (= **PONT**) on left. *Gold aureus. Cyrene, autumn 31* BC (Crawford 546/5; RIC 533; CBN p. 141, *: all citing unique specimen formerly in Narbonne).

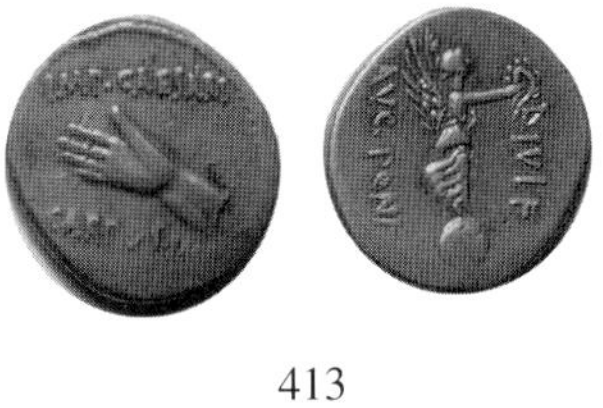
413

413 Similar to preceding, but the **MP** of **SCARPVS IMP** is sometimes ligatured. *Silver denarius. Cyrene, autumn 31 BC* (Crawford 546/6; RIC 534; CBN 894; AMC 327; Sydenham 1282; BMCRE 689 = BMCRR Cyrenaica 5; Babelon Julia 142; RSC/Cohen 500, 500a).

414

414 Open right hand, **SCARPVS** above, **IMP** below. *Reverse:* Victory standing right on globe, holding wreath in extended right hand and palm-branch in left, **CAESARI** on right, **DIVI F** on left. *Silver denarius. Cyrene, autumn 31 BC* (Crawford 546/7; RIC 531; CBN 891; Sydenham 1283; BMCRE 686 = BMCRR Cyrenaica 6; Babelon Julia 143; Cohen 498).

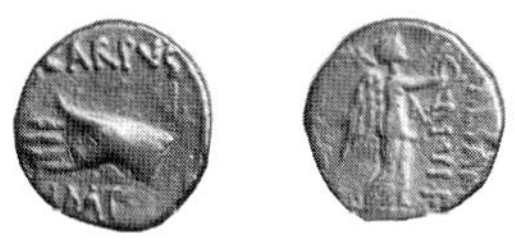
415

415 Open right hand, **SCARPVS** above, **IMP** below. *Reverse:* Victory standing right, holding wreath in extended right hand and palm-branch in left, **CAESARI / DIVI F** on right. *Silver quinarius. Cyrene, autumn 31 BC* (Crawford 546/8; RIC 532; CBN 892; Sydenham 1284; BMCRE 687 = BMCRR Cyrenaica 7; Babelon Julia 144; Cohen 499).

As soon as Scarpus felt confident that his switch in allegiance had been favourably received by the victor of Actium the head of Jupiter Ammon, symbolic of Africa, disappeared entirely from his coinage. It was replaced by the conciliatory type of an open right hand extended in a gesture of friendship. The change may also be indicative of the closure of the mint at Cyrene and the transfer of operations to a mobile establishment travelling with Scarpus' legions. However, this is based on nothing more than conjecture as no major change is discernible in the style of the coinage itself. Scarpus' own name now reappears after having been omitted from the initial issue in honour of Octavian. Once again, as under Antony, the commander-in-chief's name appears in the dative case, indicating the dedicatory nature of the issue. Remarkably, coins of this new design were struck in three denominations – aureus, denarius, and silver quinarius. The gold type is represented by a single surviving specimen. The half denarius was a denomination not normally associated with north Africa, though one and a half decades before M. Porcius Cato had issued it from Utica at the time of the civil war between Caesar and the Pompeians (see no. 47). At first, the names of both imperators appear on the obverse, but Scarpus then takes sole possession of this position relegating Octavian – now lacking his *praenomen imperatoris* and priestly titles – to the reverse. At this point the untrustworthy Scarpus was probably relieved of his military command, his legions being incorporated into the army of Octavian's lieutenant Cornelius Gallus. The rarity of Scarpus' coinage, both in Antony's name and for Octavian, attests to the brevity of the issue and it is doubtful whether the entire series extended over more than a few months in the second half of 31 BC, preceding and following the battle of Actium.

CHAPTER 6

The Pre-eminence of Octavian – Prelude to Empire, 30–27 BC

The executions in Alexandria of the eldest sons of both Antony and Cleopatra, together with a number of the late Triumvir's closest political adherents, brought to an end the initial phase of Octavian's political career. Over the preceding fourteen years he had gained a reputation for cruelty which made men nervous for a future in which his authority would no longer be questioned or challenged. But in the event these fears proved to be unfounded for Rome's master now appeared to go through a metamorphosis which resulted in his emergence as a gentle and beneficent ruler, a true father-figure to his people. The Augustus of the principate appeared to bear little resemblance to the Octavian of the civil wars. It must be assumed that his nature had always been one of kindness and forgiveness which makes it all the more remarkable that he was able to play the power game so effectively when it was vital for his very survival. He had never lost sight of his goal and he pursued it with an astonishing persistence, undaunted by countless setbacks, until it had been achieved. Only then was he able to revert to his true nature and, with infinite patience, lay the solid foundations for his new imperial state. His work was well done and was to endure for many centuries; had all his successors been endowed with similar gifts the future of Rome would have been blissful indeed. Unfortunately, the fatal weakness of an autocratic system of government lies in its inability to guarantee the continuity of excellence in the succession to the supreme office. In a dynastic arrangement the son may so easily prove to be unworthy of the father, and when the throne changes hands by other means strength and cruelty will often prevail over virtue. So it was to be with the history of imperial Rome.

Once affairs had been settled in Egypt Octavian gave his attention to the other territories of the East which had been so disrupted by the upheavals caused by two decades of civil war. He travelled through both Syria and Asia meeting with the client kings and petty dynasts, most of whom were confirmed in the positions to which they had been appointed by Antony (this despite the earlier Caesarian condemnation of the eastern Triumvir's handling of these matters). The Phoenician cities regained their freedom and extensive honours were granted to other communities which had been wise enough to declare their loyalty to Octavian, even before the issue with Antony had been finally decided. Such places included Berytus in Phoenicia, which had revolted from Cleopatra prior to Actium; Sparta in the Peloponnese, which was also given the prestigious stewardship of the quinquennial Actian games; and the Cretan towns of Cydonia and Lappa. The island of Cyprus and the Cyrenaica in north Africa, both of which been involved in Antony's 'Donations of Alexandria', were now restored to provincial status. Very special honours were reserved for Actium, the site of the great naval engagement on 2 September 31 BC. The temple of Apollo of Actium, the deity to whom Octavian ascribed his success, was enlarged and embellished, whilst the Actian games were given equal status with the Olympian festival. In addition, an 'Actian era' was established, commencing 31/30 BC, by which many local coinages in the East were dated. Near the site of Octavian's camp, on the promontory to the north of the entrance to the Ambracian Gulf, was founded the city of Nicopolis. Named in honour of the famous victory, the new settlement was populated by citizens from many of the surrounding communities and the place quickly grew in importance. It was here that the Actian games were celebrated.

On Rome's eastern frontier Octavian decided to reverse the aggressive policy which had proved so costly to Antony. Armenia, which had only recently been reduced to provincial status by the eastern Triumvir, managed to regain its independence during the War of Actium. Octavian did not attempt to recover it. He had no need of this costly burden as he had already determined to pursue a strategy of peaceful co-existence with Parthia and, if possible, to achieve by diplomatic means the goals which had proved so elusive by force of arms. Octavian's main concerns were with the West and the North, scarcely surprising in one whose sphere of influence had hitherto been confined to those regions. At the time of his initial rise to power the East had been controlled by the republican tyrannicides Brutus and Cassius and after the battle of Philippi in 42 BC the government of the area had been claimed by Antony. Now, for the first time, it came under Octavian's rule. But Caesar's heir had no particular concerns with the Hellenistic East other than the maintenance of peace which would allow its communities to recover their former prosperity.

In the summer of 29 BC Octavian returned to Rome. Ever since he had left Italy the previous spring affairs in the capital had been in the capable hands of Maecenas and little had occurred to distract Octavian's attention during his settlement of the East. Now he was at last able to celebrate his magnificent triple triumph for his victories in Illyricum and the Wars of Actium and Alexandria. On August 13th, 14th, and 15th the city witnessed the kind of pomp and pageantry which was reminiscent of Caesar's great quadruple triumph seventeen years before. On August 18th the dedication of the long-delayed Temple of Divus Julius took place. Much construction and restoration of public buildings and roads was already under way at this time, all financed by the immense wealth of Egypt which had flowed into the state's coffers by virtue of the 'victory' over Cleopatra. So great was the impact of the injection of this capital into the economy that interest rates in Rome dropped to just one-third of their former level. Furthermore, Octavian was able to pay off in full some 100,000 legionary veterans and settle them in colonies not just in Italy but in strategic locations all over the Roman world. The standing army was now reduced from an unwieldy and impossibly expensive level of some sixty legions to the twenty-eight which Octavian considered sufficient to maintain the security of the state.

By such means Octavian re-established confidence in a world which had been shattered by endless civil conflict over the preceding twenty years. But despite the outward show of assurance and success Rome's leader must have felt serious concern over the lack of a constitutional basis for the exercise of his authority. That authority was very real but it was also strictly personal to him and for the sake of the future security of the state his position had to be regularized. For the moment peace in the Roman world hung by a slender thread, for if anything had happened to Octavian (and his health had always been delicate) civil war would almost certainly have flared up again. He had worked too hard for peace to allow this to happen so he now gave his full attention to the matter of a constitutional settlement. The year 28 BC saw the preparations for this proceed apace. Octavian and Agrippa were colleagues in the consulship and for the first time in two decades Rome witnessed the spectacle of two chief magistrates exercising the powers of their office together in the city for the full twelve-month span. Under their auspices a census of the people was held, the first in more than forty years, and the membership of the Senate was reduced by some 20% to about 800. There was a general consensus that due to the disruption of the civil wars the number of senators had been allowed to grow unchecked and that in consequence the assembly now included some who, in more settled times, would have been deemed unworthy. Later, the number of senators was reduced still further to about 600. In recognition of his attention to the quality of the membership of that august body Octavian received the honorific title of 'Princeps Senatus'.

All was now ready. The first day of the new year (27 BC) saw a renewal of the joint consulship of Octavian and Agrippa. The time had come to unveil the plan which had been so carefully devised by Octavian in consultation with his closest associates. Undoubtedly, a considerable number of the most favoured senators had been briefed in advance so as to ensure the desired reaction in the chamber at the critical moment. The full membership of the Senate was convened on January 13th to hear a special address by the 'Princeps Senatus'. It must have come as quite a shock to those senators who were unaware of the contents of the speech. Octavian announced his intention of resigning all his powers, together with the provinces under his control, and transferring the State to the free disposal of the Senate and People, *i.e.* a full restoration of the Republic. The assembly was obviously stunned by this news, but even while he was speaking cries of protest began to be heard (no doubt the 'favoured' senators were performing according to plan). The saviour of Rome was implored not to abandon his country at this critical time and he was ultimately 'persuaded' to accept a special ten-year commission during which time he would exercise proconsular authority over a special *provincia* comprising Spain, Gaul, and Syria (in addition to Egypt). And it just so happened that these areas contained the bulk of the Roman army. On January 16th, at another meeting of the Senate, an unprecedented series of honours was heaped on the reluctant autocrat. These included a wreath of laurel to be placed above the door of his house, and a magnificent golden shield, inscribed with the full catalogue of his virtues, to be hung in the Senate-house.[174] But perhaps most significant of all, on a decree proposed by Antony's former general L. Munatius Plancus Octavian was granted the title 'Augustus', the name by which he is best known to history. Further, the name of the month Sextilis was changed to Augustus, just as Quintilis had become Julius (hence July and August).

So the Senate could congratulate itself on the restoration of the Republic and feel magnanimous in its generous bestowal of honours on the saviour of the state. Of course, the conscript fathers had been hoodwinked by their artful master who, not wishing to tread the same path that had proved so fatal to his great-uncle, had given the appearance of resigning his powers whilst still retaining the control over the armed forces which was so vital to his interests. The Senate was now satisfied that Augustus was exercising his authority in a fully constitutional manner by their special dispensation. The reality, for sure, was quite different, for oaths of allegiance had been sworn to him in the West at the time of the war with Antony and Cleopatra and the same thing was now happening in the other provinces. The East had its own traditions and there the cult of Augustus was already being associated with that of Roma. There could be no doubt that the army would always be totally loyal to him, both because of his name and out of regard for his record as a generous benefactor.

Ever since his third consulship in 31 BC Augustus had held the supreme magistracy. In fact, he continued to do so without interruption until 23 BC when he celebrated his eleventh consulship, even though under the constitutional settlement of 27 BC he was also in possession of proconsular authority in his special 'province'. The consulship provided him with a temporary validation for the exercise of power in Rome and Italy, but as it was merely an annual office it did not meet the long-term requirements for a head of state. The problem was resolved in 23 BC when Augustus resigned the consulship, receiving in its place proconsular *imperium* over all of Rome's territories. At the same time he obtained a lifetime grant of the tribunician power (*tribunicia potestas*), thereby acquiring the absolute right of veto. These developments were of immense importance for they gave Octavian (and his successors) complete control of the state. Despite the outward appearance of constitutionality in the form of his authority Augustus had effected a revolution in the government of the Roman Empire. What was even more remarkable was that he had accomplished the transformation almost imperceptibly, so awed were the Roman people with the personal *auctoritas* of their leader, now generally referred to as the 'Princeps'.

The tribunician power was first granted to Augustus on 1 July 23 BC. It was subsequently assumed by each of his successors at the time of accession, if not before, and the reign was dated by the anniversary of its initial conferment. The military title of *imperator* was also of great importance in imperial times. As early as 38 BC Octavian had taken the significant step of adopting it as his *praenomen* (*Imperator Caesar*) instead of following the traditional practise of using it as a *cognomen* (*Caesar Imperator*). This personalized his position as overall head of the armed forces, a prerequisite for any autocratic ruler. Surprisingly, the next three emperors did not follow Augustus' example in the employment of the *praenomen imperatoris*. But the last of the Julio-Claudians, the notorious Nero, resumed its use towards the end of his reign (*c.* AD 66). It was eagerly adopted by the rulers of the second great imperial dynasty, the Flavian, and thereafter *imperator* came to denote the supreme power. The English word 'emperor' is ultimately derived fom this source.

So it was that after two decades of civil wars the last of the Roman Imperators, great-nephew and adopted son of the Divine Julius, a mere youth of eighteen at the time of the dictator's assassination, against seemingly overwhelming odds brought about the completion of the transformation of the Roman state from a republic to an autocracy. As one great era ended another began, and just fifteen years after the death of the celebrated orator, statesman, and patriot the Emperor Augustus reigned in Cicero's Rome. Ahead lay the long centuries of Rome's imperial history and an autocratic succession which was to stretch in an unbroken line for five hundred years in the West and almost three times as long in the East.

COINAGE OF THE PERIOD

Issues of the Final Phase of the Pre-Augustan Coinage

The IMP CAESAR coinage was a celebration of the final triumph of the Caesarian cause. It addressed the many themes of the 'new order' – the recent military and naval victories over the enemies of Rome; Octavian's work of settlement in the East and the restoration to the Roman people of the rightful boundaries of their state; the building programme in Rome; the foundation of Nicopolis in Epirus and the establishment of new colonies in various parts of the Roman world; and the earlier milestones in Octavian's military career which had led to Actium and the conquest of Egypt, bringing peace at last to a world grown weary of conflict. It was a most appropriate coinage for the period preceding Octavian's magnificent triple triumph in mid-August 29 BC. Its large volume was made possible by the wealth of the Ptolemaic treasury, now safely in Roman hands, and was necessary for the recompense of soldiers retired from the disbanded legions and the financing of the lavish festivities in the capital.

416

416 Victory standing right on prow of galley, holding wreath in extended right hand and palm-branch over shoulder in left (no legend). *Reverse:* Octavian in triumphal quadriga right, the car ornamented with figures on its front and side panels, holding branch in extended right hand and reins in left, IMP CAESAR in exergue. *Silver denarius. Italian mint (possibly Rome), autumn 30 BC* (RIC 264; CBN 98; AMC 206; BMCRE 617 = BMCRR 4343; Babelon Julia 154; Cohen 115).

It seems probable that this was the first type to be issued in the IMP CAESAR series as it replaces an identical denarius with the earlier CAESAR DIVI F legend (see no. 410). It has already been suggested that the reverse type commemorates Octavian's victorious entry into Alexandria, whilst the obverse looks back to Actium. The IMP CAESAR variety was struck in much greater quantities than its predecessor, presumably from the first batch of bullion received in Italy from the recently captured Ptolemaic treasury.

Later Roman walls pierced by rounded-headed gateways are the most substantial remains now of Octavian's city of Nicopolis, founded to commemorate Actium. On the nearby headland are the remains of the temple of Apollo of Actium, who appears on the reverse of some later coins of Augustus.

417

417 Bare head of Octavian right (no legend). *Reverse:* Victory standing facing on globe, looking left, her wings spread, holding wreath in extended right hand and vexillum over shoulder in left, **IMP – CAESAR** across field. *Gold aureus. Italian mint (possibly Rome), autumn 30–summer 29* BC (RIC 268; CBN 85; BMCRE 622 = BMCRR 4356; Babelon Julia 152; Cohen 113).

This type is based on the post-Actian **CAESAR DIVI F** denarius with Victory standing on a celestial globe, the symbol of world dominion (see nos. 406–8). However, on this aureus in place of the palm-branch the goddess holds a vexillum, a military standard in the form of a flag suspended from a horizontal cross bar at the top of a pole. This specific reference to the legions makes perfect sense when viewed in the context of an issue struck for the payment of retiring veterans and in anticipation of Octavian's great military triumph. Once thought to represent the celebrated golden statue of Victory in the chamber of the Senate House it has now been demonstrated that this type actually shows the ornament which was placed on the roof of the building at the apex of the pediment (see commentary on no. 421).

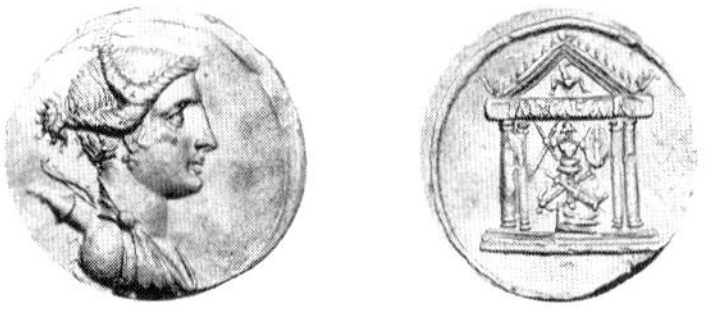

418

418 Draped bust of Diana Siciliensis right, her shoulders bare, the hair drawn back and coiled into two rolls on top and at back of head, bow and quiver behind neck (no legend). *Reverse:* IMP CAESAR on frieze of tetrastyle temple containing trophy set on prow, triskeles within the pediment above the extremities of which are two aplustra. *Gold aureus. Italian mint (possibly Rome), autumn 30–summer 29* BC (RIC 273; CBN 91; BMCRE 643 = BMCRR 4355; Babelon Julia 160; Cohen 121).

The naval victory over Sextus Pompey at Naulochus six years before is here commemorated on this attractive aureus type, an interpretation which is confirmed by the Sicilian triskeles in the pediment of the temple. Following the battle a shrine was erected to Diana Siciliensis at Naulochus and the distinctive head of the goddess appears as the obverse type. Naulochus had been a turning point in Octavian's career. It eliminated the troublesome Sextus Pompey as a political factor in the western Mediterranean area and led indirectly to the downfall of the scheming and resentful third Triumvir, Aemilius Lepidus. These important developments, taken in combination with the disastrous outcome of Antony's invasion of Parthia, were to set the western Triumvir firmly on the path to world domination.

A trophy of similar form to the one depicted in the temple of Diana (though the rudder and anchor at the base are transposed and the shape of the shield is different) appears on the following denarius type. As the imagery lacks the specificity of the aureus it may be taken as a general reference to the various naval victories achieved by Octavian (or rather by Marcus Agrippa), most notably at Naulochus in 36 BC and at Actium in 31.

419

419 Bare head of Octavian right (no legend). *Reverse:* trophy, composed of helmet, cuirass, shield, and crossed spears, set on prow of galley right, crossed rudder and anchor at base, IMP – CAESAR across field. *Silver denarius. Italian mint (possibly Rome), autumn 30–summer 29* BC (RIC 265a; CBN 57; AMC 222; BMCRE 625 = BMCRR 4352; Babelon Julia 158; Cohen 119).

420 Similar to preceding, but Octavian's head is to left. *Silver denarius. Italian mint (possibly Rome), autumn 30–summer 29* BC (RIC 265b; CBN 64; BMCRE 626 = BMCRR 4353; Babelon Julia 159; Cohen 120).

In addition to the aureus honouring Diana and her Sicilian shrine the IMP CAESAR series includes three further depictions of buildings as reverse types, all of them featuring structures in Rome having special associations with the events of this period. These were to mark the beginning of a long tradition of architectural designs on the Roman imperial coinage.

421

421 Bare head of Octavian right (no legend). *Reverse:* IMP CAESAR on the architrave of the Roman Senate House (*Curia Julia*), showing central door with three windows above, porch supported by four short columns along front, statue of Victory on globe surmounting apex of roof, statues of standing figures, each holding parazonium (?) and spear, at the extremities of the architrave, bas-reliefs of seated figure between animals or birds in pediment. *Silver denarius. Italian mint (possibly Rome), autumn 30–summer 29 BC* (RIC 266; CBN 52; AMC 217; BMCRE 631 = BMCRR 4358; Babelon Julia 161; Cohen 122).

The identification of the porched edifice as the *Curia Julia*, Caesar's new Senate House, appears to have received universal scholarly acceptance over the past few years.[175] Indeed, it bears an obvious resemblance to the structure presently occupying the site (formerly the church of S. Adriano) though Mussolini's renovation in 1935–8 was based on Diocletian's early 4th century restoration of the Caesarian building.[176] The dictator had commenced construction shortly before his assassination in 44 BC and completion was delayed for one and a half decades by the civil wars of the triumviral period. The official dedication of the *Curia Julia* finally took place on 28 August 29 BC, barely two weeks after the festivities of Octavian's triple triumph. The exterior features of the building had obviously been completed some time before as its image had already been appearing on the coinage over the preceding months. Of particular interest is the figure of Victory on the roof. Sutherland[177] and Hill both noticed that on well preserved specimens this figure may be seen to be identical to the reverse type of the contemporary aureus (see no. 417). It had previously been thought that the aureus depicted the famous 'Tarentine Victory' which Octavian had placed on an altar within the main chamber of the new Senate House, eventually to become a major bone of contention between pagans and Christians in the closing years of the 4th century. It now seems clear that in reality the aureus shows the principal roof ornament of the *Curia Julia*. The actual 'Tarentine Victory' may be shown on some of the post-Actian denarii of the CAESAR DIVI F series (see nos. 406–8).

422

422 Bare head of Octavian right (no legend). *Reverse:* IMP CAESAR on the architrave of Octavian's Actian arch (*arcus Octaviani*), showing a single span surmounted by large group of statuary depicting Octavian in facing triumphal quadriga. *Silver denarius. Italian mint (possibly Rome), autumn 30–summer 29 BC* (RIC 267; CBN 66; AMC 213; BMCRE 624 = BMCRR 4348; Babelon Julia 162; Cohen 123).

Prior to excavations in the Roman Forum in 1950–53 the site of the arch depicted on the second of the architectural denarii in the IMP CAESAR series remained uncertain.[178] It is known that the Senate had decreed arches at Rome and Brundisium to commemorate Octavian's victory at Actium,[179] but the remains discovered in 1888 near the temple of Divus Julius were of a triple arch which did not accord well with the appearance of the coin type. Further investigation on the site eventually revealed traces of an earlier single span structure which may be identified as Octavian's Actian ach. This had evidently been demolished little more than a decade after its erection when the much larger triple span *arcus Augusti* was constructed in 19 BC in honour of Augustus' recovery from the Parthians of the legionary standards lost by Crassus and Antony.[180]

423

423 Laureate head of Octavian, as Apollo, right (no legend). *Reverse:* statue of Octavian, naked but for cloak over left shoulder and holding spear and parazonium, standing facing atop rostral column ornamented with two anchors and six beaks of galleys, IMP – CAESAR across field. *Silver denarius. Italian mint (possibly Rome), autumn 30–summer 29 BC* (RIC 271; CBN 68; AMC 233; BMCRE 633 = BMCRR 4349; Babelon Julia 163; Cohen 124).

The combination of Apollo with the theme of naval victory immediately brings Actium to mind. In fact, two rostral columns had been decreed by the Senate in Octavian's honour, one for the victory over Sextus Pompey at Naulochus in 36 BC, the other for the defeat of Antony and Cleopatra at Actium.[181] The former was located in the Forum, the latter on the Palatine in the piazza before the temple of Apollo.[182] The evidence would strongly suggest that the depiction on this denarius is of the Actian column and as such it would complement the type of the arch appearing on no. 422.

424

424 Laureate head of Apollo of Actium right, with features resembling Octavian (no legend). *Reverse:* Octavian, as city founder, veiled and in priestly robes, ploughing right with yoke of oxen, holding whip in left hand, IMP CAESAR in exergue. *Silver denarius. Italian mint (possibly Rome), autumn 30–summer 29 BC* (RIC 272; CBN 92; AMC 227; BMCRE 638 = BMCRR 4363; Babelon Julia 156; Cohen 117).

The foundation of Nicopolis in Epirus, on a site close to Octavian's military camp during the Actian campaign, clearly provided the inspiration for this type.[183] Here were settled large numbers of people from all the neighbouring communities of Epirus and Acarnania and work on the new city seems to have commenced very soon after the great event which had been responsible for its birth. The actual dedication probably took place in 29 BC, by which time these coins would already have appeared in circulation. At Actium itself the temple of Apollo, the god to whom Octavian ascribed his success, was enlarged and embellished, hence his depiction as the obverse type. The founder ploughing with oxen refers to the Roman custom (inherited from the Etruscans) of fixing the boundary (*pomoerium*) of a new city by marking it with a furrow. This ceremony possessed a deep religious significance, hence the founder's priestly garb. Many Roman colonies during the imperial period adopted this reverse type for their coinage.

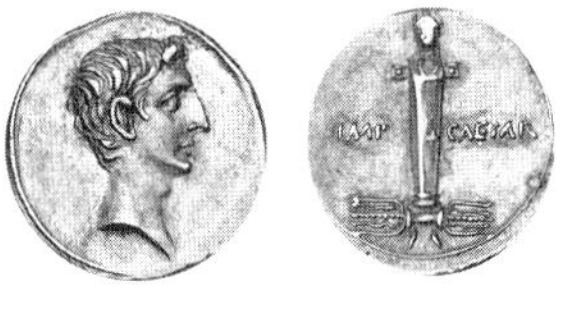

425

425 Bare head of Octavian right (no legend). *Reverse:* ithyphallic boundary-stone of Jupiter Terminus, surmounted by laureate head of Octavian facing, winged thunderbolt below, IMP – CAESAR across field. *Silver denarius. Italian mint (possibly Rome), autumn 30–summer 29 BC* (RIC 269a; CBN 49; AMC 224; BMCRE 628 = BMCRR 4360; Babelon Julia 153; Cohen 114).

The Senate House, the Curia Julia, in the Roman Forum, begun by Caesar and completed by Octavian, was dedicated on 28 August 29 BC.

426 Similar to preceding, but Octavian's head is to left. *Silver denarius. Italian mint (possibly Rome), autumn 30-summer 29 BC* (RIC 269b; BMCRE 630 = BMCRR 4361; RSC/Cohen 114a).

427 Laureate bust of Octavian, as Jupiter Terminus, right, thunderbolt behind (no legend). *Reverse:* Octavian, togate, seated left on curule chair, holding Victory on extended right hand, IMP – CAESAR across field. *Silver denarius. Italian mint (possibly Rome), autumn 30–summer 29 BC* (RIC 270; CBN 43; AMC 226; BMCRE 637 = BMCRR 4362; Babelon Julia 155; Cohen 116).

427

These intriguing types provide yet another example of the curious antithetical relationship already observed on both the pre- and post-Actian phases of the CAESAR DIVI F coinage (see nos. 395–8 and 399–400, and nos. 406–9). The message which they convey clearly relates to Octavian's activities in the East where the structure of the administration required regulation following the downfall of the regime of Antony and Cleopatra. In urgent need of review was the system of client kings established by the eastern Triumvir, though ironically this resulted in Octavian's confirmation of many of his former colleague's appointments. The cities of Asia, whose wealth had been so mercilessly pillaged by republicans and Antonians alike, required help to begin the process of recovery and Octavian lost no time in initiating this. Of a more symbolic nature was the cancellation of the disgraceful assignments of Roman territory to Cleopatra and her children,[184] though in truth even while the Ptolemaic kingdom still existed these had never represented any real threat to Roman interests in the East.

The god Terminus, here equated with Jupiter through the symbolism of the accompanying thunderbolt, was a personification of the concept of boundaries, hence his representation in the form of a pillar or boundary-stone.[185] The boundaries in question were, of course, those of Rome's eastern possessions which were now being regularized by the vanquisher of Rome's insidious enemy, the queen of Egypt. Jupiter Terminus has the features of Octavian himself, yet another example of the imperator's appearance in the guise of a deity,[186] a sure sign that he was actively encouraging the notion of his own divinity. The form of the pillar, with male genitals on its front, indicates assimilation with the Greek herm, an aniconic representation of the god Hermes.

428

428 Head of youthful Mars right, usually with slight beard, wearing crested Corinthian helmet, IMP below. *Reverse:* circular shield, inscribed CAESAR around upper part of rim, the boss ornamented with star, lying on top of sword and spear in saltire. *Silver denarius. Italian mint (possibly Rome), autumn 30–summer 29 BC* (RIC 274; CBN 87; AMC 314; BMCRE 644 and note * = BMCRR 4368 and note 2; Babelon Julia 164; RSC/Cohen 44, 44a).

This type differs from the others in the IMP CAESAR series through its separation of the two elements of the legend – IMP on obverse, CAESAR on reverse. The symbolism may simply be commemorative of the military success of the young imperator, personified as the god of war, over his adversaries Antony and Cleopatra. However, there is a strong likelihood of a deeper meaning here. Just as the aureus featuring Diana Siciliensis (see no. 418) celebrated the victory over Sextus Pompey at Naulochus six years before, so this denarius would appear to relate to the other pivotal battle of the triumviral period, the victory over the republican 'liberators' at Philippi in 42 BC. As the conqueror of Antony and Cleopatra Octavian could conveniently overlook the facts of history and portray himself as the true architect of the defeat of Brutus and Cassius and the avenger of his slain adoptive father, represented by the *sidus Iulium* at the centre of the shield.[187]

Over the three-year period autumn 32 to summer 29 BC the extraordinary expenses of the Actian campaign, the conquest of Egypt, the settlement of the legionary veterans, and the triple triumph had been been met by the large scale CAESAR DIVI F and IMP CAESAR issues. Immediately following this spell of intense activity there was a dramatic diminishment in the output of coinage down to the time of the constitutional settlement of January, 27 BC, under which Octavian received the title Augustus. This was a difficult transitional time during which Octavian's constitutional position remained undefined, though no one dared question his authority. The same could have been said of the final stages of the triumviral rivalry, after the lapse of the temporary emergency arrangements at the end of 33 BC, but now that Octavian was the sole possessor of power attention became focused on the basis of his authority and the situation cried out for some form of regularization. These final seventeen months of the Roman imperatorial period saw the production of the following coin types in Italy and in Asia.

429 Bare head of Octavian right, **CAESAR IMP VII** around. *Reverse:* Victory standing left, holding wreath and palm-branch, on cista mystica flanked by two interlaced snakes with heads erect, **ASIA** on right, **RECEPTA** on left. *Silver quinarius. Italian mint (possibly Rome), 29–28 BC* (RIC 276; CBN 899; AMC 237; BMCRE 647 = BMCRR East 240; Babelon Julia 145; Cohen 14).

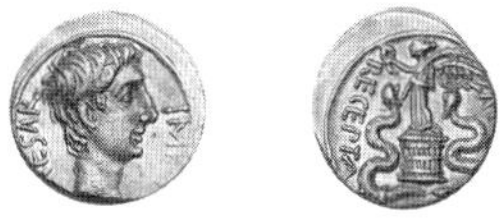
429

Because of its reverse type this quinarius – the only coin of the period to be struck in appreciable quantity – has traditionally been assigned to a mint in Asia.[188] Sutherland,[189] however, correctly perceived that the style closely resembles the aurei and denarii of the **CAESAR DIVI F** and **IMP CAESAR** series and pointed out that the half denarius is not a denomination normally associated with the eastern provinces. Moreover, these coins are frequently found in western hoards.[190] For these reasons the **ASIA RECEPTA** quinarius should be regarded as the immediate successor of the **IMP CAESAR** coinage at the Italian mint (possibly Rome) which had been so active over the preceding three-year period. The message of the reverse, obviously intended for the eyes of a western audience, is unequivocal in its proclamation of the extension of Octavian's authority to *provincia Asia* which, until his recent downfall, had been under Antony's rule ever since Philippi in 42 BC. The type of a Dionysiac cista, or basket, with snakes was the traditional one for the coinage of the Roman province just as it had been for its predecessor, the kingdom of Pergamum. The surmounting Victory refers to Octavian's recent successes at Actium and Alexandria which had brought the eastern provinces under his control.

The obverse legend records Octavian's seventh imperatorial acclamation (**IMP VII**) behind which lies an intriguing story which throws much light on the political confusion of this transitional period. The occasion for this salutation was not a victory won by Octavian himself but the spectacular successes of M. Licinius Crassus,[191] proconsul of Macedonia, who pacified Thrace and even killed with his own hands a certain Deldo, king of the Bastarnae. For this rare distinction Crassus claimed the ancient honour of the *spolia opima*, spoils offered by a Roman general who had slain an enemy leader in single combat. This came at a bad time for Octavian who, without constitutional backing for his authority, was not anxious to see another military leader achieve fame superior to his own. Accordingly, Octavian produced evidence (undoubtedly spurious) which denied Crassus his unique honours. Even his triumph was postponed to July, 27 BC, and as a final insult he was not allowed to accept his acclamation as *imperator* which Octavian simply added to the six which he had already received. Crassus then disappears into obscurity, a victim of the relentess ambition of Caesar's heir which would brook no rivalry.

Doubtless, the entire episode, unimportant in itself, hastened the constitutional settlement of January, 27 BC.

430

430 Bare head of Octavian right, lituus behind, CAESAR COS VI around. *Reverse:* crocodile standing right, AEGVPTO / CAPTA above and in exergue. *Silver denarius. Italian mint (possibly Rome), 28 BC* (RIC 275a; CBN 905; AMC 255; BMCRE 650 = BMCRR East 243; Babelon Julia 148; Cohen 2).

431

431 Similar to preceding, but Octavian's head is to left. *Silver denarius. Italian mint (possibly Rome), 28 BC* (RIC 275b; CBN 907; AMC 257; BMCRE 652 = BMCRR East 245; Babelon Julia 149; Cohen 3).

The subjugation of the Ptolemaic kingdom of Egypt in August of 30 BC provides the theme for these denarii of Italian mintage dated by Octavian's sixth consulship to 28 BC. As in the case of the ASIA RECEPTA quinarii this issue has often been deemed to be of eastern origin, but the style of the engraving is purely Italian and there seems no valid reason to regard them as anything other than a continuation of the large scale issues of 32–29 BC. The lituus appearing behind Octavian's head draws attention to his association with the priestly college of augurs. Antony had given great prominence on his coinage to his membership of this exclusive body and Octavian was obviously anxious to stress his own position in this regard. The nomenclature of the new master of the Roman world has now been reduced to a simple 'CAESAR', as on the coinage of the dictator himself, a clear indication of the uncertainties surrounding his constitutional position at this time. The crocodile, the symbol *par excellence* of the 'Land of the Nile', is the sole element of the reverse design, whilst the accompanying legend conveys the simple message of the conquest of Egypt and the reduction of a once proud nation to the status of a Roman province. A similar reverse type appears on aurei and denarii of markedly different style (see nos. 432 and 434). These should probably be attributed to an eastern mint, possibly in Asia.

432

432 Bare head of Octavian right, small capricorn right below, CAESAR DIVI F COS VI around. *Reverse:* crocodile standing right, AEGVPTO / CAPTA above and in exergue. *Silver denarius. Uncertain eastern mint, 28 BC* (RIC 545; CBN 928; AMC 315; BMCRE 653 = BMCRR East 246; Babelon Julia 150; Cohen 4).

In addition to the obvious difference in style coins of this issue vary from the contemporary Italian denarii of the AEGVPTO CAPTA type through the addition of DIVI F to the obverse legend, the omission of the augural symbolism behind Octavian's head, and the appearance of a small capricorn below his neck. Their place of mintage remains uncertain, though Giard[192] has attributed them to Pergamum on the basis of similarities in portrait style to some of the provincial 'C A' bronzes which he gives to this mint. Unfortunately, however, the origin of the 'C A' coinage is wholly uncertain,[193] so the argument loses much of its validity. I will not attempt any further speculation on the subject in the present state of our knowledge. The capricorn represents Octavian's birth sign[194] and was to appear frequently as a coin type during his reign.

433

433 Laureate head of Octavian right, IMP CAESAR DIVI F COS VI LIBERTATIS P R VINDEX around. *Reverse:* Pax standing left on parazonium (?), holding caduceus, PAX in field to left, snake emerging from cista mystica to right, all within laurel-wreath. *Silver cistophorus = three denarii. Ephesus, 28 BC* (RIC 476; RPC 2203; Sutherland 1–72; CBN 908; AMC 673; BMCRE 691 = BMCRR East 248; Babelon Julia 147; Cohen 218).

These were the first silver cistophori to be minted in Asia in over a decade, since Antony's issue depicting himself and his new bride Octavia in 39 BC. The mint was probably located at Ephesus, the likely source of the earlier series, and the issue marked the beginning of a vast output of cistophori extending over the following decade. Ephesus and Pergamum both seem to have participated in this later coinage which, interestingly, seems to coincide with the lengthy interruption in the production of aurei and denarii in Italy.[195] For the first time Octavian is depicted laureate instead of bare-headed,[196] *i.e.* as a god. It was fitting that this should have occurred first on an issue from the East where the concept of a divine monarchy was deeply rooted. The wreath of laurel doubtless refers to Apollo with whom Octavian had had a special relationship ever since Actium. The message conveyed by the legends and the reverse type leave no room for ambiguity. In a remarkably lengthy obverse inscription Octavian is proclaimed as the 'Champion of the Liberty of the Roman People', whilst the figure of Pax on reverse, firmly identified by the accompanying inscription, gives promise of the peace which will now be bestowed on a troubled world through Octavian's triumph over his enemies, who were also the enemies of Rome. The traditional cista, or snake basket, is relegated to a minor symbol in the reverse field, whilst the whole is encircled by Apollo's wreath of laurel instead of the Dionysiac garland of ivy, now tainted by its association with Antony, the 'New Dionysus'.

We finally come to the issues of Octavian's seventh consulship celebrated in 27 BC, the last year of our survey.

434 Bare head of Octavian right, small capricorn right below, CAESAR DIVI F COS VII around. *Reverse:* crocodile standing right, AEGVPT / CAPTA above and in exergue. *Gold aureus. Uncertain eastern mint, January 27 BC* (RIC 544; CBN 935; BMCRE 655 = BMCRR East 250; cf. Babelon Julia 151; Cohen 1).

434

This type is in continuation of the series of denarii produced at an unidentified eastern mint during Octavian's sixth consulship (see no. 432). The only difference, other than the denomination and the consular numbering, is the omission of the final letter from **AEGVPTO**. As Octavian entered his seventh consulship on 1 January and received the title of Augustus just sixteen days later it would appear that this issue was confined to the first half of the month. However, news of events in Rome probably took some time to reach wherever it was that this mint was located, so production may have continued for a while longer. The series appears to terminate at this point unless the enigmatic gold four-aureus piece in Madrid,[197] with obverse legend **IMP CAESAR DIVI F AVGVST COS VII** and reverse **AEGYPTO CAPTA** with hippopotamus right, should prove to be authentic. The piece appears to be highly suspect, though it is listed by both Sutherland in *RIC* (no. 546) and Giard in *CBN* (p. 147, *).

Not surprisingly, Octavian's Italian mint produced no coinage prior to him being honoured with the title of Augustus on 16 January. Thereafter, the following remarkable aureus was issued in commemoration of the momentous changes being enacted at this time, the culmination of all that had taken place since Caesar's fateful crossing of the Rubicon twenty-two years before when Octavian was just thirteen years of age.

435

435 Bare head of Augustus right, **CAESAR COS VII CIVIBVS SERVATEIS** around. *Reverse:* eagle standing facing on oak-wreath flanked by **S – C**, its wings spread and head turned to left, branches of laurel on either side in background, **AVGVSTVS** above. *Gold aureus. Italian mint (possibly Rome), 27 BC, after 16 January.* (RIC 277; CBN 911; BMCRE 656 = BMCRR 4371; Cohen 30).

This appears to represent the final issue in Octavian's extensive Italian coinage which had begun with the **CAESAR DIVI F** series in the autumn of 32 BC, almost a year before Actium. Another eight years were to elapse before the Augustan coinage recommenced in Italy, this time undoubtedly from the mint of Rome as the issues bore the names of the moneyers, as in the days prior to 40 BC. This last aureus type, prior to Augustus handing back to the Senate and Roman People the prerogative of coinage, is filled with symbolism. Of the many honours bestowed by the Senate and accepted by Octavian on 16 January several are recorded on this coin: the conferment of the civic wreath, or *corona civica*, of oak-leaves ('*ob cives servatos*'), an award originally intended to recognize the valour of one who had saved the life of a fellow-citizen in battle, but in this exceptional case extended to encompass the broader concept of having rescued the entire state; the planting of laurel-trees either side of the doorway of Augustus' house as a sign of honour and respect; and, of course, the granting of the title 'Augustus' itself, a name which was to become synonymous with the ultimate imperial authority over the centuries to follow.

The appearance of the abbreviation S[*enatus*] C[*onsulto*], 'by decree of the Senate', referred to the supposed source of the honours and privileges which were being bestowed on this 'first citizen', or *princeps*. But the reality was very different. Octavian, like Caesar before him, had built his authority on the steadfast loyalty of his army and his control over the military was retained in an undiminished form even after the so-called constitutional settlement of January, 27 BC. Whether they realized it or not (and most of them probably did in their heart of hearts) the Senate and the Roman People were now living under a military autocracy, no matter how fine was the velvet which clothed the iron fist. It was no accident that the bird of Jupiter, the sovereign god of the Romans, made his initial appearance on the coinage of Caesar's heir at this very moment of transition. Truly, the Republic of Brutus and Cicero, with all its ancient traditions and institutions, was finally dead.

The stage was now set for the evolution of the Roman imperial coinage in all its majesty. The Emperor Augustus would rule the Roman world for a further forty-one years during which time he would effect, with infinite patience and subtlety, a total transformation of the state, handing on to his successors a firmly established monarchical system of government the like of which would have been unimaginable at the time of his great-uncle's fateful crossing of the Rubicon on that January day in the year 49 BC.

APPENDIX 1

Chronological Conspectus of Roman Coin Issues, January 49–January 27 BC

The numbers in parentheses refer to the catalogue entries

49 BC The Pompeians in Rome (1–2)
The Pompeians in the East (3–8)
Caesar in Italy, etc. (9)
The moneyer Mn. Acilius in Rome (16)

48 BC Caesar in the East (10–14)
The Caesarian moneyers in Rome (17–28)

47 BC Caesar in the East (15)
The Caesarian moneyers in Rome (29–39)
The Pompeians in North Africa (40–7)
Caesar in Sicily and North Africa (54–5)

46 BC Caesar in North Africa (57)
Aurei of A. Hirtius in Rome (56)
The Caesarian moneyers in Rome (63–81)
The Pompeians in Spain (48–53)
Caesar in Spain (58–9)

45 BC The Caesarian moneyers in Rome (82–97)
Gold of L. Plancus and *aes* of C. Clovius in Rome (60–2)
Sextus Pompey in Spain (232–4)

44 BC Lifetime and posthumous issues of the Roman moneyers for Caesar (98–112)
Aurei of Rome commemorating Caesar's fifth consulship (117)
Denarii of the moneyer P. Sepullius Macer for Antony (142)
Regular issues of the Roman moneyers (164–70)
Sextus Pompey in Massilia (235–6)

43 BC Antony in northern Italy and Gaul (118–25)
Octavian in northern and central Italy (130–5)
Emergency issues of aurei by the Senate (195–6)
Denarii of L. Flaminius honouring the memory of Caesar (113)
Regular issues of the Roman moneyers (171–4)
C. Antonius as proconsul of Macedonia (141)
Commencement of *aes* coinage of Sextus Pompey in Sicily (336)

42 BC Antony in Italy and Greece before and after Philippi (126–9)
Octavian in Italy and Greece before and after Philippi (136–8)
Lepidus in Italy prior to Philippi (139–40)
Aurei and denarii of the Roman moneyers for Antony and Octavian (143–58)

Aurei of the Roman moneyers for Lepidus (159–63)
Denarii of the Roman moneyers honouring Caesar (114–16)
Regular issues of the Roman moneyers (175–94)
Brutus and Cassius in the East (197–226)
Q. Cornuficius in North Africa (227–31)
Commencement of precious metal coinage of Sextus Pompey in Sicily (332–4, 335)

41 BC Antony in the East (237–51)
Octavian in Italy (298–9)
Regular issues of the Roman moneyers (316–24)
Staius Murcus in the region of the Ionian Sea (337)
Cn. Domitius Ahenobarbus in the region of the Adriatic and Ionian Seas (338–9)
Sextus Pompey in Sicily (334–5)

40 BC Antony in Greece (252–8)
Antony's issues in Italy in commemoration of the Pact of Brundisium and his marriage to Octavia (259–61)
Denarii issued in Italy by Q. Salvidienus for Octavian (300)
Octavian's issues in Italy in commemoration of the Pact of Brundisium (301–3)
Issues of the Roman moneyers for Octavian (325–31)
Sextus Pompey in Sicily (334a–b, 335b)
Q. Labienus in Syria or S.E. Asia Minor (340–1)
Aes of L. Atratinus as augur, possibly of Asia (264)

39 BC Cistophori of Ephesus honouring Antony and Octavia (262–3)
Denarii issued in the East by P. Ventidius for Antony (265)
Issue of quinarii by Octavian in Gaul on the occasion of his visit (304)
Cn. Domitius Calvinus in Spain (342)

38 BC Antony in Athens (266–8) and in Syria (269–72)
'Fleet coinage' (*aes*) of Bibulus, Atratinus, and Capito in Syria and Greece (273–90)
Aurei and denarii of Octavian commemorating Agrippa's designation to his first consulship (305–7)
Italian *aes* of Octavian and Divos Iulius (308–9)

37 BC Denarii of Octavian issued prior to and following the renewal of the Triumvirate (310–13)
'Fleet coinage' (*aes*) of reduced weight of Atratinus and Capito in southern Italy (291–6)
Denarii of Antony issued in Syria or Armenia commemorating Canidius Crassus' defeat of Artavasdes (297)

36 BC Aurei, denarii and quinarii of Octavian issued prior to the war against Sextus Pompey (314–15a)

35 BC Octavian in Illyricum (392–3)

34 BC Aurei of Antony and Antyllus in Syria or Armenia (343–4)
Denarii of Antony and Cleopatra at Alexandria (345)

33 BC (no coinage attributable to either Triumvir in this year)

32 BC Denarii issued at Athens by M. Junius Silanus for Antony (346–7)
'Legionary coinage' (aurei and denarii) of Antony at Patrae (348–86)
Octavian's pre-Actian CAESAR DIVI F coinage in Italy (394–401)

31 BC Denarii issued at Actium by D. Turullius for Antony (387–8)
Denarii issued in the Cyrenaica by Pinarius Scarpus for Antony (389–91)
Aurei and denarii issued in the Cyrenaica by Pinarius Scarpus for Octavian (411–15)
Octavian's post-Actian CAESAR DIVI F coinage in Italy (402–10)

30 BC Octavian's IMP CAESAR coinage in Italy commencing after the conquest of Egypt (416–28)

29 BC ASIA RECEPTA quinarii issued by Octavian in Italy (429)

28 BC AEGVPTO CAPTA denarii issued by Octavian in Italy (430–31) and in the East (432)
LIBERTATIS P R VINDEX / PAX cistophori issued by Octavian at Ephesus (433)

27 BC AEGVPT CAPTA aurei issued by Octavian in the East (434)
Aureus issued in Italy in commemoration of the bestowal of the title *Augustus* on Octavian on 16 January (435)

APPENDIX 2

Local Coinages of the Imperatorial Period

Based on the listings in *Roman Provincial Coinage*

436. SPAIN, BAETICA: Carteia. Æ 20–21 (semis). CARTEIA, turreted head of Fortuna right, trident behind. *Reverse:* P FALCIDI IIII VIR, winged thunderbolt between lines. *Circa 40* BC. (RPC 111; Chaves 944–6).

437. – *Obverse:* same as preceding. *Reverse:* P FALCIDIVS IIII VIR [EX S C] F C, club, bow, and quiver. *Circa 40* BC. (RPC 112; Chaves 947–57).

438. – CARTEIA EX D D, turreted head of Fortuna right. *Reverse:* C MAIVS C F POLLIO IIII VIR, winged caduceus. *Circa 35* BC. (RPC 113; Chaves 959–98).

439. – EX D D, winged head of Victory right. *Reverse:* L ATINI C NVCIA IIII VIR, cornucopiae. *Circa 30* BC. (RPC 114; Chaves 999–1021).

440. – EX D D, head of Apollo right. *Reverse:* L ATINI C NVCIA IIII VIR, lyre. *Circa 30* BC. (RPC 115; Chaves 1022–45).

441. SPAIN, TARRACONENSIS: Carthago Nova. Æ 20–22 (semis). P ATELLI (or ATELLIVS), coiled snake. *Reverse:* L FABRIC on upper of two crossed rectangular tablets. *Date uncertain.* (RPC 146; Beltran 1).

442. – C CAEDI T POPILI, dolphin right. *Reverse:* II VIR QVIN, palm-branch. *Date uncertain.* (RPC 147; Beltran 2).

443. – HEL POLLIO ALBINVS II Q (or QV), or ALBINVS HEL POLLIO II QV, veiled and diademed head of Concordia right. *Reverse:* SABINVS C M IMP, trophy. *Date uncertain.* (RPC 149; Beltran 3–4).

444. – Head of Minerva right, in crested Corinthian helmet (no legend). *Reverse:* C V I N, pedestal surmounted by statue of figure standing left. *After 42* BC. (RPC 151; Beltran 6).

445. – L IVNIVS II VIR QVIN (or QVINQ) AVG (or AVGVR), eagle standing right on thunderbolt, looking back, lituus to right. *Reverse:* L ACILIVS II VIR QVIN (or QVINQ) AVG (or AVGVR), patera, jug and lituus. *Date uncertain.* (RPC 152; Beltran 10).

446. – C MAECIVS QVINQ, vexillum. *Reverse:* L ACILIVS II VIR QVINQ, legionary eagle. *Date uncertain.* (RPC 154; Beltran 12).

447. – L APPVLEI RVF QVINQ, legionary eagle between two standards. *Reverse:* C MAECI QVINQ (or QVINIQ or QVINQV), galley right. *After 31* BC. (RPC 155; Beltran 13).

These types are, of course, closely modelled on Antony's 'legionary' coinage issued in 32–31 BC.

448. – P BAEBIVS POLLIO II VIR QVIN, Victory walking right, holding wreath and palm-branch. *Reverse:* C AQVINVS MELA II VIR QVIN, two standards. *After 31* BC. (RPC 157; Beltran 9).

449. – CONDVC (or CONTVC) MALLEOL, open right hand. *Reverse:* II VIR QVINQ, bull standing right. *After 31* BC. (RPC 158; Beltran 15).

This distinctive obverse type was likely inspired by the Cyrenaican coinage of Pinarius Scarpus issued in the name of Octavian shortly after Actium.

450. Æ 16–18 (quadrans). CAED, stem of prow. *Reverse:* POPI, anchor. *After 38 BC.* (RPC 148).

451. – HEL POLLI II QVI across field, small snake above. *Reverse:* ALBINVS II QVI across field. *Date uncertain.* (RPC 150; Beltran 5).

452. – L IVNIVS, jug. *Reverse:* L ACILIVS, patera and lituus. *Date uncertain.* (RPC 153; Beltran 11).

453. – II L APPVLEI QVINQ across field. *Reverse:* II C MAECI QVINQ across field. *After 31 BC.* (RPC 156; Beltran 14).

454. – COND MALL, hammer. *Reverse:* II VIR QVINQ, circular shield. *After 31 BC.* (RPC 159; Beltran 16).
In common with many other mints of this region the remarkably extensive coinage of this city (if all the issues given to it are correctly attributed) exhibits the interesting phenomenon of having numerous types which appear to be copied from Roman issues of the late Republican and Imperatorial periods. For a full listing of the examples from Carthago Nova, including the two noted above, see RPC, p. 91.

455. **Ilici.** Æ 20 (semis). Q TERENTIVS II VIR, simpulum, inscribed MO. *Reverse:* C SALVIVS II VIR, clasped right hands. *After 42 BC.* (RPC 187; Llorens 2).
This reverse type and the next were probably inspired by the triumviral aurei of the moneyer C. Vibius Varus issued at Rome in 42 BC.

456. – C SALVIVS II VIR, simpulum. *Reverse:* Q TERENT MONT II VIR, clasped right hands. *After 42 BC.* (RPC 188; Llorens 1).

457. **Ilerda.** Æ 24 (denomination uncertain). IMP CAESAR DIVI F, bare head of Octavian right. *Reverse:* MVN ILERDA, she-wolf standing right. *Late triumviral or early post-triumviral period.* (RPC 260; NAH 956).

458. **Lepida-Celsa.** Æ 28–30 (as). COL VIC IVL LEP (or C V I L), winged bust of Victory right, palm over shoulder. *Reverse:* M FVL C OTAC PR QVIN, priest ploughing right with yoke of oxen. *Circa 44–36 BC.* (RPC 261; GMI 433).

459. – C V I L PR II VIR, bust of Victory right, palm over shoulder. *Reverse:* C BALBO L PORCIO, bull standing right. *Circa 44–36 BC.* (RPC 262; GMI 434).

460. – COL VIC IVL LEP, draped (or undraped) female bust (Venus?) right. *Reverse:* L NEP L SVRA (RA ligatured) PR II VIR, bull standing right. *Circa 44–36 BC.* (RPC 263; GMI 432).

461. – COL VIC IVL LEP, head of Minerva (?) right, wearing crested helmet. *Reverse:* P SALPA M FVLVI PR II VIR, bull butting (or running) right. *Circa 44–36 BC.* (RPC 264; GMI 435–6).

462. – COL V I CELSA II VIR, bare head of Octavian right. *Reverse:* L POMPE (MP ligatured) BVCCO L CORNE (NE ligatured) FRONT (or FRONTO, NT ligatured), bull standing right. *Before 27 BC.* (RPC 269; GMI 438).

463. Æ 19–21 (semis). C V I L, head of Hercules right, club behind. *Reverse:* L SEMP (MP ligatured) MAX (MA ligatured) M CAEC AED, bull standing right. *Circa 44–36 BC.* (RPC 265; NAH 897).

464. – C V I L, radiate and draped bust of Sol facing. *Reverse:* L CAL SEX NIG AED, sheep standing right. *Circa 44–36 BC.* (RPC 266; NAH 898).

465. – COL VIC IVL LEP, radiate head of Sol right. *Reverse:* L CA . . . . . , sheep standing right. *Circa 44–36 BC.* (RPC 267).

466. Æ 15 (quadrans). C V I L . . . . . , boar standing right. *Reverse:* . . . . . SEX NIG AED, crescent. *Circa 44–36 BC.* (RPC 268).

467. **Osca.** Æ 29 (as). VRB VICT, bare head of Octavian right. *Reverse:* OSCA, horseman galloping right, holding spear. *Before 27 BC.* (RPC 281; GMI 604).

468. Æ 14 (quadrans). MV (ligatured), bare head of Octavian right. *Reverse:* OSCA, Pegasus running right. *Before 27 BC.* (RPC 282; GMI 610).

469. **Turiaso.** Æ 29 (as). SILBIS, laureate female head right. *Reverse:* TVRIASO, rider on horseback pacing left, his right hand raised. *Triumviral period, date uncertain.* (RPC 401; GMI 361).

470. – Similar to preceding, but with reverse type horseman galloping right. *Triumviral period, date uncertain.* (RPC 402; GMI 360).

471. Calagurris. Æ 29 (as). NASSICA, bare head of Octavian right. *Reverse:* CALAGVRRI IVLIA, bull standing right. *Late triumviral or post-triumviral period.* (RPC 431; GMI 682).

472. Æ 21 (semis). NASSICA, bare head of Octavian right. *Reverse:* C VAL C SEX AEDILES, bull's head facing. *Late triumviral or post-triumviral period.* (RPC 432; GMI 683).

473. GAUL: Treviri. Æ 16. A HIRTIVS, elephant standing right. *Reverse:* emblems of the pontificate – simpulum, aspergillum, axe and apex. *50 BC, just prior to Caesar's invasion of Italy.* (RPC 501; Scheers, no. 162, class I).
This remarkable type appears to provide evidence that Caesar's first issue of denarii (from which it is clearly imitated) commenced in Gaul prior to the crossing of the Rubicon in January, 49 BC. The mint for these little bronzes was probably located in the Belgic oppidum of the Tetelbierg, in present-day Luxembourg, as large numbers have been recovered there. Caesar's lieutenant Aulus Hirtius is known to have been in Gaul in 51–50 and in December of the latter year he was sent as an envoy to Pompey.

474. – Similar to preceding, but with legend CARINA (retrograde) on obverse. *30–29 BC.* (RPC 502; Scheers, no. 162, class II).
Carinas was proconsul of Gallia Comata in 30–29 BC and it is tempting to see in this issue a twentieth anniversary revival of the coinage of Hirtius marking the end of two decades of civil wars. A much rarer issue than its prototype, once again most of the known specimens come from the Tetelbierg (Luxembourg).

475. Uncertain tribe of central Gaul. Æ 14. AΘIIDIAC, head of tribal chief Athediac right. *Reverse:* A HIR IMP, lion running right. *45–44 BC.* (RPC 503; BN 8086A).
This series belongs to the time of Hirtius' later presence in Gaul when he governed the new province of Gallia Comata which he had helped to conquer.

476. – Similar to preceding, but with head of tribal chief Inecriturix and legend INIICRITVRIX on obverse. *45–44 BC.* (RPC 503).

477. – Similar to preceding, but with head of tribal chief Coriarcos and legend CORIARCOS on obverse. *45–44 BC.* (RPC 503; BN 8093).

478. – Similar to preceding, but with head of tribal chief . . . carius and legend . . . CARIVS on obverse. *45–44 BC.* (RPC 503; BN 8092).

479. The Ruteni. Æ 16. L MVNATI, head (of Attalus?) left, X beneath. *Reverse:* ATTALVS, bird right, seizing snake, palm and S above. *Uncertain date in the late 40s or 30s BC.* (RPC 504; BN 4792–6).
Formerly considered to have been issued by a tribal chief 'Attalus' in honour of the proconsular governor L. Munatius Plancus, it is now thought that 'L. Munatius Attalus' had received Roman citizenship and taken his praenomen and gentilicium from Plancus and that the issue may, therefore, be of a somewhat later date (cf. RPC pp. 148–9).

480. Æ 14. L MVNAT, laureate head (of Plancus?) right. *Reverse:* ATTALVS, lion running right. *Uncertain date in the late 40s or 30s BC.* (RPC 505; BN 4797).

481. Lugdunum. Æ 15. COPIA FELIX, turreted bust of city-goddess right, cornucopiae behind. *Reverse:* MVNATIA, bull charging left, restrained by Hercules, club in field to right. *Late 43 BC.* (RPC 511; FITA pp. 206–7).
This represents the foundation issue of the Colonia Copia Felix Munatia Lugdunum, founded in 43 BC by L. Munatius Plancus during his governorship of Gallia Comata.

482. Æ 30–32 (dupondius). IMP CAESAR DIVI F DIVI IVLI, back to back heads of Caesar left, wearing wreath, and Octavian right, bareheaded. *Reverse:* COPIA, prow of galley right, *meta* above. *Circa 38 BC.* (RPC 514; FITA p. 207).

483. – Similar to preceding, but with palm-branch between the heads on obverse, and with star superimposed on globe to left of the *meta* on reverse. *Circa 36 BC.* (RPC 515; FITA p. 207).

484. Æ 17 (semis). CAESAR DIVI F, bare head of Octavian right. *Reverse:* COPIA, bull charging right, snake beneath. *Circa 36 BC.* (RPC 516; FITA p. 208).

485. Vienna. Æ 29–31 (dupondius). IMP CAESAR DIVI F DIVI IVLI, back to back heads of Caesar left and Octavian right, both bareheaded. *Reverse:* C I V, prow of galley right, with elaborate superstructure. *Circa 36 BC.* (RPC 517; FITA p. 337).

Colonia Iulia Viennensis was founded about 50 BC and was the civitas-capital of the Allobroges.

486. Narbo. Æ 28–30 (dupondius). CAESAR, bare head of Octavian right. *Reverse:* prow of galley right, with superstructure and mast (no legend). *Circa 40 BC.* (RPC 518; FITA pp. 41–3).

Founded in 118 BC Narbo was the first Roman colony in Gaul. The mint attribution rests on the discovery of a small hoard of these coins at Narbonne in 1973 (cf. RPC p. 152).

487. Nemausus. Æ obol (0.4 gm). Helmeted and draped bust right (no legend). *Reverse:* NEM COL within wreath. *Circa 40 BC.* (RPC 519; Giard 6).

Colonia Nemausus was probably founded by Tiberius Claudius Nero, first husband of Livia and father of the future emperor Tiberius, at the time of his settlement of Caesarian veterans in Narbonese Gaul between 46 and 44 BC.

488. Æ 15–16 (semis). Helmeted and draped bust right, S behind. *Reverse:* NEM COL, Valetudo standing left, holding patera over two snakes and resting on column. *Circa 40 BC.* (RPC 520; Giard 7).

489. Æ 13–14 (quadrans). Helmeted and draped bust right, Q behind. *Reverse:* NEM COL, inverted urn between two palms. *Circa 40 BC.* (RPC 521; Giard 8).

490. Cabellio. Æ diobol or hemidrachm (1 gm). CABE, head of Apollo right, hair in ringlets. *Reverse:* LEPI and cornucopiae within wreath. *44–43 BC.* (RPC 527; BMCC 601).

This type and the next were struck under M. Aemilius Lepidus (the possible founder of the colony) during his governorship of Gallia Narbonensis prior to the establishment of the Second Triumvirate with Antony and Octavian at Bononia in November of 43 BC.

491. Æ obol (0.45 gm). Same as preceding. *44–43 BC.* (RPC 528; BMCC 602–5).

492. Æ 14–16 (semis). COL, helmeted head right. *Reverse:* CABE, head of Apollo right, hair in ringlets, all within wreath of myrtle. *Uncertain date in the late 40s or 30s BC.* (RPC 529; BMCC 242–52).

493. Antipolis. Æ 15. ΙΣΔΕΜ, diademed head of Venus right. *Reverse:* ANTIΠ ΛΕΠΙ, Victory standing right, crowning trophy. *44–43 BC.* (RPC 531; BMCC 260).

The coinage of Antipolis also originates from the time of the governorship of Aemilius Lepidus. However, because of the variety of names (?) appearing on the obverses of this issue it may have extended beyond the time of the governorship into the period of the Triumvirate.

494. Æ 10–13. Similar to preceding, but with legend AI MAI on obverse. *44–43 BC and later.* (RPC 532; BN 2185).

495. – Similar to preceding, but with legend ANTI. *44–43 BC and later.* (RPC 532; BN 2206).

496. – Similar to preceding, but with legend KAN (N retrograde). *44–43 BC and later.* (RPC 532; BN 2195).

497. – Similar to preceding, but with legend ΛΑΚΑ. *44–43 BC and later.* (RPC 532; SNG Cop. 857).

498. – Similar to preceding, but with legend ΛΑ ΤΕ. *44–43 BC and later.* (RPC 532; BN 2196).

499. – Similar to preceding, but with legend ΝΙΔΙ. *44–43 BC and later.* (RPC 532; SNG Cop. 856).

500. – Similar to preceding, but with legend ΠΑΚΟΡ. *44–43 BC and later.* (RPC 532; BN 2193).

501. – Similar to preceding, but with legend TEP AIM. *44–43 BC and later.* (RPC 532: Fréjus find).

502. – Similar to preceding, but with legend TI Δ KOP. *44–43 BC and later.* (RPC 532; BN 2194).

503. Arausio (?). Æ 27–28 (dupondius). IMP DIVI F, back to back heads of Octavian right and Agrippa left, both bareheaded. *Reverse:* prow of galley right, with superstructure, circular medallion above apparently bearing a ram's head device (no legend). *Circa 30–29 BC.* (RPC 533; FITA pp. 208–10).
Grant's tentative mint attribution of this type is based on the identification of the ram's head as the emblem of Legio II Gallica whose veterans formed the original colony about 35 BC.

504. Forum Iulii. AR drachm (2.22 gm). Prow left, with rostrum. *Reverse:* capricorn right, O beneath. *Circa 31–27 BC.* (RPC 536; Deroc 289 and fig. 5).
The attributions of this, and the following two uninscribed types in bronze, rest on the evidence of finds from Fréjus and its vicinity. After Actium the military harbour of Forum Iulii became the base for the 300 Antonian warships captured in the battle.

505. Æ 10–14 (semis). Laureate head right. *Reverse:* capricorn right, with cornucopiae. *Circa 31–27 BC.* (RPC 535; Deroc 288 and fig. 4).

506. Æ 10–12 (semis). Prow left, with rostrum. *Reverse:* capricorn right, with globe. *Circa 31–27 BC.* (RPC 534; Deroc 288 and fig. 3).

507. ITALY: uncertain mint. Æ 27 (dupondius?). Diademed head of Venus right, varying symbol/s in field (crescent or star in crescent before; capricorn behind, sometimes with crescent before. *Reverse:* Q OPPIVS PR, Victory advancing left, looking right, her wings spread, holding palm-branch and bowl of fruit, sometimes with symbol beneath (thunderbolt or vine-leaf). *Date uncertain, possibly mid-40s BC.* (RPC 602; Crawford 550/2).
Widely varying attributions and chronologies have been proposed by different scholars for this enigmatic coinage. It appears to resemble the bronzes in Caesar's name issued in Italy in 45 BC by the prefect C. Clovius (see no. 62), but Oppius' coins are a good deal scarcer and the evidence of provenances is unfortunately scant. Crawford preferred to assign them to Cilicia in 88 BC, though without conviction, whilst Grant (FITA p. 61) attributed them to Syria in the late triumviral period. The authors of RPC have adopted the Italian attribution which is followed here, but final resolution of the problem will have to await the appearance of new evidence.

508. – Similar to preceding, but the head of Venus is to left (with star before, sometimes also with ram's head behind); on reverse, the only symbol so far recorded is a vine-leaf. *Date uncertain, possibly mid-40s BC.* (RPC 603; Crawford 550/3).

509. – Diademed head of Venus right. *Reverse:* Q OPPIVS PR, Victory standing facing, her wings uplifted, holding wreath and palm-branch. *Date uncertain, possibly mid-40s BC.* (RPC 602A; Crawford 550/1).

510. Uncertain mint. Æ dupondius. Laureate head of Janus, II above. *Reverse:* two galleys right, side by side, ROMA above, CN PISO FRVGI beneath. *Date uncertain, possibly of the triumviral period.* (RPC 619; Crawford 547).
Represented by a unique specimen in Pesaro, the origin of this type is even more uncertain than the coinage of Q. Oppius. Even the authenticity of the piece is not beyond question and the present writer believes that it belongs to a much earlier period than the one here under consideration. However, as it is included by both Crawford and RPC (though with reservations) it seems better not to omit it from this listing.

511. SARDINIA: Turris Libisonis (?). Æ 27–28 (as?). M L S C P, bare male head (the colony's founder, M. Lurius?) right. *Reverse:* Q A M P C II V, hexastyle temple. *Circa 40 BC.* (RPC 622; FITA pp. 205–6).
M. Lurius was Octavian's governor on the island from circa 42–40 BC. He was ousted by Sextus Pompey's legate Menodorus.

512. Æ 24–25 (semis?). Q A M L C VE (ligatured) II V, helmeted head of Sardus Pater right. *Reverse:* D D, plough. *Circa 40 BC.* (RPC 623; FITA pp. 205–6).

513. Caralis. Æ 30–32 (dupondius?). ARISTO MVTVMBAL RICOCE SVF, conjoined male heads right. *Reverse:* VENERIS, tetrastyle temple, KAR in exergue. *Circa 40 BC.* (RPC 624; FITA pp. 149–50).
The portraits on this type are probably merely those of local officials. The

Caesarian connection with this town – the dictator visited it following Thapsus – is perhaps illustrated by the temple of Venus. The former attribution to Carthage has been discredited by the evidence of provenances.

514. Uselis (?). Æ 22–24 (semis?). M ATTIVS BALBVS PR, bare head of M. Atius Balbus left. *Reverse:* SARD PATER, helmeted head of Sardus Pater right, spear at shoulder. *Circa 38–36 BC.* (RPC 625; FITA pp. 150–52).

M. Attius Balbus was, presumably, Octavian's governor on the island following its liberation from the control of Sextus Pompey in 38 BC (cf. RPC pp. 162–3).

515. SICILY: island of Lipara. Æ 19 (triens?). ΛΙΠΑΡΑΙΩΝ, head of Hephaestus left, wearing pilos. *Reverse:* Γ ΜΑΡΚΙΟϹ ΛΕΥ (?), Λ ΑVϹWΝΕΥϹ, ΔΥΟΑΝΔΡ (ΜΑΡ, ΛΕ, ΑV, ΝΕ, ΑΝ and ΔΡ all ligatured), tongs. *Circa 44–37 BC.* (RPC 626; BMCG 81–4).

516. Halaesa. Æ 21 (semis?). HAL ARCH (AL ligatured), laureate head of Apollo left. *Reverse:* CÆC RVF II VIR (VF also ligatured), tripod. *Uncertain date, possibly of the triumviral period.* (RPC 628; BMCG 15).

517. Æ 20 (semis?). HAL ARCH (AL ligatured), laureate head of Apollo right. *Reverse:* CÆC RVF II VIR (VF also ligatured), lyre. *Uncertain date, possibly of the triumviral period.* (RPC 629; BMCG 16).

518. Cephaloedium. Æ 23 (semis?). C Æ (?) DOM, laureate head of Heracles right. *Reverse:* KE ΦA, Heracles standing left, holding club and lion's skin. *Uncertain date, possibly of the triumviral period.* (RPC 634; FITA p. 192).

519. Æ 22 (semis?). C CANINIVS [II VIR?], bare head (of Caninius?) right. *Reverse:* KE FA, Heracles standing left, as preceding. *Uncertain date, possibly of the triumviral period.* (RPC 635; FITA p. 192).

520. Panormus. Æ 21 (semis?). Laureate head of Zeus right, sceptre behind. *Reverse:* ΠΑΝΟΡΜΙΤΑΝ, tetrastyle temple, C D in exergue. *Uncertain date, possibly of the triumviral period.* (RPC 636; Gabrici 98–108).

521. Æ 17 (triens?). D D, pharos or tower. *Reverse:* rectangular altar, with horns. *Uncertain date, possibly of the triumviral period.* (RPC 637; BMCG 22).

522. Æ 14 (sextans?). D D, pharos or tower. *Reverse:* L M, palm-tree. *Uncertain date, possibly of the triumviral period.* (RPC 638; FITA p. 28).

523. Segesta. Æ20 (semis?). M VIPSANO ATHENAEO . . . (HE ligatured), conjoined heads of the Dioscuri right, surmounted by stars. *Reverse:* C IVLIO DIONYSIO IIVIRIS EX D D (VL ligatured), dolphin right, and aplustre. *Uncertain date, possibly of the triumviral period.* (RPC 648; FITA p. 189).

524. – C IVLIVS C F LONGVS II VIR (VIR ligatured), caps of the Dioscuri surmounted by stars. *Reverse:* EX D D, dolphin right. *Uncertain date, possibly of the triumviral period.* (RPC 649; FITA p. 190).

525. – Similar to preceding, but with obverse legend M VIPS DOSS . . . . *Uncertain date, possibly of the triumviral period.* (RPC 650; Gabrici 57).

526. Æ 16 (triens?). Caps of the Dioscuri surmounted by stars (no legend). *Reverse:* D D, rudder. *Uncertain date, possibly of the triumviral period.* (RPC 651; FITA p. 194).

527. Entella. Æ 19 (semis?). ΑΤΡΑΤΙΝΟΥ, radiate head of Helios right. Reverse: ΕΝΤΕΛΛΙΝWΝ, Tyche standing left, holding corn-ears and cornucopiae. *36 BC.* (RPC 653; BMCG 8).

Antony's lieutenant L. Sempronius Atratinus was at this time assisting Octavian against Sextus Pompey in accordance with the terms of the Pact of Tarentum (see also no. 529 below).

528. Æ 17 (triens?). ΑΤΡΑΤΙΝΟΥ, head of Dionysus right, wreathed with ivy. Reverse: ΕΝΤΕΛΛΙΝWΝ, bunch of grapes. *36 BC.* (RPC 654; SNG Cop. 239).

529. Lilybaeum. Æ 26 (as?). ΛΙΛΥΒΑΙΙΤΑΙϹ, turreted and veiled female head right, within triangular enclosure. *Reverse:* ΑΤΡΑΤΙΝΟ ΠΥΘΙΩΝ, snake-entwined tripod. *36 BC.* (RPC 655; BMCG 4).

530. Agrigentum. Æ 22 (semis?). ΑΚΡΑΓΑΝΤΙΝΩΝ, bare head of Octavian right. *Reverse:* ΑΚΡΑΓΑΝΤΙΝΩΝ, bare head (of Agrippa?) right. *Uncertain date, probably of the later triumviral period.* (RPC 658; BMCG 165).

531. Henna. Æ 30 (as?). L MVNATIVS M CESTIVS, veiled head of Ceres left, wreathed with corn, torch behind. *Reverse:* MVN HENNAE, Pluto abducting Proserpina in fast quadriga right. *Circa 44–36 BC.* (RPC 661; BMCG 9).

532. Æ 20 (semis?). MVN HENNAE, head of Proserpina (?) right. *Reverse:* M CESTIVS L MVNATIVS II VIR, Triptolemus standing left, naked but for chlamys over left arm, right hand extended. *Circa 44–36 BC.* (RPC 662; BMCG 11).

533. Æ 17 (triens?). MVN HENNAE, head of Dionysus right, wreathed with ivy. *Reverse:* M CESTIVS L MVNATI . . , bull butting left. *Circa 44–36 BC.* (RPC 663; Gabrici 14).

534. Æ 12 (sextans?). MVN HEN, laureate head of Apollo right. *Reverse:* M CES L MVN (MV ligatured) II VIR, swan right. *Circa 44–36 BC.* (RPC 664).

535. Assorus. Æ 22 (semis?). ASSORV, laureate head of Apollo right. Reverse: CRVSAS, river-god Crusas standing left, holding amphora and cornucopiae. *Uncertain date, possibly of the triumviral period.* (RPC 665; BMCG 1).

536. Æ 18 (triens?). Female head right, wearing stephane. *Reverse:* ASSORV, yoke of oxen ploughing right. *Uncertain date, possibly of the triumviral period.* (RPC 666; BMCG 2).

537. Centuripae. Æ 10 (uncia?). Monogram of uncertain form. *Reverse:* CENTVR, branch. *Uncertain date, possibly of the triumviral period.* (RPC 667; Gabrici 39).

538. Island of Melita. Æ 20 (triens?). ΜΕΛΙΤΑΙΩΝ, veiled and diademed head of Astarte (?) left. *Reverse:* C ARRVNTANVS BALB PROPR, curule chair. *Uncertain date, probably of the triumviral period.* (RPC 672; Gabrici 17).

539. Æ 22 (triens?). Veiled and diademed head of Astarte (?) right. *Reverse:* MELITAS, tripod. *Uncertain date, possibly of the triumviral period.* (RPC 673; SNG Cop. 471).

540. – Similar to preceding, but head of Astarte is to left. *Uncertain date, possibly of the triumviral period.* (RPC 674; Hunterian 33).

541. Island of Cossura. Æ 27 (semis?). Head of Isis (?) right, crowned by Nike flying right behind, uncertain object before. *Reverse:* sign of Tanit and COSSVRA within wreath. *Uncertain date, possibly of the triumviral period.* (RPC 675; SNG Cop. 451).

542. Æ 22 (triens?). Head of Isis (?) left, crowned by Nike flying right before. *Reverse:* COSSVRA within wreath. *Uncertain date, possibly of the triumviral period.* (RPC 676; SNG Cop. 452).

543. AFRICA: Juba, king of Numidia (60–46 BC). Æ denarius. REX IVBA, diademed and cuirassed bust of Juba right, with long beard, sceptre over right shoulder. *Reverse:* Punic legend IOBAI HMMLKT, octastyle temple on podium with flight of steps, sometimes with pellet at centre. *Utica (?), 47–46 BC.* (RPC 717; Mazard 84–6).

An implacable enemy of Caesar, Juba of Numidia lent his considerable support to the Pompeian cause in the period prior to the battle of Thapsus in 46 BC. His extensive output of denarii (with much rarer fractions) may have been issued from Utica, capital of the Roman province of Africa, rather than from his own capital city of Zama.

544. Æ quinarius. REX IVBA, winged and draped bust of Victory right. *Reverse:* Punic legend IOBAI HMMLKT, free horse galloping right. *Utica (?), 47–46 BC.* (RPC 718; Mazard 87).

545. – Diademed and cuirassed bust of Juba right, with long beard, sceptre over right shoulder (no legend). *Reverse:* free horse galloping right. *Utica (?), 47–46 BC.* (RPC 719; Mazard 88).

546. Æ sestertius. Bust of Africa right, wearing elephant's skin headdress. *Reverse:* lion walking right, head facing, S (retrograde) above. *Utica (?), 47–46 BC.* (RPC 720; Mazard 89).

547. WESTERN MAURETANIA: King Bogud (49–38 BC). Æ denarius. Head of Africa left, wearing elephant's skin headdress. *Reverse:* REX BOCVT (VT ligatured), griffin standing right, *mihir* (winged solar disk) above. *47–46 BC.* (RPC 853; Mazard 103).

Bogud supported the Caesarians against the Pompeians at the time of the civil war in north Africa which culminated in Thapsus. Like Juba, who was on the Pompeian side, Bogud struck silver denarii as his contribution towards the expenses of the war. No fractional silver was issued, but there are associated bronzes (probably semisses).

548. – Griffin left, attacking kneeling stag. *Reverse:* REX BOCVT (VT ligatured), griffin standing right, *mihir* (winged solar disk) above, thunderbolt beneath. *47–46 BC.* (RPC 854; Mazard 104).

549. – *Obverse:* same as preceding. *Reverse:* REX BOCV, griffin standing left, *mihir* (winged solar disk) above. *47–46 BC.* (RPC 855; Mazard 105).

550. Æ 25 (semis?). Bearded head (of Bogud?) right. *Reverse:* REX BOCVT (VT ligatured), prow of galley left. *47–46 BC.* (RPC 856; Mazard 106).

551. Tingi. Æ 28. IVL TINGI, IV VIR IVR D EX D D, two ears of corn. *Reverse:* Q FABIVS FABVLLVS L AVRELIVS (AV ligatured) SENECA, bearded head of Baal-Melqart facing, transverse sceptre behind. *Circa 38–33 BC.* (RPC 857; Mazard 612).

552. Æ 18–19. Ear of corn. *Reverse:* IVL TINGI across field. *Circa 38–33 BC.* (RPC 858; Mazard 621).

553. Æ 24–26. EX D D, diademed female head (Venus-Astarte?) right, all within laurel-wreath. *Reverse:* L ÆMI L VAL ÆD, Q FAB FABVL C IVL ATTIC IV, two ears of corn. *Circa 38–33 BC.* (RPC 859; Mazard 614–17, and 619).

554. Æ 23. COL IVL TINGI FABVLLVS ANTISTIVS IV VIR (ANT ligatured), female head (Ceres?) left, wreathed with corn. *Reverse:* L BAEBIVS COSA M CVRIVS L M AID, two ears of corn. *Circa 33–27 BC.* (RPC 860; Mazard 618).

555. Æ 25–26. TING MAIOR SIMINT II VIR (MA and NT ligatured), two ears of corn. *Reverse:* ÆMIL POL ÆD (MIL also ligatured), bearded head of Baal-Melqart right. *Circa 33–27 BC.* (RPC 861; Mazard 613).

556. Zilil. Æ 26. CAESAR DIVI F CONST, bare head of Octavian right. *Reverse:* ANI AR . . . . . . , trophy between two captives seated at base. *Circa 33–27 BC.* (RPC 866A).

No coins of Colonia Iulia Constantia Zilil had been recorded until recent excavations on the site brought to light several specimens of two denominations from which, unfortunately, it has not been possible to fully reconstruct the legends (cf. RPC pp. 211–12 and 722). The reverse type of no. 556 is clearly inspired by the Caesarian denarii issued in Spain in 46–45 BC for the Munda campaign (see no. 58).

557. Æ 23. CAESAR DIVI F CONST, bare head of Octavian right. *Reverse:* ANI (AN ligatured) AR POM . . . . . D D, diademed female head right. *Circa 33–27 BC.* (RPC 866).

558. Lixus. Æ 28–29. LIXS, two ears of corn. *Reverse:* Punic legend LKS MBAL, two fishes, pellet at centre. *After 38 BC?* (cf. RPC p. 212; Mazard 638).

559. – LIX, large ornamented altar. *Reverse:* Punic legend LKS MBAL, two bunches of grapes. *After 38 BC?* (cf. RPC p. 212; Mazard 639.)

560. – Head of Chusor–Phtah right, wearing conical headdress to top of which is attached long cord terminating in ring-ornament. *Reverse:* LIX, large ornamented altar. *After 38 BC?* (cf. RPC p. 212; Mazard 640).

561. Æ 21–22. LIX, head of Chusor-Phtah left, wearing conical headdress to top of which is attached long cord terminating in ring-ornament. *Reverse:* Punic legend LKS MBAL, two bunches of grapes. *After 38 BC?* (cf. RPC p. 212; Mazard 641).

562. – Similar to preceding, but the head of Chusor-Phtah is to right. *After 38 BC?* (cf. RPC p. 212; Mazard 642).

563. Babba. Æ 15. IVLIA CAMP (AM ligatured), tunny fish right. *Reverse:* head of Ceres (?) right, wreathed with corn. *After 33 BC.* (RPC 867).

564. EASTERN MAURETANIA: King Bocchus II (49–33 BC). Æ 26–31 (as). REX BOCCHVS SOSI F, janiform head (possibly with features of Octavian and Bocchus), floral ornament above. *Reverse:* Punic legend BQS HMMLKT, head of Africa right, wearing elephant's skin headdress. *38–33 BC.* (RPC 873; Mazard 118).

In 49 BC Bocchus II, son of Sosus (= Mastanesosus), and Bogud became the rulers of eastern and western Mauretania respectively, each receiving from Caesar the title of ally and friend of the Roman people. Eleven years later Bogud was overthrown and Bocchus, a friend of Octavian, received the government of the entire kingdom which he retained until his death in 33 BC (cf. RPC pp. 210 and 213).

565. Æ 24–28 (semis). REX BOCCHVS SOSI F, bearded head of Bocchus II right. *Reverse:* Punic legend BQS HMMLKT, elephant walking right. *38–33 BC.* (RPC 874; Mazard 119).

566. Æ 18–22 (triens). *Obverse:* same as preceding. *Reverse:* Punic legend BQS HMT, lion walking right, head facing. *38–33 BC.* (RPC 875; Mazard 120 *bis).*

567. – Similar to preceding, but the lion stands to right with its left forepaw raised. *38–33 BC.* (RPC 875; Mazard 120).

568. Æ 14–15 (sextans). *Obverse:* same as preceding. *Reverse:* Punic legend BQS HMT, horse (?) right. *38–33 BC.* (RPC 876; Mazard 121).

569. Cartenna. Æ 29–31. A POMP MI (retrograde), bearded head right, partially surrounded by palm-branch. *Reverse:* C AL (ligatured) POMP M F VIC Q A F C KAR (AR ligatured), diademed head (of Venus?) right. *After circa 30 BC.* (RPC 884).

570. – Similar to preceding, but the bearded head is to left. *After circa 30 BC.* (RPC 885).

571. Arsennaria (?). Æ 21–22. Head of Hercules right, club behind. *Reverse:* N P AD (ligatured) D (possibly P or R) AR (ligatured), diademed head right. *After circa 30 BC?* (RPC 886).

572. ROMAN PROVINCE OF MAURETANIA (33–25 BC). Æ 33–34. IMP CAESAR, bull butting right. *Reverse:* DIVI F, lion prowling right. *33–28 BC.* (RPC 877; Mazard 124).

On the death of Bocchus II in 33 BC the Mauretanian kingdom was constituted a Roman province. Eight years later, however, Augustus restored the monarchy in the person of his young friend Juba II, son of Juba I of Numidia.

573. Æ 24–25. IMP CAESAR, bare head of Octavian right. *Reverse:* DIVI F, head of Africa right, wearing elephant's skin headdress. *33–28 BC.* (RPC 878; Mazard 122).

574. Æ 21–22. IMP CAESAR, head of Zeus Ammon left. *Reverse:* DIVI F, elephant right, trampling on dragon. *33–28 BC.* (RPC 879; Mazard 123).

The reverse type is clearly inspired by Caesar's initial issue of silver denarii.

575. CYRENAICA AND CRETE: P. Lepidius P.f. Æ 14–19. P LEPIDIVS PRO Q, bust of Libya right, ΛΙΒ–ΥΗ across field. *Reverse:* P LEPIDIVS P F PRO Q (or similar), bust of Artemis right, with bow and quiver, ΚΡ–ΗΤΑ across field or ΚΡΗΤΑ beneath. *Cretan mint, circa 40 BC.* (RPC 907; FITA pp. 35–6).

576. L. Lollius. Æ 30–32 (unit). Diademed head of Zeus Diktaios right, B and sceptre before. *Reverse:* L LOLLIVS, curule chair, variable Greek letter-numeral between legs. *Cnossus (?), circa 37–34 BC.* (RPC 908; BMCG Cyrenaica p. 114, 3).

577. – Head of Zeus Ammon right, B behind, sceptre before. *Reverse:* ΛΟΛΛΙΟΥ, curule chair, variable Greek letter-numeral between legs or in field to left. *Cyrene, circa 37–34 BC.* (RPC 911; BMCG Cyrenaica p. 116, 19–20).

578. Æ 26–28 (half unit). Head of Artemis Diktynna right, bow and quiver at shoulder, sometimes with B or G beneath chin. *Reverse:* L LOLLIVS, stag standing right, usually with variable Greek letter-numeral beneath belly. *Cnossus (?), circa 37–34 BC.* (RPC 909; BMCG Cyrenaica pp. 114–15, 4–16).

579. – Head of Apollo right, bow and quiver at shoulder, B beneath chin. *Reverse:* ΛΟΛΛΙΟΥ, dromedary standing right, variable Greek letter–numeral beneath belly. *Cyrene, circa 37–34 BC.* (RPC 912; BMCG Cyrenaica p. 116, 21–3).

580. Æ 15–18 (quarter unit). L LOLLIVS, club, B or Γ in lower field to left. *Reverse:* laurel-wreath containing Γ or Δ. *Cnossus (?), circa 37–34 BC.* (RPC 910; BMCG Cyrenaica p. 115, 16 *bis*-18).

581. – Head of Libya right, Α or Β behind or beneath chin. *Reverse:* ΛΟΛΛΙΟΥ, caduceus between poppy and ear of corn, Α or Β in field to left or to right. *Cyrene, circa 37–34 BC.* (RPC 913; BMCG Cyrenaica p. ccvi, 23a and 23 *bis* a).

582. Crassus. Æ 28–30. ΠΤΟΛΕΜΑΙ, head of city-goddess right, wearing turreted crown. *Reverse:* ΚΡΑΣ, crocodile right. *Ptolemais, circa 37–34 BC.* (RPC 916; BMCG Cyrenaica p. ccvi, 25 *bis* a)..

583. – ΚΥΡΑ, head of Libya right. *Reverse:* ΚΡΑΣ, crocodile right. *Cyrene, circa 37–34 BC.* (RPC 917; BMCG Cyrenaica p. ccvii, 25 *bis* b).

584. Æ 25–26. Crocodile right. *Reverse:* CRAS, beak of war-galley right. *Cnossus (?), circa 37–34 BC.* (RPC 914; BMCG Cyrenaica p. 117, 24).

585. Æ 21. Laureate head of Apollo right, hair in ringlets. *Reverse:* CRA, fasces. *Cnossus (?), circa 37–34 BC.* (RPC 915; BMCG Cyrenaica p. 117, 25–25 *bis).*

586. Æ 14–15. ΚΡΑ, diademed head of Libya right. *Reverse:* ΚΥΡΑ, silphium plant. *Cyrene, circa 37–34 BC.* (RPC 918; BMCG Cyrenaica p. 117, 26).

587. CYRENAICA: A. Pupius Rufus. Æ 26–28. ΑΥΛΟC ΠΟΥΠΙΟC L, head of Zeus Ammon right. *Reverse:* ΤΑΜΙΑΣ ΑΝΤΙCΤΡΑ, sella castrensis and fasces, L–Λ in field. *Circa 34–31 BC.* (RPC 919; BMCG Cyrenaica p. 118, 32).

588. – Similar to preceding, but with legends ΚΑΙ ΤΑΜΙΑC L on obverse, and ΠΟΥΠΙΟC ΑΝΤΙCΤΡΑΤ on reverse. *Circa 34–31 BC.* (RPC 920; BMCG Cyrenaica pp. 117–18, 27–31).

589. Æ 21. ΠΟΥΠΙΟC, ram standing right, L beneath belly. *Reverse:* ΡΟΥΦΟC ΤΑΜΙΑC, sella quaestoria, viewed from the left, with hasta and sacculus, L in field to right. *Circa 34–31 BC.* (RPC 921; BMCG Cyrenaica p. 118, 33).

590. – ΑΝΤΙCΤΡΑ, ram standing left, L beneath belly. *Reverse:* ΠΟΥΠΙΟC ΤΑΜΙΑC, sella quaestoria, similar to preceding, but viewed from the right. *Circa 34–31 BC.* (RPC 922; BMCG Cyrenaica p. 118, 34).

591. Æ 14–15. Diademed head of Libya right, L behind. *Reverse:* ΠΟΥΠΙΟC, coiled snake. *Circa 34–31 BC.* (RPC 923; BMCG Cyrenaica p. 119, 35).

592. Cleopatra VII of Egypt and M. Antony. Æ 26–27. ΒΑCΙΛ ΘΕΑ ΝΕ in three lines across field. *Reverse:* ΑΝΤΩ ΥΠΑ Γ in three lines across field. *31 BC.* (RPC 924; Svor. Ptol. 1899).

593. Æ 18. Same as preceding. *31 BC.* (RPC 925; Svor. Ptol. 1900).

594. CRETE: Kydas the Cretarch. Æ cistophorus (= 3 denarii). Cista mystica with open lid, from which snake emerges, all within ivy-wreath. *Reverse:* ΚΥΔΑΣ ΚΡΗΤΑΡΧΑΣ, ΚΡΗΤΑΙΕΩΝ, Zeus standing right, holding thunderbolt and eagle, flanked by two interlaced snakes with heads erect. *Gortyn, 43 BC.* (RPC 926). *Kydas was a friend of M. Antony who appointed him to office at the time of a change in the status of Crete (cf. RPC p. 222).*

595. Cnossus. Æ 20–22. Bust of Artemis right. *Reverse:* ΚΝΩΣΙΩΝ, bow and quiver crossed. *Late 40s BC.* (RPC 928; Svor. Crete 171–2).

596. Æ 13–14. Similar to preceding, but with reverse type winged caduceus. *Late 40s BC.* (RPC 927; Svor. Crete 173).

597. Æ 25–29. ΚΝΩΣΙΩΝ, laureate head of Zeus right, thunderbolt before. *Reverse:* ΜΝΗΣΙΘΕΟΣ, eagle standing right, wings spread. *Circa 37/36 BC.* (RPC 929; Svor. Crete 138–41).

598. – Similar to preceding, but with legend ΚΝΩΣΙΩΝ ΜΝΗ (ΝΗ ligatured) or ΝΜΗ on reverse. *Circa 37/36 BC.* (RPC 929; Svor. Crete 133–7).

599. – Laureate head of Zeus right. *Reverse:* ΘΑΡΣΙΔΙΚΑΣ, eagle standing right, wings spread. *Circa 36/35 BC.* (RPC 930; Svor. Crete 152–8).

600. Æ 19–21. Head of Artemis right. *Reverse:* ΘΑΡΣΙΔΙΚΑΣ, quiver. *Circa 36/35 BC.* (RPC 931; Svor. Crete 170).

601. Æ 25–26. Laureate head of Zeus right, thunderbolt before. *Reverse:* ΤΑΥΡΙΑΔΑΣ, eagle standing right, wings spread. *Circa 35/34 BC.* (RPC 932; Svor. Crete 160–64).

602. Æ 20–22. Head of Artemis right. *Reverse:* ΤΑΥΡΙΑΔΑΣ, quiver. *Circa 35/34 BC.* (RPC 933; Svor. Crete 167–9).

603. Æ 25–27. Laureate head of Zeus right, thunderbolt before. *Reverse:* ΚΥΔΑΣ, eagle standing right, wings spread. *Circa 34/33 BC.* (RPC 934; Svor. Crete 142–51).

604. Æ 25–26. Similar to preceding, but with legend ΣΑΥΡΟΜΑΤΑΣ on reverse. *Circa 33/32 BC.* (RPC 935).

605. Æ 26–29. Similar to preceding, but without thunderbolt on obverse, and with legend ΑΡΙΣΤΙΩΝ on reverse. *Circa 32/31 BC.* (RPC 936; Svor. Crete 159).

606. Æ 23. Similar to preceding, but with legend . . . . . ΜΕΝΙΣ on reverse. *Circa 31/30 BC.* (RPC 937).

607. SOUTHERN GREECE (later the province of Achaea): Sparta. Æ 19. ΑΤΡΑΤΙΝΟC, bare head of L. Sempronius Atratinus right. *Reverse:* ΛΑ ΦΙΔΙ, eagle standing right, wings closed. *Circa 38 BC.* (RPC 1101; BMCG Peloponnesus p. 128, 69).

Antony's general Atratinus was at this time stationed in southern Greece with the rank of legatus pro praetore, as attested by an inscription from Hypata (cf. FITA p. 382).

608. Æ 27. ΣΠΑΡΤΗ, diademed head of Sparta left. *Reverse:* ΛΑ ΕΠΙ ΕΥΡΥΚΛΕΟΣ (ΛΕ ligatured), the Dioscuri galloping right, all within wreath. *After 31 BC.* (RPC 1102; SNG Cop. 602).

C. Julius Eurycles ruled Sparta and its territory for almost three decades, from 31–32 BC. As it is not possible to differentiate between early and late issues all of the varieties listed by RPC have been included here.

609. Æ 20. Head of Zeus right. *Reverse:* ΛΑ ΕΠΙ ΕΥΡΥΚΛΕΟΣ (ΛΕ ligatured), club, all within wreath. *After 31 BC.* (RPC 1103; BMCG Peloponnesus p. 127, 63).

610. Æ 16. ΚΑΙC, bare head of Octavian/Augustus right. *Reverse:* ΛΑ ΕΠΙ ΕΥΡΥΚΛΕΟΣ (ΛΕ ligatured), eagle standing right, wings closed. *After 31 BC.* (RPC 1104; BMCG Peloponnesus p. 128, 70).

611. Æ 15. Female head (Livia?) right. *Reverse:* ΛΑ ΕΥΡΥΚΛΕΟΣ in four lines within wreath. *After 31 BC.* (RPC 1105; SNG Cop. 605).

612. – ΑΓΡ, bare head of Agrippa right. *Reverse:* ΛΑ ΕΥΡΥΚΛΕ (ΡΥ ligatured), caduceus. *After 31 BC.* (RPC 1106).

613. – ΛΥCΙΞΕΝΙΔΑ (ΝΙΔΑ ligatured), head of Lysixenidas right. *Reverse:* ΛΑ ΕΥΡΥΚΛΕ (ΡΥ ligatured), caduceus. *After 31 BC.* (RPC 1107).

614. Corinth. Æ 22–24 (as). LAVS IVLI CORINT (INT ligatured), wreathed head of Caesar right. *Reverse:* L CERTO ÆFICIO C IVLIO II VIR, Bellerophon on Pegasus flying right, thrusting with spear. *44/43 BC.* (RPC 1116; BMCG Corinth p. 58, 485–9; Amandry Corinth pp. 120–22, I).

Colonia Laus Iulia Corinthiensis was founded by Julius Caesar in 44 BC more than a century after the destruction of the ancient city of Corinth by L. Mummius in 146.

615. – CORINTHVM, Bellerophon striding right, seizing Pegasus by the bridle, arched porch on right. *Reverse:* P TADI CHILO C IVLI NICEP II VIR, naked Poseidon seated right on rock resting on long trident. *43/42 BC.* (RPC 1117; BMCG Corinth p. 58, 483–4; Amandry Corinth pp. 123–4, II).

616. Æ 18–22 (as). CORINT (NT ligatured), laureate head of Zeus right. *Reverse:* INST L CAS II VIR, Athena advancing right, brandishing thunderbolt and holding shield. *42/41 BC.* (RPC 1118; BMCG Corinth p. 64, 525; Amandry Corinth pp. 124–5, IIIa).

617. Æ 17–20 (semis). CORINT (NT ligatured), Nike advancing right, carrying palm, Q in field to right. *Reverse:* INST L CAS II VIR, chimaera left. *42/41 BC.* (RPC 1119; BMCG Corinth p. 64, 526–8; Amandry Corinth pp. 126–7, IIIb).

618. Æ 15–17 (quadrans). INTS (INT ligatured) CAS II VIR in two lines within wreath. *Reverse:* CORINT (NT ligatured), dolphin left, trident behind. *42/41 BC.* (RPC 1120; Amandry Corinth p. 127, IIIc).

619. Æ 15 (sextans). INTS (INT ligatured) CAS II VIR, trident. *Reverse:* CORINT (NT ligatured), Pegasus flying left, Q beneath. *42/41 BC.* (RPC 1121; BMCG Corinth p. 65, 529; Amandry Corinth p. 128, IIId).

620. Æ 15–20 (semis). CN PVBLILI M ANT OREST II VIR QVIN (NT ligatured), head of Saturn right. *Reverse:* CORINT (NT ligatured), Dionysus standing left, holding cantharus and thyrsus. *40 BC.* (RPC 1122; Amandry Corinth pp. 128–9, IVa).

621. Æ 10–11 (sextans). C PVBL ANT OR (PVBL and ANT ligatured), urceus (one-handled jug). *Reverse:* CORIN in two lines within wreath. *40 BC.* (RPC 1123; Amandry Corinth pp. 129–30, IVb).

622. Æ 22 (as). CORINT (NT ligatured), bare head of M. Antony left. *Reverse:* P AEBVTIO C PINNIO II VIR, prow of galley left. *Circa 39–36 BC.* (RPC 1124; BMCG Corinth p. 59, 490; Amandry Corinth pp. 130–31, Va).

623. – CORINT (NT ligatured), head of Poseidon right. *Reverse:* P AEBVTIO C PINNIO II VIR, chimaera left. *Circa 39–36 BC.* (RPC 1125; BMCG Corinth p. 59, 493; Amandry Corinth pp. 131–2, Vb).

624. Æ 16–17 (semis). *Obverse:* same as preceding. *Reverse:* P AEBVTIO C PINNIO II VIR in three lines within wreath of pine. *Circa 39–36 BC.* (RPC 1126; Amandry Corinth pp. 132–3, Vc).

625. Æ 21–22 (as). Head of Aphrodite right, sometimes with legend CORINT (NT ligatured). *Reverse:* Q CAECIL NIGR C HEIO PAM II VIR (AM ligatured), Pegasus flying right. *Circa 34–31 BC.* (RPC 1127; BMCG Corinth p. 60, 498–9; Amandry Corinth pp. 133–6, VIa–b).

626. – *Obverse:* similar to preceding (with legend). *Reverse:* Q CAECIL NIGR C HEIO PAM II VIR (AM ligatured), Bellerophon on Pegasus prancing right, striking with spear at chimaera left before them. *Circa 34–31 BC.* (RPC 1128; BMCG Corinth p. 60, 496–7; Amandry Corinth pp. 136–8, VIc).

627. Æ 14–16 (semis). M ANTONIVS II VIR QVINQ, wreath on four-legged table. *Reverse:* P AEBVTIVS II VIR QVINQ, urceus (one-handled jug). *30 BC.* (RPC 1129; Amandry Corinth pp. 138–9, VIIa).

628. – M ANT THEOPHIL II VIR QVINQ (ANT, THE and PHIL ligatured), bucranium. *Reverse:* same as preceding. *30 BC.* (RPC 1130; Amandry Corinth pp. 138–9, VIIb).

629. Æ 11 (sextans). M ANT THEOPHIL II Q (ANT, THE and PHIL ligatured), dolphin right. *Reverse:* P AEBVTIVS II Q, trident. *30 BC.* (RPC 1131; Amandry Corinth p. 140, VIIc).

630. Æ 15–17 (semis). Bust of Poseidon right, trident over left shoulder. *Reverse:* CORINT (NT ligatured), hippocamp right. *Circa 44–31 BC.* (RPC 1225; Amandry Corinth pp. 237–8, C1).

631. – Similar to preceding, but with reverse type Pegasus flying right. *Circa 44–31 BC.* (RPC 1226; Amandry Corinth p. 238, C2).

632. – Similar to preceding, but with obverse type radiate bust of Helios right. *Circa 44–31 BC.* (RPC 1227; Amandry Corinth p. 238, C3).

633. – Similar to preceding, but with reverse type Pegasus walking right. *Circa 44–31 BC.* (RPC 1228; Amandry Corinth p. 238, C4).

634. – Bust of Poseidon right. *Reverse:* COR within wreath. *Circa 44–31 BC.* (RPC 1234; BMCG Corinth p. 90, 678; Amandry Corinth p. 242, H).

635. – Bust of Poseidon right, trident over left shoulder. *Reverse:* COR, Pegasus flying right. *Circa 44–31 BC.* (RPC 1235; Amandry Corinth p. 242, I).

636. Æ 12–16 (quadrans). Head of Poseidon right, trident behind neck. *Reverse:* CORINT (NT ligatured), dolphin right. *Circa 44–31 BC.* (RPC 1223; Amandry Corinth pp. 236–7, A).

637. – CORINT (NT ligatured), dolphin right. *Reverse:* trident. *Circa 44–31 BC.* (RPC 1229; BMCG Corinth p. 91, 687–8; Amandry Corinth pp. 238–9, D).

638. – Similar to preceding, but with reverse type wreath. *Circa 44–31 BC.* (RPC 1230; Amandry Corinth p. 239, E).

639. – COR, rudder left. *Reverse:* dolphin left. *Circa 44–31 BC.* (RPC 1231; Amandry Corinth p. 240, F1).

640. – COR, rudder right. *Reverse:* trident. *Circa 44–31 BC.* (RPC 1232; BMCG Corinth p. 91, 684; Amandry Corinth p. 240, F2–4).

641. Æ 11–12 (sextans). CORINT (NT ligatured), Pegasus flying left. *Reverse:* trident. *Circa 44–31 BC.* (RPC 1224; BMCG Corinth p. 91, 686; Amandry Corinth p. 237, B).

642. – Chimaera right. *Reverse:* CORINT (NT ligatured), Pegasus flying right. *Circa 44–31 BC.* (RPC 1233; Amandry Corinth pp. 241–2, G).

643. Patrae. Æ 21 (as). ΒΑCΙΛΙCCΑ ΚΛΕΟΠΑΤΡΑ, diademed bust of Cleopatra VII of Egypt right. *Reverse:* ΑΓΙΑC ΑΥCΩΝΟC ΠΑΤΡΕΩΝ, headdress of Isis. *32–31 BC.* (RPC 1245; BMCG Peloponnesus p. 23, 14–15; Svor. Ptol. 1905).
Struck while Antony and Cleopatra were wintering in Greece prior to Actium.

644. Dyme. Æ 20 (as). C ARRI A F C I D C IVL TANG, wreathed head of Caesar right. *Reverse:* II VIR QVINQ EX D D, plough. *40 BC.* (RPC 1283; FITA p. 264).
The Colonia Iulia Dumaeorum was founded by Julius Caesar in 44 BC.

645. Æ 17–20 (semis). C ARRI A F C IVL TANG C I D, head of Athena right, in crested Corinthian helmet. *Reverse:* II VIR QVINQ EX D D, fasces either side of curule chair. *40 BC.* (RPC 1284; FITA p. 264).

646. – M ANT ARIST. . . . CN OCTA (ANT ligatured), type as preceding. *Reverse:* C I A DVM in two lines within wreath. *39–36 BC.* (RPC 1285; FITA p. 264).

647. Æ 21 (as). C IVLI CALAMO L AEMIL LA. . . . , bare head of Octavian right. Reverse: II VIR. . . . DIMEN. . . . , wreathed head of Caesar right. *31–27 BC.* (RPC 1286).

648. Zacynthus. Æ 19–21 (as). IMP, bare head of M. Antony right. *Reverse:* C SOSIVS Q, eagle standing right on thunderbolt, wings closed, caduceus and ZA before. *39 BC.* (RPC 1290; FITA p. 40; Sydenham 1271).
The island of Zacynthus was the home of an important naval station established by Antony following the Pact of Misenum in 39 BC. It would seem that Gaius Sosius was given command of the fleet there and charged with the task of ensuring that Sextus Pompey did not gain a firm footing in the region. Thereafter, Antony's lieutenant appears to have maintained close links with the island, hence his later issues down to 32 BC.

649. Æ 19 (semis). ZA, bare head of M. Antony right. *Reverse:* C SOSIVS IMP, two captives seated at foot of trophy. *36 BC.* (RPC 1291; Sydenham 1272).
This type commemorates Sosius' capture of Jerusalem in July 37 BC.

650. Æ 17 (quadrans). ZA, laureate head of Apollo right. *Reverse:* C SOSIVS COS DESIG, tripod. *Circa 34 BC.* (RPC 1292; Sydenham 1273).

651. Æ 15–16 (sextans). ZA, laureate head of Neptune right. *Reverse:* C SOSIVS COS, dolphin right, encircling trident. *32 BC.* (RPC 1293; Sydenham 1274).

652. Athens. Æ 19–20. Head of Athena right, wearing crested Corinthian helmet. *Reverse:* ΑΘΕ, Demeter standing right, holding torch, kernos in field to right. *Circa 31–27 BC.* (RPC 1306).

653. – Helmeted head of Athena Parthenos right. *Reverse:* ΑΘΕ, Nike advancing right, holding fillets, all within wreath. *Circa 31–27 BC.* (RPC 1307).

654. – Similar to preceding, but with reverse type Zeus standing right, holding thunderbolt. *Circa 31–27 BC.* (RPC 1308).
For a detailed survey of earlier Athenian issues, attributed to the triumviral and pre-triumviral periods, cf. the publication of the Chaidari and Ag. Varvara hoards by J. H. Kroll (Archaiologikon Deltion 27, 1972, Mel., pp. 86–120).

655. Chalcis. Æ 23 (as). ΧΑΛΚΙΔΕΩΝ, Hera in slow quadriga right. *Reverse:* ΘΕΟΚΛΗΣ ΠΑΥΣΑΝΙΟΥ in four lines within wreath. *Circa 42–31 BC.* (RPC 1343; BMCG Central Greece p. 115, 89–91).

656. Cephallenia (?). Æ 21–22 (as). Terminal bust of Jupiter right, Greek monogram (of Cephallenia?) behind. *Reverse:* C PROCVLEI L F, skate fish. *Circa 30–28 BC.* (RPC 1359; BMCRR East 232–3).
Gaius Proculeius, Octavian's emissary to Antony and Cleopatra after Actium, seems to have been given the task of demobilizing the massive concentration of troops in western Greece in the post-Actian period.

657. Cranium (?). Æ 15–16 (quadrans). Head of Jupiter right, Greek monogram (of Cranium?) behind. *Reverse:* C PROCVLEI L F, double-axe. *Circa 30–28 BC.* (RPC 1360; BMCRR East 234–5).

658. Æ 12–13 (sextans). Turreted head of Tyche right, Greek monogram (of Cranium?) behind. *Reverse:* C PROCVLEI L F, column on base. *Circa 30–28 BC.* (RPC 1361; BMCRR East p. 534, Type III).

659. Pronni (?). Æ 18 (quadrans). Laureate head of Apollo (?) left. *Reverse:* C PROCVL L F, double-axe. *Circa 30–28 BC.* (RPC 1362).

660. Buthrotum. Æ 21–22 (as). P DASTIDIVS L CORNELIVS, laureate head of Zeus right. *Reverse:* D D II VIR Q A, bull standing right. *Triumviral period.* (RPC 1378; SNG Cop. 41–2).

661. Æ 17 (quadrans). C I BVT, veiled and wreathed head of Caesar right. *Reverse:* ... SVRA II VIR ITER (IR ligatured), club and snake-entwined staff of Aesculapius. *Triumviral period.* (RPC 1379).

The Colonia Iulia Buthrotum was planned by Caesar and founded by L. Plautius Plancus in 44 BC. Under Augustus it was renamed Colonia Augusta Buthrotum.

662. MACEDONIA: Dium. Æ 13–15 (quadrans). DIANA BAPHYR, Diana Baphyras advancing right, trampling on vexillum. *Reverse:* COL DIENSIS, plough. *Circa 43 BC.* (RPC 1503; FITA pp. 272–3).

663. Cassandrea (?). Æ 25 (dupondius?). Q HORTENSI PROCOS, bare head of the proconsul Hortensius right. *Reverse:* PRAEF COLON DEDVC, yoke for oxen, plough, and measuring-rod with vexillum. *43–42 BC.* (RPC 1509; FITA p. 33).

The mint attribution for this type and the next are not certain and there is a possibility that they were issued at Dium rather than Cassandrea.

664. Æ 19 (as?). COLONIA . . . . . . , female head right. *Reverse:* Q HORT XV VIR COLON DEDVX, tripod. *43–42 BC.* (RPC 1510; FITA pp. 278–9).

665. Æ 15 (semis?). HAMMO[N?], head of Zeus Ammon right. *Reverse:* HORT COL D, two ears of corn. *43–42 BC.* (RPC 1511; FITA p. 272).

666. Pella. Æ 26–28 (dupondius). ΠΕΛΛΑΙΩΝ, bust of Eleutheria (?) right. *Reverse:*ΠΕΛΛΑΙΩΝ, Nike advancing left, holding wreath and palm. *42 BC.* (RPC 1545; cf. BMCG Macedonia p. 92, 31 – obverse misdescribed).

667. Æ 22–23 (as). ΠΕΛΛΗΣ, bust of Eleutheria (?) right. *Reverse:* ΠΕΛΛΗΣ in two lines within laurel-wreath. *42 BC.* (RPC 1546; cf. BMCG Macedonia p. 92, 32 – obverse misdescribed).

668. Æ 20 (semis?). ΠΕΛΛΗΣ, laureate head of Zeus right. *Reverse:* ΠΕΛΛΗΣ, eagle standing right, wings spread. *42–32 BC.* (RPC 1547; AMNG II p. 96, 18).

669. Æ 23–26 (as). IMP DIVI F, ACTIO, Octavian, in military attire, standing left, right foot set on prow, resting on spear held in right hand. *Reverse:* NONIVS SVLPICIVS II VIR QVINQ, wreath on curule chair. *Circa 29 BC.* (RPC 1548; AMNG II p. 97, 21).

RPC dates this issue and the following types to circa 26 BC. However, the absence of the title AVGVSTVS and the specific reference to Actium would appear to point to a slightly earlier date.

670. Æ 19–20 (semis). CAESAR FLARVNT N S II VIR QVIN, bare head of Octavian right. *Reverse:* COLONIAE PELLENSIS, SPES, Spes standing left, holding wreath. *Circa 29 BC.* (RPC 1549; AMNG II p. 97, 20).

671. Æ 16–17 (triens?). NONIVS SVLPICIVS II VIR QVINQ, curule chair. *Reverse:* COLONIA PELLA, plough. *Circa 29 BC.* (RPC 1550; AMNG II p. 97, 22).

672. Thessalonica. Æ 27 (dupondius). ΘΕΣΣΑΛΟΝΙΚΕΩΝ ΕΛΕΥΘΕΡΙΑΣ, bust of Eleutheria right, E behind or before. *Reverse:* M ANT AYT Γ KAI AYT, Nike advancing left, holding wreath and palm. *38/37 BC.* (RPC 1551; BMCG Macedonia p. 115, 62–3).

The E *in obverse field is probably the Greek letter-numeral '5' representing the year of the Antonian era commencing from the battle of Philippi.*

673. Æ 23 (as). ΑΓΩΝΟΘΕΣΙΑ, head of Agonothesia right, sometimes with E behind. *Reverse:* ANT KAI in two lines within laurel-wreath. *38/37 BC.* (RPC 1552; BMCG Macedonia p. 115, 64).

674. Æ 20 (semis). ΟΜΟΝΟΙΑ, head of Homonoia right. *Reverse:* ΘΕΣΣΑΛΟΝ ΡΩΜ, free horse galloping right. *Circa 38/37 BC.* (RPC 1553; BMCG Macedonia p. 113, 43).

675. Æ 21 (as). ΘΕΟΣ, wreathed head of Caesar right. *Reverse:* ΘΕΣΣΑΛΟΝΙΚΕΩΝ, bare head of Octavian/Augustus right, Δ beneath. *28/27 BC.* (RPC 1554; BMCG Macedonia p. 115, 58).

The Δ on reverse is probably the Greek letter-numeral '4' representing the year of the Actian era.

676. Amphipolis. Æ 21 (as). ΚΑΙΣΑΡ ΘΕΟΥ ΥΙΟΣ, bare head of Octavian right. *Reverse:* ΑΜΦΙΠΟΛΕΙΤΩΝ, Artemis Tauropolos, with billowing veil, on bull galloping right. *Circa 32–30 BC.* (RPC 1626; BMCG Macedonia p. 52, 73).

677. Philippi. Æ 20–23 (as?). A I C V P, bare head of M. Antony right. *Reverse:* Q PAQVIVS RVF LEG C D, priest ploughing right with yoke of oxen. *42–41 BC.* (RPC 1646; FITA p. 274).

The Colonia Victrix Philippensis was founded by Antony soon after the battle of Philippi. It was later (30 BC) refounded by Octavian and after 27 BC came to be known as Colonia Augusta Iulia Philippensis.

678. – Similar to preceding, but with reverse type togate figure seated left, holding writing-tablet (?) before him, urn at his feet. *42–41 BC.* (RPC 1647; FITA p. 274).

This remarkable reverse illustrates the actual process of the apportionment of land in the new colony by lot.

679. Æ 15–17 (semis?). A I C V P, facing head, of uncertain identity. *Reverse:* Q PAQVIVS RVF LEG C D, plough. *42–41 BC.* (RPC 1648; FITA p. 274).

680. Æ 12 (triens?). A I C V P, urn. *Reverse:* Q PAQVI RVF LEG C D in three lines within wreath. *42–41 BC.* (RPC 1649; FITA p. 274).

681. THRACIAN KINGS: Koson. AV stater (8.42 gm). Procession of three togate figures moving left, the first and last each carrying axe over his shoulder, ΚΟΣΩΝ in exergue, sometimes with monogram (of ΟΛΒ) in field. *Reverse:* eagle standing left, wings spread, holding wreath in one claw and sceptre in the other. *Before circa 29 BC.* (RPC 1701; BMCG Thrace p. 208, 1–2).

The obverse of this enigmatic issue is copied from the denarius of M. Junius Brutus issued circa 54 BC when the later tyrannicide held the office of moneyer (Crawford 433/1). The eagle was one of the standard types on the coinage of the northern Black Sea mint of Olbia. Koson (or Kotison) must have ruled in Scythia rather than Thrace (cf. RPC p. 312).

682. Rhaescuporis I. Æ 18–19 (unit). ΒΑΣΙΛΕΥΣ ΚΟΤΥΣ, diademed and draped bust of Kotys II right. *Reverse:* ΒΑΣΙΛΕΩΣ ΡΑΙΣΚΟΥΠΟΡΙΔΟΣ, Victory advancing left, holding wreath and palm. *42 BC.* (RPC 1702; Youroukova 153–6).

Rhaescuporis I, a loyal ally of Brutus, ruled in Thrace from circa 48 BC until the disaster of Philippi in 42. His coin types are, in fact, copied from two of the issues of Brutus (cf. nos. 202 and 207).

683. Æ 17–18 (half unit). Similar to preceding, but with reverse type trophy. *42 BC.* (RPC 1703; Youroukova 157).

684. THRACIAN CITIES: Byzantium. Æ 18. Bare head of M. Antony left (no legend). *Reverse:* ΒΥΖΑΝΤΙΩΝ, trophy set on prow right between rudder and anchor. *Circa 38–37 BC.* (RPC 1770; BMCG Thrace p. 99, 60).

The identification of the obverse portrait seems reasonably secure, and the type appears to be loosely based on denarii issued by the eastern Triumvir in the late summer or autumn of 38 BC (see nos. 271–2 and commentary thereon).

685. KINGDOM OF BOSPORUS: Asander. AV stater (8.1 gm). Bare head of Asander right. *Reverse:* ΑΡΧΟΝΤΟΣ ΑΣΑΝΔΡΟΥ ΒΟΣΠΟΡΟΥ, Nike standing left on prow, holding wreath and palm, regnal date and monogram in field. *47/6–45/4 BC.* (RPC 1842–4).

Asander ruled the kingdom of Bosporus for about three decades, first as archon (47/6–45/4 BC), then as king (44/3–18/17 BC). His staters as archon bear the regnal dates 1–3 (ΕΤ Α–Γ).

686. Diademed head of Asander right. *Reverse:* ΒΑΣΙΛΕΩΣ ΑΣΑΝΔΡΟΥ, Nike standing left on prow, holding wreath and palm, regnal date in field. *44/3–18/17 BC.* (RPC 1847–63; BMCG Pontus, etc. p. 48, 2–3).

Asander's staters as king have been recorded with regnal dates 4, 6, 7, 9, 10, 14, 16, 17, 18, 20–23, 25, and 27–9 (Δ–ΘΚ).

687. Æ 25. Head of Asander (?) right. *Reverse:* ΑΡΧΟΝΤΟΣ ΑΣΑΝΔΡΟΥ, prow left and trident. *47/6–45/4 BC.* (RPC 1845; SNG Cop. 13).

688. Æ 20. Winged head of Nike right. *Reverse:* ΑΡΧΟΝΤΟΣ ΑΣΑΝΔΡΟΥ, prow left. *47/6–45/4 BC.* (RPC 1846; BMCG Pontus, etc. p. 48, 1).

689. BITHYNIA AND PONTUS: Apamea. Æ 15–16. Head of Hermes right, wearing winged petasus. *Reverse:* C I C A D D, winged caduceus. *Triumviral period, after circa 42 BC.* (RPC 2001; RG 32; BMCG Pontus, etc. p. 111, 18).
The Colonia Iulia Concordia Apamea was planned by Caesar but probably not founded until after Philippi by M. Antony.

690. – Similar to preceding, but with reverse type cornucopiae. *Triumviral period, after circa 42 BC.* (RPC 2002; RG 33; SNG v. Aul. 6919).

691. – Similar to preceding, but with reverse type three standards. *Triumviral period, after circa 42 BC.* (RPC 2003; RG 34; BMCG Pontus, etc. p. 111, 19).

692. – Similar to preceding, but with reverse type Victory standing left on globe, holding wreath and palm. *Triumviral period, after circa 42 BC.* (RPC 2004; RG 35).

693. – Dolphin right. *Reverse:* C I C A D D, Victory advancing left, holding wreath and palm. *Triumviral period, after circa 42 BC.* (RPC 2005; RG 36).

694. – C I C A D D, Victory advancing left, holding wreath and palm. *Reverse:* C I C A D D, winged caduceus. *Triumviral period, after circa 42 BC.* (RPC 2006).

695. Cius (Prusias ad Mare). Æ 22. ΒΑΣΙΛΙΣΣΗΣ ΟΡΣΟΒΑΡΙΟΣ ΜΟΥΣΗΣ, diademed head of Queen Orsobaris Musa left. *Reverse:* ΠΡΟΥΣΙΕΩΝ ΤΩΝ ΠΡΟΣ ΘΑΛΑΣΣΗΙ, head of Heracles left. *Triumviral period (?).* (RPC 2020; RG 26).
Orsobaris Musa was the daughter of Mithradates VI of Pontus. This type and the next are perhaps best dated to the decade of Antony's rule in the East following the triumviral victory at Philippi (cf. RPC p. 344).

696. Æ 20. ΩΡΟΔΑΛΤΙΔΟΣ ΒΑΣΙΛΕΩΣ ΛΥΚΟΜΗΔΟΥΣ ΘΥΓΑΤΡΟΣ, diademed bust of Orodaltis right. *Reverse:* ΠΡΟΥΣΙΕΩΝ ΠΡΟΣ ΘΑΛΑΣΣΗ, winged thunderbolt, all within wreath. *Triumviral period (?).* (RPC 2021; RG 27).
Orodaltis was the daughter of king Lycomedes who had been placed on the throne of Pontic Comana by Caesar.

697. Nicaea. Æ 25. ΝΙΚΑΙΕΩΝ, bare head of Julius Caesar right. *Reverse:* ΕΠΙ ΓΑΙΟΥ ΟΥΙΒΙΟΥ ΠΑΝΣΑ, Nike advancing right, holding wreath and palm, ϛΛΣ (= 236) beneath, two monograms in field. *47/46 BC.* (RPC 2026; RG 11; BMCG Pontus, etc. p. 153, 8–9).
C. Vibius Pansa was proconsular governor of Bithynia and Pontus in 47/46 BC. The date appearing on the reverse is according to an era commencing with the death of king Lysimachus of Thrace. This would appear to be the earliest portrait of Caesar and is of excellent style.

698. Amastris. Æ 21. Turreted head of Tyche right. *Reverse:* ΑΜΑΣΤΡΕΩΣ, crossed torches, date above, all within wreath. *33–31 BC.* (RPC 2105; RG 20).
The dates recorded for this type are 32 (ΒΛ) and 33 (ΓΛ) reckoned from a Pompeian era of 64/63 BC.

699. Sinope. Æ 24–25. COLON FEL SIN, P SVLP, turreted head of Tyche right. *Reverse:* . . . DIC (?) Q F RVF PROCOS PONTIFE . . , emblems of the pontificate – aspergillum, simpulum, axe and apex. *Circa 46/45 BC.* (RPC 2107; RG 75a; FITA pp. 251–2).
Caesar's foundation of Colonia Iulia Felix Sinope seems to have taken place in 46 BC when P. Sulpicius Q.f. Rufus was proconsul of Bithynia and Pontus (see also no. 706).

700. – C VIBI L PONTI II VIR C F I, veiled head of Ceres (?) right, wreathed with corn. *Reverse:* L PONTI C VIBI II VIR C F I, crescent with projections above plough. *Late 40s BC (?).* (RPC 2108; FITA pp. 258–60, attributed to Berytus).

701. – C F I AN (ligatured) VIII, wreathed head (of Caesar?) right. *Reverse:* EX D D, clasped hands holding cornucopiae. *39/38 BC.* (RPC 2109; FITA p. 253, no. 1).
This and the following are dated according to the era of the colony's foundation.

702. – C F I AN (ligatured) VIII, bare head right, of uncertain identity. *Reverse:* EX D D, bare head right, of uncertain identity. *39/38 BC.* (RPC 2110; RG p. 203 note).

703. – C F I AN (ligatured) XI, turreted head of Tyche right. *Reverse:* EX D D, emblems of the pontificate – aspergillum, simpulum, axe and apex. *36/35 BC.* (RPC 2111; cf. FITA p. 253, no. 3).

704. Amisus. Æ 27. Laureate head of Apollo right, monogram beneath. *Reverse:* ΑΜΙΣΟΥ, Amisus standing right, facing Roma, helmeted, standing left, holding spear and shield. *Triumviral period (?).* (RPC 2143; RG 47).

705. Æ 20. Bare head (of Roman general or governor?) right. *Reverse:* FETIA, two togate (?) figures standing facing each other, sacrificing pig. *Triumviral period (?).* (RPC 2156).
The attribution of this type to Amisus has not been proven, though one of the nine recorded specimens was acquired there. The fetiales belonged to the Roman college of priests who represented the Roman people in their dealings with other nations. The ceremonial sacrifice of a pig was used to sanctify the oaths taken in a treaty.

706. Uncertain Pontic or Paphlagonian mint. Æ 26. PROPR, turreted head of Tyche right. *Reverse:* P SVLPICIVS Q F RVFVS, owl, with wings spread, standing facing on crab. *Circa 46/45 BC.* (RPC 2155; FITA pp. 11–13; SNG v. Aul. 6732, misnumbered on plate).
P. Sulpicius Q.f. Rufus was proconsul of Bithynia and Pontus circa 46/45 BC and is known from the coinage of Sinope (see no. 699). Grant attributed the type to Amisus and Sinope was suggested by RPC, but both attributions have significant problems and the question is regarded as unresolved in RPC.

707. PAPHLAGONIA: King Deiotarus Philadelphus (37–6 BC). AR drachm of Gangra. ΒΑΣΙΛΕΩΣ ΔΗΙΟΤΑΡΟΥ ΦΙΛΑΔΕΛΦΟΥ, diademed head of Deiotarus right, Λ ΚΖ behind. *Reverse:* ΒΑΣΙΛΙΣΣΗΣ ΠΡΟΥΣΙΑΔΟΣ ΑΔΟΒΟΓΩΝΙΑΣ, diademed and draped bust of Queen Adobogonia right. *37 BC?* (RPC 3508; SNG v. Aul. 151).
The letters behind the head on obverse may indicate a date (year 27) reckoned according to the Pompeian era commencing in 64 BC. If so, then this type would be a coronation issue following Deiotarus' elevation by Antony. Pompey had annexed the coastal area of Paphlagonia to the province of Pontus, whilst the inland region had been placed under the care of native rulers (cf. RPC p. 537).

708. Æ 21–22 of Gangra. ΒΑΣΙΛΕΩΣ ΔΗΙΟΤΑΡΟΥ ΦΙΛΑΔΕΛΦΟΥ, diademed head of Deiotarus right, monogram behind. *Reverse:* ΒΑΣΙΛΕΩΣ ΔΗΙΟΤΑΡΟΥ ΦΙΛΟΠΑΤΟΡΟΣ, caps of the Dioscuri, monograms between. (RPC 3509; RG 6).
The identity of Deiotarus Philopator is uncertain. Possibly, he was a brother of Philadelphus.

709. PROVINCIA ASIA (CONVENTUS OF ADRAMYTEUM): Parium. Æ 14. C G P I, diademed female head (Venus?) right. *Reverse:* MVC PIC IIII I D D D, urceus (one-handled jug). *Circa 45 BC.* (RPC 2253; FITA p. 248, 1; BMCG Mysia p. 102, 77).
The Colonia Gemella Iulia Pariana seems to have been founded by Caesar about 45 BC as the twin of the foundation at nearby Lampsacus.

710. – Similar to preceding, but with reverse legend PIC MVC IIII I D D D. *Circa 45 BC.* (RPC 2254; FITA p. 248, 1; BMCG Mysia p. 102, 78–9).

711. Æ 17. Similar to preceding, but with reverse legend C MATVINVS T ANICIVS AED. *Circa 45 BC.* (RPC 2255; FITA p. 248, 2).

712. – Similar to preceding, but with reverse legend C MATVINO T ANICIO AED. *Circa 45 BC.* (RPC 2256; FITA p. 248, 2).

713. Æ 14. C G I P, plough, ear of corn beneath. *Reverse:* T ANICIO C MATVINO AED in three lines across field. *Circa 45 BC.* (RPC 2257; MG p. 251, 124).

714. – Similar to preceding, but with reverse legend C MATVIN T ANICI AED. *Circa 45 BC.* (RPC 2258; MG p. 251, 125).

715. Æ 13. C G I P, diademed female head (Venus?) right. *Reverse:* D D, urceus (one-handled jug). *Triumviral period, after 43 BC.* (RPC 2259; BMCG Mysia p. 102, 80–82).

716. Æ 27–28. IMP CAESAR DIVI F C G I P, bare head of Octavian right. *Reverse:* M AGRIPPA, bare head of Agrippa right. *Circa 29 BC.* (RPC 2260; FITA p. 249, 1; BMCG Mysia, p. 103, 85).

Although a date of circa 29 BC is assigned to this and the following two types by Grant (in FITA) RPC considers them to be of slightly later date (after 27 BC).

717. Æ 23. C G P I, bare head of Octavian right. *Reverse:* M BARBATIO MN (ligatured) ACILIO II VIR, priest ploughing right with yoke of oxen. *Circa 29 BC.* (RPC 2261; MG p. 255, 136).

718. – M BARBATIO MN (ligatured) ACILIO II VIR C G I P, bare head of Octavian right. *Reverse:* P VIBIO SAC CAES Q BARBA PRAEF PRO II VIR, priest ploughing right with yoke of oxen. *Circa 29 BC.* (RPC 2262; FITA p. 249, 2; BMCG p. 103, 84).

719. Lampsacus. Æ 22. C G I L, wreathed head of Caesar right. *Reverse:* Q LVCRETIO L PONTIO II VIR M TVRIO LEG, priest ploughing right with yoke of oxen. *Circa 45 BC.* (RPC 2268; FITA p. 246, 1).
This colony appears to have been established by Caesar as a 'twin' of the neighbouring foundation at Parium. The abbreviation C G I L may be expanded as Colonia Gemella Iulia Lampsacus.

720. – Similar to preceding, but with reverse legend Q LVCRETIVS L PONTIVS II VIR COL DED PR. *Circa 45 BC.* (RPC 2269; FITA p. 246, 2).

721. Æ 19. C G I L, head of Ceres right, wreathed with corn. *Reverse:* Q LVCRETIO L PONTIO II VIR M TVRIO LEG, female figure (Fortuna?) standing left, extending right hand over amphora and holding cornucopiae in left. *Circa 45 BC.* (RPC 2270).

722. – Similar to preceding, but with reverse legend Q LVCRET L PONT II VIR COL DED PR. *Circa 45 BC.* (RPC 2271; cf. FITA p. 246, 6).

723. Æ 16. C G I L, head of Janus. *Reverse:* Q LVCRETI L PONTI II VIR M TVRIO LEG, prow of galley right. *Circa 45 BC.* (RPC 2272; FITA p. 246, 4).

724. – Similar to preceding, but with reverse legend Q LVCRET L PONT II VIR COL DED PR. *Circa 45 BC.* (RPC 2273; FITA p. 246, 5).

725. PROVINCIA ASIA (CONVENTUS OF SMYRNA): Magnesia ad Sipylum. Æ 23. ΜΑΡΚΟΣ ΤΥΛΛΙΟΣ ΚΙΚΕΡΩΝ, bare head of M. Tullius Cicero (son of the orator) right. *Reverse:* ΜΑΓΝΗΤΩΝ ΤΩΝ ΑΠΟ ΣΙΠΥΛΟΥ ΘΕΟΔΩΡΟC, right hand holding wreath, two ears of corn, and vine-branch with grapes. *Circa 29 BC.* (RPC 2448; FITA p. 385; BMCG Lydia p. 139, 13–15).
Marcus Tullius Cicero the younger, born in 65 BC, was consul suffectus in 30 and probably began his term as proconsular governor of Asia on Octavian's departure from the East in 29.

726. PROVINCIA ASIA (CONVENTUS OF EPHESUS): Ephesus. Æ 16. Conjoined bare heads of the three Triumvirs right (no legend). *Reverse:* ΕΦΕ, cult-statue of Ephesian Artemis facing. *Early triumviral period, after 42 BC.* (RPC 2569; BMCG Ionia p. 71, 191).

727. – Similar to preceding, but with reverse legend ΑΡΧΙΕΡΕΥΣ ΓΡΑΜ (ΑΜ ligatured) ΓΛΑΥΚΩΝ ΕΦΕ ΑΣΚΛΗΠΙΑΔΗΣ (ΚΛ ligatured). *Early triumviral period, after 42 BC.* (RPC 2570; BMCG Ionia p. 71, 192).

728. – Similar to preceding, but with reverse legend ΑΡΧΙΕΡΕΥΣ ΓΡΑΜ (ΑΜ ligatured) ΓΛΑΥΚΩΝ ΕΦΕ ΕΥΘΥΚΡΑΤΗΣ. *Early triumviral period, after 42 BC.* (RPC 2571; BMCG Ionia p. 71, 193).

729. – Similar to preceding, but with reverse legend ΑΡΧΙΕΡΕΥΣ ΓΡΑΜ (ΑΜ ligatured) ΓΛΑΥΚΩΝ ΕΦΕ ΘΕΟΝΑΤΑΣ. *Early triumviral period, after 42 BC.* (RPC 2572; KM p. 55, 47).

730. – Similar to preceding, but with reverse legend ΑΡΧΙΕΡΕΥΣ ΓΡΑΜ (ΑΜ ligatured) ΓΛΑΥΚΩΝ ΕΦΕ ΜΑΖΖΑΣ (?). *Early triumviral period, after 42 BC.* (RPC 2573; cf. BMCG Ionia p. 71, 194).

731. Æ 13. Draped bust of Octavia (?) right (no legend). *Reverse:* ΑΡΧΙΕ ΓΡΑΜ (ΑΜ ligatured) ΓΛΑΥΚΩΝ ΕΦΕ, bee. *Circa 39 BC.* (RPC 2574).

732. Tralles (Caesarea). Æ 22. Bare head of Octavian right (no legend). *Reverse:* ΚΑΙΣΑΡΕΩΝ ΜΕΝΑΝΔΡΟΥ ΠΑΡΡΑΣΙΟΥ, octastyle temple, caduceus to right. *Circa 30 BC.* (RPC 2633; LS p. 173, 23).

733. – ΠΩΛΛΙΩΝ ΚΑΙΣΑΡΕΩΝ, bare head of Vedius Pollio right, object of uncertain identity behind. *Reverse:* similar to preceding, but with legend

ΜΕΝΑΝΔΡΟΣ ΠΑΡΡΑΣΙΟΥ. *Circa 30* BC. (RPC 2634; BMCG Lydia p. 338, 74–5).

Augustus' cruel and wealthy friend P. Vedius Pollio is known to have been active in Asia, both in an official capacity following Actium and as a private benefactor.

734. Æ 19. ΟΥΗΙΔΙΟΣ ΚΑΙΣΑΡΕΩΝ, bare head of Vedius Pollio right, as preceding. *Reverse:* ΜΕΝΑΝΔΡΟΣ ΠΑΡΡΑΣΙΟΥ, laureate head of Zeus right. *Circa 30* BC. (RPC 2635; BMCG Lydia p. 338, 76–8).

735. Æ 16. ΜΕΝΑΝΔΡΟΣ ΠΑΡΡΑΣΙΟΥ, laureate head of Apollo right. *Reverse:* ΚΑΙΣΑΡΕΩΝ, Hermes standing left, holding purse and caduceus. *Circa 30* BC. (RPC 2636; BMCG Lydia p. 338, 79–80).

736. Æ 14–15. ΚΑΙΣΑΡΕΩΝ, bare head of Octavian right. *Reverse:* ΜΕΝΑΝΔΡΟΣ ΠΑΡΡΑΣΙΟΥ, clasped right hands holding caduceus. *Circa 30* BC. (RPC 2637; LS p. 174, 24).

737. – Bare head of Octavian right (no legend). *Reverse:* ΚΑΙΣΑΡΕΩΝ, type as preceding, monograms of ΜΕΝΑΝΔ and ΠΑΡΥ in field. *Circa 30* BC. (RPC 2638; LS p. 174, 25).

738. Æ 11. ΚΑΙΣΑΡΕΩΝ, humped bull standing right. *Reverse:* ΜΕΝΑΝΔΡΟΣ, eagle standing right, wings spread. *Circa 30* BC. (RPC 2639; GM p. 203, 643a).

739. PROVINCIA ASIA (CONVENTUS OF HALICARNASSUS): Cos. Æ 31 (drachm?). ΝΙΚΙΑΣ, wreathed head of Nikias right, with slight beard. *Reverse:* ΚΩΙΩΝ ΑΝΤΙΟΧΟΣ, laureate head of Aesculapius right. *Circa 30* BC. (RPC 2724; BMCG Caria p. 213, 196).

Nikias was the ruler of the Carian island of Cos from circa 50 BC *down to the time of Augustus. This issue of large bronzes likely belongs to the period following the downfall of Antony and Cleopatra at Actium. Nikias' head appears to be strongly influenced by the contemporary portraits of Octavian.*

740. – Similar to preceding, but with magistrate's name ΔΙΟΦΑΝΤΟΣ on reverse. *Circa 30* BC. (RPC 2725; SNG v. Aul. 2764).

741. – Similar to preceding, but with magistrate's name ΕΙΡΗΝΑΙΟΣ. *Circa 30* BC. (RPC 2726).

742. – Similar to preceding, but with magistrate's name ΕΥΚΑΡΠΟΣ. *Circa 30* BC. (RPC 2727; BMCG Caria p. 213, 197).

743. – Similar to preceding, but with magistrate's name ΚΑΛΛΙΠΠΙΔΗΣ. *Circa 30* BC. (RPC 2728; BMCG Caria p. 213, 198).

744. – Similar to preceding, but with magistrate's name ΟΛΥΜΠΙΧΟΣ. *Circa 30* BC. (RPC 2729).

745. – Similar to preceding, but with magistrate's name ΠΟΛΥΧΑΡΗΣ. *Circa 30* BC. (RPC 2730).

746. – Similar to preceding, but with magistrate's name ΧΑΡΜΥΛΟΣ. *Circa 30* BC. (RPC 2721; BMCG Caria p. 213, 199–200).

747. PROVINCIA ASIA (CONVENTUS OF ALABANDA): Rhodes. Æ 35 (drachm?). Radiate head of Dionysus right, wreathed with ivy. *Reverse:* ΡΟΔΙΩΝ ΤΑΜΙΑ ΤΕΙΜΟΣΤΡΑΤΟΥ, rose viewed in profile, poppy on left, ear of corn on right. *After circa 31* BC. (RPC 2748; BMCG Caria p. 265, 377).

748. – Similar to preceding, but with reverse type Nike standing right on prow, holding aplustre and palm. *After circa 31* BC. (RPC 2749; BMCG Caria p. 265, 376).

The Nike reverse on the large bronzes of Rhodes was probably initially introduced in celebration of Octavian's victory at Actium.

749. Æ 17–18 (obol?). Radiate head of Helios left. *Reverse:* ΡΟΔΙѠΝ, rose viewed in profile, caduceus (sometimes with dolphin and palm-branch) in field. *After circa 31* BC. (RPC 2746; BMCG Caria p. 265, 382).

750. – Similar to preceding, but head of Helios is to right, and with symbols caduceus and dolphin, or poppy, in reverse field. *After circa 31* BC. (RPC 2747; SNG Cop. 879).

751. Plarasa and Aphrodisias. AR drachm/denarius. Veiled and draped bust of Aphrodite right. *Reverse:* ΠΛΑΡΑΣΕΩΝ ΚΑΙ ΑΦΡΟΔΕΙΣΙΕΩΝ, eagle standing (right or left) on thunderbolt, wings closed, magistrates' names across field, sometimes with symbol in field (*e.g.* caduceus, wreath, or cornucopiae). *Series* *commencing circa 39–35 BC (?).* (RPC p. 466; cf. BMCG Caria pp. 26–7, 6–13 and p. 271, 6A–10A).

The occasion for the introduction of this remarkable series may have been Antony's conferment on this Carian community of the rights of ελευθερια and ατελεια by a Senatusconsultum between 39 and 35 BC. The veiled female head and the bird of Zeus certainly hint at some connection with the Ptolemaic kingdom of Egypt. For the purposes of this issue the towns of Aphrodisias and Plarasa were united, though under Augustus Plarasa was absorbed by its larger neighbour and its name disappears from the coinage. It is difficult to estimate how long this issue of silver coins extended but it may have been well into the reign of Augustus. There are also bronzes associated with the joint coinage of Plarasa and Aphrodisias. Remarkably, two varieties of the silver type bear the distinctive star-shaped XVI monogram on reverse indicating that, despite their lower weight (c. 3.55 gm), these pieces may have been tariffed as the equivalent of the Roman denarius.

752. Æ 13. Bare head of Octavian right (no legend). *Reverse:* ΠΛΑΡΑ ΑΦΡΟ, diademed head of Aphrodite right. *After circa 31 BC.* (RPC 2837; SNG Cop. 76). *Doubtless struck soon after Actium to reflect the change in regime.*

753. PROVINCIA ASIA (CONVENTUS OF APAMEA): Fulvia (Eumenea). Æ 18. Head of Fulvia (wife of Antony), as Nike, right, top of her wings visible behind (no legend). *Reverse:* ΦΟΥΛΟΥΙΑΝΩΝ ΖΜΕΡΤΟΡΙΓΟΣ ΦΙΛΩΝΙΔΟΥ, Athena advancing left, holding spear and shield. *Circa 41 BC.* (RPC 3139; BMCG Phrygia p. 213, 20–21).

At the time of Antony's journey to the East following his great victory at Philippi the name of the Phrygian city of Eumenea was changed to Fulvia in honour of the Triumvir's wife. Bronze coins were struck on this occasion which provide valuable evidence for the identification of similar female heads appearing on certain Roman aurei, denarii, and quinarii over the period 43–41 BC (see nos. 122, 126, 186, and 321).

754. Æ 16. *Obverse:* same as preceding. *Reverse:* ΦΟΥΛΟΥΙΑΝΩΝ ΖΜΕΡΤΟΡΙ in three lines within ivy-wreath. *Circa 41 BC.* (RPC 3140; KM p. 231, 2).

755. Æ 14. Diademed female head right. *Reverse:* ΖΜΕΡΤΟΡΙΓΟΣ, bunch of grapes. *Circa 41 BC.* (RPC 3141).

756. LYCIAN LEAGUE: district of Cragus. Ꜳ hemidrachm (quinarius). ΛΥ, laureate head of Apollo right. *Reverse:* ΚΡ, cithara, all in shallow incuse square. *48–42 BC.* (RPC 3301; Troxell 84.2–45).

757. – Similar to preceding, but without LY on obverse, and with ΛΥΚΙΩΝ ΚΡ on reverse. *48–42 BC.* (RPC 3301 note; Troxell 84.1).

758. – Laureate head of Apollo right (no legend). *Reverse:* ΛΥΚΙΩΝ ΚΡΑ, cithara, all in shallow incuse square. *42 BC.* (RPC 3302; Troxell 88).

759. – Similar to preceding, but with ΛΥ on obverse, and with reverse legend ΚΡ and filleted branch to right of cithara. *42 BC.* (RPC 3302; Troxell 89).

760. – Similar to preceding, but with reverse legend ΚΡΑ and tripod to left of cithara. *42 BC.* (RPC 3302; Troxell 90).

761. – LY, laureate head of Apollo right. *Reverse:* ΚΡ, cithara, eagle on omphalos to left, all in shallow incuse square. *Early 30s BC.* (RPC 3303; Troxell 93).

762. – Similar to preceding, but with symbol ear of corn to left of cithara. *Early 30s BC.* (RPC 3303; Troxell 94).

763. – Similar to preceding, but without inscription on obverse and no symbol on reverse. *Early 30s BC.* (RPC 3303; Troxell 95).

764. – Head of Apollo right, wearing taenia (no legend). *Reverse:* ΛΥΚΙΩΝ ΚΡΑΓ, cithara, all in shallow incuse square. *Late 30s BC.* (RPC 3304; Troxell 102).

765. – ΛΥ, laureate head of Apollo right. *Reverse:* ΚΡ, cithara, branch (usually filleted) to left, all in shallow incuse square. *Late 30s–27 BC.* (RPC 3305; Troxell 104–5).

766. – Similar to preceding, but with symbol ear of corn to left of cithara. *Late 30s–27 BC.* (RPC 3305; Troxell 106).

767. Ꜳ quarter-drachm (sestertius). Diademed head of Artemis right, quiver behind neck. *Reverse:* ΛΥ ΚΡ, quiver, stag's head to left (sometimes to right), all in shallow incuse square. *48–27 BC.* (RPC 3306; Troxell 124).

768. – Similar to preceding, but with symbol filleted branch to left of quiver. *48–27 BC.* (RPC 3306; Troxell 125).

769. – Similar to preceding, but with legend ΛΥ ΚΡΑΓ (ΑΓ ligatured) and symbol star to right of quiver. *48–27 BC.* (RPC 3306; Troxell 126).

770. Æ 17–20 (semis). ΔΙ, diademed head of Artemis right, quiver behind neck. *Reverse:* ΛΥ ΚΡ, stag standing right, plectrum in exergue. *Late 30s–27 BC.* (RPC 3314; Troxell 159).

771. – Similar to preceding, but with magistrate's name ΕΠ on obverse. *Late 30s–27 BC.* (RPC 3314; Troxell 160).

772. Æ 14 (quadrans). ΔΙ, laureate head of Apollo right. *Reverse:* ΛΥΚΙ ΚΡ, bow and quiver in saltire, all in shallow incuse square. *Late 30s–27 BC.* (RPC 3315; Troxell 161).

773. – Similar to preceding, but with magistrate's name ΕΠ on obverse. *Late 30s–27 BC.* (RPC 3315; Troxell 162).

774. Æ 10–11 (11/2 unciae). ΔΙ, diademed head of Artemis right, quiver behind neck. *Reverse:* ΛΥ ΚΡ, quiver. *Late 30s–27 BC.* (RPC 3316; Troxell 163).

775. – Similar to preceding, but with magistrate's name ΕΠ on obverse. *Late 30s–27 BC.* (RPC 3316; Troxell 164).

776. – Similar to preceding, but without magistrate's name on obverse. *Late 30s–27 BC.* (RPC 3316; Troxell 173).

777. **District of Masicytus.** AR hemidrachm (quinarius). ΛΥ, laureate head of Apollo right. *Reverse:* ΜΑ, cithara, all in shallow incuse square. *48–42 BC.* (RPC 3301; Troxell 85.5–28).

778. – Similar to preceding, but with star above cithara. *48–42 BC.* (RPC 3301; Troxell 86).

779. – Similar to preceding, but with plectrum to left of cithara. *48–42 BC.* (RPC 3301; Troxell 87).

780. – Similar to preceding, but without ΛΥ on obverse, and with ΛΥΚΙΩΝ ΜΑ on reverse (no symbol). *48–42 BC.* (RPC 3301 note; Troxell 85.1–4).

781. – Laureate head of Apollo right (no legend). *Reverse:* ΛΥΚΙΩΝ ΜΑΣ, cithara, all in shallow incuse square. *42 BC.* (RPC 3302; Troxell 91).

782. – Similar to preceding, but with ΛΥ on obverse, and with reverse legend ΜΑ and filleted branch to right of cithara. *42 BC.* (RPC 3302; Troxell 92).

783. – ΛΥ, laureate head of Apollo right. *Reverse:* ΜΑ, cithara, snake coiled around omphalos to left, all in shallow incuse square. *Early 30s BC.* (RPC 3303; Troxell 97).

784. – Similar to preceding, but with symbol owl to left of cithara. *Early 30s BC.* (RPC 3303; Troxell 98).

785. – Similar to preceding, but with symbol torch to left of cithara. *Early 30s BC.* (RPC 3303; Troxell 99).

786. – Head of Apollo right, wearing taenia (no legend). *Reverse:* ΛΥΚΙΩΝ ΜΑΣΙ, cithara, all in shallow incuse square. *Late 30s BC.* (RPC 3304; Troxell 103).

787. – ΛΥ, laureate head of Apollo right. *Reverse:* ΜΑ, cithara, branch (sometimes filleted) to left, all in shallow incuse square. *Late 30s–27 BC.* (RPC 3305; Troxell 107–8).

788. – Similar to preceding, but with symbol caduceus to left (sometimes to right) of cithara. *Late 30s–27 BC.* (RPC 3305; Troxell 109).

789. AR quarter-drachm (sestertius). Diademed head of Artemis right, quiver behind neck. *Reverse:* ΛΥ ΜΑ, quiver, stag's head to left, all in shallow incuse square. *48–27 BC.* (RPC 3306; Troxell 130).

790. – Similar to preceding, but with symbol filleted branch to left of quiver. *48–27 BC.* (RPC 3306; Troxell 131).

791. – Similar to preceding, but with symbol torch to left of quiver. *48–27 BC.* (RPC 3306; Troxell 132).

792. – Similar to preceding, but with reverse legend ΜΑ and symbol crescent to right of quiver. *48–27 BC.* (RPC 3306; Troxell 133.1–2).

793. – Similar to preceding, but with reverse legend ΛΥ and symbol crescent to right of quiver. *48–27 BC*. (RPC 3306; Troxell 133.3).

794. – Similar to preceding, but the crescent is to left of quiver. *48–27 BC*. (RPC 3306; Troxell 133.4).

795. – Similar to preceding, but with reverse legend ΜΑ and symbols crescent and star to left and right of quiver. *48–27 BC*. (RPC 3306; Troxell 134).

796. Æ 26 (as). ΛΥ, laureate head of Apollo right. *Reverse:* ΜΑ ΙΠΠΟΛΟ, cithara, all within wreath. *Late 30s–27 BC*. (RPC 3313; Troxell 168).

797. Æ 17–20 (semis). ΛΥ, diademed head of Artemis right, quiver behind neck. *Reverse:* ΜΑ (or ΜΑϹΙ) ΙΠΠΟ (or ΙΠΠΟΛΟ), stag standing right on torch. *Late 30s–27 BC*. (RPC 3314; Troxell 169).

798. Æ 14 (quadrans). ΛΥ, laureate head of Apollo right. *Reverse:* ΜΑ ΙΠ (or ΙΠΠΟ), bow and quiver in saltire, all in shallow incuse square. *Late 30s–27 BC*. (RPC 3315; Troxell 170).

799. – Similar to preceding, but without legend on obverse, and with legend ΛΥΚΙ ΜΑ on reverse. *Late 30s–27 BC*. (RPC 3315; Troxell 174).

800. – Similar to preceding, but with legend ΜΑ on obverse, and ΑΠΟ on reverse. *Late 30s–27 BC*. (RPC 3315; Troxell 176).

801. Æ 10–11 (11/2 unciae). ΛΥ, diademed head of Artemis right, quiver behind neck. *Reverse:* ΜΑ ΙΠ, quiver. *Late 30s–27 BC*. (RPC 3316; Troxell 171).

802. – Similar to preceding, but usually with ΜΑ on obverse, and with ΛΥ ΜΑ on reverse. *Late 30s–27 BC*. (RPC 3316; Troxell 175).

803. – Similar to preceding, but legend (if any) uncertain on obverse, and with ΑΠΟ on reverse. *Late 30s–27 BC*. (RPC 3316; Troxell 177).

804. Pinara. Æ hemidrachm (quinarius). ΛΥ, laureate head of Apollo right. *Reverse:* ΠΙ, cithara, all in shallow incuse square. *Early 30s BC*. (RPC 3303; Troxell 96).

805. Cyaneae. Æ hemidrachm (quinarius). ΛΥ, laureate head of Apollo right. *Reverse:* ΚΥ, cithara, helmet to left, all in shallow incuse square. *Early 30s BC*. (RPC 3303; Troxell 100).

806. Tlos. Æ 26 (as). ΛΥ, laureate head of Apollo right. *Reverse:* ΤΛΩ ΚΡ, cithara, all within wreath. *Late 30s–27 BC*. (RPC 3313; Troxell 165).

807. Æ 17–20 (semis). ΛΥ, diademed head of Artemis right, quiver behind neck. *Reverse:* ΤΛΩ ΚΡ, stag standing right. *Late 30s–27 BC*. (RPC 3314; Troxell 166).

808. Æ 14 (quadrans). ΛΥ, laureate head of Apollo right. *Reverse:* ΤΛ ΚΡ, bow and quiver in saltire, all in shallow incuse square. *Late 30s–27 BC*. (RPC 3315; Troxell 167).

809. Myra. Æ hemidrachm (quinarius). ΛΥ, laureate head of Apollo right. *Reverse:* ΜΥΡΑ, cithara, bee to left, all in shallow incuse square. *Early 30s BC*. (RPC 3303; Troxell 101).

810. GALATIA: King Amyntas (37/36–25 BC). Æ tetradrachm of Side in Pamphylia. Head of Athena right, wearing crested Corinthian helmet. *Reverse:* ΒΑΣΙΛΕΩΣ ΑΜΥΝΤΟΥ, Nike (sometimes with elephant's skin headdress) advancing left, holding sceptre (or sometimes sword in sheath) bound with diadem. *Circa 37/36 BC*. (RPC 3501; BMCG Galatia, etc. p. 2, 1 and 5–7).

811. – Similar to preceding, but with ΑΔ behind head of Athena, and with ΙΒ (= regnal year 12?) in reverse field to left. *26/25 BC?* (RPC 3501; BMCG Galatia, etc. p. 2, 2–4).

Prior to the formation of the new province of Lycia-Pamphylia under Claudius in AD 43 Pamphylia had formed part of the territory of Galatia.

812. Æ 22. Head of bearded Heracles right, club over left shoulder, Ɛ Ϛ behind. *Reverse:* lion prowling right, Β above, monogram of ΑΜΥΝΤΟΥ in exergue. (RPC 3505; BMCG Galatia, etc. p. 3, 12–13).

813. Æ 19–22. Similar to preceding, but with monogram behind head of Heracles, and reverse legend ΒΑΣΙΛΕΩΣ ΑΜΥΝΤΟΥ. (RPC 3502; BMCG Galatia, etc. p. 3, 8–9).

814. Æ 19. Diademed and draped bust of Artemis right, bow and quiver at shoulder, Ɛ – Ϛ behind and before. *Reverse:* stag standing right, Β above, monogram of ΑΜΥΝΤΟΥ in exergue. (RPC 3506).

815. Æ 17–19. Similar to preceding, but with monogram before head of Artemis, and reverse legend ΒΑΣΙΛΕΩΣ ΑΜΥΝΤΟΥ. (RPC 3503; BMCG Galatia, etc. p. 3, 14).

816. Æ 15. Draped bust of Hermes right, wearing petasus, caduceus at shoulder, Ε Ϛ before. *Reverse:* winged caduceus, Β in field to left, monogram of ΑΜΥΝΤΟΥ beneath. (RPC 3507).

817. Æ 14–15. Similar to preceding, but without Ε Ϛ on obverse, and with reverse legend ΒΑΣΙΛΕΩΣ ΑΜΥΝΤΟΥ. (RPC 3504; BMCG Galatia, etc. p. 4, 16).

818. **Isinda.** Æ 16. Laureate head of Zeus right, sceptre at shoulder. *Reverse:* ΙΣΙΝΔΕΩ, warrior galloping right, brandishing spear, snake beneath, variable Greek letter-numeral (Α, Β, Γ or Δ = 1, 2, 3, 4) in field. *39–36 BC?* (RPC 3510; v. Aul. Pisidia 497, 501–14).
The letters in reverse field on this type and the next would appear to be dates of the era of King Polemo, corresponding to 39, 38, 37 and 36 BC.

819. Æ 14. Head of Artemis right, bow at shoulder. *Reverse:* ΙΣΙΝΔΕ, ear of corn, variable Greek letter-numeral (Α or Δ = 1 or 4) in field. *39–36 BC?* (RPC 3511; v. Aul. Pisidia 498–500, 515).

820. Æ 16–19. Laureate head of Zeus right. *Reverse:* ΙΣΙΝ, warrior galloping right, brandishing spear, snake beneath, palm-branch before, variable Greek letter-numeral (Α–ΚΓ = 1–23) in field. *36–14 BC?* (RPC 3512; v. Aul. Pisidia 516–38, 551–76, 580–688).
The era by which this and the following type are dated remains uncertain. The accession of Amyntas to the Galatian throne is one possibility, but the provincial era (25 BC) or an era commencing in 9 BC have also been proposed (cf. H. von Aulock, Münzen und Stadte Pisidiens).

821. Æ 14. Head of Artemis right, bow at shoulder. *Reverse:* ΙΣΙΝ, crested helmet, variable Greek letter-numeral (Α or Γ = 1 or 3) in field. *36–34 BC?* (RPC 3513; v. Aul. Pisidia 539–50, 577–9).

822. **Termessus.** Æ 17–19. Laureate head of Zeus right. *Reverse:* ΤΕΡ, free horse galloping left, variable Greek letter-numeral (Α–ΚΔ = 1–24) above. *71–48 BC?* (cf. RPC p. 538; BMCG Lycia, Pamphylia, and Pisidia pp. 268–9, 3–13).
This series appears to have been initiated at the time of Rome's recognition of Termessus' status as a free city under the terms of the Lex Antonia de Termesibus (circa 71 BC). The series as a whole extends down to year 32 (ΛΒ = 39 BC), the year of Polemo's appointment as ruler of this territory.

823. – Similar to preceding, but the head of Zeus is to left, and with Greek letter-numeral ΚΕ or ΚS (= 25 or 26) on reverse. *47–46 BC?* (cf. RPC p. 538; BMCG Lycia, Pamphylia, and Pisidia p. 269, 15–16).

824. – Laureate head of Zeus right. *Reverse:* ΤΕΡ, forepart of bridled horse galloping left, thunderbolt behind, variable Greek letter-numeral (ΚΒ–ΛΒ = 22–32) above. *50–39 BC?* (cf. RPC p. 538; BMCG Lycia, Pamphylia, and Pisidia pp. 269–70, 18–23).

825. Æ 20. Laureate head of Zeus right. *Reverse:* ΤΕΡΜΗ, forepart of bridled horse galloping left, Greek letter-numeral Γ (= 3) behind. *37 BC?* (BMCG Lycia, Pamphylia, and Pisidia p. 269, 17).
The era employed on this type and the next would appear to be that of King Polemo, commencing in 39 BC.

826. Æ 15. Laureate head of Zeus right. *Reverse:* ΤΕΡΜΗΣΣΕΩΝ, forepart of zebu (humped ox) kneeling left, Greek letter-numeral Γ (= 3) behind. *37 BC?* (cf. RPC p. 538; SNG v. Aul. 5338).

827. **Cremna.** Æ 16. Head of Artemis right, bow and quiver at shoulder. *Reverse:* ΚΡΗ, winged thunderbolt, variable Greek letter-numeral (Γ or S = 3 or 6) in field. *29–26 BC?* (RPC 3518; v. Aul. Pisidia 954–6, 1007–8).
The era in use here is probably that of Amyntas' rule in Cremna which extended from 31 BC until his death in 25 BC.

828. – Laureate head of Zeus right. *Reverse:* same as preceding: the date numerals range from Δ to Ζ (= 4 to 7). *28–25 BC?* (RPC 3519; v. Aul. Pisidia 957–8, 974–1006, 1014–47).

829. Æ 15. Turreted head of Tyche right, spearhead behind. *Reverse:* ΚΡΗ, forepart of lion right, variable Greek letter-numeral (Γ, Ε or Ζ = 3, 5 or 7) in field. *29–25 BC?* (RPC 3520; v. Aul. Pisidia 943–53, 965–73, 1009–13).

830. Æ 10–12. Bust of Hermes right, wearing petasus. *Reverse:* ΚΡΗ, caduceus, variable Greek letter-numeral (Β–S = 2–6) in field. *30–26 BC?* (RPC 3521; v. Aul. Pisidia 933–42, 962–4).

831. Æ 9. Facing female head. *Reverse:* ΚΡΗ, cornucopiae, Greek letter-numeral Δ (= 4) in field. *28 BC?* (RPC 3522; v. Aul. Pisidia 959–61).

832. **COMMAGENE: Samosata.** Æ 23. Eagle standing facing, wings spread, looking right. *Reverse:* ΣΑΜΟΣΑΤΩ ΠΟΛΕΩΣ, Tyche seated right on rock, holding palm-branch. *Circa 38 BC.* (RPC 3848; BMCG Galatia, Cappadocia, and Syria p. 117, 15).
The occasion for the issue of this and the following type may have been the Roman siege of Samosata in 38 BC initiated by Antony's general P. Ventidius and continued by the Triumvir himself.

833. – Lion walking right. *Reverse:* same as preceding. *Circa 38 BC.* (RPC 3849; BMCG Galatia, Cappadocia, and Syria p. 116, 4–6).
RPC also records a variant of this and the following on which 'the type is to left'. However, it is not specified whether this refers to the obverse or reverse, or both.

834. Æ 18. Same as preceding. *Circa 38 BC.* (RPC 3850; BMCG Galatia, Cappadocia, and Syria p. 116, 7–8).

835. **KINGDOM OF CILICIA: Tarcondimotus (circa 39–31 BC).** Æ 20 of Hieropolis (?). Diademed head of Tarcondimotus right. *Reverse:* ΒΑΣΙΛΕΩΣ ΤΑΡΚΟΝΔΙΜΟΤΟΥ ΦΙΛΑΝΤΩΝΙΟΥ, Zeus enthroned left, holding Nike and sceptre. (RPC 3871; BMCG Lycaonia, Isauria, and Cilicia p. 237, 1–4).
Tarcondimotus, who owed his royal title to Antony's patronage, met his death at Actium on 2 September 31 BC.

836. **CYPRUS UNDER PTOLEMAIC RULE: Cleopatra VII and Ptolemy XV Caesarion.** Æ 29–30 of Paphos. Diademed bust of Cleopatra, as Aphrodite, right, sceptre at shoulder, holding in her arms the infant Caesarion, as Eros. *Reverse:* ΚΛΕΟΠΑΤΡΑΣ ΒΑΣΙΛΙΣΣΗΣ, double cornucopiae bound with fillet, ΚΥΠΡ monogram in field to right. *Paphos, after 47 BC.* (RPC 3901; Svor. Ptol. 1874).
Cyprus, a Roman province from 59 BC, was restored to the Egyptian kingdom by Caesar in 48 BC and remained under Ptolemaic rule down to the time of the Roman conquest of Egypt eighteen years later.

837. Æ 27–28 of Paphos. Head of Zeus Ammon right. *Reverse:* ΠΤΟΛΕΜΑΙΟΥ ΒΑΣΙΛΕΩΣ, two eagles standing left on thunderbolt, sceptre (?) under wing of bird on right, ΚΥΠΡ monogram in field to right. *Paphos, after 47 BC.* (RPC 3902; Svor. Ptol. 1876–7).

838. Æ 25–26 of Paphos. Similar to preceding, but on reverse only one eagle with palm under wing. *Paphos, after 47 BC.* (RPC 3903; Svor. Ptol. 1875).

839. **SYRIA (CILICIA PEDIAS): Aegeae.** AR tetradrachm. Turreted and veiled head of Tyche right. *Reverse:* ΑΙΓΕΑΙΩΝ, Athena standing left, holding wreath-bearing Nike and shield, spear resting against left arm, club and letters or monogram in field, Greek letter-numeral (Δ, ΙΓ, ΙS, ΙΖ or ΙΗ = years 4, 13, 16, 17 or 18) in exergue. *44–29 BC.* (RPC 4025–9; SNG Levante 1655–6).
The era used to date this issue would appear to be the Caesarian of 47/46 BC (cf. A. Houghton and S. Bendall, 'A Hoard of Aegean Tetradrachms and the Autonomous Tetradrachms of Elaeusa Sebaste', in ANSMN 33, 1988, pp. 71–89 and pl. 19).

840. **CILICIA/SYRIA: uncertain colonial mint.** Æ 22–23 (as?). PRINCEPS FELIX, bare head of Octavian right. *Reverse:* VE TER (both ligatured) COLONIA IVLIA II VIR (IR ligatured), Athena standing left, holding Nike. *31–30 BC?* (RPC 4082; FITA pp. 13–15 and 244–5).

841. Æ 19–20 (semis?). Similar to preceding, but with reverse type two humped oxen pulling plough to left. *31–30 BC?* (RPC 4083; FITA pp. 244–5).

842. Uncertain Greek mint. Æ tetradrachm. ΒΑϹΙΛΙϹϹΑ ΚΛΕΟΠΑΤΡΑ ΘΕΑ ΝΕѠΤΕΡΑ, diademed and draped bust of Cleopatra VII of Egypt right. *Reverse:* ΑΝΤѠΝΙΟϹ ΑΥΤΟΚΡΑΤѠΡ ΤΡΙΤΟΝ ΤΡΙѠΝ ΑΝΔΡѠΝ, bare head of M. Antony right. *Circa 36* BC. (RPC 4094; BMCG Galatia, Cappadocia, and Syria p. 158, 53–6).

The mint and date of this celebrated issue remain uncertain. Antioch has been a popular choice of many scholars, but convincing arguments against this attribution have been advanced in RPC (cf. pp. 601–2) where it is suggested that the mint should perhaps be sought further south in Cleopatra's 'Phoenician' kingdom. Tyre appears to have a break in the sequence of its dated silver shekels between years 89 (38/37 BC*) and 92 (35/34* BC*) which at least raises the possibility of the production of the Antony and Cleopatra coinage at this important Phoenician mint. Cleopatra's portrait on these tetradrachms bears a striking resemblance to that on an issue of bronze coins from Damascus which is dated by the Seleucid era to 37/36* BC *(see no. 930), though it is uncertain which served as the prototype.*

843. – Similar to preceding, but with horse's head right behind head of Antony. *Circa 35–34* BC. (RPC 4095; Svor. Ptol. 1898).

844. – Similar to preceding, but with R• behind head of Antony. *Circa 35–34* BC. (RPC 4096: Sarnakounk hoard 372).

845. NORTHERN SYRIA: Antioch. Æ tetradrachm of the 'posthumous Philip' series. Diademed head of King Philip Philadelphus right. *Reverse:* ΒΑΣΙΛΕΩΣ ΦΙΛΙΠΠΟΥ ΕΠΙΦΑΝΟΥΣ ΦΙΛΑΔΕΛΦΟΥ, Zeus enthroned left, holding Nike and sceptre, monogram (of ΑΥΤΟΝΟΜΟΥ) in inner field to left, Greek letter-numeral (Γ, Δ, Ε, S, Η, Ι, ΒΙ, ΘΙ, Κ, ΑΚ, or ΒΚ = years 3, 4, 5, 6, 8, 10, 12, 19, 20, 21, or 22) in exergue, traces of surrounding wreath. *47–27* BC. (RPC 4127–34, 4136–9).

Philip Philadelphus, son of Antiochus VIII, had ruled the Seleucid kingdom during the 80s BC *and had issued coinage on a massive scale. Shortly before Pompey's annexation of Syria in 64* BC *Philadelphus' son, also named Philip, had been proclaimed king by the citizens of Antioch and for this reason it seems that the Romans decided to resume issues in the name of King Philip when they revived silver coinage in the newly constituted province of Syria in the early 50s* BC *(cf. RPC p. 606). The listing here commences with the series of 'posthumous Philips' which are dated according to the Caesarian era commencing in 49/48* BC*. The significant gap in the dates between years 12 and 19 (37–31* BC*) is generally accounted for by the production of the Cleopatra and Antony tetradrachms during this period. The series extends well into the reign of Augustus, the latest securely attested date being year 33 = 17/16* BC*.*

846. Æ drachm. Turreted and veiled head of Tyche right. *Reverse:* ΑΝΤΙΟΧΕΩΝ ΤΗΣ ΜΗΤΡΟΠΟΛΕΩΣ ΚΑΙ ΑΥΤΟΝΟΜΟΥ, tripod, ΚΛ monogram in inner field to left, Greek letter-numeral Η (= year 8 of the Caesarian era = 42/41 BC) in exergue. (RPC 4131A).

The Antiochene drachms of this period are of considerable rarity, this type and the next currently existing only in single specimens.

847. – Bare head of M. Antony right (no legend). *Reverse:* ΑΝΤΙΟΧΕΩΝ ΜΗΤΡΟΠΟΛΕΩΣ, turreted and veiled head of Tyche right. *Circa 37–36* BC. (RPC 4135; BMCG Galatia, Cappadocia, and Syria p. 157, 52).

This appears to belong to the period of Antony's preparations for the invasion of Parthia when he was wintering in the Syrian capital.

848. Æ 23–24. Laureate head of Zeus right. *Reverse:* ΑΝΤΙΟΧΕΩΝ ΤΗΣ ΜΗΤΡΟΠΟΛΕΩΣ, Zeus enthroned left, holding Nike and sceptre, cornucopiae in inner field to left, Greek letter-numeral ΙΘ or ΘΙ (= year 19 of the Pompeian era = 48/47 BC) in exergue, traces of surrounding wreath. (RPC 4216; BMCG Galatia, Cappadocia, and Syria p. 155, 33–5).

Earlier Antiochene bronze coins dated according to the Pompeian era were issued from 64/63 to 50/49 BC*.*

878. Æ 16. Turreted and veiled bust of Tyche right. *Reverse:* ΛΑΟΔΙΚΕΩΝ ΤΩΝ ΠΡΟΣ ΘΑΛΑΣΣΗ, Nike advancing left, holding wreath and palm, date numeral Z (= year 7 of the Caesarian era) to left, AN in exergue. *42/41 BC.* (RPC 4403A; BMCG Galatia, Cappadocia, and Syria p. 247, 1–2).
This legend may be associated with Cassius' occupation of the city in 43 BC (cf. RPC p. 635). See also no. 881.

879. – Similar to preceding, but with reverse legend ΙΟΥΛΙΕΩΝ ΤΩΝ ΚΑΙ ΛΑΟΔΙΚΕΩΝ, date numerals H, IB, IΓ, IE, IS, or ΘI (= years 8, 12, 13, 15, 16, or 19 of the Caesarian era) to left, and KΛ(?), Θ, or ME in exergue. *41–29 BC.* (RPC 4404–9; SNG Cop. 326).
This series extends down to year 32 = 17/16 BC with a late revival in year 58 = AD 10/11.

880. Æ 13. Head of Nike right, sometimes winged. *Reverse:* ΙΟΥΛΙΕΩΝ ΤΩΝ ΚΑΙ ΛΑΟΔΙΚΕΩΝ, dolphin right, date numerals A, Z, H, or ΘI (= years 1, 7, 8, or 19 of the Caesarian era) beneath. *47–29 BC.* (RPC 4437–40; SNG Cop. 327).
This series extends down to year 47 = 2/1 BC.

881. Æ 12. Bust of Athena right, in crested Corinthian helmet. *Reverse:* ΛΑΟΔΙΚΕΩΝ ΤΩΝ ΠΡΟΣ ΘΑΛΑΣΣΗ, owl standing right, head facing, date numeral Z (= year 7 of the Caesarian era) and AN or ...Π beneath. *42/41 BC.* (RPC 4419).
This legend may be associated with Cassius' occupation of the city in 43 BC (cf. RPC p. 635). See also no. 878.

882. – Similar to preceding, but with reverse legend ΙΟΥΛΙΕΩΝ ΤΩΝ ΚΑΙ ΛΑΟΔΙΚΕΩΝ, and date numerals A, E, IA, IΓ, ΔI, EI, ZI, ΘI, or KA (= years 1, 5, 11, 13, 14, 15, 17, 19, or 21 of the Caesarian era) beneath, with no additional letters. *47–27 BC.* (RPC 4417–18, 4420–26).
This series extends down to year 47 = 2/1 BC.

883. Gabala. Æ 20. Turreted and veiled head of Tyche right. *Reverse:* ΓΑΒΑΛΕΩΝ, Astarte (?) seated left, holding poppy and sceptre, forepart of sphinx at her feet, Greek letter-numeral SI (= year 16 of the Caesarian era) to left, ZM in exergue. *31/30 BC?* (RPC 4449).

884. Balanea. Æ 23. Bare head of M. Antony right (no legend). *Reverse:* ΒΑΛΑΝΕΩΤΩΝ, male deity in quadriga galloping left, holding sceptre, AΦ CY behind, ΔI in exergue. *37/36 BC?* (RPC 4456).

885. Æ 20. Turreted and veiled head of Tyche right. *Reverse:* ΒΑΛΑΝΕΩΤΩΝ, Nike standing right, holding wreath and palm, AΦ CY or AIZH in field, ΔI in exergue. *37/36 BC?* (RPC 4457).

886. Æ 17. Radiate head of Helios right. *Reverse:* ΒΑΛΑΝΕΩΤΩΝ, cornucopiae, AΦ CY to left. *37/36 BC?* (RPC 4458).

887. Æ 15. Bust of Hermes right, wearing petasus, caduceus at shoulder. *Reverse:* ΒΑΛΑΝΕΩΤΩΝ, ear of corn, AΦ CY to left. *37/36 BC?* (RPC 4459).

888. Aradus. AR tetradrachm. Veiled, turreted and draped bust of Tyche right. *Reverse:* ΑΡΑΔΙΩΝ, Nike standing left, holding aplustre and palm, Greek letter-numerals CIA, CIΓ, CIΔ, or CIS (= years 211, 213, 214, or 216 of the city's autonomy) to left, Phoenician and Greek letters in field, all within laurel-wreath. *49–43 BC.* (RPC p. 641; BMCG Phoenicia p. 35, 290–91).
These issues represent the end of an extensive series which had commenced in the early 130s BC soon after the Aradians had succeeded in overcoming the rival city of Marathus.

889. Æ 20–22. Bare head of M. Antony right (no legend). *Reverse:* humped bull galloping left, head facing, CWM above, date numeral CKB (= year 222) with M and ΔI beneath. *38/37 BC.* (RPC 4466; BMCG Phoenicia p. 44, 355).

890. – Similar to preceding, but with date numeral CKΔ (= year 224) above bull and MH beneath. *36/35 BC.* (RPC 4467).

891. – Bare head of M. Antony left (no legend). *Reverse:* urn between two palm-branches and two sphinxes, date numeral CKE (= year 225) in field. *35/34 BC.* (RPC 4468).

The existence of this type is open to some doubt as it suspiciously resembles types struck three-quarters of a century later under Caligula and Claudius (cf. RPC 4487 and 4489–90).

892. – Veiled and diademed bust of Astarte (?) right, sometimes with sceptre over shoulder. *Reverse:* humped bull galloping left, head facing, Greek and Phoenician letters above, date numerals CIΔ or CKΘ (= years 214 or 229) beneath. *46/45 and 31/30 BC.* (RPC 4473; BMCG Phoenicia p. 42, 341–5).

893. – Radiate and draped bust of Helios right. *Reverse:* APAΔIΩN, two ears of corn and vine-branch with bunches of grapes, date numeral CΛA (= year 231) and Phoenician letters in field. *29/28 BC.* (RPC 4478).

894. Marathus. Æ 20. Bare head of M. Antony right (no legend). *Reverse:* humped bull seated left on ground, IAN (AN ligatured) and Phoenician letter above, Greek letter-numeral CKΓ (= year 223 of the city's autonomy) and M in exergue. *37/36 BC.* (RPC 4494).

The era used by Marathus is the same as that of Aradus (commencing 259 BC). In the absence of an ethnic the mint attribution is based on the reverse type which is clearly distinct from the galloping bull of the Aradian coinage.

895. Æ 25. Veiled head right. *Reverse:* humped bull seated right on ground, ΔI above, date numeral CKΘ (= year 229) and Phoenician letter in exergue. *31/30 BC.* (RPC 4495).

896. Orthosia. Æ 19–20. Diademed bust of Cleopatra VII of Egypt right. *Reverse:* OPΘΩCIEΩN, Baal of Orthosia in car drawn right by two griffins, regnal date LB or LΓ (= years 2 or 3 of Cleopatra's rule in Phoenicia) behind. *36–34 BC.* (RPC 4501–2; SNG Cop. 174).

897. Æ 22. Turreted bust of Tyche right. *Reverse:* similar to preceding, but with Greek letter-numeral SΛ (= year 36 of the Pompeian era) above. *29/28 BC.* (RPC 4503).

This series extends down to year 41 = 24/23 BC.

898. Tripolis. Æ 21. Bare head of M. Antony right (no legend). *Reverse:* TPIΠOΛITΩN, draped bust of Fulvia right, date LΓK (= year 23 of the Pompeian era) behind. *42/41 BC.* (RPC 4509; cf. BMCG Phoenicia p. 204, 20).

Antony's third wife died in 40 BC. She appears also on coins of Eumenea in Asia (see nos. 753 and 754).

899. – Diademed bust of Cleopatra VII of Egypt right. *Reverse:* TPIΠOΛITΩN, Nike standing right on prow of galley, holding wreath and palm, regnal date LB (= year 2 of Cleopatra's rule in Phoenicia) and star before. *36/35 BC.* (RPC 4510; BMCG Phoenicia p. 203, 19).

900. Botrys. Æ 20. Turreted head of Tyche right. *Reverse:* BOTPYHNΩN, shield, date LHK (= year 28 of the Pompeian era) to left, all within wreath. *37/36 BC.* (RPC 4523).

901. Æ 13. Similar to preceding, but with reverse type Baal in car drawn right by two griffins. *37/36 BC.* (RPC 4524).

902. Berytus. Æ 23. Diademed bust of Cleopatra VII of Egypt right, regnal date LB (= year 2 of Cleopatra's rule in Phoenicia) behind, Θ/A before. *Reverse:* Baal of Berytus standing in facing quadriga of hippocamps, BH in field to left, ΔIO to right. *36/35 BC.* (RPC 4529).

903. – Diademed bust of Cleopatra VII of Egypt right. *Reverse:* Baal of Berytus standing in quadriga of hippocamps left, BH with regnal dates LS and LAK (= year 6 of Cleopatra's rule in Phoenicia and year 21 of her rule in Egypt) in field. *31 BC.* (RPC 4530; Svor. Ptol. 1886).

904. Æ 21. Laureate head of Baal of Berytus right, trident at shoulder. *Reverse:* BHPYTI, Baal of Berytus in quadriga of hippocamps left, date LΓN (= year 53 of the city era) above. *28/27 BC.* (RPC 4531; BMCG Phoenicia pp. 54–5, 17–22).

The era is reckoned from 80 BC. This and the following represent the last issue of Greek coinage from Berytus prior to the establishment of the Roman colony during the principate of Augustus.

905. Æ 18. Turreted and veiled head of Tyche right. *Reverse:* BHPYTIωN, Nike standing right on prow of galley, holding wreath and palm, date LΓN (= year 53 of the city era) above. *28/27 BC.* (RPC 4532; BMCG Phoenicia p. 55, 23–5).

906. Æ 14. Turreted head of Tyche right. *Reverse:* dolphin and trident between pilei of the Dioscuri, ΒΗ in field to right, date LΓΝ (= year 53 of the city era) above. *28/27 BC.* (RPC 4533; BMCG Phoenicia p. 54, 16).

907. Sidon. AR shekel. Veiled, turreted and draped bust of Tyche right, sometimes with palm-branch and X behind. *Reverse:* ΣΙΔΩΝΙΩΝ ΤΗΣ ΙΕΡΑΣ ΚΑΙ ΑΣΥΛΟΥ, eagle standing left on beak of galley, palm-branch under right wing, date numerals LSΞ, LΗΞ, LΑΟ, LΒΟ, LΟΕ, LΘΟ, LΠ, LΑΠ, or LΒΠ (= years 66, 68, 71, 72, 75, 79, 80, 81, or 82 of the city's autonomy) and monogram/s in field. *46–29 BC.* (RPC 4548–56; BMCG Phoenicia p. 159, 106–10).

The era of Sidon's independence from Seleucid rule commenced in 111/110 BC.

908. AR half shekel. Similar to preceding, but sometimes with monogram behind head of Tyche, and with date numerals LSΞ or LΑΠ (= years 66 or 81) and letters or monogram in reverse field. *46–30 BC.* (RPC 4557–8; BMCG Phoenicia p. 160, 112).

The production of Sidonian half shekels continued intermittently down to the reign of Claudius, the latest recorded date being year 154 = AD 43/44.

909. Æ 22. Laureate head of Zeus right. *Reverse:* ΣΙΔΩΝΙΩΝ, Europa seated facing on bull running left, holding billowing veil, date numerals LΟ, LΓΟ, LSΟ, LΖΟ, or LΠ (= years 70, 73, 76, 77, or 80) above, Phoenician inscription below. *42–31 BC.* (RPC 4562–6; BMCG Phoenicia p. 166, 144–6).

The latest recorded date for this type is year 117 = AD 6/7.

910. Æ 20–21. Turreted and veiled head of Tyche right. *Reverse:* ΣΙΔΩΝΙΩΝ, Astarte standing on galley left, date numeral LΟ (= year 70) in field. *42/41 BC.* (RPC 4597).

The latest recorded date for this type is year 101 = 11/10 BC.

911. – Similar to preceding, but with legend ΣΙΔΩΝ, date numeral LΒΠ (= year 82) in field, and Phoenician inscription below the galley. *30/29 BC.* (RPC 4599; BMCG Phoenicia p. 168, 161).

912. Æ 17–18. Head of young Dionysus right, wreathed with ivy, sometimes with letter behind. *Reverse:* ΣΙΔΩΝΟΣ, cista, date numerals LΞS, LΖΞ, or LΗΞ (= years 66, 67, or 68) in field, all within ivy-wreath. *46–43 BC.* (RPC 4572–4; BMCG Phoenicia p. 167, 149).

This series extends down to the reign of Nero, the latest recorded date being year 169 = AD 58/59.

913. – Conjoined heads right of Tyche, turreted and veiled, and Zeus. *Reverse:* ΣΙΔΩΝΟΣ ΘΕΑΣ, galley left, date numeral LΗΞ (= year 68) above, Phoenician inscription below. *44/43 BC.* (RPC 4595; cf. BMCG Phoenicia p. 165, 141).

The latest recorded date for this type is year 110 = 2/1 BC.

914. Tyre. AR shekel. Laureate head of Heracles/Melqart right, lion's skin knotted about neck. *Reverse:* ΤΥΡΟΥ ΙΕΡΑΣ ΚΑΙ ΑΣΥΛΟΥ, eagle standing left on beak of galley, palm-branch under right wing, club and date numerals ΟΘ, Π, ΠΑ, ΠΒ, ΠΓ, ΠΔ, ΠΕ, ΠS, ΠΖ, ΗΠ, ΠΘ, ϘΒ, ϘΓ, ϘΔ, ϘΕ, ϘS, ϘΖ, or ϘΘ (= years 79, 80, 81, 82, 83, 84, 85, 86, 87, 88, 89, 92, 93, 94, 95, 96, 97, or 99 of the city's autonomy) in left field, Greek letters or monogram to right, Phoenician letter between eagle's legs. *48–27 BC.* (RPC 4619–34 and 4629A; BMCG Phoenicia pp. 245–7, 166–80).

The era of Tyre's independence from Seleucid rule commenced in 126/125 BC when its celebrated series of silver shekels and half shekels was initiated. The shekels extend down to the reign of Nero, the latest recorded date being year 184 = AD 58/59. The break in the sequence of dates between years 89 (38/37 BC) and 92 (35/34 BC) might possibly be interpreted as evidence favouring Tyre as the mint for the tetradrachms of Cleopatra and Antony (see note following no. 842).

915. AR half shekel. Similar to preceding, with date numerals ΠΖ, ΠΗ, ϘS, or ϘΘ (= years 87, 88, 96, or 99) in left field. *40–27 BC.* (cf. RPC 4681–2, giving date 'ΠΕ = 41/40 BC' (*sic*), apparently in error, and 4681A–C; BMCG Phoenicia p. 252, 231–2).

The series of half shekels also extends down to the reign of Nero, the latest recorded date being year 191 = AD 65/66, the year of the outbreak of the Jewish 'First Revolt'.

916. Æ 21. Laureate head of Heracles/Melqart right, lion's skin knotted about neck. *Reverse:* club surmounted by ΤΥΡ monogram, date numeral LϘ (= year 90) on left, Phoenician legend on right, all within oak-wreath. *37/36 BC.* (RPC 4707; BMCG Phoenicia p. 257, 268).
Production of this type continued beyond the Julio-Claudian period into Flavian times.

917. Æ 19. Turreted and veiled head of Tyche right, palm-branch behind. *Reverse:* galley left, date numeral LϘ (= year 90), ΤΥΡ monogram, and ΙΕΡΑ ΑΣΥ above, Phoenician legend below. *37/36 BC.* (RPC 4720).
Production of this type also continued into Flavian times.

918. Ptolemais. Æ 24. Bare head of M. Antony right, within laurel–wreath. *Reverse:* Tyche standing left on blade of rudder, on handle of which she rests her right hand, holding aplustre and cornucopiae, ΠΤΟΛΕΜΑΕΩΝ ΙΕΡΑΣ in right field, date numeral LΙΑ (= year 11 of the Caesarian era) and ΚΑΙ ΑΣΥΛΟΥ in left. *39/38 BC.* (RPC 4740; BMCG Phoenicia p. 130, 14).
As at Antioch, the Caesarian era is reckoned from 49/48 BC. This is confirmed by the double-dating on the following types.

919. – *Obverse:* same as preceding. *Reverse:* diademed and draped bust of Cleopatra VII of Egypt right, ΠΤΟΛΕΜΑ and regnal date LΓ (= year 3 of Cleopatra's rule in Phoenicia) behind, ΙΕΡΑϹ ΑϹΥΛΟΥ and date numeral ΙЄ (= year 15 of the Caesarian era) before. *35/34 BC.* (RPC 4741).

920. – Similar to preceding, but with reverse legend ΠΤΟΛЄΜΑΙЄΩΝ ΤΟΥ ΚΑΙ around, and with date numerals ΙЄ (= year 15) behind head of Cleopatra and LΓ (= year 3) before. *35/34 BC.* (RPC 4742).

921. Dora. Æ 23. Conjoined busts right of Cleopatra VII of Egypt, diademed and draped (in foreground), and M. Antony, bareheaded (no legend). *Reverse:* Tyche standing left, holding palm-branch and caduceus, regnal date LΘΙ (= year 19 of Cleopatra's rule in Egypt) and ΔΩ in field. *34/33 BC.* (RPC 4752).
Another, less likely, interpretation of this type is that the era is Pompeian (= 46/45 BC) and the male bust on obverse is of Ptolemy XV.

922. Æ 22. Laureate head of bearded Doros right. *Reverse:* similar to preceding, but with date numerals LΒΛ (= year 32 of the Pompeian era) and ΔΩΡΙΤΩΝ in left field. *33/32 BC.* (RPC 4755; BMCG Phoenicia p. 116, 24).
***NB.** The attributions of RPC 4753 and 4754 to Dora appear too conjectural to warrant their inclusion here.*

923. ANTILEBANON: Chalcis. Æ 20. Diademed male head right, ΠΤΟ monogram behind. *Reverse:* ΛΥϹΑΝΙΟΥ ΑΡΧΙЄΡЄ ΤЄ (ligatured), or ΛΥϹΑΝΙΟΥ ΤЄΤΡ ΑΡΧ ΙΦ (ΤЄΤΡ and ΑΡΧ both in monogram form), or similar more abbreviated legend (sometimes retrograde), Nike standing left, holding wreath and palm, ΒΟϹ (= year 272 of the Seleucid era) in field. *40 BC.* (RPC 4768).
Specimens of this type are generally of crude style. The issue was made under Lysanias, tetrarch and high-priest of Chalcis from 40–36 BC, though it is uncertain whether it is his portrait which appears on the obverse. The accompanying monogram seems to indicate that the head is rather of Lysanias' father, the tetrarch Ptolemy.

924. – Female head right. *Reverse:* ΛϹΑ ΤЄΤΡ ΑΡΧ ΦΙ (all but ΦΙ in monogram form), double cornucopiae. *40–36 BC.* (RPC 4769).
These are also of crude style and the identity of the female head on obverse is wholly uncertain.

925. – Diademed male head right, ΠΤΟ monogram before. *Reverse:* ΛΥΣΑΝΙΟΥ ΤΕΤΡΑΡΧΟΥ ΚΑΙ ΑΡΧΙΕΡΕΩΣ, Athena standing left, holding Nike, spear and shield, ΦΙΛ monogram in field to right. *40–36 BC.* (RPC 4770; BMCG Galatia, Cappadocia, and Syria p. 280, 6).
Although usually identified as Lysanias the obverse portrait could just as easily be that of his father, the late tetrarch Ptolemy (see note following no. 923).

926. – ΒΑϹΙΛΙϹϹΗϹ ΚΛΕΟΠΑΤΡΑϹ, diademed and draped bust of Cleopatra VII of Egypt right. *Reverse:* ЄΤΟΥϹ ΚΑ ΤΟΥ ΚΑΙ S ΘЄΑϹ ΝЄѠΤЄΡΑϹ, bare head of M. Antony right. *32/31 BC.* (RPC 4771; Svor. Ptol. 1887; BMCG Phoenicia p. 54, 15).

*The double-dating in the reverse legend records Cleopatra's regnal years in Egypt (**KA** = 21) as well as in Phoenicia (**S** = 6). There is no reference to Antony other than his portrait and even that disappears on the smaller denominations.*

927. Æ 17. Similar to preceding, but with reverse type Nike advancing right, holding long palm-branch, all within wreath. *32/31 BC.* (RPC 4772; Svor. Ptol. 1888; BMCG Phoenicia p. 53, 14).

928. Æ 16. Similar to preceding, but with reverse type Athena advancing left, holding shield and spear. *32/31 BC.* (RPC 4773).

929. Æ 20. Bare head of Octavian right, **NE** behind, Seleucid date **BΠΣ** (= year 282) before. *Reverse:* **ZΗΝΟΔΩΡΟΥ ΤΕΤΡΑΡΧΟΥ ΚΑΙ ΑΡΧΙΕΡΕΩΣ**, bare head of Zenodorus left. *31/30 BC.* (RPC 4774).

Zenodorus, son of Lysanias, was awarded the tetrarchy of Chalcis by Octavian following the downfall of Cleoptra and Antony at Actium. A later issue bears the Seleucid date 286 = 27/26 BC.

930. Damascus. Æ 25. Diademed and draped bust of Cleoptra VII of Egypt right (no legend). *Reverse:* **ΔΑΜΑΣΚΗΝΩΝ**, Tyche seated left on rock, her right arm extended and holding cornucopiae in left hand, river-god swimming at her feet, ear of corn and **SOΣ** (= year 276 of the Seleucid era) in left field, all within wreath. *37/36 BC.* (RPC 4781; Svor. Ptol. 1890; SNG Cop. 419).

The obverse portrait on this issue bears a striking resemblance to that on the silver tetradrachms of Cleopatra and Antony of uncertain mintage (see no. 842), though it is uncertain which coinage was earlier and served as the prototype.

931. Æ 21–22. Similar to preceding, but with sistrum (?) instead of ear of corn in reverse field to left, and with Seleucid date **LΠΣ** (= year 280). *33/32 BC.* (RPC 4783; Svor. Ptol. 1893).

932. – Turreted head of Tyche right. *Reverse:* **ΔΑΜΑΣΚΗΝΩΝ**, Nike advancing right, holding wreath and palm, Seleucid date **SOΣ** (= year 276) in right field, all within wreath. *37/36 BC.* (RPC 4782).

The victory type is doubtless in anticipation of Antony's success in his invasion of Parthia.

933. Æ 18. Helmeted head of Athena (?) right. *Reverse:* **ΔΑΜΑΣΚΗΝΩΝ**, Hermes standing left, holding purse and caduceus, sistrum (?) and Seleucid date **LΠΣ** (= year 280) in left field, all within wreath. *33/32 BC.* (RPC 4784).

934. Æ 14. Turreted head of Tyche right. *Reverse:* **ΔΑΜΑΣΚΗΝΩΝ**, eagle standing right, wings closed, Seleucid date **LΠS** (= year 280) in field, all within wreath. *33/32 BC.* (RPC 4785).

935. Æ 21. Bare head of Octavian right (no legend). *Reverse:* **ΔΑΜΑΣΚΗΝΩΝ**, Tyche seated left on rock, her right arm extended and holding cornucopiae in left hand, river-god swimming at her feet, **LΓΠΣ** (retrograde = year 283 of the Seleucid era) in left field, all within wreath. *30/29 BC.* (RPC 4786).

936. Æ 15. Bust of Artemis right, with bow at shoulder. *Reverse:* **ΔΑΜΑΣΚΗΝΩΝ**, Athena standing facing, head right, holding spear and shield, **LΓΠΣ** (retrograde = year 283 of the Seleucid era) in left field, all within wreath. *30/29 BC.* (RPC 4787).

937. – Radiate bust of Helios right. *Reverse:* **ΔΑΜΑΣΚΗΝΩΝ**, Hermes standing left, his right hand extended and holding caduceus in left, **LΓΠΣ** (retrograde = year 283 of the Seleucid era) in left field, all within wreath. *30/29 BC.* (RPC 4788).

938. JUDAEA & PALESTINE: Gaba. Æ 16. Head of Athena right, wearing crested helmet. *Reverse:* **ΓΑΒΗΝΩΝ**, bull walking left, date numeral **KE** (= year 25) in field. *37/36 or 36/35 BC.* (RPC 4855).

The era used by this obscure mint appears to have commenced in either 61 or 60 BC.

939. Ascalon. Æ tetradrachm. Diademed and draped bust of Cleopatra VII of Egypt right (no legend). *Reverse:* **ΑΣΚΑΛΩΝΙΤΩΝ ΙΕΡΑΣ ΑΣΥΛΟΥ**, eagle standing left on thunderbolt, palm-branch under right wing, dove and monogram in left field, date numerals **LNЄ** or **LΞS** (= years 55 or 66 of the city's autonomy) in right. *50/49 BC, 39/38 BC.* (RPC 4866, 4868; Svor. Ptol. 1885; BMCG Palestine p. 108, 20).

The dates on this remarkable series are reckoned from Ascalon's achievement of freedom from Seleucid rule in 104 BC. Other dates probably exist: RPC 4867 records two specimens with uncertain date, possibly year 56 (49/48 BC).

940. – Diademed and draped bust of Ptolemy XIII of Egypt right (no legend). *Reverse:* similar to preceding, but with date numeral LNS (= year 56 of the city's autonomy) in right field. *49/48 BC.* (cf. RPC p. 724; cf. Svor. Ptol. 1881; cf. BMCG Palestine p. 107, 19).

Ptolemy XIII, the younger brother of Cleopatra VII, shared the Egyptian throne with his sister (to whom he was married) from 51 to 47 BC. He made the mistake of opposing Caesar in the Alexandrian War and paid the price with his life. The date on this coin was formerly incorrectly read as year 50 (LN).

941. Æ 21–22. Bare male head right, bearded. *Reverse:* eagle standing left, palm-branch under right wing, ΑΣ and dove in left field, date numerals ΔΟ or SΟ (= years 74 or 76 of the city's autonomy) in right. *31/30 BC, 29/28 BC.* (RPC 4869–70; BMCG Palestine p. 106, 16).

942. JUDAEAN KINGDOM: Herod the Great (40–4 BC). Æ 22. Couch upon which pileus surmounted by star and flanked by two palm-branches. *Reverse:* ΒΑΣΙΛΕΩΣ ΗΡΩΔΟΥ, tripod, regnal date LΓ (= year 3) in left field, TP monogram in right. *37 BC.* (RPC 4901; Meshorer 1; BMCG Palestine pp. 220–21, 1–10).

Uncertainty still surrounds the precise date of this and the following types. However, it seems best to regard them as issues of the time of Herod's recovery of the Judaean throne from the Parthian nominee Antigonus Mattathias in 37 BC. This must have taken place before the end of Herod's third regnal year (38/37 BC) reckoned from his elevation by Antony and the Senate in 40 BC. The obverse type is often described as a helmet with cheek pieces, but the above interpretation is preferred in RPC.

943. Æ 20. Circular shield, elaborately decorated with pattern of crescents in angles of a cross. *Reverse:* ΒΑΣΙΛΕΩΣ ΗΡΩΔΟΥ, crested helmet, regnal date LΓ (= year 3) in left field, TP monogram in right. *37 BC.* (RPC 4902; Meshorer 2; BMCG Palestine p. 221, 11–13).

944. Æ 17. Poppy-head on stalk. *Reverse:* ΒΑΣΙΛΕΩΣ ΗΡΩΔΟΥ, winged caduceus, usually with regnal date LΓ (= year 3) in left field and TP monogram in right. *37 BC.* (RPC 4903; Meshorer 3–4; BMCG Palestine pp. 221–2, 14–17).

945. Æ 14. Palm-branch. *Reverse:* ΒΑΣΙΛΕΩΣ ΗΡΩΔΟΥ, aplustre, usually with regnal date LΓ (= year 3) in left field and TP monogram in right. *37 BC.* (RPC 4904; Meshorer 5–6; BMCG Palestine p. 222, 18–19).

946. PTOLEMAIC KINGDOM OF EGYPT: Cleopatra VII (51–30 BC). Ꞩ tetradrachm of Alexandria. Diademed head of Ptolemy I right, the hair arranged in tiers above the diadem (years 1–11) or in long undulating locks radiating from a central point on top of head (years 12–22). *Reverse:* ΠΤΟΛΕΜΑΙΟΥ ΒΑΣΙΛΕΩΣ, eagle standing left on thunderbolt, palm-branch under right wing, regnal dates LB, LΓ, LΔ, LH, LΘ, LI, LIA, LIB, LIΓ, LIΔ, LIE, LIS, LIZ, LIH, LIΘ, LK, or LKB (= years 2, 3, 4, 8, 9, 10, 11, 12, 13, 14, 15, 16, 17, 18, 19, 20, or 22) above headdress of Isis in left field, ΠΑ in right. *51–48 BC, 45–32 BC, 31/30 BC.* (Svor. Ptol. 1817–20, 1822–35; BMCG Ptolemies pp. 115–16, 2–26; Mørkholm pp. 16–19, 22–3).

The two gaps in the sequence of regnal dates (years 5–7 and year 21) doubtless reflect the economic disruption associated with the Alexandrine War and the preparations for the Actian campaign. Occasionally a star appears above the date numeral in left field.

947. Ꞩ drachm of Alexandria. Diademed head of Cleopatra VII right. *Reverse:* ΚΛΕΟΠΑΤΡΑΣ ΒΑΣΙΛΙΣΣΗΣ, eagle standing left on thunderbolt, palm-branch under right wing, regnal dates LS or LIA (= years 6 or 11) above headdress of Isis in left field, ΠΑ in right. *47/46 BC, 42/41 BC.* (Svor. Ptol. 1853; BMCG Ptolemies p. 122, 1; Mørkholm p. 22).

The production of these rare portrait coins on two separate occasions seems to be associated (a) with Cleopatra's assertion of her supremacy in Egypt following the downfall of her brother Ptolemy XIII in 47 BC, and (b) her fateful meeting with Antony at Tarsus six years later, a theatrical encounter in anticipation of which the year 11 drachms may have been struck.

948. Æ 25–27 (80 bronze drachmas = 1 silver obol) of Alexandria. Diademed and draped bust of Cleopatra VII right. *Reverse:* ΚΛΕΟΠΑΤΡΑΣ ΒΑΣΙΛΙΣΣΗΣ, eagle standing left on thunderbolt, double cornucopiae in left field, mark of value Π (= 80) in right. *Date uncertain, probably late in reign.* (Svor. Ptol. 1871; BMCG Ptolemies p. 123, 4–5).

At some point in her reign – probably in her final years – Cleopatra undertook a reform of the Ptolemaic bronze coinage. Two denominations are represented, both undated but bearing the marks of value 'Π' (= 80) and 'M' (= 40). The ratio between the silver and bronze drachma at this time was probably 480:1, so the piece of 80 drachmas may be regarded as the equivalent of a silver obol and the 40 drachmas a hemiobol.

949. Æ 20–22 (40 bronze drachmas = 1 silver hemiobol) of Alexandria. Similar to preceding, but with mark of value M (= 40) in reverse field to right. *Date uncertain, probably late in reign.* (Svor. Ptol. 1872; BMCG Ptolemies p. 123, 6–11).

950. Ptolemy XV Caesarion (37–30 BC). Æ tetradrachm of Alexandria. Diademed head of Ptolemy I right, the hair in long undulating locks radiating from a central point on top of head. *Reverse:* ΠΤΟΛΕΜΑΙΟΥ ΒΑΣΙΛΕΩΣ, eagle standing left on thunderbolt, palm-branch under right wing, regnal dates LA or LZ (= years 1 or 7) above headdress of Isis in left field, ΠΑ in right. *37/36 BC, 31/30 BC.* (Svor. Ptol. 1821; Mørkholm pp. 16–19, 22–3).

The distinctive form of the obverse hairstyle would seem to confirm the validity of this remarkable attribution as it corresponds to that found on the Cleopatra tetradrachms dated between years 12 and 22 = 41/40 to 31/30 BC. Ptolemy XV Caesarion, claimed by Cleopatra to be her son by Julius Caesar, appears to have been elevated to the status of co-regent with his mother at the time of her marriage to Antony in 37 BC. The coins of year 1 would thus be a coronation issue, whilst those of year 7 would belong to the period of crisis following Actium when Cleopatra was hoping to persuade Octavian to allow her son to take her place on the Egyptian throne. Cleopatra tetradrachms of year 7 (46/45 BC) seem to be unknown, whilst those of year 1 (if they exist) are indistinguishable from coins of her father's last regnal year '30' (unfortunately there is no distinction between the letters Λ and A in Ptolemaic inscriptions at this time).

951. ROMAN PROVINCE OF EGYPT: Alexandria. Æ 25–27 (80 bronze drachmas = 1 silver obol). Bare head of Octavian right, ΘΕΟΥ – ΥΙΟΥ either side of neck. *Reverse:* ΚΑΙΣΑΡΟΣ ΑΥΤΟΚΡΑΤΟΡΟΣ, eagle standing left on thunderbolt, double cornucopiae in left field, mark of value Π (= 80) in right. *30–27 BC.* (RPC 5001; BMCG Alexandria p. 1, 1–2).

This type and the next represent Octavian's initial local coinage in Egypt following his conquest of the Ptolemaic kingdom. They are closely modelled on Cleopatra's bronze issues (see nos. 948–9) which would appear to confirm that her currency reform took place late in the reign. In place of the royal name and title on reverse Octavian is styled ΚΑΙΣΑΡΟΣ ΑΥΤΟΚΡΑΤΟΡΟΣ, the equivalent in Greek of the Latin legend IMP CAESAR. I have already proposed that the change from CAESAR DIVI F to IMP CAESAR on Octavian's Roman gold and silver issues took place following the conquest of Egypt and the evidence of his first Alexandrian coinage would appear to support this view. The obverse legend, simply proclaiming their new Roman master the 'son of god', was clearly intended to appeal to the religious sensibilities of the Egyptian populace.

952. Æ 20–22 (40 bronze drachmas = 1 silver hemiobol). Similar to preceding, but with mark of value M (= 40) in reverse field to right. *30–27 BC.* (RPC 5002; BMCG Alexandria p. 1, 3).

953. UNCERTAIN MINTS: Uncertain Gallic mint. Æ 28–29 (dupondius?). Bare head of Octavian right (no legend). *Reverse:* prow of galley right, with ram and superstructure (no legend). *After circa 30 BC (?).* (RPC 5416; FITA pp. 82–4).

954. Parium in Asia (?). Æ 12. Bare head of Hercules right. *Reverse:* M IA . . . . L LIC . . . . AED in three lines across field. *Triumviral period (?).* (RPC 5404).

955. Uncertain colony in Pisidia. Æ 25. CAESAR IMP DICT COS, wreathed head of Caesar right. *Reverse:* IVL GEM M FERIDIVS II VIR EX D D (*reading uncertain*), Athena standing left, holding Nike and spear. *Triumviral period.* (RPC 5407).

956. Æ 18. M RVTILVS PRO COS COL IVL . . . . , bare head of the proconsul M. Rutilus right. *Reverse:* . . . . FERIDIVS II VIR EX D D, colonist ploughing left with two hump–backed bulls. *Triumviral period.* (RPC 3517; FITA p. 238).

957. Uncertain Syrian mint. Æ 24–28 (dupondius?). Bare head of Octavian right (no legend). *Reverse:* sella quaestoria between hasta, on left, and fiscus, Q below. *Circa 30 BC.* (RPC 5409; AMNG III p. 74, 226–7; FITA pp. 13–19).
Although usually attributed to Macedonia, no specimens of this or the following two types are recorded as having been found in the area. In fact, the evidence of provenance would appear to point rather to a Syrian origin and, as noted in RPC (p. 715), the obverse portrait bears a striking resemblance to that on the 'PRINCEPS FELIX' series of Cilicia/Syria (see nos 840–41). The types would appear to reflect the governmental changes now taking place in the East as a result of the defeat of Antony and Cleopatra at Actium.

958. Æ 20–22 (as?). Same as preceding. *Circa 30 BC.* (RPC 5410; AMNG III p. 74, 228; FITA pp. 13–19).

959. Æ 19–20 (semis?). *Obverse:* same as preceding. *Reverse:* prow of galley right, Q below. *Circa 30 BC.* (RPC 5411; FITA pp. 13–19).

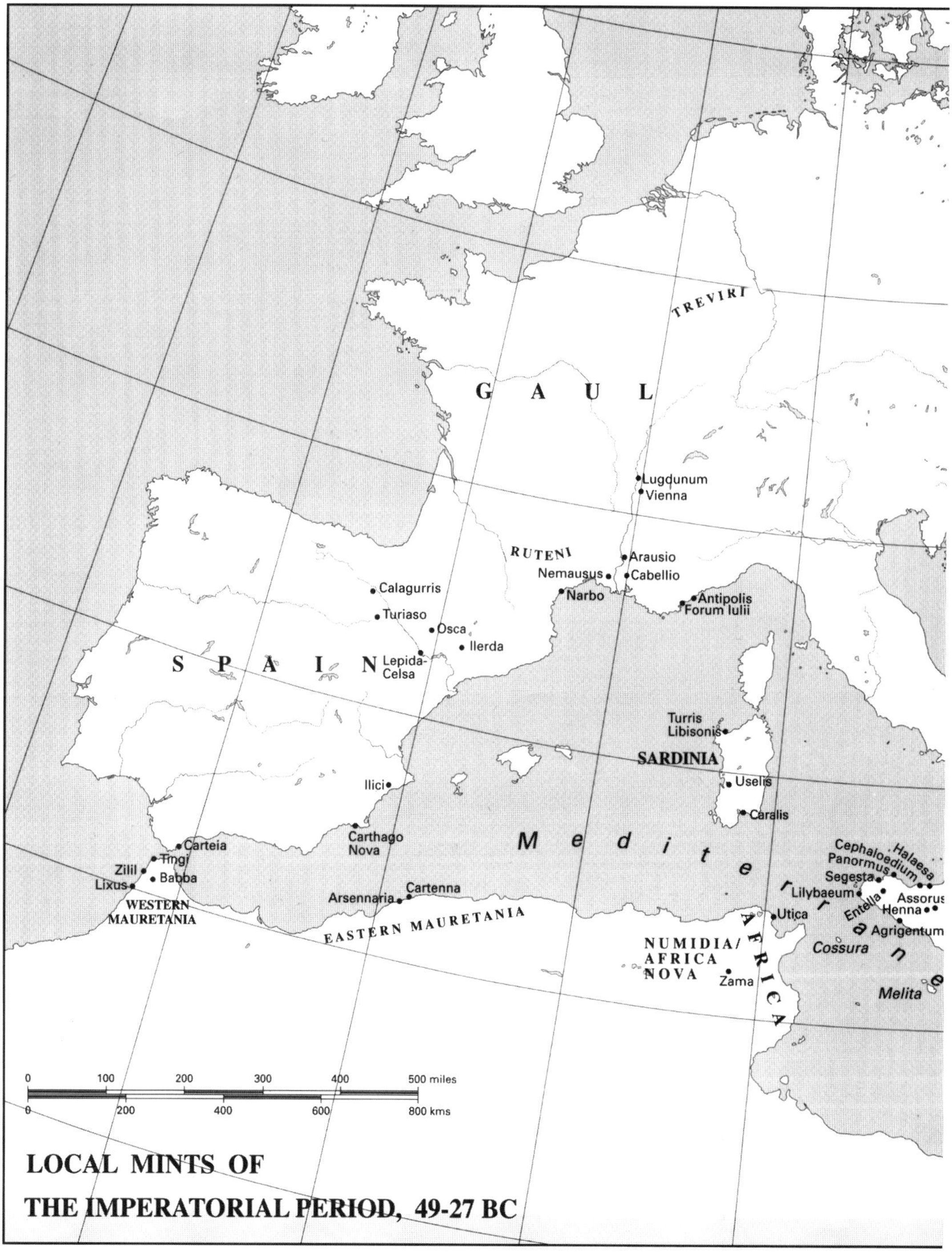

LOCAL MINTS OF THE IMPERATORIAL PERIOD, 49-27 BC

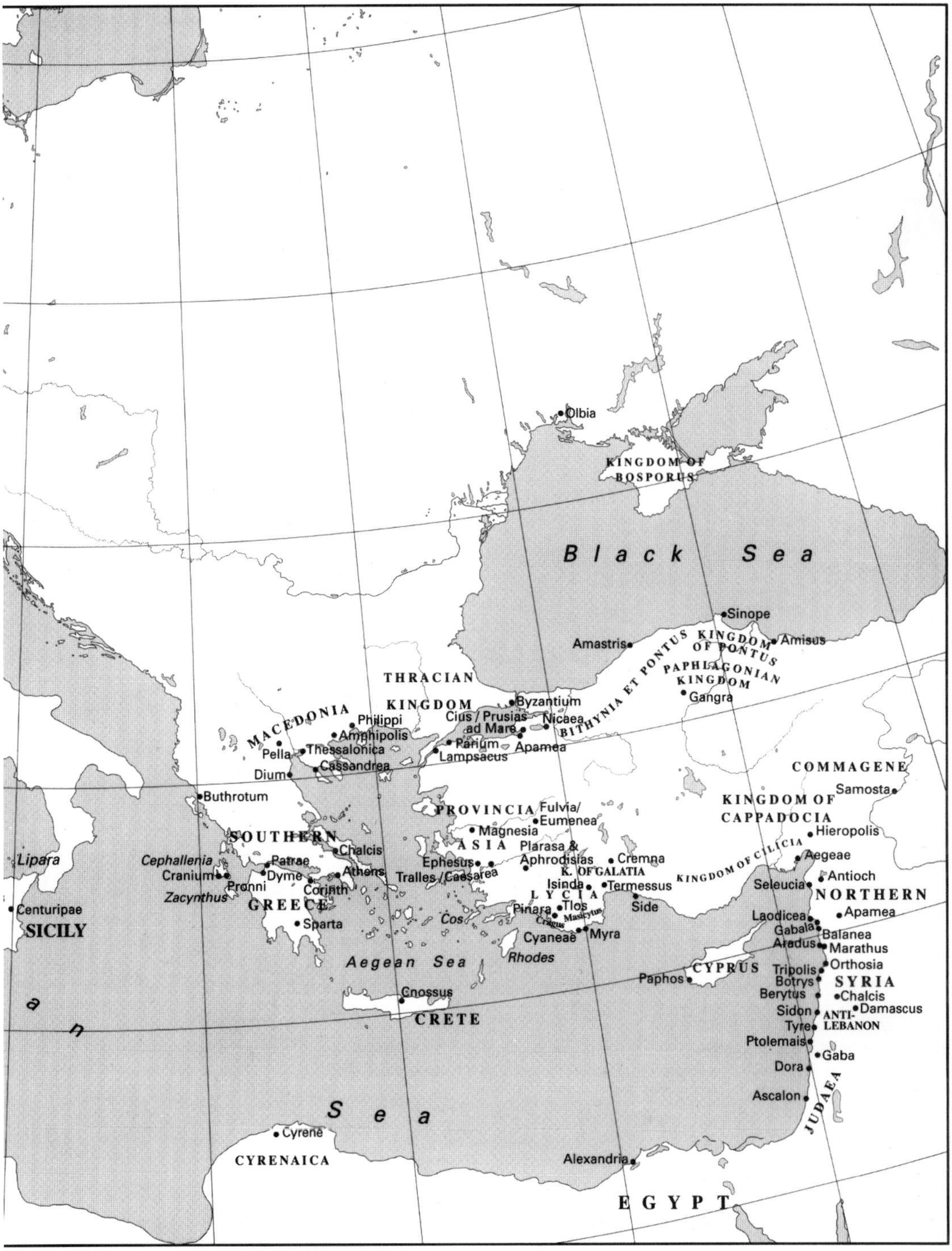
Olbia
KINGDOM OF BOSPORUS
Black Sea
Sinope
Amastris
Amisus
KINGDOM OF PONTUS
PAPHLAGONIAN KINGDOM
Gangra
BITHYNIA ET PONTUS
THRACIAN KINGDOM
Byzantium
Cius / Prusias ad Mare
Nicaea
Apamea
Philippi
Amphipolis
MACEDONIA
Pella
Thessalonica
Cassandrea
Dium
Parium
Lampsacus
COMMAGENE
Samosta
KINGDOM OF CAPPADOCIA
Hieropolis
Buthrotum
PROVINCIA ASIA
Fulvia/ Eumenea
Magnesia
Plarasa & Aphrodisias
Cremna
K. OF GALATIA
Isinda
Termessus
KINGDOM OF CILICIA
Aegeae
Antioch
Seleucia
NORTHERN SYRIA
Apamea
Laodicea
Gabala
Balanea
Aradus
Marathus
Orthosia
Tripolis
Botrys
Berytus
Chalcis
Damascus
Sidon
ANTI-LEBANON
Tyre
Ptolemais
Gaba
Dora
Ascalon
JUDAEA
SOUTHERN GREECE
Chalcis
Lipara
Cephallenia
Patrae
Cranium
Dyme
Athens
Pronni
Corinth
Zacynthus
Sparta
Ephesus
Tralles / Caesarea
Cos
LYCIA
Pinara
Tlos
Cragus
Masicytus
Side
Cyaneae
Myra
Rhodes
Aegean Sea
CYPRUS
Paphos
Cnossus
CRETE
Centuripae
SICILY
a n
S e a
Cyrene
CYRENAICA
Alexandria
EGYPT

Table of Comparative Rarities and Values

Crawford (*Roman Republican Coinage*, 1974) has attempted to compute the number of dies used for precious metal issues (*i.e.* '129/143' = 129 obverse dies and 143 reverse dies; '<30/<33' = less than 30 obverse dies and less than 33 reverse dies). This data is generally more useful for determining the relative size of mass produced issues than in estimating degrees of rarity for small coinages. For struck bronzes Crawford has simply recorded the number of pieces of each issue in the Paris collection, the largest and most representative assemblage for this period (*i.e.* '14' = 14 specimens in the Cabinet des Médailles, Bibliotheque Nationale).

For certain provincial issues (usually in bronze), most notably the 'fleet coinage' of Antony, Octavian and Octavia (unlisted by Crawford), reference has been made to the number of specimens recorded for each type in **RPC** (*Roman Provincial Coinage, Volume I*, 1992).

Crawford's listing of the coinage of Octavian ceases with the issues of 36 BC and thereafter reference is made to Volume I of **RIC** (*The Roman Imperial Coinage*, 1984), the standard work on the coinage of the Roman Empire. This estimates the frequency or rarity of the coins listed on the basis of the numbers of specimens in major collections — "a rough and ready method but the ony one generally possible." 'C' may represent common, very common, or extremely common; 'S' is scarce; 'R' (rare) up to about 20 or somewhat more specimens; 'R2' up to about 15; 'R3' up to about 10; 'R4' up to 5; and 'R5' unique.

Sydenham (*The Coinage of the Roman* Republic, 1952) estimates degrees of rarity on a scale of one to ten: 1 = extremely common; 2 = very common; 3 = common; 4 = scarce; 5 = very scarce; 6 = rare; 7 = very rare; 8 = extremely rare; 9 = exceedingly rare; 10 = of the greatest rarity.

Babelon (*Description Historique et Chronologique des Monnaies de la République Romaine*), published in Paris in 1885-6, provides actual market valuations in French francs. The work of **Cohen** (*Description Historique des Monnaies Frappées sous l'Empire Romain*, 1880) generally covers the same material as Babelon for this period, with the notable exception of the regular issues of the Roman moneyers down to 40 BC. Cohen's valuations in French francs are added in parentheses only where they differ from those of Babelon.

Current Value (summer 1997) is based on specimens in high collectors' grade, *i.e.* extremely fine ('EF') for gold and silver denominations and very fine ('VF') for *aes* (except where stated). These valuations are intended as a general guide only. Actual prices of individual specimens offered on the market may vary significantly on the basis of other vital factors (style of engraving, attractiveness of toning and patination, regularity of flan, importance of pedigree, etc.) and it should be borne in mind that the majority of coins available to collectors are of a lesser grade and consequently of significantly lower value than the figures quoted here. Also, the degree of competence of the various minting establishments was extremely variable, the standard of production normally being finer at Rome than at the military mints operating in the field. The valuations have been calculated in pounds sterling and the U.S. dollar equivalents are based on an approximate exchange rate of $1.60 to the £. Given the volatility of the currency market this rate may well change significantly over the coming months and years and this should be taken into account by those utilizing the dollar amounts in the table.

Catalogue no.	*Crawford/RPC/RIC*	*Sydenham*	*Babelon/Cohen*		*Current Value* (EF for precious metals, VF for bronze)	
1	129/143	3	4 fr.		£275	($450)
2	<20/<22	4	12 fr.		£325	($525)
3	105/117 (including 3a & 3b)	3	3 fr.		£250	($400)
3a		4			£650	($1,050)
3b		5	30 fr.		£850	($1,350)
4	<30/<33	4	4 fr.		£350	($550)
5	<30/<33	3	4 fr.		£375	($600)
6	<30/<33	7	50 fr.		£1,500	($2,400)
7	<30/<33	4	15 fr.		£650	($1,050)
8	<30/<33	4	12 fr.		£750	($1,200)
9	750/833	1	2 fr.		£275	($450)
10	4/3	8	500 fr.		£16,000	($25,500)
11	63/70	2	3 fr. (2 fr.)		£325	($525)
12	<30/<33	8	80 fr.		£1,800	($2,900)
13	<30/<33	8	80 fr.		£1,600	($2,550)
14	<10/<11	6	30 fr.		£1,000	($1,600)
15	3/1 (including 15a)	7	500 fr.		£14,000	($22,500)
15a		7			£14,000	($22,500)
16	651/723 (including 16a)	2	2 fr.		£150	($240)
16a		2			£275	($450)
17	99/110	2	3 fr.		£250	($400)
18	57/63	3	3 fr.		£1,100	($1,750)
19	126/140	3	3 fr.		£325	($525)
20	279/310 (incl. 20a & 20b)	2	2 fr.		£225	($350)
20a		2			£250	($400)
20b		4			£550	($875)
21	54/60	1	1 fr.		£275	($450)
22	<30/<33 (including 22a)	2	3 fr.		£350	($550)
22a		2	3 fr.		£350	($550)
23	33/37	3	8 fr.		£450	($725)
24	3/3	10	100 fr.	Very fine ('VF')	£1,000	($1,600)
25	69/77	2 & 4	4 fr.		£300	($475)
26	171/190	2	4 fr.		£275	($450)
27	51/57	2-4	6 fr.		£325	($525)
28	<30/<33	3	6 fr.		£350	($550)
29	195/217 (including 29a)	3-4	1 fr.		£250	($400)
29a		3	1 fr.		£275	($450)
30	66/73	3	6 fr.		£325	($525)
30a	<30/<33	5	25 fr.		£475	($750)
31	<10/<11	7	60 fr.	Very fine ('VF')	£400	($650)
32	4/5	8	80 fr.	Very fine ('VF')	£800	($1,275)
33	1/2	8	80 fr.	Very fine ('VF')	£900	($1,450)
34	33/37	4	10 fr.		£550	($875)
35	<30/<33	4	10 fr.		£450	($725)
36	<10/<11	5	10 fr.	Very fine ('VF')	£350	($550)
37	6/5	7	80 fr.	Very fine ('VF')	£700	($1,125)
38	1/1	8	100 fr.	Very fine ('VF')	£900	($1,450)
39	2/2	6	60 fr.	Very fine ('VF')	£800	($1,275)
40	1/1	10	800 fr.		£100,000	($160,000)

Catalogue no.	*Crawford/RPC/RIC*	*Sydenham*	*Babelon/Cohen*		*Current Value*	
41	<30/<33	6	25 fr.		£1,750	($2,800)
42	<30/<33	6	25 fr.		£1,500	($2,400)
43	<30/<33	6	25 fr.		£2,000	($3,200)
44	<30/<33	5	15 fr.	(large hd.)	£500	($800)
				(small hd.)	£400	($650)
45	93/103	3	6 fr.		£300	($475)
46	<30/>33 (incl. 46a & 46b)	2	3 fr.		£350	($550)
46a		2	2 fr.		£325	($525)
46b		2	2 fr.		£300	($475)
47	50/56	2	2 fr.		£160	($250)
48	42/47 (including 48a)	3	4 fr.		£450	($725)
48a		3	4 fr.		£500	($800)
49	5/8 (including 50, 51, & 52)	8	300 fr.		£3,500	($5,500)
50		8	300 fr.		£3,750	($6,000)
51		9			£4,000	($6,400)
52		8	300 fr.		£3,750	($6,000)
53	6 [RPC: 20 specimens]	4	20 fr.		£450	($725)
54	<30/<33	7	80 fr.		£2,000	($3,200)
55	390/433	1	2 fr.		£275	($450)
56	100/100	3–4	50-60 fr.		£1,750	($2,800)
57	123/137 (including 57a)	3	2 fr.		£300	($475)
57a		3	2 fr.		£300	($475)
58	135/150	3	2 fr.		£300	($475)
59	<30/<33	3	2 fr.		£400	($650)
60	50/50 (including 60a)	5	100 fr.		£3,000	($4,800)
60a		6	100 fr.		£3,500	($5,500)
61	<10/<10	8	350 fr.		£6,000	($9,500)
62	9 (incl. 62a) [RPC: 72 spec.]	3	4 fr. (5 fr.)		£350	($550)
62a	RPC: 27 specimens	3	4 fr. (5 fr.)		£400	($650)
63	549/610 (including 63a)	2	3 fr.		£175	($275)
63a		3–4	3 fr.		£175	($275)
64	51/57	3	3 fr.		£350	($550)
65	108/120	2	3 fr.		£300	($475)
66	<10/<11 (including 66a)	6		Very fine ('VF')	£400	($650)
66a		8	60 fr.	Very fine ('VF')	£550	($875)
67	11/14	5	30 fr.	Very fine ('VF')	£375	($600)
68	8/8 (including 68a)	5	30 fr.	Very fine ('VF')	£400	($650)
68a		5		Very fine ('VF')	£425	($675)
69	117/130	4	5 fr.		£400	($650)
70	120/133	3	3 fr.		£275	($450)
71	102/113 (including 71a	2–3	2 fr.		£225	($350)
71a	& 71b)	2–3	2 fr.		£225	($350)
71b		2–3	2 fr.		£225	($350)
72	75/83	3	2 fr.		£275	($450)
73	186/207	2	2 fr.		£225	($350)
74	<10/<11	7	80 fr.	Very fine ('VF')	£500	($800)
75	5/5 or 4	8	100 fr.	Very fine ('VF')	£750	($1,200)
76	13/15 (including 76a)	5	30 fr.	Very fine ('VF')	£375	($600)
76a		5	30 fr.	Very fine ('VF')	£400	($650)
77	45/50 (including 77a)	2	3 fr.		£275	($450)
77a		2	3 fr.		£275	($450)
77b	93/103 (including 77c)	2	2 fr.		£250	($400)
77c		2			£250	($400)
78	33/37	2	1 fr.		£275	($450)
78a	63/70	3	1 fr.		£250	($400)
79	42/47	2	1 fr.		£250	($400)

Catalogue no.	*Crawford/RPC/RIC*	*Sydenham*	*Babelon/Cohen*		*Current Value*	
80	<10/<11 (including 80a)	4	25 fr.	Very fine ('VF')	£350	($550)
80a		4		Very fine ('VF')	£375	($600)
80b	<10/<11 (including 80c)	4	3 fr.	Very fine ('VF')	£350	($550)
80c		4		Very fine ('VF')	£375	($600)
81	13/14 (including 81a)	6	25 fr.	Very fine ('VF')	£375	($600)
81a		6	25 fr.	Very fine ('VF')	£425	($675)
82	48/53	3	6 fr.		£325	($525)
83	<30/<33	4	6 fr.		£375	($600)
84	<10/<11	6	50 fr.	Very fine ('VF')	£425	($675)
84a	<10/<11	6		Very fine ('VF')	£425	($675)
85	5/5 (including 85a & 85b)	8	80 fr.	Very fine ('VF')	£750	($1,200)
85a		9	80 fr.	Very fine ('VF')	£825	($1,325)
85b		9	80 fr.	Very fine ('VF')	£825	($1,325)
86	39/43	4–5	8 fr.		£400	($650)
87	<30/<33	4	10 fr.		£375	($600)
88	2/2	8	60 fr.	Very fine ('VF')	£500	($800)
89	2/4	8	100 fr.	Very fine ('VF')	£800	($1,275)
90	72/80 (including 90a)	3	5 fr.		£350	($550)
90a		4	6 fr.		£375	($600)
91	<30/<33 (including 91a & 91b)	5			£475	($750)
91a		5	10 fr.		£450	($725)
91b		5	10 fr.		£475	($750)
92	<30/<33 (including 92a)	7	50 fr.		£1,100	($1,750)
92a		8	80 fr.		£1,400	($2,250)
93	<30/<33	9	100 fr.		£3,500	($5,500)
94	<30/<33	2	3 fr.		£350	($550)
95	<10/<11	6	60 fr.	Very fine ('VF')	£450	($725)
96	3/3	7	100 fr.	Very fine ('VF')	£750	($1,200)
97	1/1				(false)	
98	8/7 (including 99)	5	40 fr.		£4,000	($6,400)
99					£4,250	($6,800)
100	36/45	3	15 fr. (12 fr.)		£1,500	($2,400)
101	28/40	3	15 fr.		£1,500	($2,400)
102	36/36	3	12 fr.		£1,500	($2,400)
103	11/17	5	25 fr.		£3,250	($5,200)
104	1/2		20 fr.		£2,500	($4,000)
104a	76 (incl. 105, 107, 107a, & 107b)/15	4	20 fr.		£2,250	($3,600)
105	(see above)/28	3	10 fr.		£1,500	($2,400)
106	45/42 (including 106a)	4			£2,000	($3,200)
106a		3	8 fr.		£1,500	($2,400)
107	(see above)/1	3			£2,000	($3,200)
107a	(see above)/23	3	8 fr.		£1,400	($2,250)
107b	(see above)/24	3	8 fr.		£1,400	($2,250)
107c	81 (incl. 107d & 107e)/1				£2,000	($3,200)
107d	(see above)/76	3	8 fr.		£1,250	($2,000)
107e	(see above)/9	3			£1,600	($2,550)
108	6/8	3	12 fr.		£1,600	($2,550)
109	1/1	7	80 fr.		£6,500	($10,500)
110	5/6	6	60 fr.		£1,800	($2,900)
111	10/13	5	35 fr.		£2,000	($3,200)
111a	5/13	5	30 fr. (20 fr.)		£2,250	($3,600)
112	14/14	4	20 fr.		£2,500	($4,000)
113	<30/<33	5	15 fr.		£5,000	($8,000)
114	<30/<33	6	100 fr.		£3,500	($5,500)
115	<30/<33	5	12 fr.		£2,250	($3,600)

Catalogue no.	*Crawford/RPC/RIC*	*Sydenham*	*Babelon/Cohen*	*Current Value*	
116	<30/<33	4	12 fr.	£2,000	($3,200)
117	20/20	7	150 fr.	£5,500	($8,800)
118	<30/<33	5	10 fr.	£1,600	($2,550)
119	<30/<33	6	40 fr. (30 fr.)	£1,250	($2,000)
119a	<30/<33	5	30 fr.	£1,100	($1,750)
120	14/15	4	3 fr.	£275	($450)
121	52/58	4	4 fr.	£250	($400)
122	10/11 [RPC: 42 specimens]	4	4 fr.	£300	($475)
123	<30/<33	5	10 fr.	£1,400	($2,250)
124	2/2	8	300 fr.	£12,000	($19,000)
125	2/1	9	2,500 fr.	£100,000	($160,000)
126	14/15 [RPC: 32 specimens]	4	4 fr.	£300	($475)
127	<30/<33	4	6 fr.	£1,500	($2,400)
128	<30/<33	4	5 fr.	£650	($1,050)
129	<30/<33	5	10 fr.	£1,250	($2,000)
130	<30/<33	9	200 fr.	£8,000	($12,800)
131	<30/<33	5	8 fr.	£850	($1,350)
132	25/25	8	500 fr.	£15,000	($24,000)
133	<10/<10	8	250 fr.	£10,000	($16,000)
134	<30/<33	6	25 fr.	£1,000	($1,600)
135	1/1	Unique		£10,000	($16,000)
136	<10/<10	7	100 fr.	£10,000	($16,000)
137	<30/<33 (including 137a)	3	4 fr.	£650	($1,050)
137a				£700	($1,125)
138	<30/<33	4	5 fr.	£600	($950)
139	1/1	Unique	— (2,000 fr.)	£125,000	($200,000)
140	<30/<33 (including 140a)	6	40 fr.	£2,250	($3,600)
140a				£2,500	($4,000)
141	<30/<33	8	300 fr.	£6,500	($10,500)
142	10/12	4	10 fr.	£1,250	($2,000)
143	4/1	9	1,000 fr.	£25,000	($40,000)
143a	4/3	9	1,000 fr.	£25,000	($40,000)
144	1/2	8	400 fr.	£27,500	($44,000)
145	2/2	7	500 fr.	£25,000	($40,000)
145a	2/1		500 fr.	£25,000	($40,000)
146	2/4	7	500 fr.	£25,000	($40,000)
147	1/1	8	1,500 fr.	£30,000	($48,000)
148	<30/<33	4	40 fr.	£1,500	($2,400)
149	<30/<33	5	10 fr.	£1,100	($1,750)
150	2/1	9	40 fr. (= 400 fr.?)	£20,000	($32,000)
150a	2/1	9	40 fr. (= 400 fr.?)	£20,000	($32,000)
151	1/1	8	600 fr.	£25,000	($40,000)
151a	1/1		600 fr.	£25,000	($40,000)
152	1/1		250 fr.	£18,000	($29,000)
152a	1/1	7		£18,000	($29,000)
153	2/3	7	350 fr.	£20,000	($32,000)
154	1/1	8	800 fr.	£22,500	($36,000)
155	<30/<33	5	8 fr. (80 fr.)	£1,500	($2,400)
156	<30/<33	9	300 fr.	£2,500	($4,000)
157	<30/<33	4	20 fr.	£850	($1,350)
158	<30/<33	7	200 fr.	£2,000	($3,200)
159	1/1	9	1,000 fr. (2,000 fr.)	£90,000	($145,000)
160	2/1	10		£95,000	($152,000)
161	1/2	9	1,000 fr. (2,000 fr.)	£95,000	($152,000)
161a	1/1			£95,000	($152,000)
162	2/3	9	1,200 fr. (2,000 fr.)	£95,000	($152,000)

Catalogue no.	*Crawford/RPC/RIC*	*Sydenham*	*Babelon/Cohen*		*Current Value*	
163	1/1	10	2,500 fr. (—)		£100,000	($160,000)
164	7/7	7	100 fr.		£2,500	($4,000)
165	<10/<11	6	60 fr.	Very fine ('VF')	£425	($675)
166	2/2	7	80 fr.	Very fine ('VF')	£700	($1,125)
167	<10/<11	5	50 fr.	Very fine ('VF')	£375	($600)
168	1/1	7	80 fr.	Very fine ('VF')	£900	($1,450)
169	<10/<11	10	100 fr.	Very fine ('VF')	£1,000	($1,600)
170	5/6	5	30 fr.	Very fine ('VF')	£500	($800)
171	<30/<33	4	20 fr.		£350	($550)
172	84/93 (including 172a)	3	3 fr.		£400	($650)
172a		4	5 fr.		£450	($725)
173	34/45	3	6 fr.		£400	($650)
174	85/74 (including 174a	3	6 fr.		£325	($525)
174a	& 174b)	4	6 fr.		£350	($550)
174b		4	6 fr.		£350	($550)
175	3/4	8	600 fr.		£30,000	($48,000)
176	<30/<33	4	5 fr.		£375	($600)
177	<30/<33	4	5 fr.		£350	($550)
178	<30/<33	4	5 fr.		£375	($600)
179	36/40	6	6 fr.		£750	($1,200)
180	<30/<33	4	6 fr.		£400	($650)
181	30/30 (including 181a)	6	200 fr.		£5,500	($8,800)
181a		6	200 fr.		£5,500	($8,800)
182	<30/<33	2	6 fr.		£325	($525)
183	1/1	10	500 fr.		£40,000	($64,000)
184	363/403	1	3 fr.		£200	($320)
185	<10/<10 (including 185a)	8	300 fr.		£7,500	($12,000)
185a		8	300 fr.		£7,750	($12,400)
185b	<10/<10	8	300 fr.		£7,500	($12,000)
185c	1/1	8			£8,000	($12,800)
186	<30/<33	3	10 fr.		£550	($875)
187	<30/<33	3	8 fr.		£325	($525)
188	87/97 (including 188a	3	3 fr.		£325	($525)
188a	& 188b)	3	3 fr.		£300	($475)
188b		3	3 fr.		£300	($475)
189	51/57 (including 189a)	3	4 fr.		£400	($650)
189a		4			£425	($675)
190	40/40	8	400 fr.		£5,500	($8,800)
191	<10/<10	8	400 fr.		£8,500	($13,500)
192	75/83	2	2 fr.		£250	($400)
193	<30/<33	3	3 fr.		£450	($725)
194	30/33	3	5 fr.		£400	($650)
195	30/30 (including 195a)	6	200 fr.		£5,000	($8,000)
195a		6	200 fr.		£5,000	($8,000)
196	25/25	6	200 fr.		£5,000	($8,000)
197	<10/<10	8	500 fr.		£12,000	($19,000)
198	<30/<33	3	20 fr.		£1,000	($1,600)
199	<30/<33	4	10 fr.		£850	($1,350)
200	2/2	8	600 fr.		£22,500	($36,000)
201	<30/<33	5	25 fr.		£1,100	($1,750)
202	<10/<11	7	100 fr.		£1,500	($2,400)
203	<10/<11	4	30 fr.		£750	($1,200)
204	<30/<33	9	150 fr.		£3,000	($4,800)
205	<30/<33	7	80 fr.		£2,000	($3,200)
206	20/20	7	600 fr.		£10,000	($16,000)
207	2/3		50 fr.		£5,000	($8,000)

Catalogue no.	*Crawford/RPC/RIC*	*Sydenham*	*Babelon/Cohen*	*Current Value*	
208	<10/<13	9	1,500 fr.	£85,000	($135,000)
209	<30/<33	5	20 fr.	£900	($1,450)
210	<10/<11	3	6 fr.	£375	($600)
211	<10/<10 (including 211a)	9	1,500 fr.	£75,000	($120,000)
211a		9	1,500 fr.	£75,000	($120,000)
212	<30/<33	6	25 fr.	£1,200	($1,900)
213	1/2	8	600 fr.	£25,000	($40,000)
214	<30/<33	6	20 fr.	£1,500	($2,400)
215				£200,000	($320,000)
216	<30/<33	9	350 fr.	£40,000	($64,000)
217	<10/<10	8	500 fr.	£12,000	($19,000)
218	<10/<10	8	500 fr.	£12,000	($19,000)
219	<30/<33	9	200 fr.	£3,500	($5,500)
220	10/10	7	300 fr.	£8,000	($12,800)
221	<30/<33	3	4 fr.	£600	($950)
222	<10/<10	7	300 fr.	£8,000	($12,800)
223	<30/<33	3	4 fr.	£600	($950)
224	20/20	8	300 fr.	£10,000	($16,000)
225	<30/<33	7	150 fr.	£2,000	($3,200)
226	<30/<33	8	120 fr.	£2,500	($4,000)
227	1/2	10	3,000 fr.	£125,000	($200,000)
228	<30/<33	9	500 fr.	£15,000	($24,000)
229	1/1			£150,000	($240,000)
230	<30/<33	9	500 fr.	£15,000	($24,000)
231	<30/<33	9	400 fr.	£12,500	($20,000)
232	6/9 (incl. 232a-c & 233)			£2,750	($4,400)
232a		7	120 fr.	£2,500	($4,000)
232b		7	120 fr. (200 fr.)	£2,500	($4,000)
232c		7	120 fr.	£2,500	($4,000)
233		8	— (200 fr.)	£7,500	($12,000)
234	12 (including 234a) [RPC:	5	25 fr.	£450	($725)
234a	41 specimens]			£500	($800)
235	33/37	6	25 fr.	£2,250	($3,600)
236	1/2	10	500 fr.	£15,000	($24,000)
237	10/10	7	200 fr.	£10,000	($16,000)
238	<30/<33	4	10 fr.	£1,100	($1,750)
239	1/1			£2,000	($3,200)
240	10/10	8	300 fr.	£12,000	($19,000)
241	<30/<33	4	15 fr.	£1,250	($2,000)
242	15/15	6	200 fr.	£8,000	($12,800)
243	129/143	3	30 fr.	£850	($1,350)
244	1/1		100 fr.	£2,500	($4,000)
245	2/2 (including 245a)	10	2,000 fr.	£35,000	($55,000)
245a				£30,000	($48,000)
246	<30/<33 (incl. 246a & 247)	5	40 fr.	£1,400	($2,250)
246a				£1,600	($2,550)
247		7		£2,000	($3,200)
248	1/1		100 fr.	£1,500	($2,400)
249	1/1 (3 now known)	9	300 fr.	£12,000	($19,000)
250	<30/<33	5	20 fr.	£1,400	($2,250)
251	<30/<33	5	6 fr.	£950	($1,500)
252	1(?)/1(?)		600 fr.	£50,000	($80,000)
253	<30/<33	7	50 fr.	£1,600	($2,550)
254	1/1			£50,000	($80,000)
255	<30/<33	7	40 fr.	£1,500	($2,400)
256	<30/<33	6	40 fr.	£1,500	($2,400)

Catalogue no.	*Crawford/RPC/RIC*	*Sydenham*	*Babelon/Cohen*		*Current Value*	
257	2/3	8	500 fr.		£25,000	($40,000)
258	<30/<33	6	25 fr.		£1,500	($2,400)
259	1/1		3,000 fr.		£150,000	($240,000)
260	<10/<10 (including 260a)	6	250 fr.		£9,000	($14,500)
260a					£10,000	($16,000)
261	<30/<33 (including 261a)	5	8 fr.		£950	($1,500)
261a		5	6 fr.		£1,000	($1,600)
262	RPC: 98 specimens	5	35 fr.		£1,200	($1,900)
263	RPC: 139 specimens	5	35 fr.		£1,000	($1,600)
264	1 [RPC: 11 specimens]	7	50 fr.		£750	($1,200)
265	2/2	9	800 fr.		£10,000	($16,000)
266	1/1		1,500 fr.		£200,000	($320,000)
267	<30/<33	3	4 fr.		£450	($725)
268	4/2	9	2,500 fr.		£100,000	($160,000)
268a	1/1	9	2,500 fr.		£110,000	($175,000)
269	<30/<33	4	10 fr.		£1,200	($1,900)
270	<30/<33	4	10 fr. (15 fr.)		£1,200	($1,900)
271	<30/<33				£1,400	($2,250)
272	<30/<33	4	10 fr.		£1,300	($2,100)
273	RPC: 5 specimens	9	100 fr.	Fine ('F')	£1,500	($2,400)
274	RPC: 4 specimens	9		Fine ('F')	£1,500	($2,400)
275	RPC: 6 specimens	9	100 fr.	Fine ('F')	£850	($1,350)
276	RPC: 3 specimens	9		Fine ('F')	£600	($950)
277	RPC: 30 specimens	5	30 fr.	Fine ('F')	£275	($450)
278	RPC: 1 specimen	9		Fine ('F')	£325	($525)
279	RPC: 13 specimens	8	100 fr.	Fine ('F')	£1,250	($2,000)
280	RPC: 7 specimens	8		Fine ('F')	£1,350	($2,150)
281	RPC: 15 specimens	8	100 fr.	Fine ('F')	£800	($1,275)
282	RPC: 15 specimens	8		Fine ('F')	£500	($800)
283	RPC: 1 specimen			Fine ('F')	£450	($725)
284	RPC: 2 specimens			Fine ('F')	£275	($450)
285	RPC: 4 specimens	8		Fine ('F')	£1,500	($2,400)
286	RPC: 22 specimens	8	150 fr.	Fine ('F')	£1,250	($2,000)
287	RPC: 31 specimens	5	60 fr.	Fine ('F')	£750	($1,200)
288	RPC: 30 specimens	5		Fine ('F')	£450	($725)
289	RPC: 4 specimens	9	40 fr.	Fine ('F')	£350	($550)
290	RPC: 3 specimens	10		Fine ('F')	£250	($400)
291	RPC: 16 specimens	8		Fine ('F')	£750	($1,200)
292	RPC: 11 specimens	8	50 fr.	Fine ('F')	£500	($800)
293	RPC: 7 specimens	8		Fine ('F')	£300	($475)
294	RPC: 12 specimens	8	60 fr.	Fine ('F')	£750	($1,200)
295	RPC: 29 specimens	5		Fine ('F')	£400	($650)
296	RPC: 116 specimens	5	40 fr.	Fine ('F')	£150	($240)
297	<30/<33	6	40 fr.		£1,800	($2,900)
298	8/6	4	10 fr.		£900	($1,450)
299	11/12	5	10 fr.		£750	($1,200)
300	<30/<33	3	5 fr.		£550	($875)
301	15/15	7	200 fr.		£8,000	($12,800)
302	<30/<33 (incl. 302a & 302b)	4	4 fr.		£600	($950)
302a		4	4 fr.		£600	($950)
302b		4	4 fr.		£650	($1,050)
303	<30/<33	5	6 fr.		£1,100	($1,750)
304	148/172 (including 304a)	3	4 fr.		£225	($350)
304a					£275	($450)
305	1/1	8	500 fr.		£30,000	($48,000)
306	<30/<33	7	80 fr.		£3,000	($4,800)

Catalogue no.	*Crawford/RPC/RIC*	*Sydenham*	*Babelon/Cohen*	*Current Value*	
307	<30/<33	4	20 fr.	£900	($1,450)
308	14 [RPC: 62 specimens]	3	6 fr.	£750	($1,200)
309	3 [RPC: 39 specimens]	5	8 fr.	£650	($1,050)
310	<30/<33	6	40 fr.	£1,200	($1,900)
311	<30/<33	8	100 fr.	£2,000	($3,200)
312	39/43	3	4 fr.	£550	($875)
313	<30/<33	8	100 fr.	£2,250	($3,600)
314	<10/<10	8	200 fr.	£10,000	($16,000)
315	<30/<33	3	4 fr.	£600	($950)
315A		6	50 fr.	£1,250	($2,000)
316	10/10	7	250 fr.	£6,500	($10,500)
317	30/33	3	6 fr.	£225	($350)
318	<10/<10	9	500 fr.	£20,000	($32,000)
319	<30/<33	7	120 fr.	£2,750	($4,400)
320	1/1	9	300 fr.	£10,000	($16,000)
321	<10/<10	9	600 fr. (700 fr.)	£30,000	($48,000)
322	<30/<33	8	150 fr.	£3,000	($4,800)
323	<10/<10	10	600 fr.	£35,000	($55,000)
324	<30/<33	6	60 fr.	£2,500	($4,000)
325	<10/<10	8	400 fr.	£12,500	($20,000)
326	<30/<33	5	30 fr.	£1,200	($1,900)
327	<30/<33	5	12 fr.	£2,000	($3,200)
327a	<30/<33	5	12 fr.	£2,000	($3,200)
328	<10/<10	8	500 fr.	£14,000	($22,500)
329	<30/<33	5	20 fr.	£2,500	($4,000)
330	<10/<10	8	500 fr.	£14,000	($22,500)
331	<30/<33	5	12 fr.	£2,000	($3,200)
332	15/15	7	600 fr.	£30,000	($48,000)
333	<30/<33	5	30 fr. (12 fr.)	£850	($1,350)
334	51/57 (incl. 334a & 334b)	4	15 fr.	£1,250	($2,000)
334a		6	30 fr.	£1,400	($2,250)
334b			30 fr.	£1,500	($2,400)
335	<30/<33 (incl. 335a & 335b)	4	30 fr. (12 fr.)	£750	($1,200)
335a				£850	($1,350)
335b		6	30 fr. (12 fr.)	£800	($1,275)
336	44 [RPC: 185 specimens]	3	6 fr.	£300	($475)
337	<30/<33	8	40 fr.	£7,500	($12,000)
338	<10/<10	9	800 fr. (1,800 fr.)	£75,000	($120,000)
339	<30/<33	5	20 fr.	£1,250	($2,000)
340	2/3	9	1,500 fr. (3,000 fr.)	£125,000	($200,000)
341	<30/<33	9	400 fr. (600 fr.)	£25,000	($40,000)
342	<30/<33	6		£750	($1,200)
343	1/1	9	— (3,500 fr.)	£125,000	($200,000)
344	3/5	9	2,500 fr.	£110,000	($175,000)
345	<30/<33	7	40 fr.	£2,500	($4,000)
346	<30/<33	3	6 fr.	£1,000	($1,600)
347	<30/<33	4	6 fr.	£1,000	($1,600)
348	864/960 (for all varieties of	8	500 fr.	£12,500	($20,000)
349	the 'legionary' silver)	2	2 fr.	£275	($450)
349A	7 (?) obverse dies for all varieties of the 'legionary' gold/1			£20,000	($32,000)
350		2	2 fr.	£275	($450)
351	1 reverse die	8	800 fr.	£20,000	($32,000)
352		2	2 fr.	£275	($450)
353		2	3 fr.	£325	($525)

Catalogue no.	*Crawford/RPC/RIC*	*Sydenham*	*Babelon/Cohen*	*Current Value*	
354		2	2 fr.	£275	($450)
355	1 reverse die	8	800 fr.	£20,000	($32,000)
356		2	2 fr.	£275	($450)
357		2	2 fr.	£275	($450)
358		2	2 fr.	£275	($450)
359		2	2 fr.	£275	($450)
360		3	3 fr.	£350	($550)
361		2	2 fr.	£275	($450)
362		2	2 fr.	£275	($450)
363		4	6 fr.	£500	($800)
364	1 reverse die			£20,000	($32,000)
365		2	2 fr.	£275	($450)
366	1 reverse die	Unique		£20,000	($32,000)
367		2	2 fr.	£275	($450)
368	1 reverse die		800 fr.	£20,000	($32,000)
369		2	3 fr.	£325	($525)
370		3	6 fr.	£425	($675)
371		2	2 fr.	£275	($450)
372		2	2 fr.	£275	($450)
373		4	9 fr.	£550	($875)
374		2	2 fr.	£275	($450)
375		4	12 fr.	£600	($950)
376		2	3 fr.	£325	($525)
377	1 reverse die		800 fr.	£20,000	($32,000)
378		2	2 fr.	£275	($450)
379		6	10 fr.	£750	($1,200)
380		2	2 fr.	£300	($475)
381		2	2 fr.	£300	($475)
382		2	3 fr.	£325	($525)
383		2	6 fr.	£425	($675)
384	3 (?) reverse dies	7	800 fr.	£22,500	($36,000)
385		4	6 fr.	£650	($1,050)
386		4	6 fr.	£650	($1,050)
387	<30/<33	7	60 fr.	£1,800	($2,900)
388	<30/<33	7	50 fr.	£1,600	($2,550)
389	1/1	8	200 fr.	£5,000	($8,000)
390	13/28	4	12 fr.	£850	($1,350)
391	1/6	4	12 fr.	£950	($1,500)
392	RIC: S		5 fr.	£750	($1,200)
393	RIC: S		5 fr.	£800	($1,275)
394	RIC: R2		80 fr.	£5,500	($8,800)
395	RIC: S		10 fr.	£650	($1,050)
396	RIC: S		— (6 fr.)	£700	($1,125)
397	RIC: S		4 fr.	£600	($950)
398			20 fr.	£1,000	($1,600)
399	RIC: S		5 fr.	£650	($1,050)
400	RIC: S		4 fr.	£600	($950)
401	RIC: C		6 fr.	£650	($1,050)
402	RIC: R2		80 fr.	£6,000	($9,500)
403	RIC: R3			£7,000	($11,200)
404	RIC: R3		80 fr.	£6,500	($10,500)
405	RIC: R2		80 fr.	£6,000	($9,500)
406	RIC: S		10 fr.	£700	($1,125)
407	RIC: S		4 fr.	£650	($1,050)
408	RIC: S		12 fr.	£750	($1,200)
409	RIC: S		6 fr.	£650	($1,050)

Catalogue no.	*Crawford/RPC/RIC*	*Sydenham*	*Babelon/Cohen*	*Current Value*	
410	RIC: R4		20 fr.	£1,800	($2,900)
411	4/11 [RIC: R3]	7	120 fr.	£2,400	($3,850)
412	1/1 [RIC: R5]			£125,000	($200,000)
413	7/10 [RIC: R3]	6	60 fr.	£2,000	($3,200)
414	1/4 [RIC: R3]	6	60 fr.	£2,200	($3,500)
415	1/5 [RIC: R2]	6	60 fr.	£1,500	($2,400)
416	RIC: C		5 fr.	£550	($875)
417	RIC: R		50 fr.	£7,500	($12,000)
418	RIC: R3		200 fr.	£17,500	($28,000)
419	RIC: S		5 fr.	£600	($950)
420	RIC: C		5 fr.	£625	($1,000)
421	RIC: C		5 fr.	£750	($1,200)
422	RIC: C		5 fr.	£700	($1,125)
423	RIC: S		5 fr.	£650	($1,050)
424	RIC: C		5 fr.	£600	($950)
425	RIC: S		5 fr.	£750	($1,200)
426	RIC: R2			£900	($1,450)
427	RIC: S		8 fr.	£800	($1,275)
428	RIC: C		10 fr.	£650	($1,050)
429	RIC: C		4 fr.	£250	($400)
430	RIC: S		25 fr.	£1,600	($2,550)
431	RIC: S		25 fr.	£1,800	($2,900)
432	RIC: R3		30 fr.	£2,000	($3,200)
433	RIC: C [RPC: 80 specimens]		40 fr.	£1,250	($2,000)
434	RIC: R4		200 fr.	£20,000	($32,000)
435	RIC: R		Cohen: 100 fr.	£8,500	($13,500)

Concordances

1. Crawford—Sear

Crawford	*Sear*	*Crawford*	*Sear*
440/1	1	453/1a	29
441/1	2	453/1b	29
442/1a	16	453/1c	29a
442/1b	16a	453/1d	29a
443/1	9	453/1e	29a
444/1a	3	454/1	30
444/1b	3a	454/2	30a
444/1c	3b	454/3	31
445/1a	4	454/4	32
445/1b	4	454/5	33
445/2	5	455/1a	34
445/3a	6	455/1b	34
445/3b	6	455/2a	35
446/1	7	455/2b	35
447/1a	8	455/3	36
447/1b	(ancient forgery)	455/4	37
448/1a	17	455/5	38
448/1b	17	455/6	39
448/2a	18	456/1a	15
448/2b	18	456/1b	15a
448/3	19	457/1	54
449/1a	20	458/1	55
449/1b	20a	459/1	45
449/1c	20b	460/1	40
449/2	21	460/2	41
449/3a	22	460/3	42
449/3b	22a	460/4	43
449/4	23	461/1	44
449/5	24	462/1a	46a
450/1a	25	462/1b	46b
450/1b	25	462/1c	46
450/2	26	462/2	47
450/3a	27	463/1a	63
450/3b	27	463/1b	63a
450/3c	27	463/2	64
451/1	28	463/3	65
452/1	10	463/4a	66a
452/2	11	463/4b	66
452/3	14	463/4c	66
452/4	12	463/4d	66
452/5	13	463/5a	67

Crawford	*Sear*
463/5b	67
463/6a	68
463/6b	68a
464/1	69
464/2	70
464/3a	71a
464/3b	71b
464/3c	71
464/4	72
464/5	73
464/6	74
464/7a	75
464/7b	75
464/8a	76
464/8b	76a
465/1a	77
465/1b	77a
465/2a	77b
465/2b	77c
465/3	78
465/4	78a
465/5	79
465/6a	80c
465/6b	80b
465/6c	80b
465/6d	80b
465/7a	80a
465/7b	80
465/8a	81
465/8b	81a
466/1	56
467/1a	57
467/1b	57a
468/1	58
468/2	59
469/1a	48
469/1b	48
469/1c	48
469/1d	48
469/1e	48a
470/1a	49
470/1b	52
470/1c	50
470/1d	51
471/1	53
472/1	82
472/2	83
472/3	84, 84a
472/4a	85a
472/4b	85
472/4c	85b
473/1	86
473/2a	87
473/2b	87
473/2c	87
473/2d	87
473/3	88

Crawford	*Sear*
473/4	89
474/1a	90
474/1b	90a
474/2a	91
474/2b	91a
474/2c	91b
474/3a	92
474/3b	92a
474/4	93
474/5	94
474/6	95
474/7	96
474/8	97 (modern forgery)
475/1a	60
475/1b	60a
475/2	61
476/1a	62
476/1b	62a
477/1a	232
477/1b	232a
477/2	233
477/3a	232b
477/3b	232c
478/1a	234
478/1b	234a
479/1	336
480/1	164
480/2a	98
480/2b	98
480/2c	99
480/3	100
480/4	102
480/5a	106
480/5b	106a
480/6	103
480/7a	104
480/7b	104a
480/8	105
480/9	107
480/10	107a
480/11	107b
480/12	107c
480/13	107d
480/14	107e
480/15	111a
480/16	111
480/17	101
480/18	108
480/19	112
480/20	109
480/21	110
480/22	142
480/23	167
480/24	165
480/25	169
480/26	166
480/27	170

Crawford	*Sear*
480/28	168
481/1	117
482/1	130
483/1	236
483/2	235
484/1	141
485/1	113
485/2	171
486/1	172, 172a
487/1	173
487/2a	174
487/2b	174a
487/2c	174b
488/1	118
488/2	123
489/1	119
489/2	119a
489/3	120
489/4	121
489/5	122
489/6	126
490/1	131
490/2	132
490/3	134
490/4	135
491/1a	195
491/1b	195a
491/2	196
492/1	124
492/2	125
493/1a	133
493/1b	133
493/1c	133
494/1	159
494/2a	143
494/2b	143a
494/3a	150a
494/3b	150
494/4	160
494/5	144
494/6a	151
494/6b	151a
494/7a	161a
494/7b	161
494/8a	145a
494/8b	145
494/9a	152a
494/9b	152
494/10	163
494/11	147
494/12	154
494/13	162
494/14	146
494/15	153
494/16	114
494/17	148
494/18	155
494/19	156
494/20a	181a
494/20b	181
494/21	182
494/22	183
494/23	184
494/24	115
494/25	157
494/26a	175
494/26b	175
494/27	176
494/28	177
494/29	178
494/30	179
494/31	180
494/32	149
494/33	158
494/34	190
494/35	191
494/36	192
494/37	193
494/38	194
494/39a	116
494/39b	116
494/40	186
494/41	187
494/42a	188
494/42b	188a
494/42c	188b
494/43a	189
494/43b	189a
494/44a	185
494/44b	185a
494/45	185b
494/46	185c
495/1	139
495/2a	140
495/2b	140
495/2c	140
495/2d	140a
496/1	128
496/2	127
496/3	129
497/1	136
497/2a	137
497/2b	137
497/2c	137
497/2d	137a
497/3	138
498/1	217
499/1	218
500/1	219
500/2	220
500/3	221
500/4	222
500/5	223
500/6	197

Crawford	*Sear*
500/7	198
501/1	199
502/1	200
502/2	201
502/3	202
502/4	203
503/1	204
504/1	205
505/1	224
505/2	225
505/3	226
505/4	206
505/5	207
506/1	208
506/2	209
506/3	210
507/1a	211a
507/1b	211
507/2	212
508/1	213
508/2	214
508/3	216
509/1	227
509/2	228
509/3	229
509/4	230
509/5	231
510/1	337
511/1	332
511/2a	333
511/2b	333
511/2c	333
511/3a	334
511/3b	334a
511/3c	334b
511/4a	335
511/4b	335
511/4c	335a
511/4d	335b
512/1	316
512/2	317
513/1	318
513/2	319
513/3	320
514/1	321
514/2	322
515/1	323
515/2	324
516/1	240
516/2	241
516/3	239
516/4	237
516/5	238
517/1a	242
517/1b	242
517/2	243
517/3	244

Crawford	*Sear*
517/4a	245
517/4b	245a
517/5a	246
517/5b	246a
517/5c	247
517/6	248
517/7	249
517/8	250
518/1	298
518/2	299
519/1	338
519/2	339
520/1	256
521/1	257
521/2	258
522/1	252
522/2	253
522/3	254
522/4	255
523/1a	300
523/1b	300
524/1	340
524/2	341
525/1	325
525/2	326
525/3	327
525/4a	327a
525/4b	327a
525/4c	327a
526/1	328
526/2	329
526/3	330
526/4	331
527/1	259
528/1a	260a
528/1b	260
528/2a	261
528/2b	261a
528/3	251
529/1	301
529/2a	302
529/2b	302b
529/2c	302a
529/3	303
529/4a	304a
529/4b	304
530/1	264
531/1a	265
531/1b	265
532/1	342
533/1	266
533/2	267
533/3a	268
533/3b	268a
534/1	305
534/2	306
534/3	307

Crawford	*Sear*	*Crawford*	*Sear*
535/1	308	544/26	365
535/2	309	544/27	367
536/1	269	544/28	370
536/2	271	544/29	369
536/3	272	544/30	371
536/4	270	544/31	372
537/1	310	544/32	374
537/2	311	544/33	376
538/1	312	544/34	379
538/2	313	544/35	378
539/1	297	544/36	380
540/1	314	544/37	381
540/2	315	544/38	382
541/1	343	544/39	383
541/2	344	545/1	387
542/1	346	545/2	388
542/2	347	546/1	389
543/1	345	546/2a	390
544/1	384	546/2b	390
544/2	351	546/2c	390
544/3	355	546/2d	390
544/4	364	546/3a	391
544/5	366	546/3b	391
544/6	368	546/3c	391
544/7	377	546/4	411
544/8	385	546/5	412
544/9	363	546/6	413
544/10	373	546/7	414
544/11	375	546/8	415
544/12	386	547/1	510
544/13	348	548/1a	(earlier date)
544/14	349	548/1b	(earlier date)
544/15	350	549/1	(earlier date)
544/16	353	550/1	509
544/17	352	550/2a	507
544/18	354	550/2b	507
544/19	356	550/2c	507
544/20	357	550/2d	507
544/21	358	550/2e	507
544/22	360	550/2f	507
544/23	359	550/3a	508
544/24	361	550/3b	508
544/25	362	550/3c	508

2. Babelon/RSC—Sear

Babelon/RSC		*Sear*	*Babelon/RSC*		*Sear*
Accoleia	1	172	Antia	4	37
Acilia	8	16, 16a		5	38
Aemilia	12	164		6	39
	18	165	Arria	1	318
	19	166		2	319
Antia	1	34		3	320
	2	35	Caecilia	47	45
	3	36		48	40

Babelon/RSC		*Sear*
Caecilia	49	41
	50	44
	51	43
	52	42
Carisia	1	70
	2	72
	3	73
	4	71, 71a-b
	5	71, 71a-b
	6	74
	7	76
	8	76a
	9	76a
	10	69
	11	69
	12	75
	13	75
Cestia	1	195
	2	195a
	3	196
Claudia	12	316
	13	317
	14	183
	15	184
	16	181, 181a
	17	182
Considia	2	77b
	2a	77c
	3	77a
	4	77
	5	79
	6	78
	7	78a
	8	80
	8a	80a
	9	80b
	9a	80b
	9b	80b
	9c	80c
	10	81
	11	81a
Cordia	1	63a
	2	63
	3	65
	4	64
	5	66a
	5b	66
	5c	66
	6	67
	7	67
	8	68
	9	68
Cornelia	64	4
	65	5
	66	6
	67	6
Cornuficia	1	227

Babelon/RSC		*Sear*
Cornuficia	2	228
	3	231
	4	230
Domitia	20	338
	21	339
Flaminia	2	171
Hostilia	2	18
	4	19
	5	17
Licinia	23	30a
	24	30
	25	31
	26	32
	27	33
Livineia	8	180
	9	175
	10	176
	11	177
	12	179
	13	178
Lollia	1	87
	2	86
	3a	88
	4	89
Mettia	1	167
	2	168
Mussidia	1	185
	2	185a
	3	185b
	4	186
	5	187
	6	188–188b
	7	189
Neria	1	2
Numonia	1	321
	2	322
Papia	2	82
	3	83
	4	84
	4a	84a
	5	85
	6	85b
	7	85a
Petillia	1	173
	2	174
	3	174a
	4	174b
Plautia	14	29a
	15	29
Porcia	9	46
	10	46a
	10a	46b
	11	47
Postumia	10	26
	11	25
	13	27
	14	27

Babelon/RSC		*Sear*
Sepullia	9	169
	11	170
	12	170
Sicinia	1	3
	2	3a
	4	3b
	5	1
Statia	1	337
Sulpicia	9	323
	10	324
Valeria	14	92
	15a	92a
	16	90a
	17	90
	18	91a
	18a	91
	19	91b
	20	94

Babelon/RSC		*Sear*
Valeria	21	93
	22	95
	23	96
	23a	97 (modern forgery)
Vibia	16	21
	17	22, 22a
	18	20
	19	20a
	20	23
	21	24
	22	28
	23	193
	24	192
	25	191
	26	194
	27	190

3. Cohen/RSC—Sear

Cohen/RSC		*Sear*
Pompey the Great	1	48 (Gnaeus Pompey Junior)
	1a	48a (Gnaeus Pompey Junior)
	2	234 (Sextus Pompey)
	3	8
	3a	(ancient forgery)
	4	7
	5	49 (Gnaeus Pompey Junior)
	6	49 (Gnaeus Pompey Junior)
	7	49 (Gnaeus Pompey Junior)
	8	49 (Gnaeus Pompey Junior)
	9	52 (Gnaeus Pompey Junior)
	9a	52 (Gnaeus Pompey Junior)
	9b	52 (Gnaeus Pompey Junior)
	9c	52 (Gnaeus Pompey Junior)
	10	52 (Gnaeus Pompey Junior)
	11	50 (Gnaeus Pompey Junior)
	11a	50 (Gnaeus Pompey Junior)
	11b	50 (Gnaeus Pompey Junior)
	11c	50 (Gnaeus Pompey Junior)
	11d	51 (Gnaeus Pompey Junior)
	12	232c (Sextus Pompey)
	12a	(does not exist)
	12b	232 (Sextus Pompey)
	13	232b (Sextus Pompey)
	13a	(does not exist)
	14	232a (Sextus Pompey)
	15	233 (Sextus Pompey)
	16	336 (Sextus Pompey)
	17	334 ((Sextus Pompey)
	18	334a (Sextus Pompey)
	18a	334b (Sextus Pompey)
	19	(earlier date)

Cohen/RSC		*Sear*
Pompey the Great	20	235 (Sextus Pompey)
	20a	235 (Sextus Pompey)
	21	236 (Sextus Pompey)
	22	(Trajanic restoration)
Julius Caesar	1	54
	2	56
	3	56
	4	57a
	4a	57
	5	(reign of Augustus)
	6	(reign of Augustus)
	7	62, 62a
	8	112
	8a	112
	8b	112
	9	111
	10	111a
	11	(does not exist)
	12	55
	13	58
	14	59
	15	130 (Octavian)
	16	14
	17	10
	18	11
	19	13
	19a	12
	20	117
	21	15
	22	102
	23	105
	24	104, 104a
	25	103
	26	113
	27	115
	28	(modern forgery)
	29	116
	30	60a
	31	60
	32	61
	33	305
	34	100
	35	101
	36	98
	36a	99
	37	114
	38	107, 107a
	39	107d
	39/40	107e
	40	107b
	41	106a
	41a	106
	42	108
	43	109
	44	110
	44a	110
	44b	110

Cohen/RSC		*Sear*
Julius Caesar	45	331
	46	329
	47	327a
	47a	327a
	47b	327a
	48	327
	48a	(does not exist)
	49	9
	50	(altered)
	51	(uncertain colonial)
	52	(Trajanic restoration)
	53	(Trajanic restoration)
	54	(Trajanic restoration)
	55	(Trajanic restoration)
	56	(Trajanic restoration)
J. Caesar & Mark Antony	1	(modern forgery)
	2	118
	2a	118
	3	123
	3a	123
J. Caesar & Octavian	1	(reign of Augustus)
	2	132
	3	308
	4	308
	5	306
	6a	135
Brutus	1	213
	2	214
	3	212
	4	209
	5	199
	5a	210
	6	198
	7	205
	8	204
	9	206
	9a	207
	10	200
	11	201
	12	202
	13	203
	14	211a
	15	216
	16	208
Cassius	1	218
	2	217
	3	220
	4	221
	4a	221
	5	222
	6	223
	7	219
	8	224
	9	225
	10	226
Domitius Ahenobarbus	1	338
Labienus	1	340

Cohen/RSC		*Sear*
Labienus	2	341
Sextus Pompey	1	333
	1a	333
	1b	333
	1c	333
	1d	333
	2	335
	2a	335
	2b	335a
	3	335b
	3a	335b
	4	(modern forgery)
Sextus, Pompey & Pompey Jr.	1	332
Lepidus	1	162
	2	161
	3	159
	4	490 (Cabellio)
Lepidus & Mark Antony	1	125
	2	119a
	2a	(does not exist)
	3	120
	3a	120
	3b	120
	3c	120
	4	119
	4a	119
	4b	119
	5	120
	6	(ancient forgery)
	6a	(ancient forgery)
	6b	(does not exist)
Lepidus & Octavian	1	139
	2	140
	2a	140
	2b	140
	2c	140a
	2d	140
Mark Antony	1	390
	1a	390
	1b	390
	1c	391
	1d	391
	2	347
	3	264
	4	149
	5	303
	6	386
	7	385
	8	384
	9	257
	10	258
	10a	258
	10b	258
	10c	258
	11	387
	12	128
	12a	128

Cohen/RSC		*Sear*
Mark Antony	13	267
	13a	267
	14	(modern forgery)
	15	266
	16	269
	17	(wrongly described)
	17a	270
	18	272
	18a	272
	18b	272
	18c	272
	18d	271
	19	297
	20	146
	21	145, 145a
	22	255
	23	252
	24	253
	25	143, 143a
	26	348
	27	349
	28	350
	29	353
	30	352
	31	351
	32	354
	33	356
	34	357
	35	358
	35a	358 note
	36	360
	37	359
	38	361
	39	362
	40	363
	41	365
	42	367
	43	370
	44	369
	45	368
	46	(altered)
	47	371
	48	372
	49	374
	50	373
	51	376
	52	376 note
	53	375
	54	379
	55	378
	56	377
	57	380
	58	381
	59	382
	60	383
	61	(does not exist)
	62	(does not exist)

	Cohen/RSC	*Sear*
Mark Antony	62a	(does not exist)
	63	(does not exist)
	63a	(does not exist)
	64	(does not exist)
	65	(does not exist)
	66	256
	66a	256
	66b	256
	67	304
	67a	304
	67b	304a
	68	127
	68a	(does not exist)
	69	(modern forgery)
	70	129
	70a	129
	71	346
	72	148
	73	144
	74	142
	75	265
	75a	265
	76	240
	77	241
	77a	239
	78	237
	79	238
	79a	238
	80	389
	81	388
	82	121
	83	(restoration by M. Aurelius)
	97	277
	98	289
Mark Antony & Octavian	1	261
	1a	(does not exist)
	1b	261a
	2	251
	2a	251
	2b	251
	2c	251
	3	133
	4	124
	5	301
	6	(ancient forgery)
	6a	248
	7	242
	8	243
	8a	243
	8b	243
	8c	243
	8d	243
	8e	243
	8f	243
	9	249
	10	250
	10a	250

Cohen/RSC		*Sear*
Fulvia	1	753 (Eumenea)
	2	321
	3	126
	4	122
Octavia & Mark Antony	1	268, 268a
	2	262
	3	263
	4	(wrongly described)
	5	279
	6	(wrongly described)
	7	281
	8	292
	9	(wrongly described)
	10	(wrongly described)
	11	296
	12	287
	13	294
Octavia, Antony & Octavian	1	286
Cleopatra	1	cf. 703 (Sinope)
Cleopatra & Mark Antony	1	345
	1a	345
	1b	345
	1c	345
	1d	345
	1e	345
Mark Antony Jr. & M. Antony	1	344
	2	343
Gaius Antonius	1	141
Lucius Antony & M. Antony	1	245
	2	246
	2a	246a
	2b	247
	2c	247
	3	244
Octavian (Augustus)	1	434
	2	430
	3	431
	4	432
	5	302b
	6	302
	6a	302a
	14	429
	30	435
	44	428
	44a	428
	55	137
	55a	137a
	55b	137
	55c	137a
	60	409
	61	401
	62	395
	63	396
	64	407
	65	406
	66	408
	67	402

	Cohen/RSC	*Sear*
Octavian (Augustus)	68	(wrongly described?)
	69	399
	70	397
	71	398
	72	400
	73	394
	74	(does not exist)
	75	410
	76	405
	77	404
	88	313
	89	314
	90	315
	90a	315
	91	312
	94	315A
	95	309
	96	(barbarous copy)
	111	311
	113	417
	114	425
	114a	426
	115	416
	116	427
	117	424
	118	(modern forgery)
	119	419
	120	420
	121	418
	122	421
	123	422
	124	423
	125	411
	126	392
	127	393
	128 = 337	310
	218	433
	227	299
	243	134
	245	136
	246	131
	248	138
	337 = 128	310
	410	155
	411	156
	412	151
	416	(modern forgery)
	417	298
	443	157
	444	150, 150a
	467	153
	468	152
	497	(does not exist)
	498	414
	499	415
	500	413
	500a	413

Cohen/RSC		*Sear*
Octavian (Augustus)	514	300
	514a	300
	514b	300
	522	325
	523	326
	539	158
	539a	(ancient forgery)
	540	154
	545	307
	546	328
	547	330
	573	(Trajanic restoration)

4. RIC—Sear

RIC	*Sear*
250a	395
250b	396
251	397
252	399
253	400
254a	406
254b	407
255	408
256	409
257	401
258	405
259	404
260	402
261	403
262	394
263	410
264	416
265a	419
265b	420
266	421
267	422
268	417
269a	425
269b	426
270	427
271	423
272	424
273	418
274	428
275a	430
275b	431
276	429
277	435
476	433
531	414
532	415
533	412
534	413
535	411
543a	392
543b	393
544	434
545	432

Footnotes

1 Suetonius, *Divus Julius*, 34.
2 *BMCRR*, vol. ii, p. 468, note.
3 *Roman Republican Coinage*, p. 89.
4 *Roman Republican Coinage*, p. 735.
5 *Roman Republican Coinage*, p. 511.
6 *Roman Republican Coinage*, p. 737.
7 *BMCRR*, vol. ii, p. 572, note 2.
8 *Roman Republican Coinage*, p. 93, no. 475.
9 *BMCRR*, vol. i, p. 538, note – 'These gold coins were struck on the occasion of Caesar's triumph in October, BC 45, after his return from Spain'.
10 On the evidence of provenance Burnett (*RPC*) and Grant (*FITA*) would prefer an attribution to a mint in northern Italy, possibly Milan.
11 Suggested by S. Cesano (*Rend. Pont. Acc. Arch*, 1947–9).
12 *BMC Greek Coins* (Troas, Aeolis, and Lesbos) p. 55 and pl. x, 12–15.
13 *Roman Republican Coinage*, p. 478.
14 *Roman Republican Coinage*, p. 483.
15 Charles Lenormant, 'Notice sur les deniers romains qui portent le nom de L. Valerius Acisculus', in *Nouvelles Annales publiées par la section française de l'Institut Archologique de Rome*, vol. ii, 1838, pp. 142–69.
16 *Roman Republican Coinage*, p. 485.
17 I am reliably informed by R. B. Witschonke that the unique example of this type (published in 1956 by I. Maull in *Blatter fur Munzfreunde* and cited by Crawford) is a modern forgery. I have retained the listing, however, on the chance that the forgery may represent an authentic prototype no specimen of which is currently known.
18 Suetonius, *Divus Julius*, 80.
19 *Civil Wars*, book ii, chaps. 115–17.
20 From the words of Edwin Stanton, Secretary of War, following the death of Lincoln.
21 Dio Cassius, xliv. 4.
22 *Roman Republican Coinage*, pp. 492–3.
23 Asconius Pedianus, *in Scaur.*, 28C (historical commentary on the orations of Cicero).
24 *Roman Republican Coinage*, p. 494.
25 *Roman Republican Coinage*, p. 494.
26 *Julius Caesar*, lvii, 32.
27 'The Triumviral Portrait Gold of the *Quattuorviri Monetales* of 42 BC' (*ANSNNM 137*), 1956, pp. 32–44.
28 *Roman Republican Coinage*, p. 510.
29 Suetonius, *Divus Julius*, 59.
30 *African War*, 89.
31 A similar feature occurs on coins of Caesar struck after his victory over Pompey at Pharsalus (see. nos. 10–14).
32 *RPC* 3139–40.
33 Cf. John Melville Jones, *A Dictionary of Ancient Roman Coins*, p. 47.
34 'A Dialogue of Power in the Coinage of Antony and Octavian (44–30 BC)', in *AJN* 2, 1990, p. 41, note 13.

35 *AMC* 1117 = *RPC* 1383.
36 Crawford assigns the issue to an 'uncertain' mint in 44 BC; Sydenham gives it to Gaul in 47 BC; and Grueber, in *BMCRR* (following Count de Salis), places it in Spain in 49 BC.
37 Newman, 'A Dialogue of Power in the Coinage of Antony and Octavian (44–30 BC)', in *AJN* 2, 1990, p. 56.
38 Formerly in the French collection, but lost in the great theft of 1831.
39 *Roman Republican Coinage*, p. 512.
40 *Roman Republican Coinage*, p. 510.
41 *Roman Republican Coinage*, p. 510.
42 The only exception being the type of L. Livineius Regulus.
43 *BMCRR*, vol. i, p. 584.
44 *The Coinage of the Roman Republic*, p. 184.
45 'The Triumviral Portrait Gold of the *Quattuorviri Monetales* of 42 BC' (*ANSNNM 137*), 1956, p. 8.
46 *Roman Republican Coinage*, p. 510.
47 *Roman Republican Coinage*, p. 510.
48 Asconius Pedianus, *in Scaur.*, 28C (historical commentary on the orations of Cicero).
49 *Sulla*, ix.
50 *Roman Republican Coinage*, p. 497.
51 *Roman Republican Coinage*, p. 498.
52 *Satirae* i, 4, 24.
53 *Roman Republican Coinage*, p. 510.
54 *Roman Republican Coinage*, p. 729.
55 *RPC* 3139–40.
56 *Roman Republican Coinage*, p. 325, 320/1.
57 *Roman Republican Coinage*, pp. 500–501.
58 Appian, *Civil Wars*, iv. 26.
59 *Roman Republican Coinage*, p. 501.
60 *Roman Republican Coinage*, p. 501.
61 Hyla A. Troxell, 'The Coinage of the Lycian League' (*ANSNNM 162*), p. 180, note 286.
62 Hyla A. Troxell, 'The Coinage of the Lycian League' (*ANSNNM 162*), pl. 16, B.
63 Cicero, *ad Brut.* i, 6, 4.
64 Cicero, *ad Brut.* i, 17, 3.
65 Plutarch, *Brutus,* 51.
66 Appian, *Civil Wars*, v. 207.
67 *Roman Republican Coinage*, p. 517.
68 *Roman Republican Coinage*, p. 408.
69 'besides, he struck coins on which were represented a pileus and two daggers, to show by this design and also by the inscription that he had in concert with Cassius given liberty to his country' (xlvii.25).
70 *Roman Republican Coinage*, p. 552, note 107.
71 *Cf. Bellum Africum*, 57, 89.
72 Plutarch, *Brutus,* 30.
73 Cicero, *ad Familiares.* xii. 7; *Philippicae*, iv. 6.
74 Cicero, *ad Familiares.* xii. 17–30.
75 Livy (xxi. 62).
76 *Roman Republican Coinage*, p. 486 (note following 477/1a).
77 Appian, *Civil Wars*, ii. 430.
78 This type has been found in significant quantities in Sicily in the excavations at Morgantina (*Morgantina Studies II. The Coins.* Princeton, 1989). However, the bevelled edges of the flans and the 9 o'clock die axis would seem to support the traditional attribution to Spain. The coins from Morgantina were probably carried to Sicily by Sextus' supporters when he took possession of the island in 43 BC.
79 Dio Cassius, xlviii. 19.
80 Horace, *Epodes* 9, 7f.
81 For the remarkable series of bronze coins known as the 'fleet coinage', initiated in the East in the summer of 38 BC in the names of three Antonian admirals (including Atratinus and Capito) and continued later in the West following the Pact of Tarentum, see nos. 273–96.

Struck in six denominations, this series anticipates many of the features of the reformed *aes* coinage introduced by Augustus some two decades later.

82 though they do show the lituus, or augur's staff, behind the head of Antony, a feature also to be found on no. 129.

83 Dio Cassius, xlviii, 5, 4.

84 See also the denarii of Q. Caecilius Metellus Pius, as imperator, issued four decades earlier (Crawford 374/1 and 2).

85 Plutarch, *Antonius*, 24.

86 Crawford records 15 obverse and 15 reverse dies for the aureus, and 129 obverse and 143 reverse dies for the denarius.

87 Crawford expresses doubt regarding the authenticity of aurei of this type: 'I list 4b (unknown before 1963) with some misgivings; a specimen of 5b, with the same variant legend, was in the Lawrence sale [1950] and since then no less than four specimens of 4b, all from the same pair of dies, have appeared on the market'.

88 The one exception, the denarius with head of Octavian (no. 249), is almost certainly a hybrid piece with a reverse die belonging to the coinage of L. Gellius.

89 Generally on flans which are thinner and more spread and struck from dies which are of less elegant style.

90 In dating this type to 41 rather than 40/39 BC I follow Newman, 'A Dialogue of Power in the Coinage of Antony and Octavian (44–30 BC)', in *AJN* 2, 1990, p. 43, note 19.

91 De la Nauze, *Mém. de l'Acad. roy. des Inscr., &c.*, vol. xxx, 1764, *Le Poids de l'anc. Livre romaine*, p. 382.

92 Cf. H. Dessau, *Inscriptiones Latinae Selectae (ILS)* 886.

93 As Grueber, *BMCRR East*, p. 496, note 1; Sydenham, *The Coinage of the Roman Republic*, p. 192; and Newman, 'A Dialogue of Power in the Coinage of Antony and Octavian (44–30 BC)', in *AJN* 2, 1990, p. 45.

94 The caduceus, the winged staff of Mercury (protector of merchants and commerce) surmounts the terrestrial globe together with two cornuacopiae, emblems of plenty.

95 Compare also the undoubted portraits of Octavia on the cistophori of Asia issued in 39 BC (nos. 262 and 263) and on the aurei struck in Athens the following year (nos. 268 and 268a).

96 I have followed Burnett (*RPC*) in attributing both types in this series to the Ephesus mint. Sutherland (*The Cistophori of Augustus*), following Grueber (*BMCRR*), preferred to give no. 262 to Pergamum.

97 Dio Cassius (xlviii. 39) records that when Antony returned to Athens with Octavia towards the end of 39 BC he ordered that he should be addressed as the 'New Dionysus'.

98 Compare also the portraits on the wedding aureus (no. 259) and on the aurei struck in Athens in 38 BC (nos. 268 and 268a).

99 *RPC*, p. 285.

100 Cf. the Spanish issues of Gnaeus Pompey Junior in 46–45 BC (no. 53) and those of Sextus Pompey in 45–44 BC (nos. 234 and 234a).

101 H.A. Grueber, in *BMCRR*, vol. ii, pp. 403–4, compares them with eastern issues of Antony which he believed were struck by the Antonian generals in Cisalpine Gaul (cf. no. 241).

102 'A Dialogue of Power in the Coinage of Antony and Octavian (44–30 BC)', in *AJN* 2, 1990, pp. 45–6, note 22.

103 Marcus Antonius 'Creticus', praetor 74 BC.

104 Marcus Antonius, praetor 102 BC, consul 99 BC, censor 97 BC.

105 The single surviving specimen was formerly in the Metropolitan Museum, New York, and was sold at auction through Sotheby in Zürich, Switzerland, on 10 November 1972 (lot 11). Prior to this the coin had been in the collections of Hyman Montagu, Count Alberic du Chastel, and Lord Bagot. It was originally published by Joseph Eckhel in *Doctrina Numorum Veterum*, vol. vi, p. 46, and was mentioned by Longpérier in *Revue Numismatique*, 1856, p. 73 f.

106 Cf. *RPC* 653–4, 655, and 1101.

107 Crawford also comments on the upward-looking head of Antony on this type which he suspects is directly borrowed from the iconography of Alexander. However, the present writer fails to recognize this peculiarity, the angle of the Triumvir's gaze appearing to be no more elevated than on many other portraits of the period.

108 Cicero, *Pro Balbo*.
109 Cornelius Nepos, *Vita Attici* 21, 4.
110 The ancient Phoenician city of Gades possessed a celebrated sanctuary of Heracles-Melkart situated on the island of Cotinussa.
111 The family of Salvidienus appears to have had its roots in the country of the Vestini, a mountain tribe of central Italy. He was still a member of the equestrian order at the time of his designation as consul in 40 BC.
112 Cf. *ILLRP* 1113 and 1120. Examples have also been found at Leucopetra, south of Rhegium, occupied by Salvidienus at the time of his war against Sextus Pompey in 42 BC.
113 A similar representation of the young Julius occurs two decades later on aurei and denarii of Augustus commemorating the *Ludi Saeculares* of 17 BC. (cf. *RIC* 337–40).
114 His second and third consulships were in 28 and 27 BC.
115 The titles *divi Iuli filius* and *divi filius* had first appeared on the final issue of coinage by the Roman moneyers in 40 BC (see nos. 325–6, 328, and 330).
116 *BMCRR*, vol. ii, p. 412.
117 *Cercle d'Etudes Numismatiques Bulletin*, April–June 1986, pp. 21–34.
118 The true picture is obscured by the existence of large numbers of contemporary imitations.
119 In 1898 the base of a large, probably round, altar was discovered in a semicircular niche in the middle of the platform which fronted the temple of Divus Julius.
120 *CIL* xi, 3310a, 3311.
121 Crawford appears to be mistaken in dismissing this interpretation on the basis that the Floralia were first celebrated in 238 BC. This was, in fact, the date of the foundation of her temple close to the Circus Maximus (Pliny the Elder, *Naturalis historia*, 18. 286) which took place several years after the inauguration of the festival.
122 The other member of the college, C. Clodius Vestalis, selected a more conventional type for his issues. Either he had no strong political affiliations or his coinage may have belonged to the earlier part of the year, prior to the beginning of the conflict which culminated in the Perusine War.
123 The vowel duplication is merely an archaism, like *Feelix* on coins of Sulla's son, Faustus Cornelius Sulla (cf. Crawford 426/2).
124 This identification, suggested by Sydenham, is dismissed as unconvincing by Crawford, though he is quite prepared to accept the more problematic depiction of Brutus on the denarii of Servius Rufus.
125 near modern Frascati, fifteen miles south-east of Rome. The place was a favourite residence of Cicero who composed several philosophical treatises in his Tusculan villa.
126 Crawford dismisses the identification of this portrait as that of the fourth century tribune Servius Sulpicius Rufus on the basis that the moneyer was a Servius and not a Sulpicius.
127 Had the Antonian generals Pollio and Ventidius decided to come to Lucius Antony's aid and raise Octavian's siege of Perusia it is doubtful in the extreme whether the young Triumvir would have survived this episode.
128 The third Triumvir, M. Aemilius Lepidus, was already an irrelevance by this time.
129 He continued to use the title, however, as it appears on all his subsequent issues of precious metal coinage.
130 A prominent example was Tiberius Claudius Nero, husband of Octavian's future wife Livia and father of the future emperor Tiberius. All three of them sought refuge with Sextus in Sicily, though the fugitive later quarrelled with his host and joined Antony in Greece.
131 Curiously, despite being defeated in this engagement Salvidienus was also hailed as *imperator* (see commentary on no. 300).
132 It was to serve as the model for many such types of the imperial age, such as the coins of Augustus with heads of Julia and Gaius and Lucius Caesars on reverse, those of Vitellius with his two children, those of Vespasian with Titus and Domitian, and the extensive series of Septimius Severus depicting the various members of the imperial family.
133 *Odyssey* 12. 85 ff.
134 Grant (*FITA*, p. 22) and Sydenham (p. 174) seem to regard the entire issue as being of Spanish mintage, whilst Crawford (pp. 94 and 487) dates its commencement to 45 BC and states that it 'bridges the period during which Sex. Pompeius is moving from Spain to Sicily; pieces of fine style, presumably early in the issue, are found in Spain, pieces of degenerate style, presumably the result of production on a massive scale, are found in Sicily'.

135 *ILLRP* 444.

136 gained in recognition of his victory over the triumviral admiral Domitius Calvinus on the very day of the first battle of Philippi (early October, 42 BC).

137 Cf. Hill *The Monuments of Ancient Rome as Coin Types*, pp. 29–30. The temple is identified with the remains found in 1837 beneath nos. 9 and 10, Via S. Salvatore in Campo.

138 *In Verrem*, 2. 1. 139.

139 *Roman Republican Coinage*, p. 529.

140 *i.e.* his name should be read as Quintus Labienus Parthicus. Although 'Labienus' is often referred to as a *cognomen* of the Atia *gens* it should rather be regarded as a *gentilicium* (cf. Grueber, *BMCRR*, vol. ii, p. 500, note 1).

141 This ancient structure at the east end of the Forum traditionally occupied the site of the home of King Numa. It contained the archives of the pontifex maximus. The restoration by Domitius Calvinus followed a fire in 36 BC.

142 It is recorded, however, in an inscription found on the Palatine – CN DOMITIVS CALVINVS PONTIFEX COS ITER IMPER (*CIL* vi, 1301).

143 *Res Gestae* 25. This remarkable document had been deposited with the Vestal Virgins and was read in the Senate after the emperor's death in AD 14. It was later engraved on two bronze tablets placed outside his Mausoleum and copies of these were set up in the provinces. The finest surviving example is the celebrated *Monumentum Ancyranum* discovered in 1555 on the walls of a mosque at Ancyra in Galatia. The building had originally been the temple of Roma and Augustus.

144 The triumviral office had in any case lapsed at the end of the preceding year and Octavian was not even bothering to use the title.

145 Gaius Sosius is later heard of in Rome restoring the temple of Apollo, near the theatre of Marcellus, and participating as *quindecimvir sacris faciundis* in the Secular Games of 17 BC.

146 The series was suspended between year 12 (38/37 BC) and year 19 (31/30 BC), though Antioch may not have been the actual mint of the tetradrachms of Antony and Cleopatra (cf. *RPC*, pp. 601 and 606–7).

147 called Antyllus by the Greek writers, possibly recalling Hercules' son Anto, the family's Tiburtine ancestor (cf. *OCD*, 3rd edition, p. 116).

148 Cf. Grueber, *BMCRR East*, p. 522, note (after Cavedoni). Both were sons of a Marcus, so presumably the differentiation was deemed necessary. Other examples of this form of epigraphy are met with in inscriptions.

149 Curiously, most modern authorities have preferred alternative attributions: Grueber (in *BMCRR*) dated the issue to 32–31 BC and placed it at Ephesus; four decades later Sydenham followed suit, though he did concede the possibility of an earlier date; Crawford, whilst commenting in a note (p. 102) that 'this issue presumably follows the assignation at Alexandria late in 34 of kingdoms to Cleopatra and her children' thereupon dates it to 32 BC in the catalogue portion of the text. Newman also notices this apparent inconsistency and presents the argument for the earlier date most succinctly – 'the minting of this coin must have taken place in 34, the year of Antony's Alexandrian triumph, since it would otherwise be without context'.

150 In the catalogue entry I have followed the normal convention of placing Antony on the obverse, but on some specimens I have examined – most noticeable on those struck on unusually broad flans – there can be no doubt whatsoever that the Egyptian queen appears as the obverse type. This may, or may not, be true of the entire issue.

151 Grueber (*BMCRR*) and Sydenham place it in 34 BC, Crawford and Newman in 33.

152 *IG* ii, 2–3.4114. Newman cites this inscription (note 30) but does not make the connection with the Triumvir's arrival in the city in May of 32 BC.

153 Santamaria, 21 November 1920, lots 177 and 184.

154 Its sole previous appearance had been on a denarius issued at Massilia in 82 BC by the imperator C. Valerius Flaccus, proconsul in Gaul (Crawford 365).

155 Grueber (*BMCRR East*, p. 526, note 1) assigns the issue to Ephesus where Antony and Cleopatra wintered in 33/32 BC.

156 Sydenham (p. 196) notes 'known specimens of these coins are forgeries or very questionable. The British Museum pieces are very dubious'.

157 Cf. Michael Grant, *The Army of the Caesars*, pp. 90–2.

158 IMP IIII for an apparently fictional victory, COS TERT for a consulship which was never held, and III VIR R P C for a triumvirate which had expired.
159 The other, Cassius of Parma, was also in Antony's company at this time.
160 Presumably it is the same eighth legion which is being honoured on both this type and on Antony's 'legionary' issue (see no. 358).
161 Ammon was a Libyan god whose worship later extended into Egypt. The Greeks equated him with Zeus, hence the handsome coin types of Cyrene, Barce, and the Ptolemaic kings.
162 This is certainly true in the case of the longer version of Antony's name (see no. 391) and was probably intended in the abbreviated version (nos. 389–90). The change might have been made to clarify any confusion on this point.
163 '[He] left three-quarters of his estate, after certain legacies had been deducted, to Gaius Octavius, afterwards Augustus, and one-eighth each to Lucius Pinarius and Quintus Pedius. These were his three sororal grand-nephews' (Suetonius, *Divus Julius*, 83). Apparently Pinarius and Pedius resigned their shares to Octavian (Appian, *Civil Wars*, iii. 22 f).
164 Appian, *Civil Wars*, iv. 107.
165 Grueber (*BMCRR*) places them in Gaul and dates them to 29–27 BC; Mattingly (*BMCRE*) attributes them to Emerita in Spain, 22–19 BC; Sutherland (*RIC*) categorizes them under 'uncertain mints' before 27 BC; and Giard (*CBN*) gives them to Spain in 27–26 BC. It is difficult to understand how Mattingly and Giard could resolve the absence of the title AVGVSTVS with attributions subsequent to 27 BC.
166 It is also obvious that IMP CAESAR DIVI F contains the elements of both forms of the succeeding legends.
167 First fully comprehended by Kraft (*Zur Münzpragung des Augustus*, p. 206 ff.) and later commented on by Sutherland (*The Emperor and the Coinage*, p. 51).
168 For the cult of Augustus as Mercury, cf. the article by J.P. Six in *Revue Archéologique*, 1916, p. 257 ff; also Horace, *Odes*, i. 2, 41–4. Kraft's contention (*op. cit.*, p. 214 ff.) that the depiction is of Apollo Leucadius can scarcely be supported in the light of the prominent petasus which clearly identifies the god as Mercury. In any case, the likelihood of this issue being post-Actian seems very slight. All the other types of the final phase of the CAESAR DIVI F coinage are of a stridently military nature and an abstruse reference to a little-known local Greek deity would have been quite out of place.
169 Symbolized by the lyre with a sounding box made from the shell of a tortoise, which was invented by the god.
170 This type (see nos. 406–8) may represent the celebrated 'Tarentine Victory', the gold statue of the goddess Nike taken by the Romans from the Greek city of Tarentum. Octavian later placed this image on an altar in the meeting chamber of the new Senate House (*Curia Julia*) which he dedicated in 29 BC. It was to remain there for four hundred years until its removal by the Christian emperor Gratian.
171 Possibly derived from the early 3rd century BC coinage of Demetrius Poliorcetes or the celebrated sculptural representation known as the Victory of Samothrace, both commemorating Demetrius' victory over Ptolemy of Egypt in the battle of Salamis (306 BC). It is tempting, though perhaps fanciful, to see in Octavian's use of the type an allusion to an earlier Ptolemaic naval defeat, that of the dynasty's founder 275 years before. The idea may receive some corroboration from the similarity of another of the Octavianic types (no. 409) to the coinage of Demetrius. Here, the standing figure of Octavian as Neptune bears a striking resemblance to the pose of Poseidon on the portrait tetradrachms of the Hellenistic monarch.
172 On the occasion of the defection of two of Antony's principal allies, the dynasts Rhoemetalces of Thrace and Deiotarus of Paphlagonia, whose desertion was largely responsible for the failure of Antony's first attack on Octavian's camp.
173 The Octavianic type may depict the celebrated Tarentine Victory which was later placed in the meeting chamber of the Senate House (*Curia Julia*).
174 Several replicas of this exist indicating that they were distributed throughout the Empire: one was found at Arles dated 26 BC, another is at Potentia in Picenum.
175 Cf. Hill *The Monuments of Ancient Rome as Coin Types*, p. 44. Grueber's theory, adopted by Mattingly, that the depiction is of the temple of Divus Julius can certainly be discounted, as can O.L. Richmond's curious suggestion (mentioned by Mattingly in *BMCRE* , p. cxxiii) that it represents 'a little shrine built just outside the atrium of Augustus'. Hill states that it

was Lugli (*Roma Antica: Il centro monumentale*, Rome, 1946, p. 132 and fig. 26) who identified the coin type with the *Curia Julia*. However, as early as 1909 Huelsen (*The Roman Forum*, 2nd edition, Rome, pp. 116–22 and figs. 54–8) made the correct association and even used this denarius to illustrate the building's original appearance.

176 The Emperor Domitian had also carried out a restoration in AD 94.

177 *Quaderni Ticinesi* 1976, p. 151.

178 Cf. Hill *The Monuments of Ancient Rome as Coin Types*, pp. 52–3.

179 Dio Cassius, li. 19.

180 Cf. *RIC* 131–7 for a depiction of the *arcus Augusti* on aurei and denarii issued in Spain in 18/17 BC.

181 Cf. Hill *The Monuments of Ancient Rome as Coin Types*, p. 60.

182 Although this temple was not completed until 28 BC there can little doubt that the rostral column commemorating Actium had been erected well in advance of the official dedication by Octavian.

183 Kraft (*Zur Münzpragung des Augustus*, p. 211 ff.) has even proposed that the mint for this, and other types in the IMP CAESAR series, should be sought at Nicopolis rather than in Italy. The idea, though superficially attractive, lacks corroborative evidence other than that provided by the symbolism of the types. The style of the entire series is uniform throughout and there seems to be no valid reason to give further consideration to Kraft's contention.

184 in the 'Donations of Alexandria' (autumn 34 BC).

185 Cf. John Melville Jones, *A Dictionary of Ancient Roman Coins*, p. 300.

186 See also his representations as Neptune (no. 409) and Apollo (nos. 423–4).

187 This interpretation suggested by Sutherland in *The Emperor and the Coinage*, p. 53, note 88.

188 Most recently by Giard in *CBN*, pp. 44 and 143, who gives it to Ephesus.

189 *RIC*, vol. i, pp. 31 and 61.

190 Cf. Crawford, *Roman Republican Coin Hoards*, nos. 478–82.

191 Grandson of the M. Licinius Crassus who lost his standards, and his life, in his invasion of Parthia in 53 BC.

192 Cf. *CBN*, pp. 43–4 and 146–7.

193 Cf. *RPC*, pp. 380–81.

194 His birthday was 23 September (63 BC), which would have made him a Libra by the modern reckoning. However, it is clear from an astronomical work dating from the early part of Tiberius' reign that the moon and not the sun was used as the basis for computations at that time. The moon was in Capricorn at the time of Augustus' birth (cf. John Melville Jones, *A Dictionary of Ancient Roman Coins*, p. 47).

195 Could it be that the cistophori were produced for much wider circulation than *provincia Asia* itself? The output during this decade was certainly on an unprecedented scale.

196 The only earlier instances were on the IMP CAESAR coinage of 30–29 BC where Octavian appeared in the guise of Apollo or as Jupiter Terminus (see nos. 423–7).

197 *AIIN*, 15, 1968, p. 54 (weight 31.97 grammes).

Index of Roman Coin Legends

This index relates to the coin descriptions only and the numbers given are those of the catalogue entries. Ligatures are not indicated.

Index of Roman Coin Types

This index relates to the coin descriptions only and the numbers given are those of the catalogue entries. Subsidiary types and symbols are not included unless pertinent to the symbolism of the main type.

Index of Roman Mints

This index relates to the coin descriptions only and the numbers given are those of the catalogue entries. All mints producing regular Roman coin denominations are listed, though the precise locations of many still await certain identification. The approximate date of each issue is included.

Index to Historical Narrative

This index relates to the introductory text and the historical commentaries at the commencement of each chapter. The numbers given refer to the relevant pages. In the case of personal names of principal characters the form adopted in popular usage has been preferred to the normal convention of arrangement by *nomen* (*e.g.* Caesar, C. Julius, instead of Iulius Caesar, Gaius; Mark Antony, instead of Antonius, Marcus; and Decimus Brutus, instead of Iunius Brutus Albinus, Decimus).